THE CAMBRIDGE COMPANION
TO XENOPHON

This *Companion*, the first dedicated to the philosopher and historian Xenophon of Athens, gives readers a sense of why he has held such a prominent place in literary and political culture from antiquity to the present and has been a favorite author of individuals as diverse as Machiavelli, Thomas Jefferson, and Leo Tolstoy. It also sets out the major problems and issues that are at stake in the study of his writings, while simultaneously pointing the way forward to newer methodologies, issues, and questions. Although Xenophon's historical, philosophical, and technical works are usually studied in isolation because they belong to different modern genres, the emphasis here is on themes that cut across his large and varied body of writings. This volume is accessible to students and general readers, including those previously unfamiliar with Xenophon, and will also be of interest to scholars in various fields.

Michael A. Flower is Professor of Classics at Princeton University. His major research and teaching interests are in ancient Greek history, historiography, and religion. He is the author of *Theopompus of Chios: History and Rhetoric in the Fourth Century* B C (1994), *Herodotus, Histories, Book IX* (with John Marincola, 2002), *The Seer in Ancient Greece* (2008), and *Xenophon's Anabasis, or the Expedition of Cyrus* (2012) and the co-editor (with Mark Toher) of *Georgica: Greek Studies in Honour of George Cawkwell* (1991).

A complete list of books in the series is at the back of this book.

THE CAMBRIDGE
COMPANION TO
XENOPHON

EDITED BY

MICHAEL A. FLOWER
Professor of Classics
Princeton University

CAMBRIDGE
UNIVERSITY PRESS

CAMBRIDGE
UNIVERSITY PRESS

University Printing House, Cambridge CB2 8BS, United Kingdom
One Liberty Plaza, 20th Floor, New York, NY 10006, USA
477 Williamstown Road, Port Melbourne, VIC 3207, Australia
4843/24, 2nd Floor, Ansari Road, Daryaganj, Delhi – 110002, India
79 Anson Road, #06-04/06, Singapore 079906

Cambridge University Press is part of the University of Cambridge.

It furthers the University's mission by disseminating knowledge in the pursuit of
education, learning, and research at the highest international levels of excellence.

www.cambridge.org
Information on this title: www.cambridge.org/9781107050068
DOI: 10.1017/9781107279308

© Cambridge University Press 2017

First published 2017
Printed in the United Kingdom by Clays, St Ives plc

A catalogue record for this publication is available from the British Library

Library of Congress Cataloging-in-Publication Data
Names: Flower, Michael A., editor.
Title: The Cambridge companion to Xenophon / edited by Michael A. Flower.
Description: Cambridge, United Kingdom; New York: Cambridge University Press, 2016. |
Series: Cambridge companions to literature
Identifiers: LCCN 2016036442| ISBN 9781107050068 (hardback) |
ISBN 9781107652156 (paperback)
Subjects: LCSH: Xenophon–Criticism and interpretation. |
Greece–History–To 146 B.C.–Historiography.
Classification: LCC PA4497 .C434 2016 | DDC 938/.007202–dc23
LC record available at https://lccn.loc.gov/2016036442

ISBN 978-1-107-05006-8 Hardback
ISBN 978-1-107-65215-6 Paperback

CONTENTS

CONTENTS

MAPS AND ILLUSTRATIONS

Maps

Illustrations

CONTRIBUTORS

EMILY BARAGWANATH (Associate Professor of Classics, The University of North Carolina at Chapel Hill) has research interests in Greek literature and culture, and especially historiography. She is the author of *Motivation and Narrative in Herodotus* (2008), co-author of the *Herodotus Oxford Bibliography Online*, and co-editor of *Myth, Truth, and Narrative in Herodotus* (2012) (both with Mathieu de Bakker).

EWEN BOWIE (formerly Praelector in Classics at Corpus Christi College, Oxford and Professor of Classical Languages and Literature in the University of Oxford; now an Emeritus Fellow of Corpus Christi College) has published articles on early Greek elegiac, iambic, and lyric poetry; on Aristophanes; on Hellenistic poetry; and on many aspects of Greek literature and culture from the first century BC to the third century AD. He co-edited (with Jaś Elsner) *Philostratus* (Cambridge University Press, 2009) and (with Lucia Athanassaki) *Archaic and Classical Choral Song* (2011). He is currently completing a commentary on Longus, *Daphnis and Chloe* for Cambridge University Press.

RICHARD FERNANDO BUXTON (Visiting Assistant Professor, Colorado College) is interested in the history, historiography, and economy of Classical Greece. He has authored articles on Herodotus, Xenophon, and Athenian coinage.

PAUL CHRISTESEN (Professor of Classics, Dartmouth College) has research interests in ancient Greek history (with a particular focus on Sparta), sport history (including the ancient Olympics), and the relationship between sport and political systems. He is the author of *Olympic Victor Lists and Ancient Greek History* (Cambridge University Press, 2007) and *Sport and Democracy in the Ancient and Modern Worlds* (Cambridge University Press, 2012). He is also co-editor, with Donald Kyle, of *The Wiley-Blackwell Companion to Sport and Spectacle in Greek and Roman Antiquity*. He is currently working with Paul Cartledge of Cambridge University on the *Oxford History of the Archaic Greek World*.

GABRIEL DANZIG (Senior Lecturer in the Departments of Classics and Philosophy at Bar Ilan University) has research interests that include Socratic literature, Greek political and economic thought, Plato, Aristotle, and especially Xenophon. He has also published on the influence of Greek philosophical themes on ancient and medieval Jewish literature. He has published a Hebrew translation of Xenophon's Socratic dialogues and an English volume entitled *Apologizing for Socrates: How Plato and Xenophon Created our Socrates* (2010). He is currently editing a volume of essays entitled "Plato and Xenophon: Comparative Studies."

JOHN DILLERY (Professor of Classics, University of Virginia) has research interests in Greek history and historiography of the Classical and Hellenistic periods, as well as in Greek and non-Greek interaction and papyrology. He is the author of *Xenophon and the History of His Times* (1995) and *Clio's Other Sons: Berossus and Manetho, with an Afterword on Demetrius* (2015). He revised, updated, and contributed a new introduction and notes to Brownson's translation for the Loeb Library of Xenophon's *Anabasis*.

LOUIS-ANDRÉ DORION (Professor of Philosophy, Université de Montréal) teaches ancient philosophy. Since publishing his doctoral thesis, a translation and commentary on Aristotle's *Sophistic Refutations* (1995), most of his research pertains to Socrates and Socratic literature. He has translated Xenophon's *Memorabilia* for the Collection des Universités de France (3 vols, 2000–11), and he has published a collection of his articles on the Socratic works of Xenophon, *L'Autre Socrate: Études sur les écrits socratiques de Xénophon* (2013). He is presently working on a translation of Xenophon's *Hieron* for the Collection des Universités de France.

MICHAEL A. FLOWER (Professor of Classics, Princeton University) has research interests in Greek history, historiography, and religion. He is the author of *Theopompus of Chios: History and Rhetoric in the Fourth Century B.C.* (1994), *Herodotus, Histories, Book IX* (with John Marincola, Cambridge University Press, 2002), *The Seer in Ancient Greece* (2008), *Xenophon's Anabasis, or the Expedition of Cyrus* (2012), and co-editor (with Mark Toher) of *Georgica: Greek Studies in Honour of George Cawkwell* (1991).

SARAH BROWN FERRARIO (Associate Professor of Greek and Latin, The Catholic University of America) is a specialist in Greek history and literature, particularly of the fifth and fourth centuries BC. She is the author of *Historical Agency and the 'Great Man' in Classical Greece* (Cambridge University Press, 2014). Her recent and forthcoming publications include projects on the reception of Aeschylus in western opera and on Thucydidean leadership.

VIVIENNE GRAY (Emeritus Professor of Classics at the University of Auckland) has research interests in Xenophon, historiography, and other genres of Greek prose writing. She is the author of various books including most recently *Xenophon on Government* (Cambridge University Press, 2007), *Xenophon: Oxford Readings in Classical Studies* (2010), and *Xenophon's Mirror of Princes* (2011).

EDITH HALL (Professor of Classics, King's College London) has published widely on ancient Greek culture and its reception. She has particular interests in ethnicity, gender, and class. Her publications include *Inventing the Barbarian* (1989), an edition of Aeschylus' *Persians* (1996), *The Theatrical Cast of Athens* (2006), and *The Return of Ulysses* (2008). Her most recent books are *Adventures with Iphigenia in Tauris: Euripides' Black Sea Tragedy* (2013) and *Introducing the Ancient Greeks* (2014).

FIONA HOBDEN (Senior Lecturer in Greek Culture, University of Liverpool) is a cultural historian whose interests range from ancient Greek drinking parties to the reception of Classical antiquity on television. She is the author of *The Symposion in Ancient Greek Society and Thought* (Cambridge University Press, 2013) and co-editor of *Xenophon: Ethical Principles and Historical Enquiry* (2012) with Christopher Tuplin. She teaches on topics in ancient Greek history, politics, and society including myth, gender, democratic Athens, and religion, and on receptions of the ancient world in popular culture today.

NOREEN HUMBLE (Associate Professor, Dept. of Classics and Religion, University of Calgary) researches primarily on Xenophon and Plutarch, both in their contemporary setting and in the early modern period. She is the editor of *Plutarch's Lives: Parallelism and Purpose* (2010) and co-editor (with Pat Crowley and Silvia Ross) of *Mediterranean Travels* (2011).

DAVID M. JOHNSON (Associate Professor of Classics, Southern Illinois University Carbondale) devotes most of his research to the Socratic works of Xenophon. He has translated and edited Socratic texts in his *Socrates and Athens* (Cambridge University Press, 2011) and *Socrates and Alcibiades: Four Texts* (2003), and published a number of articles on Xenophon's Socratica and related topics.

JOHN W. I. LEE (Associate Professor of History, University of California, Santa Barbara) has research interests in Greek and Achaemenid Persian history and the history of warfare. He is the author of *A Greek Army on the March: Soldiers and Survival in Xenophon's Anabasis* (Cambridge University Press, 2007).

NINO LURAGHI (D. Magie Professor of Classics, Princeton University) has worked on various subjects in Greek social and cultural history and ancient historiography. He is the author of *The Ancient Messenians: Constructions of Ethnicity and Memory* (Cambridge University Press, 2008) and the editor of *The Historian's Craft in the Age of Herodotus* (2001) and *The Splendors and Miseries of Ruling Alone: Encounters with Monarchy from Archaic Greece to the Hellenistic*

Mediterranean (2013), as well as the author of over sixty articles in journals and collective volumes.

JOHN MARINCOLA (Leon Golden Professor of Classics, Florida State University) has interests in Greek and Roman historiography, rhetoric, and literary criticism. Among his publications are *Authority and Tradition in Ancient Historiography* (1997), *Greek Historians* (2001), and an edition, co-edited with Michael A. Flower, of *Herodotus: Histories Book IX* (2002). He is currently at work on monographs on Polybius and Plutarch.

CHRISTOPHER PELLING (Emeritus Regius Professor of Greek at Oxford University) is the author of *Literary Texts and the Greek Historian* (2000), *Plutarch and History* (2002), and, with Maria Wyke, *Twelve Voices from Greece and Rome* (2014), together with commentaries on Plutarch, *Antony* (Cambridge University Press, 1988), *Philopoemen and Flamininus* (in Italian, 1997), and *Caesar* (2011); he also edited or co-edited *Characterization and Individuality in Greek Literature* (1990), *Ethics and Rhetoric* (1995), *Greek Tragedy and the Historian* (1997), and *Ancient Historiography and its Contexts* (2010). He is now working with Simon Hornblower on a commentary on Herodotus 6 (Cambridge University Press).

TIM ROOD (Professor of Greek Literature at the University of Oxford, and Dorothea Gray Fellow and Tutor in Classics at St Hugh's College) has research interests in Greek historiography and its reception. His first book, *Thucydides: Narrative and Explanation* (1998), was a revision of his doctoral thesis. Since then, he has written two books on the reception of Xenophon's *Anabasis*: *The Sea! The Sea! The Shout of the Ten Thousand in the Modern Imagination* (2004) and *American Anabasis: Xenophon and the Idea of America from the Mexican War to Iraq* (2010).

MELINA TAMIOLAKI (Assistant Professor of Classics, University of Crete) has research interests in Greek historiography, Greek political thought, and the theory of history. She is the author of *Liberté et esclavage chez les historiens grecs classiques* (2010), co-editor (with A. Tsakmakis) of *Thucydides between History and Literature* (2013), and editor of *Comic Wreath: New Trends in the Study of Ancient Greek Comedy* (2014, in modern Greek).

CHRISTOPHER TUPLIN (Professor of Ancient History, University of Liverpool) is the author of *Failings of Empire* (1993) and *Achaemenid Studies* (1996), co-author (with J. Ma, D. G. K. Taylor, and L. Allen) of *The Arshama Letters from the Bodleian Library* (2014, on-line), editor of *Pontus and the Outside World* (2004), *Xenophon and his World* (2004), and *Persian Responses: Cultural interaction (with)in the Achaemenid Empire* (2007), and co-editor (with T. E. Rihll) of *Science and Mathematics in Ancient Greek Culture* (2002) and (with F. E. Hobden) of *Xenophon: Ethical Principles and Historical Enquiry* (2012). He has also published numerous research papers, chiefly on Xenophon, Classical Greek history, and the Achaemenid Empire.

KOSTAS VLASSOPOULOS (Assistant Professor in Greek History, University of Crete) has research interests in Greek economic, social, and political history, the history of slavery, and the history of historiography and political thought. He is the author of *Unthinking the Greek Polis: Ancient Greek History beyond Eurocentrism* (Cambridge University Press, 2007), *Politics: Antiquity and its Legacy* (2010), and *Greeks and Barbarians* (Cambridge University Press, 2013) and co-editor (with Claire Taylor) of *Communities and Networks in the Ancient Greek World* (2015).

PREFACE

Given the central place of Xenophon's writings in literary and political culture from antiquity to the present, it is surprising that he has not previously been the subject of a companion or handbook. It is my hope that this volume will both fill this gap and appeal to general readers, students, and scholars in a range of fields (Classics, Political Science, Philosophy, History, English, Reception Studies, and Comparative Literature, to name the most obvious). The aim of this Companion is first and foremost to give readers a sense of why Xenophon has been a favorite author of individuals as diverse as Machiavelli, Thomas Jefferson, and Leo Tolstoy. It also sets out the major problems and issues that are at stake in the study of his writings, while at the same time pointing the way forward to newer issues and questions. Although Xenophon's works are usually studied in isolation because they belong to different modern genres, each chapter looks at themes that run across his large and diverse body of writings. One very special feature of Cambridge Companions is that they are not meant to close subjects down but to open them up by stimulating further interest among scholars, students, and general readers alike.

In the best of all possible worlds, another consequence of this volume would be to advance the timely return of Xenophon's writings to the university curriculum both in translation and in the original Greek. It was only relatively recently, in fact, that Xenophon was mostly dropped from the college curriculum in Classical Greek, having been replaced by authors (primarily Plato) who are significantly more difficult to read at the intermediate level. The diversity of Xenophon's subjects, the accessibility of his manner of exposition, and his value as a window into almost every aspect of Greek culture recommend him as an author to be read not only by students of ancient Greek, but in courses in translation on Greek history, civilization, political thought, and philosophy. The revival of Julius Caesar (whose range of subject matter is far more limited than Xenophon's) is well underway, and surely it is now Xenophon's turn.

I owe many debts for assistance with this volume. I could not have completed it without a sabbatical leave from Princeton University and a generous grant from the Classics Department's Magee Fund. Harriet Flower has had to live with Xenophon, in one form or another, for many years now, and her encouragement and advice have been, as always, invaluable. My daughter Isabel Flower took time off from her own editing duties to improve my introduction and chapter. One of the more tangible benefits of editing a volume such as this is working closely with fellow specialists in one's field and, above all else, making new friends (a sentiment with which Xenophon would certainly have agreed). All of the contributors have gone beyond the call of duty in lending assistance, but I would especially like to thank John Lee for choosing and modifying the maps, as well as revising the timeline, and Tim Rood for assistance in selecting and obtaining images. John Marincola, Christopher Pelling, John Dillery, and Nino Luraghi have given me helpful advice at every stage.

Alex Petkas assisted me with editing the manuscript and he shares the credit for this volume's publication on schedule. Kim Richardson was an exemplary copy-editor and Judy Oliver provided an impressively thorough index. Last, but hardly least, Michael Sharp and Elizabeth Hanlon of Cambridge University Press are editors without peer, and I am deeply grateful to them for their assistance and advice at every stage, as well as to Michael for the original invitation to edit this volume.

ABBREVIATIONS

The following abbreviations and titles are used for Xenophon's works. *The Oxford Classical Dictionary* has generally been followed for the abbreviations of other ancient works and authors.

Ages.	*Agesilaus*
Anab.	*Anabasis (Expedition of Cyrus)*
Apol.	*Apology (Defense of Socrates)*
Ath. Pol.	*Athenaion Politeia (Constitution of the Athenians)*
Cyn.	*Cynegeticus (On Hunting)*
Cyr.	*Cyropaedia (Education of Cyrus)*
Eq.	*De re equestri (On Horsemanship)*
Hell.	*Hellenica*
Hier.	*Hiero*
Hipp.	*Hipparchicus (How to Be a Good Cavalry Commander)*
Lac. Pol.	*Lacedaemonion Politeia (Constitution of the Spartans)*
Mem.	*Memorabilia (Conversations with Socrates)*
Oec.	*Oeconomicus (Household Management)*
Por.	*Poroi (Ways and Means)*
Smp.	*Symposium*

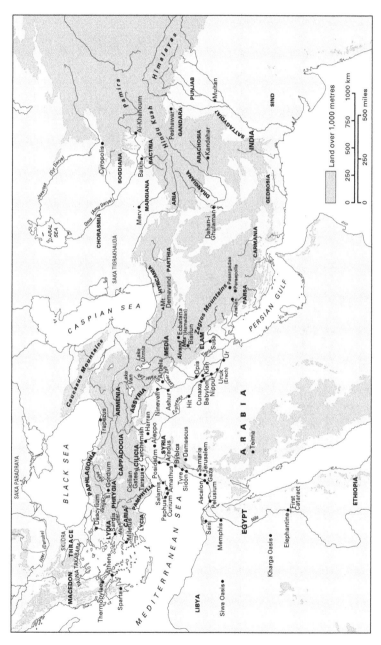

Map 1 The Achaemenid Empire

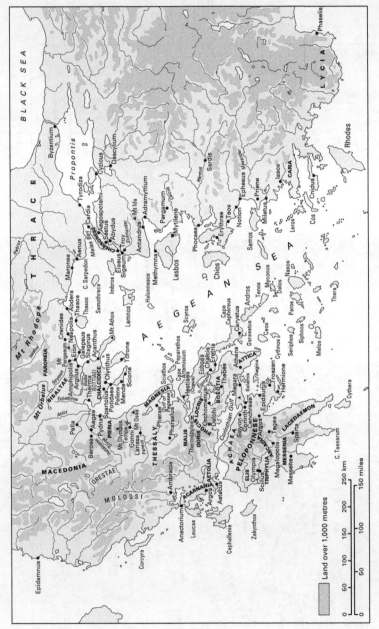

Map 2 Greece and western Asia Minor

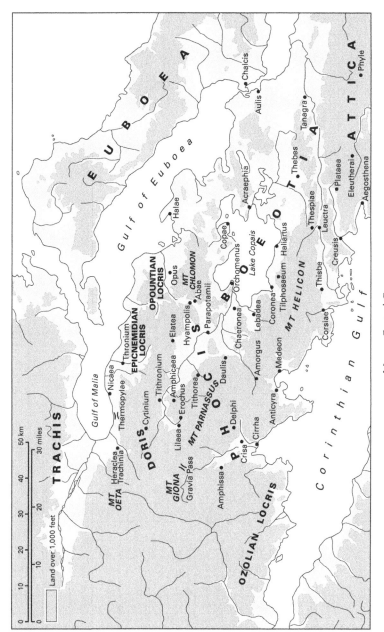

Map 3 Central Greece

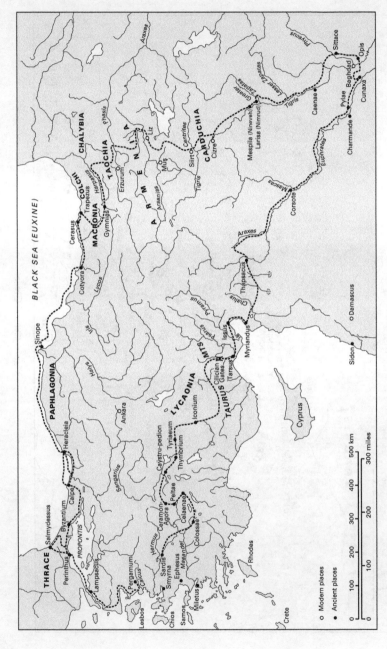

Map 4 The March of the Ten Thousand, 401–399 BC

MICHAEL A. FLOWER

Introduction

Your Latin & Greek should be kept up assiduously by reading at spare
hours ... I would advise you to undertake a regular course of history &
poetry in both languages, in Greek, go first thro' the Cyropaedia, and
then read Herodotus, Thucydides, Xenophon's Hellenics & Anabasis,
Arrian's Alexander, & Plutarch's lives ...
Thomas Jefferson to his grandson Francis Eppes, October 6, 1820

It may seem surprising to most readers of this book, including professional
classicists, that Xenophon's *Cyropaedia* (or *Education of Cyrus*) is at the
top of President Jefferson's "must read" list of ancient Greek prose literature. Perhaps even more surprising is Jefferson's recommendation in a letter to his nephew Peter Carr that for moral instruction he read Xenophon's
Memorabilia as well as the Socratic dialogues of Plato.[1] But to the educated
Europeans and Americans of Jefferson's own time, this was, if anything, very
conventional advice. And this advice was not restricted to a white upper-
class elite. When the coeducational Institute for Colored Youth was established in Philadelphia in 1837, one of its purposes was to provide a classical
education to African-American students; the two Greek texts selected for
study were the New Testament and Xenophon's *Anabasis*. The *Cyropaedia*,
Memorabilia, and *Anabasis*, along with Xenophon's many other works in
various genres, were standard reading and were thought to impart moral
and political lessons of considerable value. If this were true today as well,
it would be to our profit, as I hope the present volume will go some way
towards demonstrating.

In his autobiography, *The Life of Henry Brulard*, Stendhal (whose real
name was Marie-Henri Beyle) informs us: "My moral life has been instinctively spent paying close attention to five or six main ideas, and attempting
to see the truth about them."[2] The same might be said of Xenophon, and

---

[1] Dated August 19, 1785.
[2] This work was written in 1835–6, but only published in 1890.

that would not be a criticism in the case of either author. Like Stendhal, Xenophon wrote in an array of different genres and paid close attention to some half dozen "main ideas" that engaged him over the span of his long life (ca. 430–350 BC). More importantly, those ideas are no less relevant today for "the moral life" of individuals, families, cities, and nations than they were two and a half thousand years ago. As essential as his ideas are, of equal significance is Xenophon's contribution to the forms of literature in which those ideas were expressed. Stendhal, for his part, arguably invented the realist novel. Xenophon either invented or reconfigured several new types of literature. But whereas Stendhal began many books that he left unfinished, Xenophon has bequeathed us a substantial body of finished works. He wrote the first memoir (the *Anabasis*) and the first historical romance (the *Cyropaedia*), he contributed to the genre of Socratic literature (*Memorabilia, Symposium, Defense of Socrates, Oeconomicus*), he wrote technical treatises (on horsemanship, hunting, leadership, finance, and the Spartan constitution), one of the very first prose encomia (*Agesilaus*), and he may have been the earliest continuator of Thucydides (the *Hellenica*). It would be difficult to name a classical author who experimented in so many different genres and achieved success (both during his lifetime and afterwards) in all of them.

Changing Fortunes

Despite his literary versatility and his focus on questions that should be of interest to modern readers (What is the best way to organize a community, to exercise leadership, to live a good life, to treat one's friends?), Xenophon's popularity suffered during much of the twentieth century. His philosophy was seen as inferior to that of Plato, and as a historian he seemed far less capable than either Herodotus or Thucydides. It was not always so. Amongst the Romans his *Cyropaedia* was held in special regard, since it seemed to offer such useful paradigms of behavior for statesmen and monarchs. Scipio Aemilianus (the adopted grandson of Scipio Africanus) is reported by Cicero to have kept a copy of it with him at all times.[3] The historian Sallust knew the works of Xenophon well. The speech of Micipsa in his *Jugurtha* (10.3–6) is closely modeled on that of Cyrus to his sons in the *Cyropaedia* (8.7.13–16).[4] The *Cyropaedia*'s general popularity among Roman elites is revealed by Cicero's complaint (*Brutus* 111–12) that his contemporaries were reading about "the life and training of Cyrus" rather

---

[3] *Letter to His Brother Quintus* 1.1.23; *Tusculan Disputations* 2.62.
[4] See Münscher 1920: 82–3.

than the utterly neglected, but more suitable, memoirs of Marcus Aemilius Scaurus.

Renaissance writers were especially attached to Xenophon and his *Cyropaedia* was considered essential reading for princes.[5] Edmund Spenser, in his introduction to *The Faerie Queene*, ranked Xenophon even above Plato. Machiavelli cites Xenophon more frequently in *The Prince* and the *Discourses* than Plato, Aristotle, and Cicero combined.[6] Moreover, he is the only one of the four and, apart from Virgil, the only classical author, to be even mentioned in *The Prince* (in chap. 14, discussing how Scipio Africanus imitated Xenophon's Cyrus the Great). But the *Cyropaedia*'s popularity did not end in the sixteenth century (as the quotation from Thomas Jefferson reveals). In fact, the *Cyropaedia* was the first book printed in America from Greek type made in that country.[7]

During the eighteenth century Xenophon's most popular work was the *Memorabilia*. Although his reputation as a philosopher declined steeply after the publication of Schleiermacher's influential 1818 attack on Xenophon's portrait of Socrates ("Über den Werth des Sokrates als Philosophen"), Nietzsche did not hide his admiration for the *Memorabilia*, calling it in 1879 "the most attractive book of Greek literature."[8] Yet just when appreciation of the *Memorabilia* was waning, the *Anabasis* came to be considered Xenophon's masterpiece and one of the greatest works of Greek prose. Lord Macaulay, after reading it for the third time, wrote at the end of his personal copy: "One of the very first works that antiquity has left us. Perfect in its kind. – *October* 9, 1837." Such praise from a fellow historian is perhaps not unexpected; more surprising perhaps is that Leo Tolstoy listed the *Anabasis* (which he taught himself Greek in order to read) as one of the fifty books which had most influenced him. It is no wonder then that "X is for Xenophon" appeared in so many nineteenth-century alphabet books.[9]

Over the past twenty years there has been a resurgence of interest in Xenophon that has involved new ways of reading his works and understanding his significance as a historian, philosopher, and political theorist. No area of Xenophontic studies has been more significantly reappraised in recent years than his relationship to Socrates and Plato. A huge body of scholarship (most of it in French) has shown that Xenophon should be

---

[5] See the contribution of Humble in this volume.

[6] Newell 1988.

[7] *Xenophontis De Cyri institutione libri octo*, published by Wm. Poyntell, Philadelphia, Pennsylvania, 1806.

[8] Schleiermacher 1818/1879 (1879 is an English translation) and Nietzsche 1967: vol. IV.3: 442; posthumous fragment 41 [2] 1879. See further Dorion 2009 and his chapter in this volume.

[9] See Rood in this volume and Figure 22.1.

taken seriously as a philosopher and that his version of "Socrates" is well worth studying in its own right (and not just for the sake of comparison with Plato's). The *Cyropaedia* has been the subject of a series of important studies (principally in English), and Xenophon's place in the development of historical writing is currently undergoing a major reappraisal, with a flurry of publications on the *Anabasis* in particular.

Xenophon's literary and linguistic style has also received renewed appreciation. Xenophon was famous in antiquity as the "Attic bee" and "Attic Muse" whose style and diction were as sweet as honey. Yet his reputation as a thinker has suffered in modern times, ironically enough, as a very consequence of his style. His apparently artless eloquence and simplicity of expression have wrongly been taken as a sign of simplicity of thought, in contrast to the complex linguistic and conceptual brilliance of Thucydides and to the wonderfully varied, yet often difficult, style of Plato. It might be going too far to deny the link completely between complexity of thought and complexity of style, but it is certainly the case that complex ideas can be expressed effectively in straightforward language.

Linguistic style aside (that is, his manner of expression and choice of words), Xenophon is a master of narrative style second to none. This is evident whether he is providing the telling vignette or creating suspense before a major battle. Many of his narrative techniques cut across genres and indeed serve to blur the boundaries between them. Yet despite Xenophon's fame during his lifetime (as attested by Diogenes Laertius) he employs a highly reticent literary persona, perhaps even suppressing his identity as the author of his own works or publishing under a pseudonym, as may have been the case with the *Anabasis*. His narrative voice, so different from that of Herodotus and Thucydides, requires careful analysis.

In antiquity Xenophon was chiefly known as a philosopher first and a historian second, whereas now the situation is reversed. Ironically, the opposite fate befell David Hume, who wished to be remembered as a historian, and was indeed best known as a historian in the eighteenth and nineteenth centuries (for his massive six-volume *History of England*), but is now almost exclusively known as a philosopher. As is the case with Hume (whose philosophic and historical thinking inform each other), the historical and the philosophical aspects of Xenophon's writings are not so easy to disentangle.[10]

It cannot be denied that Xenophon has little interest in epistemology or metaphysics, and in those areas cannot compete with Plato or Aristotle, and that the speeches in his historical works lack the highly abstract *Realpolitik*

---

[10] On this aspect of Hume, see Spencer 2013.

theorizing of Thucydides. But there is still much of philosophical value. Because of the prevalent modern assumption that Xenophon was not a philosopher, even when he does make an original argument he is seldom given credit for it. Near the beginning of the *Memorabilia* and once again near its end (1.4 and 4.3), Xenophon gives the first ever account of a theory that still has currency in certain sectors of contemporary society – that is, the theory of intelligent design. Xenophon's Socrates attempts to prove that the gods have designed the universe for the benefit of humankind. Given the fictional nature of the genre of the Socratic dialogue (see below), this is likely to be Xenophon's own personal contribution to a theological and philosophical debate that has had a very long history.[11]

Moreover, his ethical teaching is still of immense value for anyone who wishes to improve their managerial style or their interpersonal relationships; his political theory offers a powerful alternative to the realist foreign policy of Thucydides;[12] and his economic ideas, anticipating those of some modern economists, could benefit both small businesses and large corporations, as well as governments. Indeed, Xenophon anticipated, and even influenced, Adam Smith's insight that the division of labor is determined by the extent of the market, and he aptly has been called "the earliest extant management consultant or managerial *guru*."[13]

But perhaps the most radical and unusual idea to be found in Xenophon's writings is the belief (articulated especially in his *Oeconomicus* and *Poroi*) that the same capacity for virtue can be found in all human beings – that is, in men and women, in free people and in slaves, and in Greeks and non-Greeks.[14] Xenophon, to be sure, did not advocate the abolition of slavery or the extension of political rights to women; yet the truly radical notion that they were fully capable of moral and intellectual virtue makes him look much more forward-thinking than Aristotle, whose theories of natural slavery and of women's defective rationality have had such a long and pernicious afterlife.

When making the case for the contemporary relevance of an author or subject, it strikes me as a mistake to appeal to precise contemporary events, since such references, however pressing at the moment, become dated sooner

---

[11] See especially McPherran 1996: 279–91 and Sedley 2007: 75–92, who, however, attribute the theory to the historical Socrates rather than to Xenophon. But note Dorion in this volume.

[12] Lendon 2006.

[13] So Figueira 2012: 683–4, a fundamentally important study of Xenophon's economic thought. For Xenophon's influence on Adam Smith, see Lowry 1987: 68–73, with *Cyro.* 8.2.5–6.

[14] See especially Baragwanath 2012b, and note Jansen 2012.

than one might imagine at the time. Nonetheless, one sweeping generalization seems to me to be valid. The problems facing contemporary democratic states, especially in terms of effective and morally responsible corporate and political leadership, find practical and realistic solutions in the works of Xenophon. To express his theory very concisely: his ideal leader secures consent to his leadership, treats his followers as friends, shares their toils, solicits their advice, and works for their mutual success as a group with shared interests. This theory can be applied equally to one's relations with co-workers, friends, and family. The value of Xenophon's theory of leadership was recognized for centuries by political leaders in every type of polity, ranging from the monarch Queen Elizabeth I to the democratically elected president Thomas Jefferson. In today's world, his model has an important place in current management theory.[15]

I think that it would be very instructive to undertake a wide-ranging comparison of the reception, for good and ill, of Xenophon's *Cyropaedia* and Plato's *Republic*, the former currently of interest only to a limited number of specialists and the latter a staple of university reading lists in at least a half dozen different disciplines.[16] Yet it was not without good reason that Karl Popper gave the title "The Spell of Plato" to the first volume of his seminal work *The Open Society and Its Enemies*. I doubt if one could find a similar denunciation of the *Cyropaedia*, given that it promotes a particular style of leadership, in which leaders govern willing followers for their mutual benefit, rather than advocating monarchy per se.

The value in reading Xenophon, taken for granted for so many centuries, becomes apparent to those who take the trouble to become acquainted with his works at first hand. But to get the most benefit out of this experience, one must read across genres. Since he was both a philosopher and a historian, his many works are all too often examined in isolation because they fall into different genres that now come under the purview of distinct academic specializations. The contributors to this volume have cut across those generic boundaries in order to give a more holistic view of Xenophon's methods and concerns. This way of examining Xenophon, with a marked emphasis on intertextuality, opens up new avenues of research and new types of questions. Vivienne Gray, of course, has already pioneered this method of reading Xenophon – but much more can be done.[17]

---

[15] See, for instance, O' Flannery 2003 and Field 2012, both cited by Tamiolaki in this volume.
[16] For the reception of Plato, see Lane 2001. Pontier 2006 compares the solutions that they offered to the political crisis of their own times.
[17] Especially in her magisterial 2011 book.

Irony and the Reader

Given that the same themes, with the quest for effective leadership heading the list, appear again and again throughout his corpus, this has prompted two different ways (they could even be called schools) of how to read Xenophon's works: one that sees a consistent message, to be taken at face value, that is repeated in all of his writings, and another that stresses "irony" and a need to read between the lines. As it happens, none of the essays in this volume propose an "ironic" reading in the tradition of the influential political philosopher Leo Strauss; that is, a reading according to the principle that what Xenophon says is consistently the opposite of what he means for those clever enough to read between lines or to perceive the tension between passages that convey conflicting messages. Of course, as David Johnson has proposed in another venue, one does not need to be a follower of Leo Strauss to perceive that actions narrated by Xenophon sometimes are at variance with explicit authorial evaluations.[18] It is in that spirit that Paul Christesen, in his chapter, says that "the reading of Xenophon's views on Sparta presented here might be described as Neo-Straussian or perhaps Straussian-lite." More radically, I have elsewhere argued that although Cyrus the Younger is almost always taken by modern scholars to be a latter-day version of Cyrus the Great, he lacks certain of his namesake's virtues, such as self-control, humanity (*philanthropia*), and, most noteworthy of all, piety. In my opinion Xenophon intended his readers to notice the difference between the two men and to reach the conclusion that the younger Cyrus was a greatly inferior version of his namesake.[19]

I will not press that interpretation here and I only mention it by way of example, since the dangers of this kind of reading are apparent and I am fully aware that many readers of the *Anabasis* will understand Xenophon's portrait of Cyrus the Younger very differently. This is because reading against the grain always entails jettisoning some statements that point in the other direction, such as the narrator's claim in Cyrus' obituary that "no one has been more beloved either by Greeks or non-Greeks" (1.9.28). Xenophon, if nothing else, is a subtle and discreet writer, and that can lead to the related dangers of "overreading" (seeing in a text things that are not signified within it) and "underreading" (missing things that are signified).[20]

The best way to negotiate these two poles is by being an informed reader – one who can relate any particular passage to similar passages throughout

---

[18] Johnson 2012a.

[19] See Flower 2012: 188–94 and, more fully, 2016. Higgins 1977: 82–6 is especially good on Xenophon's treatment of Cyrus the Younger.

[20] For these terms see Kermode 1983: 138–9 and Abbott 2008: 86–90.

Xenophon's corpus and who can place them in their broader historical context.[21] Moreover, one has to be an imaginative reader, one who can think deeply about the implications of a text, but not so imaginative as to make Xenophon consistently mean the opposite of what he explicitly says in violation both of common sense and of the narrative logic of the text. For instance, to read the *Agesilaus* as a subversive critique of its honoree is to ignore the generic conventions of encomia and to render Xenophon's opening statement that Agesilaus was "a perfectly good man" spectacularly hypocritical. If the work glosses over Agesilaus' failures and faults, it is because Xenophon chooses to ignore them in this particular literary context and rather stresses his virtues.[22] Contemporary readers would not have been surprised, or disturbed, to read a more critical treatment in the *Hellenica*.

The power of a work of literature resides not only in the meanings assigned to it by readers but also in its capacity (or potential) to create (or stimulate) meanings. Xenophon's various works have elicited vastly different, and often diametrically opposed, interpretations by scholars over the past fifty years. That is surely a sign of their continuing vitality. And it may not be going too far to say (and not too anachronistic to suggest) that if Xenophon sometimes leaves implicit the lessons that his narrative seems designed to convey, prompting his readers to do some of the interpretative work themselves, such was his "intention." As Fiona Hobden has argued (2005: 105), in many of his works, and particularly in his *Symposium*, *Cyropaedia*, *Anabasis*, and *Hellenica*, "Xenophon displays a propensity for writing which stimulates its reader towards intellectual endeavor instead of offering straightforward lessons." Or as John Marincola suggests in this volume, "Like Herodotus and Thucydides before him, Xenophon expected his readers to be engaged constantly in the work of interpretation."

Unanswerable Questions

The task of interpretation, however, is made more difficult by our ignorance or uncertainty in regard to several essential matters. One of these is the relative chronology of Xenophon's works and the other is the concept of genre that both he and his readers were working with. Scholars tend to group most of his writings after 371, the year in which he fled his idyllic estate at Scillus near Olympia for the life of an exile at Corinth.[23] It is possible that he could have produced this large and varied body of work late in life, but perhaps

---

[21] See further the insightful remarks of Hobden and Tuplin 2012b: 31–7.

[22] A recent subversive reading is Harman 2012; Pontier 2010 rightly stresses the encomium's emphasis on Agesilaus' civic virtues.

[23] Thomas 2009a: xxii–xxiii is typical.

not very likely. As far as we know, Xenophon may have circulated, revised, and then recirculated some of his works over the course of his long career before they reached a final form.[24] It is difficult to imagine that he wrote nothing at all during his many years at Scillus, and then became a prolific author only after he began his exile at Corinth. In any case, we simply do not know enough about the editing, manufacture, and circulation of books (or rather "papyrus rolls") in antiquity to be able to say how Xenophon produced and then distributed his writings. It might be better, therefore, to lay aside the question of chronology, and concentrate on the construction of meaning across the corpus. That would also avoid the temptation to read these works in terms of the author's assumed life story.

The question of generic expectations is rather more vexed. In antiquity, or at least by the time of Dionysius of Halicarnassus writing in the first century B C, Xenophon was known as both a philosopher and as a historian. Indeed, our main source of information about his life, apart from what he tells us explicitly or what we can infer from his writings, is the brief biography of him that Diogenes Laertius, a writer of the third century A D, includes in his lives of famous philosophers.[25] We tend to assume that Xenophon used different methodologies when writing "history" and "philosophy," since they belonged to two different genres each with its own set of more or less implicit rules. So when the anonymous narrator of the *Anabasis* says that Xenophon was a participant in Cyrus' expedition, we take that as a fact. But when in the *Memorabilia* and *Symposium* the narrator (presumably Xenophon) says that he witnessed certain conversations of Socrates, we assume that to be one of the fictional narrative devices of the genre of the Socratic dialogue.[26] And when the proem to the *Cyropaedia* mimics the language of historical inquiry (1.1.6), most, but not all, scholars do not take those words literally, but again as a literary or rhetorical device.

There is, however, a serious problem with this set of assumptions. What if all of these statements of method and claims to autopsy are equally fictional? What if the set of generic expectations that we moderns take for granted did not exist in the same form, or, if they did (which is unlikely), Xenophon is purposefully subverting them? If the Socratic dialogue is essentially a work of fiction (albeit one in which the characters are actual people as in some modern historical novels), then can we take as a historical fact the interchange between Xenophon and Socrates in the *Anabasis* (3.15–7)

---

[24] For one possible scenario, see Kelly 1996.
[25] See Dion. Hal. *Letter to Pompeius* 4; Diog. Laert. 2.48; Cicero, *de orat.* 2.58.
[26] See Danzig and Pelling in this volume. Kahn 1996: 29–35 makes the larger argument that the Socratic dialogue, as composed by all of the Socratic writers including Plato, was a genre of literary fiction.

in which Socrates advised Xenophon to consult the Delphic oracle about joining Cyrus' expedition? Could Xenophon keep his generic boundaries so well fenced that there was no slippage from one into the other?

By the middle of the fourth century BC the Greeks seem to have developed a notion of historical writing as a particular genre of prose literature.[27] But even so, the expectations of a historical work's various audiences were not the same as those of modern readers, at least since the emergence of "scientific," evidence-based history during the nineteenth century.[28] As Christopher Pelling has aptly pointed out, generic expectations, especially for prose literature, were never totally fixed in antiquity, and readers had only general expectations of what they would find when they picked up a work. So a reader "will have a provisional idea of what may be expected, but will not be surprised to find one or several of the usual features to be absent, or present in an unusual or off-key way."[29] To judge from his penchant for literary innovation, Xenophon certainly was not worried about breaking any tacit rules or normative expectations. Yet unlike Isocrates, who highlights his generic innovations, Xenophon lets his speak for themselves without any cues from the author that the reader is about to experience something new.[30]

One huge question remains unanswered and, if the truth be known, unanswerable. Why did Xenophon write anything at all, much less a huge corpus of varied works: five volumes in the Oxford Classical Texts series (in Greek), six volumes in the Loeb Classical Library (facing Greek and English), and four volumes of Penguin paperbacks (minus the *Cyropaedia*)? There is a concern with practical ethics that underpins nearly all of his writings, even the technical ones such as his treatises on commanding cavalry (*Hipparchicus*) and on hunting (*Cynegeticus*). And this ethical dimension is very likely to have its origin in his attachment to Socrates. But we simply do not know which came first, his historical narratives (especially the "continuation" of Thucydides' unfinished history of the Peloponnesian War which comprised the first part of his *Hellenica*) or his Socratic essays (his *Defense of Socrates* is probably the earliest of them). And thus it is probably overly speculative to see his interest in Socratic moral philosophy as the key to understanding the genesis of and motivation behind his entire literary production, including his historical works.[31] As Melina Tamiolaki well observes

---

[27] See Isocrates, *Antidosis* 45–6, *Panathenaicus* 1–2; Aristotle, *Poetics* 1451a36–b11, *Rhetoric* 1.4.1360a36–7; Theopompus, *FGrH* 115, F 25; and Ephorus *FGrH* 70, F 111.

[28] Tucker 2004: 44–5.

[29] Pelling 2007: 80.

[30] See *Antidosis* 10 with Nicolai 2014b: 77–84.

[31] Hobden and Tuplin 2012b: 20–39 suggest that he was drawn to the presentation of the past by the fate of Socrates.

in her chapter: "It should be born in mind, when studying Xenophon, that he was not only a Socratic, but also a historian. Hence it would be risky to reduce possible influences on his thought *only* to Socratics or *only* to historians." The *Cyropaedia* has every appearance of being the summation of his life's work: it is both the longest of his writings and contains within it a treatment of the major themes and subjects that are explored in his other works. Not surprisingly, the *Cyropaedia* is just as difficult to categorize (or pigeonhole) as is Xenophon himself.

Why then did Xenophon write? A whole range of motives and concerns, stemming from his experience as a professional soldier, wealthy landowner, and devotee of Socrates, may well have coalesced and combined. Xenophon may have needed to justify his participation in Cyrus the Younger's expedition, he may have wanted to explain his attachment to King Agesilaus of Sparta, he may have felt compelled to defend the memory of his teacher Socrates, and he may have been disillusioned, as was Plato, with the political and social condition of Greece in his own time, and used his various writings both to reflect on what went wrong and to suggest various solutions. But he was not alone. Other elite Greek males had served as officers under Cyrus, been intimate with elite Spartans, been followers of Socrates, and had a passion for horses and hunting. Some of them wrote about their experiences in one genre or another, most of them never penned a word. Something more was at play in Xenophon's decision to create his works – whether he began writing early or late in his long life – and something impelled him to innovate in the production of new genres and in the manipulation of existing ones. The psychological underpinnings of his urge to create may elude us, but we should be grateful that he wrote and wrote extensively. Not every reader, past or present, will see the same strengths and weakness in his abilities as writer and thinker, but one thing is indisputable. Xenophon's influence on western culture from antiquity to the present has been both substantial and sustained, with only a short intermission in the middle of the twentieth century.

One last thing needs to be stressed. At least seven of Socrates' followers wrote Socratic dialogues, but of these only the works of Plato and Xenophon survive.[32] Between Thucydides' unfinished history of the Peloponnesian War (431–404) and Polybius' account of the period 264–146 BC (only partially preserved) hundreds of Greek histories were written, but only Xenophon's *Hellenica* and *Anabasis* are extant. For no other reason than this, Xenophon is an author whom no scholar of antiquity can afford to ignore. Yet, as I have tried to suggest in this introduction, if his importance rested solely on

---

[32] The fragments of the others are succinctly discussed by Döring 2011.

his survival or on his historical influence, then his readership could justifiably be restricted to the circle of his modern academic devotees, whose numbers are, in any case, on the rise. The reason why Xenophon merits a wide readership is the fact (and I believe it is a fact) that his ideas still have the power to engage us in profound and useful ways. The essays in this volume hopefully will contribute towards making that wider readership a reality.

PART I

CONTEXTS

I

JOHN W. I. LEE

Xenophon and his Times

> Xenophon the philosopher, a man who alone out of all philosophers
> adorned philosophy with both words and deeds.
>
> Eunapius (ca. AD 347–414), *Lives of the Sophists* 453

Virtually every volume devoted to Xenophon begins with a discussion of his life and times. The more you investigate Xenophon, though, the more you realize how little is known for certain about his personal history.

One thing we can say: Xenophon wrote prolifically. His works, fourteen in all, often cross genre lines.[1] *Anabasis*, a mix of memoir, leadership manual, and travelogue, records his years (401–399) with the mercenaries whom Cyrus the Younger (ca. 424–401) enlisted to help seize the Achaemenid Persian throne from King Artaxerxes II (405/4–359/8). *Hellenica* examines war and politics in the Greek world from 411 to 362 BC, picking up where the historian Thucydides left off. *Cyropaedia*, an account of how Cyrus of Anshan (r. ca. 550–530) founded the Persian Empire, stirs together biography, romance, and political philosophy.[2] *Agesilaus* offers an idealized portrait of Xenophon's Spartan benefactor, King Agesilaus II (r. 400–359), while *Lacedaimonion Politeia* (*Constitution of the Spartans*) does something similar for the Spartan way of life. Xenophon's mentor Socrates (469–399) is at the heart of a quartet of texts that blend dialogue and narrative: *Memorabilia*, *Oeconomicus*, *Symposium*, and *Apology*. Dialogue appears again in *Hiero*, a fictionalized encounter between the Syracusan tyrant Hiero (r. 478–466) and the poet Simonides of Ceos (ca. 566–465).

---

[1] A fifteenth work once ascribed to Xenophon, *Athenaion Politeia* or *Constitution of the Athenians*, is now attributed to another author. Doubts have also been expressed about Xenophon's authorship of *Cynegeticus* (*On Hunting*): Breitenbach 1967: 1920–1.

[2] Cyrus was king of Anshan in what is today southwestern Iran. We call the Persian Empire Cyrus founded "Achaemenid" because the Persian king Darius I (522–486) claimed that he and Cyrus shared a common ancestor named Achaemenes. For a brief overview of Achaemenid Persia see Waters 2014, for full discussion Briant 2002.

In *Hipparchicus* (*Cavalry Commander*), *De re equestri* (*On Horsemanship*), and *Cynegiticus* (*On Hunting*) Xenophon displays his expertise in warfare, horses, and hunting. And in *Poroi* (*Ways and Means*) he turns his attention to the public finances of Athens.

All Xenophon's works survive. Yet, wresting biographical detail from his writings is difficult. *Anabasis* offers a sometimes day-by-day picture of Xenophon's life during 401–399, but for the decades before and after we get only snippets of personal information. Modern authors often mold their interpretations of these snippets to fit their own preconceptions about Xenophon's character.[3] Some infer his presence at specific events from the vividness of his narrative, especially in *Hellenica*. Others contend that vividness and detail could result as much from Xenophon's access to talkative eyewitnesses as from his being there, for his works include vivid descriptions of events at which he was clearly not present. There is also the challenge – some might say the impossibility – of disentangling Xenophon the historical person from Xenophon the textual character.[4]

To supplement Xenophon's words we must rely on a scattering of other sources. Most important is a short biography written by Diogenes Laertius in the later second or early third century AD, part of a series of philosophers' lives.[5] Diogenes probably relied on a now-lost first-century BC account by the grammarian Demetrius of Magnesia, though he also read some of Xenophon's writing.[6] Diogenes provides more chronological narrative about Xenophon than is usual in his lives, yet some of it is manifestly incorrect.[7] Moreover, Diogenes no less than modern authors shaped his portrait of Xenophon to suit his own purposes.

The Age of Xenophon, ca. 430–350 BC

Diogenes does not say when Xenophon was born, only that he was at his peak (*akme*) in the fourth year of the ninety-fourth Olympiad (401–400 BC). Since the ancients often judged one's *akme* as about age forty and Xenophon does write in *Symposium* that he was present at a party whose dramatic date is 422 BC, some have concluded he was born ca. 440. Others argue that we need not take the *Symposium* passage literally.[8] Likewise, in *Anabasis* the Thracian king Seuthes thinks Xenophon might have a

---

[3] Humble 2002b offers an excellent discussion of modern portrayals of Xenophon.
[4] Flower 2012.
[5] Date of Diogenes: Mejer 1978: 57–8.
[6] Diogenes' sources: Badian 2004.
[7] Hägg 2012: 313–14.
[8] Xen. *Smp.* 1.1, Waterfield 2004: 87.

marriageable daughter but that could just as well mean he looked or seemed older to Seuthes.[9] We can also discount Diogenes' report that some believed Xenophon was at his peak in the eighty-ninth Olympiad (424–420), tying him with older followers of Socrates such as the aristocrat Alcibiades (ca. 450–404/3) and Plato's maternal uncle Critias, for that would put him in his sixties in 401 BC.[10]

Xenophon himself writes in *Anabasis* of being at his peak or prime of strength in 401, in a speech meant to convince Cyrus' mercenaries he is suited for command despite his youth. After taking command he describes himself as one of the youngest of the generals. He also describes a Persian emissary addressing him as a young man (*neaniskos*), which in the military context of the *Anabasis* could mean someone under thirty. Possibly Xenophon was younger than his friend Proxenus, who was about thirty in 401 BC.[11] That would make Xenophon one of the younger men in the army, which included many soldiers over thirty and some over forty-five.[12] While some still prefer an older Xenophon and others go for a much younger one, most scholars these days concur that he was born sometime between 430 and 425 BC.[13]

Diogenes is more precise about when Xenophon died: the first year of the hundred and fifth Olympiad or 360/59 BC.[14] In his *Poroi*, though, Xenophon references the Social War (357–355) between Athens and its allies. And in *Hellenica* he mentions events in Thessaly that may have happened as late as August 353.[15] So, he was alive until the mid to late 350s.

What we might call the Age of Xenophon, then, stretches from about 430 to 350 BC, cutting across the artificial split into "fifth" and "fourth" centuries that standard histories of Classical Greece often employ. His lifetime saw rapid change in mainland Greece and the wider West Asian world. The bipolar divide between Athens and Sparta that had structured Greek politics for generations broke down, to be replaced by multiple regional powers and complex interstate rivalries. "Common peace" and "autonomy"

---

[9] Seuthes: Xen. *Anab.* 7.2.38; Xenophon had no children at the time: Xen. *Anab.* 7.6.34.

[10] Diog. Laert. 2.55, 2.59.

[11] At his peak: Xen. *Anab.* 3.1.25. Youngest of generals: *Anab.* 3.2.37. *Neaniskos*: *Anab.* 2.1.12–13, *Mem.* 1.2.36. Some manuscripts name the young man Theopompus rather than Xenophon, on which see Farrell 2012: 49–51 and Rood 2004a: 321–2. Proxenus: Xen. *Anab.* 2.6.20.

[12] Ages of Cyrus' mercenaries: Lee 2007: 74–6.

[13] Younger Xenophon: Gray 2010b: 8 n. 34 suggests a possible birthdate as late as 420, Farrell 2012: 51–2 suggests 427/6–418/17; see also Nails 2002: 301, Stronk 1995: 3–4.

[14] Diog. Laert. 2.56.

[15] Social War: Xen. *Por.* 4.40, 5.9, 5.12. Thessaly: Xen. *Hell.* 6.4.33–7, Green 2010: 493, Tuplin 1993: 30.

became political buzzwords, alongside the reality of more intense, more professionalized warfare. Light troops and cavalry became ever more important, and mercenaries became ordinary sights even in the Spartan army. Exiles remained a source of political instability, while wealth concentration and economic inequality increased.[16]

During Xenophon's life, Athens suffered defeat at Spartan hands, the loss of its empire, and civil war, then managed gradually to recover a modicum of power and prosperity before again losing much of it. Xenophon saw Sparta rise to hegemony over Greece only to find its supremacy continually challenged abroad, while at home Spartan society faced serious demographic problems. He served with the Spartan army and became close with the Spartan king Agesilaus. He witnessed Thebes rise to new heights as it defeated a Spartan army in battle and invaded the Peloponnese, threatening Sparta itself. He saw federal leagues, which promised to transcend the limitations of individual Greek city states, arise in Boeotia, Arcadia, Thessaly, and the Chalcidice. And, after taking part in the civil war between Cyrus and his older brother Artaxerxes II, Xenophon survived to see Achaemenid Persia, which had for a generation kept out of Greece, become a major force in mainland Greek affairs. Under Artaxerxes, the longest-ruling Achaemenid king, a Persian fleet cruised Aegean waters for the first time in nearly a century; the empire re-established undisputed control over Asia Minor and repeatedly dictated terms to the Greeks. While lack of evidence keeps many details of Xenophon's life uncertain, it is still possible to sketch the outlines of his personal history against the broader backdrop of these momentous developments.

Xenophon the Athenian, ca. 430–401

Few people flying into Athens these days realize it, but as their aircraft descends for a landing over the olive trees and houses of eastern Attica they are passing above the ancestral lands of Xenophon. Ancient Erchia, Xenophon's home deme or district, lies in the Mesogeia plain near modern Spata, north of the international airport. From Erchia it is about twenty kilometers west to the Agora of ancient Athens; the way there skirts the north slopes of Mount Hymettus. Little remains at Erchia today but scattered potsherds and stone blocks.[17]

---

[16] For an overview of "common peace" (*koine eirene*) and "autonomy" (*autonomia*) as slogans see Rhodes 2010. Mercenaries in Spartan army: Xen. *Hell.* 7.5.10. Economic changes: Davies 2007: 357–9, Von Reden 2007: 399–402.

[17] Erchia: Dow 1965: 181–2, Osborne 1985: 192, Vanderpool 1965: 23.

Xenophon, relates Diogenes, was the son of Gryllus of Erchia. The name Xenophon was not uncommon at Athens, but his father's name is rare and was perhaps in origin a nickname ("Porky" or "Grunter").[18] His mother, whose name may have been Diodora, must have been a freeborn Athenian for Xenophon to be a citizen.[19] We know nothing of siblings or other relatives. Nor are we sure Xenophon was born in Erchia, for many Athenians did not reside in their ancestral demes. We can say that Xenophon was younger than his demesman Isocrates, born in 436/5, and about the same age as Plato, born around 429–427. Athenian citizens were divided into ten civic tribes and both Plato's urban deme Collytus and the rural deme Erchia belonged to the same tribe: Aegeis, named after its eponymous hero Aegeus, mythical king of Athens. Xenophon, Plato, and Isocrates thus shared a common civic identity. A deme such as Erchia counted only a few hundred citizens, so Xenophon and Isocrates probably knew each other from childhood. It may be that Xenophon and Plato also met as children, for while tribes were much larger than demes, festivals, civic duties, and other events often brought tribesmen together.

Plato, whose family had been prominent in Athens for centuries, and Isocrates, whose father rose from modest beginnings to become one of the richest men in the city, both came from the wealthiest stratum of Athenian society. Their fathers were liable for liturgies, a form of taxation through which rich men paid for public expenses such as warships and religious festivals.[20] Xenophon's father Gryllus, though, apparently was not wealthy enough to perform a liturgy.

In *Anabasis*, Xenophon mentions owning horses and cavalry armor, most likely an indication that his family kept horses in Athens.[21] Maintaining horses was expensive and many have inferred that Xenophon's father belonged to the second-highest Athenian property class, the *hippeis* or Knights. That did not necessarily make Xenophon naturally anti-democratic. Popular Athenian stereotypes linked horse owning with free-spending, dim-witted aristocrats, yet many prosperous Athenians supported democracy. Cavalry was also glamorous and appealing enough to feature prominently on the public democratic sculpture of the Parthenon frieze. Furthermore,

[18] Xenophon's name: *LGPN* s.v. Ξενοφῶν. Gryllus: *SEG* 17.97 (ca. 350–300 BC), *LGPN* s.v. Γρύλλος, Herchenroeder 2008.

[19] Diodora: Breitenbach 1967: 1571. The name is attested once at Athens, on a late fifth-century lead curse tablet from the Kerameikos: Peek 1957: 59–60 (no. 206).

[20] Plato: Davies 1971: 322–33; Isocrates: Davies 1971: 245–8.

[21] Xen. *An.* 3.3.19. Xenophon explicitly distinguishes the horses he has at his quarters (παρ᾽ ἐμοί: *LSJ* s.v. παρά B.II.2) from others that had belonged to Clearchus' Thracian cavalry and yet others captured from the enemy. Cavalry armor: Xen. *Anab.* 3.4.48; see also *Eq.* 12.1–2, *Mem.* 3.10.

probably in the 440s the Athenians had begun subsidizing the costs of horses and fodder, so less wealthy men could serve in the cavalry.[22] Not until later in Xenophon's life would cavalrymen be seen as especially hostile to democracy.[23] Indeed, Xenophon's own writings reveal a sympathy for democracy that is at odds with the modern stereotype of him as a born oligarch.[24]

Athens at Xenophon's birth was still near its height of power. In 480–479 BC the city had joined with Sparta to defend against an Achaemenid Persian invasion of Greece. Afterwards Sparta turned to isolationism while Athens took over the Delian League, a Greek alliance meant to forestall Persian attack. As the Persian threat receded, the Athenians during the mid-fifth century transformed this league into a maritime empire run for their own benefit. Meanwhile, the Persian Empire, stretching from the Mediterranean coast all the way to central Asia, remained powerful under the long-lived Artaxerxes I (r. 465–424). In the 450s, the Persians suppressed a major revolt in Egypt and crushed an Athenian force sent to aid the rebels. After about 450, open hostilities between Athens and Persia ceased.

Back in Greece, Athenian imperialism made enemies of the Boeotians and their chief city Thebes, and led to outbursts of open war with Sparta. Following a brief rapprochement, tensions with Sparta grew anew in the 430s. By now, democracy had brought Athens decades of internal political stability and prosperity. With their fleet of three hundred war galleys called triremes, the Athenians held a firm grip on an empire that stretched across the Aegean. Imperial tribute paid for the Parthenon and the gleaming chryselephantine statue of Athena. It was with great confidence that Athens went to war with Sparta in 431 BC. This conflict, the Peloponnesian War (431–404), defined the first third of Xenophon's life.

From 431 to 425 the Spartan army invaded Attica every summer. If they were not already living in town, young Xenophon and his family may have moved there for safety.[25] Refugees crowded within Athens's walls and plague followed, killing thousands. After that, word of relatives and friends slain in battle probably arrived with sad frequency. Even if family circumstances sheltered Xenophon from the worst, the war must always have colored his early years. Fortunately the Spartans left Attica each winter. When they left, Xenophon could return to the country, where there was space to ride and hunt. Judging from the superb knowledge of horses he displayed later in

[22] Spence 1993: 10, 164–211.
[23] Farrell 2012: 90–5, Spence 1993: 216–24.
[24] Gish 2012, Kroeker 2009.
[25] Living in town: Xen. Oec. 11.14–18.

life, it is likely that Xenophon learned to ride young. Indeed, we are told his demesman Isocrates rode horses as a boy.[26]

The war continued as Xenophon grew, though neither Athens nor Sparta could gain a decisive edge. A peace of exhaustion in 421 was followed by a gradual slide back into open hostilities. Then, in 415 BC the Athenians decided to attack Syracuse, far away in Sicily. Just before the Athenian fleet sailed, the herms of Athens – religious markers that stood before house doors and temples – were defaced during the night and Alcibiades, the expedition's driving force, was accused of mocking the sacred Eleusinian Mysteries. Nonetheless the expedition went forward. Xenophon, now aged ten to fifteen, would have been old enough to join the crowd that went down to the port of Piraeus to watch the magnificent armada depart.[27]

Alcibiades fled into exile, the Athenians fumbled their best chance to take Syracuse, and in 413 the Spartans re-entered the war. This time they built a fort at Decelea, about twenty kilometers north of Erchia, from which to ravage the Attic countryside year-round. Thousands of slaves escaped to Decelea. Some Athenians, amongst them Isocrates, lost everything. Xenophon's family may have suffered as well, although it would come out of the war still able to maintain horses.[28] By now Xenophon was entering his teens. Possibly he got his first sight of combat as early as 413, helping guard Attica against Spartan raiders. Memories of Decelea certainly stuck with him into old age.[29]

The Sicilian expedition ended in catastrophe for Athens in 413, with thousands of men and hundreds of ships lost. Widespread uprisings against the Athenian Empire ensued. Even privileged allies such as Chios revolted. Worse, the Persian king Darius II (r. 424–405/4), working through his satraps Tissaphernes and Pharnabazus in Asia Minor, began to support Sparta. Persian funds helped Sparta build ships and hire rowers to challenge the Athenian navy, threatening the imported grain supply that kept Athens alive. A misguided attempt, instigated by the still-exiled Alcibiades, to win Persian favor led the Athenians to overthrow their own democracy. From summer 411 to spring 410 a series of oligarchic governments held a shaky grip on Athens.

Sometime between 412 and 407 Xenophon turned eighteen. It was an important milestone, for at this age male Athenians were formally enrolled

[26] Isocrates: Plut. *Mor.* 839c. Farrell 2012: 84 speculates Xenophon might only have learned to ride in Anatolia, but the skill Xenophon shows in *Anab.* 3.4.49 reveals many years' experience.

[27] Thuc. 6.27–30.

[28] Isocrates' property: Isoc. 15.161. Xenophon's horses: Xen. *Anab.* 3.3.19.

[29] Decelea and Athenian cavalry: Thuc. 7.27. Memories: *Por.* 4.25.

as citizens.[30] Five years, though, is a long time for a teenager. If Xenophon was born in 430, he would have been just old enough to participate in the events of 411–410. Some associate Xenophon with the armed youths and young cavalrymen who supported the Four Hundred, one of the oligarchic regimes that ruled Athens in 411–410, but that requires assuming he opposed democracy.[31]

Xenophon probably served in the cavalry even before turning eighteeen; Athens needed every soldier it could get during these years. Details from *Hellenica* may suggest he participated in the Athenian attack on Ephesus in 409, under the general Thrasyllus.[32] Interestingly, *Hellenica* omits a battle near Megara that occurred around the same time, in which Plato's older brothers took part; was it because Xenophon was not there?[33] Thrasyllus went on to join forces with Alcibiades – now rehabilitated and leading Athenian forces – in the Hellespont, not returning home until spring 407.[34] If he indeed accompanied Thrasyllus, Xenophon perhaps also served under Alcibiades, taking part in sieges and plundering forays as well as pitched battle. That might explain the military expertise he displays in *Anabasis*. On the other hand, *Anabasis* gives no sense Xenophon had previously seen the Hellespont. In any case, Thrasyllus returned to Athens ahead of Alcibiades, so Xenophon could have been in the crowd that came down to Piraeus to see Alcibiades briefly return from exile in 407.

It is to these years we might assign a passing remark by the early third-century AD Athenian writer Philostratus, who says Xenophon spent time as a prisoner in Boeotia, during which he heard the philosopher Prodicus of Ceos.[35] Xenophon's works show a familiarity with Prodicus but that does not confirm the story, for Prodicus was no stranger to Athens.[36] Still, a sojourn in Thebes could explain how Xenophon met the Theban Proxenus, whom he describes in *Anabasis* as an old friend. Philostratus presents himself as a careful researcher, but he also wrote in an era when invented traditions about figures such as Xenophon circulated widely.[37] Did Philostratus or one of his sources make up Xenophon's time at Thebes to explain his friendship with Proxenus, or do we trust Philostratus?

---

[30] Rhodes 1981: 496–8.

[31] Youths and cavalry: Thuc. 8.69.4 (compare Xen. *Hell.* 2.3.23), 8.92.6.

[32] Xen. *Hell.* 1.2.1–1.4.10, Anderson 1974a: 18.

[33] Megara: Pl. *Resp.* 368a, *Hell. Oxy.* F4 Chambers (Florence A.1), Diod. 13.65, Green 2010: 223.

[34] On the chronology of this period see Krentz 1989: 11–14, Lazenby 2004: 208–15, Thomas 2009b. I follow the low chronology outlined by Thomas 2009b: 339.

[35] Philostr. *VS* 1.12.

[36] Xen. *Mem.* 2.1.21; Xen. *Smp.* 1.5, 4.62.

[37] Hägg 2012: 322–4.

However much he was out of Athens, Xenophon still had plenty of opportunity to meet Socrates. In Diogenes' telling, Socrates encounters Xenophon in a narrow alley, stretches out a walking stick to bar the way, and quizzes him on where to find various kinds of food.[38] Socrates finally stumps Xenophon by asking where men can become noble and good (*kaloi kagathoi*).[39] "Follow me and learn," Diogenes has Socrates say, after which Xenophon becomes a devoted follower. Whether or not this story is true, and despite the doubts of modern scholars who would dismiss Xenophon simply because he is not Plato, Xenophon seems to have been among the close associates of Socrates in the last decade of the 400s.[40] Diogenes claims Xenophon and Plato were rivals, but his main reason is that they both wrote about Socrates.[41] While Plato never explicitly names Xenophon, Xenophon mentions Plato by name in passing. There is evidence that the two read and responded to each others' writing, though the nature of their literary interactions is much disputed.[42]

Diogenes asserts Xenophon was extremely handsome, which if true may have played a role in his first meeting with Socrates. Although Socrates was famous for controlling his sexual impulses, he did not deny his erotic attraction to youths. Xenophon too recognized the power of same-sex desire. He admired Socrates' abstinence, while allowing that not everyone could live up to the rigorous Socratic ideal.[43] Although his writings stress the dangers of uncontrolled lust, Xenophon acknowledges same-sex relations as a normal part of life, including military life. He relates how same-sex desire or relationships sometimes distracted soldiers from duty, but also notes how they inspired courage.[44] And, in *Memorabilia* Xenophon depicts himself – or at least the textual character bearing his name – becoming aroused at the possibility of kissing a beautiful youth.[45]

The war went on. In 407, Darius II sent his teenaged son Cyrus the Younger out to coordinate Achaemenid activities on the western frontier. Athens was now fighting for survival. In summer 406 the Spartans defeated the Athenian fleet, trapping the survivors at Mytilene on Lesbos. The Athenians scraped together a rescue force, melting down gold statues

---

[38] Diog. Laert. 2.6.48; compare Xen. *Mem.* 4.4.5.

[39] On the term καλὸς κἀγαθός see Donlan 1973, Pomeroy 1994: 259, Roscalla 2004.

[40] Dillery 2001: 5–6, Gray 1998: 2–6, Gray 2010b: 8–10, Humble 2002b: 72–4.

[41] Diog. Laert. 2.57, 3.34.

[42] Critique of *Cyropaedia*: Plat. *Laws* 694c–695b. Xenophon names Plato: *Mem.* 3.6.1. Literary interactions: Danzig 2002, Danzig 2005, Waterfield 2004.

[43] Hindley 1999: 85.

[44] Distracted: Xen. *Hell.* 4.8.18, 5.4.57; *Anab.* 4.1.14–15, 5.8.4. Courage: *Hell.* 4.8.39, 5.4.33; *Anab.* 7.4.7–9; Hindley 2004.

[45] Kissing: Xen. *Mem.* 1.3.8–14.

from the Acropolis for an emergency coinage and conscripting slave rowers. Xenophon notes that even some of the cavalry – was he among
them? – took ship as rowers or marines. Near the Arginusae Islands east
of Lesbos the Athenians managed a victory, but a storm afterwards forced
the Athenians to abandon the crews of their own damaged ships. Probably
several thousand men perished.[46]

Two of the fleet's eight generals did not bother returning to Athens. The
others came back to rough justice: the Athenian Council's inquiry degener-
ated into a mass trial before the Assembly. Since by any reckoning Xenophon
was now of citizen age, he may well have attended the Assembly meetings
where the matter was debated, an angry scene of shouting and threats as he
describes it. Both Xenophon and Plato remembered that Socrates, one of the
Assembly's fifty-member presiding committee (*prytaneis*) and perhaps even
its chair (*epistatês*) for the day, refused to do anything contrary to the law
despite the uproar.[47] Nonetheless all the generals were found guilty and the
six who came back were executed.

Arginusae was only a temporary reprieve. Late in 405 BC, the Spartan
commander Lysander caught the entire Athenian fleet on the beach at
Aegospotami in the Hellespont. Only nine of the 180 Athenian ships escaped,
one reaching Athens after dark with word of the calamity. Xenophon may
have heard the lamentations spreading up from Piraeus as people learned
the news; he tells us no one in Athens slept that night.[48] The city resolved
to hold on, but the Spartans set up a blockade and food began to run low.
Early in 404 the starving Athenians surrendered. A Spartan fleet sailed into
Piraeus, exiled oligarchs returned, and the city's walls were demolished – to
the music of flute girls, writes Xenophon, again perhaps a detail from his
own memory.[49]

Thebes and Corinth wanted Athens destroyed. Instead the Spartans
installed thirty commissioners, including Plato's uncle Critias, to chart the
city's future. The Thirty soon turned to tyranny. They got garrison troops
from Sparta, disarmed most citizens, and arbitrarily executed as many as
1500 people. Democratic insurgents gathered at the mountain fortress
of Phyle, beat back troops sent to quell them, then reclaimed Piraeus for
the democrats. After fierce street fighting in Piraeus in which Critias was

[46] Arginusae: Lazenby 2004: 227–34.
[47] Xen. *Hell.* 1.5.15; Xen. *Mem.* 1.1.18, 4.2.2; Plat. *Apol.* 32b–c; Krentz 1989: 163–4,
Rhodes 1981: 533–4. The fifty *prytaneis* were chosen by lot from one of the ten tribes
and served for a month. The *epistatês* held office only for a single night and day.
[48] Xen. *Hell.* 2.2.3. Compare the sleepless night after the execution of the Cyrean
generals: Xen. *Anab.* 3.1.3.
[49] Xen. *Hell.* 2.2.21–3.

killed, the Spartan king Pausanias intervened and brokered a settlement. In spring 403 Athens returned to democracy and a general amnesty was declared, though some supporters of the Thirty went to live apart at Eleusis in Athenian territory.[50]

Most scholars these days believe Xenophon served in the cavalry under the Thirty and that he sympathized with their cause. It is true that the cavalry were strongly associated with the Thirty and that *Hellenica* spends a lot of time on the activities of the cavalry.[51] Xenophon, though, portrays the Thirty very negatively and depicts the cavalry as ambivalent.[52] He shows Critias forcing cavalrymen and hoplites to vote for the execution of fellow citizens from Eleusis, and describes how some cavalrymen objected when their commander cut the throats of prisoners.[53] Perhaps he is just covering his tracks. Yet, he need not have been a wholehearted oligarch.[54] Civil wars are filled with people who fight for causes or leaders they do not believe in. Family obligations, loyalty to cavalry comrades, or plain reluctance to seem cowardly could have kept Xenophon in the ranks just as much as sincere political belief.

Xenophon emphasizes how well the amnesty worked, even excusing the democracy's forcible reincorporation of Eleusis in 401. The amnesty was indeed remarkable, for Athens never again saw such an oligarchy. Even so, horsemen who had sided with the Thirty suffered financial penalties, and when in 399 the Spartans demanded three hundred riders for service in Anatolia, the Athenians sent men who had fought for the Thirty. Xenophon writes that the people thought it would be a good thing if these men went abroad and perished.[55] Moreover, Athens in the wake of military defeat and civil war faced an uncertain future.[56] Its population was perhaps half or two thirds of what it had been at Xenophon's birth, the Attic countryside was wrecked, and the city remained beholden to Spartan power. Xenophon was probably not the only young Athenian wondering what to do next.

---

[50] On the Thirty see Krentz 1982.
[51] *Ath. Pol.* 38.2; Rhodes 1981: 458.
[52] Xenophon on the Thirty: Krentz 1982: 145, Tuplin 1993: 43–7.
[53] Forced to vote: Xen. *Hell.* 2.4.9. Prisoners killed: Xen. *Hell.* 2.4.26.
[54] It has even been suggested Xenophon could have fought against the Thirty. After Critias was killed, people apparently defected to the democrats (Diod. 14.33.4) and some cavalry fought for the democrats (Xen. *Hell.* 2.4.25).
[55] Penalties: Lys. 16.6, 26.10, Spence 1993: 217–18. Three hundred cavalry: Xen. *Hell.* 3.1.4. Krentz 1995: 159 notes this figure might represent half the horsemen who served under the Thirty.
[56] Letter: Xen. *Anab.* 3.1.4. Proxenus: Xen. *Anab.* 1.2.11, 2.1.10, 2.6.16–20.

The Mercenaries of Cyrus, 401–399

The rest of Xenophon's life began with a letter from his *xenos* or ritualized guest friend, Proxenus of Thebes.[57] Athens and Thebes had been enemies during the Peloponnesian War, so how did Xenophon and Proxenus become *xenoi*? As noted earlier, perhaps Xenophon was a prisoner in Boeotia during the war. Another possibility is that they inherited the relationship, for guest friendships could cross generations. Proxenus, a pupil of the rhetorician Gorgias of Leontini who had taken service with the Achaemenid prince Cyrus, had an offer for Xenophon: join Cyrus' expedition against rebellious Pisidian highlanders in Anatolia. Cyrus, said Proxenus, was worth more to him than his native Thebes. If Xenophon came along he too could become a friend of Cyrus.[58]

In a famous *Anabasis* passage, Xenophon recalls how he consulted Socrates, who, worried that joining Cyrus might get him in trouble at Athens, told him to go to Delphi.[59] There, instead of asking the oracle whether or not he should go, Xenophon asked to which of the gods he should sacrifice and pray in order to make the journey worthily and, having done well, to get home safely. When Xenophon returned to Athens, Socrates chided him that he had not really consulted the oracle, but made up his mind to go and then asked the god the best way of going. Some would take this story as evidence Xenophon learned nothing from Socrates, but it is better read as an older and wiser Xenophon looking back on his impulsive younger self. Exactly what motivated him to accept Proxenus' invitation remains unknown, but we are fairly sure he was unmarried at the time and had no family to keep him at home.[60] Xenophon sailed from Athens to join Cyrus early in 401 BC. It would be decades before he returned. He would never see Socrates again.

Unbeknownst to Proxenus and Xenophon, Cyrus' real goal was to unseat his older brother, King Artaxerxes II (405/4–359/8). Darius II had groomed Artaxerxes as his successor, but also displayed early confidence in Cyrus, sending him out west in 407 BC as regional overlord. Late in 405 Darius called the two to his deathbed, perhaps reminding them that he had fought his brothers for power and admonishing them not to do likewise. Barely had Darius breathed his last and Artaxerxes become king, though, than the brothers were at odds. Xenophon says Tissaphernes falsely accused Cyrus of

57 For more on the Thirty and their aftermath, see Wolpert 2002, Shear 2011.
58 "Worth more to him": could this suggest Proxenus was an exile from Thebes? If so, he and Xenophon could have become friends in Athens. It is worth noting that Isocrates also studied with Gorgias of Leontini.
59 Xen. *Anab.* 3.1.4–10.
60 Unmarried: Anderson 1974a: 162–3. For another view see Pomeroy 1994: 3.

conspiracy; others claim Cyrus did really try to kill Artaxerxes.[61] Whatever the truth, their mother Parysatis intervened and Cyrus returned to Sardis, where he began plotting to usurp the throne.

Cyrus' plan included recruiting more than twelve thousand Greek and non-Greek mercenaries to supplement his satrapal troops. Achaemenid commanders had long employed mercenaries, but never before in such numbers. Proxenus brought two thousand men to join Cyrus at Sardis, where Xenophon caught up with them just as they were setting out, ostensibly against the Pisidians.[62] Xenophon says he went along as neither general nor captain nor ordinary soldier, but he clearly got to know Proxenus' officers and met Cyrus himself.

Across Anatolia the army marched, as the mercenaries became increasingly wary of Cyrus' true aims. A few deserted, but the prince kept the rest going with new cover stories and promises of extra pay. Finally, at Thapsacus on the upper Euphrates River, Cyrus revealed the true objective. More promises – a year's extra pay in silver! – got the mercenaries across the Euphrates. Then they headed downriver towards Babylon, where Artaxerxes waited with his army.

The two brothers and their armies met at Cunaxa northwest of Babylon, sometime in August or September 401. Cyrus and Artaxerxes got within spear's reach and Cyrus wounded Artaxerxes before being killed. The mercenaries swept their part of the field, but the rest of Cyrus' army disintegrated. In the days that followed Cyrus' erstwhile Persian supporters began to reconcile with Artaxerxes, who soon held the upper hand. The mercenary commanders, now led by the Spartan Clearchus, tried negotiating their way out. The Persians invited Clearchus, Proxenus, and the other generals to a conference, then seized and executed them. That might have been the end of it, but Xenophon, as he tells it, helped the army rally and select new generals, amongst them himself.

Unable to return along the Euphrates, the mercenaries fought their way up the Tigris valley, then slogged across rugged mountains and frozen plains to reach the Black Sea near Trapezus early in 400 BC. About a quarter of them perished along the way.[63] West along the Pontic coast they went on foot and by sea, their numbers steadily dwindling as generals and men fell to squabbling amongst themselves. Xenophon, offered sole command, declined the post.[64] The army held together just barely, reaching Byzantium in autumn 400.

[61] Xen. *Anab.* 1.1.3–5; Plut. *Artax.* 2.3–5, 3.3–6.
[62] Xen. *Anab.* 1.2.3, 3.1.4, 3.1.8–9.
[63] Xen. *Anab.* 1.7.10, 5.3.3.
[64] Xen. *Anab.* 6.1.21–31.

Xenophon claims he wanted to return to Athens as early as summer 400, and he actually sailed out from Byzantium late in 400 before deciding to rejoin the mercenaries, who now went to work for the Thracian dynast Seuthes.[65] After a cold winter in Thrace, he again planned to go home, but again ended up sticking with the army. Along with about five thousand other survivors, Xenophon returned to coastal Anatolia in spring 399. Probably he did not know that back in Athens his mentor Socrates was about to go on trial. Socrates was executed in late May or early June; how long afterwards Xenophon got the news is unknown.[66]

If Athens defined Xenophon's early life, the years 401–399 shaped his outlook for decades afterward. To begin with, marching with Cyrus gave Xenophon in-depth exposure to the Persians and their empire. Greeks had gone into the Achaemenid realm before, but few – notably Ctesias of Cnidus, court physician to Artaxerxes II – had such a sustained opportunity to interact with Persians from the highest levels of Achaemenid society. Through them Xenophon gained access to the wealth of information on Persian culture, traditions, and practices that shows up in his writings.[67]

Furthermore, during these years Xenophon got to know men from across West Asia: Greeks and non-Greeks, exiles, ex-slaves, even a former professional boxer. There were a few Athenians in the ranks but half the Cyreans, as the mercenaries of Cyrus came to be called, were from rugged Arcadia and coastal Achaea in the Peloponnese. Some of the close comrades Xenophon names in Anabasis, such as Eurylochus of Lusi, who saved his life in battle, and the loyal captain Agasias of Stymphalus, were Arcadians. He also emphasizes his good relations with the Spartan Cheirisophus, even presenting the pair ribbing each other about hometown customs.[68] Other men he recognizes as brave commanders became rivals by the end of the expedition.[69] One of them, Sophaenetus of Stymphalus, may have composed a competing account of the march (about which more later). Xenophon's diverse comrades opened his eyes to the world beyond Athens, a world in which humble mercenaries and even slaves could count as good and noble.[70]

Religion was another key part of Xenophon's Cyrean life. He made sure to perform the proper rituals, regularly looked to the gods for guidance, and

[65] Return home: Xen. Anab. 6.2.15, 7.1.4, 7.1.8, 7.1.39, 7.6.11, 7.7.57.
[66] Socrates' trial took place in the Athenian month Thargelion (late April–late May) and about thirty days separated his conviction and execution: Plat. Phaed. 58a–c, Xen. Mem. 4.8.2.
[67] Hirsch 1985, Parpola 2003, Tuplin 2004b.
[68] Cheirisophus: Xen. Anab. 4.6.2–3, 4.6.10–21.
[69] For example, Callimachus of Parrhasia: Xen. Anab. 4.7.8–12, 6.2.9.
[70] Xen. Anab. 4.1.19; Oec. 14.9–10, Pomeroy 1994: 259, 321–2.

even took his dreams seriously.[71] It is common to dismiss this religiosity as "conventional" or "traditional," as if Xenophon's piety rendered him somehow less intelligent or admirable, or to see religion as a tool used to manipulate superstitious common soldiers. Yet religion helped Xenophon and the Cyreans endure weather and hunger, cope with death, and make sense of uncertainty. If Xenophon was as religious as he portrays himself, his belief deserves our understanding, even respect, as a genuine human response.[72] Indeed, the extraordinary experience of surviving the march to Babylonia and back may have led Xenophon to emphasize religion (and its connections with good leadership) in a way that might not have happened had he stayed in Athens. Another way to think of it: secular academia often prefers Thucydides, but in the context of his age Xenophon was not exceptionally religious.

Agesilaus and Exile, 399-ca. 394

Anabasis ends with the return to the west coast of Anatolia, today western Turkey, and Xenophon picks up events in *Hellenica*. After the sharp focus of the *Anabasis* years, the next phase of his life emerges only in blurred outlines.

From 399 to 394, Xenophon served in western Anatolia under a series of Spartan commanders, campaigning against the Persian satraps Tissaphernes and Pharnabazus. At first Xenophon led the surviving Cyreans, but after King Agesilaus came out to take charge of Sparta's forces in 396 he moved to another role, perhaps helping improve Agesilaus' cavalry.[73] Sparta's quest to "liberate" western Anatolia from the Achaemenids proved quixotic. Agesilaus won battles, but never truly controlled anything. Meanwhile, Sparta's disgruntled allies Thebes and Corinth joined forces with Athens to challenge Spartan hegemony. In spring 394 Agesilaus and his army had to march back to Greece and confront the threat; Xenophon went too.[74]

That August, near the Boeotian town of Coronea, Agesilaus narrowly defeated an allied Greek army that included Athenians. Xenophon was there, although whether he actually bore arms against his countrymen is debated.[75] Agesilaus then headed to Delphi to dedicate the spoils of victory.

---

[71] Sacrifices: Xen. *Anab.* 5.6.16, 5.6.29, 7.8.1–6. Divine guidance: Xen. *Anab.* 6.1.22–4, 6.2.15, 7.6.44. Dreams: Xen. *Anab.* 3.1.12, 4.3.8, 6.1.22.

[72] On Xenophon and religion see Bowden 2004, Flower 2012: 203–16 and 2016 Parker 2004.

[73] Xen. *Hell.* 3.2.7, 3.4.20, Diod. 14.37.1; Krentz 1995: 189–90.

[74] Xen. *Anab.* 5.3.6; *Hell.* 4.2.1–4.

[75] Coronea: Xen. *Hell.* 4.3.15–20, Plut. *Ages.* 18.2. We can place the battle soon after August 14, 394 BC thanks to the partial solar eclipse Xenophon mentions (*Hell.* 3.4.10).

Probably at this time Xenophon made his own offering at Delphi, using his portion of the tithe to Apollo that the Cyrean generals had set aside nearly six years before on the Black Sea coast. Inscribing the votive with his and Proxenus' names, he dedicated it in the Treasury of the Athenians.[76] The decisive battle had already taken place on the other side of the Aegean, where the Persians destroyed the Spartan fleet off Cnidus in southwest Anatolia. Agesilaus had gotten this news just before Coronea but lied to his army by proclaiming a Spartan victory. The truth could not long be concealed. Without a fleet, Spartan hopes of controlling Anatolia were finished. While the Persians reasserted their hold there, the Spartans faced one battle after another in mainland Greece. This struggle, called the Corinthian War because much of the fighting took place around Corinth, would drag on until 386.

By then, Xenophon had been exiled from Athens. When and why has been endlessly debated. Socrates had worried that associating with Cyrus might get Xenophon in trouble at Athens, and many ancients took that worry as the actual reason. Joining Cyrus, though, could not have been the cause of Xenophon's exile, for he was still planning to go home in spring 399.[77] Diogenes says Xenophon was sentenced to exile for "Laconizing" – siding with Sparta – but the specific charges are unknown, and Xenophon's own writings reveal he was not mindlessly pro-Spartan.[78] Since Athens was formally still allied with Sparta until 395, Xenophon may not have been exiled until 394–393.[79]

The Scillus Years, ca. 392–371

Xenophon perhaps stayed in the field with Agesilaus for some years after Coronea, but by the late 390s the Spartans had given him a new home at Scillus just south of Olympia in the Peloponnese. The location was no accident: Scillus lay in the strategic region of Triphylia, which the Spartans had recently wrested from neighboring Elis.[80] Within a few days' walk lay the hometowns of many Cyreans. Xenophon may have found himself amidst a network of fellow veterans. By now he also had a wife, Philesia, and two sons, Gryllus and Diodorus.[81] We know nothing of Philesia's origins or how

[76] Delphi: Xen. *Hell.* 4.3.21, *Anab.* 5.3.5; see also Badian 2004: 41, Tuplin 1987: 64–6.
[77] Xen. *Anab.* 3.1.4, Diog. Laert. 2.58, Dio Chrys. *Or.* 8.1, Paus. 5.6.5.
[78] Diog. Laert. 2.51, but cf. 2.58. Not pro-Spartan: Tuplin 1993: 41.
[79] Humble 2002b: 81–2, Badian 2004: 42. Farrell 2012: 95–108 offers an exhaustive discussion.
[80] Scillus: Xen. *Anab.* 5.3.7–13, Paus. 5.6.4–6, Nielsen 2004: 545–6. Triphylia: Nielsen 2004: 540–1.
[81] Diog. Laert. 2.52.

she met Xenophon. Her name is attested at Athens but is not distinctively Athenian, and that her sons later served in the Athenian cavalry does not prove she was an Athenian citizen.[82] Gryllus and Diodorus were born after 399 and probably before Xenophon arrived at Scillus. Possibly Xenophon left his wife and children at the Spartan base of Ephesus while he was campaigning in Anatolia.[83] Later authors claim the boys were sent to Sparta for education, but even if the story is true it seems unlikely they went through the full Spartan upbringing.[84]

Scillus' proximity to Olympia must have brought Xenophon visitors and probably made it easy for him to send and receive correspondence. It is tempting to wonder how much contact he had with Plato, who did a fair amount of traveling in these years, or with Isocrates, who had become a hugely successful rhetorician back in Athens.[85] He certainly got a visit from Megabyzus, the *neokoros* (temple warden) of Ephesian Artemis, who brought with him the tithe Xenophon had deposited at Ephesus before marching back with Agesilaus. With the money Xenophon bought a rural estate for Artemis, building an altar and temple in emulation of the great temple at Ephesus. In *Anabasis* he gives an idyllic description of the fertile landscape, with meadows, tree-covered hills, a stream, and abundant wildlife, and of the festivals and hunting the whole community enjoyed.[86]

While Xenophon found respite at Scillus, Sparta's wars continued. Athens, its walls and fleet rebuilt, and the Theban-led federal state of Boeotia were Sparta's main rivals. The Spartans reached for Persian support, resulting in the King's Peace of 386, which recognized Persian authority over the Greeks of Anatolia.[87] The remaining Greeks were supposed to be "autonomous," a term which immediately became the cause of dispute. The King's Peace was a triumph for Artaxerxes II and set a pattern for repeated Achaemenid

---

[82] Philesia: *SEG* 21.855 (fourth century BC) attests a Philesia at Rhamnous in Attica, as does *Agora* XVII.712 (Bradeen 1974: 135–6), a fourth-century funeral stele from the Athenian Agora. Interestingly, *SEG* 11.1174b (second century BC) attests a Philesia at Letrinoi in Elis, about 15 km northwest of Scillus. See also Anderson 1974a: 162–3. Letrinoi: Xen. *Hell.* 3.2.25, 3.2.30, 4.2.16; Paus. 6.22.8–11.

[83] Wife and children: compare Xen. *Anab.* 1.4.8.

[84] Plut. *Ages.* 20.2, Diog. Laert. 2.54; Humble 2004b. Could Gryllus and Diodorus have been old enough to be among the foreign companions or foster children (*trophimoi xenoi*: Xen. *Hell.* 5.3.9) who volunteered for military service with Sparta in 381?

[85] Isocrates' *Panegyricus*, written in 380, references the Cyreans, as do several of his later works: Isoc. *Paneg.* 4.146–8, 5.89–96, *Letter* 9.9.

[86] Megabyzus and the sacred precinct: Xen. *Anab.* 5.3.6–13. Megabyzus came for the Olympics, but which one is uncertain; perhaps 392 or 388? Hunting: Xen. *Cyn.* 13.18 alludes to women hunting; one wonders whether Philesia hunted, as Persian noblewomen did. For more on Scillus, see Tuplin 2004b.

[87] King's Peace: Xen. *Hell.* 5.1.31.

intervention in Greek affairs in the 370s and 360s. Still, Artaxerxes had bigger problems elsewhere. Egypt had rebelled around 400 BC, and Artaxerxes could not recover it despite trying in the 380s and 370s.[88] Many Greek mercenaries served in these Egyptian wars. Even Agesilaus found himself there at the end of his life, working for one Egyptian king then another.[89] Egypt remained independent when Artaxerxes II died in 359/8, and only in 343/2 did his son Artaxerxes III (r. 359/8–338) retake it.

Back in Greece, Sparta used "autonomy" as an excuse to consolidate power: breaking up the Boeotian league (386), dismembering neighboring Mantinea (385), and subduing Olynthus in northern Greece (382–379). En route north in 382, a Spartan commander took it on himself to seize Thebes, an action the Spartan government confirmed and Xenophon severely criticized.[90] Sparta now stood at its acme, but not for long. In winter 379/8 Theban patriots liberated their city and refounded the Boeotian league, now more democratic and more Theban-dominated. The next spring the Athenians founded a new naval confederacy, attracting allies by abjuring the garrisons and tribute that had marked the empire of Xenophon's youth.[91]

The Spartans sent armies against Boeotia and ships into the Aegean. But, off Naxos in 376 the Athenians defeated the Spartan fleet.[92] Worse came on land, where the Thebans under their leaders Epaminondas and Pelopidas were developing new battle formations and tactics. At Leuctra in Boeotia during summer 371 the Thebans inflicted a stunning defeat on the Spartans, killing King Cleombrotus and up to a third of the entire Spartan citizenry.[93] The next year the Arcadians, led by a refounded Mantinea, broke with Sparta. The Arcadians created a federal state of their own, built an entirely new capital city at Megalopolis only 50 kilometers northwest of Sparta, and allied with the Thebans. The Thebans then repeatedly invaded the Peloponnese. They liberated the Messenian helots whose labor had underpinned the Spartan system for centuries, and helped the Messenians found a new capital city, Messene. The Theban Pelopidas even won the favor of Artaxerxes.[94] Sparta's day was done.

---

[88] On the Achaemenids and Egypt see Ruzicka 2012.

[89] Xen. Ages. 2.28–31; Plut. Ages. 36–40.

[90] Thebes: Xen. Hell. 5.2.29, 5.3.5–6, 5.4.1.

[91] Xenophon never describes the foundation of the league. For an overview of the league see Buckler 2003.

[92] Naxos: Xen. Hell. 5.4. 61. Buckler 2003: 247–9.

[93] Leuctra: Xen. Hell. 6.4.4–15. Xenophon never mentions that Thebans had already beaten Spartans in a skirmish at Tegyra in 375 (Plut. Pel. 17).

[94] Xenophon says nothing about the foundations of Megalopolis and Messene. Pelopidas: Xen. Hell. 7.5.33–7.

At Scillus, Xenophon had kept track of events through the 380s and 370s. During this time he had also begun writing. When he wrote what, for whom he wrote, whether he worked from notes or a diary – especially for *Anabasis* – whether individual works were composed as a whole or in pieces, when and why he revised or rewrote, and how his works circulated are all subjects of discussion.[95] There are a few secure points: *Agesilaus* records the king's death, so it must have been finished after 360/59. *Hellenica* mentions the Thessalian dynast Tisiphonus, active ca. 357–353. The last book of *Cyropaedia* refers to a Persian satraps' rebellion in 362/1.[96] On the other hand, *Lacedaimonion Politeia* is variously dated to the late 390s, 378–377, and to the 360s or early 350s.[97]

Agesilaus and *Hellenica* show mutual influence, but it is hard to tell which was worked into the other. Possibly *Agesilaus* was written at least before the second part of *Hellenica*.[98] The first part of *Hellenica*, up to the end of the Peloponnesian War, was written earlier, perhaps in the mid–380s; the rest in sections during the 360s and 350s.[99] *Anabasis* perhaps appeared in the interim, in the early 360s; perhaps earlier written or oral versions circulated in the network of Cyrean veterans around Scillus.[100] Xenophon may have written to correct other writers' misrepresentations. His old rival Sophaenetus of Stymphalus, for example, is said to have written an *Anabasis* of his own. And in *Hellenica*, Xenophon refers to an account of the Cyreans written by Themistogenes of Syracuse: was this a pseudonym for Xenophon himself, or the name of an actual author whose work does not survive?[101]

With Xenophon's Socratic writings, particularly *Apology* and *Symposium*, there is also the question of date relative to Plato's works. Plato is often assumed to have written first, with Xenophon's writings following, perhaps sometime in the 380s or 370s, but some have argued the opposite.[102] If so, *Symposium* could have been written as early as the 390s. *Memorabilia*

---

[95] Thomas 2009a: xxii–xxiii offers an accessible summary of one set of views about the order of composition, with references to variant positions. Notes or diary: Cawkwell 2004: 54–6.

[96] Agesilaus: Xen. *Ages.* 10.3, 11.15. Tisiphonus: Xen. *Hell.* 6.4.35–7. Satraps' revolt: Xen. *Cyr.* 8.8.4.

[97] Cartledge 2009: 348, Lipka 2002: 9–13, Thomas 2009a: xxiv.

[98] Thomas 2009a: xxiii–xxiv, Tuplin 1993: 30.

[99] *Hellenica*: Badian 2004: 43–51, Thomas 2009a: xxxiv, Tuplin 1993: 29–33. *Anabasis*: Cawkwell 2004: 47–8.

[100] Kelly 1996 suggests the possibility of oral transmission and small private reading groups, but in a context that disparages Xenophon as a stereotypical close-minded aristocrat.

[101] Themistogenes: for a variety of views see Pitcher 2014, Flower 2012: 53–5.

[102] Relationship between the two *Symposia*: Danzig 2005.

may refer obliquely to the Spartan defeat at Leuctra in 371, meaning that Xenophon completed or revised the text after that battle.[103]

Athenian Again, ca. 371–350

Xenophon did not do all his writing at Scillus, for after Leuctra the Eleans reclaimed Triphylia. Pausanias (a late second-century AD travel writer) claims the Eleans pardoned Xenophon after a trial and let him stay at Scillus, but Diogenes says he fled with his family to Corinth.[104] Diogenes also says the Athenians pardoned Xenophon.[105] Since some of his later works, notably *Hipparchicus* and *Poroi*, focus on hometown issues of the late 360s and 350s, he may well have visited Athens. Although any family property in Erchia had probably long since been sold, it is not impossible Xenophon had maintained connections with relatives or friends during the long years of his exile – one wonders again about contacts with Plato and Isocrates. Diogenes and Pausanias agree that Xenophon's sons served in the Athenian cavalry in the late 360s.

The last years of Xenophon's life brought Greece a dizzying succession of shifting alliances. Theban military supremacy led the Athenians to support Sparta and to renew their old imperialistic ways. By the mid–360s Athens and Thebes were at war and the Thebans were trying to expand into the Aegean. The Thebans also attempted to gain influence in Thessaly and Macedon, but Pelopidas was killed in Thessaly. The only lasting result of the push north was that a young Philip of Macedon spent time as a hostage in Thebes, where he likely observed Theban military practices. In the Peloponnese the Arcadians, Eleans, Achaeans, and others took turns fighting for Thebes, against Thebes, against Sparta, and amongst each other. The Olympics of 364 were interrupted mid-pentathlon, as the Eleans and Arcadians fought a battle within the sacred precinct, the Arcadians tearing up the wooden bleachers to build barricades.[106] In 362 Epaminondas and the Thebans again invaded the Peloponnese, assaulting Sparta itself before being turned back. At Mantinea the Thebans met an army of Spartans, Athens, Eleans, and Mantineans; Arcadians and mercenaries stood on both sides. Epaminondas' innovative tactics won the battle, but the Theban leader fell mortally wounded.[107]

[103] Xen. *Mem.* 3.5.
[104] Xen. *Hell.* 6.5.2, Paus. 5.6.6, Diog. Laert. 2.53.
[105] Athenian pardon: Diog. Laert. 2.59.
[106] Xen. *Hell.* 7.4.27–32.
[107] Mantinea: Xen. *Hell.* 7.5.19–25, Diod. 15.84–9.

Xenophon ends his *Hellenica* with the battle of Mantinea, commenting that "there was more uncertainty and disturbance after the battle than there had been before."[108] He does not mention that Mantinea was also a personal loss: his son Gryllus, serving with the Athenian cavalry, died in a skirmish just before the decisive clash.[109] In one final twist to Xenophon's eventful life, his fallen son became a public hero. The Mantineans paid for Gryllus' funeral and set up a sculpted stele in his honor.[110] Cavalry made a comeback in popularity at Athens.[111] Later, perhaps as late as the 340s, a painting in the Painted Stoa at Athens depicted Gryllus actually wounding Epaminondas.[112] By the time Pausanias traveled Greece nearly five centuries later, even the Thebans agreed with this story, although the Mantineans and Spartans had their own versions.[113]

Xenophon lived to see Philip II become king of Macedon in 360/59, but perhaps he paid more attention to the news the next year, when Artaxerxes III, son of the Artaxerxes he had fought to dethrone so many years ago at Cunaxa, became Great King. As the Greek cities staggered on into the 350s, Xenophon saw Athens again lose power over its allies in the Social War of 357–355, after which he wrote his last datable work, *Poroi*, with recommendations on how Athens could restore its battered finances. He was dead by the late 350s, at Corinth says Diogenes, though in the second century AD locals at Scillus showed Pausanias "the tomb of Xenophon."[114] His tribesmen from childhood, Plato and Isocrates, survived him. Plato died around 347; Isocrates made it to 338.

The Limits of Biography

Every generation writes its own Xenophons. British writers used to cram him into the stereotypical molds of the retired brigadier, country squire, or dunderheaded Colonel Blimp. In the United States there are visions of Xenophon as inspired amateur, citizen-soldier, or symbol of manifest destiny and imperialism. My interpretation of Xenophon's life is likewise shaped by my own circumstances and experiences. For someone raised on Confucian

---

[108] Xen. *Hell.* 7.5.27 (transl. Marincola).
[109] Xen. *Hell.* 7.5.17.
[110] Funeral: Paus. 8.11.6. Stele: Paus. 8.9.5, 8.11.6. Pausanias does not say he saw the tomb of Gryllus at Mantinea: was he buried at Athens, Corinth, Scillus, or elsewhere?
[111] Spence 1993: 224–6.
[112] Painted Stoa: Paus. 1.3.4, 9.15.5; Plut. *Mor.* 346b–e, Plin. *HN* 35.129, Humble 2008. The painting proved so popular a copy was made at Mantinea: Paus. 8.9.8.
[113] Paus. 8.11.6.
[114] Diog. Laert. 2.56, Paus. 5.6.6.

values, Xenophon's emphasis on proper ritual and behavior carries an appealing familiarity. Marrying into a farming, hunting, riding family has given me a deep appreciation for aspects of Xenophon's writing that are generally foreign to U.S. academia. And my understanding of Xenophon has been shaped over the past decade by reading him with student veterans, women and men who like Xenophon saw war in Mesopotamia, who have returned home physically yet sometimes still find themselves exiles metaphorically, their military service setting them apart from the carefree innocence of their classmates' college lives.

Realizing how little we know for certain about Xenophon's personal history is but one element of the general reassessment of Xenophon that has occurred over the past few decades. Instead of the stereotyped aristocrat, Laconophile, and country gentleman we now have a much more nuanced Xenophon to consider. Above all, realizing the uncertainties of his biography reminds us that if we cannot pin down Xenophon the individual, we are fortunate that so much of his writing has survived. His many and varied works, rather than his person, are the true focus of this volume.

Further Reading

On Xenophon's personal history see especially Humble 2002b, Badian 2004, Gray 2010b, Flower 2012; Anderson 1974a remains an engaging book-length study. The essays in Strassler 2009 offer helpful introductions to many aspects of Xenophon's life and times. For a fuller picture of Greek and Achaemenid history during Xenophon's lifetime see Briant 2002, Buckler 2003, Rhodes 2010, Waters 2014.

2

LOUIS-ANDRÉ DORION

Xenophon and Greek Philosophy

Xenophon was a wide-ranging author who wrote in a great variety of literary genres. He published historical and biographical works, political, economic, and technical treatises, and philosophical dialogues as well, refusing to confine himself to any one genre in particular. To the extent that he was a "philosopher" – a title that the ancients never denied him – even a *serious* philosopher – something that very few moderns have been willing to concede – his relation to the philosophical tradition is quite significant. The goal of the following study is to highlight the depth and diversity of Xenophon's philosophical connections both to his predecessors and to his contemporaries, and to briefly indicate the reception of his work among philosophers connected with Stoicism.

The Presocratics[1]

Contrary to Plato, who mentions nine Presocratic philosophers,[2] Xenophon explicitly mentions only one, Anaxagoras (*Mem.* 4.7.6). It would be an error, however, to take this passage in the fourth book of the *Memorabilia* as the only reference to the Presocratics in Xenophon's philosophical writings, especially since they are the central theme in a long passage in the first book of the *Memorabilia*:

> 11 Nobody ever saw Socrates do, or heard him say, anything that was impious or irreverent. He did not discourse about the nature of the physical universe, as most other philosophers did, inquiring into the constitution of the cosmos, as the sophists (τῶν σοφιστῶν) call it, and the causes of the various celestial phenomena; on the contrary, he pointed out the foolishness of those who concerned themselves with such questions. 12 In the first place, he inquired

---

[1] For the purposes of this study, I distinguish the Presocratics from the sophists, who are the theme of the next section.

[2] Thales of Miletus, Pythagoras, Heraclitus, Parmenides, Zeno of Elea, Empedocles, Anaxagoras, Democritus, and Hippocrates.

whether they proceeded to these studies only when they thought they had a sufficient knowledge of human problems, or whether they felt that they were right in disregarding human problems and inquiring into divine matters. 13 He expressed surprise that it was not obvious to them that human minds cannot discover these secrets, inasmuch as those who claim most confidently to pronounce upon them do not hold the same theories, but disagree with one another just like lunatics 14 ... [H]e said ... some of those who ponder about the nature of the universe think that reality is one, and others that it is infinitely many; some think that everything is always in motion, and others that nothing can ever be moved; some think that everything comes to be and passes away, and others that nothing can come to be or pass away. 15 He also raised this further question about them: whether, just as those who study human nature expect to achieve some result from their studies for the benefit of themselves or of some other selected person, so these students of divine matters expect that, when they have discovered the laws that govern the various phenomena, they will produce at will winds and rain and changes of season and any other such required effect; or whether they have no such expectation, but are content with the mere knowledge of how these various phenomena occur. 16 That is how he spoke about people who occupied themselves with these speculations. He himself always discussed human matters, trying to find out the nature of piety and impiety, beauty and ugliness, justice and injustice, prudence and madness, courage and cowardice, State and statesman, government and the capacity for governing. (*Mem.* 1.1.11–16)[3]

This important passage calls for several remarks:

a) The "sophists" (τῶν σοφιστῶν) in question in *Mem.* 1.1.11 are not the itinerant teachers from the Classical period who came to Athens where they could charge fees for their lessons, but rather the philosophers who have come to be known as the "Presocratics" (although some were in fact contemporaries of Socrates), that is, those sixth- and fifth-century Greek philosophers who were interested in studying nature (φύσις) as a whole.

b) Socrates categorically condemns those who are interested in questions dealing with "divine things," that is to say, cosmogonical and cosmological questions, and he shows no hesitation about saying that they have lost their reason and resemble fools. Moreover, according to Xenophon, Socrates condemned the research of Anaxagoras using the same terms:

In general, he dissuaded them [i.e., his companions] from concerning themselves with the way in which the divinity regulates the various heavenly bodies; he thought that these facts were not discoverable by human beings, and he did not consider that a man would please the gods if he pried into things that they had not chosen to reveal. He said that a person who bothered about

---

[3] Trans. Tredennick 1970, revised by Waterfield (*Penguin Classics*) 1990, slightly modified.

these things would run the risk of going just as crazy as Anaxagoras, who prided himself enormously on his exposition of the workings of the gods. (*Mem.* 4.7.6)[4]

In this passage, Anaxagoras is clearly depicted as a thinker whose extravagant theories, about things that are beyond the scope of human understanding, run the risk of leading men to atheism. This criticism of Anaxagoras probably has an apologetic dimension to the extent that, according to certain accounts, Socrates was a pupil of Anaxagoras[5] and/ or Archelaus,[6] the latter having been himself a disciple of Anaxagoras (DK 59 A 7). Xenophon's judgment of Anaxagoras is much more critical and negative than Plato's, who has Socrates credit Anaxagoras with the idea that the νοῦς is the cause of the organization and the ordering of all things (*Phd.* 97b–c). Xenophon's attitude towards Anaxagoras recalls his attitude towards Alcibiades: Plato makes no attempt to conceal Socrates' interest in the research of Anaxagoras, or even his love for Alcibiades,[7] but Xenophon makes every effort to dissociate Socrates from anyone – and in particular from Alcibiades[8] and Anaxagoras – who might damage the reputation of his teacher and stand in the way of his apologetic enterprise.

c) Socrates condemns this type of research because he considers that it lays claim to forms of knowledge that are inaccessible to human beings and that the gods have reserved for themselves,[9] the implication being that it is impious to seek to reveal nature's secrets. Since (as Xenophon reminds his readers at the beginning of *Mem.* 1.1.11) Socrates was never guilty of impiety, he necessarily turned away from such questions.

d) At the beginning of *Mem.* 1.1.14, Xenophon mentions certain positions of the Presocratics and opposes them to each other in such a way as to have them cancel each other out and demonstrate, by their very opposition, that the phenomena that they supposedly explain are in fact unknowable. This way of setting the positions in opposition to each other, in order to neutralize them, is a striking anticipation of the argumentative strategy of the Sceptics.

e) The end of *Mem.* 1.1.14, where Xenophon cites three pairs of contradictory theses defended by philosophers who speculate about the nature of

---

[4] Trans. Tredennick 1970, revised by Waterfield (*Penguin Classics*) 1990, slightly modified.
[5] D.L. 2.19 and 2.45.
[6] Cicero, *Tusc.* 5.4.10–11; D.L. 2.16, 2.19, 2.23, 10.12; Theodoret of Cyrus, *Gr. aff. Cur* 12.67; Clement of Alexandria, *Strom.* 1.14, 63, 3.
[7] *Prt.* 309a–b; *Grg.* 481d–482a; *Alc.* I 103a, 131d–132a.
[8] See *Mem.* 1.2.16 and 1.2.39–47.
[9] See *Mem.* 1.1.13 and 4.7.6.

the universe, has all the appearances of a doxographical passage and most likely derives from Gorgias.[10] Indeed, there are very important similarities between *Mem.* 1.1.14 and a passage from *On Melissus, Xenophanes, and Gorgias* (5, 979a14–18). The positions mentioned in *Mem.* 1.1.14 were defended by different Presocratics, and each of the three oppositions exposed by Xenophon contains an Eleatic thesis. Moreover, Xenophon and the author of the Pseudo-Aristotelian *On Melissus, Xenophanes, and Gorgias* both fail to name the philosophers whose doctrines they cite.

f) One reason that Socrates condemns the study of nature is that, in his view, it has no practical utility whatsoever (*Mem.* 1.1.15). He sees the study of nature as completely useless, in comparison to the study of human matters, because it is impossible for men to apply such knowledge to produce natural phenomena (such as wind, rain, and the seasons)[11] for their own purposes. However, given that modern natural science has allowed men to recreate certain natural phenomena for the benefit of human beings (through assisted reproduction, organ transplants, artificial limbs, etc.), it seems likely that Socrates would approve of the study of nature if he were alive today. Finally, the question raised at the end of *Mem.* 1.1.15 clearly shows that Socrates rejects the disinterested perspective that Aristotle sees as founding the superiority of the theoretical sciences. While Aristotle bases the prestige of the theoretical sciences, in particular physics, on the fact that they have no other finality than that of the pursuit of knowledge in and for itself,[12] Socrates criticizes disciplines that have no other ambition than to pursue disinterested and useless knowledge.

g) The interpretation of Socrates' exclusive interest in questions dealing with human matters (*Mem.* 1.1.16) has to be nuanced to the extent that, even in the *Memorabilia*, he also shows interest in cosmology and astronomy.[13] Diogenes Laertius saw that Socrates' interest in human matters is not as exclusive as Xenophon claims.[14] No matter how one interprets this wavering in position that is manifest in the text itself of the *Memorabilia*, the passage at *Mem.* 1.1.11–16 enjoyed considerable success among later

---

[10] Mansfeld 1986: 37: "[T]here can be no doubt that what is in Xenophon [*sc. Mem.* 1.1.14] derives from Gorgias, although there are some minor differences."

[11] Is Xenophon thinking of Empedocles here? Certain fragments, in which Empedocles is said to be able to control wind and rain, may suggest that he is (see DK B 111, A 1.60, A 13, and A 14).

[12] *Metaph.* A 2.982b22–8.

[13] See *Mem.* 1.4, 4.3, and 4.7.5.

[14] D.L. 2.45: "In my opinion Socrates discoursed on physics as well as on ethics, since he holds some conversations about providence, even according to Xenophon, who, however, declares that he only discussed ethics" (trans. Hicks 1925).

philosophers. For it is the text that has contributed the most to creating the image of a Socrates who turns away from the study of nature in order to focus exclusively on ethical questions.[15]

The Sophists

Xenophon's position on the sophists is fairly equivocal: sometimes he treats them with outright hostility, whereas at other times his attitude towards them is more conciliatory, even to the point of apparently sharing some of their theses. It is best to begin with the thirteenth and final chapter of Xenophon's treatise on hunting, the *Cynegeticus*, since this chapter alone contains half of the occurrences of the term σοφιστής to be found in his works. It consists of a full-on attack on the sophists in which Xenophon presents numerous criticisms of them:

- They do not lead the young to virtue (*Cyn.* 13.1)
- They have written nothing promoting virtue (*Cyn.* 13.1)
- Their writings are empty, and it is a waste of time to read them: their research concerns nothing but words (*Cyn.* 13.2–3)
- They are masters of the art of deception (*Cyn.* 13.4)
- They pretend to be clever with words, but express no real thoughts (*Cyn.* 13.6)
- They attempt to deceive for their personal gain (*Cyn.* 13.8)
- They are of no use to anyone (*Cyn.* 13.8)
- None of them is wise (*Cyn.* 13.8)
- They chase after the rich and the young (*Cyn.* 13.9 and 12)
- They steal the property of private citizens and plunder the state (*Cyn.* 13.11)
- They are not physically fit and have no capacity for hard work (*Cyn.* 13.11)
- They hunt friends (*Cyn.* 13.12) and attempt to triumph over them (*Cyn.* 13.15)
- They seek to satisfy selfish desires (*Cyn.* 13.15)
- They are impious (*Cyn.* 13.16)

In his other works, Xenophon never repeats any of these criticisms and he even contradicts some of them in what he says about individual sophists. For example, he says in the *Cynegeticus* that no sophist is wise (σοφός, 13.8),

---

[15] See, among others, Cicero, *Tusc.* 5.4.10–11, *Rep.* 1.10.15, *Fin.* 5.29.87–8, *Acad. poster.* 1.4.15–18; Seneca, *Ep.* 71.7; D.L. 2.20–1; 45; Long 1988: 153: "I call attention to the passage from Xenophon, *Mem.* 1.1.11–16, which by the Hellenistic period had become the principal authority for Socrates' exclusively ethical orientation."

but elsewhere he acknowledges on two separate occasions that Prodicus is wise (σοφός),[16] and there is no indication that this repeated affirmation is ironical. Moreover, as we have just seen, he says in the *Cynegeticus* that the sophists' writings have no other aim than to provide "empty pleasures" (ἡδοναὶ κεναί) (*Cyn.* 13.2), that reading them is a waste of time (*Cyn.* 13.2), that they like to play far-fetched word games (*Cyn.* 13.3), that they are of no help when it comes to making the young virtuous (*Cyn.* 13.1), and that they are not physically fit and have no capacity for hard work (*Cyn.* 13.11); and yet, in the *Memorabilia* (2.1.21–34), he has Socrates quote a long excerpt from the fable of Heracles at the crossroads precisely because Prodicus – who is the author of this fable that Socrates praises for expressing thoughts in such a splendid way (*Mem.* 2.1.34) – combats the search for immediate pleasures and urges young people to engage in strenuous training, to apply themselves with diligent effort, and to set out on the road to virtue. The opposition between *Cyn.* 13.3 and *Mem.* 2.1.34 is particularly striking. In the *Cynegeticus*, Xenophon criticizes the sophists for limiting themselves to studying words (*rhêmata*) and neglecting the importance of thoughts (*gnômai*) that have the potential to lead young people to virtue, but in the *Memorabilia*, Socrates exhorts Aristippus to choose the road that leads to virtue by taking to heart the thoughts (*gnômai*) that Prodicus has expressed using such magnificent words (*rhêmata*).

The discrepancy between *Cyn.* 13 and the rest of Xenophon's works disappears if, as some commentators have argued,[17] the *Cynegeticus* is spurious; however, there exists no convincing reason to question the authenticity of the *Cynegeticus*.[18] Since the chronology of Xenophon's works is uncertain, it is not at all appropriate to appeal to it and invoke a hypothetical evolution in Xenophon's thought to explain the discrepancy between *Cynegeticus* 13 and the rest of his works. Perhaps the solution to this problem consists in emphasizing that the sophists criticized by Xenophon in chapter 13 of the *Cynegeticus* are not the same ones that he evokes in his other works. In fact, he twice employs the expression "the sophists of today" (οἱ νῦν σοφισταί, *Cyn.* 13.1 and 6) to refer to the sophists that he vehemently attacks, as if he found it necessary to distinguish them from the late fifth-century sophists.

Protagoras,[19] Gorgias,[20] and Prodicus[21] are briefly mentioned in Xenophon's Socratic writings, but they do not take part in discussions with

[16] *Mem.* 2.1.21 and *Smp.* 4.62.
[17] See, among others, Nestle 1939/1948: 430; Classen 1984/1986: 175.
[18] Gray 1985.
[19] *Smp.* 1.5.
[20] *Smp.* 1.5; *Anab.* 2.6.16.
[21] *Smp.* 1.5, 4.62; *Mem.* 2.1.21–34.

Socrates; however, as we shall see in a moment, this should not lead to the conclusion that Xenophon is indifferent to them and that his thought does not overlap in remarkable ways with the thought of the sophists. Antiphon[22] and Hippias[23] are not only mentioned by Xenophon, they are also Socrates' interlocutors in the *Memorabilia*. And Xenophon's judgment of Hippias is not as negative as one might suppose. Far from depicting him as an adversary who is mercilessly refuted by Socrates, Xenophon represents him as a docile and cooperative interlocutor who adopts Socrates' position all the more voluntarily since he himself has no position to put forward.

As for Antiphon, he is the only sophist mentioned by Xenophon whose portrait is negative. At the beginning of his conversation with Socrates, Antiphon pokes fun at his poverty, reproaches him for not using his knowledge to earn money, and describes him as a "teacher of misery"[24] (*Mem.* 1.6.3). Antiphon's criticism of Socrates for not earning money from his teaching is in fact the exact opposite of the one that Xenophon addresses to the sophists when he blames them for taking payment for their lessons.[25] Whereas the dialogue between Socrates and Hippias does not involve a refutation of the latter, the conversation reported in *Mem.* 1.6 can be read as a demonstration of the inanity of Antiphon's criticisms of Socrates.

As for Prodicus, he is the sophist who receives the most distinguished treatment from Xenophon. It is true that Xenophon fails to grant him the honor of conversing directly with Socrates; however, he does show him a great deal of consideration. For Xenophon's Socrates (henceforth Socrates[X]) does not express the same irony with respect to Prodicus as Plato's Socrates (henceforth Socrates[P]) does when he claims that he was a pupil of Prodicus, but that he settled for his one-drachma course instead of his exhaustive fifty-drachma course.[26] Admittedly, both Socrateses send Prodicus potential disciples who are not gifted enough to belong to their circle of friends,[27] but contrary to Socrates[P], Socrates[X] does not appear to depreciate Prodicus' teaching. There is no detectable irony on the two occasions when Socrates[X] describes Prodicus as "wise," and the fact that he adapts a very long passage from one of his writings, with manifest approval, confirms that he holds Prodicus in high esteem.[28]

---

[22] *Mem.* 1.6.
[23] *Mem.* 4.4; *Smp.* 4.62.
[24] Trans. Tredennick 1970, revised by Waterfield (*Penguin Classics*) 1990.
[25] *Mem.* 1.2.6; 1.5.6; 1.6.3–5; 1.6.11–13; *Ap.* 16.
[26] *Cra.* 384b.
[27] See *Smp.* 4.62 and *Tht.* 151b.
[28] *Mem.* 2.1.21 and *Smp.* 4.62.

The passages in which Xenophon mentions the sophists in general, or certain sophists in particular, are far from exhausting the connections between his thought and theirs. Indeed, by comparing passages in Plato, where certain ideas and theses are attributed to sophists, and passages in Xenophon, where the same ideas and theses are attributed to Socrates, it is possible to establish that Socrates[X] and the sophists have several positions in common. Four of them are especially worthy of mention: 1) the relativist position that Socrates presents in *Mem.* 3.8.7 is identical to the one that Plato attributes to Protagoras (*Prt.* 334a–c) – what is good for one thing can be bad for another thing, so that the good cannot be determined independently of the relation between a thing and its use; 2) Socrates was reputed to teach his disciples the ability to speak and to act (ἱκανοὶ λέγειν τε καὶ πράττειν).[29] Given that this ability amounts to political competency,[30] it follows that his teaching aimed at training future political leaders, as he himself boasts (*Mem.* 1.6.15). Judging from a passage in the *Protagoras* (318e–319b), where Protagoras employs nearly the same expression (τὰ τῆς πόλεως δυνατώτατος ἂν εἴη καὶ πράττειν καὶ λέγειν, 319a) to explain his commitment to teaching political competency to his disciples, a competency which Socrates[P] doubts can be taught, the position of Socrates[X] is closer to the one held by Protagoras than to the one held by Socrates[P]; 3) Plato represents Protagoras, Prodicus, and other sophists as claiming that they can teach the *tekhnê politikê* ("art of politics"), the art of managing one's household and of governing the city.[31] But the *basilikê tekhnê* ("art of kingship") taught by Socrates[X] consists in precisely that – managing one's *oikos* well and governing the city well.[32] The notion that the *tekhnê politikê* of the sophists and the *basilikê tekhnê* of Socrates[X] are the same thing is all the more relevant given that Plato employs the two expressions interchangeably in the *Euthydemus* (291c); 4) Protagoras maintains that acquiring virtue depends on diligence (*epimeleia*), exercise (*askêsis*), and study (*mathêsis*).[33] This view of the conditions for acquiring virtue conflicts with the view held by Socrates[P] because it is not at all intellectualist; however, it corresponds very closely to the one that Socrates[X] presents on numerous occasions in the *Memorabilia*.[34]

A passage in the *Cyropaedia* provides unexpected confirmation of the strong similarity between Socrates[X] and the sophists. While conversing

---

[29] *Mem.* 1.2.15; 2.9.4; 3.6.16; 4.2.1; 4.2.4; 4.2.6; 4.3.1; *Smp.* 8.23.

[30] Dorion and Bandini 2000: ccvi–ccix.

[31] *Prt.* 319a–b; *Resp.* 10.600c–d.

[32] *Mem.* 2.1.17; 4.2.11.

[33] *Prt.* 323c–324a.

[34] See *Mem.* 2.6.39; 3.9.2–3; 3.9.14; 4.2.40; 4.5.10. It is also Xenophon's position in his non-Socratic works (see, for example, *Cyr.* 7.5.74–7).

with Tigranes, Cyrus realizes that the young man greatly admires a sophist (*sophistês*, *Cyr.* 3.1.14) who is among his circle of friends. However, this sophist is no longer alive because Tigranes' father has had him put to death for supposedly corrupting (*diaphtheirein*, *Cyr.* 3.1.38) Tigranes and stealing away the admiration that his son should have reserved for him. (*Cyr.* 3.1.39). These motives for killing the sophist are extraordinarily similar to the ones used to justify the condemnation of Socrates, and Xenophon's intention to identify the sophist with Socrates becomes manifest when he has him say the following just before he dies: "Do not be angry with your father, Tigranes, for putting me to death; for he does it, not out of malice, but out of ignorance, and I believe that any wrong that men do out of ignorance is involuntary" (*Cyr.* 3.1.38).[35] Since Xenophon has no hesitation about depicting a sophist as a victim of the same type of injustice as Socrates suffered at his trial, nor about attributing positions to Socrates that Plato attributes to the sophists, it is clear that the final chapter of the *Cynegeticus* is not at all representative of Xenophon's general attitude towards the sophists.

Plato and the Socratics

In his *Lives and Opinions of Eminent Philosophers*, Diogenes Laertius presents the life of Xenophon (2.47–59) immediately after the life of Socrates (2.18–47) – a resounding confirmation of his recognition of Xenophon's status as a Socratic. Moreover, he states that Xenophon "took Socrates as a model to be rigorously imitated" (Σωκράτην ζηλώσας ἀκριβῶς, 2.56). Numerous other ancient authors corroborate this judgment.[36] Notwithstanding the opinion of certain modern commentators,[37] there is no valid reason to question Xenophon's status as a disciple of Socrates who belonged to his circle of friends. It is true that Plato never mentions Xenophon, while the latter does in fact mention Plato on one occasion;[38] but the silence on the part of Plato with respect to Xenophon is probably a result of the rivalry that opposed these two disciples of Socrates.

Given that our sources provide no reliable biographical information about the relations between Plato and Xenophon as disciples of Socrates, the best way to study the differences between their approaches to him is

---

[35] Trans. Miller 1914, slightly modified.
[36] See Cicero, *Off.* 2.87, *Div.* 1.25.52, *Tusc.* 2.26 and 62, *Orat.* 2.14 and 58; Seneca, *Tranq.* 7.3; Plutarch, *Cons. Ap.* 33 and 118f, *Apoph.* 50 and 212b; Sextus Empiricus, *Adv. Math.* VII 8, etc. See also Giannantoni, *SSR* I H (= *De philosophis qui Socratici appellati sunt*) 2, 3, 5, 7, 12, 17.
[37] See Burnet 1911: xiv–xv, xviii–xx; Maier 1913: 6–11; Taylor 1932: 16; Vlastos 1991: 99, 103.
[38] *Mem.* 3.6.1.

to compare their representations of the Socratic themes that are common to both of them, beginning with the two dialogues to which they gave the same titles, namely the *Apology of Socrates* and the *Symposium*. Most of the comparative studies on these works have concluded that Plato's *Apology* and his *Symposium* were written before Xenophon's. Fewer and fewer commentators are reluctant to admit that Xenophon borrowed many elements from Plato's versions of these dialogues when he wrote his own versions of them. Is this to say that Xenophon relied entirely on Plato, that he copied him, and that he does not constitute an independent and original source for our knowledge of Socrates? Far from it! For Xenophon's more or less incontestable borrowings from Plato are not synonymous with plagiarism, nor do they indicate a lack of originality; for it was quite possible for Xenophon to borrow elements from Plato and use them in ways that run counter to Plato's intentions in his dialogues. In other words, he was able to insert elements borrowed from Plato into his own original interpretation of the philosophy of Socrates in order to contest Plato's interpretation of it. The process of reinterpreting a borrowed element is magnificently illustrated by Xenophon's version of the episode of the Delphic oracle about Socrates that was given to Chaerephon, an episode that he probably borrowed from Plato, but one that he interprets quite differently from him.[39]

There are two fundamental approaches that commentators who interpret Xenophon's Socratic writings can use to highlight the originality of Socrates[X]: on the one hand, they can analyse his philosophical positions in and for themselves, and on the other hand, they can do a comparative exegesis of Socratic themes that are common to both Plato and Xenophon. The goal of comparative exegesis is not to determine the most faithful or the most exact version of a common theme from a historical perspective,[40] but instead to record the differences and indicate how they fit into each author's philosophically coherent representation of the character of Socrates. Much recent work has focused on restoring Xenophon's Socratic works to favor, and it is now possible to specify the character traits and the philosophical doctrines of Socrates[X] that distinguish him from his Platonic twin. Very often, it has become manifest that the two Socrateses approach the same philosophical issues from very different perspectives. Indeed, with respect to at least twenty philosophical questions,[41] Socrates[X] holds a position that is irreducible, even radically opposed, to that of Socrates[P]; and many key notions on which he relies in his philosophizing have little or no importance

---

[39] Compare Xen. *Apol.* 1.14 with Plato *Apol.* 21a. See Vander Waerdt 1993.
[40] Elsewhere (Dorion 2011) I have explained why the famous "Socratic problem" is destined to remain unsolvable.
[41] See Dorion 2013a: xiv–xviii.

for his Platonic twin. For example, it is extremely surprising to note that *enkrateia* ("self-control"), which he sees as the foundation of virtue (*Mem.* 1.5.4), plays almost no role in the ethics presented in Plato's early dialogues.

The most important disciples of Socrates appearing in Xenophon's dialogues are incontestably Antisthenes and Aristippus. They receive, however, very different treatment from Xenophon. Antisthenes, who is one of Socrates' closest friends,[42] plays a major role in the *Symposium*, and he is also Socrates' interlocutor in a brief discussion of friendship.[43] In the *Symposium*, he acknowledges that he is indebted to Socrates for that which constitutes his greatest pride, namely his wealth, which consists in his having no needs.[44] Given that self-sufficiency is one of the principal qualities of Socrates[45] and that it is through self-sufficiency that men can liken themselves to the gods,[46] the fact that Socrates could show Antisthenes how to become self-sufficient is a confirmation, not only of just how close a connection the two men have to one other, but also of Socrates' tremendous utility. But besides being a character in Xenophon's Socratic dialogues, Antisthenes is a disciple of Socrates who wrote a great number of Socratic works himself,[47] although there only remain fragments of them today.

An interpretation that had its hour of glory at the end of the nineteenth century, when *Quellenforschung* held sway, would have it that Xenophon's representation of Socrates relies entirely on the Socratic works of Antisthenes. Despite K. Joel's attempt to justify this audacious hypothesis in a work more than 1700 pages long,[48] it remains extremely fragile, for given that practically none of Antisthenes' writings has survived, there is no way to verify it. In other words, Taylor's caution with respect to this question is completely appropriate: "Modern speculations about possible borrowings in Xenophon from the *writings* of Antisthenes are, of course, only speculations."[49] This does not exclude the possibility that Xenophon may have been greatly inspired by the *logoi sokratikoi* of other disciples of Socrates; however, the disappearance of these texts makes it impossible to determine, with any degree of exactitude, the extent and the importance of such borrowings. Besides, the example of Xenophon's borrowings from Plato should put commentators on their guard. Xenophon takes over elements from Plato's representation of Socratics, but this does not prevent him

[42] *Mem.* 3.11.17.
[43] *Mem.* 2.5.
[44] *Smp.* 4.43.
[45] *Mem.* 1.2.1, 1.2.14, 1.2.60, 4.7.1, 4.8.11.
[46] *Mem.* 1.6.10.
[47] D.L. 6.15–18.
[48] Joel 1893–1901.
[49] Taylor 1932: 33 n. 1. Cooper holds the same position (1999: 9–10 and 27 n. 48).

from integrating them into his own profoundly original representation of Socrates, so that it is completely reasonable to assume that he would have been capable of the same degree of originality in the event that he borrowed from other authors of Socratic dialogues.

In the *Memorabilia*, Aristippus converses with Socrates twice (2.1 and 3.8), and on both occasions Xenophon does not present him in a favorable light. His hostility to Aristippus is confirmed by other ancient authors, including Diogenes Laertius (2.65), who probably alludes to *Mem.* 2.1 when he says, "Xenophon was no friend to Aristippus; and for this reason he had Socrates direct against Aristippus the discourse against pleasure (τὸν κατὰ τῆς ἡδονῆς λόγον)."[50] However, it is inexact to describe *Mem.* 2.1 as a "discourse against pleasure," for Socrates does not object to pleasure *tout court*. He is strongly opposed to the pursuit of immediate pleasures (*Mem.* 2.1.20), but otherwise persuaded that the *enkrateia* ("self-control") that he himself possesses to the highest degree, and which he urges others to strive to develop, has the effect of procuring the greatest pleasure (*Mem.* 4.5.9–10). The immediate pleasures that Socrates condemns are precisely the ones that Aristippus seeks.[51] Moreover, it is also interesting to note that Socrates' two conversations with Aristippus (*Mem.* 2.1 and 3.8) provide the structural frame for two blocks of successive discussions, the first block dealing with the theme of *philia* or "friendship" (*Mem.* 2.2–10), and the second one, with the theme of public offices (*Mem.* 3.1–7). It is as if Aristippus – who argues for a life on the fringes of the city – served as a foil for Socrates' arguments and helped to highlight, by way of the contrast between their positions, Socrates' useful role in strengthening the bonds between men, whether it be those of *philia* or the ones of political community for which political leaders are responsible.

Xenophon's severe judgment of Aristippus is not only at the opposite extreme of his positive judgment of Antisthenes, it is also more negative, in many respects, than his stance on the sophists. In his first conversation with Aristippus, Socrates tries to convince him to renounce his dissolute way of life by telling him a fable composed by the sophist Prodicus. Thus Xenophon openly acknowledges that a sophist's writings can be used to criticize the way of life of a Socratic and set him on the road to virtue. Moreover, when Socrates tells Aristippus the fable of Heracles at the crossroads, he clearly identifies Aristippus' position with that of the character Vice.[52] In his second appearance in the *Memorabilia*, Aristippus becomes *the only one of Socrates'*

---

[50] Trans. Hicks 1925, modified.
[51] D.L. 2.66; Aelianus, *VH* 14.6; Athenaeus 12. 544A–B = *SSR* IV A 174.
[52] See Dorion and Bandini 2011a, Appendix 1: 407–13.

interlocutors in the entire work who openly attempts to refute him.[53] It is important to add that Antiphon and Hippias, the only two sophists who participate in discussions with Socrates in the *Memorabilia*, never attempt to refute him. Finally, there is every reason to believe that Xenophon has Aristippus in mind when he reports with disapproval that some of Socrates' disciples charged fees for passing on the teachings that they had received for free from Socrates.[54] It is as if the author of the *Memorabilia* wanted to accuse this Socratic of one of the cardinal sins of the sophists.

Aristotle

Aristotle probably wrote one of his early works, the *Gryllus*, in honour of Xenophon's son who was killed at the battle of Mantinea (362 BCE). But given that Aristotle's goal in writing the *Gryllus* was probably to criticize Isocrates' work of the same title,[55] it would provide us, even if it were not a lost work, with little or no information about the connections between his philosophy and the works of Xenophon. Besides, is there any proof that Aristotle actually read Xenophon? Completely opposed positions have been defended in response to this question. Burnet, whose hostility to Xenophon is well known,[56] claims in the introduction to his 1911 edition of Plato's *Phaedo* that Aristotle never did.[57] H. Maier argues,[58] in his great work on Socrates published two years later, not only that Aristotle read Xenophon, but also that *Mem.* 4.6 is the principal source for his representation of Socrates as a philosopher who is primarily concerned with definitions and with the question of essence (*ti esti*).[59] Faced with these two diametrically opposed positions, it is necessary to begin by examining the texts that support the idea that Aristotle did in fact read Xenophon's *Memorabilia*.

There are three passages in the *Memorabilia* with parallels in Aristotle that are sufficiently precise to warrant the idea that they are based on his reading of Xenophon's text. The first one is *Mem.* 1.2.9, where Xenophon explains Socrates' criticism of the practice of appointing citizens to positions of civic responsibility by drawing lots. This passage appears to be the source for Aristotle's summary of Socrates' criticism of this practice in the *Rhetoric* (2.20, 1393b4–8). This criticism has no direct parallel in Plato, so that the

[53] *Mem.* 3.8.1.
[54] *Mem.* 1.2.60.
[55] Thillet 1957.
[56] Burnet 1914: 150: "It is really impossible to preserve Xenophon's Sokrates, even if he were worth preserving."
[57] Burnet 1911: xxiv.
[58] Maier 1913: 93–102.
[59] See *Metaph.* M 4.1078b23–30.

probability that Aristotle relies on Xenophon here is very high, despite the fact that the wording in the *Rhetoric* differs significantly from the wording in the *Memorabilia*. The second passage is *Mem.* 1.2.54, where Xenophon states that Socrates maintained that people show no hesitation about ridding their bodies of what seems useless, namely fingernails, hair, and saliva. In the *Eudemian Ethics* there is a passage (7.1, 1235a37–b2) that faithfully summarizes the content of *Mem.* 1.2.54, and most commentators acknowledge that the latter is its source.[60] The third passage is *Mem.* 2.6.35, where Socrates says that "the best quality in a man is to outdo his friends in acts of kindness and his enemies in acts of hostility (τοὺς μὲν φίλους εὖ ποιοῦντα, τοὺς δ᾽ ἐχθροὺς κακῶς)."[61] This should be compared with the passage in the *Rhetoric* where Aristotle refers to the reason that Socrates gave for his decision not to go to the court of Archelaus, king of Macedon: "He [Socrates] said that 'one is insulted by being unable to requite benefits, as well as by being unable to requite injuries (εὖ παθόντας ὥσπερ καὶ κακῶς)' " (*Rh.* 2.23, 1398a24–6).[62] To the extent that this position is directly opposed to the position that Plato attributes to Socrates,[63] namely that one must never harm another person, even an enemy, the passage from the *Rhetoric* suffices to demonstrate that Aristotle's statements about Socrates are not always based on Plato's representation of him.

In addition to the three passages from the *Memorabilia* just discussed, there are three others that present striking parallels with passages in Aristotle, although they do not have an absolutely certain connection to them. The first one is *Mem.* 1.4.6, where Socrates states that "our foreheads have been fringed with eyebrows that jut out like a cornice (ἀπογεισῶσαι) to prevent damage even from the sweat of the head."[64] This teleological explanation of the function of eyebrows is astonishingly similar to a passage in *De partibus animalium*:

> Both eyebrows and eyelids exist for the protection of the eyes; the former that they may shelter them, like the eaves of a house (οἷον ἀπογείσωμα), from any fluids that trickle down from the head; the latter to act like the palisades which are sometimes placed in front of enclosures, and keep out any objects that might otherwise get in. (*PA* 2.15, 658b14–18)[65]

[60] See, among others, Taylor 1911: 59 and 63; Chroust 1945: 66 n. 81; Mingay and Walzer 1991 ad loc.; Kahn 1996: 82 n. 22.
[61] Trans. Tredennick 1970, revised by Waterfield (*Penguin Classics*) 1990. This position is frequently stated in the *Memorabilia* and in Xenophon's other works (see Dorion and Bandini 2011a: 44 n. 3).
[62] Trans. Roberts in Barnes 1984, vol. II.
[63] See *Cri.* 49c–d; *Resp.* 1.332d–336a.
[64] Trans. Tredennick 1970, revised by Waterfield (*Penguin Classics*) 1990, modified.
[65] Trans. Ogle in Barnes 1984, vol. I.

These two texts not only share the same teleological perspective with respect to the function of eyelids and eyebrows, they also make use of the same metaphor, that of the cornice, to which Xenophon (ἀπογεισῶσαι) and Aristotle (ἀπογείσωμα) both compare eyebrows. Does this constitute proof that Aristotle borrowed from Xenophon when he wrote the above text from *On the Parts of Animals*? It is obviously impossible to establish with certainty that his text has its source in Xenophon's; moreover, we cannot exclude the possibility that Xenophon's and Aristotle's texts may both have their source in a third text that is no longer extant.

The second passage is *Mem.* 3.6, where Socrates undertakes to test Glaucon's knowledge in four areas: revenues and expenses (3.6.4–6 and 12); war and peace (3.6.7–9); defending the city's territory (3.6.10–11); and supplying the city with food (3.6.13). These four areas of knowledge reappear in the fourth chapter of the first book of the *Rhetoric* (1.4, 1359b19–1360b3), where Aristotle says, "The main matters on which all men deliberate and on which deliberative speakers make speeches are five in number: revenues and expenses, war and peace, national defence, imports and exports, and legislation" (1.4, 1359b19–21).[66] The close similarity between *Mem.* 3.6 and *Rh.* 1.4 is not limited to the enumeration of the important matters that politicians must deliberate over and give opinions on. Xenophon and Aristotle present these matters in the same order, and the arguments that they use are sometimes very similar. The resemblance between *Mem.* 3.6.5–6 and the parallel passage in *Rh.* 1.4 dealing with the matter of revenues and expenses (1.4, 1359b23–30) is particularly striking. Together with the points already mentioned, this suggests that once again there are two alternative and equally plausible explanations: either Xenophon's text is the source for the parallel text in the *Rhetoric*, or Xenophon and Aristotle both depend on a common source.

The third passage is *Mem.* 3.9.8, where Xenophon gives Socrates' definition of envy (Φθόνον):

> Considering the nature of envy, he [Socrates] concluded that it was a species of distress (λύπην μέν τινα), but not the sort that arises over the misfortunes of friends or the good fortune of enemies; he said that only those people were envious who were distressed at the success of their friends (ἐπὶ ταῖς τῶν φίλων εὐπραξίαις).[67]

Commentators have often compared this definition to Plato's definition of envy in the *Philebus* (48b–50a). Indeed, it has been argued that Xenophon was likely acquainted with the passage in question from the *Philebus* and

[66] Trans. Roberts in Barnes 1984, slightly modified.
[67] Trans. Tredennick 1970, revised by Waterfield (*Penguin Classics*) 1990.

that *Mem.* 3.9.8 is probably his corrected version of Plato's definition.[68] However, the differences between the two definitions are too significant to warrant such an interpretation. Plato does not define envy as a type of *distress* (λύπη) caused by the *success* of one's friends, but rather as a type of *pleasure* caused by their *misfortune* (*Phlb.* 48b, 50a). Therefore, it appears quite excessive to speak of Xenophon's probable dependence on Plato; and in fact, the definition of envy in *Mem.* 3.9.8 should not be compared to the definition of envy in the *Philebus*, but instead to the one in Aristotle's *Rhetoric*:

> To take envy (φθόνος) next: we can see on what grounds, against what persons, and in what states of mind we feel it. Envy is pain (λύπη) at the sight of such good fortune (ἐπὶ εὐπραγίᾳ) as consists of the good things already mentioned; we feel it towards our equals; not with the idea of getting something for ourselves, but because the other people have it. (*Rh.* 2.10, 1387b22–5)[69]

In light of the above passages, there seems little doubt that Aristotle did in fact read Xenophon's *Memorabilia*,[70] which obviously raises the question of whether the latter had an influence on his general portrait of Socrates. Just over a century ago, Maier argued that we should attach great importance to *Mem.* 4.6, which he considered the principal source of the Aristotelian representation of Socrates, most notably in *Metaphysics* M.4, 1078b17–30, where Aristotle credits Socrates with two important philosophical discoveries: inductive reasoning and the use of universal definitions to determine the essence (*ti esti*) of things.[71] However, since Taylor, the majority of commentators have maintained that Aristotle's view of Socrates is mostly based on Plato.[72] Besides, if Maier was right to insist on Xenophon's numerous borrowings from Plato in *Mem.* 4.5.11–12 and 4.6,[73] then why would Aristotle have contented himself with using Xenophon as an intermediary if he realized that the latter was merely borrowing from Plato? A close examination of the general portrait of Socrates that emerges from Aristotle's writings reveals that the influence of the *Memorabilia* on Aristotle is marginal and that his conception of Socrates' philosophy derives essentially, if not exclusively, from Plato's early dialogues.

---

[68] Kahn 1996: 395–6.

[69] Trans. Roberts in Barnes 1984.

[70] *Mem.* 1.6 may also be the source of fr. 75 Rose (= D.L. 2.46), but this remains very hypothetical (see Deman 1942: 48–9).

[71] Maier 1913: 96–102.

[72] See Taylor 1911: x and 40–90; Kahn 1996: 79–87; Beversluis 1993: 298–301; Vander Waerdt 1993: 3 n. 7.

[73] Maier 1913: 57–62.

Finally, it is important to stress that on various philosophical issues Xenophon and Aristotle have very similar positions. They both consider that virtue results above all from exercise and training,[74] that self-knowledge consists in taking the measure of one's own capacities and abilities,[75] that a good dialectician leads a discussion by seeking support from the most widely held opinions,[76] that speech is indispensable to all that touches on community life,[77] that tyranny can be reformed,[78] and that animals exist for the sake of human beings (*anthrôpôn heneka*).[79] These parallels and others certainly deserve to be emphasized; however, they do not justify the conclusion that Aristotle's positions on the points in question are based on his reading of Xenophon.

After Aristotle

The influence that *Mem.* 1.1.10–16 had on the Hellenistic philosophers' representation of Socrates has already been mentioned. However, the importance of the *Memorabilia* for the philosophers who came after Aristotle is far from being limited to this one passage. At the beginning of book 7 of his *Lives and Opinions of Eminent Philosophers*, Diogenes Laertius tells an anecdote about Zeno of Citium, the founder of Stoicism, which reveals the interest that the Stoic philosophers had in the *Memorabilia*:

> Having gone up to Athens, he sat down in a bookseller's shop, being then a man of thirty. The bookseller was reading out the second book of Xenophon's *Memorabilia*, and Zeno was so pleased by it that he inquired where men like Socrates were to be found. Crates was passing by at just the right moment, and the bookseller pointed to him and said: "Follow that man." From that day he became Crates's pupil, showing in other respects a strong bent for philosophy, though with too much native modesty to assimilate Cynic shamelessness. (D.L. 7.2–3)[80]

From a strictly biographical perspective, this anecdote is patently false. It is clear that Diogenes Laertius uses it simply to establish a line of descent between Socrates and Stoicism through the intermediary of Cynicism. Nevertheless, it provides striking evidence of the influence that the *Memorabilia* had on the Stoics. Above all, they were influenced by the two

---

[74] See *Mem.* 1.1.2.19–23 and *EN* 2.1–2.
[75] See *Mem.* 4.2.24–30 and *EN* 4.9, 1125a27–9.
[76] See *Mem.* 4.6.15 and *Top.* 1.1, 100a18–21; *SE* 34, 183b6.
[77] See *Mem.* 3.3.11; 4.3.12 and *Pol.* 1.2, 1253a9–19.
[78] See the parallels indicated by Luccioni (1947b: 30) in his edition of the *Hiero*.
[79] See *Mem.* 4.3.8; 10 and *Pol.* 1.8, 1256b15–22.
[80] Trans. Hicks 1925, modified.

passages in which divine providence and the theo-teleological conception of nature are discussed (*Mem.* 1.4 and 4.3). In fact, it was long believed that Xenophon could not have been the author of what appears to be one of the first expositions of the idea of divine providence. At the end of the nineteenth century, some commentators went so far as to say that these "theological" chapters of the *Memorabilia* were so profoundly original that they must be stoic interpolations.[81] However, there is no valid reason for questioning Xenophon's authorship of these two chapters that had such a significant influence on the Stoics,[82] and especially on Zeno of Citium who, according to Sextus Empiricus, took his starting point from Xenophon (ἀπὸ Ξενοφῶντος τὴν ἀφορμὴν λαβών, 9.101). Demonstrating his knowledge of Xenophon's text, Sextus Empiricus makes this claim after quoting extensively from the beginning of *Mem.* 1.4.[83] It is also important to mention that *Mem.* 1.4 and 4.3 greatly influenced Cicero's exposition of Stoic theology in book 2 of *De natura deorum*;[84] moreover, the fact that Panaetius considered Xenophon's Socratic writings to be genuine (see D.L. 2.64) is another confirmation of Xenophon's importance for the Stoics. Thus, contrary to Schleiermacher's claim that Stoicism had no philosophical debt to Socrates[X],[85] there is absolutely no question that the *Memorabilia* had a profound influence on this famous school of ancient philosophy.

Indeed, the philosopher on whom Xenophon had the greatest influence was a Stoic. Arrian of Nicomedia (ca. AD 85–165) took Xenophon as his model, writing both as a philosopher and as a historian, just as the author of the *Memorabilia* and the *Hellenica* had done. And just as Xenophon had done for Socrates, he chose to preserve the memory of a philosopher by recording in his works (the *Discourses* and the *Manual*) the lectures of his teacher Epictetus, who left no written account of his philosophy himself. Therefore, it is no surprise that these two works contain numerous passages with echoes of Xenophon's *Memorabilia*.[86] But Xenophon's influence on his other writings is also manifest. The title of his most well-known work,

---

[81] On this point, see Dorion 2000: 33 n. 231.
[82] On the influence of *Mem.* 1.4 and 4.3 on Stoic theology, see above all Sedley 2007: 212–25.
[83] M. 9.92–101.
[84] See Dorion 2016. Cicero greatly admired Xenophon and was an avid reader of his works. Indeed, he translated the *Oeconomicus* (see *Off.* 2.24, 2.87).
[85] Schleiermacher 1818/1879: 3–4.
[86] The following passages in the *Memorabilia* have echoes in Epictetus: 1.1.1 (= *Diss* 3.23.20); 1.1.6–9 (= *Ench.* 32.3); 1.1.18 (= *Diss* 4.1.64); 1.1.19 (= *Diss* 1.12.3); 1.3.3 (= *Ench.* 31.5); 1.4 (= *Diss* 2.14.11); 1.4.7 (= *Diss* 1.6.3–11 and fr. 23 Schenkl); 1.6.14 (= *Diss* 3.5.14); 2.2 (= *Diss* 4.5.3); 3.7.4 (= *Diss* 2.13.2); 3.9.8 (= *Diss* 2.12.7); 4.1.1 (= *Diss* 4.1.69); 4.3.16–17 (= *Ench.* 31.5); 4.6.1 (= *Diss* 1.17.12 and 4.1.41); 4.7.10 (= *Ench.* 32.3).

the *Anabasis of Alexander*, is clearly inspired by Xenophon's *Anabasis of Cyrus*, a work whose fame is stressed by Arrian in an important passage in book 1;[87] moreover, the fact that the *Anabasis of Alexander* has seven books is another parallel with Xenophon's *Anabasis*. In his *Cynegeticus*, Arrian stresses that his goal is to update Xenophon's work of the same title by discussing certain breeds of hunting dogs that were unknown to him.[88] His *Tactica*, a work that mostly deals with the tactics used by the Roman cavalry, recalls Xenophon's *Hipparchicus*. Since Arrian made such a point of imitating him, it is little wonder that he became known as the "new Xenophon."[89]

Conclusion

The ancients never questioned Xenophon's status as a Socratic philosopher. Why then has he been so frequently denied the title of philosopher? For Schleiermacher (1818/1879), one of the first to deny him this title, Xenophon's Socratic writings are of so little interest that Socrates' immense reputation as a philosopher would be impossible to understand if it were based on nothing more than the depiction of him as a pedantic moralizer in the *Memorabilia*. This scathing assessment of Xenophon's Socratic writings has been repeated by all of his detractors since the beginning of the nineteenth century, and some recent commentators continue to lend it credence.[90] Indeed, it underlies the peremptory attitude of those who still maintain that the only Socrates who has any philosophical merit is the one depicted in Plato.[91]

Yet there are compelling reasons to contest this cruel belittlement of Xenophon's contribution to philosophy: a) The very fact that no one ever doubted the importance of Xenophon's contribution to philosophy before the beginning of the nineteenth century deserves reflection. On the basis of what conception of philosophy did this astonishing prejudice against Xenophon become so widespread? It would appear that it is rooted in the idea of philosophy as an essentially critical and/or speculative activity. Since Xenophon's Socratic works have little to do with critical or speculative

---

[87] Arrian, *Anab.* 1.12.3.
[88] See *Cyn.* 1.4–5; 2.1–5; 16.7.
[89] Photius, *Bibliotheca* 58, 17b14–15; Suidas, s.v. Ἀρριανός, no. 3868 Adler.
[90] Brickhouse and Smith 2000: 38 and 42–3.
[91] See, among others, Vlastos 1971: 2: Plato's Socrates is "in fact the only Socrates worth talking about"; Santas 1979: x: "[I]t is only Plato's Socrates that is of major interest to the contemporary philosopher"; Kahn 1981: 319: "As far as we are concerned, the Socrates of the dialogues [*sc.* Plato's] *is* the historical Socrates. He is certainly the only one who counts for the history of philosophy."

philosophy, those who accept this hyper-modern view of philosophy draw the conclusion – as if it were self-evident – that these writings are of no philosophical value. But what if it were more legitimate to see philosophy as the ancients did – as *a way of living one's life*?[92] How then could Xenophon – whose Socrates strives to make human action and speech consistent with one another[93] in order to help other men improve their lives[94] – be denied the title of philosopher? b) If, on the basis of an anachronistic conception of philosophy, it were in fact legitimate to deny Xenophon the title of philosopher, then it would be extremely difficult to explain the tremendous influence that his Socratic writings had on so many authors in antiquity,[95] and especially on Cicero, Plutarch, and the Stoics. c) A number of modern and contemporary philosophers do not subscribe to the scathing assessment of Xenophon that Schleiermacher and his epigones have used to undermine his philosophical credibility. For example, Nietzsche greatly admired the *Memorabilia*, which he described as "the most attractive book in Greek literature."[96] Recent scholarship has restored Xenophon's Socratic writings to favor and finally made it possible to evaluate their influence on the philosophers of his time as well as on those who came later.

Further Reading

The work of Münscher 1920 has not been superseded and it remains the comprehensive overview of the reception of Xenophon's writings in ancient authors. We nonetheless hope that the rehabilitation of Xenophon's philosophical works will stimulate new studies of the influence of those writings in antiquity. For the relationship between Xenophon and Plutarch, see the recent article of Stadter (2012), but much still remains to be said on the subject. Stadter (1976) has likewise devoted a study to the influence of Xenophon on the *Cynegeticus* (*On Hunting*) of Arrian. Finally, many recent studies (Erler 2002, Sedley 2005 and 2007, Dorion 2016) have focused on the considerable influence that Xenophon exercised on the Stoics.

---

[92] Hadot 2002.
[93] *Mem.* 1.2.18; 1.3.1; 1.5.6.
[94] *Mem.* 1.4.1; 1.4.19; 1.5.1; 1.6.14; 1.7.1; 2.1.1; 4.3.1–2; 4.3.18; 4.4.25; 4.5.1; 4.8.7; 4.8.10–11.
[95] Münscher 1920.
[96] "Das anziehendste Buch der griechischen Litteratur: Mem<orabilia> Socr<atis>" (Nachgelassenes Fragment 41 [2] 1879, in *Kritische Gesamtausgabe*, IV 3, Berlin, 1967: 442). See also Nachgelassenes Fragment 18 [47] 1876, in *Kritische Gesamtausgabe*, IV 2, Berlin, 1967: 423.

3

SARAH BROWN FERRARIO

Xenophon and Greek Political Thought

Introduction: "Greek Political Thought" and Xenophon in the Fourth Century

Our modern definitions of "the political" embrace far too narrow a semantic and intellectual field to adequately describe this concept in ancient Greece.[1] Although individual thinkers naturally varied in their perspectives,[2] what the ancient Greeks viewed as "political" interactions encompassed nearly the whole sphere of human activity, from the level of the family up to the level of the culture. Perhaps the best way to describe ancient Greek political thought, then, is to claim for it a profound interest, both descriptive and prescriptive, in human relationships.[3] In sum, how *do* human relationships work, and how *should* they work?[4]

There may be no richer time in the history of ancient Greece for the consideration of these questions than the fourth century. In the first place, this was a period of extraordinary upheaval. The victory of the Spartan side in the Peloponnesian War (431–404) temporarily created the prospect of a new hegemony that was poised to control most of the Greek-speaking

---

[1] Balot 2006: 3–8. All dates in this chapter are BC; all literary citations are to works of Xenophon (whose authorship is therefore not reiterated in the references) unless otherwise noted.

[2] In an oft-cited passage near the opening of the *Politics* (1252a7–16), for example, Aristotle contends that different qualities are required for different varieties of leadership, with the result that a household steward does not occupy a position precisely analogous to that of a miniature king. But as Gray 2007: 3 and Reeve 1998: 1 n. 2 ad loc. observe, Xenophon holds almost precisely the opposite view in the *Memorabilia*, most notably when Socrates argues that scale is the only substantive difference between private and public activities (*Mem.* 3.4.12). See also Buxton's contribution in this volume.

[3] Balot 2006: 3–6, 12.

[4] See Xenophon's summary of Socrates' interests at *Mem.* 1.1.16.

I remain very grateful to my research assistant for this project, B. Lewis (PhD student, Department of Greek and Latin, The Catholic University of America), and especially to this volume's editor, M. Flower, for his thoughtful comments and generous support.

lands of the Aegean. But Sparta became a burdensome leader and proved unable to sustain both its internal political and economic system and the many external pressures that arose against it. Athens and Thebes were well positioned, both together and separately, to take advantage of Sparta's increasingly obvious weakness, but while Athens concentrated upon trying to rebuild its lost naval empire, Thebes focused more significantly upon conquests by land – and upon the utter destruction of Sparta. By 362, after the battle of Mantinea, Sparta was no longer a factor in Greek geopolitics. Athens was preoccupied with the northward expansion of its new alliances; Thebes, having achieved the dissolution of Sparta's old network of Peloponnesian allies, was forging relationships with them on its own. For both aspiring imperial powers, serious conflict with Philip II of Macedon lay just over the horizon. Up to this point, however, most interference in Greek affairs from abroad had come from Persia, which had changed the course of the Peloponnesian War by bankrolling a Spartan fleet and had been shifting its own support from state to state in Greek quarrels ever since.

In significant part as a response to these large-scale developments, the fourth century witnessed a flowering of Greek literature about politics. At Athens, the experience of the Peloponnesian War (and of the brief reign of the Thirty afterwards) prompted not only a major revision of the legal code (403–399) but also a series of thoughtful considerations, couched in the literature of both philosophy and law, about the nature of democracy and its feasibility as a form of effective government. Beyond Athens, historical writing in particular flourished as authors strove to understand the present by linking it with the past, and sometimes even to contextualize the story of "Greece" as a whole within a universalizing narrative that also embraced material from the wider world.[5] Most of the rich historiography of this era has not been preserved beyond fragments, but the Athenian literature in other genres has fared better, with the best-known exponents of what we might recognize as "political theory" being Plato, Isocrates, and Aristotle.[6]

Straddling these several categories of discussion is another important writer whose political ideas have sometimes received less attention: Xenophon. Born, raised, and educated in late fifth-century Athens during the Peloponnesian War, Xenophon saw military service both with

[5] On the evolution of "universal" historiography in Greek, e.g. Alonso-Núñez 2002 and Marincola 2007b.
[6] The first two of these are Xenophon's rough contemporaries and will receive some brief comparative attention in this chapter. Aristotle (b. 384) was still a much younger man when Xenophon died (at some point after 362, perhaps ca. 354).

a multi-polis Greek force in Babylonia and with the Spartans in western Anatolia; benefited from elite patronage and cultivated an aristocratic life-style on his estate in the Peloponnese; and sent two grown sons back to Athens for military service in the turbulent interstate conflicts that charac-terized most of his own adult life.[7] Xenophon's political experiences, there-fore, were not confined to his home state of Athens, and this may have helped to invite especially intensive reflection on his part as to the many possibilities – both good and bad – immanent in all human communities, from *oikos* (household) to empire.

With his Socratic education and his democratic background, Xenophon was from the time of his youth steeped in discussions about the ideal politi-cal life. He seems to have had some exposure to certain of Plato's writings, although in most cases he arrives at his own versions of "Socratic" ideas.[8] He also read at least some of Isocrates' work,[9] and in fact shares certain intellectual concerns with him.[10] Some especially important concepts that were at stake in these and other entries into fourth-century Athenian politi-cal discourse included the appropriate relationship between citizens and the law; the viability of various constitutions; the potential efficacy of dem-ocratic decision-making; the recognition and propagation of appropriate social and other structures to support a functioning and successful state; the nature of effective leadership; and the shape and scope of interstate relations, including the concept of panhellenism and dealings with for-eign powers. Xenophon addressed all of these subjects – and many more, although these are the ones that will receive chief attention here – in his own writings.[11]

Although Xenophon engaged with the major political issues of his day, his own particular perspective upon them was both coherent and distinctive. Xenophon is wide-ranging in his authorship: one would be hard-pressed to find another writer from any portion of antiquity from whom we possess

[7] On Xenophon's biography, see Lee in this volume.
[8] Comparisons between Plato's and Xenophon's versions of Socrates and his teachings are abundant in the scholarship. On some key intertextual questions, see Danzig 2005, with expansion in Danzig 2010; on the problem of the historical Socrates, see Dorion 2011, and (on broader issues) see also Dorion's contribution to this volume.
[9] As witnessed at a minimum by the links between Xenophon's *Agesilaus* and Isocrates' encomiastic *Evagoras*: see at note 77.
[10] On connections between the political thought of Xenophon and Isocrates, see Azoulay 2006b; Azoulay 2006a (also noting some potential personal connections, including Isocrates' eulogy for Xenophon's son Gryllus); de Romilly 1954. For more on Isocrates and Gryllus, see Wareh 2012: 103–4, 144–6.
[11] These topics can be easily rearranged into different – and equally productive – categories. Gray 2000, for example, examines Xenophon's (and Isocrates') political thought under four headings: democracy, rulership, Sparta, and panhellenism.

historiography, autobiography, encomium, novel, philosophical dialogue, and essay.[12] Nevertheless, his exploration of *ta politika* (political matters) may safely be said to extend across the full corpus of his works, and his discussions display remarkable consistency, especially in the areas that seem to have mattered most to him. A most important recurring and unifying theme both for Xenophon and for this chapter is the cultivation, practice, and consequences of good leadership,[13] which may be manifested in any context from household guidance to imperial reign, and which is present in works deriving from throughout Xenophon's authorial career.[14]

This chapter, then, treats Xenophon's perspectives on a number of important political issues. I also occasionally note, at the ends of subsections, some ways in which Xenophon's thought seems to converge with or diverge from the ideas of his contemporaries Plato and Isocrates. Before proceeding, it is important for me to note two brief points. Firstly, I treat the work of Xenophon as a unity. This is not to deny him the possibility of intellectual growth and change, only to acknowledge that the chronology of his works is not entirely secure and that there is probably more to be gained here by unification than by atomization.[15] Secondly, I take an essentially non-Straussian approach:[16] that is, I read Xenophon's political analyses as being largely un-ironic, although, as will emerge below, Xenophon's ideas can be not only explicitly discussed, but also implicitly demonstrated, especially through anecdotes and set scenes.

Xenophon's Socratic and other philosophical and prescriptive writings – and indeed, the *Cyropaedia*, as well – are clearly possessed of paradigmatic qualities for the remainder of his body of work.[17] Unencumbered by the need to record historical events, these projects permit the airing of Xenophon's political perspectives with greater creative license, and so with Gray, I too employ Socrates as the initial point of departure for my larger discussion.[18]

---

[12] The closest comparand in terms of sheer generic diversity might be Cicero.

[13] A seminal treatment of this subject is Breitenbach 1967; more recently, see Gray 2011.

[14] The precise order of Xenophon's literary output remains unclear, although certain works are thought to be earlier or later than others, and Xenophon seems to have done most of his writing rather later in his life: see Lee in this volume.

[15] *Pace* Rahn 1971 on developments in Xenophon's historiographic perspectives, since once the other works are added the timeline becomes considerably less clear; see, for example, Aalders 1953.

[16] On Straussian readings of Xenophon, see the bibliography collected by Kroeker 2009: 197 n. 3. Tamiolaki 2014b provides a lucid summary of Straussian methodologies and their intellectual consequences.

[17] Gray 2011: 7–30; Gray 2004a: 171; Gray 2000: 144.

[18] See note 17, above.

Citizenship and the Law: Xenophon on Rights, Responsibilities, and Constitutions

Xenophon's Socrates in the *Memorabilia* emphasizes his obedience, even above the value of his own life, to the laws of Athens,[19] due at least in part to the apologetic qualities of the work as a whole. And yet, Socrates' reasons for this obedience are far from mindless or slavish. He argues that laws promote justice and confidence between citizens (*Mem.* 4.4.13, 17) and internal unity for the state (*Mem.* 4.4.16), a condition that has positive consequences both in peace and in war (*Mem.* 4.4.15). Law, therefore, is an eminently practical creation, whether it is brought into being by human effort (*Mem.* 4.4.13) or laid down by divine providence (*Mem.* 4.4.19)[20] – and there is more than one useful way to structure it. In conversation with Alcibiades in the *Memorabilia*, for example, Pericles gradually arrives at the idea that law can be created by a populace, an oligarchy, or a tyrant, but that it cannot reasonably be called "law" if it is imposed by force without the consent of the governed (*Mem.* 1.2.40–6).[21] While the democratic *politeia* of Athens is therefore one possible constitutional model, just monarchy (*Mem.* 4.6.12) and the special governmental system of Sparta also provide productive examples, especially since Sparta's citizens are notably adherent to the unique code of their state (*Mem.* 4.4.15; *Lac. Pol.* 8.1).

This may help to explain why Xenophon dedicates an entire separate essay, the *Lacedaemonion Politeia*, to the "constitution" of Sparta, a concept that extends in Xenophon's view not only to Spartan governmental structure, but to the elaborate rules and social mechanisms that seem in his account to function as virtual "laws" to guarantee that citizens will be productive contributors to the state in all phases of life (*Lac. Pol.* 10.1; see also 1.3–4.7, 5.1). In this sense, the laws and institutions of Sparta protect not only the people and the polis, but also the very Spartan system itself. Tight organizational control over the cultivation – and exploitation – of ideal citizens, coupled with the deliberate loosening of bonds to what might be perceived as competing political units (even down to the level of the family) and social temptations (such as individual economic advancement), produces a degree of stability that Xenophon both notes and admires (*Lac. Pol.* 1.1–2).[22]

---

[19] Gray 2007: 9, citing *Mem.* 4.4.1–4. See also Pangle 1994: 132–5.
[20] Gray 2007: 9–10 (see esp. 9 n. 15) notes that there seems to be no disconnect between Socrates' respect for written vs. unwritten law.
[21] For a more complex reading of this passage that demonstrates the important flaws in both interlocutors' arguments, see Gray 2004a: 145–6.
[22] Family: *Lac. Pol.* 1.5–10 (elaborate rules regarding marriage, cohabitation, and childbearing), 2.10 and 6.2 (men have control over all children, not only their

He is (rhetorically) surprised that other states do not adopt at least some of the measures of the Spartan code, given its success (*Lac. Pol.* 10.8).[23]

What others should certainly aspire to, Xenophon seems to believe, is the outcome that Sparta produces: a body of citizens who live in temperate harmony with one another, subordinating their baser impulses and personal desires in favor of the needs of a just society.[24] (Even the two hereditary kings are on some level subject to Sparta itself: they exchange a monthly oath of loyalty with the ephors, who represent the polis, *Lac. Pol.* 15.7.) That such an accomplishment as Sparta's is actually possible in other contexts, at least on the individual level, is implicitly argued by Xenophon's own characterization of Socrates in the *Memorabilia*, where the philosopher displays many qualities in common with the Spartans.[25]

Sparta provides Xenophon's most unusual specimen of monarchy (*Lac. Pol.* 15.1–9), but there are other notable examples in his writings of properly ordered kingship. Socrates in the *Memorabilia* (in a recalled conversation) offers careful distinctions: "For he [Socrates] deemed monarchy to consist of rule over willing people in conformity with the laws of their poleis, and tyranny to consist of rule over unwilling people not in conformity with the laws, but in whatever way the ruler might prefer it" (*Mem.* 4.6.12). Xenophon's chief exemplar of good monarchy is Cyrus the Great in the *Cyropaedia*, although material located elsewhere in Xenophon's body of work reveals that the lessons of Cyrus' reign as Xenophon sketches them may be applied to other monarchies, and indeed to other leadership situations.

The prologue to the *Cyropaedia* famously reflects upon different types of government, ranging from democracy to monarchy to oligarchy, and analogizes between stable, effective government and the effective management of farms and households (*Cyr.* 1.1.1–2). For Xenophon, Cyrus proves to be exceptional, as witnessed by the outcome of his reign: not only did he expand his empire to include many lands beyond those he inherited (*Cyr.* 1.1.4), but, far more significantly, he enjoyed the ready submission and respect both of his own people and of those whom he conquered (*Cyr.* 1.1.3, 5). This, then,

---

own), 2.13 (relationships between men and boys so important for the cultivation of aristocratic values in other states reduced in Sparta to mentorship only), 5.2–7 (state messes), 7.1–2 (no mercantile pursuits for citizens, which would also remove the possibility of e.g. guilds). Economic advancement: *Lac. Pol.* 7.1–6; 6.3 notes the common use of personal property like household staff, dogs, and horses.

23 Kroeker 2009: 202–6, outlining some reasons why not only this comment, but many structural and rhetorical features of the *Lac. Pol.* may perhaps be taken as criticism of Athens.

24 See note 25, below, and *Mem.* 3.5.15–16.

25 Lipka 2002: 18–19, with references.

is the signature achievement of Cyrus' kingship, almost precisely as laid out in the *Memorabilia*: that people wanted to follow him.

The remainder of the work endeavors, among other goals, to examine *why* Cyrus flourished as he did. His personal qualities and the virtues that he cultivated are the most critical ingredients in his success, but the structure of his society is also important. The unwritten "constitution" of Cyrus' Persia in fact has a number of features in common with Sparta,[26] most significantly its focus on collective, rather than individual, good (*Cyr.* 1.2.2). The training of Persian citizens (for whom Xenophon uses the word *politai*, the same employed of the members of Greek poleis) by age-classes begins in childhood, and expectations continue into adult life, through military service and into old age (*Cyr.* 1.2.6–16); as in Sparta, moderation and discipline are prioritized (*Cyr.* 1.2.8, 9, 11, 16). But there is an overarching theme in Xenophon's Persia that may be considered distinctive: the pursuit of virtue. Xenophon depicts this not only as the objective of all Persian education (*Cyr.* 1.2.3, 6, 7, 15), but as a central goal of Cyrus himself (especially *Cyr.* 7.5.70–85, 8.1.21–33). Whether this ambition can be wholly maintained as Cyrus converts his kingdom into an empire, however, is a question that has preoccupied modern scholars, who have sometimes seen the idealizing system of Cyrus' Persia as buckling, in spite of Cyrus' apparent high aspirations, under the weight of conquest and rule.[27]

In addition to these "positive" examples of the relationships between citizens and the law (in the widest possible sense), Xenophon also provides one particularly cutting analysis of the negative, mirror image of monarchy. This is tyranny, the exercise of arbitrary, unconstitutional power by an individual who does not enjoy the support of his citizens (*Mem.* 4.6.12). Xenophon's *Hiero*,[28] a fictitious conversation between the poet Simonides of Ceos and the despot Hiero of Syracuse, concentrates initially upon debunking various popular myths about the experience of being a tyrant. Tyrants, for example, are constantly fawned upon by their subjects, which Simonides assumes would be a pleasurable experience, but Hiero reminds him that not only is such praise empty, but, ironically, its absence breeds further suspicion (*Hier.* 1.14–16; see also 7.1–10). Suspicion, in fact, is a significant theme in the *Hiero*, since a tyrant is unable to trust his people (*Hier.* 1.12, 2.7–11, 4.1–5,

---

[26] Azoulay 2007a; cf. also Kroeker 2009: 206, citing (n. 34) Christesen 2006, who reads the *Cyr.* as an imaginary template for the reform of the Spartan military. Tuplin 1994 urges more caution, recommending that perceived similarities between different societies (particularly Sparta and Persia) may be due to the fact that Xenophon's ideas about virtue and leadership are applied across his body of work.

[27] These, of course, represent more subversive readings: see e.g. Nadon 2001; Carlier 1978/2010; but contrast Gray 2011: 246–90, esp. 264–5.

[28] See Dillery in this volume.

5.1–2, 6.1–8); he even fears that those whom he loves may return his affections out of a sense of obligation or dread rather than out of mutual feeling, or worse, that they may turn against him and destroy him (*Hier.* 1.33–8, 3.7–8). Tyranny, therefore, poisons human relationships at every level, from the domestic up to the national.

Perhaps most damagingly of all, the tyrant is unable to interact productively with his own citizens to cultivate the best circumstances within his own state, for his safety and continuance depends upon their subordination, a condition that can only be fostered through disenfranchisement (*Hier.* 6.3–4). A tyrant's citizens, and indeed his very office, are therefore something like Athens's fifth-century empire: dangerous when under control, but also dangerous or well-nigh impossible to release (Thuc. 2.63.2; *Hier.* 6.15–16, cf. 7.11–12).

But there does exist a remedy for the ills of tyranny, and Xenophon places it here in the mouth of Simonides (*Hier.* 9.1–11, 10.2–11.15). The poet's prescriptions contain many suggestions for effective leadership, but of particular importance is the idea that the tyrant should turn the services of his personal guard over to the protection of the entire populace (*Hier.* 10.2–8). This recalls a complaint by Hiero earlier in the dialogue that his guards cannot be trusted, in contrast to the watchmen of Greek military camps (*Hier.* 6.9–11). Hiero argues that the laws of their states shield the watchmen, with the result that they are concerned both for themselves and for their fellow-citizens, but that his guards are prevented from killing him only by their dubious loyalty to the money that they are paid. Law, then, is a literal protector of those who live under it (Hiero goes so far as to use the verb *prophulattousin*, saying that the laws "stand guard before" people, *Hier.* 6.10), and its lack not only endangers civic stability, but affects the value placed upon people's lives.

Xenophon's larger perspectives on law and constitutions display some important similarities with those of his contemporaries Plato and Isocrates, most significantly in their shared respect for civic order and their desire for education, governmental structures, and regulations that will maintain it.[29] Where they differ is in precisely how they feel that order is to be realized. All three writers believe, for example, that grooming for ethical citizenship is critical. Exactly what an appropriate education should contain, however, and in what kind of political system such well-equipped citizens might most productively participate varies amongst the three authors, all of whom explore a range of governmental structures, whether real or potential, in their writings.[30]

[29] See e.g. Schofield 2006: 30–50, 155–93, 203–49 (Plato); de Romilly 1954 (commonalities in the political and social views of Xenophon, Isocrates, and Aeschines); see also Gray 2000 *passim* (Xenophon and Isocrates).
[30] On Plato, e.g. McCoy 2007; Schofield 2006 in n. 29, above; on Isocrates e.g. the essays in Poulakos and Depew 2004, esp. Morgan 2004, and Gray 2000; for a comparison of

Plato's *Republic* and *Laws* describe speculative, utopian societies (Callipolis and Magnesia, respectively) that aim for good government in part by placing those who are possessed of the necessary knowledge in positions of authority.[31] The *Republic* imagines a state in which every individual is trained from youth to assume a carefully defined civic role, with the highest power vested in elite "philosopher-kings"; the *Laws* constructs an elaborate network of legislation to be protected by a class of "guardians" and supported by a "nocturnal council." Although the social and political visions represented by the two works differ significantly on the surface, they share some important intellectual priorities, including their convictions that leaders must be able to think beyond particular experiences to general principles, and must be readied for this by their education;[32] and that the very structure of the state contributes to the cultivation of good citizens.[33]

Isocrates, like Plato, proposes in his writings more than one version of improved civic life, but a significant difference is Isocrates' interest in realia, rather than in abstract ideals.[34] He focuses many of his criticisms and observations upon Athens itself,[35] including the educational system and its practical public import.[36] Particularly later in his life, when the geopolitical situation had changed, his emphasis seems to have rested more significantly upon panhellenism, which while it remained an unrealized possibility was at least portrayed in Greek rhetoric as having significant potential consequences.[37] A disposition that remains common amongst Isocrates, Plato, and Xenophon, however, is a bias in favor of the political dominance of elites. All three of these authors offer in their writings both implicit and explicit criticisms of the Athenian democracy, in the sense that they harbor a certain distrust in the ability of the *dêmos* – or any group like it – to make good decisions without the guidance of leaders from the upper classes.[38]

Isocratean and Platonic paideutic philosophies, see Johnstone 2009: 146–87; a more general treatment of education is Morgan 1999.

[31] Saunders 1992: 464–7.

[32] Saunders 1992: 467. See also Stalley 1983: 8–22, esp. 14–15.

[33] Stalley 1983: 8.

[34] See note 96, below.

[35] Davidson 1990 esp. 20.

[36] Too 1995; see also the essays in Poulakos and Depew 2004.

[37] On Isocratean panhellenism, see Perlman 1976: 25–9, discussing in particular Isoc. *Panegyricus* and *To Philip*; see also Isoc. *Panathenaicus*. On panhellenism in general, see below.

[38] On Xenophon, see above; on Plato and Isocrates, see Ober 1998: 156–289; Roberts 1994: 65–92.

Democracy and Democratic Athens

Many of Xenophon's political ideas can be observed and discussed in relation to non-democratic constitutions,[39] but certain aspects of his thought do apply directly to democracy, and more specifically to Athens. Xenophon's interests in this regard are diverse: three of his most important areas of concern are the ideas of Socrates regarding the positive cultivation of the democratic citizenry and particularly of its leadership (covered in most detail in the *Memorabilia*); the ways in which Athens as a political society can sustain and improve its way of life (again, an important theme in the *Memorabilia*, and the central subject of the *Poroi*); and the capacity of democracy to produce effective decisions and good government (particularly visible through a number of anecdotes in the *Anabasis* and *Hellenica*).

The *Memorabilia* is *de facto* set in democratic Athens, but within that framework Socrates' conversations and comments reveal important ideas that reach beyond signature democratic political structures. Qualities of ideal leaders, for example, are repeatedly discussed, likely in large part because of the growing dependence of the Athenian democracy – and indeed of other Greek states – upon such eminent individuals.[40] But the general rights and responsibilities of prominent democratic citizens are also treated, since Xenophon's Socrates views himself not as being politically active, but rather as a teacher of those who ultimately will be.[41] Those who aspire to political distinction should not only cultivate virtue in themselves, but should also, for the good of the city, associate peacefully and productively with others who are like-minded (*Mem.* 2.6.24–5), rather than struggling against them. Their reputations should be founded upon substance rather than upon false rhetoric (*Mem.* 2.6.38–9; this was a highly sensitive issue in the debates over the role of sophism in education).[42] A citizen, particularly an influential one, necessarily has a symbiotic relationship with the city, receiving praise in return for the benefits he renders (*Mem.* 3.6.3), and his very membership in the polis obligates him to political participation and to action if he is able to do his city some good (*Mem.* 3.7.1–9).[43] Similarly, like members of all constitutions, the democratic citizen is obligated to obey his city's laws, both written and unwritten (*Mem.* 4.4.17–21), and will fare best if he controls his personal impulses (*Mem.* 4.5.1–12). But in the Socratic worldview, personal moderation is equated not merely with virtue, but with

[39] Seager 2001: 396.
[40] Ferrario 2014; Stadter 2009: 457, 459.
[41] McNamara 2009: 223–4; see also *Apol.* 1.21, 25–6.
[42] Blanchard 1994; Johnstone 1994: 226, 228–9, 239.
[43] See Kroeker 2009: 210.

freedom (*Mem.* 4.5.2) – a concept that when transferred from the personal to the political becomes a central pillar of Greek democratic thinking.[44]

One recent analysis shows that the political advice that Socrates gives in *Memorabilia* 3.1–7 (especially 5–7) focuses, against a sobering background, upon improving the status of Athens itself, for "Socrates' Athens is a city in decline."[45] Socrates' prescriptions are in many ways encapsulated in his suggestion that Glaucon, as an aspiring leader, requires above all else deep knowledge of the operation of the city (*Mem.* 3.6.18): its finances (*Mem.* 3.6.5–7), its military strength in comparison with that of its enemies (*Mem.* 3.6.8–9), its defenses (*Mem.* 3.6.10–11), its natural resources (i.e. its silver mines, *Mem.* 3.6.12), its food supply (*Mem.* 3.6.13–14). And Socrates' practical recommendations in the *Memorabilia* are also in many ways consonant with those made in Xenophon's own narrative voice in the *Poroi*. The *Memorabilia*'s emphases may be summarized thus: "Socrates' policy recommendations favor a militarily independent, fiscally responsible, economically self-sufficient, politically moderate and non-imperial regime for Athens."[46] In the case of the *Poroi*, Xenophon places food independence at the very beginning of his argument (*Por.* 1.1), and then moves on to iterate some of the resources of Attica, including, again, its silver mines (*Por.* 1.5, treated in great detail at *Por.* 4.1–52). He next discusses ways in which Athens's population of metics could be put to better use for the good of the state: they should be released from mandatory military service and allowed to operate their businesses for the good of the general economy (*Por.* 2.1–4), and at the same time should be allowed to increase the ranks of the cavalry (*Por.* 2.5), a form of service that carries with it overtones of elite pride. Athens should increase its mercantile interests, which will have a positive ripple effect on revenue (*Por.* 3.1–14), and should, most importantly, refrain from war unless absolutely necessary (*Por.* 5.1–13).[47]

But is the Athenian government, in Xenophon's view, capable of the kind of effective decision-making that such forward-thinking policies would require? Xenophon's Socrates in the *Memorabilia* is sketched as being distrustful of, or perhaps even opposed to, the system of random draw that determined so many of the political offices under the Athenian democracy, arguing instead that rulership should belong to those who are intellectually

---

[44] Compare Plato's version of the elderly Sophocles liberated from physical impulses: Pl. *Rep.* 1.329b–d. On *eleutheria* ("freedom") in Greek thought, see Tamiolaki 2010; Raaflaub 2004; Raaflaub 1983.

[45] McNamara 2009: 240–1, quote at 241. This is perhaps most visible in the conversation between Socrates and the younger Pericles at *Mem.* 3.5.1–28.

[46] McNamara 2009: 241.

[47] Lewis 2009 summarizes and explicates the policies that Xenophon proposes. On the avoidance of warfare, see esp. Dillery 1993.

prepared for it.[48] But this single sentiment does not capture the complexity of the views espoused either by Xenophon's Socrates (who elsewhere in the *Memorabilia* is at pains to provide the education that he believes rulers require, while highlighting for them the need to obey the laws of the state)[49] or by Xenophon himself. Two of Xenophon's works in particular provide historical case studies of this type of Greek governance in action: the *Anabasis* and (especially) the *Hellenica*.

The *Anabasis*, it must be stated outright, is not a study of democracy. The governmental "system" in effect during the journey of the Ten Thousand out of Babylonia is dictated by two major factors: firstly, traditional military hierarchy; and secondly, the use of military assemblies, at which arguments are ventured by leaders and votes taken by those present. Although this elemental structure has certain features in common with those of a fully developed polis,[50] the soldiers, when questions are put to them, most often ratify their commanders' decisions rather than establishing policies or determining between courses of action. Even a brief factional split in the army ultimately leads to a reunion and a renewed expression of dependence upon its generals (*Anab.* 6.2.4–4.11).[51] The fourth century did tend to elevate and lionize prominent leaders even in democratic contexts, but Xenophon's Ten Thousand subject themselves to their commanders, and in particular to Xenophon himself, to a degree that suggests they are likely incapable of independent decision-making. Perhaps no moment in the *Anabasis* is more illustrative of this than when Xenophon's men are hoping to invade Byzantium – but approach him to ask for his leadership (*Anab.* 7.1.21): "When the soldiers spotted Xenophon, many of them hurried towards him and said, 'Now, Xenophon, you can become a man. You have a city, warships, resources, so many troops. Now, if you want to, you could help us and we would make you great.'"

The *Hellenica*, in contrast, furnishes a number of opportunities to observe the Athenian democracy in action, and on some important occasions the *dêmos* is depicted as lacking in its capacity for good government or even for right thinking.[52] These episodes, as might be expected, are concentrated in the large first section of the work (*Hell.* 1.1.1–2.3.10), which represents

---

[48] Gray 2004a: 152, citing *Mem.* 3.9.10 and (n. 1) Vlastos 1994a: 89, who in turn cites *Mem.* 1.2.9.

[49] Gray 2004a: 153–4.

[50] On the Ten Thousand as a quasi-polis, see Hornblower 2004: 244–5; Dillery 1995: 69–90. On democratizing features of the military assemblies in the *Anabasis*, see Nussbaum 1967: 48–68.

[51] Ferrario 2014: 195–9.

[52] Forsdyke 2009: 240, citing both the Arginusae episode and the quotation of *Hell.* 1.7.12 referenced immediately following note 54, below.

a conclusion of the narrative of the Peloponnesian War.[53] Most illustrative as negative examples are the affair of Arginusae (*Hell.* 1.6.24–7.35) and the treatment of Alcibiades (distributed throughout books 1 and 2). The former is quickly explained: after an Athenian naval victory, although the generals planned to go to the rescue of those injured and stranded, their efforts were prevented by bad weather (see especially *Hell.* 1.6.35). The *boulê* responded by detaining for trial in the Assembly those of the commanders who came back to Athens (*Hell.* 1.7.1–4), and while the mode of the proceedings was under discussion, fraudulent mourners and bribery swayed the *boulê* to propose to the Assembly an unconstitutional mass trial (*Hell.* 1.7.7–16). Despite objections, some popular (*Hell.* 1.7.12) and some from governmental officials, including Socrates (*Hell.* 1.7.14–16), the generals were condemned and those within the reach of the law were executed (*Hell.* 1.7.34).

Particularly chilling notes in Xenophon's account of these events are sounded by two features: the shout of *to plêthos*, "the masses" in the Assembly,[54] who supported the collective attack on the leaders outside of the law, saying that "if anyone hindered the *dêmos* from enacting its wishes, it would be a horrific thing" (*Hell.* 1.7.12), and the extensive speech placed by Xenophon into the mouth of Euryptolemus, who argues the more moderate side of the question at length, but to no avail (*Hell.* 1.7.16–33). The inability of such an accomplished speaker to rein in the destructive impulses of the *dêmos* may perhaps be taken as a meditation upon the unique leadership capacities of the deceased Pericles.[55] But it may also, from Xenophon's perspective at least, serve as a larger symbol of the governmental crisis into which wartime Athens, bereft of a guiding hand that can both coddle and channel the collective emotions of the *dêmos*, has sunk.[56]

The treatment of the notoriously disloyal Alcibiades by his countrymen in the *Hellenica* also invites reflective criticism of the efficacy of Athenian democracy.[57] While "commander narrative," where the name of a leader stands in for the movements of his troops, becomes more prominent in Greek historical writing over time,[58] the exiled but militarily active Alcibiades is

---

[53] Even other democracies are not exempt from criticism in this part of the *Hellenica*: at *Hell.* 1.1.27–31, Syracuse is deprived of a highly competent core of leaders and commanders (most notably Hermocrates), who are exiled through the political action of the Syracusan *dêmos*. On the possibility that this section of the *Hellenica* is designed to finish the work left incomplete by Thucydides, see Luraghi in this volume.

[54] On the potentially problematic nature of this term, e.g. Ober 1989: 11 n. 15.

[55] Thuc. 2.65.1–13.

[56] *Pace* Gish 2012, who reads the *dêmos* in this episode as defending its sovereignty and therefore the very concept of democracy itself.

[57] For more detail on Xenophon's version of Alcibiades, see Ferrario 2014: 184–90.

[58] Dillery 2001: 14 and n. 13, citing Connor 1984: 54–5.

featured in the narratives of the conflicts at Abydus (*Hell.* 1.1.4–6), Cyzicus (*Hell.* 1.1.9–18), and Calchedon (*Hell.* 1.3.1–8) in a manner that paints him almost as Athens's savior. And his homecoming soon thereafter (*Hell.* 1.4.12–21) shows the viewing public literally marveling at him (*Hell.* 1.4.13). In this section, Xenophon presents bystander comments from both Alcibiades' critics and his supporters. Most notably, the latter suggest that Alcibiades as an individual leader harbored the capacity to help his city to an extraordinary degree, since before he had been exiled "more [esteem] came to him from the *dêmos* than did to his peers, nor was he outranked by those who were his senior" (*Hell.* 1.4.16). Afterwards, however, "although he watched those closest to him, countrymen and relatives and the whole *polis*, acting in error, he had no way of assisting them, since he was banned due to his status as an exile" (*Hell.* 1.4.15). Similarly, his detractors argue that Alcibiades alone was responsible for all of the troubles that his city had recently experienced (*Hell.* 1.4.17).

Xenophon's critical term for the watching crowd in this scene, *ho ochlos* (*Hell.* 1.4.13), carries a negative sense not unlike that of *to plêthos* in the Arginusae episode,[59] and the treatment that this "mob" furnishes to this extraordinary individual demonstrates both its fickleness and its lack of forethought. The credulous Assembly names Alcibiades as "high commander with sole authority," *hapantôn hegemôn autokratôr* (*Hell.* 1.4.20), a position of extraordinary influence and power, but quickly turns on him when his subordinate, in his absence, provokes and loses an ill-conceived battle (*Hell.* 1.5.10–16). Alcibiades is deposed and withdraws to the Chersonese (*Hell.* 1.5.17); when the desperate fighting near the end of the war verges close to his own residence he recommends that the Athenians make their base at Sestus, but is rebuked by the active generals (*Hell.* 2.1.25–6). His advice is ironically prescient, for the imminent Athenian loss at the battle of Aegospotami opens the way for the final Spartan siege of Athens. The Athenian *dêmos*, therefore, has been wrong about Alcibiades on nearly all accounts, having trusted him far too deeply in the earlier years of the war and having been unable to harness his expertise appropriately in the later ones.

Is Xenophon, then, an anti-democrat? As is frequently observed, Xenophon meditated abundantly upon the ways in which Socrates was misunderstood and underappreciated by his people. The *Memorabilia* and *Poroi* also reflect significant disappointment with the current state of Athenian affairs, and it is not clear whether even Xenophon believes that their proposals can actually be meaningfully realized. His *Anabasis* shows a general dependence

---

[59] See note 54, above.

upon the individual leader that is both shared and extended in the *Hellenica*, which also casts democracy in an occasionally poor light. It is small wonder that Xenophon has in the past been branded an elitist and an oligarch.[60] But the explanation is not quite so simple.[61] The very existence of prescriptive qualities in Xenophon's writings suggests a fundamental interest in the operation and improvement of Athens, rather than a wholesale rejection of its systems and values.[62] The problem for Xenophon is not necessarily democracy, but rather the ability of *to plêthos* to govern without the interdependent guidance of truly capable leadership.[63] And as will be discussed further below, Xenophon is aristocratic in his background and often in his thinking, but he also sees elites as bearing significant social, political, and economic responsibilities as a result of their positions of privilege. For Xenophon, those who would seek political prominence, under any constitution, must have the requisite background in education and in character to fulfill the duties thereby placed upon them, in order to sustain and enhance both their own positions and those of their states.

This vision bears certain resemblances to the imaginary society sketched in Plato's *Republic*, where citizens at every level are groomed and educated for the permanent positions that they are destined to fulfill. There are, however, some important differences. Plato's prescriptions, as observed above, are idealized;[64] Xenophon's are at least nominally intended for more practical application. Plato's Callipolis is, of course, a non-democratic regime; Xenophon's views suggest that some variety of democracy might be possible if it is appropriately guided. But both of these perspectives, along with Isocrates' clear preference for a democracy steered by educated aristocrats,[65] implicitly demonstrate the increasing reliance of fourth-century Athens – and indeed, of fourth-century Greece – on individual leaders.[66] For

---

[60] Kroeker 2009: 198–9, with references. So has Socrates, including Xenophon's own particular version of him: e.g. (cited *ibid.* 209 n. 49) Vlastos 1994a: 87–108, arguing that Xenophon's Socrates is "subversive," while Plato's is supportive of the Athenian democracy and closer to the historical version of the philosopher.

[61] Gray 2004a: 167–9, for example (cited in Kroeker 2009: 199 n. 14), reads Socrates as being quite positively disposed towards democracy, and Xenophon himself even more so.

[62] Gray 2004a: 169–71.

[63] This is the interpretation of M. Tamiolaki, to whom I am also grateful for additional discussion that helped to clarify my thinking on this subject.

[64] On whether Plato considered an actual realization of his "Callipolis" to be feasible, see e.g. Morrison 2007.

[65] Ober 1998: 285; see also Roberts 1994: 66–9, noting that Isocrates nowhere provides a detailed explication of his precise prescriptions for the Athenian democracy, although he abundantly contrasts the present with the past.

[66] See note 40, above.

all of these thinkers, the "quality of the management" still remains the key to a successful society, regardless of the precise nature of the constitution.[67]

Other Ways of Organizing People: Elite Life and the Estate as City

The role of the aristocracy within a productively functioning state is therefore one of Xenophon's significant political interests.[68] And the preparation of that aristocracy to assume its leading role is part of the prompt for some of Xenophon's shorter writings, most notably the *Cavalry Commander* and *On Hunting*. These are prescriptive essays, significantly concerned with technical recommendations. Their contributions to an understanding of Xenophon's wider political thinking, however, run far deeper than the selection of revealing comments that they contain, for they both connect in meaningful ways with the rest of Xenophon's corpus.

The *Cavalry Commander*, for example, stresses regard for military structure and emphasizes that subordinates in positions of authority should share the convictions of the leader (*Hipparch.* 1.8, 24), not unlike the issues explored in the *Anabasis*. Also represented in more specific situations in the *Anabasis* are the ideas that a commander should be able to do with distinction anything that he asks his men to do (*Hipparch.* 1.25, 6.3; compare, for example, *Anab.* 3.4.47–9), that he should avoid unnecessary danger (*Hipparch.* 4.13, 6.2–3, with *Anab.* 4.6.10), and that he should be pious (*Hipparch.* 1.1, 7.1, with *Anab.* 3.2.9). In short, a commander who sets a good example and guides with a firm hand is likely to gain both human and divine favor, and to create a stable and productive military "society," which while not identical to a polis may share certain positive characteristics with it.

The essay *On Hunting* holds that hunting generates two positive outcomes: firstly, it creates readiness for warfare; and secondly, through the various kinds of work that it demands, it promotes the development of good character (*Cyn.* 1.1–8, 12.1–9). An important observation is that Xenophon sees *ponos*, "toil," as a means for the cultivation of virtue since it involves not only physical effort, but also self-control.[69] For this reason, he both advocates hunting as an aristocratic exercise and writes positively of its presence in the rituals of the other societies that have captured his greatest interest: Sparta,

---

[67] Quotation from Gray 2000: 146, speaking explicitly of Xenophon and Isocrates; see also Stadter 2009: 457, 469; cf. Johnstone 1994: 222, and note 63, above.
[68] Johnstone 1994: 219 makes a similar generalization regarding "the lifestyle of elites," but my concerns here are somewhat broader.
[69] Johnstone 1994 esp. 219, 221, 227–8.

where it is encouraged by Lycurgus (*Lac. Pol.* 4.7), and Persia, where it is modeled with especial skill by Cyrus (*Cyr.* 1.4.5–15, 8.1.35–9).

The *Oeconomicus* shows Xenophon imagining the structure of a different kind of political association: not a state or an empire like Athens, Sparta, Syracuse, or Persia; and not a military unit like the Ten Thousand or a cavalry detachment; but rather an estate settled by a landowner, his wife, and their workers and slaves (and presumably later on, their children). At the same time, however, Xenophon also provides a discussion of the social and political value of farming. In the extensive framing portion of the dialogue, where Socrates converses with Critobulus, a more specific set of principles is again connected with a larger context, not unlike the links already observed between the *Cavalry Commander* and the *Anabasis*. Here, however, what is at issue is the activity of agriculture itself, which Socrates claims has broad consequences in application – so much so, in fact, that it even attracts the attention of the king of Persia, who prioritizes it on a level similar to his interest in war (*Oec.* 4.5–25). Farming, like hunting, is another means of cultivating virtue, since it demands the same kind of honorable work (*Oec.* 5.1–17);[70] further, like military life, it demands appropriate "command" over obedient subordinates (*Oec.* 5.14–16).

Socrates' case study, on the estate of Ischomachus, occupies the remainder of the dialogue. The transition is accomplished through a summary of the preceding discussion, highlighted by some reasons why farming creates good citizens: it fosters loyalty to the land, promotes physical vigor (and hence readiness for warfare), allows time for engagement in political concerns, and demands courage (*Oec.* 6.6–10). The succeeding conversation between Socrates and Ischomachus (here reported by Socrates) next demonstrates some important ways in which Xenophon sees the small community of the *oikos* as mirroring the larger one of the polis. The union of spouses, with their respective masculine and feminine duties to land and home, exterior and interior life, warfare and family, is viewed as a divinely ordained service to society (*Oec.* 7.17–30), which implicitly requires all of these responsibilities to be well executed if orderly prosperity is to be achieved.

So important is the household, therefore, that Ischomachus sketches its internal operation as if it were a city in miniature. The housekeeper that he hires and trains (*Oec.* 9.11–13) displays many of the same capacities that a good citizen shows in the *Memorabilia*,[71] and the regulations of the home

---

[70] Johnstone 1994: 229–32. And indeed, Socrates sees hunting as itself dependent upon farming: *Oec.* 5.5–8.

[71] E.g. self-control (*Mem.* 1.5.1, 2.1.1–7), the desire for honor (*Mem.* 3.7.1–2), a sense of communal responsibility (*Mem.* 3.7.2), the drive to increase the general lot (*Mem.* 3.6.4), and a commitment to justice (*Mem.* 4.2.11).

are analogized with law (*Oec.* 9.14–15). Servants, too, are inculcated with important citizen virtues, such as self-restraint (*Oec.* 12.11–14) and justice (*Oec.* 14.3–9, where this quality is said to be taught using principles derived from Draco, Solon, and the king of Persia). Ischomachus' own aristocratic background and prior experience with the positive outcomes produced by farming has therefore, at least according to his own vision, implicitly prepared him not only for good citizenship in the polis, but also for leadership of his own domain, his *oikos* and his estate.[72]

While it has been argued that Ischomachus' view of the world may be incomplete or inadequate from Socrates' perspective,[73] its portrayal nevertheless allows Xenophon to sketch out how aristocrats of his era may have viewed themselves.[74] There is no denying that Xenophon's social elitism is similar in many ways to that displayed by other political writers and thinkers of the fourth century.[75] But his generally pro-aristocratic perspective tends often to manifest itself in a call to class-appropriate political and social responsibility.

Effective Leadership

As has already been suggested, this topic is perhaps the most important of all to Xenophon, and is addressed throughout his corpus. Interesting case studies, however, are represented by the *Agesilaus*, the *Cyropaedia*, and the *Anabasis*. Each of these works has a unique story to tell: the *Agesilaus* is an essay project born of Xenophon's admiration for a single figure; the *Cyropaedia*, which may be characterized as a wisdom novel, foregrounds the grooming – in family circumstance, in education, in military service, and in life experience – of a successful king and explores his relationship with his people; and the *Anabasis* finally represents Xenophon's account of himself in a position of leadership. The latter work, perhaps an apologia, allows potential observation of how Xenophon would prefer that he himself be acknowledged and remembered as a leader.[76]

Xenophon's *Agesilaus* is to some extent characteristic of its time. While it is believed to have been inspired by Isocrates' *Evagoras*, the latter is actually far from being an isolated literary event. Instead, the *Evagoras* is possessed both of historiographic antecedents and of successor projects, often by

[72] On Ischomachus as an aristocrat, see Johnstone 1994: 225, 229.
[73] See Nee 2009, but contrast Dorion 2008; Danzig 2003 offers a moderate reconciliation.
[74] Johnstone 1994: 230, observing that "the *Oeconomicus* shows how elites stylized mundane, productive activities by making them the object of self-conscious reflection."
[75] See Ober 1998 and 1989.
[76] E.g. Flower 2012: 31–8; Cawkwell 2004: 59–67.

Isocrates' own former students, that demonstrate a growing interest during the fourth century in encomium and in its generic sibling, biography.[77] But Xenophon's own encomium for the Spartan king who had been his friend and supporter is also a demonstration of the writer's regard for the Spartan way of life and especially for the particular personal qualities that Agesilaus displayed. By Xenophon's account, Agesilaus was a military commander with a good appreciation of social psychology, capable simultaneously of treating enemies humanely when the circumstances invited it (*Ages.* 1.20–2) and of using strong rhetorical displays to inspire his men (*Ages.* 1.25–7, 1.28). He was willing and able to sacrifice personal gain for the good of his state (note in particular his obedient and selfless response to his recall from his Asian expedition, *Ages.* 1.36, 2.16). He promoted peace and unity in the lands that he conquered (*Ages.* 1.37–8), and displayed notable piety (*Ages.* 2.13, 3.2). Agesilaus was immune to the influence of money (*Ages.* 4.1), moderate in his personal life (*Ages.* 5.1–2, 5.4, 8.6–7), courageous (*Ages.* 6.1), wise (*Ages.* 6.4), gifted with military skill (*Ages.* 6.5–8), and a lover of his polis and an honorable politician (*Ages.* 7.1).

This picture provides a compact iteration of some of the virtues that Xenophon seems to believe a good leader should possess, but it is indisputably idealized.[78] The Agesilaus of Xenophon's *Hellenica* differs in a number of ways, both clear and subtle, from the subject of the encomium. The greater detail present in the longer historical account, coupled with Xenophon's need to provide background and motivations for various actions there, creates a much more complex character. The Agesilaus of the *Hellenica* can be both immoderate and impetuous (e.g. *Hell.* 3.4.4, 4.5.6, 4.5.10), and personally ambitious beyond the level that the encomium seems to allow. This is perhaps best observed in the narrative of the withdrawal from Asia (*Hell.* 4.2.1–5). In the *Agesilaus*, as observed above, the cancellation of the king's grand expedition is nobly borne as a sacrifice for the good of Sparta (*Ages.* 1.36–8); in the *Hellenica*, however, Agesilaus is filled with regret at the loss to his honor (*Hell.* 4.2.3), and his allies weep openly (*Hell.* 4.2.3–4). Agesilaus musters troops from the Asian cities, offering lavish rewards in return, and then follows the same path homeward that the Persian king Xerxes had employed when attacking Greece a hundred years before (*Hell.* 4.2.5–8). The deep irony of this reversal – Agesilaus' "answering" invasion of Asia against the Persians, after all, has essentially proven a failure[79] – is entirely omitted from the encomium.

[77] Wareh 2012: 140–9.
[78] For more realistic treatments of Agesilaus, see Hamilton 1991 and Cartledge 1987; for an ironic reading of Xenophon's *Agesilaus*, see Harman 2012.
[79] Dillery 1995: 107–8, 113–19.

A similar situation occurs in the *Cyropaedia*, where open discussions of idealized leadership and rather more complex depictions of character take place not in separate literary works, but within the same project. Physical and temporal remove, however (Cyrus the Great ruled in Persia from 559 until his death in 530), here allow Xenophon license to craft his material with almost complete freedom, since the historical Cyrus had long since been subsumed into a paradigm in Classical Greece.[80] The *Cyropaedia* furnishes a model of leadership that focuses upon the cultivation of necessary virtues and the acquisition of appropriate knowledge in order to inspire ready obedience and support from followers.[81] Whether this leadership is read positively, as rooted in honor, or negatively, as grounded in deception,[82] it is objectively effective. Cyrus takes what he learns during his youth and education, as well as from meaningful conversations during his young adulthood (e.g. the extensive instruction furnished by his father, Cambyses, at *Cyr.* 1.6.1–46), and uses it to build an empire that is reliably loyal. The fact that the text as transmitted has this empire failing after Cyrus dies (*Cyr.* 8.8.1–27) has disturbed many readers, but in any case it may be taken as demonstrating the extraordinary dependence of the machine upon the man, whether for good or for ill.[83]

What, then, distinguishes Xenophon's Cyrus and marks him for success? Cyrus' chief qualifications for leadership have been characterized as a love of humanity, a love of learning, and a love of honor.[84] But Cyrus' pursuit of happiness and prosperity for his followers is also critically important, since (in Xenophon's Socratic worldview) the betterment of self and others is one of the chief functions of good leadership.[85] Although Xenophon clearly composed Cyrus as a model rather than a man, the king is also consistent in a number of ways with Xenophon's presentations of other important leaders. Just as the Persian way of life shows certain features in common with the Spartan one,[86] some of Cyrus' personal qualities and experiences again overlap with references in Xenophon's other projects.

[80] Sandridge 2012: 2; on Xenophon's rhetorical liberties, see also note 17, above.

[81] See Tamiolaki 2012: 567 on knowledge and virtue as important qualities for leadership in Xenophon. The followers will ideally in turn find themselves, their affairs, and their country developed to fullest potential through the leader's example and skill: Gray 2011: 24.

[82] See Reisert 2009: 296–8. A positive interpretation represents a more direct reading; a negative one requires a more ironic and subversive approach. Tamiolaki 2012: 565 offers appropriate caution and recommends a middle course; Gray 2011: 246–90 is a recent argument that Xenophon really is praising Cyrus.

[83] For opposing perspectives, see Reisert 2009: 297 nn. 10–11; Browning 2011, citing Gray 2011 (there, see esp. 246–63).

[84] Sandridge 2012.

[85] Gray 2011: 25–30.

[86] See note 26, above.

Cyrus excels in horsemanship and in the hunt from the days of his youth (*Cyr.* 1.4.5–15), and he subordinates his own desires to the summons of his father and his country when he leaves his grandfather's court in Media to return to Persia (*Cyr.* 1.4.25–6; Agesilaus' return to Sparta from his Asian expedition, discussed above, demands similar selflessness, particularly in the *Agesilaus*). Cyrus holds that virtue begets virtue within the army (*Cyr.* 2.2.23–5), just as Lycurgus believed that it would do within the Spartan state (*Lac. Pol.* 10.4–7). Like Agesilaus, Cyrus can be merciful towards his enemies if it suits his purposes (*Cyr.* 7.1.40–6, on the Egyptians). Certain of his actions, however, are best paralleled by situations – both negative and positive – discussed in the *Hiero*. Like the defensive and paranoid Hiero, Cyrus forms a bodyguard after he has conquered Babylon (along with posting guards for the palace and the city, as well, *Cyr.* 7.5.58–69; *Hier.* 5.3, 6.4, 6.10–11, 10.1–3). He also seeks safety by binding his nobles to him rather than encouraging their alliances with one another.[87] In other regards, however, Cyrus seems to be partaking of many of the prescriptions for good rulership offered by Simonides at *Hiero* 11.1–15:[88] serving not just as a leader but as an instructor for his people (*Hier.* 11.2; compare, for example, *Cyr.* 3.3.49–55), honoring the best amongst his subjects (*Hier.* 11.2, 6–10, with *Cyr.* 2.2.20), cultivating his people's and his nation's success (*Hier.* 11.1, 7, with *Cyr.* 8.1.9–39, 8.6.10–18), and distributing benefits to those whose loyalty he seeks (*Hier.* 11.13–15, with *Cyr.* 8.2.1–28, 8.6.23), so that all desire to obey him freely (*Hier.* 11.8–12, with *Cyr.* 4.1.19 on the army, 1.1.3–6 on the empire in general).

Cyrus, therefore, like all leaders in Xenophon, is more complex than he may seem at first glance–and also necessarily imperfect.[89] Agesilaus is so selectively represented in his eponymous encomium that the contrasting picture in the *Hellenica* cannot but be taken by modern readers as a corrective. Hiero understands the problems inherent in tyranny but has not worked out solutions of his own accord. The interlocutors of the *Memorabilia* who are in (or who aspire to) preferential positions in Athenian politics are in need of extended instruction by Socrates.[90] And even Socrates himself, who might on some level be construed as Xenophon's ideal leader, does not actually apply his own moral virtues directly to active political life, in spite of prescribing that his students should do so.[91]

---

[87] *Cyr.* 8.1.48. Compare the somewhat different but related ideas at *Hier.* 5.1–4, 6.13–16.
[88] On some of the thematic links between the *Hiero* and the *Cyropaedia*, see Aalders 1953 (arguing that the former postdated the latter).
[89] Tamiolaki 2012.
[90] See McNamara 2009.
[91] Tamiolaki 2012: 580–7.

What happens, then, when Xenophon becomes a leader himself? Is he, too, imperfect? It is highly unlikely that Xenophon, even if using the *Anabasis* as a defense of his own actions and ideas,[92] would style himself as being superior to Socrates, and indeed he does not. On the contrary, his coverage of his departure for the expedition of the rebel Persian prince Cyrus the Younger includes an account of the ways in which he failed to correctly interpret Socrates' advice (*Anab.* 3.1.5–7). But the very placement of his entry into his own narrative also implies that he is destined to take the place of Cyrus,[93] who is often characterized in an idealizing manner, as if possessing qualities in common with the famous ancestor whose name he shares (note especially his eulogizing obituary at *Anab.* 1.9.1–31, in comparison with the extended treatments of the leadership of Cyrus the Elder in *Cyr.* 8).[94] But Cyrus the Younger is killed in battle at *Anabasis* 1.8.27. Into this breach (eventually) steps Xenophon. *Anabasis* 3.1.4–26 contains the coverage of Xenophon's rise from rank to command, introduced by a prophetic dream (*Anab.* 3.1.10–12) and concluded with Xenophon's modest – and moderate – suggestion that he is willing either to follow or to lead (*Anab.* 3.1.25).

As a commander, Xenophon the character does exhibit a number of the positive characteristics that Xenophon the writer seems to espouse in other contexts. He is willing and able to lead both by encouragement and by example, as when he cheers on his men, then leaps from his horse and takes up the shield of an exhausted soldier (*Anab.* 3.4.46–9), or chops wood in the snow (*Anab.* 4.4.12–13). He places the requirements of his army ahead of his own, not prioritizing his physical needs for meals and rest (*Anab.* 4.3.10). He is pious, as witnessed by his gifts, sacrifices, and other attendances upon the gods (*Anab.* 3.1.5–7, 3.1.10–12, 4.3.13, 5.3.5, 5.6.15–16), and he is willing to sacrifice his own potential glory to the will of his men.[95] He is not immune to criticism by the army, although this situation typically arises when the men misunderstand Xenophon's actions or intentions. The soldiers are unwilling to follow Xenophon when he aspires to found a colony, for example, because they receive inaccurate reports about his motivations (*Anab.* 5.6.15–35), and they also bristle at reports that he has dispensed beatings, until it emerges that this has been done for the good

[92] See note 76, above.

[93] Ferrario 2014: 193.

[94] But cf. Flower 2012: 188–94, arguing that the younger Cyrus fails to measure up to the elder in several important respects, most notably piety, and is not presented as an exclusively positive figure.

[95] See esp. *Anab.* 5.6.15–31, where Xenophon abandons the idea of becoming a colonial founder under pressure from his troops, and 6.1.7–31, where Xenophon rejects the possibility of sole command because it seems to oppose divine will. For more on these passages, see Ferrario 2012: 368–9.

of their military "society," to punish a man who tried to bury an injured comrade alive (*Anab.* 5.8.1–12). Xenophon here defends the discipline that he has rendered to those who deserved it, in the manner that a teacher would for a student or a parent for a child, and offers equal reminders of the services and honors that he has dispensed. As might be expected under the circumstances of the character, the author, and the work, this précis of Xenophon's leadership philosophy is warmly received by the assembled soldiers, and Xenophon *qua* author reports that "things ended well" (*Anab.* 5.8.13–26, quote at 26).

As noted above, the fourth century in general, and fourth-century political thought in particular, was especially interested in the role of the outstanding individual in civic affairs. Plato, Isocrates, and Xenophon were all key intellectual contributors to this perspective, but while Plato concentrated centrally upon formulating principles,[96] the other two authors focused at various points in their work upon historical leaders, past and present, from a variety of political and cultural contexts, with virtue remaining a central concern.[97] Isocrates even composed a series of addresses to contemporary political figures that offered not only recommendations on policy and action, but also moral prescriptions: his *Epistles* 1–9 are addressed to Dionysius of Syracuse, Philip II of Macedon (who receives not one but two epistles), Antipater, Alexander III of Macedon, the children of Jason of Pherae, Timotheus of Heracleia, those in power in Mytilene, and Archidamus III of Sparta.[98] This prioritization, even in politically oriented discourse, of individuals' *tropoi* (manners of living) ahead of (for example) the structures of constitutional systems can be viewed as anticipating the personality-centered monarchical politics of the Hellenistic age.[99] Certainly, Isocrates' advocacy of a potential Panhellenic expedition against Persia to be led by Philip seems to point in this direction, calling as it does for the charismatic leadership of a single powerful man.[100]

Interstate Relations

Associations between states were of great interest to Xenophon: they comprise central themes in his longest works, the *Cyropaedia*, *Anabasis*, and *Hellenica*, although for very different reasons. In the *Cyropaedia*, Cyrus is the leader in his people's progression, both diplomatic and military, towards

---

[96] See the compact summary of Forsdyke 2009: 242–3; see also Johnstone 2009: 146–87, contrasting Platonic idealism with Isocratean practicality.

[97] Azoulay 2006b: 152.

[98] Isoc. 2 and 3 furnish further examples of Isocratean moral advice on good leadership.

[99] Azoulay 2006b *passim*, but summarized at 152–3.

[100] See esp. Isoc. 5 and 12.

empire, and the loyalty of his subjects both old and new is portrayed as one of his major priorities.[101] He is interested not only in the treatment of individuals, but further in the lessons that such treatment can provide for interstate relationships.[102] In this, the character Cyrus demonstrates a way of thinking that Xenophon may also be seen employing elsewhere, namely a predilection for understanding large-scale political interactions on human – and humane – terms.[103] The household-as-polis model described in the *Oeconomicus*,[104] the argument of Socrates in the *Memorabilia* that public and private undertakings can be construed as being very similar in their methods,[105] and even the inextricable intimacy between personal experience and rulership in the *Hiero* represent varied examples of Xenophon's work with this same general concept.

The extent to which analyses like Xenophon's may then be read as incorporating morals or values into political thinking in general and into international relations in particular becomes, for a number of scholars, a way of describing the distance of any given interpretation from the *Realpolitik* of Thucydides,[106] a worldview in which, even within the ethical framework of Greek culture, the calculation of advantage and disadvantage centrally determines the interactions of states.[107] While Xenophon does share Thucydides' awareness of, for example, the negative impact that irrational emotion can have upon political decision-making,[108] he tends to invest more deeply in human factors and to moralize much more frequently than did his predecessor, an attitude that also characterizes much fourth-century thinking about history, both distant and recent.[109] This ethical turn, in which Xenophon seems to have been an active participant, may help to explain why scholars of the *Cyropaedia* have sometimes wondered, particularly in light of the work's criticisms of later Persian mores, whether the imperial version of Cyrus' kingdom actually demands – or permits – the kind of virtuous leadership to which both Persia and Cyrus himself (in Xenophon's depiction)

---

[101] E.g. *Cyr.* 3.1.9–43 (mercy shown to the royalty of Armenia), 7.1.40–6 (settlement with the Egyptians on the basis of their merits), 8.2.1–28, 8.6.23 (Cyrus cultivates his people through beneficence).

[102] See esp. Lendon 2006, analyzing *Cyr.* 3.1.14–31.

[103] Low 2007: 173 (generalizing about classical Greek thought), cited in Christ 2012: 121.

[104] Lendon 2006: 83.

[105] See note 2, above.

[106] Christ 2012: 120–2.

[107] Lendon 2006: 96 sees this as taking place against a background of fear; Grissom 2012 (see e.g. 3–6) reads Thucydides as distinguishing between two types of fear: a productive aversion to risk and a hazardous "fear of loss of honor and status" (3).

[108] Lendon 2006 esp. 95–8.

[109] Pownall 2004.

aspired.[110] The apparent internal conflict between the vision and the outcome, particularly in an imagined "history" like this one whose content is independent of the burden of documentation,[111] may actually show Xenophon grappling with his own ideals.

The subject matter of the *Cyropaedia*, broadly defined, is perhaps partially explained by the fact that the position of Persia was a major preoccupation of the Greeks during Xenophon's lifetime. There was no consensus, however, on how this problematic neighbor was to be handled. The Greeks of the fifth century, especially the Athenians, in many ways defined themselves by the experience of the Persian Wars,[112] but by the fourth century it was unclear whether Persia was to be managed or attacked. One notable response – again, with potential ethical overtones – was panhellenism, which advocated the unification of Greeks across polis boundaries and against outsiders, especially the Persians.

Isocrates, for example, called for an alliance amongst ethnic Greeks to invade Persia, liberate the Greek-speaking cities of Asia Minor that were ruled and taxed by the Persians, and annex Persian territory.[113] But Persia was a complicated foe: not only had it long supported various Greek states in their constant conflicts with one another, but it had also brokered and even forced the conclusion of peace treaties. It had also hired Greek mercenaries for its own purposes, most notably during the attempted coup of Cyrus the Younger that initially brought Xenophon and the Ten Thousand into Persian service in 399. One way of reading the Ten Thousand, then, once the army's purposes were changed, was as a kind of *de facto* Panhellenic expedition that simply had to fight its way *out* of Persian-controlled territory, rather than into it. Isocrates did not view the experiences of the Ten Thousand in quite this way, interpreting them variously as a sign of Persian weakness and even as part of a Spartan plan for wide-ranging conquest,[114] but it can be argued that panhellenism did inform Xenophon's presentation of some important thematic material in the *Anabasis*,[115] including negative depictions of Persia and Persians and the praise of Greek "freedom."[116]

[110] See note 27, above.
[111] See note 80, above, and Lendon 2006: 82.
[112] On the relationship (which involved both fascination and hostility) between Athens and Persia during this time, see Miller 1997.
[113] Flower 2012: 170; Flower 2000: 65–6, cited in Mitchell 2007: xvii; see also Mitchell 2007: xv–xx for a brief survey of the history of scholarship on this topic.
[114] Perlman 1976–7: 247–9, citing Isoc. 4.145–9 on Persia and Isoc. 8.98, 12.98–105 on Sparta.
[115] Flower 2012: 170–201; Rood 2004a; Laforse 2000 esp. 85–7; Laforse 1998: 56; Moles 1994.
[116] Dillery 1995: 41–98, esp. 60–3.

Regardless of whether it might be desirable, is true panhellenism possible in Xenophon's vision of the world outside of the unique environment of the *Anabasis*? It has been argued that panhellenism in general during the fourth century was a powerful rhetorical tool (as opposed to a practical one), and that, ironically, it was most often wielded as a weapon by Greeks against one another.[117] While the natural optimism of the *Agesilaus* seems to advocate panhellenism at various points, the *Hellenica*, which reveals the interactions between the Greek states of Xenophon's day in greatest historiographic detail, seems in sum to recommend more guarded prospects.[118] Historical circumstances dictate some of the coverage: Athens's empire dissolves with its walls at the conclusion of the Peloponnesian War (*Hell.* 2.2.23), and Sparta's grand expedition to Asia, a kind of symbolic response not only to the expedition of Xerxes but also to the march of the Ten Thousand, is recalled due to strife within Greece (*Hell.* 4.2.1–8). Although Panhellenic sentiments do surface in the *Hellenica*, most notably in speeches,[119] the ending, commonly characterized as being pessimistic, simply abandons the narrative at the close of the Pyrrhic battle of Mantinea with no conclusive assessment of the large-scale outcome (*Hell.* 7.5.27). The speeches that surround Xenophon's account of the pivotal battle of Leuctra in book 6 may be said to sketch out a vision of the wide-ranging benefits to be gained should Athens and Sparta be able to put aside their differences,[120] but there is no such actual consummation by the end of the *Hellenica*. Instead, the constant Greek-on-Greek conflicts of the earlier fourth century have worn down all of the combatants, and despite the fact that certain individual figures have emerged for notice and praise, in the end all of the states, in some way, have lost.

Conclusion

It has become commonplace to note that Xenophon has in more recent years enjoyed redemption both as a writer and as a thinker, but it is worth remarking that this also includes his ideas about politics. This chapter has argued that Xenophon's thoughts in this area range widely over many different kinds of human communities, incorporate both the diagnosis of

---

[117] Laforse 1998: 56–7.
[118] Laforse 1997: 216–61 (cited in Laforse 1998: 58 n. 9), contrasting the portrayal of the subject in the *Agesilaus* with his depiction in the *Hellenica*.
[119] Laforse 1998 esp. 65, and see note 120, below.
[120] Dillery 1995: 242–9, examining *Hell.* 6.3–5; see also the *Poroi*, which concludes, save for its brief coda, with an argument for the economic blessings wrought by peace (*Por.* 5.1–13).

difficulties and the imagination of ideals, and remain remarkably consistent throughout his body of work. Xenophon is significantly the product of his own epoch and of his own experiences, and yet despite all that he shares with (for example) Plato and Isocrates in terms of aristocratic background, education, and interests, he is still able to fashion a distinctive view of the Greek world that is at once pragmatic and idealistic, and occasionally quite innovative. To imagine, as Xenophon clearly did from time to time, a fourth century where the Greek states were at peace with one another and their inhabitants cultivated to their best potential may be all but alien to our longer knowledge of their history, but it represents an experiment in thought that the modern world might occasionally do well to imitate.[121]

Further Reading

I confine my suggestions here to works written in English. Useful surveys dealing with Greek ideas about politics include Balot 2006 and Ober 1989 and 1998. On Xenophon in particular, Gray 2007 has a valuable introduction. Of her many other writings, especially recommended is Gray 2011, which treats Xenophon's ideas about leadership in a unified approach to the corpus. *Polis* 26.2 (2009, ed. Gish and Ambler) is a special issue dedicated to "The Political Thought of Xenophon," and many of its individual articles are cited here and listed in the bibliography.

Kroeker 2009, Gray 2004a, and Seager 2001 are useful for their examinations not merely of the institution of democracy, but of Xenophon's complex relationship to it. However, all view Xenophon as being at least somewhat optimistic regarding this form of government; for a slightly more critical view, see Tamiolaki 2012.

On interstate relations and panhellenism, Flower 2000 provides useful background; for more specific readings of Xenophon's own attitudes, see Dillery 1995. Laforse 1998 distills some of the content from the broader treatment of Laforse 1997; Perlman 1976–7 is wider-ranging even than the title would suggest and provides much comparative material. The edited volumes by Lane Fox 2004 and Hobden and Tuplin 2012a furnish good points of entry into topics further afield.

---

[121] This concept is owed to Breebaart 1983: 134, who characterizes the treatment of the Persian empire in the *Cyropaedia* as "a mental experiment" on Xenophon's part.

4

NINO LURAGHI

Xenophon's Place in Fourth-Century Greek Historiography

Xenophon lived in interesting times: he saw the end of the Peloponnesian War (431–404 BC) and, as a young adult, was involved in the terror regime imposed by the Spartans on the Athenians after the latter capitulated. Leaving aside his greatest adventure, narrated in his *Anabasis*, Xenophon witnessed the rise and fall of Spartan naval power, the Diktat that goes by the name of the "King's Peace" and represented the high point of Persian dominance in the Aegean, the astonishing defeat that the army of the Boeotian League inflicted upon the Spartans at Leuctra in 371 BC, and then, immediately thereafter, the foundation of the Arcadian "big city," Megalopolis, and of Messene, which crippled Spartan power once and for all. In many cases he was very close to key events as they unfolded – he saw the battle of Coronea, some scholars think he even fought in it, and was probably personally present at Sparta, when the envoys of the Greeks swore allegiance to the King's Peace, and later, when the news came of the defeat at Leuctra.[1]

His lifespan also coincided with one of the most crucial periods in the history of Greek historiography, a period that saw momentous developments in aspects ranging from the use of source material and research techniques in general to the thematic definition of historiography, the purposes and style of history writing. To mention but the tip of the iceberg, Xenophon was a contemporary or a near-contemporary of two of the most widely acclaimed historians of ancient Greece, Ephorus of Cyme and Theopompus of Chius. His activity as a historian could hardly have taken place in a more vibrant context.[2]

For us, modern readers of his works, the task of appreciating Xenophon's specific place in the general trajectory of Greek historiography is made more

[1] On Xenophon's life and times, see Lee in this volume. All the relevant evidence is collected and discussed in Breitenbach 1967: 1571–8.

[2] A recent and sympathetic overview of fourth-century historiography is offered by the contributions assembled in Parmeggiani 2014; in particular, on Ephorus see Parmeggiani 2011, on Theopompus Flower 1994.

difficult by the loss of almost the whole of Greek historical writing between Thucydides (died ca. 399 BC) and Polybius (died ca. 118 BC). With one partial exception, namely the so-called *Hellenica Oxyrhynchia* (see below), the works of Xenophon's contemporaries and immediate successors are known to us only indirectly, thanks to later authors' references to such works that go by the somewhat misleading name of fragments and, even more hypothetically, through the works of later authors who are supposed, generally not without good reason, to have made use of these earlier, lost authors.[3] Accordingly, in the pages that follow the attempt to compare and contrast Xenophon's historical writings, and in particular his *Hellenica*, with those of other historians operating around the same time or soon thereafter will be of necessity speculative. This is after all, more often than not, the plight of the ancient historian.

The Legacy of Thucydides

Xenophon's *Hellenica* famously starts, without a proem, where Thucydides' book 8 ended – almost in mid-sentence. The joint is not perfect, and yet there can scarcely be any doubt that, unless what we read is not the real beginning of *Hellenica*, Xenophon's narrative emphatically presented itself as a continuation of Thucydides.[4] In antiquity, Xenophon was even said to have published and promoted Thucydides' history, which had hitherto remained unknown, having been left incomplete at the death of the author. This notion may be no more than a product of inference, of course, although it has to be said that if it were merely an inference, it would be surprisingly circumstantial.[5] In any case, it serves at least to underline the fact that for ancient readers a close connection between Xenophon and Thucydides was a given. Xenophon, on the other hand, signaled in various ways his relationship to his predecessor. Apart from the direct link suggested by the opening of his *Hellenica*, the use of arranging the narrative of the last years of the

---

[3] For general orientation on the problem of historical fragments and on using indirect evidence to reconstruct lost works of ancient historiography, see Brunt 1980.

[4] See the discussions of Canfora 1970: 65–70, MacLaren 1979: 228–32, and Dover 1981: 439–40. Note that there is reason to believe that some ancient manuscripts of Thucydides actually included *Hellenica* books 1 and 2 up to the capitulation of Athens; see recently Nicolai 2006: 715–16 with further references.

[5] The reference to Xenophon promoting the circulation of the text of Thucydides comes in his short biography by Diogenes Laertius, 2.57, without any source attribution; it may (or may not) go back to Demetrius of Magnesia, a scholar of the time of Cicero (see Nicolai 2006: 705 with further references). It should not be confused with the speculation (Marcellinus, *Vita Thucydidis* 43) that Xenophon had edited book 8 of Thucydides (cf. Breitenbach 1967: 1672): the same was attributed also to Theopompus and to Thucydides' daughter.

Peloponnesian War according to a division in summers and winters is an explicit nod to Thucydides' narrative layout, and the tendency not to give an introduction to characters who had already appeared in Thucydides further underscores the intended continuity between *Hellenica* and the predecessor.[6]

In emphatically presenting himself as Thucydides' heir, Xenophon was by no means unique, or even untypical, among the historians of his age. Greek historiography of the first half of the fourth century appears to have been literally dominated by the influence of Thucydides, as shown by the fact that in these decades at least three and possibly more historians wrote continuations of his work.[7] Now, even though in hindsight it may seem otherwise, there was nothing accidental or obvious in the choice of continuing the unfinished historical work of a predecessor, nor more broadly in the notion, which would become more common only later, of starting one's historical narrative from the point where a predecessor had stopped – nobody had continued Herodotus, after all. Accordingly, we need a special explanation for this phenomenon. It seems reasonable to recognize that the continuators of Thucydides were responding to the extraordinary intellectual prestige of their predecessor – while at the same time also contributing to establishing it. Competitive differentiation between the continuators is a safe assumption, much as it is difficult to flesh out, for the simple reason that Xenophon's *Hellenica* is the only continuation that has come down to us, as far as we can tell, in complete form.

Besides Xenophon, continuators of Thucydides known by name include Cratippus of Athens and Theopompus of Chius, the former probably a younger contemporary of Thucydides, the latter born in the last years of the fifth century or at the beginning of the fourth.[8] In both cases, we can formulate informed guesses, and in the case of Theopompus something more than that, as regards the size of their works and the extension of time covered in them, which, as we shall see in a moment, is a very important aspect.

[6] In antiquity, this way of subdividing the narrative was seen as characteristic of Thucydides, see Dion. Hal. *de Thucydide* 9; it is important to realize that the references to summers and winters in Xenophon are independent of the extended chronological references that accompany the beginning of each year; the latter have often been thought to be interpolated. For a complete list of indications of change of year and of change of season in Xenophon's *Hellenica*, see Breitenbach 1967: 1656–7.

[7] For a concise synopsis of the evidence on the continuators of Thucydides, see Schepens 1993: 173–6.

[8] The date generally assigned to Cratippus results from Dionysius of Halicarnassus' statement that he was a contemporary of Thucydides (Dion. Hal. *de Thuc.* 16 = *FGrHist* 64 T 1). Theopompus' date of birth is a more complex problem, due to inconsistencies in the evidence; recent scholarship has been increasingly tending to an early date, in the very last years of the fifth century (see Flower 1994: 11–23, Billows 2009: 226–9, Carlucci 2013).

However, in both cases the evidence for the actual contents of the works in question is extremely thin – again, the situation is somewhat better for Theopompus, by far the better known of the two.[9] On the other hand, book 14 of Diodorus Siculus' *Historical Library* includes a narrative of mainland Greek political history that derives, directly or not, from the work of a continuator of Thucydides, and three large fragments of papyrus, or possibly four, have preserved remains of another work of Greek history that appears to have been a continuation of Thucydides as well.[10] This work goes by the conventional name of *Hellenica Oxyrhynchia* and is by most scholars taken to be the direct or ultimate source from which Diodorus derived his own narrative.[11] Its author cannot be identified with certainty, but it is virtually certain that he must be looked for among the historians who are already known to us as having written histories of the years after 411 BC. Unsurprisingly, and not without good reason, Theopompus and Cratippus are the two main candidates.[12]

It appears that in each of the continuations of Thucydides engagement with the model took different forms, mixing in various proportions imitation and criticism, as we would expect. The Athenian Cratippus, we are told by Dionysius of Halicarnassus, criticized his predecessor for the use of long and convoluted speeches, which, according to Cratippus himself, ended up being an obstacle to the narrative of events and an annoyance for the reader. Cratippus further speculated that the absence of long speeches from book 8, where passages in direct speech, while by no means absent, never

---

[9] We have all in all nineteen fragments of Theopompus' *Hellenica*, ranging from an isolated word to a few sentences (*FGrHist* 115 F 5–23). On the character of Theopompus' *Hellenica*, see esp. Momigliano 1982: 180–7.

[10] Alongside the London, Florence, and Cairo papyri that are included in the recent editions of the *Hellenica Oxyrhynchia*, a persuasive case can be made for the so-called Theramenes papyrus (PMich 5982 + 5797b) also originating from the same work; see most recently Vannini 2012, with a new edition of the fragments, and the discussion in Bearzot 2001.

[11] On the *Hellenica Oxyrhynchia* as the indirect source of the narrative of Greek history in Diodorus' book 14, see Hornblower 1994: 37; Diodorus' direct source is generally thought to be Ephorus.

[12] These two names were proposed almost immediately when the first papyrus of the *Hellenica Oxyrhynchia* was published, in the early twentieth century. It is fair to say that nowadays scholars are divided between the two of them, with a moderate prevalence for Cratippus; see especially Schepens 2001 and Magnelli 2007 for Cratippus, Billows 2009 and Canfora 2013 for Theopompus. Herbert Bloch's suggestion (Bloch 1940) that the author of the *Hellenica Oxyrhynchia* might be one whose memory has not otherwise survived in ancient literature becomes less likely with every new papyrus: late in his life, Bloch himself abandoned it and propended for Theopompus (personal communication). In spite of the high authority of its proponent, the theory of Jacoby 1950, which identified the author with the otherwise almost unknown historian Daemachus of Plataea, is nowadays generally rejected.

run for more than a few lines, showed that Thucydides himself had come to the same conclusion.[13] Interestingly from the point of view of a modern reader, Dionysius shared Cratippus' suggestion that uneasiness about this compositional feature explained the fact that Thucydides had not been able to complete his work.[14]

But Cratippus' criticism should not be taken as a complete devaluation of Thucydides – far from it: for ancient writers, showing that you had improved upon your model was commonsense and did not imply a negative judgment of the model as a whole. A poor model would not be worth imitating. As a matter of fact, the high authority of Thucydides was a cornerstone of the whole enterprise of continuing his work, and for Xenophon, Cratippus, and Theopompus, presenting themselves as continuators of Thucydides was certainly a way of laying claim to what they understood to be his intellectual heritage. At the same time, a scrutiny of the evidence gives a strong impression that all three of them were also in a sense trying to harness the authority of their model for ulterior purposes. Let us see how this may have been the case.

We should start with a very simple fact, which does not always receive the attention it deserves: none of the continuators of Thucydides we know of actually brought to completion the work of the prestigious predecessor in the framework that the latter had himself announced, that is, none of them ended with the surrender of Athens in the spring of 404.[15] This is all the more noteworthy considering Thucydides' insistence on precisely defining the chronological boundaries of the Peloponnesian War and on the fact that, notwithstanding the Peace of Nicias in 421, one really had to think in terms of one single war from 431 to 404.[16] By itself, the act of crossing the threshold so emphatically announced by Thucydides could not but imply the claim that the surrender of Athens in 404 could not be regarded as "the end of the story." With this move, the continuators of Thucydides implicitly called the

[13] Cratippus *FGrHist* 64 F 1 = Dion. Hal. *de Thuc.* 16. Cratippus' negative views of book 8 are probably the reason why ancient scholarship excluded him from the role of editor of that book, see above, n. 5.

[14] Dionysius is the last historian from whom one would expect such criticism, considering that his *Roman Antiquities* have the highest proportion of speeches to narrative of any work of ancient historiography.

[15] Thucydides refers to the surrender of the Athenians as the endpoint of his work in 5.26.1.

[16] Thuc. 5.26.2–3. Thucydides' insistence on his notion of one single war lasting from 431 to 404, in spite of the temporary interruption represented by the Peace of Nicias in 421, may point to his awareness that such a notion was contentious, as pointed out to me by John Marincola; see on this Strauss 1997: 168–9. Strauss's discussion of Thucydides' periodization of the Peloponnesian War sheds light on the importance of the endpoints chosen by his continuators.

attention of the reader to the endpoint chosen for their works: if the story did not end with the surrender of the Athenians, when did it end, really? Ancient readers of historiography, at a later time at least, were definitely sensitive to an author's choice of beginning and end.[17] In such a choice, narrative economy and political interpretation are inseparably entangled with one another. As a mental experiment, a modern reader might think of an incomplete history of the French Revolution that stopped with the Thermidorian Reaction in 1794, and then of works that continued it and ended, respectively, with the coup d'etat of Brumaire 18, 1799 and with the battle of Waterloo in 1815. Surely, each of them would convey a rather different message and suggest, or propose, a different interpretation of the historical trajectory it enclosed. We have every reason to think that the several endpoints chosen by the continuators of Thucydides should be interpreted along similar lines.

The Athenian Cratippus, according to Plutarch's pamphlet *On the Glory of the Athenians*, talked about the re-establishment of Athenian naval power by Conon, the Athenian admiral-at-large, and the layout of Plutarch's passage suggests that that may have been the endpoint of his work. Most likely, we should take this as a reference to the reconstruction of the Long Walls that connected Athens to its military harbor and ensured undisturbed access to the sea; we would then be looking at the fall or winter of 393 BC.[18] Clear in itself, from the very words used by Plutarch, the meaning of this cutoff point becomes even clearer if we remind ourselves that the Long Walls had been demolished after the capitulation of Athens in 404, and Thucydides, in the prospective passage just mentioned, had referred precisely to the fall of the Long Walls as the endpoint of the war and of his own work.[19] By extending his narrative to include the reconstruction of the Long Walls, Cratippus transformed a story of Athenian defeat into one of Athenian recovery from defeat.

Theopompus on the other hand, writing almost certainly later than Cratippus and Xenophon, although possibly not much later, seems to have concluded his twelve books of *Hellenica* with the victory of Conon over the Spartan admiral Pisander at the battle of Cnidus in 394, which represented

---

[17] See Dionysius of Halicarnassus' discussion of the respective starting and endpoints of Herodotus and Thucydides at *ad Pomp.* 3.

[18] Plut. *de glor. Athen.* 1 (345C–E) = Cratippus *FGrHist* 64 T 2. For a detailed commentary on this passage, see Schepens 1993: 173–82, and particularly 180–1 for a precise interpretation of the endpoint of Cratippus' work; Canfora 1990: 75 speaks a not unnecessary word of caution regarding the possibility of reading Plutarch's passage in such a specific way.

[19] Thuc. 5.26.1; the dismantling of the Long Walls is described memorably in Xen. *Hell.* 2.2.23.

the end of Spartan naval power and was construed by Theopompus himself as the end of the Spartan hegemony. In this way, he could take a much more Panhellenic perspective, or at any rate a bipartisan one that showcased the successive failures of both the Athenians and the Spartans in their imperial projects, while at the same time stopping short of what could be construed as the rebirth of Athenian power signaled by the reconstruction of the Long Walls.[20] Beyond that Theopompus, who went on to write his *Philippica* centering around the figure of the Macedonian king Philip II, Alexander's father, may well have thought that the eighties and seventies, with the King's Peace and the Theban hegemony, were really the beginning of a new historical development that culminated in the establishment of Macedonian supremacy and were a prelude to the final confrontation with the Persian Empire.[21]

Xenophon's endpoint, the battle of Mantinea in 362 BC, may seem at first sight less obviously meaningful, although it has to be recognized that such an impression stems largely from what Xenophon himself says: after a gripping narrative of the battle, Xenophon comments that the outcome was undecided, and accordingly the expectation that the battle, to which the main players in Greek power politics participated, would decide the balance of power in Greece was disappointed. At which point, Xenophon declares that his narrative ends here, and another historian will perhaps take up from where he left off.[22] Such an innocent-sounding statement from as shrewd an author as Xenophon must arouse suspicion, and in fact a credulous reader might be somewhat surprised to learn that soon after the battle, apparently still in the year 362, most of the Greeks concluded a common peace, and possibly even an alliance, from which the Spartans alone were excluded because they were not willing to accept the Messenians as a party to the treaty, which would have meant finally acknowledging their independence.[23] Quite apart from the fact that a modern historian would be much more likely to take the conclusion of the peace, rather than the battle, as an endpoint, it is clear that the peace was a heavy political defeat for the Spartans, effectively putting an end to their hopes ever to recover Messenia, which had formed part of their territory from the Archaic period until 370. By concluding his narrative

---

[20] On the extension of Theopompus' *Hellenica*, see FGrHist 115 F 14 = Diod. 14.87.4. On the meaningfulness of the endpoint, see Momigliano 1982: 181–5 and Schepens 1993: 186.

[21] Momigliano 1982: 186; on Theopompus' *Philippica*, see Flower 1994: 29–36.

[22] Xen. *Hell.* 7.5.26–7. Interestingly, nobody did: no narrative of Greek history, as far as we know, started from the point where Xenophon ended – so much for the conception of *Hellenica* as continuing each other (see below, n. 49).

[23] Diod. 15.89.1–2; on the peace of 362, see Jehne 1994: 96–115.

with the battle rather than extending it to the peace, Xenophon was able to give his narrative a somewhat misleading sense of open-endedness as regarded the future of Spartan power, which is by any assessment the central theme of his *Hellenica*.[24] If we now step back and look at the complete picture, as it were, Xenophon's *Hellenica*, combined with Thucydides' incomplete history of the Peloponnesian War, covered a historical trajectory that allowed the author to write a story of multiple successes and failures of Athens and Sparta, a story in which both had had moments of glory and moments they would have rather liked to forget about. Sparta's somewhat spotty record in terms of defending the freedom of the Greeks would be counterbalanced by the notorious oppressiveness of imperial Athens.[25] The story would then very appropriately culminate in a battle fought by Spartans and Athenians side by side, against a coalition led by the old Medizers, the Thebans – whose record of treason of the Greek cause Xenophon makes sure to mention with due emphasis.[26]

Apart from the broader trajectory that the continuations of Thucydides created, each one of them must have also engaged in other ways with the model set by the predecessor. In the case of Xenophon's *Hellenica* and in that of the *Hellenica Oxyrhynchia*, which may well be the work of Cratippus or Theopompus, the two most obvious features of Thucydides' historical narrative, the extensive use of speeches rendered in direct form and the temporal subdivision of the wars into winters and summers, ignoring the actual calendar of the poleis involved, are addressed and transformed in interesting ways.[27] We have already seen that Cratippus criticized quite outspokenly Thucydides' use of speeches, and indeed the preserved portions of the *Hellenica Oxyrhynchia*, coincidentally or not, include very little in terms of direct speech, and absolutely nothing that might be compared to Thucydides. Xenophon, while giving up Thucydides' penchant for employing speeches in order to explore fundamental political issues, does not renounce them entirely, and in one case he uses the typically Thucydidean expedient of reporting multiple speeches delivered on the same occasion as a way of exploring different views of a political issue. Overall it is fair to say, however, that Xenophon, too, seems to have shared Cratippus' misgivings

---

[24] Jehne 1994: 112 has perceptive remarks on the implicit tendentiousness of Xenophon's assessment of the situation in 362.
[25] Tuplin 1993 offers a book-length exploration of the criticism of Spartan imperialism by Xenophon.
[26] Note especially Xenophon's report on the embassy of the Theban Pelopidas at the Persian court in Susa in 367, Xen. *Hell.* 7.1.34.
[27] For an explanation of the Thucydidean year, see Thuc. 5.20.2–3.

regarding Thucydides' use of speeches.[28] As for the chronological structure, as mentioned above, Xenophon's *Hellenica* essentially follows Thucydides' pattern until the end of the Peloponnesian War, and abandons it after the fall of the Thirty – but sporadic seasonal indications in books 3 to 7 detract from the sharpness of the difference.[29] In between, the narrative of the Thirty and their overthrow (*Hell.* 2.3.11–2.4.43) acted as a pivot, forming a vivid transition where the level of detail of the narrative increased, and with it the level of authorial participation. The author of the *Hellenica Oxyrhynchia*, for his part, followed the division in summers and winters, at least in the fragments that are preserved, and mentioned Thucydides by name at one point in the narrative.[30] On the other hand, he seems to have been one of the originators, or possibly the single originator, of the tendency of later historians to question the unity of the Peloponnesian War as defined by Thucydides and to divide it into separate wars – Archidamian, Decelean, Ionian.[31] It scarcely needs to be underlined that such an analytical view of the Peloponnesian War must have been an integral part of the historical interpretation that resulted from the choice of endpoint for the *Hellenica Oxyrhynchia*, whatever this might have been.

More specific connections are difficult to appreciate. A recent study has drawn attention to a high density of allusions to Thucydides to be found both in Xenophon's *Hellenica* and in Diodorus, whose narrative of early fourth-century mainland Greek history is generally thought to derive ultimately, though possibly not directly, from the *Hellenica Oxyrhynchia*.[32] Particularly striking are the different ways in which key moments of the story are rendered, in implicit dialogue with Thucydides. For Xenophon, after the final defeat of their fleet at Aegospotami in 405, the Athenians were terrified because they feared that now the Spartans would visit upon them the same fate that the Athenians themselves had meted out to the Melians in 416; the reader of Thucydides' Melian Dialogue will have realized that the Athenians' fear was ultimately misguided, for back then, their

---

[28] Gray 1989: 79–140 provides an extended discussion of speeches in Xenophon's *Hellenica*, underlining their different function compared to Thucydides' speeches – "the celebration of moral qualities through the characterizations of the speakers" (p. 137). See also Baragwanath in this volume. For an example of multiple speeches, see the speeches of Critias and Theramenes in *Hell.* 2.3.24–49 – but note that it is a rather exceptional case in terms of length.

[29] Dover 1981: 442 with refs.: sporadic indications of time in *Hell.* books 3–7 show that books 1–2 are not so strongly different as sometimes maintained.

[30] On the chronological layout of the *Hellenica Oxyrhynchia*, see Bruce 1967: 8–9.

[31] Schepens 2007: 65 n. 15; the Decelean War is mentioned twice in the extant portions of the *Hellenica Oxyrhynchia*, at 7.3 and 19.2.

[32] Rood 2004b.

minds not misled by fear, the Athenians had seen clearly that Sparta, itself an imperial power, had no interest in their annihilation. The same reader will also be prepared to see through the Spartans' claim that they spared Athens for the sake of the merits of the Athenians at the time of the Persian Wars.[33] Diodorus, on the contrary, picks up Thucydides' appreciation of the resilience of the Athenians by stressing their willingness to fight on even after Aegospotami.[34] In the words of Tim Rood, "The presence of so many Thucydidean allusions in Xenophon and Diodorus suggests that Thucydides' continuators (and imitators) responded (perhaps even in competition to one another) not just to the broad outlines of his historical vision, but also to fine points of textual detail."[35] Nonetheless, in their creative engagement with the model, they were at the same time undermining its fundamental tenets, in ways that deserve our attention.

The World of the Three-Headed Monster

Visiting Olympia at some point during the second century AD, Pausanias saw a statue of the orator and historian Anaximenes of Lampsacus, dedicated by his fellow citizens in gratitude for saving them from mass enslavement at the hands of Alexander the Great. The monument provokes Pausanias to a brief digression, which ends with a curious anecdote – curious and very revealing. Anaximenes, says Pausanias, bore a grudge against his colleague Theopompus, and decided to take revenge in a particularly sophisticated way, by composing in the style of Theopompus a pamphlet in which he slandered Athenians, Spartans, and Thebans, and then sending copies to the respective cities passing it off as a genuine work of Theopompus, with the result that Theopompus himself, says Pausanias, came to be hated throughout Greece.[36] Scholars have long recognized that the pamphlet in question is the one referred to by other authors under the title of *Trikaranos*, or "The Three-headed Monster" – the three heads being Athens, Sparta, and Thebes, at that time the three most powerful cities of the Greek world, that had been vying for supremacy ever since the Peloponnesian War. Even though both Pausanias and Aelius Aristides, who also refers to the pamphlet providing us with its title, describe it as a general indictment of the Greeks, obviously because of their penchant for

---

[33] Compare Xen. *Hell.* 2.2.3 (Athenians' fear) and 2.2.22 (Spartans spare the Athenians) with Thuc. 5.91.1; see Rood 2004b: 351–6.

[34] Compare Diod. 13.107.1 with Thuc. 8.1.3 (after the disaster of the Athenian expedition to Sicily was announced).

[35] Rood 2004b: 365.

[36] Paus. 6.18.5 (= Anaximenes *FGrHist* 72 T 6).

internecine war, it seems clear that most criticism must have concentrated on the three main offenders.[37]

The story of the *Trikaranos*, be it a work of Anaximenes or one of Theopompus, as some have suspected, casts an oblique and all the more revealing light on the practice of historiography during the fourth century, illuminating for us a context in which historians were acutely aware of each other's work and jealousies ran rampant, possibly stimulated also by competition for incipient royal patronage.[38] It also points to a way of conceptualizing Greek history that is typical of fourth-century historiography, a conception in which events were organized around the fortunes of the most powerful cities, seen as competitors in an intra-Greek struggle for leadership, that is, hegemony. The succession of the hegemonies of the several cities then functioned as a way of periodizing history. Aspects of this conception are familiar to readers of Xenophon's *Hellenica*, of course, and the succession of hegemonies appears to have been prominent in Theopompus' *Hellenica*, too; some scholars find trace of it even in Cratippus.[39] Furthermore, it largely underpins the work that can be termed the most ambitious product of fourth-century historiography, the thirty-book *Histories* of Ephorus of Cyme. Besides being the structuring principle of Ephorus' narrative of Greek political history of the fifth and fourth centuries, the notion had an impact even on the way that Ephorus dealt with the most distant past: in his *Histories*, the origins and early history of Athens, Thebes, and Sparta each received its own book. Interestingly, and diametrically opposite of Anaximenes, Ephorus appears to have offered sympathetic views of all three contenders.[40]

Even though this way of seeing Greek history, in slightly modified form, still constitutes the backbone of most modern treatments of this period, there is nothing obvious in interpreting Greek history from, say, 431 to 357 as a succession of phases in which different poleis in turn occupied an individual position of leadership. For one thing, only Sparta's hegemony was recognized by all the Greeks, de facto or officially, and that only for very short periods of time, immediately after the end of the Peloponnesian War

---

[37] See Ael. Arist. 26.50–1 = Anaximenes *FGrHist* 72 F 31. For a recent discussion of the *Trikaranos*, including the question of authorship, see Parmeggiani 2012.

[38] Anaximenes, Callisthenes, and Theopompus were all variously associated with the court of the Macedonian kings; see Meissner 1992: 383–7, 395–9, 417–19. Theopompus' presence at the court of Philip II of Macedonia is memorably addressed in the *Letter of Speusippus to Philip*, whose authenticity has been endlessly debated; see recently Natoli 2004.

[39] See especially Schepens 1993.

[40] Luraghi 2014: 148. On the importance of hegemony as a structuring principle in Ephorus, see the extended discussion in Wickersham 1994: 119–77.

and immediately after the King's Peace.[41] More importantly, at any given point the situation on the ground was vastly more complicated. Other trends and factors, such as the progressive expansion of federal systems, arguably had a more important long-term impact, and in any case, the most powerful player, incomparably superior in terms of resources to any Greek polis, was the Great King. Nobody could hope to maintain a position of preeminence without his financial support, as even the Thebans quickly realized. Finally, every one of the major players was in most cases, if not always, following a much more regional agenda, one in which long-established territorial interests and aspirations arguably had a more prominent role than leadership over the Greeks, however construed.[42]

Surely the polarized view of the Greek world that underpins and structures Thucydides' history of the Peloponnesian War, with its exclusive focus on the conflict between Athens and Sparta, had already laid the groundwork for conceptualizing the history of the Greeks in such a simplified way, in terms of a succession of hegemonies of individual poleis, and the very way that the Greeks narrated political history led in that direction.[43] One could of course say that authors of Greek history in the generation of Xenophon, to the extent that they did not decide to jettison the Thucydidean paradigm entirely – which none of them actually did – were bound to extend the theme into a sequence of successes and failures for the main powers. To be sure, this had to come at the cost of sacrificing Thucydides' notion of the uniqueness of "his" war, which he saw as the culmination of the whole of Greek history, but such a sacrifice would have been inevitable anyway, inseparable as it was from the very project of continuing Thucydides' work, rather than just completing it. And yet, limiting the intellectual contribution of the historians of the fourth century to a declension of a Thucydidean paradigm, adding only the necessary modifications, would be unduly reductive.

Thucydides' uncompromising focus on the structural factors that made Athens' hegemony inevitable and predicted its final victory, barring mistakes

---

[41] Xenophon's reference to the Spartans as the enforcers of the King's Peace (*Hell.* 5.1.36) has often been interpreted as indicating an official role accorded to them, but see Jehne 1994: 41. On the "acknowledged hegemony" of Sparta after the Peloponnesian War, see Polyb. 1.2.3, Diod. 14.10.1, 13.1, and Schepens 1993: 171–2.

[42] For a striking exemplification, see Xenophon's narrative of the diplomatic exchanges at the court of the Satrap Tiribazos in Sardis in 392, *Hell.* 4.8.12–15. Jehne 1994: 31–135 offers the most helpful guide to the intricacies of mainland Greek politics from the King's Peace to the Sacred War, and at the same time shows how that story can be told other than as a succession of hegemonies. For standard treatments of the Spartan hegemony and of the Theban hegemony, see Hamilton 1979 and 1991 and Buckler 1980, respectively.

[43] Already, Herodotus saw Greek history after the Persian Wars as characterized by the struggle for supremacy between the major Greek powers, see Hdt. 6.98.2.

in its internal leadership, was based on the assumption that the Persian Empire would not have been able to influence in a decisive way the balance of power within the Greek world.[44] By the early fourth century, such an assumption had proven untenable, and everybody knew that hegemony over the Greeks came at the price of a pact with the devil – that is, with the Persians. Under such circumstances, in order to construe the history of the Greeks as a succession of hegemonies of Greek poleis, in which very few of them rose, seized hegemony, fell, and then rose again, fourth-century historians were in a sense compelled to look for new categories of historical explanation and especially of evaluation, focusing on what it took to be the hegemon of the Greeks, and on who actually, at any given point, deserved that position, and why.[45] By regarding hegemony as contingent and volatile, as they had to do in order to conceptualize Greek politics in those terms, Xenophon and his contemporaries were confronted with a new set of problems, and bringing ethics back into politics, turning their back on Thucydides' uncompromising political realism, was a rather natural step. Granted that a pact with the devil had to be struck, one could still turn a blind eye to its realities and focus on the moral qualifications of the Greeks who from time to time signed it.[46]

If we look back at the historical trajectories that we can surmise, based on the chronological boundaries of the several *Hellenica*, a moral interpretation, and one that occasionally pointed out the ironies of history when seen in the long term, seems like a very likely assumption. In this respect, Xenophon was certainly not alone. Modern scholars have long found fault with fourth-century historians, accusing them of having learned from the school of Isocrates rather than from Thucydides – of having traded historical analysis for rhetorical embellishment.[47] But a more sympathetic

---

[44] This view is implicit in what Thucydides says at 2.65.12; see Luraghi 2013: 82–3.
[45] For a fascinating exploration of the nexus of hegemony and virtue in Theopompus' views on the Spartan hegemony, see Schepens 2004.
[46] Indeed, not all Greeks enlisted Persian support with the same dignity: Xenophon is ready to characterize the Thebans as traditional traitors of the Greek cause when Pelopidas shows up at the Persian court at Susa in 367, but the fact that the Spartans sold off the freedom of the Greeks of Asia in order to regain the upper hand in Greece and put an end to the Corinthian War receives no comparable scorn. For Xenophon's criticism of Spartan imperialism and moral decadence, see Tuplin 1993, and note that, if it had been obvious for every reader that Xenophon indeed criticizes the Spartans, Tuplin would not have needed a whole book to make his point.
[47] For the traditional view of fourth-century historiography as fundamentally inspired and dominated by rhetoric, see e.g. Meister 1990: 83–94. This view is partly based on ancient sources that describe Ephorus and Theopompus, the two most prominent historians of this period, as pupils of the Athenian orator Isocrates; whether or not this piece of information is accurate, it cannot by itself characterize their activity as historians; see Flower 1994: 42–62 for Theopompus and Parmeggiani 2011: 34–66 for Ephorus.

approach to their intellectual and political world suggests that it may be at least worth exploring the notion that it was precisely the attempt at mustering and mastering unsavory historical facts within a specific ideological framework, much more than the dangerous liaison with the methods of rhetoric, that induced Xenophon and Theopompus to depict events with the moralizing attitude that so much puzzles and annoys many of their modern readers. The Thucydidean moment with its political Darwinism, itself the product of a highly selective approach to reality, was over, and in many ways historians were now turning back to Herodotus, turning to divine intervention and moral exemplarity as parameters for evaluating history – and yet, it was really the shadow of Thucydides that dictated to them what counted as historical subject matter.[48]

By the next generation, the principle was well established whereby *Hellenica*, far from being just segments of a history conceived of as essentially continuous, tended to select an arbitrary chronological framework with an eye to political and moral interpretation.[49] Callisthenes of Olynthus, Aristotle's relative and collaborator, opened his ten books of *Hellenica* with the King's Peace of 386, concluding with the Sacred War in 346, thereby following the complete trajectory of the Theban hegemony and the early stages of the rise of Macedon under Philip II, and mercilessly exposing the political, and most likely also moral, bankruptcy of Sparta.[50] At the same time, the independent position of his narrative of the Sacred War, which is thought to have circulated as an autonomous work in antiquity, announced the new age of Philippic history – an age of kings that the Greeks would emerge from only with the Roman conquest and the end of the autonomous polis.

Xenophon and Greek Historiography

Regardless of whether the interpretation presented here is found persuasive or not, there is no doubt that Xenophon's *Hellenica* embodies important trends in post-Thucydidean historiography. To what extent Xenophon

---

[48] Tamiolaki 2008 provides a very helpful and even-handed discussion of the relationship of Xenophon to Herodotus and Thucydides.

[49] The reader should be alert to the fact that here I am parting ways with the common interpretation of *Hellenica* as conceived of by their authors as notional segments of a continuous history, as found for instance in Tuplin 2007d. The evidence for the chronological boundaries of *Hellenica* seems to contradict this view – which is not to say that ancient historians could not occasionally take as the starting point of their works the endpoint of a predecessor, but this does not appear to have been particularly typical of authors of *Hellenica*.

[50] On Callisthenes' *Hellenica*, see especially Prandi 1985: 35–6 (layout and contents), 36–68 (commentary on the fragments), 69 (anti-Spartan tendency).

himself contributed to establishing such trends depends in part on when we think *Hellenica* was written.[51] Many scholars have thought, for very good reasons, that the narrative of the final years of the Peloponnesian War in books 1 and 2 of *Hellenica* was composed before, possibly even long before, the five books that follow it. Furthermore, it is hard to deny that, when Isocrates wrote his *Panegyricus* in 380, he had read Xenophon's judgment on the position of Sparta after the King's Peace, in *Hellenica* book 5.[52] On the other hand, *Hellenica* refers indirectly to events as late as the 350s.[53] It seems at least possible that parts of *Hellenica* were circulating in some form before the final version was completed, a procedure that would by no means be without parallels even among the earlier Greek historians. In any case, we can indicate only a rather broad span of time during which Xenophon formed his vision of Greek history. All we can say, therefore, is that Xenophon's *Hellenica* is clearly part of a broader intellectual discussion. Even though it did not become the standard work of reference on the period, due if nothing else to its conciseness, and possibly to its several loud silences, it is rather likely to have had an impact, and probably a decisive impact, in contributing to the moral turn of Greek historiography of the fourth century. After all, nothing in the *Hellenica Oxyrhynchia* points to a clear awareness of the renewed interest for moral parameters in the interpretation of the unfolding of historical events – but then again, we ought not to forget that all we have is rather scanty fragments of what must once have been a sizable work.

In his old age, Xenophon was a famous man, and Greek literati competed with one another to write in praise of his son Gryllus, who died fighting in the Athenian cavalry at the battle of Mantinea. We can surmise that his fame was to a significant extent due to his writings, and his historical works certainly had generated no less interest than the rest of his highly diverse corpus, and probably more, at least up to then. Things may have changed in later periods. Even though Xenophon was included in the canon of the Greek historians, a list of must-read works that was formulated in the early Hellenistic period, his impact on the development of Greek historiography is most clearly recognizable in his own times and immediately thereafter, as far as we can tell. His younger contemporaries, Theopompus, Ephorus,

---

[51] For a clear discussion of the various views on this topic, see Dillery 1995:12–14.

[52] Compare Xen. *Hell.* 5.1.36 with Isocr. 4.139. Tuplin 1993: 31 n. 74 states, without any further argument, that it is actually Xenophon who refers to Isocrates; but this is possible, and still by no means proved, only if one accepts Tuplin's general interpretation of Xenophon's *Hellenica* as a pamphlet criticizing Spartan imperialism.

[53] See Lee's contribution in this volume.

Callisthenes, Anaximenes, knew his historical works and silently reacted to them in various ways.[54]

For Hellenistic scholars and for the learned men of the Roman Republic, on the other hand, Xenophon was far more prominent as a political philosopher than as a historian. Cicero praised his *Cyropaedia*, and there was general agreement on its importance. In a similar vein, in his *Institutio oratoria* Quintilian, in the course of a catalogue of historians, said in so many words that Xenophon was to be counted among the philosophers, not among the historians (10.1.81ff). While we have every reason to believe that Xenophon's historical prose continued being read, the influence of Xenophon the historian on the works of other Hellenistic and Roman historians is more difficult to trace. Overall, among his historical works it was the *Anabasis* that had the strongest long-term impact, meeting the sympathies of other historians/politicians for centuries to come. Tacitus is the first Roman historian who certainly read it.[55] In the time of the emperor Hadrian, the governor of the province of Cappadocia Lucius Flavius Arrianus, commander of the Roman legions on the Upper Euphrates border and better known to classicists as the historian Arrian of Nicomedia, author of the *Anabasis of Alexander*, was seen and saw himself as a new Xenophon, who construed his relationship to the stoic philosopher Epictetus in parallel with that of Xenophon and Socrates, and personally retraced some segments of the march of the Ten Thousand.[56]

Very typically, even Arrian saw Xenophon first and foremost as a man of action and a philosopher, not so much as a historian. Generations of modern scholars shared this judgment, considering Xenophon's *Hellenica* essentially as a memoir that did not achieve a valid historical understanding of the period it dealt with. Of course, there is no denying the political agenda of Xenophon the historian, but the same is true of probably all ancient authors of political history, as far as we can tell, including Thucydides: tendentiousness is not Xenophon's special defect. On the other hand, a more fine-grained understanding of the major authors and trends in fourth-century historiography, as achieved thanks to the scholarship of the last decades or so, has finally paved the way for a more balanced understanding of Xenophon the historian, of his place in post-Thucydidean historical writing, and of his impact on the development of Greek historiography.

---

[54] See Münscher 1920: 24–32.
[55] Tac. *Ann.* 13.35 and Xen. *Anab.* 4.5.3; see Münscher 1920: 93.
[56] On Arrian and Xenophon, see Ameling 1984 and Rood 2011, with further references.

Further Reading

Times are ripe for a new synthesis on fourth-century historiography. Currently, individual authors have been dealt with in great detail, but the reader would be hard-pressed to find an overview that reflects the state of the art. Guido Schepens, the scholar who more than any other has contributed to the progress of our understanding of this field, has authored many articles in five different languages. The English-speaking reader will find Schepens 1977, 2001, and 2012 particularly helpful. Parmeggiani 2014 offers a selection of studies by scholars, most of whom do not usually publish their works in English. Beyond the titles mentioned in the footnotes, Lewis 1977 is illuminating on the political history of the early fourth century.

PART II

INDIVIDUAL WORKS

5

JOHN MARINCOLA

Xenophon's *Anabasis* and *Hellenica*

Xenophon's Historical Works

The Augustan-era critic Dionysius of Halicarnassus, in praising Xenophon, says that "the historical subjects which he chose are fine and impressive and appropriate to a philosopher" (*Letter to Pompeius* 4). Perhaps somewhat surprisingly, Dionysius included the *Cyropaedia* among Xenophon's "historical" works, although modern scholars, when they evaluate Xenophon as a historian, generally limit themselves to the *Anabasis* and the *Hellenica*.[1] This seems a sensible approach, since the two works have much in common. Both employ the techniques developed by Herodotus and Thucydides in the fifth and earlier fourth century, namely the use of a largely third-person mimetic narrative that treats political and military events, has multiple focalizations, employs direct (and indirect) speech by the characters, constructs characterizations (both explicit and implied) of individuals, including the attribution of motive and intention to those individuals, and offers occasional comment by the narrator in his own person on the people and events that his history comprises.[2] In addition, there are certain idiosyncratic features of these works that unite them: both lack a preface of the sort that introduces and explains the work before the reader and both feature a narrator who only rarely interrupts the narrative to speak in the first person; both are marked too by an especial concern to maintain anonymity.[3]

There are, nonetheless, important differences between the two works. First is scope. The *Hellenica* is a narrative that plunges *in medias res*, beginning with the words, "And after these things" (*Hell.* 1.1.1), clearly portraying

---

[1] On the genre of the *Cyropaedia* see Tamiolaki and Flower in this volume.
[2] On the narrative manner of Xenophon see Pelling and Rood in this volume.
[3] Xenophon's unusual anonymity *might* be seen if: (1) he means himself when he refers to the "leader of the Cyreans" (*Hell.* 3.2.7); (2) he is actually the "character" Theopompus (*Anab.* 2.1.12–3); and (3) he published the *Anabasis* pseudonymously as by Themistogenes of Syracuse (which last I believe he did, mainly to avoid the ill will attendant upon self-praise; but see most recently Flower 2012: 52–5).

itself as a "continuation" of Thucydides' history of the Peloponnesian War, since it assumes an advanced knowledge in the reader of what has gone before (characters, places, and situations are not explained). But it then goes well past the end of that war for some forty more years, and ends abruptly, with an explicit remark by the narrator that what everyone *thought* would be a decisive, perhaps concluding, event was nothing of the sort. And his final remark, that someone after him may care to record subsequent history, leaves the "story" even more open and unfulfilled (*Hell.* 7.5.26–7).[4] The *Anabasis*, by contrast, is more tightly focused around a series of particular events in a mobile, but limited, theater, i.e. the gathering of a Greek mercenary force to assist Cyrus, their march into the heart of the Persian Empire, and their struggle to survive and return to Greece.[5] Although it seems at times to be a "homecoming" story, the latter books end in disarray and uncertainty. Even so, the *Anabasis* as a whole has a much clearer beginning, middle, and end.[6] A second difference is that the *Hellenica* has many theaters of operation, focalizing events now from the perspective of the Spartans, now from the Athenians, now from the Persians or the Corinthians or Thebans or even the Eleans or Phleiasians. The *Anabasis* focuses on far fewer places and characters, and much of the narrative is focalized through the Greek mercenaries and their leaders, especially, as the narrative progresses, through one in particular, Xenophon.[7] Finally, the *Hellenica* shows people and leaders in a greater *variety* of action: in political assemblies and courts as well as in battles of varying kind on land and sea. The *Anabasis*, on the other hand, shows mostly an army on the march, with leaders, to be sure, but the give and take of the political fighting and plotting is more narrowly focused on the generals and their men, and one does not see the different kinds of battles that are found in the *Hellenica*. Yet even with this limitation, the army of the *Anabasis* has some characteristics of a typical Greek community.[8]

It is worthwhile, therefore, to treat the *Anabasis* and *Hellenica* together, since both are recognizable historical narratives,[9] even if Xenophon does not give us much help in interpreting these works. No major ancient historian

---

[4] On the historical nature of the *Hellenica*, see Giraud 1999: 55–92; on the ending of the *Hellenica* see below.

[5] See Xenophon's own "summation" of the subject matter of the *Anabasis* at *Hell.* 3.1.2.

[6] On the ending of the *Anabasis* see Ma 2004; Rood 2004a: 320 ("an escape story that subverts itself"); Purves 2010: 163–4; Bradley 2011; Flower 2012: 45–7.

[7] Xenophon's increasing role: Dillery 1995: 71; Dorati 2007; Bradley 2001; Grethlein 2012.

[8] For the community of the *Anabasis*: Dalby 1992; Dillery 1995: 59–94; Lee 2007; Hornblower 2004.

[9] Flower 2012: 48 calls the *Anabasis* microhistory, the *Hellenica* macrohistory.

is more reticent about the nature and purpose of his history (and history in general), and whereas both Herodotus and Thucydides had prefaced their works with the reasons for their writing – memory and glory in the case of the former (*praef.*), learning and understanding of the human condition in the latter (1.22) – in neither *Hellenica* nor *Anabasis* does Xenophon explain his motives. Aside from a few explicit remarks,[10] Xenophon's views and interests must be determined from the way in which the stories he tells unfold, or the characters behave and/or meet particular challenges; and also by the sorts of things he focuses on, the kinds of incidents that recur in the narrative, the places where he fleshes out his account to explore in more detail, or stops the narrative movement of his history to dwell on particular actions or people.

Xenophon is a hedgehog in fox's clothing: he has a consistent overriding theme, "an ethical interest throughout his works … in the Socratic search for the best life,"[11] but he does not explore this theme in only one area or in one genre alone, as he well might have. Rather, he employed a wide range of sometimes very different kinds of writing, of which historical narrative was merely one.

Generic Considerations

For the ancients, Xenophon was one of the three great historians, together with his predecessors, Herodotus and Thucydides, yet in modern scholarship he is often ranked a distant third, judged harshly in light of those predecessors.[12] Yet such judgments, when they are not based on the presumed superficiality of Xenophon's thought or the bias believed to be contained in his historical narratives, often arise from the notion that Herodotus and Thucydides had somehow already defined the genre of historiography, such that wherever Xenophon takes a different approach, he is to be faulted. Yet the actual situation as regards the writing of history in the fifth and fourth centuries is likely to have been more complicated. While it is certainly true that the value (and perhaps even excellence) of Herodotus' and Thucydides' works were immediately recognized by contemporaries and the next generation,[13] the notion that their particular ways – and *only*

---

[10] Fundamental for Xenophon's historiographical remarks is Breitenbach 1950; for first-person remarks in the *Hellenica* see Giraud 1999: 338–50; cf. also Gray 2003 for narrative interruptions.

[11] Gray 2010a: 3.

[12] On Xenophon's place in the ancient canon, see Nicolai 1992: 311–39.

[13] On the reception of Herodotus see Riemann 1967; Hornblower 2006; for Thucydides in the fourth century Hornblower 1995.

their particular ways – of writing history were already sacrosanct in the fourth century is hardly likely. Not to mention the fact, of course, that Herodotus' narrative is quite different from Thucydides' in many fundamental ways, such that the notion of an ideal type of historical narrative, which Xenophon was expected somehow to follow exactly, becomes quite uncertain.

There is thus no reason to believe that in Xenophon's time the genre of history had been fixed with exact and invariable "rules." On the contrary, the genre was relatively new, and its orientation, purposes, and subject matter(s) were still being determined. This is not to say, of course, that historiography was an amorphous mass. When, for example, Xenophon explicitly comments several times on the subject matter of *his* history, as he does for example in quoting the remarks of Theramenes before his death, or in praising Teleutias for the devotion he inspired in his men, or his praise of the city of Phleious for its actions,[14] he shows simultaneously an awareness of what one usually found in a work of history and a desire to create space within the genre for his own approach: in other words, his own historical narratives manipulate, challenge, and extend conventions (not "rules") employed by Herodotus and Thucydides.

In formal terms, both the *Anabasis* and the *Hellenica* represent new developments in Greek historiography. Much ink has been spilled on determining the exact genre of the former, with the usual problems that the notions of "genre" tend to be Procrustean and the terms employed wholly modern.[15] The work can be described as a historical narrative tightly focalized around a few characters, with some (but only minimal) consideration of the opposing side, though whether this limited perspective entails striking it from the rolls of "history" is debatable. As for the *Hellenica*, here Xenophon has inaugurated a type of history that was to become enormously popular in the ancient world, the "continuous history," which picks up events from a predecessor and carries the story forward, usually through the author's own time.[16] In both works Xenophon bends the genre to his own needs and interests.

In this act of bending, Xenophon's historical works incorporate features generally associated with other genres. Speech, for example, had been an important part of historiography from its inception, but in Xenophon we see

---

[14] *Hell.* 2.3.56; 5.1.3–4; 7.2.1.

[15] See, e.g., Bradley 2001.

[16] On the genre of the *Hellenica* see Tuplin 1993: 167–8; for Xenophon's continuation of Thucydides, Rood 2004b; on the legacy of continuous history see Marincola 1997: 237–41. But cf. Luraghi in this volume.

new uses. Although dialogue had not been wholly absent from Herodotus or Thucydides, Xenophon employs it to a much greater extent. The formal, antithetical speeches of Thucydides are not to be found in Xenophon, who prefers shorter speeches in general, and very frequently enacts in his narrative the give and take of speaker and audience, where speakers, having made assertions that are immediately challenged, are compelled to address individual points or modify their earlier remarks. Good examples are found in *Hellenica* where Cephisodotus questions Timocrates in a scene reminiscent of Attic oratory, or Orontas' "trial" before Cyrus in *Anabasis* which displays the Socratic question-and-answer format, the hapless Orontas being led, like a Socratic interlocutor, to convict himself.[17]

The *Anabasis* presents yet other interesting variations from earlier historiographical narratives. The enumeration in the march up-country of stages and parasangs, features that seem dull to many moderns, impart useful information to the reader and graft the features of geographical writing onto a traditional historical narrative so as to provide a complex exploration of space.[18] The ethnographic observations that one finds here and throughout the narrative, and the interest in great buildings and marvels (even if humble) of all sorts, link the *Anabasis* to Herodotus' history and integrate knowledge of foreign peoples and customs into the narrative. Nor is mythographical comment absent.[19] The innovative nature of the *Anabasis* can also be seen in its presentation of itself not as a comprehensive history: at 1.8.27 Xenophon notes that Ctesias provides the number of those of the King's bodyguard who fell at Cunaxa, but the narrator himself does not tell us what that was! It seems clear that we are to read the *Anabasis*, then, not as comprehensive, but as offering an independent if limited perspective on this particular set of historical events.

An openness to the generic innovation present in Xenophon's historical works allows us to appreciate the ways in which he took historical narrative in different directions – indeed he was in no small measure responsible for bequeathing to historiography many of what were to become its salient characteristics – as well as to see those particular matters that he wished to explore in both *Anabasis* and *Hellenica*. To these we now turn.

---

[17] *Hell.* 7.1.13; *Anab.* 1.6.1–11; cf. *Hell.* 4.1.4–15; *Anab.* 3.1.15–30, 4.6.14–19, and 5.8.2–11. On Xenophon's "conversationalized narratives" see Gray 1981 and 1989: 11–64 for detailed and incisive analysis.

[18] Breitenbach 1967: 1650–5 on possible periegetic sources; Purves 2010: 168–77; Rood 2010b, esp. 55–7.

[19] Ethnographical observations: *Anab.* 1.4.9, 1.5.1–3, 2.3.15–16, 3.5.14–16, 4.4.13, 4.5.25–7, 4.7.15–16, 4.8.20–21, 5.4.12–14, 5.4.32, 6.1.5–11, 6.4.1–8 (with geographical observations as well); mythographical: 1.2.8, 1.2.13, 6.2.1–2.

Themes and Interests

A full treatment of Xenophon's themes and interests in *Anabasis* and *Hellenica* cannot, of course, be attempted here, so what follows is a mere overview.[20]

Leaders and Followers. One can hardly overestimate Xenophon's interest in leadership, whether in the political, military, or private realm: it is present in all of his works, sometimes explicitly stated, sometimes implicitly adumbrated.[21] He displays an intense and detailed interest in the way in which leaders interact with those over whom they are given rule or command. In the *Anabasis*, of course, this can be easily seen in the constant maneuvering by the generals, whether as a group or acting as individuals, with respect to their soldiers, and it is on display also in the *Hellenica*, especially in the figure of Agesilaus, although in this latter work we find also the relationship of civic leaders to their fellow citizens, as they seek to offer the best counsel and then persuade them of the wisdom of their advice.

The commander in the field, however, seems to be Xenophon's touchstone, and it has often been noted that his time as a soldier must have informed his worldview. Xenophon devotes an extraordinary amount of detail to the various roles that any successful general must play. The absolute importance of the commander is made clear by a remark in the *Hellenica* where the Spartan envoys marvel at the improved performance of the army under Dercylidas' leadership and are told by "the leader of the Cyreans" – Xenophon, surely – that there is an easy explanation: "We are the same, it is the leader who is different" (*Hell.* 3.2.6–7). In the *Anabasis* the character Xenophon assures his audience that without leaders nothing good can be accomplished (*Anab.* 3.1.38), and part of the "story" in that work traces the way in which Xenophon himself develops into a leader.[22]

[20] I have not dealt here with Xenophon's frequent and detailed narratives of military tactics and procedures. Xenophon regularly gives specific details of how success on the battlefield was achieved, and it is very clear that such detail was thought to be part of the usefulness of his history, and the way in which it could have educative value quite apart from specific situations: cf. *Hell.* 4.2.18–22, 5.1.8, 5.4.44, 6.5.26, 6.5.51–2, 7.1.21, 7.5.8, 7.5.21–4; *Anab.* 3.4.33, 3.5.8–11, 4.2.1–23, 7.3.36ff.; Gray 1989: 146–53 on stratagem narratives; more generally Whitby 2004, esp. 225–42 and Lee 2007. Nor do I treat the consistent dichotomy drawn between Greeks and barbarians (*Hell.* 3.4.19, 4.1.29–40, 7.1.38; *Anab.* 1.2.14–18, 1.5.9, 1.7.37, 2.1.12, 3.1.23, 3.2.25, 4.4.21), which is also of great importance (see Rood 2004a; Brock 2004; Harman 2012 and 2013), though this too often becomes associated with the question of Xenophon's panhellenism.

[21] Fundamental now is Gray 2011. For Xenophon and leadership see Buxton in this volume; this section should ideally be read with his remarks there.

[22] Cf. *Anab.* 2.2.6, where at the outset the men trust Clearchus alone because he is experienced.

Xenophon presents commanders in a variety of situations, and he shows, either explicitly or implicitly, what characteristics he thought necessary for success. He not infrequently shows them "manipulating" their troops – for the troops' own good, of course – with word or deed. If a false report is necessary to maintain morale, then the general must employ that.[23] A leader encourages positive rivalry among the soldiers, either by offering rewards or prizes, or simply by the attraction of good repute, with the result that the soldiers will be bold and brave,[24] but he cannot shrink from imposing penalties when needed.[25] He will himself be energetic and consistently exhort his troops to action where they have a reasonable chance of success,[26] and he will not be slow to share in the dangers and work of war.[27]

Above all he will be constantly monitoring their morale, keeping them from becoming over-confident or unnecessarily fearful. The former will lead to carelessness, and both works contain numerous examples of soldiers endangered or killed when acting with overconfidence or disdain for the enemy: such contempt often meets its match and swiftly.[28] On the opposite side, dispirited soldiers must be encouraged, especially when they suffer from despondency (*athumia*) after a setback or loss, or when the situation seems desperate; good leaders in both works consistently encourage the men to be reasonably confident.[29]

[23] Agesilaus conceals the Spartan defeat at Cnidus, telling them but part of the truth. He then sacrificed as if Cnidus had been a victory "with the result that the troops fought well and were victorious because of the report that the Spartans had won the naval battle" (*Hell.* 4.3.13–14).

[24] Cf. *Hell.* 3.2.10 (Dercylidas), 4.2.5 and 3.4.16–19 (Agesilaus), 6.1.6 (Jason), 6.2.27–30 (Iphicrates); *Anab.* 4.1.26–8, 4.7.10–12, 4.8.26–8.

[25] See *Anab.* 5.8.13–22 for Xenophon's defense of punishment; cf. Buxton, below, pp. 332–3.

[26] *Hell.* 6.2.13–14 (Iphicrates), 6.4.21 (where Jason's action shows "speed often accomplishes more than force"; 7.5.8 (Epaminondas' daring); *Anab.* 2.3.11 (Clearchus), 3.1.24 and 6.5.12–21 (Xenophon; cf. his explicit remark at 3.1.42 that stoutness of heart, not numbers or strength, wins victories).

[27] Cf. *Hell.* 1.1.30 where Hermocrates is missed by his men for (*inter alia*) his affability (*koinotēs*); *Anab.* 3.4.47–8 and 7.3.45 show Xenophon dismounting from his horse to share in the dangers; at 4.4.12–19 he rises in the cold and chops wood, leading his men to imitate him.

[28] Care: *Hell.* 6.2.31; *Anab.* 5.2.15–16, 5.8.20 ("in dangers even small blunders bring disaster"). Carelessness: *Hell.* 3.4.22, 4.1.17–18, 4.8.18, 6.2.17; this is less pronounced in the *Anabasis* because of good leadership: cf. 5.1.5–9 where Xenophon details the care necessary when foraging. Contempt: *Hell.* 2.1.27 (Athenians at Aegospotami), 4.5.12, 4.8.18 (where it is joined with lack of proper formation), 7.1.18–19 (Thebans at Corinth).

[29] Cf., e.g., *Hell.* 1.1.24 (Pharnabazus!), 3.5.21–2 and 3.5.24 (viewpoints of different sides), 5.1.27 (Antalkidas induces *athumia* in the enemy by bold action); *Anab.* 1.4.9, 3.1.2–3, 3.3.11, 3.5.2–7, 4.3.7–9. Cf. *Hell.* 7.1.31, where Archidamus must restrain his troops' enthusiasm.

The good commander must, of course, pay heed to the will of the gods, especially by frequent sacrificing, and must exhibit an unwavering obedience to what the gods indicate through the sacrificial victims or birds or even dreams (although the last are sometimes hard to interpret),[30] and he will skillfully invoke the gods in his speeches to encourage his men.[31] Xenophon's works do not examine or analyze the relationship between gods and men (still less do they question it), but presume it already to be in effect. Xenophon seems rather to be trying to explore how exactly the piety of leaders interacts with the favor of heaven: at the most basic level, it's not enough for a leader to be pious; he must also plan well, be alert, and do all those human things that contribute to success. Piety is a necessary but not sufficient condition for success.

An important element of piety is faithfulness, being true to one's promises and oaths (especially since in the latter the gods are witnesses). Tissaphernes is marked out in both *Anabasis* and *Hellenica* as particularly faithless, an element exploited by the Greek leaders.[32] Towards the end of the *Anabasis*, in the lengthiest speech of that work, the character Xenophon calls on Seuthes to be a man of his word, since trustworthiness is not only right, it is practical: "the words of untrustworthy men wander here and there without result," while "if men are seen to practice truth, their words ... have power to accomplish no less than force in the hands of other men" (7.7.24).

Homeric models of leadership are never far from Xenophon's thoughts, and just as leaders are expected to be brave fighters, they are also expected to have some of Odysseus' resourcefulness and cunning, and to use guile and ruses when those will accomplish more than force.[33] Successful generals are adaptable and can learn from their mistakes, sometimes on the go.[34] The good commander is tough but sympathetic, and he is not hesitant to join the troops in whatever role when needed, as a way of inspiring them and making them confident in him.[35] If their trust in him is gone, the outlook is not good: the Spartan Mnasippus withholds pay from his mercenaries and

---

[30] Cf., e.g., *Hell.* 3.1.17–18 and 4.8.36ff., where disregarding of omens leads to disaster; in the *Anabasis*, by contrast, omens are almost always followed; on the importance of sacrificing and the gods throughout the *Anabasis* see below, n. 42.

[31] *Hell.* 2.4.13–17 (Thrasybulus says the gods showed favor by a sudden snowfall); 3.4.11 (Agesilaus on Tissaphernes' perfidy); *Anab.* 3.1.22 and 3.2.10 (perjury of Persians).

[32] See previous note.

[33] *Hell.* 1.6.19–20, 2.4.29, 3.1.8 (Dercylidas nicknamed "Sisyphus"), 3.4.15 (Agesilaus' makeshift cavalry: cf. Xenophon's similar action at *Anab.* 3.3.19–20), 4.5.4, 4.6.8–12, 5.1.27, 5.4.48, 6.5.18–19; *Anab.* 1.3.3–19 (Clearchus fools his troops: but is this praiseworthy?), 2.1.23, 2.2.19–21, 2.3.3ff., 3.5.17–18, 4.7.1–14.

[34] *Hell.* 6.2.27–30 (Iphicrates' innovation on voyage to Corcyra); *Anab.* 3.3.12–18, 3.4.19–23 (hollow-square formation abandoned), 5.8.14–15.

[35] See Buxton, below, pp. 332–4.

strikes one of his company commanders who warns him about this, but he pays no heed: "his men marched out dispirited and hating him: a state of affairs least helpful when men go into battle" (*Hell*. 6.2.19). Sure enough, he is killed and his troops are soundly defeated.

Not least important is the general's mastery of himself. It is not only that this too can serve as a model for his soldiers, but also that as the person in command, everything he does has outsized consequences and affects all the others. Xenophon's particularly emphatic condemnation of Teleutias' anger at the siege of Olynthus, which led to his death and the destruction of "the most valuable part of the army," is motivated in part by this reality, that the commander's momentary anger was disastrous for Sparta as a whole.[36]

The soldiers' response to effective leadership is obedience to authority (*peitharchia*), which leads to effectiveness and good order (*eutaxia*).[37] Procles claims that *peitharchia* is the most important aspect of military success (*Hell*. 7.1.8) and Xenophon, in his famous description of Agesilaus' "workshop for war" at Sardis, joins piety, preparedness, and *peitharchia* as foundations for success: "For whenever men honor the gods, prepare themselves vigorously for war, and obey their commanders, how is it not reasonable for everyone to have good hopes?" (*Hell*. 3.4.18; cf. *Ages*. 27).[38] The necessity for an army to function as a cohesive unit is frequently invoked.[39]

The role of rhetoric in Xenophon's vision of leadership is paramount, and both *Anabasis* and *Hellenica* are full of speeches, short and long, and in many different situations. Speech, of course, was essential in the ancient city state for anyone who wished to take part in public life, and ancient historical narratives reflect this; speech is a dominant mode in the *Cyropaedia*, again revealing its importance in the inculcation of leadership. Particularly

---

[36] Similarly, Cheirisophon's striking of the village chief (*Anab*. 4.6.1–3), which causes him to desert the Greek forces. Cf. *Hell*. 4.8.22, where Diphidas is characterized as more resolute and enterprising than Ekdikos because he is not beholden to bodily pleasures. On emotions in *Hellenica* see Giraud 1999: 226–60.

[37] This is but one response: see Buxton, pp. 326–8 for other practical advantages gained by good leadership.

[38] Cf. also *Hell*. 1.1.26 (the Syracusan generals obey the command of their fellow citizens back home); 5.2.6 (Spartan restraint in the treatment of their enemies is marked as an exceptional example of *peitharchia*); 7.5.19 (Epaminondas' army ready to obey his every command); cf. *Anab*. 5.4.16–18 where some Greeks forage without the orders of their generals and must retreat from the enemy with heavy losses (the first time in the entire expedition, according to the narrator); Xenophon says to his men that he punished lack of order (*ataxia*) because it leads to death for all (*Anab*. 5.8.13).

[39] It can be seen in scenes as different as *Hell*. 1.1.28, where the Syracusan generals mention their courage in commanding and the men's skill in obeying, and *Anab*. 6.1.18–6.4.11, where the Ten Thousand split up, fare poorly, and eventually reunite. Note too *Anab*. 1.5.7–8 where the Persian nobles get down in the mud for Cyrus.

noteworthy, however, in Xenophon's historical works, and only rarely found in his predecessors, is the give and take between speaker and audience: arguments used by the speakers are immediately taken up by the audience, with the result that not only speech but a kind of dynamic of leadership through speech is illustrated.[40]

Leadership in Xenophon is on display not only on the battlefield but also in the assembly and the polis in general, where the *Hellenica* especially comes to the fore. The first incident written up at length by Xenophon is the trial of the generals after Arginusae, where the absence of leadership is at its starkest. Despite the impassioned pleas of Euryptolemus, who urges patience and adherence to established custom, no general or orator can restrain the lawlessness of the Athenian *demos*, nor curb its insistence on the immediate gratification of its revenge. The Athenians' self-destructive action comes back to haunt them only when it is, of course, too late.[41]

Nor is leadership just about individuals: states as leaders also interest Xenophon, especially in the *Hellenica*, where Sparta cannot maintain her success and dominance over the Greek world. Here, of course, the issues are somewhat more complex, lacking the stark necessity of the battlefield and involving, as they do, whole states and competing powers with their own interests. But there can be little doubt that the Spartans "fail" as leaders, and there is no reason to think that those qualities necessary in an individual for effective leadership were any different in Xenophon's mind from those necessary in a state; the disorder (*tarachē*, 7.5.26) that existed in Greece before and after Mantinea will, in his mind, have been largely a function of poor and inadequate leadership.

Humans and the Divine. Xenophon's piety has been much and well treated, and little need here be added. Suffice it to say that the gods play a much larger role in Xenophon than they did in Thucydides and somewhat more than in Herodotus. Divination is everywhere, and Xenophon consistently mentions the pre-battle or border-crossing sacrifices, the singing of the paean, the fulfilment of vows. The divine is present not only in sacrifices but also in omens seen and interpreted, and, less frequently but no less dramatically, in dreams. Specific actions are motivated by attempts to discover the gods' will, although (again) this does not eliminate the need for good human planning. But human planning cannot be employed unless approval from the gods is evident. The breaking of oaths as an offense against the gods has a particular role in both *Anabasis* and *Hellenica*, and in both works,

[40] See below; and for set speeches in Xenophon, Baragwanath in this volume.
[41] *Hell.* 1.7.1–35, a much discussed episode: see (*inter alia*) Due 1983; Gray 1989: 83–91; Pownall 2000; Rood 2004b: 374–80; Gish 2012.

oath-breaking allows the other side to claim the gods' support, just as the success of these parties may be said to demonstrate that support.[42]

Character. It is often said that Xenophon wrote "ethical" history: as a Socratic, he was deeply interested in human character, and the explicit delineation and evaluation of the character of historical figures is one of his lasting legacies to later historiography. The construction of character was by no means new to historiography: it can be found in Herodotus, of course, and Thucydides. Much of the characterization that we find in these historians is "indirect," revealed either by characters in the work expressing views about individuals or by the author's assumption that his readers will be cumulatively evaluating figures based on their deeds and words. And indeed, Xenophon is no stranger to this sort of characterization.[43] Direct characterization, however, is much more common in Xenophon, of the sort that Thucydides famously gives Pericles when he narrates his death (2.65). Thucydides' remarks on Pericles are focused very much on the specific ways in which his character affected his public actions and allowed him to manipulate the Athenian democracy: such "virtues" as, for example, his imperviousness to bribery, are not told merely as praise of an abstract quality but as an explanation for why the people were willing to entrust their affairs to him. With Xenophon and with fourth-century historiography in general, this "pragmatic" interest in character does not disappear, but praise of virtues in the abstract now plays a greater role.[44]

The other change is in scale. The long obituary notice for Cyrus at *Anabasis* 1.9.1–31 is unparalleled in earlier historiography, as are the notices given at the deaths of the generals at 2.6.1–30. Some of this indeed may seem to concern matters not directly relevant to the narrative, but the other way to look at it is that Xenophon thought character essential for good leadership: even the apparently gratuitous detail that Menon engaged in shameful sexual practices (2.6.28) would be relevant to the question of his self-control, and thus his ability to command the respect and loyalty of his troops.

For indeed one of the concerns that Xenophon continues from his predecessors, though now on a much greater scale, is the relationship between the

---

[42] On religion and the divine in Xenophon see Dillery 1995: 179–94; Parker 2004; Flower 2012: 203–16.

[43] *Hell.* 5.3.20 (Agesilaus weeps for Agesipolis' death); *Anab.* 2.5.29 (Clearchus too trusting of Tissaphernes), 3.1.4–7 and 5.3.5–13 (Xenophon's piety towards Apollo and Artemis), 4.3.10 (Xenophon's approachableness; cf. 7.6.3–5), 7.8.23 (Xenophon given the pick of the booty, an implicit acknowledgment by others of his leadership). On indirect characterization in *Hellenica* see Flower 2015.

[44] Some examples of explicit character evaluation: *Hell.* 2.3.56, 3.4.29, 4.4.3, 6.1.2–3, 6.4.28, 6.5.6–7; *Anab.* 6.4.8 and two notices of fighters at their death: *Anab.* 4.1.18, 4.7.14.

personal and the public. Thucydides had treated such a theme in his account of the tyrannicides as well as in his delineation of Alcibiades' character,[45] and Xenophon continues and expands this theme, whether it be Cyrus' unrestrained and fatal attack on his brother at Cunaxa (*Anab.* 1.8.23–6), the Spartan Alcetas' excessive focus on a beautiful boy from Oreos which allows the acropolis to be won back, leading to the city's revolt from Sparta (*Hell.* 5.4.57), or Sphodrias' acquittal at Sparta, where the personal affection of young men leads Agesilaus to artful action in defending Sphodrias, and this action in turn has the much larger consequence of alienating further the Spartans from the rest of Greece, and "seemed to many the most unjust verdict ever given at Sparta."[46]

Justice. The character Xenophon[47] is ridiculed in the *Anabasis* for "resembling a philosopher" in his speech (2.1.13), and it is very clear that Xenophon has an overt interest in justice, in the sense of right action, fair dealing, and the observance of appropriate reciprocity towards individuals, states, and, of course, the gods. In the *Anabasis* Orontes' "trial" before Cyrus is delineated in terms of reciprocity and justice (1.6.1–11), while in the *Hellenica*, the trial of Euphron's murderers at Thebes has each side plead the justice of their case (7.3.4–12), and Xenophon's speech to Seuthes, mentioned above, reminds that leader to fulfil his obligations, noting that there is no finer possession than excellence (*aretē*) and justice (*dikaiosynē*, *Anab.* 7.7.41). In the trial of the generals, Euryptolemus invokes the injustice of Athenian behavior (*Hell.* 1.7.16–33, esp. 19, 20, 23, 24, 33), and after Aegospotami, the Athenians remember their injustices (*ēdikoun*, 2.2.10) against fellow Greeks and expect a similar punishment. There is much talk of justice as well in the conflict between Theramenes and Critias (*Hell.* 2.3.37–49, esp. 26, 27, 28, 29, 37, 43, 49), but the theme is perhaps most brilliantly treated in the exchange of Dercylidas with Meidias, the son-in-law of Mania, who had murdered her and seized her property (3.1.16–28). Xenophon brings out clearly both the absolute control that Dercylidas has over Meidias without ever resorting to violence, and the re-establishment by Dercylidas of an equitable situation. It all hangs on justice: when Meidias asks for control of Gergis, Dercylidas says that Meidias would "not fail to receive what was just" (3.1.22). While dinner is being prepared, Dercylidas says to Meidias that they should discuss "how we can behave justly towards each other" (3.1.24). And at the very end, when Meidias asks, now that the Spartans

---

[45] Thuc. 6.53–9 on the tyrannicides; on Alcibiades, Gribble 1999.
[46] For Agesilaus and Sphodrias, *Hell.* 5.4.25–33, with Gray 1989: 327–8. Dillery 1995: 6 notes that Xenophon did not perceive "complex chains of causation working through time" but "relied on signal, benchmark events to interpret the history of his age."
[47] If it is Xenophon: see above, n. 3.

have appropriated what was once Mania's property, where he is to live, Dercylidas says, "in that very place where it is most just (*dikaiotaton*, 3.1.28) for you to live, Meidias – in your hometown of Scepsis and in your father's house."

Why Historical Narrative?

If it is the case that Xenophon pursued his themes in various genres, the question arises as to why he chose historical narrative as one of the means of conveying these themes. Why show an ideal leader in the narrative of the *Anabasis* when such a man could just as easily be delineated in the *Cyropaedia*? Why show the virtues of a commander such as Agesilaus when an explicit encomium could do (and did) that just as well?[48] Why pursue questions of justice and piety in history when such matters could be more clearly articulated in philosophical dialogue? Why, in short, history?[49]

To begin with, if the works of Herodotus and Thucydides had shown anything, it was that history could immortalize deeds and could do so by telling their story in an elevated way and with an eye towards posterity. In both *Anabasis* and *Hellenica* there are indications that Xenophon was very much aware of this capacity of history.[50] There are, first of all, the remarks that show he was working in the "memorializing" tradition of historiography: the description of Coronea as like no other battle of his time (4.3.16), or his naming those in Greece who took bribes from the Persians (3.5.1), or his praise of the Athenian cavalry at Mantinea (7.5.15–17) all show this realization. When Tissaphernes is checked from attacking Dercylidas because he remembers the Cyreans' success against the Persians (*Hell.* 3.2.18), we see a very clear example of the power of history. It is noteworthy how often in the *Anabasis* Xenophon can be seen to be thinking of the future, not least in the early scene where Phalinus is urged by Clearchus to give good advice to the Greeks, "advice which will bring you honor in future time when it is reported in this way: 'Once upon a time Phalinus, when he was sent by the King to order the Greeks to surrender their arms, gave them, when they

---

[48] On the *Agesilaus* see Dillery in this volume.
[49] It goes without saying that my answers that follow are suggestive and partial, not definitive or comprehensive.
[50] See Rood 2004a: 318 on the commemorative aspect of Xenophon's *Anabasis*; Flower 2012: 62 has sophisticated remarks on how memory works; Cawkwell 2004: 60–5 is also relevant here. Questions of memorialization in Xenophon quickly become discussions of apologetic, whether for himself in *Anabasis* or the Spartans in *Hellenica*. If I choose not to engage with such issues, it is not because I think them unimportant but because they have little bearing on how Xenophon's themes play out in his historical narratives, which is my concern here.

sought his counsel, the following advice'" (2.1.17). Similarly Xenophon's repeated injunctions to his troops to consider and remember the good repute that they wish to win in Greece shows the effect that a consideration of history can have on all people's behavior.[51]

A second opportunity afforded by history was the ability to create a more nuanced and complicated picture. Xenophon's didacticism is well known and he can quite often leave little to the imagination. But as much recent scholarship has shown, neither the *Hellenica* nor the *Anabasis*, for all of their "artless" narration, should be assumed to be wholly straightforward and uncomplicated (or uncomplicating). The Agesilaus of Xenophon's encomium is openly praised,[52] while the *Hellenica* reveals him to be a much more problematic character;[53] Xenophon's portrait of Callicratidas is nuanced and thought-provoking,[54] as is his treatment of the trial of the generals after Arginusae, which has been seen both as condemnatory of the Athenians and as defending democracy.[55] Not everything is fulfilled as promised – in the *Anabasis* the Euphrates' appearance of "retreat" before Cyrus as if he were destined to be king (1.4.18) turns out to be an incorrect inference, and Cyrus' claim (1.7.4) that the Persians will begin the battle with shouting is not correct – or things come out in an unexpected way: Xenophon's concern that the Greeks will be like the Lotus-Eaters and wish to stay in Asia is, ironically, most evident in Xenophon's longing to found a colony at Calpe Harbor.[56] Finally, in both works there are noticeable differences between what characters claim and what the narrator himself maintains.[57] Like Herodotus and Thucydides before him, Xenophon expected his readers to be engaged constantly in the work of interpretation.

Third, historical narrative offered the possibility of showing how idealized notions might work out in the "real world," and this must have appealed to Xenophon's practical and pragmatic side. Now it is of course the case that in the *Anabasis* we have a highly idealized leader who rarely makes mistakes; but he does make some and, more to the point, he is often shown under attack and the narrative must then work out how such conflict is resolved. The dynamic of leadership through speech, mentioned above, here often

---

[51] *Anab.* 5.7.33, 6.3.17, 6.5.24. For the *Anabasis* as an attempt to influence the Greeks' collective memory of the expedition see Flower 2012: 7. Note also *Hell.* 4.8.4, where Dercylidas tells the people of Abydus that loyalty in misfortune is remembered for all time, the truth of which Xenophon himself ensures for Phleious (above, n. 14).

[52] Although even here there are problems: see Harman 2012.

[53] Tuplin 1993: 164.

[54] Moles 1994.

[55] See the references in n. 41 above.

[56] *Anab.* 3.2.25; 6.4.1–6, with Ma 2004: 339–40.

[57] Ferrario 2012.

comes into play. The soldiers, the generals, or other leaders often interrupt speeches (by Xenophon and others), and make counter-charges or counter-arguments, which the speaker must then address. We see a bit of this in earlier historians[58] but nothing on this scale or with this depth. Nor is the internal audience the only one: the external audience of the history is also engaged in evaluation, examining the speaker's effectiveness, given his circumstances at the time, but also his success or failure, given that they, unlike the internal audience, know future events.[59]

Finally, history allowed a writer to tell a story, and to tell it over time, and with various characters having different roles and different interests (complexity again).[60] The success of the Ten Thousand is shown to be dependent on many factors, including the favor of the gods, the good leadership of those in command, the bravery of the common soldiers, and the errors and weaknesses of the barbarians, while the latter books show the gradual breakdown of the cohesiveness on display earlier. In the *Hellenica* the author explores how it was that the Spartans managed to lose their leadership over Greece and exchange their success and power for failure and a threat to their very existence. Like Herodotus and Thucydides, Xenophon was of course interested in what could be learned from history – the general truths that could be "extracted" from historical events and that gave history its value and meaning – but like them as well, he had an interest in how such events played out *specifically*. The trajectory that Sparta follows from the peak of her power to the final episode at Mantinea was perhaps not surprising to anyone who had learned from Herodotus and Thucydides that all empires rise and fall, but the *particular* way in which the Spartans lost their control over the Greek world could not, and did not, exactly match onto earlier powers, such as the Median or the Athenian.

The fourth century did not, like the fifth, have two superior powers who commanded great resources and allies, such that their conflict could be considered a Panhellenic "face-off"; on the contrary, the inability of any power to attain, let alone maintain, a position of pre-eminence meant an entirely different kind of story. Xenophon's delineation of how the Spartans squandered their advantages allows him to narrate their *peripeteia* while simultaneously showing the ways in which the actions of other states played into this.[61] This multi-focalized narrative brings out the special virtues of the

---

[58] See Thuc. 4.28 where Nicias and Cleon engage in debate in the Assembly; or the Melian Dialogue (5.84–116), although this is behind closed doors and somewhat abstract in its thought.

[59] See Marincola 2010: 269–79 for some suggestions how this works in the *Hellenica*.

[60] Tuplin 1993: 168 notes that storytelling is the most effective method of persuasion.

[61] Tuplin 1993: 165 points out that there are no heroes in the *Hellenica*.

genre of history, where the viewpoints, aims, and ambitions of the different protagonists (who likewise hardly come off well) can be explored and considered. Xenophon's frequent recourse to the divine as the narrative moves towards its end[62] does not in any way eliminate the need to consider purely human motivations: the seizure of the Cadmeia, the high-handed treatment of allies, Sphodrias' attack on the Piraeus, the excellence of Theban forces and strategy are all elements contributing to the Spartans' ultimate undoing. In narrating the rise and fall of the great power of his era, Xenophon was doing for his own time what Herodotus and Thucydides had done for theirs. Even if the end of the *Hellenica* is not exactly a climax,[63] the fact that Xenophon tells the story allows for the possibility that future generations can themselves try to unravel what for Xenophon and his times were seen only as mystery and uncertainty.

Further Reading

The past decades have seen extremely fruitful readings of both of Xenophon's historical works. Dillery 1995 looks at Xenophon's entire historical output and throws much light on his interests and aims, and is particularly valuable for setting Xenophon in his contemporary context. Gray 1989 and Tuplin 1993 give excellent analyses, from different angles, of many episodes in the *Hellenica*. Cawkwell 1972 and 1979 are still worth reading, the former with the (not quite) second thoughts of Cawkwell 2004. For the *Anabasis* there are very good essays in Lane Fox 2004, while Flower 2012 is a comprehensive examination and analysis of many of the themes of the *Anabasis*, the more valuable in that it is accessible also to the non-expert. Gray 2010b has a good introduction and collects recent scholarship that touches on most of Xenophon's vast oeuvre.

---

[62] See *Hell.* 6.4.2–3, 6.4.6–7, 6.4.24, 7.4.3, 7.4.9, 7.4.32, 7.5.10, 7.5.12–13, 7.5.26.
[63] On the importance of the final battle of Mantinea to Xenophon's thought see Dillery 1995: 17–38; cf. Rood 2004a: 350 on the theme of disorder as paramount in the work; cf. Moles 1994: 84; and, for similar disarray at the end of the *Anabasis*, Flower 2012: 196–201.

6

DAVID M. JOHNSON

Xenophon's *Apology* and *Memorabilia*

Defending Socrates: Audience, Tone, and History

Xenophon regarded Socrates as the best and happiest of men (*Mem.* 4.8.11). But he tried to reach readers indifferent or even hostile to Socrates. This explains as well as anything why Xenophon's Socratic works differ from Plato's.[1] An author writing about a man he admires for readers who do not yet admire that man must write defensively, and Xenophon's *Apology* and *Memorabilia* are above all defenses of Socrates. They differ little in substance; both *Apology* and *Memorabilia* start with a defense against the charges in court but broaden to include a vigorous argument that Socrates was not only innocent but supremely virtuous. They do differ considerably in tone, because their projected audiences are at different stages in their responses to Socrates.

In his *Apology*, Xenophon addresses readers who are already sympathetic enough to Socrates to wonder why he did not defend himself well; this is not a question one normally asks about a guilty man. Xenophon therefore explains to such readers that Socrates spoke boastfully at his trial because he was confident that he had lived a just and altogether superlative life, and thus was now, at his advanced age, ready to die (*Apology* 1). The audience Xenophon imagines for the *Memorabilia*, on the other hand, presumably includes readers still open to the attacks against Socrates; otherwise Xenophon would not spend so much time summarizing and refuting such arguments. To convince these readers, Xenophon mounts a lengthy direct defense of Socrates (*Mem.* 1.1–1.2), and does a much better job of defending Socrates than he allows Socrates to do on his own behalf in the *Apology*. Once this defensive case is made, the *Memorabilia* can go over to the positive case for Socrates. Thus while Socrates boasts in the *Apology* that he is superior to others, in the *Memorabilia* Xenophon praises him because he is

---

[1] I owe this observation – though it took years for it to bear fruit with me – to Roderick Long of Auburn University.

most helpful to others – a rather more attractive character to present to a wider range of readers. By the time we reach the end of the *Memorabilia*, Xenophon has converted his critical audience so that it resembles the audience he starts with in *Apology*, and can again discuss why Socrates did not mount an effective defense. Thus the *Memorabilia* ends by addressing the question, and the audience, that the *Apology* began with. The two works differ not so much because Xenophon has changed his views as because he has changed his readers.[2]

Xenophon's Socrates makes no effort to avoid the death penalty, and indeed provokes it through his boasting (*Apology* 32), but his *Apology* does not only show Socrates committing suicide by jury. Rather, Socrates wanted to demonstrate that he was neither impious nor unjust (*Apology* 22). He did so not only by addressing the legal charges against him – that he did not acknowledge the gods of Athens, but introduced new divinities, and corrupted the young – but by arguing that he was the most just and most pious of men.[3] In the fuller defense in the *Memorabilia* Xenophon brings more arguments against Socrates on to the stage. Some of those arguments reflect complaints about Socrates going back to Aristophanes' *Clouds* (including Socrates' tendency to alienate sons from their fathers); others will have been raised at the trial; and still others may reflect arguments made years later by the Athenian sophist Polycrates.[4] Whatever the ultimate source of these attacks on Socrates, it is clear that Xenophon manipulates the rhetoric of the accusers to his own ends, showing them progressively beaten down by his aggressive defense of Socrates.[5] Xenophon aims to prove not only that Socrates was religiously orthodox (though he does claim this, largely by citing Socratic orthopraxy), but that Socrates was the most pious of men. So too he did not corrupt the youth. How could he, given how self-controlled he was? Rather, he benefited them, and even in the case of his scandalous young charges Alcibiades and Critias, he deserves credit for taming them as long as he did. Far from being guilty of a capital offense, he was in fact worthy of honor by the city.

Unlike Xenophon's Socratic dialogues, the *Oeconomicus* and *Symposium*, and indeed unlike all the other early Socratic literature that has come down to us, *Memorabilia* and *Apology* have a clear authorial voice, a relatively clear audience, and an overt agenda, the defense of Socrates. But just who

---

[2] For a rather different effort to untangle the chronology of the two works, see Stokes 2012.

[3] More than suicide by jury: Pangle 1985: 101–2; Vander Waerdt 1993: 19–21.

[4] Livingstone 2001: 28–40 has, however, raised important doubts about making Polycrates the source for these arguments.

[5] Gray 1998: 70–93.

is this Socrates that Xenophon is defending? Is this the historical Socrates, Socrates as a fictional Xenophontic ideal, or something in between? Whether we want to or not, we had better confront the Socratic Question, which in practice means not so much asking who the historical Socrates was as asking whether pursuit of the historical Socrates is practicable. Especially among students of Xenophon's Socrates, the trend has been to characterize historical approaches to Xenophon's Socratica (his texts featuring Socrates) as a waste of time.[6] This is not the place to refight that question, but let us at least glance at the beginning of Xenophon's *Apology*, which may be our single most important piece of evidence regarding the Socratic Question.

> It seems to me worthwhile also to recall how, when he'd been summoned to trial, Socrates deliberated about his defense and about the end of his life. Others, too, have indeed written about this, and all of them have captured his boasting, which makes it clear that Socrates really spoke like this. But they have not made it clear that he believed that at this point death was preferable to life for him, and as a result his boasting appears rather foolish. Now Hermogenes was a companion of his, and by reporting the following about him he made it clear that Socrates' boasting was fitting, given his intention. (1–2)

Xenophon appears to be approaching his task like a historian.[7] He makes the agreement of his predecessors grounds for an historical inference (that Socrates really was boastful); he characterizes his task as correcting their failure to explain Socrates' motivation, a historical enough endeavor; and he cites his source, Hermogenes, a necessary move given that Xenophon was off with the Ten Thousand in Asia at the time of Socrates' trial. As the trial of Socrates is one of the most important and controversial events in Athenian history, we should be relieved to see that Xenophon presents his intentions as historical in this sense. And given that many of Xenophon's works are "historical" in some sense of that fraught word, his remarks here may help us to link Xenophon's procedure in his Socratica to that in his other works.

In the case of the trial, of course, we have an extant alternative account of the events Xenophon describes, Plato's *Apology*. Plato must be one of the other authors Xenophon here criticizes. Xenophon found Plato's Socrates boastful enough, as have most if not all modern readers, and Plato's Socrates does allude to the evils of old age, but only vaguely and late in his *Apology* (41d). Xenophon's correction of Plato's account consists in putting Socrates'

---

[6] So Dorion 2013a: 27–49.
[7] So too Brickhouse and Smith 1989: 6–7, though they regularly discount Xenophon's evidence, and argue that Socrates, rather than boasting, made the best forensic defense he could, given his philosophical scruples.

readiness to die front and center, as an explanation for how the trial unfolded. Other divergences between our two sources are more striking, and thus make historical reconstruction harder, but also provide insight into the particular character of Xenophon's work. Whereas in Plato the Delphic oracle reported that no man was wiser than Socrates (Plato, *Apology* 21a), when Xenophon presents the story, he has Apollo give the more fulsome response that no man was more free, more just, or more moderate than Socrates (*Apology* 14).[8] Later, after Socrates had been convicted of impiety, and it was time for the defendant to suggest an alternative to the death penalty the prosecution was asking for, Plato's Socrates allowed his friends to volunteer to pay a substantial fine on his behalf (*Apology* 38b). Xenophon, on the other hand, tells us that Socrates explicitly refused to suggest any penalty at all, as doing so would amount to an admission of guilt (*Apology* 23). Both differences highlight the boastfulness of Xenophon's Socrates. He is not merely wiser than other men in knowing that he knows nothing important, à la Plato's Socrates: he is so self-controlled and self-sufficient that no man could be more free or more just. So too his refusal to even suggest a counter-penalty highlights his uncompromising nature.

But these differences, while substantive and striking, are not perhaps as weighty as they may seem. Xenophon's Socrates does also argue, as part of his examination of what the oracle means, that he is wiser than anyone else (*Apology* 16); and Plato's Socrates, while yielding to his friends' suggestion that he offer a counter-penalty, does so only after inflaming the jury by saying that what he really deserved was a permanent place of honor at state banquets (*Apology* 36d). A deeper difference comes in the divine mission that Plato's Socrates somehow derives from the oracle, the mission that led him to question his fellow Athenians and exhort them to pursue virtuous souls rather than wealth or glory. There is no hint of any such mission in Xenophon's *Apology*. Nor, it should be said, is Socrates' mission explicitly discussed in any other Socratic work by Xenophon or Plato, raising the possibility that Plato invented it for the special circumstances of his *Apology*.[9] That mission reflects a more general distinction between Plato's Socrates and Xenophon's. Plato's sees himself as devoted to a special way of life, that of philosophy; and his conversations are more limited to topics we would recognize as philosophical. His mission is thus part of Plato's proselytizing for philosophy – promotion of the very way of life Plato was leading in the Academy. Xenophon's Socrates has no special mission. He is more integrated with the rest of society, and discusses a far wider range of topics. It is

[8] For a full reading of the oracle stories, see Vander Waerdt 1993.
[9] For doubts about the historicity of the Platonic mission, see Danzig 2010: 49–53.

tough to say whether Plato has imprinted his own notion of philosophy as a way of life on to Socrates, or Xenophon has downplayed this aspect of the historical Socrates to bring him more in sync with Xenophon's own, wider range of interests. But both could be true: Socrates could well have been both more practical than Plato presents him, and more philosophical than Xenophon implies. It is often the case that Xenophon's portrait of Socrates is compatible with Plato's, even where they emphasize different things. This suggests that historical reconstruction need not be vain – though it is certainly perilous enough, given the complex relationship between our sources.[10]

The Structure and Genre of the *Memorabilia*

After the direct defense of Socrates, Xenophon introduces the rest of the *Memorabilia* as follows: "He also seemed to me to really benefit his companions, sometimes in deed, by showing the sort of man he was, sometimes in conversation. I will write up as much of this as I remember" (*Mem.* 1.3.1). The second sentence, a typical bit of Xenophon's humility as an author, is a fitting introduction to the rest of the *Memorabilia*. The problem, initially, is that the bulk of the *Memorabilia* seems something of a mess, featuring multiple conversations, some very short, across a tremendous range of topics. Absent the chronological framework of *Anabasis*, *Hellenica*, or *Cyropaedia*, the dramatic unity of his Socratic dialogues (*Oeconomicus* and *Symposium*), or the clear argumentative structure of his treatises, Xenophon might be thought to have lost his way. It was long thought that the *Memorabilia* fell into two unequal parts published at different times: a relatively coherent defense, then a long collection of isolated passages, drawn perhaps from notes Xenophon happened to make of Socrates in action.[11]

Such developmental hypotheses are now largely discounted, however, and there is more structural integrity here than meets the eye. Xenophon demonstrates Socrates' usefulness first by alternating sections depicting his piety and self-control, Socrates' chief characteristics in Xenophon (1.3–2.1). We then move on to a series of conversations in which Socrates benefits first family and then friends (2.2–2.10). The third book shows him providing benefits to would-be leaders (3.1–7), then, following a pair of more philosophical chapters on the good, the beautiful, virtue, and knowledge (3.8–9), we turn to practical advice to artisans and others (3.10–3.14). Book

---

[10] For a considerably more skeptical take on the possibility of historical reconstruction based on comparisons between Plato and Xenophon, see Dorion in this volume.

[11] Dorion 2000: clxxxiii–cclii summarizes these criticisms, then provides a lengthy account of the unity and plan of the *Memorabilia*.

4 illustrates Socrates' approach to his companions (4.1), largely through his education of Euthydemus, which starts with a humbling philosophical seduction of the young lad (4.2), followed by more positive lessons (4.3; 4.5–4.6). A passage on law and justice with the sophist Hippias intervenes in the midst of this (4.4). A chapter on the proper limits of learning and a concluding chapter returning to the trial and culminating in a panegyric to Socrates' virtues wrap up the work (4.7–4.8).

The basic structure of the *Memorabilia* thus resembles a structure common in Greek forensic oratory, in which a section devoted to meeting the specific charges at hand (1.1.–1.2) is followed by another section, often longer, which lays out the virtues of the defendant (1.3–4.8).[12] Xenophon returns to and amplifies his treatment of key themes, beginning in the defense itself and continuing throughout the work; this is particularly clear with piety and self-control. What has struck many readers as a confused pastiche of more or less random minor conversations, then, Xenophon more likely considered a proof of the range of Socrates' beneficence. In the fourth book, rather than showing Socrates' breadth, Xenophon aims to show Socrates' depth, as we see a detailed picture of Socrates' education of a single model student. It is not surprising, then, that the fourth book contains many of the most philosophically substantive passages in the *Memorabilia*, including the discussion of the divine order in 4.3 (though this topic is introduced at 1.4) and of natural (unwritten) law in 4.4. The *Memorabilia* moves from a defensive to a more positive posture, from apology towards philosophy.

The *Memorabilia* is an example of Xenophon's flexibility when it comes to genre. It is a *Sokratikos logos*, a work of Socratic literature, but Xenophon's authorial voice, as well as the work's episodic structure and range in subject matter and interlocutors, distinguish it from all other such works known to us – though the loss of so much Socratic literature makes it impossible to be certain about Xenophon's originality here. Xenophon provides almost no dramatic context within the individual vignettes that make up the *Memorabilia*, no dramatic dates, scenery, or overt characterization. This makes the *Memorabilia* seem a pale shadow of more dramatic Socratic dialogues – including Xenophon's own *Symposium* and *Oeconomicus*. That contrast within Xenophon's own body of work shows that Xenophon chose to omit such dramatic effects in the *Memorabilia*, rather than being incapable of them. Xenophon is up to something else, a new kind of Socratic work, potentially unlimited in scope, not so much a distinct and unified literary whole as the frame through which Xenophon

---

[12] Erbse 1961.

would have readers view Socrates, even when they read of him in other works.[13] This is explicitly true of Xenophon's other Socratic works, each of which begins with Xenophon saying that he *also* found their topic worth discussing (light moments in *Symposium*, the trial in *Apology*), or had *also* heard Socrates talking about a certain topic (*oikonomia* in the *Oeconomicus*.) The *Memorabilia*, perhaps, is to be not just one Socratic work among others, but the introduction to Socrates, or at least to Socrates as benefactor (*Mem.* 1.3.1).

In its breadth the *Memorabilia* resembles a biography of Socrates, or, better, an encomium of him. While Xenophon does not give a full account of Socrates' life, he does cover some of the most famous events: Socrates' opposition to the illegal trial of the Arginusae generals, his refusal to participate in the murder of Leon of Salamis by the Thirty Tyrants, and his trial. Compare Xenophon's encomium of Agesilaus, which is limited to his patron's accomplishments after he became king, around the age of forty, and is explicitly intended to display his character (*Agesilaus* 1.6). The *Cyropaedia* is another encomium of sorts, meant not to tell the tale of Cyrus' life but to demonstrate his success at ruling men. One way of addressing Xenophon's evidence for the historical Socrates is to ask which Xenophontic biography is closer in spirit to Xenophon's Socratic works. The trend has been to make Xenophon's Socratic works no more Socratic than his *Cyropaedia* is historical, but this surely goes too far; the differences between Xenophon's Socrates and Plato's Socrates are far less than those between Xenophon's Cyrus and Herodotus' Cyrus. There is, however, considerable slippage between Xenophon's encomiastic account of Agesilaus in *Agesilaus* and his account of Agesilaus in the *Hellenica*; while these differences do not reduce Agesilaus to a fictional ideal, they provide us with something of a minimum estimate for the degree of historical latitude Xenophon would have felt in writing about Socrates.[14]

Vivienne Gray, in the fullest literary analysis of the *Memorabilia*, has argued that wisdom literature was "the chief generic influence on Xenophon's work."[15] The basic unit of such wisdom literature was the *chreia*, a brief account of a wise man's practical instruction, via words or deeds, sometimes presented in a dialogue form, and usually conventional in substance. A collection of such anecdotes came to be known as *Memorabilia* (ἀπομνημονεύματα), perhaps due to the influence of Xenophon himself. Wisdom literature aimed for breadth rather than depth, and prized

[13] For the metaphor of a frame, see Gray 1998, though I use the term rather differently here.
[14] For differences between the two accounts of Agesilaus, see Dillery 1995: 114–19.
[15] Gray 1998: 176.

innovation in form rather than in subject matter. In wisdom literature one tool we would expect, Gray notes, is amplification, a speaker's tendency to return to the same topic again and again, with each new attempt building on prior ones. In this sort of work, no individual account of a topic gives us the whole teaching, and the loose structure and seemingly conventional subject matter of the *Memorabilia* are par for the course. A passage like 3.13.1 nicely exemplifies this sort of thing:

> Once someone was angry, because after he greeted a man he was not greeted in return. "It's funny," he [Socrates] said, "that you wouldn't get angry if you met someone whose body was in a poor condition, but it does irk you when you meet someone with a boorish soul."

Xenophon's contribution, for Gray, was to "socraticize" the genre, not only by often expanding a *chreia* to a lengthy conversation, but by introducing Socratic modes of argumentation and unconventional elements in Socrates' thinking. As passages like that above are relatively rare, it is probably better to accord wisdom literature a secondary influence on Xenophon and on his reader's expectations rather than the chief one. Even this secondary influence, however, distinguishes Xenophon from Plato, who is so often at pains to distance himself from the rhetorical tradition, alluding to and parodying it in order to carve out out philosophy as a new way of life with its distinct literary genre.[16] Xenophon was less worried about distancing Socrates from the sophistic and rhetorical competition, going so far as to have Socrates happily adopt Prodicus' rhetorical set piece "Heracles at the Crossroads" (*Mem.* 2.1.21–33).[17]

As its traditional title implies, the *Memorabilia* is also a sort of memoir. Justification for the title comes above all from the five occasions on which Xenophon claims to be recalling Socratic conversations that he himself had heard (1.4.2, 1.6.14, 2.4.1, 2.5.1, 4.3.2). Once upon a time, Xenophon's claims to be present were taken at face value, as part of an argument for the historicity of his account of Socrates.[18] This is pretty clearly wrong; Xenophon also claims autopsy for the drinking party he depicts in his *Symposium*, which is set at a date at which he could not have attended such an affair. In the *Oeconomicus*, Xenophon overhears Socrates mentioning the death of Cyrus the Younger, an event which took place after Xenophon left to join Cyrus in 401, never to see Socrates again.

---

[16] Nightingale 1995.

[17] Though Xenophon may have significantly adapted Prodicus' original: see Dorion 2013a: 219–246. For Xenophon's general attitude towards the sophists, see Dorion's chapter in this volume.

[18] See Dorion 2000: xxxix–lii.

The second anachronism is particularly glaring, given the notoriety of Xenophon's service with Cyrus, so it is clear that Xenophon wasn't trying to fool anyone. It makes more sense to consider these part of Xenophon's effort to claim responsibility for what he has written; as John Cooper has argued, Xenophon's account of Socrates is "controlled by his personally acquired sense of who Socrates was and what he stood for."[19] Of course this claim to authority may be no more worthy of being taken at face value than the claim to historical veracity that others have seen in such remarks. But when we do have one of Xenophon's sources, as we have seen in discussing his *Apology* in light of Plato's, we can certainly see that he did feel free to differ from his fellow Socratic. One of the traditional criticisms of Xenophon was that he was the captive of his sources. Despite the convenient fact that Xenophon's sources, other than Plato, are now lost, and thus can be reconstructed as models of perfection from which the hapless Xenophon strayed, this view is not tenable, given Xenophon's free hand in recasting Plato.[20] But it is a view that Xenophon himself seems to have anticipated and attempted to meet by characterizing his work as his own memoir of Socrates.

Xenophon clearly sees himself as contributing to an ongoing conversation about Socrates. Consider the following passage, which serves as a third introduction to the *Memorabilia*, alongside Xenophon's wonder at the charges against Socrates at the outset of the work and his telling us that he plans to show all he can remember of Socrates' helpfulness at 1.3.1.

> And if some people make conjectures on the basis of what others write and say about him, and believe that he was the best at turning people towards virtue, but not capable of leading them to it, let them consider not only what he said to those who thought they knew everything when he refuted them by questioning and correcting them, but also what he said all day long with those who spent their time with him. Let them then judge whether he was capable of making those with him better. (*Memorabilia* 1.4.1)

Xenophon is going to improve on other accounts about Socrates, but he does so not by rejecting them but by adding to them. Readers will be aware of how Socrates refuted know-it-alls – above all from reading Plato; Xenophon calls their attention to another sort of conversation. Scholarship emphasizing differences between Plato and Xenophon has done much to help us understand both authors,[21] but the essential Socrates is an intertextual Socrates, the character who consists of the amalgam of different images

---

[19] Cooper 1999: 14.
[20] So Cooper 1999, and cf. Dorion in this volume.
[21] Above all, the papers gathered in Dorion 2013a.

of Socrates projected by the Socratics. "Xenophon's Socrates" is not the Socrates who appears in Xenophon and only in Xenophon: he is Socrates as he is reshaped by Xenophon.

Benefits, Pleasure, and Subtlety

In Xenophon's view, the best way to demonstrate Socrates' usefulness is to show him engaged with numerous interlocutors on a wide range of topics. These topics include philosophical concepts we would have expected from Plato's Socrates, as efforts at defining justice (especially in 4.2) and other key philosophical terms (1.1.16, 3.8, 3.9, 4.6); here Xenophon's Socrates is usually successful, while Plato's Socrates regularly fails, though Xenophon's definitions will not strike many as profound. But Xenophon's Socrates is more often shown teaching or giving advice than philosophizing.[22] The topics he discusses are often what we would expect from the author of works on politics, military affairs, leadership, and economics. But Xenophon's Socrates brings a certain amount of intellectual rigor to his advice through a focus on what is useful.[23] Good generals battle not for personal glory, or victory, or in defense of freedom, but for the well-being of those they lead (3.2). Familial discord can be resolved when relatives recognize how useful they can be to one another (2.3, 2.7). Friends are our most valuable possessions (2.4, 2.5), in friendships that aren't exploitative but are rather based on reciprocity and designed for the long term.[24] Dialectic is the ability to make distinctions helpful in deliberations (4.5.12). Socrates makes the intelligent design argument – our first extant example of this argument – not to prove the existence of God but to benefit his interlocutors by making them more pious and more moderate (1.4; 4.3).[25] His objection to natural philosophy is primarily its uselessness, as practiced by the Presocratics (1.1.15); so too he rejects advanced study of mathematics as idle (4.7).[26] Sometimes the emphasis on the beneficial gives the *Memorabilia* the air of a paperback from the Self-Help section, but concentration on the advantageous is intellectually substantive, as the pursuit of advantage is distinct from pursuit of glory, honor, freedom, truth, or other possible goals. It is also arguably Socratic enough. Socrates' contribution to philosophy was after all to bring it down to earth and focus on practical, human things (*Mem.* 1.1.16; cf.

[22] Morrison 1994.
[23] Danzig forthcoming.
[24] Van Berkel 2010.
[25] On these passages see Sedley 2007: 75–92 and Powers 2009.
[26] For more on Xenophon's relationship to Presocratic science, see Vander Waerdt 1994b and Dorion's chapter in this volume.

Cicero, *Tusculans* 5.4.10). The standard reading of Plato's Socrates holds that he too bases his ethics on the well-being of the individual; this reading has been critiqued of late,[27] but if it is correct, then Plato's Socrates, for all his talk of definitions, virtues, and justice, has the same sort of goal in mind that Xenophon's Socrates does.

The mixture of philosophy and practicality that makes Xenophon's Socrates so difficult to pin down is nowhere more evident than in a strange chapter in the middle of the *Memorabilia*, where Socrates is asked to name something good or beautiful (3.8). Examination of this passage will also show the sorts of subtleties some find in Xenophon – though others argue that they have been imported into the text by overly imaginative readers.[28]

Socrates is asked to name something good by Aristippus, the hedonist, whom he had earlier refuted by demonstrating that self-control was necessary to any worthwhile life (2.1).[29] Aristippus thinks he can trap Socrates by showing that whatever good Socrates suggests, it will always be bad in some circumstances: "Socrates, wishing to profit those with him, did not answer like those who are guarding against their argument being overthrown, but like those who are convinced that they must do what is right." Socrates therefore refuses to say that anything is good *tout court*, and instead asks if Aristippus wants to know what is good for a fever, or ophthalmia, or hunger. He answers Aristippus' question about the good and his parallel question about the beautiful precisely as Protagoras does in Plato, by saying that a thing advantageous for one end may be disadvantageous for another (*Protagoras* 334a–c). Perhaps this just shows Xenophon failing to understand Plato – and Socrates. But there may be something more interesting going on. As a hedonist, Aristippus would presumably have to be content with the answer that the pleasant was good, but he also apparently knew that Socrates would not provide this answer, so believed he had Socrates cornered. Socrates presumably thought that saying that pleasure was good would not profit his companions. This may be because such an answer would be false. But elsewhere Xenophon's Socrates is quite willing to argue that a course of action is good because it is pleasant. He argues, including in an argument directed to Aristippus (2.1.30), that the self-controlled life is ultimately the most pleasant life, and he has with some good reason been called a "moderate hedonist."[30] Given this, Socrates may have refused to

[27] For an attempt to defend the standard view, with references to doubters, see Bobonich 2011.
[28] A more elaborate version of this argument can be found in Johnson 2009: 213–19. For Xenophontic subtlety, contrast Higgins 1977 (pro) and Gray 2011 (con).
[29] For more on Xenophon's attitude towards Aristippus, see Dorion in this volume.
[30] Gosling and Taylor 1982: 38–40. Cf. *Mem.* 1.3.5–6, 3.11.13–14, 3.13.2, 4.5.9.

name pleasure as the good not because this is false but because it is in some important sense true.

This is a rather speculative reading, but consider the following. Leo Strauss, the controversial conservative thinker whose admiration for Xenophon has perhaps done Xenophon as much harm as good, pointed out that we had some reason to expect that 3.8 would be a conversation between Socrates and Plato rather than one between Socrates and Aristippus.[31] For at the beginning of 3.6, Xenophon shows us how Socrates tried to prevent Glaucon from making a fool of himself with a premature entry into politics, due to his friendship with Glaucon's relatives Charmides and Plato. In 3.7 Socrates talks with Charmides, so in 3.8 it would be Plato's turn. But perhaps we do get a conversation with Plato, if at a certain remove. In 3.8 Xenophon has Socrates play the role of a relativist in order to avoid appearing to be a hedonist. This neatly reverses the strategy of the *Protagoras*, where Plato has Socrates develop a theory in which the good is defined as the pleasant. The hedonism of the *Protagoras* has scandalized Socratics to this day, driving scholars to various efforts to disassociate Socrates from the argument. Xenophon here would appear to be the first such critic. But his criticism is not based on a fault in doctrine (he too makes Socrates out to be something of a hedonist), but a disagreement about how best to approach one's students: an open avowal of hedonism would not serve Socrates' students well, Xenophon seems to believe, as they need to learn self-control first. He corrects Plato not on doctrine but on pedagogy.

Consider, finally, the last section of 3.8, a very strange appendage in which Xenophon has Socrates describe the best design for houses and the best placement for altars. Though he had been unable or at least unwilling to suggest anything else good in all respects, Socrates can easily describe a house plan that is best in both summer and winter. That house plan is best because its southern exposure catches the low winter sunlight, providing pleasing warmth, while in summer the porch provides ample pleasant shade. Here the primary criterion for determining a good house plan, or the best place to locate an altar, is pleasure.

This reading of 3.8 will not convince all, but it does at least have the virtue of suggesting the wide range of interpretive approaches we can bring to bear in reading Xenophon's Socratica. As we have seen, Xenophon is certainly engaged in dialogue with Plato; his Socrates can address standard philosophical topics but also dish out eminently practical advice; Xenophon's Socrates modulates his arguments to fit the characters and circumstances in which he finds himself;

---

[31] Strauss 1972: 74. On Strauss and Xenophon contrast Johnson 2012a (mixed verdict) with Dorion 2013a: 51–92 (negative verdict).

Xenophon's text may be more subtle than it seems; and Xenophon shapes his arguments to suit his audience, while shaping his audience – at least his implied audience – by his arguments. To read the *Memorabilia* or *Apology* aright, we must approach them as texts of considerable philosophical and literary sophistication, texts engaged in deep dialogue with other texts, both the works of other Socratics and Xenophon's non-Socratic works. This essay, as is true of most scholarship on Xenophon's Socratica, has done more work comparing Xenophon to Plato than Xenophon to Xenophon. Readers of this companion, however, should be well positioned to reintegrate Xenophon's Socratic works with the rest of his writings, asking not only how much Socrates there is in Xenophon's Socratica but how much Xenophon there is in the Socratica, and how much Socrates there is in the rest of Xenophon.

Further Reading

The scholarship on Socrates is vast, but little of it directly addresses Xenophon, while scholarly work on Xenophon's Socrates tends to be scattered in obscure places. Readers of French will have access to the best edition of the *Memorabilia*, and the best overall introduction to Xenophon's Socrates, in Louis-André Dorion's edition of the *Memorabilia* (Dorion and Bandini 2000, 2011a, 2011b). Readers without French can sample Dorion's approach in his English-language essay in *The Blackwell Companion to Socrates* (Dorion 2006). Robin Waterfield (1990) provides fluent English translations of all of Xenophon's Socratic works, together with sympathetic introductions, in his Penguin version of Xenophon's Socratica. He also provides an historical account of the trial of Socrates from Xenophon's point of view (Waterfield 2009). Vander Waerdt 1993 provides a fine introduction to Xenophon's *Apology* and the question of the relationship between Xenophon and Plato; his edited volume *The Socratic Movement* (Vander Waerdt 1994a) is an excellent introduction to the Socratics beyond Plato, with several good essays on Xenophon. For the relation between Xenophon and Plato see also Danzig 2010, who emphasizes fourth-century debates about the Socratic legacy. Recent work done in Europe (in a rather different tradition from the more analytical Anglo-American approach to Socrates) can be sampled in the multilingual Socratica volumes: de Luise and Stavru 2013 is the most recent, with references to earlier work. On the *Memorabilia* in particular, see Gray 1998 for a literary reading; for soundings into its philosophy, consider Morrison 1994, Cooper 1999, Johnson 2003 and 2005a, and Powers 2009.

7

GABRIEL DANZIG

Xenophon's *Symposium*

Unlike Xenophon's other Socratic works, *Symposium* is not presented as a work about Socrates. The narrator explains the purpose of the work by saying that it is worthwhile to record not only the serious but also the light-hearted behavior of *kaloikagathoi*, a term that refers to men of good character and taste and is often translated "gentlemen."[1] Eleven adult men attend the dinner party hosted by Callias, a wealthy and good-looking man of about twenty-eight, in honor of Autolycus, a beautiful and accomplished younger man of about eighteen, victor in the *pancration* in 422 BC. In addition to enjoying the wit and wisdom of the participants, we are able to learn something from them about *kalokagathia*, a combination of personal quality and social grace. In this sense the work is a guide to good etiquette, offering both illustrations of good etiquette and numerous comments on it. It turns out that Socrates is the truest gentleman at the party (see 9.1) and a master of good etiquette, so the work does turn out to be about Socrates. His role begins small but gradually expands until he is by far the dominant figure, offering no less than four lengthy disquisitions in chapters 4, 5, 7,

---

[1] Scholars have noted that Xenophon's claim to autopsy (*Smp.* 1.1) cannot be authentic since he would have been too young in 422 to have attended the event himself. Strictly speaking, it is not Xenophon who claims to have been present, but the anonymous narrator. Again, strictly speaking this narrator cannot be identified with Xenophon, since no character named Xenophon is present. The identity of the narrator is never made clear; but he does appear to be an author of other works about the serious activities of *kaloikagathoi*, and this may be a reference to *Memorabilia*. Did readers know that Xenophon wrote *Memorabilia*? We don't know. It does appear that they knew who wrote *Apology*: the fact that Xenophon names Hermogenes as the source of his information about the trial suggests that he was known to be the author of that work and known to have been absent from Athens at the time of the trial. Bruns suggests that Xenophon should be understood to mean that he was present at similar events (1896: 386) but most scholars think the claim to autopsy is part of the fiction. One may contrast Plato's *Symposium*, where the author breaks with his usual pattern and offers an elaborate chain of transmission to explain how he knows what was said on the famous evening.

and 8 and dominating chapter 6 as well. He does not speak here as much as he does in the other Socratic works of Xenophon, but he does speak more than anyone else, and what he has to say is worth more than what the others have to say.

Callias does not make parties simply to pass the time; he has invited Autolycus because he has an erotic interest in him. But he pursues the young man in the right way, inviting him to an evening's entertainment together with his father and one Niceratus.[2] He has arranged some formal entertainment: a jester named Philippus will show up pretending that he has not been invited, and a Syracusan impresario will bring a handsome young boy and two beautiful young girls to entertain the party with music, dance, acrobatic performances, and a short erotic skit.[3] He has not, however, arranged for any other guests. As in Plato's *Republic*, a chance meeting with Socrates and his companions, Critobulus, Hermogenes, Antisthenes, and Charmides, provides an opportunity to remedy this failing.[4] As we will see, there is a striking difference between the two groups: not only has Callias hired professional entertainment, his chief guests are themselves trained in one or another performance art: Autolycus is a wrestler, Niceratus has learned Homer by heart, Callias himself has paid for a sophistic education. Socrates and his friends have no formal education, and little money either, but they are the ones to make the most impressive and memorable speeches.[5]

After sighting his potential guests, Callias approaches Socrates and his companions directly[6] and invites them in complimentary but mildly ironic terms: "I think the preparations would be far more brilliant if the room is decorated by men of purified spirits,[7] as yourselves, than by generals or

---

[2] Socrates himself never speaks to young men in the presence of their fathers, of course, but, despite accusations to the contrary, he presumably does not need any supervision to insure his honorable behavior.

[3] See Gilula 2002.

[4] As Huss 1999a has noted, the parallels to *Republic* are palpable. In both cases, a reluctant Socrates is pressured into attending an event in which he has no interest, but which he comes to dominate. In both cases the invitation is accepted only after pressure is applied, and not because of the offer of intelligent conversation. Both events take place in the house of a rich man in Piraeus, include Niceratus, and mention a horse race. As we will see below, the parallels between Callias and Cephalus are even more interesting.

[5] On the other hand, the Syracusan's performers are excellent, and in their final performance they show that art can fully imitate reality (9.5–7).

[6] Contrast Polemarchus in Plato's *Republic* who sends a slave boy to invite the philosopher (327b).

[7] Literally: souls (*psuchai*). There is no good English equivalent for this term, which in Greek can refer to the principle of life, the seat of consciousness, the character or personality, and the mind. The terms spirit, spiritual, and soul in this essay refer to the *psuche*.

cavalry commanders, or politicians." Socrates discerns a slight in this comparison with prominent figures who, Callias seems to imply, would normally be thought preferable. Just as they have no professional training or money, Socrates and his friends have no such public stature either. Or perhaps Socrates does not believe that Callias is the person to declare them pure of spirit, or doubts the sincerity of his compliment, true though it may be. He accuses Callias of thinking that Socrates and his friends are inferior not only to professional teachers, but even to the students of such teachers, such as Callias himself: they are home-made philosophers (1.5). Recognizing that Socrates thinks little of him, Callias offers to display the wisdom he has kept hidden from them if they will join his party. This does not prove an effective enticement, however, and they only accept the invitation when Callias makes a display of personal distress (1.7), something Socrates never did, not even when on trial for his life.

This introductory passage raises almost all of the important themes of the composition. The erotic theme was raised implicitly by the mention of Callias' motives for the event. A second theme is the contrast between the wealth and professional training of Callias and his people and the poverty and amateurism of Socrates and his friends. The joking, ironic, mildly insulting tone that is evident here will be present throughout the evening, except when it is not, providing a challenge to the reader and interpreter. Callias' show of distress foreshadows the theme of convivial unpleasantness that appears later in the evening (6; see also1.15). Another theme that is raised here and proves surprisingly important is the theme of decoration. We have learned that the best way to decorate a room is by inviting men of pure spirits. There will be many more tips on beautification, and they will all emphasize the prime role of spiritual qualities. Together with the larger theme of *kalokagathia* introduced by the narrator, and the controversy over the trial of Socrates, these will be the major themes of the composition as a whole.

Before exploring these themes, however, a few comments on form. Xenophon is, above all, an artist, and *Symposium* is one of his greatest artistic achievements. It is an amazingly rich work, built up of numerous short scenes and disquisitions on a variety of sympotic topics, discrete "pearls" that can easily be unstrung and rearranged in the manner of a Hellenistic compilation. There are disquisitions on the regal power of beauty, the proper use of perfume, the right way to drink wine, the benefits of dance, the use of onions, what makes for an enjoyable performance, and of course the right way to pursue a love affair. There are clever, memorable, paradoxical speeches by Socrates and his friends on beauty, wealth, poverty, the gods, and pimping, and slightly less clever short remarks by Callias and his associates on justice, the Homeric poems, laughter, and audiences. There is a beauty contest, a few quarrels, and an erotic performance. These scenes are combined into an artistic whole with a natural flow, wonderful characterization (see especially Bruns 1896), and a high degree of verisimilitude. There is also a complex net of interconnections between the different episodes in the composition, and I will make a special effort to point these out.

The work is also well organized. Most simply, it follows the chronological order of events; but these events are structured in an elaborate ring composition.

Introduction: 1.1
    A: Invitation and arrival (1.2–8)
    B: The effect of Autolycus' beauty (serious: 1.8–10)
    C: Philippus' insipid jokes (playful but neither serious nor funny: 1.11–16)
    D: Socrates criticizes the entertainment (playful and serious: 2–3.2)
    E: Contest of wisdom – or charm (playful and serious: 3.2–4.64)
    E: Contest of beauty – or wisdom (playful and serious: 5)
    D: Socrates criticizes Hermogenes (serious: 6.1–5), sings and proposes new entertainment (7)
    C: The Syracusan insults Socrates (serious: 6.6–8) humorous response (6.8–10)
    [Unparalleled element: Socrates' comments on Callias–Autolycus (serious: 8)]
    B: The effect of the erotic skit (serious: 9.1–7)
    A: Departure (9.7)

In addition to this overall structure, some of the individual themes are treated more than once, in a manner that recalls Vivienne Gray's observations (1998) about the amplification of themes in *Memorabilia*.

The composition is an early example of prose comedy, refuting the notion that the Greeks had no sense of humor aside from the rude burlesque humor of the comic stage (compare also Plato's *Euthydemos*). The balance between seriousness and playfulness is a central theme, and Xenophon exemplifies it in a variety of ways. Sometimes the humor and the seriousness alternate one after the other; but more often they appear simultaneously: a humorous statement turns out to have a serious point and a fit of despair may raise a laugh. The jokes are often subtle and some of their allusions continue to elude scholars and readers. All of these themes are expressed through the portrait of Socrates.

Socratic Etiquette

Socrates is the star of the evening, directing the evening's agenda as a kind of informal symposiarch, interacting with everyone in the room and winning the lion's share of attention. He not only provides explanations and directions on how a *kaloskagathos* must behave, he also serves as a personal model of *kalokagathia*. His first comment is made early in the evening after a musical performance by the young boy and girl: "By Zeus, Kallias, you have feasted us perfectly. Not only have you provided an unblemished meal, you have also provided the most pleasant sights and sounds" (2.2). That's a nice thing to say; and it also reminds us of the basic requirements for a good evening's entertainment. But the compliment implies that this part of the evening is over and now it is time for something else, something that does not involve sights and sounds or tastes. Coming as it does after the very first musical performance, this is an implicit criticism. Socrates seems to be hinting that these sensory pleasures are not really a satisfactory form of entertainment and perhaps also that it is time for Callias to redeem his promise to display his wisdom (1.6). Instead, Callias offers some perfume to regale the nose.

One sign of a *kaloskagathos* is that he knows how to block a misguided suggestion and move the conversation in a more promising direction. Socrates objects to the offer of perfume with humorous but serious comments, explaining that perfume is completely useless: men don't need it to attract other men, and women don't need it at all, especially if they are young brides, since they already smell so good. As for men attracting women, the best scent for this purpose is the smell of olive oil rubbed on a man who has worked out in the gym. Perfume obliterates natural distinctions, not only between men and women, but also between free and slave, by giving everyone the same scent. The smell of olive oil is attractive because it reflects admirable activities. Like a modern advertiser, Socrates knows that a good impression is made not merely by the product itself, but by its positive associations. It is not merely the raw scent of olive oil from the gym that attracts women, but its association with the admirable activities of a gentleman. In fact, it is possible to omit the scent altogether, replacing it with virtuous activity alone: for those who can no longer exercise in the gym the best perfume of all is simply good deeds themselves (2.4). Socrates has transformed a banal offer of perfume into a disquisition on virtue.

But there is a better way to look at it. Socrates is not just reminding us of the value of virtue, he is actually offering a beauty tip. His point is that impressive deeds and good character (*kalokagathia*) are more effective *at beautification* than artificial additives. His comments can be compared with those of Ischomachos concerning his wife's use of cosmetics (*Oec.* 10.2–13; see also Plato's *Gorgias* 464c–465d). Spiritual excellence provides more real charm and attraction than any material commodity can produce, a fact that Socrates demonstrates by his own charming behavior throughout the composition. This is an amplification of the principle that Callias acknowledged when he said that his room would be best decorated with men of spiritual purity (1.4). It also recalls the way that reverence and modesty enhance the beauty of Autolycus (1.8; see also 9.4). As Socrates explains in *Memorabilia*, the best art captures not just the physical qualities of the subject, but also its spiritual qualities (*Mem.* 3.10.3–8). The graceful motion of the dancing boy enhances his beauty, a tribute to the dance instructor (2.15), just as disgraceful motion disfigures Philippus. And in the final erotic performance we will see the power of training to create an imitation of lust that seems like the real thing (9.6). All these observations remind us that wisdom, skill, and virtue are valuable not just for their usefulness and their inherent value, but also for their beautification effect. Whatever the question is, for Socrates the answer is always wisdom and virtue. By offering this sublime beauty advice, Socrates is demonstrating his expertise in pimpery, as we will see below (3.10).

How much wine should one drink on this kind of occasion? Plato's super-human Socrates is famously immune to the effects of wine and hence indifferent to this question. The other participants in Plato's *Symposium* decide to limit the drinking in consideration of the doctor's advice (176a–d).[8] Xenophon's Socrates is a different creature. He enjoys wine and knows how to use it. As with plants, one should water people in small doses so that they can stand up straight and air themselves out in the breeze, and also so that they can be brought by its powers of persuasion to a friendly, playful mood (2.24–6). Overindulgence in wine would derail a very enjoyable evening. Philippus responds by insisting that the small doses be given frequently; but Charmides threatens to ruin the evening in another way. After a musical performance by the handsome young boy, he comments that just as wine awakens playfulness, the mixture of music and sexy young people awakens the desire for sexual relations (3.1), a comment which could lead to ruinous behavior. Socrates intervenes immediately, acknowledging that the young people can provide "pleasure," but challenging the guests to find other more useful amusements of their own making.

---

[8] The question of the relationship between the two *Symposia* is a subject of continued dispute. The possibility of Xenophontic priority has been discussed by Thesleff 1978 and Danzig 2005.

The Speeches

As in Plato's *Symposium* (176e), a round of speeches will replace the usual paid entertainment, but Xenophon's Socrates explains why some such program is called for: it would be shameful while we are together if we do not try to offer some benefit or cheer one to another (3.2). He suggests that Callias redeem his promise to display his wisdom, and Callias agrees on condition that the others also contribute to the feast. No single topic is proposed; rather, a broad mandate allows the speakers to offer the best thing they know, or the thing they are most proud of, to a kind of pot-luck feast of the intellect. They are asked to boast about their own best qualities or possessions.

Plato's speakers also boast about themselves while pretending to praise eros. But Xenophon's boasters use no subterfuge. Undisguised boasting means setting oneself up for a comedown, so it is not surprising that in explaining their boasts in a second round they have recourse to ironical, humorous, or even cynical explanations. This is part of the charm of Xenophon's speakers: they cheerfully set aside their bravado and openly confess to humble achievements, such as knowledge of the uses of onions (4.7) or their willingness to take the risks involved in possessing money (4.33). In this they are very different from their Platonic counterparts, all of whom, including Socrates, are involved in relentless and unironic self-promotion.

The speeches generally follow the seating order of the guests. Guests reclined on two-person couches at these parties, so where possible the speakers should be construed as couples. The two-seat arrangement explains why Niceratus was invited: Autolycus will be sitting upright beside his father (1.8), so someone else is needed to join Callias on his couch. While ten speakers offer boasts in chapter 3, only nine speak in chapter 4: Lycon and Autolycus are skipped in the second round, presumably because it would be offensive for them to explain why they are proud of each other. Given the nature of the other speeches, this would have resulted in mutual incriminations between father and son. As the young beauty, Autolycus' role is to be seen and not heard, and his father serves more as a chaperone than as a full-fledged participant. They are here to be entertained, not to entertain others. Perhaps we are meant to reflect also that neither of them has anything very clever to say.

In place of Lycon and Autolycus, the Syracusan impresario speaks in chapter 4 just after Philippus. Other changes occur as well: Charmides and Antisthenes exchange places, as do Socrates and Hermogenes. What are the reasons for these changes? Do the guests from the Socratic group feel less bound by the initial seating arrangements than the other guests?

Has Antisthenes moved closer to Socrates, forcing him to flee? Or are there purely literary reasons for these changes? Is there a hint of some equivalence between Charmides and Antisthenes, both of whom speak about wealth and poverty, and between Socrates and Hermogenes, who boasts of his Socratic-style *daimonion*? Obviously it is preferable to have Socrates speak last in the final round, because who can follow a speech by Socrates? But why then did he not speak last in the previous round? Does the change in order add to the anticipation, in the way that departure from expected word order adds emphasis? Xenophon does not highlight these changes as Plato does in the famous change of order between Eryximachus and Aristophanes,[9] but like Plato he offers few clues to explain them. In the following pages I will discuss some of the more interesting speeches.

Callias

Callias' presentation (it is not really a speech) sets a challenge for the other speeches this evening. Initially he boasts of his ability to make others better (3.4), a very ambitious boast to make in the presence of people who spend their time wondering whether virtue is teachable or not (2.6). Antisthenes suspects that he cannot uphold such a claim, and asks him to clarify whether he makes them better by teaching some base profession, or by actually teaching them virtue (*kalokagathia*). Callias insists that he teaches them *kalokagathia*, if justice is *kalokagathia*. In the second round he explains that while others debate the nature of justice, he goes ahead and makes other people just by giving them money (4.1). The claim that money instills justice is an extreme and absurd version of the sophistic claim that it is possible to acquire virtue by paying for lessons. It is also an insulting claim to all the non-wealthy members of the Socratic party, including Socrates, Antisthenes, and Hermogenes (see 4.49, *Mem.* 2.10). Xenophon even breaks with historical verisimilitude to describe Charmides as a poor man (he became poor only much later). Of the Socratic people, only Critobulus has any real means (*Oec.* 2.3), so Callias has injured quite a few.

Antisthenes returns fire, challenging Callias' claim that justice is to be found in the pocketbook (4.2). Callias admits that justice is found in the soul, but he claims that money can produce it because money enables people to purchase what they want instead of committing crimes (4.2). This argument closely resembles the claim made by Cephalus in the *Republic* that wealth is useful because it enables one to be just by paying one's debts and

---

[9] The reasons for the change in order of these speeches in Plato's *Symposium* have been discussed frequently. See recently O'Mahoney 2011.

not having to tell lies (331a–c). Cephalus' claim contains the nasty implication that Socrates, notable for his lack of wealth, cannot possibly be a just man. And it is this unfriendly implication that motivates the lengthy search for the nature of justice that occupies most of the *Republic*, where it turns out that justice is a spiritual quality that Cephalus cannot buy. Callias' words challenge his guests in two ways. Not only do they need to respond to the obvious fact that without money they cannot get the good things of life, they must also respond to a spiritual challenge that without Callias' wealth they can neither be just themselves nor make others just. The speeches of the Socratic members of the party are conceived in large part as responses to these challenges.

Absurd though the claim may seem, Callias wins his point. Antisthenes objects that recipients of Callias' generosity do not truly become just since while enabled to act justly towards others they do not act justly towards Callias, neither repaying him nor thanking him for his generosity (4.3). But Callias responds that it is often the case that a person is capable of doing things for others that he cannot do for himself. Surprisingly enough, Socrates chimes in on Callias' side, offering the example of seers who prophecy the fates of others but not of themselves (4.5). Charmides and Antisthenes will answer Callias later in their own speeches on poverty and wealth, but at this point the reader has to wonder what is the point of this little exchange? True, Socrates wins an ally, for Callias comes to Socrates' defense later in the evening (6.3). But is there nothing serious in his comment about seers? Does it refer, perhaps, to Socrates' inability to foresee the results of his own trial (see *Mem.* 4.8.1)? Does it refer, tragically, to his inability to make himself as beautiful as he makes others? We will return to this question when Socrates fails to win a beauty contest with Critobulus in chapter 5.

Critobulus

The two rounds of speeches offer a formal illustration of the method of amplification that Xenophon uses in this composition and elsewhere. But a speech is not always an amplification of the speaker's own boast. It may also be an amplification of another scene in the work or a reaction to the speech of someone else. Critobulus' great speech on beauty, for example, is both a response to Callias and an amplification of the narrator's exquisite description of the effects of Autolycus' beauty (2.8–10). The narrator claimed that beauty is something kingly by nature, but did not explain this claim in much detail. He said that Autolycus' beauty drew all eyes to him as a flame in the night, implying that no one could even see anyone else in the room. And he described the effects of this beauty on the love-possessed Callias: it gave him a friendly look in the eyes, a gentle voice, and a generous disposition.

These three elements of kingliness are the foundations of Critobulus' speech on beauty. Critobulus does not feel the effect of his own beauty of course, and cannot even know for sure that he is beautiful, since beauty is in the eye of the beholder. But relying on the oaths of the others and on his own experience of the beauty of his beloved Cleinias, he is able to draw conclusions about the effects he must have on them. Critobulus claims to be more than kingly when he says that he would not trade his beauty for the kingdom of Persia (compare Lycon, who would not sell his beautiful son for the Persian king's wealth: 3.13). Kings, of course, are unrivalled objects of attention to their courtiers and subjects; and just as Autolycus' beauty left the others in darkness, so too Cleinias' beauty makes him the unrivaled object of Critobulus' gaze. Critobulus would rather be blind to everything else than to Cleinias alone. He hates the night because it hides Cleinias from him (4.12). He can barely blink in Cleinias' presence (4.24). Secondly, a beautiful person enjoys a more-than-kingly repose: without lifting a finger (4.13) he gains all the benefits associated with kingship: wealth, slaves, and servants (4.14). Beauty makes one a fit commander of men in battle (4.16). It provides a status that one retains for all one's life (4.17). No less important, outdoing kings, the beautiful have their needs satisfied not by compulsion, but by the free will of their lovers (4.18; an obvious reference to sexual needs: see *Hiero* 1.32–8). Finally, again recalling Autolycus' beauty, Critobulus' beauty has positive effects on those around him, inspiring them to generosity, hard work, bravery in war, modesty, and self-restraint (4.14–15).

This description of the effects of beauty enables Critobulus to answer Callias' challenge: Callias with his wealth may make people just, but Critobulus with his beauty makes them virtuous in many ways (4.15).[10] This speech, too, is insulting in its implications. Just as Callias' speech insulted those without money, so too Critobulus' speech insults those lacking in good looks, especially Socrates. Together with his exaggerated intellect, these are the two traits that most distinguish Socrates. The implicit insult is compounded by Critobulus' claim that his beauty will be more effective than Socrates' wisdom in winning kisses from the attractive young performers. Socrates will have to respond to this stinging criticism of his ability to seduce beautiful young people. He does not deny that obtaining kisses is a worthy end, nor that he used his wisdom for this purpose. But he refuses to

---

[10] As Hobden 2013: 226 points out, Cleinias' beauty has not made Critobulus any better as regards erotic infatuation. In fact it is the cause of his infatuation, and Socrates is upbraided for failing to do anything about that (4.23).

admit that he is outdone by Critobulus in this vital area, and challenges him to a beauty contest (see below).

Antisthenes

Antisthenes attacked Callias both times he spoke (3.4, 4.2–3). By a fortuitous coincidence, he boasted about his "wealth" in the first round (3.8.8), even before he knew that Callias would refer to this subject in his later remarks, so he is able to use his own speech on wealth to provide a fuller response and counterattack on Callias.

Antisthenes' speech is an elaborate inversion of Callias' theory of education. Antisthenes accused Callias of believing that justice is found in the pocketbook (4.2) and now he argues in response that wealth is found in the soul. In a sense these two claims complement each other by neatly reversing the usual assumptions about where things are found. But they are not compatible. According to Antisthenes, even the largest sums of money will not guarantee wealth, and hence will not prevent injustice. Antisthenes knows brothers who inherited the same amounts of property but have completely different levels of wealth, and tyrants so poor that they must commit massive crimes for funding (4.35–6). Money does not create wealth; good character is the source of wealth.

Antisthenes also responds to the unspoken assumption that Callias' money makes his life more pleasurable. Antisthenes himself gets great pleasure from his meager possessions, even more than what Callias gets from his expensive possessions (4.37). He denigrates the expensive Thasian wine that Callias has provided for his guests (4.41). As for sexual enjoyment, Antisthenes visits women who are so unpopular that they are extremely grateful for his visits (4.38), thus equaling Critobulus as far as the willingness of his partners. He has so much pleasure in his life that he can only pray for less of it (4.39).

Antisthenes' speech has much in common with Socrates' own words (see *Mem.* 1.6.4–9, *Apol.* 16–18), and he closes by expressing his joy for the leisure he has to spend time with Socrates (as did Charmides: 4.32) and by thanking him for providing him with his wealth (4.43). In essence, by defending the life of the impoverished philosopher against the wealthy Callias, Antisthenes is performing the same task that Plato's Socrates performs in *Republic* where he defends the impoverished philosopher against the wealthy Cephalus. The difference, however, is striking. Unlike Plato, Xenophon does not advocate intellectual felicity as the alternative to material pleasure, so his Antisthenes responds to the rich man not by denigrating material pleasures but by arguing that greater material pleasure can be obtained without expense.[11] This enables him to respond to Callias much as Plato's Socrates responds to Cephalus by arguing that those who are satisfied with a little are more just and more generous than those (like Callias) who pursue riches (4.42–3).

Socrates the Pimp

The greatest performances are by Socrates himself. Continuing to demonstrate and lecture on *kalokagathia*, Socrates boasts that he is most proud of his expertise in pimpery, the only boast to raise a laugh (3.10). In the second round, he makes use of the dialectic method rather than a speech (compare Plato's *Symposium*) to explain why he is so proud of this expertise. Pimping means teaching people how to make an attractive impression on others. It involves arranging the hair and clothing, of course (4.57), but it also involves improving the qualities of the soul: making proper use of the eyes, the voice, and the power of speech (4.58). The narrator has told us that eros made Callias's eyes friendly and his voice gentle (1.10), so if Socrates accomplishes these improvements in others he plays the role of eros himself, just like Plato's Socrates.

Socrates has demonstrated his skill in pimping throughout the evening by teaching others how to employ the soul for the purpose of beautification (above). To this extent he has already lived up to his boast, and will continue to do so with the advice he offers in chapters 6–8. Socrates expresses his political orientation by arguing that a good pimp can make someone attractive not only to other individuals, but to entire cities as well (4.59–60). He will tell Callias that political accomplishments are an essential part of an honorable love affair (8.38–40). But how does this political dimension of pimping square with Socrates' own failure in his trial at Athens? If he was so good at self-presentation, why did Socrates lose his case at court? We will consider this below in discussing the beauty contest.

Since Antisthenes claimed to have gotten his spiritual wealth from Socrates (4.43), the latter returns the favor by foisting his disreputable skill as a pimp onto Antisthenes (4.61). His evidence: Antisthenes is skilled in the related area of procuring: a double insult. But both pimping and procuring, it turns out, are venerable professions. Pimping involves the transformation of the client into someone who is attractive to any number of other people, and even to the city as a whole. It is an educational activity, providing valuable

---

[11] Despite this Xenophon's Socrates does have a little of the Platonist in him, suggesting that intellectual contemplation on natural phenomena can provide an inexpensive form of entertainment (7.4).

economic and political skills (recall Theodote). Procuring on the other hand is what we would call matchmaking. It takes people as they are and finds them appropriate partners for mutual benefit. Socrates lists in ascending order friendships based on the exchange of wisdom for money, friendships based one-sided admiration, and friendships based on mutual erotic desire that Antisthenes arranged. Despite their occasional bickering, Socrates' thanks to Antisthenes for introducing him to some admirable friends seem completely sincere and are themselves an expression of a beautiful friendship. This scene reveals another side of Antisthenes, who is otherwise a very argumentative person, and foreshadows the description of erotic friendship in chapter 8.

The Beauty Contest

Socrates' position at the end of the list of speakers creates a natural glide into the beauty contest. Although the contest was inspired by Critobulus' claim to superiority in beauty, it also offers an illustration of Socrates' claim to expertise in pimpery. If he can teach others how to make themselves attractive, by making use of the soul to enhance the beauty of the body, surely he can do so for himself. Socrates' method of competing is familiar: he will rely on his spiritual qualities to enrich his personal charm, using rational arguments to demonstrate that he is more beautiful, in a sense, than the young Critobulus. Just as Antisthenes was making a semi-serious point about wealth, so too Socrates' argument that the useful is beautiful has a serious basis (see *Mem.* 3.10.9–15). The humor is found in his drawing attention to his bulging eyes and squashed nose to make the point (compare *Symp.* 2.17–19). However, when Critobulus attempts to join in the fun, suggesting that Socrates' thick lips are beautiful because of the soft kisses they can give, Socrates replies that if that were the case his lips would be uglier than those of a donkey (5.7), just as earlier his eyes were compared with those of a crab (5.5).

The beauty contest is a parody of a legal trial, complete with an *anakrisis* (5.2), an interrogation (5.3–7), and secret voting by the judges (5.8–10). Whose trial is this? In a composition laden with references to the trial of Socrates, this is the place where we see it re-enacted before our eyes. The scene makes fun of the Athenians: Was the trial of Socrates anything more than a beauty contest in which the prosecutors charmed the judges (see *Apol.* 4). It presents an image of a proud, boastful, intransigent Socrates who is not very serious about winning his case, and not the least bit disappointed with the result. Like Socrates in Xenophon's *Apology*, he blames everyone but himself for the results (*Smp.* 5.10; *Apol.* 24–5) and expresses no doubt about his personal superiority (*Apol.* 26–7).

What are we to think of Socrates' failure in the contest with Critobulus? Was he wrong in thinking that the soul provides more beauty than the body? Does he lack the ability of self-presentation or pimping that he boasted of earlier? Xenophon offers us two ways to answer this question. On the one hand, we may invoke Socrates' earlier claim that there are cases where a person is able to perform for others tasks he cannot perform for himself. This is a tragic reading of the beauty contest (see Higgins 1977): Socrates was able to make his companions, among them Plato and Xenophon, much more charming than he was able to make himself. But we may also interpret the beauty contest in terms of Socrates' first words about pimping: he could have made a lot of money if he had chosen to make use of this expertise, but he didn't (3.10). Socrates could have won his trial if he had wanted, he simply didn't want to. This is the central point of Xenophon's portrait of Socrates' defense speech (*Apol.* 1). And in any case what does it mean to lose? As Socrates said after the trial, "whichever of us has done deeds more useful and more beautiful for all time, he is the winner" (*Apol.* 29). While the judges (who, incidentally, are young and nameless slaves) may choose Critobulus, the reader is free to find Socrates more charming than Critobulus even when losing the contest, just as he proves more charming to readers than his prosecutors even when losing his trial.

Erotic Etiquette

Although eros is not the main topic of Xenophon's *Symposium* as it is of Plato's, it is certainly a very important topic, one of the crucial areas for lessons in *kalokagathia*. The theme has been raised several times, and the raw power of love was described in exaggerated terms by the narrator, by Critobulus, and even by Socrates (5.63). But Xenophon does not offer a tribute to erotic passion. Socrates intervenes when Charmides speaks of his rising erotic desires (3.1) and he criticizes Critobulus for kissing Cleinias (4.25–6; see also *Mem.* 1.3.8–15 and 2.6.30–3). His great speech in chapter 8 is the philosophic high point of the evening, and it is devoted to the theme of moderate eros.

The main point of Socrates' speech is to distinguish between honorable and dishonorable ways of pursuing a love affair with a young man.[12] Like Plato's Pausanias, whose speech he tacitly invokes at first with only minor

---

[12] The speech can be compared with Socrates' conversation with Aristippus in which he outlines two paths in life, the noble and the base (*Mem.* 2.1). There he uses the desire for happiness as an incentive to the cultivation of virtue, here and in *Mem.* 2.6 he uses the desire for love and friendship as an incentive.

reservations (8.9–10), Xenophon's Socrates advances a simple contrast between love of the soul and love of the body (compare *Cyr.* 6.1.41), arguing that sexual relations between men only spoil things. Unlike in relations between men and women, there is no mutual pleasure in a sexual relationship between an older lover and an attractive young man. There is nothing else in it for the young man either, since such a lover will not contribute to the boy's education, contrary to Pausanias' assertions. He will regard the young man the way a renter regards a field, seeking to "reap the maximum number of blossoms" and not to improve the land (8.25).

In contrast, the lover who admires the boy's character will invest in improving him (8.25). The moral benefits are mutual: the boy who knows he is admired for his virtue will exert himself to improve, and the lover who loves a virtuous boy will know that he must practice virtue if he wishes to retain the boy's affection (8.26–7). The relationship is based on mutual admiration (the word *agamai* occurs six times in chapter 8) and is "blessed by Aphrodite." In other words, it is an emotional, even erotic, relationship, despite the lack of sexual relations. Socrates thus rejects Pausanias' proposed exchange of sexual favors for educational guidance (P. *Symp.* 184d–185b), excluding sexual relations completely and insisting on the mutuality of moral improvement.[13]

The speech is of interest not only for its content but also for its dramatic role. Socrates praises Callias for being the better kind of lover, and brings as evidence the fact that he has chosen an admirable young man and invited his father along (8.10–11; see 8.37). But the praise has a motive: as Hermogenes says, Socrates educates Callias at the same time that he compliments him (8.12). If Callias still needs education, does that mean that the compliments are false? Socrates himself clearly thinks that Callias is in need of further lessons (8.37–41). He insists that Callias must show that he is genuinely cultivating virtue, reminding him that only the genuine cultivation of virtue will make his reputation more brilliant (*lamproteran*: 8.43. See Hobden 2013: 225). Callias has been criticized also for the superficial belief that his form of justice is equivalent to *kalokagathia* (Hobden 2013: 224). But all this does not show that Callias is portrayed as less than a *kaloskagathos*. He is already pursuing Autolycus in the right way: he invited Autolycus' father to the party, and the narrator himself has attested to the fact that he was possessed by moderate *eros* (1.10). While Socrates does offer him strict advice, he mainly

[13] This brief discussion offers an excellent illustration of Aristotle's mixed friendship (*EN* 8.4.1–2 1157a1–16), and of his friendship of the good (*EN* 8.3.6–8.4.1, 1156b7–35).

suggests advanced lessons in political wisdom (8.37–41). Socrates' advice does not disturb Callias, but leads to a mutual gaze between Autolycus and Callias as if to say that Socrates' program is to their liking (8.42). Since Socrates' speech makes it virtually impossible for him to convince Autolycus to sleep with him, Callias would not be happy if he were set on doing so.

As we noted, Socrates actually claims that sexual relations can and should be entirely excluded from a genuine love affair. This claim recalls the relationship between Socrates and Alcibiades reported in Plato's *Symposium* (217a–219e), and the description of the proper limits of male affection in *Republic* (403b–c). It even recalls Plato's harsh words about homosexuality in *Laws* (838e–839d). But while Plato's Socrates seems as indifferent to sexual relations as he is to the effects of wine, Xenophon's Socrates recognizes sexual desire as an essential part of human nature. While objecting to sexual relations between men, Socrates notes that sexual relations between men and women do involve mutual pleasure (8.21). His Antisthenes, whose speech is in many respects deeply Socratic, has claimed that he gains sexual satisfaction for his body, as well as very warm greetings, by visiting unwanted women (4.38). Socrates advises Aristippus that he can find outlets for his sexual needs in Athens for a reasonable fee (*Mem.* 2.1.5).[14] These suggestions should probably be taken quite seriously. Rather than recommending genuine love affairs with women of quality, Xenophon's Socrates is recommending women as sexual partners for men whose erotic interests lie elsewhere. This paradigm proposes a complete divorce between sexuality and erotic passion.[15] The composition demonstrates this divorce at the end of the evening. After a perfectly delightful and erotically charged get-together among *kaloikagathoi*, the guests, having been fired up sexually by the erotic skit, race home to enjoy their wives (9.7; Autolycus and his father have discretely made their exit beforehand: 9.1). Sexual relations are private matters between men and women. They have no place in the relations between *kaloikagathoi*.

---

[14] Socrates was familiar with *hetairai* (*Mem.* 2.11) and seems to be imitating one in his words to Antisthenes: "Just don't strike me! Your other offensive behavior I am willing to bear with a smile" (*Smp.* 8.5–6) – a scene which demonstrates his superiority in the art of imitation. For Socrates' leniency with regard to pressing needs see *Mem.* 1.3.14.

[15] There is another paradigm reflecting a closer relationship between men and women. Niceratos and his young wife love each other (8.3). Ischomachus both admires his wife and enjoys an erotic relationship with her (*Oec.* 10). And the relationship between Abradatas and Panthea is a model of erotic and high-minded inter-sexual love. But Socrates himself neither enjoys such a relationship nor recommends one to others.

Socrates and Xenophon

In Xenophon's view, the belief that Socrates had sexual relations with the young is part of what underlay the charge of corruption of the youth. The sexual nature of the charge is made clear in Socrates' conversation with the Syracusan (4.52–4), where the term *diaphtheirein* (to corrupt) describes the effects of sexual relations with the beautiful young performer.[16] Xenophon regularly defends Socrates as the most *enkrates* of men (e.g. *Mem.* 1.2.1) and his Socrates advocates complete abstention in regard to young men (see *Mem.* 1.3.8–13, 2.6.32). Did Socrates himself follow this strict advice, confining himself to necessary relations (*Mem.* 1.3.14) with his difficult wife (*Smp.* 2.10)? Or is this an extreme portrait motivated by apologetic and educational concerns? Where does Xenophon himself stand on this vital question?

In a rare personal appearance in *Memorabilia* (1.3) Socrates speaks to Xenophon in the presence of Critobulus, claiming that Critobulus has acted foolishly and dangerously. When Xenophon learns that he did this by kissing Alcibiades' son Cleinias he fails to condemn the young man, but rather says that he too would very much like to kiss a beautiful young man! This remark echoes the humorous but serious comments of Apollo and Hermes, who express a willingness to suffer humiliation for an opportunity to lie with Aphrodite (*Odyssey* 8.256–366). In response, Socrates blows his top, insulting Xenophon, warning him to stay away from young beauties, and telling Critobulus to spend a year abroad, away from Cleinias (1.3.11–13). This is not the only place where Socrates berates Xenophon. In their only other meeting, in *Anabasis* (3.1), Socrates criticizes Xenophon for misconstruing his advice and pursuing a military adventure in Persia. Both of these cases are often interpreted as tributes to Socrates' excellent advice and expressions of Xenophon's own contrition (see Gray 1998: 98–9; Flower 2012: 123–4). A recent study has argued that in *Memorabilia* Xenophon is expressing a serious disagreement with Socrates on erotic matters and that he takes a more lenient attitude than Socrates concerning erotic contact with young men.[17]

There is a third possibility: Xenophon and Socrates may not be as far apart as they seem. I will not argue that Xenophon was as strict as Socrates, but rather that Xenophon's Socrates is not as strict as he sometimes pretends. Critobulus has implied that Socrates used his wisdom as a means of getting kisses from beautiful young boys (4.18). Hermogenes has raised the

---

[16] See also Danzig 2010: 151–99.
[17] Hindley 1999. To justify his conclusion, one would need to treat Xenophon's words in *Mem.* 1.3 quite seriously, but to discount Socrates' words and behavior in *Symposium*.

charge of corrupting the youth in an even more explicit manner, blaming Socrates for Critobulus' wild infatuation with Cleinias (4.23). Socrates does not deny Critobulus' bad state or his own role as mentor, but offers excuses. Critobulus was already like this before he met Socrates; Critobulus' father deposited him with Socrates in hopes of seeing an improvement; some small, infinitesimal, improvement has occurred: while previously Critobulus stared at Cleinias without blinking, now he blinks (4.23–4). And then Socrates readily admits that things have gotten worse and that Critobulus may have actually kissed Cleinias, a very serious and dangerous transgression (4.25–6). This is the same kiss that was discussed in *Memorabilia* (1.3). Charmides takes the charge one step further, accusing Socrates of enjoying the kind of erotic contact he warns others to avoid:[18]

> Why in the world, Socrates, do you frighten us, your friends, away from the beautiful like this? I saw you yourself, by Apollo, at the schoolmaster's house, the two of you looking for something in the same book, with your head touching Critobulus' head and your bare shoulder touching his bare shoulder! (4.27)

Rubbing shoulders may be a euphemism for sexual relations.[19] It is certainly a violation of Socrates' strict principles. Socrates does not deny this charge: he exclaims that this must be why he suffers from a pain in his shoulder and a sting in his heart, and admonishes Critobulus to stay away from him until he has hair on his chin (4.28). Later, in another contradiction to his frequent warnings, Socrates insists that the reward for victory in the beauty contest be kisses from the beautiful young entertainers, and not mere ribbons (5.9).[20]

How are we to interpret Socrates' confession of personal guilt and educational disability? What kind of mentor cannot trust himself with his own charge? Most likely we do not need to take his words literally. As Huss has argued, Charmides played along with Socrates' gag earlier in the evening when Socrates claimed (falsely) that Charmides caught him dancing alone (2.17; Huss 1999b). Here Socrates returns the favor, playing along with Charmides' claim that he caught him rubbing shoulders with Critobulus. His reaction shows that this is another gag: did he really not notice the

---

[18] Charmides is an expert on hypocrisy, since he readily admits that his praise of poverty is false (4.33).

[19] See *Mem.* 1.2.30, where Socrates compares Critias to a pig rubbing himself on a stone. The image of the boy as a stone perfectly fits Socrates' description of the lack of mutual pleasure in sexual relations between an older lover and his boy. The shoulder-rubbing on the other hand appears to involve mutual pleasure.

[20] Possibly Socrates knows he will lose and wants to insure that Critobulus receives the kisses as a well-deserved punishment. But even if interpreted that way, the episode shows Socrates corrupting the youth.

supposed pain in his shoulder until now? But even if this never happened, it still contributes to the image of Socrates as indulgent of erotic misbehavior. Why, then, does Xenophon create such a portrait?

Part of the explanation is that Xenophon is engaged in a complex form of apologetics, responding not only to charges of misbehavior, but also to the charge that Socrates led a sad and joyless life (see *Mem.* 1.6.1–10). In the context of a drinking party, he prefers to highlight Socrates' pleasurable contact with beautiful young men, even if this contradicts his more prevalent apologetic tendency. Xenophon does not tell us whether Socrates really violates these principles – his superior moral character enabling him to do so with impunity (see *Mem.* 1.3.14–15) – or not. What we do see, however, is a resemblance between the portrait of Socrates and the portrait of Xenophon himself. Just like Xenophon, Socrates treats erotic temptations with humorous indulgence when the occasion warrants. The invocation of Apollo in the *Symposium* passage cited above is a sign that the same Homeric passage is on Xenophon's mind. However we understand Socrates' actual behavior, the resemblance to Xenophon is palpable: far from breaking with the master, on this point Xenophon seems to be his best student and ablest imitator.

Further Reading

German readers have access to the brilliant analysis of characterization by Bruns 1896 and to the excellent, full-length commentary by Huss 1999a. English readers will find useful material in Bowen's 1998 school text with commentary and translation. Higgins 1977 offers a brief but insightful treatment of *Symposium*, emphasizing Socrates' public-spiritedness in contrast to the private, selfish aims of others (15–20). Hobden discusses the dynamics of the social interaction in Xenophon's *Symposium* (2005) and in both Socratic *Symposia* (2013: 195–246) within the general context of sympotic literature. Gera 1993 compares this *symposion* with the *symposia* of *Cyropaedia* (132–91). Gray 1998 discusses the ironic mode of expression used by the participants. Huss 1999b offers an insightful discussion of Xenophon's sense of humor in connection with Socrates' claim to practice dance. (Although hardly emphasized by the text, Socrates not only claims to dance, he also sings, in the manner of a Hassidic Rebbe (7.1). The Hassidic *tisch*, with its alternation of singing, eating, and intellectual discourse, is probably the closest modern parallel to the Greek symposium, aside from the Passover Haggadah.) Thesleff's 1978 article is of special value, even for those who will not accept his chronological arguments, for its suggestions about the ways Plato transforms the themes of Xenophon's composition (or vice versa). Danzig adds to Thesleff's arguments for the priority of Xenophon's *Symposium* (2005) and discusses the apologetic tactics (2004). For efforts to relate the portraits found in *Symposium* to the historical individuals one may consult Ollier's introduction to his edition of the text (1961) and Huss's commentary, section five of the introduction.

8

FIONA HOBDEN

Xenophon's *Oeconomicus*

The opening sentence of Xenophon's *Oeconomicus* is concise and efficient: "I once heard him talking about household management (*oikonomia*) in this way" (1.1). As a statement of personal reflection and experience, it introduces the author and summarizes the character and content of his work: a conversation initiated by Socrates on the topic of household management, which the author allegedly heard in the past and recounts now. And yet, what follows is a series of remembered conversations set one within another; these do not all feature Socrates, nor does he always lead the debate. Furthermore, *oikonomia* may be the primary focus, but it is not the only subject addressed. While the organization, growth, and supervision of the *oikos* – in its broadest sense the physical property and human members of the household – is explored in theory and practice, insights are also developed into (for example) the nature of women, leadership skills, the gods, and the learning process itself. By listening to Socrates talking about *oikonomia*, reading across the conversations and tracing core ideas, this chapter proposes that the *Oeconomicus* offers much more than its brief opening sentence suggests. Through reported conversations, the *Oeconomicus* establishes a distinctive Xenophontic perspective on household management and how it might be learned.

Date, Setting, and Structure

In keeping with the majority of Xenophon's writings, it is impossible to establish precisely when the *Oeconomicus* was produced. As an imaginative reconstruction of the philosopher in action, the work belongs within a developing tradition that animates the person and ideas of Socrates, convicted and condemned by Athenian jurors in 399 BC for introducing new gods and corrupting the young. This development is best exemplified by Plato's massive corpus, but many others conjured up Socrates with a view to rehabilitation, explanation, and/or exploration in the years following his death.[1] With its Socratic content, the *Oeconomicus* belongs within this trend and therefore also sits together with Xenophon's *Symposium, Memorabilia,* and *Apology.* However, where it fits within this group is an open debate. Each text works with Socrates in a unique way: setting him at a symposion, sending him into conversation with young Athenians on ethical and political topics, and giving voice to his defense in court and amongst friends. Overlap and continuity in terms of outlook and theme between these works – and indeed with non-Socratic writings like *Anabasis* and *Cyropaedia* – highlight their interconnectivity, but do not necessarily shed light on the order of their composition.[2] Rather than pin down the *Oeconomicus* to a precise date, it is more useful to view it as part of Xenophon's expanding experimental oeuvre, which includes reminiscences of Socrates and develops within the intellectual environment of the first half of the fourth century.

A dramatic date is equally elusive. One reference by Socrates to the death of Cyrus the Younger (4.19) would put the conversation just before his own death. However, this is twenty years after the encounter in the *Symposium* between Socrates and Critobulus, his primary interlocutor in the *Oeconomicus.*[3] Moreover, it is well beyond the period of activity suggested by his interactions with young Athenians like Critias and Alcibiades (and again Critobulus) in the *Memorabilia.* It is in that generic moment that the conversation of the *Oeconomicus* takes place (Huss's "Golden Age of Socrates"), rather than any definable historical year.[4] Likewise, the Athens imagined is a familiar composite: of spaces (marketplace, countryside, houses, and fields) and political processes (liturgies and law courts); a city currently at peace but

[1] And possibly before: see Clay 1994, who makes Aristophanes' *Clouds* the earliest manifestation of what would become the "Socratic dialogue." Rosetti 2011: 28–31 calculates that approximately three hundred Socratic works were written by Socrates' immediate circle, concentrated in the years 394 to 370. Döring 2011 evaluates extant evidence for these early proponents; their fragments are collected by Giannantoni 1990. See also Humbert 1967.

[2] Diogenes Laertius' claim (2.48) that Xenophon was the first to give mankind Socrates' conversations through the *Memorabilia,* making it not only the first Socratic dialogue but the first Xenophontic version, need not be taken very seriously. The scheme proposed by Delebecque 1957 in which the *Oeconomicus* was first composed while Xenophon resided at Scillus ca. 381, in the same decade as the *Apology* and *Memorabilia* (plus *Constitution of the Spartans, Anabasis,* and *Art of Horsemanship*), and then worked up into its existing form after the *Symposium* (and before *Cyropaedia*) at Athens in 362/1 may be overly schematic in its combination of biography and text, and in its assumption that the *Oeconomicus* falls into two separately written parts. However, it points towards the general messiness of the problem and highlights the possibility that Xenophon's works co-existed and co-evolved during and beyond their initial conception.

[3] For the *Symposium*'s dramatic date of 422 BC see Bowen 1998: 9. Unlike present-day scholars, however, Xenophon may not have been overly concerned to locate his *Symposium,* and likewise *Oeconomicus,* in an exact year. Cf. Pomeroy 1994: 18–19.

[4] Huss 1999b: 398–401. His *Aurea Aetas Socratica* is an apologetic moment too.

potentially at war. This is Athens in overview, the city as Xenophon may have experienced it and (perhaps) in exile continues to understand it, distilled for and inhabited by participants in the *Oeconomicus*. The apparent anachronism of Socrates' awareness of Cyrus' death and other contemporary events is commensurate with this broad sweep, as Xenophon builds his knowledge and experience into a holistic world open now to analysis. The moment of recollection and retrospection initiated by the *Oeconomicus* is also one of recreation: specificity in action (Socrates talking) combines with imprecision in setting ("once upon a time": *pote*) to produce an environment conducive to an investigation into *oikonomia*.

This constructive interplay between recollection and investigation underpins the *Oeconomicus*, structuring the action and therefore also the experience of the reader who, alone or in company, may have read the work aloud and given voice to the arguments of the protagonists, or listened to others doing so.[5] After the brief authorial preface, the dialogue continues in expected fashion, with Socrates engaging Critobulus in an exploration of the chosen topic through questioning and response, starting with an attempt at definition (§§1–6).[6] However, soon Socrates introduces an earlier conversation with Ischomachus, whom he once encountered at leisure in the stoa at the temple of Zeus Eleutherius in the Athenian Agora (7.1). It is this reported conversation that comprises the bulk of the work (§§7–21). But here Ischomachus too dips out of the present, relating a previous discussion with his wife regarding her domestic duties (§§7–10), and in the process detailing an earlier encounter with the steersman of a Phoenician merchant ship, also at his leisure (8.15–16). Each "historical" conversation comprises questions and responses, as does a short discussion between the Spartan king Lysander and the younger Cyrus, which Socrates narrates (4.20–5). The *Oeconomicus* thus contains several reported conversations, each pursued in an inquisitive mode, set within each other and projected into other times and places. Hence, along with the author, the reader of the *Oeconomicus* overhears Socrates and Critobulus talking amongst friends (and through Socrates an exchange between Lysander and Cyrus in his garden at Sardis); they join Critobulus as he listens to Socrates' report of his discussion with Ischomachus; and with Critobulus and Socrates both, they hear Ischomachus speak to his wife and the steersman of the Phoenician ship. As we shall see, the result is a multi-vocal interrogation of *oikonomia* in which Socrates fluctuates between the roles of chief inquisitor and respondent, teacher and

---

[5] For reading strategies in antiquity, see Johnson 2000; Hobden 2005: 103–4, 110 n. 25 considers the implications for Xenophon's readers, regarding the *Symposium*.

[6] For the general method posited for Socrates by Xenophon and its application in *Oeconomicus*, see Natali 2001: 272–8.

pupil, expert and novice. Through the *Oeconomicus*' pocketed conversations a coherent analysis of "economic" theory and practice builds.

"Economics" in Theory and Practice

The investigation into household management begins with the following exchange: "Tell me, Critobulus, is *oikonomia* the name of some knowledge (*epistêmês*), like medicine and bronze-working and carpentry?" (1.1). Critobulus' assent to Socrates' proposition leads to the further question of whether a core activity can be identified for *oikonomia* as for these other crafts, to which he replies, "the good household manager manages his own household well" (1.2). The ability of one person to manage another's household and, understanding this craft, to make money and to grow the household is then established as Socrates questions Critobulus some more (1.3–4). The discussion continues in this back-and-forth fashion, building a definition of the *oikos* as property, and of property as whatever is useful and as wealth; hence, for something to be useful and become wealth, one must know (*epistamenôi*) how to use it (1.5–15). This conclusion is then qualified at greater length by Socrates: knowledge is of no use when a person is ruled by "deceitful mistresses pretending to be pleasures" like dicing and bad company, or he is enslaved by gluttony, lechery, wine drinking or a foolishly expensive love of honor (1.16–23). With Socrates' questions and Critobulus' answers driving the discussion forward, the conversation is productive. Together the speakers establish a way of thinking about *oikonomia* in the abstract that is grounded in practical application and outcome, within a moral frame.

The initial emphasis on knowledge becomes central to the conversation, and yet the building of knowledge is complicated by Socrates' self-styling as an economic innocent. In line with their opening discussion, Critobulus' ambition is to grow his *oikos*, and he seeks Socrates' advice on what to do (2.1). However, Socrates professes a complete lack of experience in the practicalities of household management. Economic competence is a prerequisite for political success, which Critobulus desires, but this is not a goal shared by Socrates, whose meager possessions meet his simple needs (2.1–10). Hence, the philosopher offers to show Critobulus "others far cleverer than me concerning these matters" who might make Critobulus "an extremely clever businessman" (2.16, 18). But although Socrates has no personal experience to draw upon, he has observed men who are most knowledgeable (*epistêmonestatoi*) about their particular affairs (2.17) and offers insight into their success: "For I saw those who undertook these pursuits without purpose suffered loss, and I observed those who behaved diligently (*epimeloumenous*) with earnest resolve undertook them more quickly and more easily and with greater profit" (2.18). The relevance of this hypothesis to the economic realm soon becomes apparent. Pushing Critobulus first to recognize the various activities that make up *oikonomia* – namely house-building, organizing belongings, managing slaves, farming land, keeping horses, and training a wife (§3), Socrates then conjures a Persian world in which the king adopts a hands-on approach to one aspect: farming. The king surveys his land, rewards governors who maximize its cultivation, punishes those who neglect it, and tends his gardens with his own hands, thereby providing evidence that he attends as carefully to matters of agriculture as war (§4). This diligence, which is remarked upon explicitly and represented by the younger Cyrus' award of the greatest gifts for cultivation to himself (4.4, 4.9, 4.12, 4.13, 4.14; 4.16), corresponds to Socrates' general prerequisite for success. Socrates will later introduce Critobulus to Ischomachus because he lacks direct experience of managing the *oikos*. However, at a more theoretical level he has knowledge to share. In conversation with Critobulus, Socrates demonstrates a general appreciation of necessary areas of endeavor and recommends a suitable economic style, one that Critobulus might put into practice. For his Persian digression is prefaced with a leading question: "Surely we should not be ashamed to imitate (*mimêsasthai*) the Persian king?" (4.4).

Having advanced this proposition, Socrates then drops into monologue to deliver an ethical defense of farming. Noting that even the most blessed individuals cannot avoid farming, he begins: "For diligence (*epimeleia*) in farming seems at once to be a pleasure and a means of growing the household and training the body to be capable of such as befits a free man" (5.1). By contrast to those pretended pleasures that hamper success (1.20, above), the pleasure of farming brings positive results: food to live on and luxuries to enjoy; physical adornments; sacrificial animals; endurance and strength of body through toil; horses for war and farming; an impetus to defend the land and the skills to do it; and a pleasant environment for all the family on the farm (5.1–11). Justice, survival skills for times of war, undertaking joint military action, encouraging men in battle, and steadfastness are lessons also derived from the land and its cultivation (5.12–17). The benefits are material and physical, and extend the personal to the military and beyond: "farming is the mother and nurturer of all other crafts" (5.17). The positive impact of activity in the fields is later affirmed when Socrates concludes his review of the discussion by asserting the superiority of farming, as the best activity for *kaloi kagathoi* (6.8). In addition to benefiting the individual, farming is valued by cities "because it seems to produce the best citizens, most loyal to the community" (6.10). Critobulus desires knowledge of *oikonomia* to help grow his estate and fund his political lifestyle. Here, Socrates confirms that *oikonomia* is desirable with regards to politics, but for different reasons. Because of the attributes fostered by agricultural activities (in modern terminology, "transferable skills"), knowledge of *oikonomia* is essential to anyone aspiring to be *kalos kagathos* – an accolade that combines beauty and goodness as the epitome of moral excellence – and the most valuable citizen.

By leading Critobulus through the pertinent issues, Socrates develops a theoretical perspective on the nature of *oikonomia* and the best way to approach it, whilst also outlining its general remit and extolling its benefits for the individual and community. However, for precise details of what he must undertake ("so that we might do what is good and not do what is harmful," 6.11), the philosopher presents his earlier conversation with Ischomachus, a man he sought out in order to learn the basis for his reputation as *kalos kagathos* (6.12–17). What is most striking about the following conversation is not that Socrates temporarily occupies the role of pupil to Ischomachus' teacher. It is that in content and character the vision of Ischomachus' *oikonomia* chimes with that already put forward by Socrates. Although developed through specific episodes – not just Ischomachus' exchanges with Socrates, but his reported conversations with his wife – there is a cumulative effect. Through the repetition of ideas, Socrates' earlier presentation (earlier in the format of the *Oeconomicus*, although of course later in the imagined timeframe of the reported conversations) is reinforced. Attention to their progression further highlights the central ideas underpinning Xenophon's recollection of what Socrates once said concerning *oikonomia*.

To begin, some of the core economic activities already identified by Socrates are mentioned during Ischomachus' reported instruction of his wife.[7] This section is best known for the proposal that the wife oversee her indoor realm like a "queen bee in her hive" (or more accurately, the leader, *hêgemôn*) (7.17, 32–4, 38). However, its scope extends from the supervision of household slaves and produce brought into it (7.35–43; cf. 3.4) to the storage of objects in appropriate places and good order (8.1–9.10; cf. 3.2–3), the appointment and training of subordinates in the domestic hierarchy (the housekeeper, 9.11–19; cf. the Persian king's commanders, 4.7–8, and below), and the development of a healthy body and appearance through exercise (10.1–13, esp. 11; cf. 5.4). In reporting this conversation to Socrates, Ischomachus demonstrates how to train a wife (7.4), so that she is encouraged to ask how she might contribute to growing the *oikos* (7.16).

---

[7] The identity of Ischomachus' wife and its impact on the *Oeconomicus* is addressed in the Appendix, below.

Ischomachus' description of economic industry not only corresponds with Socrates' broader vision, but his household is directed towards the same goal. Furthermore, Ischomachus possesses Socrates' awareness of the detrimental effect of pleasure on industry: the housekeeper is chosen first for her great self-control with regards to her stomach, wine, sleep, and male company (9.11; similar restraint is desirable in stewards, if they are to be taught diligence (*to epimeleisthai*), 12.9–14). Finally, the two men share a theoretical understanding of how labor within the *oikos* should be distributed. Ischomachus' advice is founded on the notion that husband and wife occupy complementary roles in the *oikos*, one inside and the other outside as determined by their divinely established natures. Thus they contribute equally to its success (7.18–28). This notion accords exactly with Socrates' comment to Critobulus on the very topic of teaching wives:

> I consider the wife who is a good partner in the *oikos* to be entirely equivalent to the husband in attaining the good, because for the most part property comes into the house through the actions of the husband, but it is mostly spent through the housekeeping of the wife. And when these things are done well households grow, and when they are managed badly households decrease. (3.15)

In retrospect, the philosopher appears to have absorbed Ischomachus' lesson. This is a lesson that Critobulus and the reader of the *Oeconomicus* receive twice, first through Socrates' brief statement (which concludes the proposal that economic success depends on how a man trains his wife, 3.10–16) and then through Ischomachus' extended reflection.

Parallels also emerge during Ischomachus' account of how he oversees and manages his fields and workers (§§11–15). Personal attendance at the estate offers an opportunity not just to observe agricultural labor in progress but for morning exercise, walking or running to and from the fields, and performing cavalry drills (11.14–18). This combination of activities delights Socrates for improving health, strength, military acumen, and wealth simultaneously, and its effectiveness is proven in the person of Ischomachus, whom he observes to be healthy and strong and whom he knows, by reputation, to be amongst the best horsemen and wealthiest men (11.19–20). Through these daily pursuits, Ischomachus embodies some of the cumulative benefits of *oikonomia* extolled by Socrates to Critobulus (5.4–8; his fondness for exercise before breakfast also matches the preference of Socrates' Cyrus, 4.24). Moreover, when training his steward, Ischomachus' primary task is to inculcate loyalty. This is achieved by rewarding the steward, so that he shares in the good things and wishes to secure them in future

(12.6–7), and by teaching him to work diligently (*epimeleisthai*) (12.9). As Ischomachus explains:

> Whenever I see men acting diligently (*epimeloumenous*), I praise and try to honor them, but whenever I see them acting without diligence (*ameloumtas*), I try to say and do the sort of thing that will sting them. (12.16)

This is exactly the method Socrates attributes to the Persian king, as he surveys his domain (4.5–16), and the underlying assumption matches Socrates' principle that diligence is key to success (2.18). And it is a point to which Ischomachus returns. If a man fails to grow corn, make wine, or get olives, in each case a single explanation suffices: "he is not diligent" (*ou gar epimeleitai*) (20.4). More generally, profit and loss are explained by a man's attitude to his laborers, whether he cares (*echêi tina epilmeleian*) that they fill their working hours, or has no care (*mê epimelêtai*) (20.16). This is a lesson learned from his father's instruction and daily practice: "To men capable of diligence (*epimeleisthai*), who farm energetically, the return from farming is rapid" (20.22). Sentiments expressed by Socrates, Socrates' Persian king, Ischomachus, and Ischomachus' father are similar in word and idea.[8]

Furthermore, the principle of reward and punishment that Ischomachus applies in the field not only mirrors the strategy of Socrates' Persian king, but also matches the strategy recommended to his wife for supervising the housekeeper (9.12–13). Its transferability across different areas of activity in the *oikos* is given wider scope by the specific recommendation that in her domestic sphere the wife – already described as the "leader" of her hive – should become like the guardians of the laws in well-ordered cities, chosen for the role because they praise whoever obey the laws and punish lawbreakers; or like a queen, who praises and honors the worthy, but rebukes and punishes those who merit it (9.14–15). A strategy applied in the economic realm is equally valid in the political, and vice versa. Indeed, for Ischomachus, it is a simple fact of existence: foals, puppies, men, and slaves can all be directed towards obedience through the promise of reward and threat of punishment (13.6–10). Hence, the steward can be taught to rule the laborers (13.3). Socrates takes this proposal seriously:

> Mark you, whoever is able to make them fit to rule men, clearly this person is also able to teach them to be masters of men, and whoever makes them masters is also able to make them fit to be kings. So the man able to do that seems to me worthy not of ridicule but of great praise. (13.5)

---

[8] A more generous interpretation than that of Chantraine 1949: 21, who identified the repetition of *epimeleisthai* and *epimeleia* as evidence of Xenophon's prosaic style.

Ischomachus thus propounds a management model that Socrates endorsed to Critobulus through his account of how the Persian king oversees his *oikos*. Indeed, he explicitly claims to implement laws of the Persian king, when using the system of reward and punishment to teach justice (14.6–7). When Socrates invites Critobulus to imitate the Persian king in his diligence to farming, he anticipates (or follows) Ischomachus' economic method. If Socrates' Persian digression is taken together with Ischomachus' advice, and viewed as a filtering and expansion of it, then the lesson strengthens. War and economics are not only mutually dependent, and so rely upon the same management techniques (4.5–12, esp. 4.10, plus 4.15), but the householder and his wife can apply the techniques of kingship to the *oikos*. A person who rules in their own domain learns how to rule beyond. According to his own evaluation, Socrates, by teaching this to Critobulus, deserves high praise. Might we then extend this praise to Xenophon?

Nestled within the conversation between Socrates and Critobulus, the discussion between Socrates and Ischomachus is thus not only rich with ideas about how to manage the *oikos*, but works in tandem with the "earlier" discussion to build a coherent set of principles upon which the would-be household manager might act to guarantee economic success and contribute to political life. A final topic that exemplifies this synergy is the role accorded to the divine. When Socrates proposes that Critobulus might become "an extremely clever businessman," he adds the qualification "if the god does not oppose you" (2.18; cf. 2.5–6). Later, he remarks:

> I thought you knew, Critobulus, that the gods are guardians of the works of farming no less than of war. And I suppose you notice that in war, before undertaking combat, men win over the gods and inquire by means of sacrifices and omens what they should or should not do. And concerning undertaking farming do you think it less necessary to supplicate the gods? Know well (he continued) that men of moderation, for prosperity of their fruits and crops and cattle and horses and sheep and for all their possessions, attend to the gods. (5.19–20)

This is a lesson Critobulus readily accepts, recognizing divine authority over peace and war and thus committing to begin every activity with the gods' help (*sun tois theois*) (6.1). Ischomachus too shares Socrates' understanding. Because the gods have the power to grant or deny happiness even to those who are knowledgeable and diligent (*epimelesi*), he always begins by attending to them (11.8; cf. 7.7, when Ischomachus postpones instructing his wife until after performing sacrifices and prayers). However, this does not mean human endeavor is entirely futile. Ischomachus explains that after caring for the gods, he tries to act in such a way as to achieve what he prays for: health, a strong body, honor in the city, loyalty from friends, safety in war, and increased wealth (11.8). Socrates accepts the efficacy of Ischomachus' measures, and at the same time ascribes their outcomes to the help of the gods (*sun tois theois*) (11.20). In their understanding of the roots of economic success, the farmer and philosopher both award priority to the gods whilst recognizing that the gods help those who help themselves.

In this paradigm, economic activity is once more intertwined with political life. Religious observance is a prerequisite for all future endeavors, and enables the type of prosperity that allows a man to be useful to his friends and the city. This is emphasized in the final chapter of the *Oeconomicus*. Having stated explicitly that the art of ruling is common to the fields of farming, politics, economics, and war (21.2), Ischomachus reiterates the notion that the style in which a man undertakes his duties determines the result. In all areas, rulers who are good and knowledgeable, who motivate their followers and achieve success, are those who are "divine" or perhaps also "under divine protection" (*theioi*) (21.5–8). The adjective *theios* holds both meanings in Homeric epic, and the duality seems to be carried forward into Ischomachus' vision of the leader who sustains his success by soliciting the favor of gods, and who attains success and favor through endeavors that elevate him above other men, which in Greek thinking means towards the divine.[9] This impression is reinforced in the closing lines:

> But I say education is necessary for whoever intends to be capable of these things and to be of a good natural disposition and above all be divine (*theion*). For this here good does not seem to me to be wholly human, but divine: the rule of the willing. Clearly it is given to those truly initiated in moderation. But they give tyranny over the unwilling, so it seems to me, to those they believe worthy of living like Tantalus in Hades, who it is said spends all eternity fearing lest he die a second time. (21.11–12)

Shortly before, Ischomachus asserted that it was not ultimately by promising reward or threatening punishment that a master enthused his subordinates, but his possession of a share in the disposition of a king (*êthous basilikou*) (21.9–11). Now, the successful ruler relies upon a triumvirate of education, innate goodness, and divinity, and rewards are granted above all to the man who practices moderation. Ultimately it is the gods who apportion leadership, deciding who deserves the more hazardous life of a tyrant, whose authority extends over unwilling subjects.[10] It is by recognizing the

---

[9] *theios*: Liddell and Scott 1996: 288. For the evaluation of leaders in Archaic and Classical Greece through the prism of the divine, see Mitchell 2013: 58–65.

[10] Cf. Arist. *Pol.* 1313a, who draws a similar distinction between monarchy and tyranny, based upon the willingness or otherwise of subjects. The idea that tyrants live in fear for their lives from rebellious subjects underpins Xenophon's *Hiero* (see 1.38, 2.7–18,

centrality of the gods to successful leadership that Ischomachus (speaking to Socrates), Socrates (conversing with Critobulus), and Xenophon (addressing the reader) end their lesson on *oikonomia*.

Look, Listen, and Learn

To summarize so far: the distinctive structure of the *Oeconomicus* is crucial to the development of a rounded discussion on *oikonomia*, placed in the mouth of Socrates. The resonances between conversations establish economic growth as a core ambition of the would-be *kalos kagathos*, as a means of helping friends and serving the polis. Approaching all aspects of household management with due diligence is essential to success, and inculcating this in subordinates is as important as displaying it oneself. To this end, a scheme of reward and punishment is most effective. Indeed, the skills developed for managing the household are eminently transferable to the political realm (and vice versa), making *oikonomia* perfect training for leadership. But those who cannot control their desires will not succeed, and diligence must be matched by care for the gods. However great an individual's knowledge, the gods ultimately determine their success. This positive conclusion stands at odds with interpretations that consider the *Oeconomicus* deeply ironic. For ironists, Socrates and Ischomachus stand in opposition; flaws in Ischomachus' reasoning are revealed through disagreement and dissonance.[11] This is not the occasion to refute any individual interpretation.[12] However, consistency in the broad pattern of thinking between Socrates and Ischomachus makes this a difficult position to maintain. Certainly, there are moments of Socratic critique, but these are productive rather than disruptive. To give one example, late in the conversation Socrates jokes that the "love of farming" Ischomachus attributes to his father is like a merchant's love of corn, because he increases his land's worth then sells it on (20.27–8). But what might be interpreted as the scorn of a man whose own needs are limited is ameliorated when Socrates concurs that men love whatever they believe to be useful (20.29).[13] And utilizing resources, the reader of the *Oeconomicus* already

---

3.7–9, 4.2–5, 4.11, 5.1–2, 6.3–7, 6.14–15, 7.8–10, 10.4). There, however, Simonides proposes that a tyrant like Hieron of Syracuse might well inculcate willing obedience through benevolent government (11.12).

[11] An approach exemplified by Strauss 1970, Pangle 1994, Stevens 1994, Ambler 1996, and Kronenberg 2009.

[12] Instead, see Gray 2011: 56–69, who addresses ironic readings of the *Oeconomicus* within a wider critique of the approach.

[13] Figueira 2012: 677–8 similarly offers a constructive reading of this exchange, describing Socrates' initial response as a "jocular analogy."

knows, is essential for economic success. Indeed, this short exchange picks up an earlier discussion on whether men who love profit can be taught diligence. After Ischomachus defends this proposal, Socrates moves the discussion forward by modifying it to cover those who are self-controlled and love profit in reasonable measure (12.15–16). In both instances, Socrates' questions and qualifications invite consideration of where the boundaries between utility, profitability, and extreme acquisitiveness lie. They do not negate Ischomachus' proposals. Socrates remains Xenophon's Socrates: a man who has mastered his desires and has no need to participate in political life, but who is nonetheless willing and able to train young men in the endeavors necessary for their own successful contribution to the polis.[14] An ironic reading is not needed to make sense of the twists and turns in the conversation.

One might take the point further by considering the continuity in thinking between the *Oeconomicus* and other works by Xenophon. For example, the transferability of techniques like "reward and punishment" between the economic, military, and political spheres and the aptitude of the "economic man" (*oikonomikos*) for managing public affairs are lessons received by Nicomachides from Socrates in the *Memorabilia* (3.4.1–12). More than most, this conversation crystallizes that work's general proposition that young men sought out Socrates "so they might become *kaloi kagathoi* and be able to serve their house and household and friends and city and citizens well" (1.2.48) – exactly the lesson Critobulus receives in the *Oeconomicus*. More broadly, "reward and punishment" features as a core leadership technique: Cyrus the Elder and Cyrus the Younger each deploy it to inculcate loyalty and high performance amongst their subordinates (e.g. *Cyr.* 4.2.47; *Anab.* 1.9.16–17), while for Simonides the system might be applied to the military, agricultural, and commercial spheres (*Hier.* 9.2–11). Amongst the benefits promised to the Sicilian tyrant Hieron are growth in revenues and the cultivation of moderation through industry (9.8).[15] Then again, the wisdom of beginning every task by seeking sacrifices and omens governs Xenophon's activities in the *Anabasis*, for example when he contemplates

---

[14] For this Socrates, distinct from the Platonic incarnation, see Waterfield 2004, Dorion 2006, and O'Connor 2011. Danzig 2003 and Dorion 2008 identify differences in the way Socrates and Ischomachus think about *oikonomia*, but likewise see this as part of a productive rather than ironic process that emphasizes Socrates' attainment of a lifestyle and morality beyond that expected for the ordinary man. Nee 2009 views perceived discrepancies more negatively, although as a condemnation of the city rather than Ischomachus *per se*.

[15] Examples from *Anabasis* and *Hiero* are given by Gray 2011: 13, who notes some other shared functions between Ischomachus' successful household manager and Cyrus in the *Cyropaedia*, at 20–5.

putting himself forward as general (6.1.21–4).[16] This is a step Cyrus the Elder also takes throughout his military campaigns, stimulated perhaps by the lesson he received from his father, Cambyses:

> Well, my son, (he said) do you remember what we once resolved, that men who learn what the gods have granted fare better than those without knowledge, and men who work accomplish more than those who are idle, and men who are diligent (*epimeloumenos*) live more securely than those who are careless about them, and so it seemed to us to be fitting for those who had prepared themselves as necessary also to ask for good things from the gods? (1.6.5)

Cambyses espouses the advantages of diligence, making it a prerequisite for soliciting divine favor. Like Socrates and Ischomachus, he proposes that the favor of the gods is essential but attendant upon the individual first maximizing their own capabilities. Cyrus agrees (1.6.6), and later, when his careful plotting with Gadatas to take over an Assyrian border fort yields success, he will credit the joy that news of success brings to the help of the gods (*sun tois theois*, 5.3.19).[17] Human endeavor and divine favor contribute to the attainment of the desired outcome. In sum, ideas proposed during the conversations of the *Oeconomicus* ripple through Xenophon's works, where they are expounded by Socrates, Persian kings and princes, the wise Simonides, and the avatar of the author himself. The *Oeconomicus* therefore contributes to Xenophon's ongoing investigations into the contemporary sociopolitical environment, revisiting and reworking issues in ways that are consonant with its author's wider patterns of thinking.

Insights in the *Oeconomicus*, furthermore, engage with longer-standing ideas about household management. The famous metaphor of wife-as-bee exemplifies this. In making Ischomachus describe his wife as queen bee, Xenophon plugs into Semonides' (fr. 7.83–93 W) praise of the woman born of the bee tribe, under whom a man's living thrives and grows.[18] The basis upon which Ischomachus' wife will merit this praise by helping the household grow is then defined according to Xenophon's model for household management and leadership more generally.[19] Extant wisdom is adapted to the immediate argument. The notion that economic success fosters political

---

[16] See Bowden 2004: 235–6 for this episode and Xenophon's approach to religion more generally; Parker 2004 offers a wider perspective on religious activity in the *Anabasis*. I am grateful to Jan Haywood for sharing his then unpublished article "Divine Narratives in Xenophon's *Anabasis*": Haywood 2016..

[17] See Tuplin 2013: 83, with n. 72, for the general sentiment and other relevant passages in the *Cyropaedia*.

[18] See for example, Pomeroy 1994: 277, citing also Phocylides 6 W (F2 Diehl).

[19] For a distinctive Xenophontic perspective, see also Glazebrook 2009, who situates Xenophon's wife-bee within broader patterns of Greek thinking about women.

competence is similarly transformed. Already in the late sixth century the Parians reportedly selected men who worked their fields well to govern strife-torn Miletus, because "these men seemed likely to attend with diligence (*epimelêsesthai*) to public affairs as if to their own" (Hdt. 5.29).[20] However, in the *Oeconomicus* the transferability of knowledge and skills is explicitly explained in terms of personal development and morality. Then again, the application of reward and punishment extends a tenet of slave-owning ideology articulated in the *Odyssey* across a spectrum of human power relationships, domestic and political.[21] And finally, the closing identification of a leader as "divine" or "under divine protection" represents a fundamental strand in thinking about kings from the *Iliad* onwards.[22] However, that state is now merited by and attendant upon (impossible without) individual endeavor. Xenophon's economic thought is at once traditional and innovative, a result of the author's profound engagement with contemporary wisdom, no doubt through the prism of his own experience and understanding: as a one-time pupil of Socrates, an estate manager at Scillus, and a leader of the Ten Thousand, which was both an army and a polity. Through the conversations of the *Oeconomicus*, Xenophon presents his expertise in *oikonomia*, an industry grounded in personal morality that blends the individual with the common good.

Furthermore, the lessons offered by the *Oeconomicus* extend beyond the economic, to include the very processes of learning. As noted already, this Socratic dialogue is distinctive for presenting a series of reported conversations, mini dramas with settings and protagonists, pocketed one inside the other. As attention shifts between the conjured worlds, the reader not only listens in on the conversations, but watches them unfold in the mind's eye.[23] They thus embark upon the learning process recommended to Critobulus by Socrates, and already practiced by the philosopher. For on promising first to show his companion people who are cleverer in the sorts of matters he wishes to learn, Socrates recommends his own method for investigation. This is evident in the description of how, having first perceived and been amazed that some were rich and poor, he then drew up a hypothesis on the importance of diligence based on what he saw (2.16–18). In sum, Socrates looks and learns. Such encounters occur across the *Oeconomicus* in episodes marked by verbs of perception (e.g. *horaô/eidon, theaomai, akouô, katamanthanô, katanoeô*)

---

[20] See Brock 2004: 247–8.

[21] On this ideology, see Hunnings 2010: 57–66. Thanks to David Lewis for pointing me in this direction.

[22] Brock 2013: 1–24.

[23] The visual dimension of the cognitive process by which words are translated into meaning is emphasized by "Text World" theorists: for example, Gavins 2007.

and wonder or amazement (*thaumazô*).[24] As described by Socrates, in the royal gardens at Sardis, Cyrus showed Lysander his garden; Lysander was amazed at what he saw and smelled, and expressed his wonder to the king. In response, Cyrus revealed how he created the garden, describing his hands-on labor and preference for diligently undertaking activities related to war and farming before eating his dinner each day. Hearing this, Lysander drew his own conclusion, that Cyrus' happiness was consonant with his goodness (4.20–5). Lysander shares Socrates' method of observation, wonder, investigation, and conclusion. The same method is implemented by Ischomachus, during his reported encounter with a Phoenician merchant vessel. Looking over the ship, he observed its organization and noticed in particular its tight storage arrangements. Then, seeing the overseer specifically reviewing the ship, he was amazed but took the opportunity to pose questions to him. Developing understanding of how and why the ship was so tightly organized through this encounter, he then drew a general hypothesis and gave it practical application through his instruction to his wife. By his own account, Ischomachus applied what he has seen and heard to the management of his household (8.11–17). Critobulus is directed by Socrates to undertake exactly this sort of activity.

So far, the underlying relationship between perception and interpretation fits with a general tendency in Greek culture to equate seeing and knowing.[25] However, if Critobulus is to learn, he must not simply look, but look in the right kind of way. His current technique, Socrates argues, is inadequate. First, Critobulus' choice of subject matter is flawed. At present, he eagerly invites Socrates to join him in watching comedies, rather than everyday activities (3.7). And secondly, he watches in the wrong way:

> For you watch them [horse breeders] in the same way as performers of tragedy or comedy, not so you might become a poet, I suppose, but to enjoy watching and listening to something. And perhaps this is right, for you do not wish to become a poet, but since you are compelled to make use of horses, do you not think it would be foolish if you did not consider how you might avoid being unskilled in this business, especially when the same horses are both good to use and profitable to sell. (3.9)

The key to Socrates' recommended learning strategy is to observe how the playwright produces his play, or how the farmer trains his horse with success (or failure). This is watching in the right way. It is interesting, then, to observe how

---

[24] "Look and learn" is not restricted to *Oeconomicus*: Baragwanath 2012b, introducing Herodotean antecedents and paying particular attention to slavery, gives examples from *Symposium*, *Oeconomicus*, and *Cyropaedia*.

[25] This is evidenced most clearly in tragedy: see, for example, Thumiger 2013; but it was also fundamental to religious experience: see Kindt 2012: 36–54, who defines "religious gazing" as "cognitive visuality" (at 53).

this approach unfolds towards the end of the conversation between Socrates and Ischomachus. In a continuation of roles, Ischomachus is instructing Socrates on some of the more practical aspects of farming. However, throughout the conversation, the teacher leads his student to realize that he already knew what he was being taught (§§16–19). This process has been identified as *anamnesis*, or "recollection," a technique deployed occasionally by Plato's Socrates to encourage companions to remember things (Forms) they inherently know, on account of the immortality of the soul.[26] By contrast, in the *Oeconomicus* recalled knowledge has a more prosaic source: prior viewing. To take Ischomachus' very first example, one can recognize what the land is capable of sustaining by looking at the crops and trees on another man's property; the land shows whether it is cultivated or not (16.3–5). "So men entirely without experience in farming are nonetheless able to recognize the nature of the soil" (16.5). Socrates agrees: even fishermen can see a land's potential, developing as good an opinion as an experienced farmer, despite merely passing by in his boat (16.7). Over the remainder of their conversation, the legitimacy of this proposition is reinforced, with Ischomachus encouraging Socrates to draw conclusions about farming based on what he has seen/knows. Socrates confirms that he has absorbed lessons without even realizing it, and wonders whether the method might be more broadly applied:

> I had forgotten my understanding of these things (I said). And for some time now I have been wondering whether I have forgotten my understanding of gold working and flute playing and painting too. For no one taught me these skills, nor taught me farming, and I watch men working at these other crafts, just as I watch them farming. (18.9)

In accordance with his advice to Critobulus, Socrates learns how to farm through observation. The *anamnesis* identified, undertaken, and theorized by Xenophon's Socrates is more pragmatic than its Platonic counterpart in both its derivation and application. Furthermore, still in conversation with Ischomachus, Socrates develops another insight into the learning process. To activate the latent knowledge acquired by looking, Socrates is dependent upon his teacher's interrogation:

> Is questioning a method of instruction, Ischomachus? I have just realized (I said) to what end you asked each question; for leading me through those things I know, and showing me they are similar to things I thought I did not know, you persuade me, I believe, that I know these things as well. (19.15)

[26] See generally Wellman 1976, and Waterfield 2004: 103–4. More specifically Allen 1959: 165 addresses the immortality of the soul (*Meno* 81b–c), while Scott 1987 describes the assimilation of perception with categories of knowing, or "*a priori* truths" (p. 351, in his discussion of *Meno*) or "innate knowledge, knowledge of the forms" (p.353, found in *Phaedo*).

Socrates' revelation articulates a dynamic learning experience, dependent upon the observations of the learner and the skill of the instructor, whose questions generate knowledge in the student. There are resonances here with the Platonic theory of recollection, in which cross-examination (*elenchos*) is essential to the recovery process.[27] However, in the *Oeconomicus*, the discussion harnesses rather than refutes the student's existing understanding: Ischomachus invites Socrates to remember what he has observed in nature and draw knowledge about sowing and planting from that (19.1–14). Furthermore, the translation of visual experience into practical know-how through interrogation might be applied to other areas of knowledge, like flute playing and painting (19.16). By outlining this method and showing it in action, Xenophon's *Oeconomicus* offers a distinctive contribution to a live philosophical debate.

To conclude, the *Oeconomicus* presents a rich and detailed investigation into the topic of household management, constructed through a series of conversations initiated or recalled by Socrates. The combination of questioning and didactic exposition facilitates a lively and above all productive examination of economic theory and practice, in which growing the *oikos* is part of an ongoing journey towards moral improvement and political leadership. However, the discourse it creates on how to learn, and the priority afforded to looking in the right sort of way, has further implications. As noted already, the *Oeconomicus* sets up an encounter between Socrates and Critoboulus for its reader's observation in their mind's eye. Like Critoboulus at the theater, that reader might take pleasure in the drama as it unfolds. However, they might also look at how Socrates carries out his conversation about *oikonomia* and apply this new-found knowledge to their own future investigations, to their benefit and promised success. Xenophon's *Oeconomicus* encourages the very mode of learning it promotes.

Appendix: Ischomachus' Wife

The present chapter argues that Xenophon's *Oeconomicus* presents a coherent and consistent exploration of economics in theory and practice and at the same time offers a model of learning that is realized within and embodied by the text. For readers of an ironic persuasion, there is one character who might undermine this conclusion: Ischomachus' wife. In the *Oeconomicus*, Ischomachus – sought out by Socrates for his renown

[27] See Fine 1992: 214.

as a *kalos kagathos* – trains his wife in the duties she must undertake and the attitude she must adopt in order to support the growth of the *oikos*. History, however, presents us with Chrysilla, the widow of Ischomachus who allegedly took up with her daughter's husband, Callias, leading that daughter to attempt suicide from shame, and bearing a child whose legitimacy was questioned. While the identification of these two women with each other cannot be firmly established, the possibility has afforded an opportunity to reconsider the effects of setting Ischomachus and his wife center stage.[28] In light of Chrysilla's misdemeanors is Ischomachus' advice suspect and his reputation exposed as false? Or alternatively, is the disgraced wife rehabilitated through the presentation of her youthful willingness to obey, with Ischomachus exonerated from responsibility on account of his excellent tuition? Or is Xenophon making a more general comment on the (un)teachability of women: you can point a woman towards virtue but you cannot make her virtuous?[29] The implication in all cases is that the association matters. However, this assumption is highly contestable when one considers the source of evidence for Chrysilla's allegedly dubious reputation and the dynamics of its reception. Imagining Chrysilla and the wife of Ischomachus in Xenophon's *Oeconomicus* to be the same woman generates interesting problems to resolve, but to make them fundamental to any reading of the work goes beyond the limits of defensible interpretation.

This becomes clear by considering i) the public reputation of Chrysilla, and ii) its potential impact on the reader of the *Oeconomicus*. For both, it is important that the allegations concerning Chrysilla survive in a forensic speech: *On the Mysteries*, made by Andocides whilst defending himself in an Athenian law court against charges purportedly concocted by Callias, around 399 BC. They follow Andocides' explanation of why Callias contrived his indictment and are central to his character assassination of that man (1.117–23, 124–31). As a member of the Ceryces family, Callias was a hereditary officiate of the cult of Demeter and Persephone at Eleusis, and it was during their Mysteries that he reportedly framed the defendant for impiety (see 1.110–16). Andocides makes great play with this in the description of Callias' home life, which introduces Ischomachus' former

---

[28] The source of the identification is outlined by Macdowell 1962: 151–2, explored in detail by Davies 1971: 264–8, and revisited by Pomeroy 1994: 261–4.

[29] Arguments presented by Stevens 1994: 214–23, Harvey 1984, and Nails 1985; cf. Mackenzie 1985, and Goldhill 1995: 140–1. Pelling 2000: 244–5 imagines the various possibilities.

wife: "the most wicked of men lived with the mother and the daughter, being the priest of the Mother and the Daughter, and kept them both in his home" (1.124). The daughter was reportedly driven to attempt suicide and afterwards left the house, allowing Andocides to claim, "the mother drove out the daughter" (1.125). Callias' priestly responsibilities are juxtaposed to maximum effect with the shameful treatment of a real-life mother and daughter in his family. Indeed, before long he will proceed to expel the mother whilst pregnant and reject their child, only to bring home Chrysilla (as she is now identified) and declare their child legitimate at a later date (1.127). All of this is pertinent to the immediate legal case, as it relates to the proposed reason for Callias' false accusations, which are signaled when the defendant observes, "The mother has driven out the daughter; and he wishes to take and live with the daughter of Epilycus, so that the granddaughter will drive out the grandmother" (1.128). Callias wants to claim the daughter of Epilycus in marriage (a contradiction, in fact, to Andocides' earlier assertion that she was wanted for his son, at 1.124). Being cousin to the *epikleros* on her father's side, Andocides had disputed this claim (1.117–21). Now Callias attempts to remove Andocides permanently from the scene by orchestrating the immediate trial.[30] This is the context for the negative depiction of Chrysilla, whose metaphorical "driving out" of her daughter foregrounds the disruption to normal family relationships that results from Callias' ambitions. Her reputation is collateral damage in the dispute between Andocides and Callias. It is worth noting that while she is named and shamed, and at one point described insultingly as "an abandoned old woman" (1.127), there is little more to her characterization. She is simply the mother-in-law and wife of Callias, and the mother of his son. Furthermore, Chrysilla's misdemeanors are all effected by Callias, who brings her into and then ejects her from the family home. He is the focus of the verbal assault, and of the juror's attention. In Andocides' defense speech, the role of Ischomachus' wife (remembering that she is never directly identified in this way) is to give the home life of the priest of the Mother and Daughter a delicious irony and to blacken his reputation.

[30] Andocides' alleged offence was to have participated in the Mysteries without being entitled to do so, leading to his indictment for *endeixis*. The placing of a supplicatory branch on the altar of the Eleusinium at Athens was ancillary to this charge, but it brought a potential penalty of death (see Andoc. 1.110–16, although the defendant argues not only that Callias put it there, but that his interpretation of the penalty was publicly disputed). For the legal indictment, the background to the trial, and the scenario involving Epilycus' daughter see MacDowell 1962: 12–14, 145–6, and Gagarin and MacDowell 1998: 99–101.

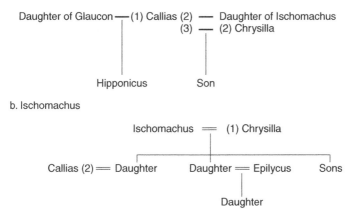

Figure 8.1. Marriages and children in the families of Callias and Ischomachus.

Furthermore, the family situation as Andocides presents it merits some review – and here the family trees in Figure 8.1 may be of some help.[31] The speaker is initially euphemistic or perhaps deliberately opaque regarding the relationship between Callias and his mother-in-law – he "takes" her, and "lives with" her (1.124) – but it becomes evident that the pair were wed ("a man married to a wife, marries besides (*epegême*) the mother of the daughter," 1.128).[32] The legitimacy of their union is emphasized by the eventual acceptance of their son by the Ceryces *genos*, confirmed by a witness. Andocides paints this scenario as stranger than myth (1.129), but it is in keeping with the sorts of strategies employed by elite families at Athens, where marriage primarily facilitated the movement of resources between

---

[31] Family trees following MacDowell 1962: 207 (Appendix L) and Davies 1971: 263–5. Note that Davies favors the possibility that the two daughters of Ischomachus may be the same person, i.e. Callias' second wife was the widow of Epilycus. This hypothesis only makes sense if that daughter had divorced Epilycus well before his death and then married Callias, to allow for the family scenario sketched by Andocides to play out. To help make it work Davies (p. 298) pushes the date of Epilycus' death back to ca. 405, but it would be odd for an *epikleros* – or more precisely her property (clearly desirable to Callias, despite Andocides' claims of her impoverishment, 1.119) – to be left unassigned for so long. Thus the "more economical" option seems unnecessary, and so the daughters are presented separately here. The family tree provided by Maidment 1941: 334 makes the widow of Epilycus a daughter of Chrysilla and Callias, so that the *epikleros* Callias seeks to claim in marriage for himself or his son is his own granddaughter. This seems most unlikely, and the timeframe implausible.

[32] Although *lambanô*, "to take" and *sunoikeô*, "to live together with" routinely connote marriage too: see Liddell and Scott 1996: 1027, 1721.

and within families.[33] Davies (1971: 264–8) convincingly argues that Callias' marriage to Ischomachus' widow was motivated by a desire to better control the patrimony inherited by her sons.[34] Having gained control of some of Ischomachus' wealth through the dowry that would have accompanied his marriage to the daughter, Callias then took Ischomachus' entire property in hand. Callias' attempt to marry himself or his son to the daughter of Epilycus and granddaughter of Ischomachus shows him consolidating the family holdings. Uncontroversial scenarios for other aspects of the family's story can similarly be imagined. Pomeroy (1994: 262) proposes that the physical consolidation of households into one place – the mother-in-law moving in with her daughter and son-in-law – could have had a very practical purpose during the Peloponnesian War.[35] And Callias might have refused to acknowledge his son by Chrysilla for financial reasons relating again to the movement of property, through inheritance. The question therefore arises of whether Callias' marriage to his wife's mother – assuming Andocides is exploiting actual circumstances and not just inventing wildly – would be a source of scandal by and of itself, that is to say before Andocides created his elaborate narrative. A suicide would certainly help make it so, but it is impossible to know where Andocides' embellishments begin and end. Andocides' focused and forceful presentation may build on existing scandal, but it is equally possible that it creates it.

These observations regarding Andocides' rhetorical manipulations have ramifications for considering the extent to which the appearance of Ischomachus' wife in Xenophon's *Oeconomicus* would have primed readers to interpret the work in a particular way. Chrysilla has certainly been exposed to the public glare, falling foul of Pericles' maxim that a woman's virtue lies in being least talked about by men (Thuc. 2.45), and in a fashion that paints her family situation as perverse. However, the attack on Callias featuring Chrysilla represents a minor charge in a lengthy forensic oration covering all manner of alleged misconduct and topical discussion. In a courtroom setting it contributed to a barrage of arguments that cumulatively denied the charges laid against Andocides and denigrated the prosecution team. There is no way of measuring either the immediate efficacy or long-lasting effects of this one particular forensic barb. Precise details might have been lost in the barrage, or an astute juror may even have seen beyond Andocides' rhetoric. Certainly,

[33] See Brulé 2003: 111–26 for some case studies, and Mitchell 2013: 96–105, citing even closer intra-familial marriages amongst elite Greeks.

[34] As he is found doing in Lysias' fragmentary speech, *Against Diogenes*, P.Oxy XXXI, 2537: see Davies 1971: 266.

[35] The discussion by Pomeroy 1994: 262 on the legitimacy of Callias' and Chrysilla's son seems to overlook Andocides' assertion that they were married; note that the Athenian law from the end of the Peloponnesian War cited as permitting men to make legitimate any sons born out of wedlock is shown by Haake 2013 to be a later fabrication.

gossip and rumor could have followed the lawcourt revelations, especially if Andocides' speech circulated soon after his acquittal, and Chrysilla's depravity might have grown in the retelling. On one level, following the trial the scandal was out there, ready to affect interpretation. However, it is quite possible that the story was partially or entirely forgotten or never heard by a good proportion of the Athenian population, or enjoyed but never taken seriously. And how far need the rumor have travelled? To Xenophon and his fellow Greek mercenaries off in Persia at the time, or later on his estate in Scillus? And even then how long might it last? Into the first, second, third, and fourth decade of the fourth century, when Xenophon composed the *Oecomonicus* and it subsequently circulated? The extent to which Callias and Chrysilla's relationship became "common knowledge" and the availability of that knowledge to readers of Xenophon's work is highly debatable. In short, a reader may or may not have been familiar with Andocides' speech or the general scenario he paints of Chrysilla's life with Callias; and Xenophon may or may not have been especially concerned with it, even if familiar with the details. Certainly, there are no pointers within the *Oeconomicus* to Chrysilla's future marital situation. The irresolvable uncertainty and lack of signaled authorial intention make problematic the assumption that Ischomachus' wife should by default be viewed through the prism of Andocides' Chrysilla. In the timeless moment in Athenian history when Xenophon's curious philosopher converses with a rich man to learn the secret of his economic success, a future in which that man is dead and his wife is remarried is of little consequence. Rather it is the future that Critoboulus and reader of the *Oeconomicus* can create by following the lessons set out in the conversations of Socrates remembered by Xenophon that matters now.

Further Reading

Pomeroy 1994 offers the best general introduction to the *Oeconomicus*, with its introduction, text, translation, and commentary. Other individual treatments might be grouped according to their primary interest in either Xenophon's depiction of Socrates (e.g. Natali 2001, Danzig 2003, and Dorion 2008), his moral and political thinking (e.g. Johnstone 1994, Stevens, 1994, Nee 2009), or his insights into aspects of economic practice and theory (e.g. Carlsen 2002 and Figueira 2012; Christophides 1992 and Alvey 2011 demonstrate the interest of *Oeconomicus* to economic historians). Ischomachus' instruction of his wife has drawn particular attention for its gender dynamics (e.g. Oost 1977/8, Murnaghan 1988, Gini 1993, Scaife 1995, Too 2001, and Glazebrook 2009). For ironic readings of the *Oeconomicus*, the logical starting point is Strauss 1970.

9

MELINA TAMIOLAKI

Xenophon's *Cyropaedia*: Tentative Answers to an Enigma

The *Cyropaedia* stands out among Xenophon's works: it is the lengthiest, the most difficult to classify in terms of genre, and the most enigmatic with regards to the author's intentions. Its designation as "the center of gravity to which everything is drawn"[1] is apposite, given the broad scope of themes it covers (leadership, military tactics, toil, happiness, Socratic ethics) and their recurrence in the whole Xenophontic corpus. Xenophon sets out to narrate certain noteworthy incidents and exceptional deeds (military and political) from the life of Cyrus the Great, the founder of the Persian Empire.[2] For the elaboration of this topic he could rely on previous authors who had also treated the life of Cyrus (Herodotus, Ctesias, and Antisthenes), as well as on Persian oral tradition, to which he was exposed during his participation in the expedition of Cyrus the Younger.[3] However, the lapse of time between his era and Cyrus' was too great to justify a proper historical account.[4] Indeed, Xenophon's aim was not to provide an up-to-date biography of Cyrus. What he found most admirable and underlines already in the prologue of this work is the fact that Cyrus managed to rule a great empire with the willing obedience of his followers.[5] The *Cyropaedia* is thus presented as having serious claims to contribute to the political discourse of Xenophon's time. It is no wonder that in antiquity it was considered a response to Plato's *Republic*, while in modern times it exerted a considerable

---

[1] Tatum 1989: 37. Cf. also Gera 1993: 25: "the *Cyropaedia* is a kind of summary of Xenophon's literary activity."

[2] The proper education of Cyrus, i.e. as a child (παῖς), covers only book 1. See Breitenbach 1967: 1707, Due 1989: 15, Tuplin 1996: 69–71.

[3] For Xenophon's literary predecessors, see Gera 1993: 1–25, Due 1989: 117–46. For the role of Persian oral tradition, see Hirsch 1985: 68–9, Tuplin 1996: 106–54, Zarghamee 2013b.

[4] Cyrus the Great lived from 598 to 529 BC. The *Cyropaedia* was written in the 360s BC. For its dating, see Gera 1993: 25, Tuplin 1996: 104.

[5] Xen. *Cyr.* 1.1.1.

influence on thinkers such as Machiavelli and Montaigne, as well as on modern management theory.[6]

The study of the *Cyropaedia* currently follows the resurgence of interest that underlies Xenophontic studies in general: although in the past it has been often considered a rather dull and tedious text, over the last few decades its sophistication and literary qualities have been brought to light.[7] This chapter outlines (albeit sketchily) the main interpretive issues raised by the study of this work.

Between Greece and Persia

The *Cyropaedia* is a selective account of episodes from the life of Cyrus, taking place mainly in Media, Persia, and Babylon. While narrating these episodes, Xenophon is inspired by, exploits, and adapts Persian material: individuals, events, customs, and practices from Persian history. The first issue that demands an explanation is the very fact that Xenophon chose a Persian leader as a paradigm. Several answers have been proposed: Xenophon was inspired by Cyrus the Younger, in whose expedition he participated; he could not find a compelling paradigm of an ideal leader from Greece; he reacted against Antisthenes, another pupil of Socrates who had also written a biography of Cyrus; he intended to send a subtle message to his contemporaries about the risks of undertaking an expedition against Persia.[8]

Although this interrogation is legitimate, it seems to have its roots in the (traditional) view and premise that the Greek and barbarian worlds were separated and mutually hostile to each other. This interpretive lens has been recently nuanced, emphasis being given on the constant and multifaceted interaction between the two worlds (in commerce, exchange of people, politics etc.).[9] With this qualification in mind, it would be fair to say that Xenophon *could have been* inspired by Cyrus the Great even without a

---

[6] Diogenes Laertius (3.34) comments on the rivalry between Plato and Xenophon. The *Cyropaedia* is interpreted as a response to the *Republic*, while Plato is considered to implicitly criticize Xenophon in the *Laws* (694c). See Danzig 2002. For the reception of the *Cyropaedia* in modern times, see Tatum 1989: 3–35. For the connections of the *Cyropaedia* with modern management theory, see O'Flannery 2003, Field 2012.

[7] For the *Cyropaedia* as a dull work, see Johnson 2012b. Monographs devoted to the *Cyropaedia* are Due 1989, Tatum 1989, Gera 1993, Nadon 2001, and Sandridge 2012; cf. also the commentary by Mueller-Goldingen 1995.

[8] For the importance of the expedition with Cyrus the Younger, see Hirsch 1985: 73–5; for the lack of a Greek paradigm, Tuplin 2013: 73–4; for competition with Antisthenes, Tuplin 1990: 28, Gera 1993: 8–10; for the Panhellenic message, see Carlier 1978/2010.

[9] See now Vlassopoulos 2013a.

personal experience of Persia (after all, Herodotus also devoted an important part of his history to Cyrus and even states that he knew more than
one version of Cyrus' life[10]). Xenophon's participation in the expedition of
Cyrus was the decisive factor that exposed him to Persian realities and royal
propaganda, but Cyrus the Younger would probably not be the ideal can-
didate for inspiration, not least because his expedition failed. Literary competition could have also played a role, but since Antisthenes' work has been
preserved only in fragments, this hypothesis cannot be verified; one should
also not exclude the possibility that Xenophon was in a state of literary
rivalry not only with the Socratics, but with other authors as well, such as,
for instance, Herodotus and Thucydides.[11] The idea of a Panhellenic intention in the *Cyropaedia* should be dismissed as an explanation of Xenophon's
inspiration: references or allusions to this topic are absent in the text. As for
the use of a Greek leader as a paradigm, it is true that it would be rather
impossible for Xenophon to find a contemporary leader with a Panhellenic
appeal and approval. But he could have had recourse to a mythical figure of
the Greek past (such as Lycurgus) and compose a quasi-historical account
similar to that about Cyrus.

Then why did he opt for Cyrus? At least two reasons can be advanced
to explain this choice: firstly, Xenophon was interested in paradigms of
successful empires; obviously he could not find such paradigms in Greece,
which experienced consecutive failures of empires. Secondly, he must have
been impressed by *specific features* on which the propaganda about Cyrus
insisted, mainly his qualities as a benevolent despot and his success in gaining the willing obedience of his followers. Greek leaders ostensibly lacked
these qualities, for the simple reason that the regime of monarchy that by
definition enables and fosters them, was absent in Greece. Xenophon wished
to underline these qualities, but without implying a suggestion about constitutional change in Greece. The prologue of the *Cyropaedia* reveals this
tension: although it starts by contemplating the failures of all regimes, this
reflection is not subsequently pursued and the paradigm of Cyrus is not used
as an indication of the superiority of monarchy.

The second issue about Persia that has attracted scholarly attention concerns the extent to which the Persian material in the *Cyropaedia* derives
from Persian evidence and/or accurately reflects Persian realities, and the
related question of whether this work can be useful for students of Persian
history. The historical value of the *Cyropaedia* has now been widely

[10] Hdt. 1.95.1.
[11] It should be born in mind, when studying Xenophon, that he was not only a Socratic,
but also a historian. Hence it would be risky to reduce possible influences on his
thought *only* to Socratics or *only* to historians.

acknowledged. Furthermore, the role of Persian oral tradition in the formation of Xenophon's account has been valorized.[12] Xenophon himself remarks that Cyrus had a reputation "in word and songs among the barbarians" (λέγεται καὶ ᾄδεται ἔτι καὶ νῦν ὑπὸ τῶν βαρβάρων) and uses the Herodotean terms "we hear" (ἀκούομεν), "it is said" (λέγεται), "we learned" (ἐπυθόμεθα), which also demonstrate his reliance upon oral tradition.[13] No doubt he got into contact with this tradition during his participation in the campaign of Cyrus the Younger and had the opportunity to exploit it creatively when writing his account about Cyrus the Great.

The search for historical accuracy in the *Cyropaedia* obviously stems from the professionalization of the discipline of history. However, despite the fascinating insights offered by Iranological studies, this line of approach tends to overlook the fact that Xenophon's aim was not so much to provide accurate information about Persian history or even Persian civilization – and he does not seem to be motivated by strong ethnographical interests, like Herodotus – but to use a historical paradigm in order to instruct (or at least provoke the reflection of) a Greek audience. The prologue of the *Cyropaedia* is again telling: it bears a striking resemblance in terms of structure with Darius' speech in the Constitutional Debate of Herodotus.[14] In both cases a theoretical approach precedes the presentation of a historical paradigm, which is used in order to verify and reinforce the aforementioned theory. Interestingly, the historical paradigm in both cases is Cyrus. Darius refers to him (though without naming him) after a theoretical introduction about the merits of monarchy, as a compelling paradigm which proves that this regime is the best. Similarly, Xenophon mentions Cyrus at the end of his prologue, after a theoretical introduction about the difficulties of all regimes in the ruling of men, in order to promote, for his part, a paradigm of successful leadership. Xenophon's prologue thus anticipates the peculiar selection and exploitation of Persian material that readers encounter in the rest of the work.

Xenophon's narrative could initially convey the impression of indifference towards Persian history. Xenophon does not hesitate to distance himself from mainstream Persian traditions concerning important events, such as Cyrus' rise to power and his death. In all other sources, Greek and non-Greek, Cyrus' ascent to kingship is depicted as the result of a conflict between Cyrus and his Median grandfather, Astyages, which ended in Cyrus' victory, with the collaboration of the Median aristocracy. Xenophon's account bears no trace of this storyline, but presents instead affectionate relations

---

[12] For the importance of Persian oral tradition, see Daryaee 2006, Shayegan 2012.

[13] Xen. *Cyr.* 1.2.1, 1.4.25, 1.1.4–6. For minstrels as carriers of Persian tradition, see Tuplin 1996: 114–16.

[14] Xen. *Cyr.* 1.1, Hdt. 3.82.

between Cyrus and Astyages.[15] Xenophon offers an alternative narrative for Cyrus' death, too: while Herodotus and Ctesias report a death in battle, Xenophon's Cyrus dies in a Socratic manner in his bed, surrounded by his friends to whom he gives his last advice.[16]

But this is not the whole story. Xenophon's *Cyropaedia* also comprises (more or less accurate) indications of Persian realities. Besides the casual occurrences of objects of Persian luxury aptly characterized by Christopher Tuplin as "Persian decor,"[17] Xenophon's portrayal of Cyrus as both benevolent and despotic has analogies with Cyrus' presentation in non-Greek sources: Persian royal propaganda as can be seen in the Cyrus Cylinder stressed his kindness and tolerance (especially religious), while the Babylonian Nabonidus Chronicle provides evidence for his despotic profile and his harsh treatment of enemies.[18] Xenophon does not seem to be interested in Cyrus' religious policy, but he narrates in the *Cyropaedia* episodes of benevolent treatment of allies, together with other incidents in which Cyrus had appeal to fear as a means to achieve his military and political goals.[19] There also seems to exist a historical kernel in Cyrus' multicultural (both Median and Persian) education: this blending reflects the interaction between the two nations, which gradually led to the rise of the Persian Empire out of the conquest of the Medes.[20] The division of the Persian people into the upper class (consisting of the king and the nobility) and the rest of the population (the commoners: δημόται) also mirrors the stratification of the Persian society.[21]

---

[15] Xen. *Cyr.* 1.4.2. For the events related to Cyrus' rise to power, see Briant 1996: 23–45.

[16] Xen. *Cyr.* 8.7.1–28. Xenophon might have been inspired by an oral (not mainstream) tradition about Cyrus' death: see Sancisi-Weerdenburg 1985/2010.

[17] Tuplin 1990: 25. These objects include metal vessels, personal adornments, garments, and jewelry. Cf. also Tuplin 2010, for the terminology of Achaemenid courts.

[18] Mallowan 1972: 11–14 comments on Cyrus' clemency towards Astyages and Croesus and his religious tolerance, as well as on his harsh treatment of Nabonidus. Cf. also Kuhrt 1984 : 157–8 for representations of Cyrus' clemency in Achaemenid art. For the Cyrus Cylinder, see now Curtis 2013 and the essays collected in Finkel 2013. For the "Nabonidus Chronicle," see Grayson 1975 and Kuhrt 2007: 176–80, who considers it a reliable source for Cyrus.

[19] The most prominent examples of benevolence are Cyrus' sparing of the life of the Armenian king (Xen. *Cyr.* 3.1.1–37) and the releasing of prisoners of war (Xen. *Cyr.* 4.4.5–9). A notable incident of appeal to fear is Cyrus' ultimatum to the Armenian king (Xen. *Cyr.* 2.4.31–2).

[20] Xenophon mentions that Cyrus was educated in Persia till the age of twelve (Xen. *Cyr.* 3.1.1), he then spent some time in Media with his grandfather and came back to Persia to complete his education (Xen. *Cyr.* 1.5.1). For the relations between Medes and Persians and the creation of the Persian Empire, see Briant 1996: 23–45, Zarghamee 2013b: 61–94.

[21] See Briant 1990, Masaracchia 1996. However, Xenophon also introduces a new term to describe the Persian nobles, the *homotimoi* (see Demont 2006) and does not use the term *doulos* for them, while also in other Greek sources the word *doulos* is used for Persian aristocrats, rendering the Persian term *bandaka*. See Missiou 1992.

The same goes for the habits of the upper class (scenes of hunting and royal banquets, which constituted important elements of the life of the Persian nobility,[22] often appear in the *Cyropaedia*) and some customs (such as the prostration or the kiss between relatives[23]). On a political level, Xenophon is interested in highlighting the expansion of Cyrus' empire and describes his military reforms concerning the reorganization of the army and the introduction of the Persian cavalry. He also mentions in detail the nations that Cyrus subjugated and gives the contours of his empire.[24] Although these descriptions are not entirely accurate, they nevertheless capture a real trait, Cyrus' imperialistic ambition, and also inform readers about some major conquests he achieved during his reign (such as the Armenians, the Lydians, and the Babylonians). Finally, Xenophon recounts several Persian practices which exist "till his own day" (ἔτι καὶ νῦν), an expression he uses very often in order to enhance the truthfulness of his Persian account.[25]

The most intriguing feature of the *Cyropaedia* is, however, the blending of Greek and Persian realities. First of all, Persia is described as a (Greek) city (polis).[26] Xenophon even relates the existence of a market (*agora*) and employs terms of Greek political vocabulary to explain political institutions in Persia: the state (τό κοινόν), the magistrates (τὰς ἀρχάς), laws (νόμοι), equality (τὸ ἴσον).[27] It is also no coincidence that Greeks and Greek or Hellenized characters figure in the narrative of the *Cyropaedia*: the Greeks of Asia, an anonymous Greek who followed Croesus (probably alluding to Bias of Priene, the advisor of Croesus in Herodotus) and the teacher of the Armenian prince Tigranes, who is not named either, but famously recalls Socrates.[28] Furthermore, Xenophon proceeds to a kind of *interpretatio graeca*: he mentions that Persians learn justice like "we (*scil.* the Greeks) learn to read" and that they train their boys in deception, "just like the Greeks teach deception in wrestling."[29] There is also an interest in analogies

---

[22] See Zarghamee 2013b: 360–1. However, the banquets in the *Cyropaedia* are sober and have a Socratic flavor. See Gera 1993: 132–91.

[23] Xen. *Cyr.* 1.4.27 (Persian kiss); Xen. *Cyr.* 4.4.9 (bowing of prisoners), Xen. *Cyr.* 8.3.14 (for the bowing of Persians).

[24] Xen. *Cyr.* 1.1.4 (nations subjugated). Cf. Mallowan 1972: 4 for the conquests of Cyrus according to Persian records. Xen. *Cyr.* 8.6.21 (contours of Cyrus' empire).

[25] For the ἔτι καὶ νῦν phrases, see Delebecque 1957: 405–8, Hirsch 1985: 92–3, Due 1989: 20–2, 35–38, Tuplin 2013: 73.

[26] Mandane says to young Cyrus that his father obeys the rules of the city (Xen. *Cyr.* 1.3.18: ὁ σὸς πρῶτος πατὴρ τὰ τεταγμένα μὲν ποιεῖ τῇ πόλει ...).

[27] Xen. *Cyr.* 1.2.2 (Persian *agora*), Xen. *Cyr.* 4.5.17 (κοινόν, ἀρχάς), Xen. *Cyr.* 1.3.18 (νόμοι, τὸ ἴσον). Cf. Tuplin 1996: 138 (on the *agora* of the Persians).

[28] Xen. *Cyr.* 1.1.4, 2.1.5, 6.2.10, 7.4.9: Greeks of Asia; 6.3.11: Greek who followed Croesus; cf. Hdt. 1.127.2–3: Bias of Priene as Croesus' advisor; 3.1.39: teacher–Socrates.

[29] Xen. *Cyr.* 1.2.6, Xen. *Cyr.* 1.6.32.

specifically with Sparta: Xenophon observes that the Persians use in war the subject people of the Hyrcanians, just like the Lacedaemonians exploit in war a people subject to them, the Sciritae, "sparing them neither in toil nor in dangers."[30] Moreover, he seems to have been inspired by military reforms in Sparta which necessitated the extension of armament to the helots. The *Cyropaedia* reflects these contemporary concerns and debates. Xenophon devotes much space to Cyrus' proposition about including the commoners in the army, and also problematizes the issue of arming slaves: Cyrus observes, for instance, that people destined to be subject to the Persians should not hold weapons and concludes that "the science of war is the means to freedom and prosperity."[31] Finally, despite its Persian setting, the *Cyropaedia* is not deprived of Greek stereotypes of oriental luxury: Xenophon stages scenes of relaxation in the Median camp and comments on the Median slaves getting drunk in the absence of their masters.[32]

In sum, notwithstanding the oriental flavor, Xenophon's overall treatment exhibits some detachment towards Persian history: he keeps some basic lines of the story of Cyrus, he uses his imagination in the elaboration of the events, and he finds ways to make his narrative attractive and familiar to his Greek audience by hinting at Greek figures or realities. It is also noteworthy that, although Xenophon praises a Persian leader and the Persian system, he does not make suggestions openly (e.g. that the Greeks should search for a leader like Cyrus or adopt Persian practices). He rather wishes to provoke the reflection of his Greek audience on the connotations of the blending between Persian and Greek material, practices, and systems of leadership.

A Work across Genres

The genre of the *Cyropaedia* is a puzzling issue. At first sight this work seems to encompass a variety of genres: biography and encomium, historiography, fiction and novel, political treatise. Depending on the perspective adopted, it has been classified in various ways. It has been labeled as the "first accomplished biography"; the loose chronological order of the events and the inclusion of novelistic elements, in combination with the prominence of the

---

[30] Xen. *Cyr.* 4.2.1.
[31] Xen. *Cyr.* 2.3.1–20, 7.5.79–80. Tuplin 1994 convincingly shows that Xenophon does not systematically model his narrative about Persia upon Spartan practices. But the resemblances concerning military reforms are hardly coincidental. Christesen 2006 goes so far as to suggest that the *Cyropaedia* is a political pamphlet aiming at the military reform of Sparta. It seems more probable that Xenophon was influenced by certain events of Spartan history, such as the armament of helots and their participation in war in exceptional circumstances. See Hunt 1998: 175–7, Tamiolaki 2010: 190–201.
[32] Xen. *Cyr.* 4.5.7, 8.

love story of Panthea, have led other scholars to stress its fictional dimension and view it as an anticipation of the ancient novel; scholars with greater sensitivity to historical issues emphasize its importance as a resource for the study of Achaemenid Empire; the political reflection of the prologue also gives justice to the claim that Xenophon intended this work to be perceived as a political treatise with (or without) a didactic dimension.[33]

This variety of approaches attests to the complex character of the *Cyropaedia* and the problems posed by its genre (or lack of). On the one hand, an attempt to single out only one element in defining its genre collides with the multifarious character of this work; on the other hand, naming it simply a blending (or mixture) of different genres is an easy (but rather unsatisfactory) way to get away from the problem. To begin with, one should take seriously into account the fact that the blending of genres does not concern *only* the *Cyropaedia*, but constitutes a distinctive feature of the whole Xenophontic corpus: the *Hellenica* and the *Anabasis* accommodate elements of encomiastic literature and Socratic-type conversations; the encomium of *Agesilaus* also consists of historiographical tints; while the *Memorabilia* are presented as a truthful (quasi-historical) account of Socrates' conversations. Nevertheless, these works have not been traditionally considered to represent a blending of genres. The *Cyropaedia* is undoubtedly a more complicated work, but the question of its genre could perhaps be better approached by answering the questions of "what is less" and "what is more," that is by trying to detect in it some more predominant elements.

In fact, it seems easier to define what the *Cyropaedia is not* (or what *is less*) than what it actually is. It bears little resemblance with Plutarch-type biographies or Isocratean *encomia*: it is much lengthier than the usual species of these genres and much less emphatically didactic.[34] Interestingly, first-person statements of the verb "praise" (ἐπαινῶ) do not occur in the *Cyropaedia*, in striking contrast with *Agesilaus* or even the *Hellenica*.[35] Its connection with the novel has been overemphasized, too: the birth of the genre of the novel is itself a controversial issue, so claiming that the *Cyropaedia* anticipates the ancient novel only adds more controversy to the already existing one. Furthermore, the story of Panthea, which has been often used to support

---

[33] Biography: Momigliano 1993: 46–57, Hägg 2012: 51–66; encomium: Zimmermann 1989; fiction: Stadter 1991/2010; connection with the novel: Tatum 1989: 36–66; source for Persian history: Tuplin 1996; political treatise with didactic dimension: Gera 1993: 11, Tatum 1989: 215–39; critical intention: Too 1998, Nadon 2001: 161–80.

[34] Tuplin 1996: 95: "there is no systematic assimilation of leadership with educative activity (even some deliberate avoidance of such an assimilation)."

[35] Xen. *Ages.* 8.4, 8.5, 10.1; Xen. *Hell.* 6.2.20, 7.5.8.

this claim, lacks important distinctive traits of the novel, such as the predominance of the love theme and the happy ending.[36] It also has an ostensibly political dimension, which is compatible with the overall content and purpose of the *Cyropaedia*,[37] but does not form a central preoccupation of the ancient novel. Finally, the political aspect of the *Cyropaedia* is undoubtedly evident, but it should not entail the characterization of the work as a political treatise. The tone of a political treatise appears more prominently in the prologue[38] and in the theoretical advice about leadership issues. However, the fact that it is not the author who gives this advice, but important characters within this work and in specific contexts situated in the plot, weakens the case that Xenophon wished the *Cyropaedia* to be read solely as a political treatise. Besides, the existence of other works (such as his works on the art of horsemanship, the *Constitution of the Spartans*, and the *Ways and Means (Poroi)*) which can be more clearly classified as treatises further proves that Xenophon was aware of this genre, but obviously did not find it appropriate for the *Cyropaedia*.

I come lastly to the historiographical claims of the work. I would like to suggest that, despite the undeniable blending of different genres, Xenophon intended the *Cyropaedia* to be conceived *more* as historiography (albeit of a peculiar sort). The prologue is again revealing: the author states that a historical (and not mythical) paradigm has triggered his reflection and goes on to give a detailed account of Cyrus' conquests. This description prepares the readers for a historiographical exposition. Two significant elements further enhance the historiographical dimension of the work: Xenophon's narratorial comments and the subtle intertextuality of the *Cyropaedia* with the historiographical tradition.

Scholars have so far focused on the expression "till my own day" (ἔτι καὶ νῦν), which Xenophon employs repeatedly when he wishes to show that a certain practice or custom (usually Persian) is followed from ancient times to his own era. But the range of narratorial interventions in the *Cyropaedia* is broader. They cover four categories: a) comments about Persian realities (which may or may not include ἔτι καὶ νῦν statements); b) comments on Cyrus' qualities in the form of comparisons; c) comments explaining the characters' motivation; d) expression of a judgment or opinion. The comparisons related to Cyrus may have poetic or specifically Homeric resonances.[39]

---

[36] For the divergences from the novel, see Reichel 1995/2010.

[37] For the political dimension of the story of Panthea, see Tatum 1989: 163–88, Tamiolaki 2010: 305–9.

[38] Expressions such as ἔννοιά ποθ' ἡμῖν ἐγένετο (we were once concerned), ἐλογιζόμεθα (we reflected), ἐνενοοῦμεν (we perceived) would point to that direction.

[39] Xen. *Cyr.* 1.4.3: compared with a lion, Xen. *Cyr.* 1.4.20: compared with a dog. For similes in the *Iliad*, see recently Ready 2011.

But the rest of these narratorial interventions add to the historiographical flavor of the work. For instance, Xenophon comments on the importance of punishing ingratitude in Persia, or on the fact that it is difficult for Persians to acquire cavalry; he even offers clarifications about Persian garments or the habits of Persian cupbearers.[40] These statements have a similar function with the expression "till my own day": they strengthen the impression that the author is interested in providing a factual account of Persian practices. The same goes for narratorial interventions referring to the attribution of motives. Xenophon can explain an attitude more assertively (for instance, Cyrus' decision to put to the vote among his peers, the Persian nobles called *homotimoi*, his suggestion about establishing rewards for bravery, is attributed to his belief that his peers would excel in battle), while other times he appears as making speculations, by using the adverb "perhaps" (ἴσως), by introducing the Herodotean formula of alternative motivation "whether … or" (εἴτε … εἴτε), or by qualifying his opinion with the use of the verb "I think" (οἴομαι).[41] These strategies again reinforce the truthfulness of the account: they indicate that the author makes sure to distinguish between reliable and less reliable information. Authorial maxims also enhance the historiographical dimension of the work, since they usually serve as a confirmation of a preceding narrative. For example, Xenophon opines that pious people are less fearful or that brave people undertake toil more gladly.[42]

The intertextual dialogue of the *Cyropaedia* with Xenophon's historical predecessors is rather underexplored in modern scholarship, attention being mainly given to the narratives of Cyrus' childhood and death, as well as to Cyrus' encounter with Croesus and their relationship with the accounts of Herodotus and Ctesias.[43] However, the engagement with the historiographical tradition is broader and covers a variety of topics: imitation of historiographical method; treatment of general historiographical themes; and adaptation of specific episodes from the historiographical tradition. Xenophon informs us on several occasions about his method of collecting and presenting his evidence, by using terms such as "we hear" (ἀκούομεν), "we will narrate" (διηγησόμεθα), "we learned" (ἐπυθόμεθα), "it is said" (λέγεται), which have a Herodotean flavor. His interest in Cyrus' genealogy

---

[40] Xen. *Cyr.* 1.2.7: punishment of ingratitude in Persia; Xen. *Cyr.* 1.3.3: Persian cavalry; Xen. *Cyr.* 1.3.2: Persian garments; Xen. *Cyr.* 1.3.9: Persian cupbearers.

[41] Xen. *Cyr.* 2.2.21, Cyrus' motives explained assertively: ὁ δὲ Κῦρος ἐβούλετο καὶ αὐτῶν ἕνεκα τῶν ὁμοτίμων γενέσθαι τοῦτο τὸ ψήφισμα (Cyrus wished that this vote take place for the sake of the peers themselves); Xen. *Cyr.* 1.4.22, 4.1.13: ἴσως statements, Xen. *Cyr.* 5.4.27, 8.3.14: formula εἴτε … εἴτε; Xen. *Cyr.* 3.3.59: οἴομαι.

[42] Xen. *Cyr.* 3.3.58, 5.4.17.

[43] See Keller 1911, Lefèvre 1971/2010, Gray 2011: 149–57, and an excellent recent treatment by Ellis (2014).

can be also traced back to Herodotus and the historiographical tradition. The chronological markers in the *Cyropaedia* are loose, but it is important that the author displays an awareness of digressions and, again in the manner of Herodotus, can pick up from previous stages of a narrative.[44] Another Herodotean feature is the inclusion of short stories in the *Cyropaedia* (mainly banquet scenes and theoretical conversations), which interrupt the main course of the plot. Of course, the distinction between novellas and anecdotes often applied to Herodotus cannot be valid for Xenophon, since in Xenophon, with the exception of the story of Panthea, there are no tragic endings. Nonetheless, the didactic and paradigmatic character of these stories is an element shared by both authors.[45] Xenophon also seems to borrow from Thucydides, when he emphasizes proofs (μαρτύρια) and when he includes a letter in his narrative.[46]

General historiographical themes in the *Cyropaedia* include the description of battles and the reporting of numbers of both camps, the measures taken for the search for allies, the pre-battle speeches and the exhortations of generals aimed at raising the morale of their soldiers, the description of motivation of characters, and the characterization of individuals before their speeches.[47] Xenophon could have borrowed these elements from epic as well, but certain themes can be characterized as *specifically* Herodotean or Thucydidean. Furthermore, the elaboration of concrete episodes from Herodotus and Thucydides points to a greater proximity with the historiographical tradition. In what follows I will confine myself to a few indicative examples which show Xenophon's dialogue with his historical predecessors.

The inspiration from Herodotus is obvious in the elaboration of some common themes (such as the mutability of fortune, the definition of human happiness from the perspective of the end, and the laughter foreshadowing

---

44 Xen. *Cyr.* 1.1.4–6: ἐπυθόμεθα, λέγεται; Xen. *Cyr.* 1.16: interest in genealogy; Xen. *Cyr.* 1.2.15–16: sense of digression (ταῦτα μὲν δὴ κατὰ πάντων Περσῶν ἔχομεν λέγειν· οὗ δ᾽ ἕνεκα ὁ λόγος ὡρμήθη, νῦν λέξομεν τὰς Κύρου πράξεις ἀρξάμενοι ἀπὸ παιδός. Translation: "this is is what we have to say with regards to the Persians in general; for this reason I began this digression. Now I am going to narrate Cyrus' deeds beginning from his childhood").

45 For the short stories in Herodotus, see Griffiths 2006. For the banquet scenes in the *Cyropaedia*, see Gera 1993: 132–91.

46 Xen. *Cyr.* 1.2.16: μαρτύρια; Xen. *Cyr.* 4.5.27 : letter of Cyrus to Cyaxares. Cf. Thuc. 1.1.3; 1.20.1 (τεκμήρια); 7.11.1–7.15.2 (letter of Nicias).

47 Battles: Xen. *Cyr.* 3.3.58–70; search for allies: 1.5.2; pre-battle speeches: Xen. *Cyr.* 3.1.2–5, 4.2.21–6, 6.2.13–20, 6.4.12–20, 7.5.19–24; encouragement to soldiers: 2.1.14–18, 2.3.1–4, 3.3.7–8, 4.1.1–6, 7.5.71–86, 8.6.10–13; 7.1.22–48; Xen. *Cyr.* 1.5.5, 5.3.24: numbers of camps; Xen. *Cyr.* 1.4.22, 3.1.1, 4.2.10, 5.1.20: motivation; 2.3.5, 2.3.7, 4.3.4, 5.1.2, 8.3.21: characterization of speakers.

disaster⁴⁸), but also in the adaptation of specific episodes. For instance, Xenophon elaborates on the topic of the poverty of the Persians. He brings out poverty as a decisive factor which motivates the Persians' decision to follow Cyrus. When Cyrus proposes the inclusion of all Persians in the ranks of the army, Xenophon makes the following comment:

> And when the Persians heard (Cyrus' speech), they thought that if they rejected his request to share the same toils (τὰ ὅμοια πονοῦντες) and enjoy the same (rewards), they would deserve to live in need for the rest of their lives (δικαίως ἂν διὰ παντὸς τοῦ αἰῶνος ἀμηχανοῦντες βιοτεύειν). (Xen. *Cyr.* 2.1.19)

Similarly, after the conquest of Babylon, Cyrus' decision to create a body of spearmen composed of two thousand Persians derives from his confidence that the Persians will be willing to abandon their poor and harsh land and move to (rich) Babylon:

> Since he knew that the Persians who lived in Persia led a most unpleasant life due to their poverty (κακοβιωτάτους μὲν ὄντας διὰ πενίαν) and, moreover, they endured the greatest toil because their land was harsh and they had to work with their hands (ἐπιπονώτατα δὲ ζῶντας διὰ τὴν τῆς χώρας τραχύτητα καὶ διὰ τὸ αὐτουργοὺς εἶναι), for these reasons he thought that they would view life with him most positively. (Xen. *Cyr.* 7.5.67)

This description picks up the Herodotean narrative. In the first book of his *Histories*, Herodotus ends his description of Cyrus' rise to power with his speech in front of the Persians. The central topic of this speech is poverty:

> Men of Persia, your situation is as follows: if you follow me willingly, these good things and ten thousand more which do not entail any slavish toil (οὐδένα πόνον δουλοπρεπέα ἔχουσι) will be at your disposal. But if you don't want to follow me, you will endure countless toils similar to those you endure every day (εἰσὶ ὑμῖν πόνοι τῷ χθιζῷ παραπλήσιοι ἀναρίθμητοι). (Hdt. 1.126.5)

The same topic is reiterated at the end of the *Histories*, in the conversation between Cyrus and Artembares. Artembares raises the issue of moving to another, more fertile land:

> Since Zeus granted the hegemony to the Persians, and among men to you, Cyrus, now that you have beaten Astyages, let us move from our land and get a better one – because our land is small and, not least, harsh (γῆν γὰρ ἐκτήμεθα ὀλίγην καὶ ταύτην τρηχέαν). (Hdt. 9.122.2)

The themes of poverty, harshness, toil, and choosing another land are echoed and reworked in Xenophon's *Cyropaedia*. But Xenophon proceeds

⁴⁸ Xen. *Cyr.* 2.1.3, 5.2.35, Xen. *Cyr.* 1.6.45, Hdt. 1.5, 1.207.2: mutability of fortune; Xen. *Cyr.* 7.3.11, Hdt. 1.32.9: reflection on endings; Xen. *Cyr.* 7.5.13–14, Hdt. 1.90, 3.22, 3.29, 3.35, 8.114: laughter foreshadowing disaster.

to an adaptation of the Herodotean narrative. In Herodotus Cyrus rejects Artembares' suggestion to abandon Persia and seek for a better land, on the grounds that soft lands produce soft and submissive people. Xenophon's Cyrus, on the contrary, believes that the life in Babylon will be much more attractive to the Persians than their life in Persia.[49]

Xenophon seems to have been also influenced by the Herodotean episode of the conversation between Xerxes and Demaratus. A significant theme that dominates this conversation is the contrast between small numbers and (great) bravery. Demaratus contrasts Spartan bravery and respect for the law with Xerxes' great numbers and the compulsion to fight that the Persian King exerts on the army.[50] Xenophon adapts this topic in the *Cyropaedia*. He does not elaborate on the respect for the law, but focuses on the issue of small numbers: in the conversation with his uncle Cyaxares, Cyrus observes that the small number of the *homotimoi* should not be viewed negatively, because, although the peers are few, they are capable of ruling many Persians (Xen. *Cyr.* 2.1.3). Moreover, before the battle with the Assyrians, Cyrus responds confidently to Gobryas' fears about the enemies' great numbers, by stating that success in battles does not rely on great numbers, but on good fighting; and he goes on to remark that "you will find more men on our side who are willing to fight than on theirs" (Xen. *Cyr.* 5.2.35).[51]

The engagement with Thucydides is equally interesting, though surprisingly overlooked.[52] Given that Xenophon deals with the empire of Cyrus, the inspiration from and the modeling upon Thucydidean themes is only to be expected. The most important Thucydidean themes exploited by Xenophon in the *Cyropaedia* are the following: the emphasis on the preservation of empire and the risks of losing it, the increase of power as a cause of war, the envy felt towards the powerful, and the conquest by the mighty as a result of an everlasting law (νόμος ἀίδιος).[53]

---

49 For the issues raised by the last passage of Herodotus's *Histories* and its (apparent) contradiction with the passage of the first book, see Flower and Marincola 2002 ad loc. and the discussion in Tamiolaki 2010: 215–19. The engagement of Xenophon with Herodotus at this point is more complex than this chapter allows me to show. I intend to offer a more systematic analysis on another occasion.

50 Hdt. 7.101–104.5. For this conversation, see Cartledge 2004: 177–8, Tamiolaki 2010: 223–8 (with previous bibliography).

51 The reference to the small size of the *homotimoi* also alludes to the famous ὀλιγανθρωπία of the Spartans.

52 Thucydides is absent from most treatments of Xenophon's literary predecessors in the *Cyropaedia*. Lendon 2006 is an exception to this trend. Cf. also the unpublished dissertation by Rinner 1981.

53 Xen. *Cyr.* 4.1.15, 4.5.15, Thuc. 2.63.2: preservation of empire; Xen. *Cyr.* 5.2.20, 5.5.24, Thuc. 1.23.6: increase of power as a cause of war; Xen. *Cyr.* 7.5.76, Thuc. 1.75.2: envy towards the mighty; Xen. *Cyr.* 7.5.73, Thuc. 5.105.1–3: everlasting law.

I have argued elsewhere, concerning the intertextual dialogue of Xenophon's *Hellenica* with Thucydides, that Xenophon draws specifically from Thucydides' Funeral Oration and the narrative of the Mytilenean Debate.[54] A similar preference can be observed in the *Cyropaedia* as well. The Funeral Oration should have attracted Xenophon's attention, not least because it is a form of praise. It should thus serve as an additional model of inspiration besides other (contemporary) *encomia*. In the prologue of the Funeral Oration Pericles states:

> By what institutions we have reached this point and by what constitution and by which way of life we have achieved greatness (ἀπὸ δὲ οἵας τε ἐπιτηδεύσεως ἤλθομεν ἐπ' αὐτὰ καὶ μεθ' οἵας πολιτείας καὶ τρόπων ἐξ οἵων μεγάλα ἐγένετο), these are the elements that I will highlight first and then I will proceed to the praise of these men. (Thuc. 2.36.4)

In a similar vein, in his prologue of the *Cyropaedia*, Xenophon states that he will narrate the nature, lineage, and education of Cyrus:

> Since this man was, in our view, worthy of admiration, we set out to investigate what was his lineage and what natural talents he possessed and what sort of education he received (τίς ποτ' ὢν γενεὰν καὶ ποίαν τινὰ φύσιν ἔχων καὶ ποίᾳ τινὶ παιδευθεὶς παιδείᾳ), so that he excelled in the ruling of men. (Xen. *Cyr.* 1.1.6)

Xenophon's singling out of three elements of praise regarding Cyrus bears a resemblance with Pericles' tripartite division in the Funeral Oration regarding the praise of the Athenians. The syntactical formulation (introduced by a verb and three indirect questions) is also the same. Xenophon seems thus to transpose the reflection on the polis to the individual. One could also observe an implicit analogy between the pedagogical function of Periclean Athens (Ἑλλάδος παίδευσιν, Thuc. 2.41.1) and Xenophon's Persia as an educational paradigm intended for the Greeks.

An inspiration from the Funeral Oration can be also detected in Cyrus' speech, in which he compares contemporary Persians with their ancestors:

> I have perceived that our ancestors were no worse than us in anything (ἐγὼ γὰρ κατενόησα ὅτι οἱ πρόγονοι χείρονες μὲν ἡμῶν οὐδὲν ἐγένοντο). Like us, they also practiced what are considered to be the deeds of virtue. However, I can no longer know whether, being virtuous, they acquired something more (ὅ τι μέντοι προσεκτήσαντο τοιοῦτοι ὄντες) either for themselves or for the commonwealth of the Persians. (Xen. *Cyr.* 1.5.8)

---

[54] Tamiolaki 2008: 34–43, Tamiolaki 2014a: 129–36.

This comparison again evokes Pericles' comparison with the Athenians' ancestors:

> I will begin with our ancestors (Ἄρξομαι δὲ ἀπὸ τῶν προγόνων πρῶτον·) ... And these men are worthy of praise, but our fathers are even worthier. For they handed down to us, contemporaries, the dominion that we have, after having expanded not without toil the empire they had received from their fathers (κτησάμενοι γὰρ πρὸς οἷς ἐδέξαντο). (Thuc. 2.36.4)

Like Pericles, Cyrus views (additional) acquisitions as a measure of success. Like Pericles, Cyrus praises his ancestors, but valorizes the present more than the past.[55]

The context of Thucydides's Mytilenean debate and the topics discussed in it also touch upon political themes which preoccupied Xenophon and can thus explain why this part of Thucydides' history could have exerted some influence on the *Cyropaedia*. Thucydides narrates the secession of the Mytileneans from the Athenian Empire in 427 BC, an important event which had triggered a heated debate in Athens: the issue at stake was whether the Athenians should punish or spare the Mytileneans. Cleon delivers a speech in favor of killing them, while Diodotus advocates a milder policy. Xenophon adapts this episode in the third book of the *Cyropaedia*. Like the Mytileneans, the Armenian king refuses to pay the tribute to Cyrus, an act which is compared with the revolt of a slave (Xen. *Cyr.* 3.1.11). Xenophon also presents a conversation between Cyrus and Tigranes, the king's son. Like the debate in Athens, this conversation revolves around the topics of crime and punishment. Tigranes' argument that the Armenian king would be more useful to Cyrus alive rather than dead (Xen. *Cyr.* 3.1.16) recalls Diodotus' arguments about the Athenians' interest in not killing the Mytileneans, because they will be useful to the empire (Thuc. 3.46.1–6). The joint reference to justice and expediency (δίκαια and σύμφορα) and the comment on human failure (Xen. *Cyr.* 5.3.31) also pick up well-known themes of the Thucydidean debate (Thuc. 3.47.5).[56]

This evidence is cumulative and discloses a continuous and creative engagement of Xenophon with his historical predecessors. It is also worth

---

[55] The verb προσκτάομαι has also Herodotean overtones: Hdt. 1.73.1, 3.21.3, 5.31.2, 7.8.α2. Again, however, Xenophon offers an adaptation: virtue in Xenophon is not an end in itself, but is linked with specific gains (often material). See further on this point Danzig 2014a.

[56] Xen. *Cyr.* 3.1.16, Thuc. 3.46.1–6: sparing is useful; Xen. *Cyr.* 5.3.31, Thuc. 3.47.5, 5.107: δίκαια καὶ σύμφορα; Xen. *Cyr.* 5.4.19, Thuc. 3.45.3: human failure. It is worth stressing that there are even more parallels between Xenophon's *Cyropaedia* and Thucydides, but limitations of space do not allow me to analyze them in the present chapter.

stressing that these elements do not occur *only* in the speeches or *only* in the narrative, but pervade the *Cyropaedia* throughout: narrative, speeches, and conversations. This is not always the case with other authors with whom Xenophon interacts: for example, his connection with Plato is more evident in the debate about *eros* and the scene of Cyrus' death, while his intertextual dialogue with Homer appears more prominently in the episode of Panthea.[57] The historiographical elements are, on the contrary, more pervasive: they are certainly not enough to prove that the *Cyropaedia* is history, but can signify that its author intended it to be conceived *more* as historiography than as any other genre.[58] However, given that the narrative of the *Cyropaedia* is very often interrupted by Socratic-type conversations, it would be tempting to consider this work as historiography of a Socratic type.

The Search for the Ideal Leader

The search for the ideal leader is a central preoccupation for Xenophon, which permeates all of his works. In the *Hellenica* he praises Agesilaus, Teleutias, Iphicrates, Jason of Pherae, and Epaminondas; in the *Anabasis* he gives a detailed necrology of Cyrus the Younger and presents nuanced portraits of all the Greek leaders who were arrested by Tissaphernes, while at the same time his self-representation is no less heroic; in the *Oeconomicus* he puts forth the qualities of the successful household leader, while in the *Memorabilia* he defends Socrates, who is not a political figure, but the epitome of virtue. The Syracusan tyrant Hiero is the anti-hero, since he incarnates all the traits that a leader should not possess. Some basic qualities are shared by all (or almost all) Xenophontic leaders: they are pious, benevolent, ingenious in military matters, capable of gaining the willing obedience of their followers; they valorize toil, orderliness, self-control, and temperance. However, subtle differentiations among them also emerge: for instance, wisdom (σοφία) is attributed only to Socrates and Agesilaus, while love of learning (φιλομάθεια) is a quality of the two Cyruses.[59] Furthermore, Socrates is an odd leader figure, since he constantly gives advice about politics (like other Xenophontic leaders), but nevertheless abstains from it.[60]

---

[57] Due 1989: 144–5, Gera 1993: 221–45.
[58] For a thesis akin to mine, about the *Cyropaedia* as ethnography, see Harman 2008.
[59] Love of learning has a more limited sense for Cyrus the Younger, since it refers only to his learning of bow and javelin (Xen. *Anab.* 1.9.5).
[60] For comparisons between Xenophontic leaders, see Due 1989: 185–206; for patterned narratives of leadership, see Gray 2011: 179–245. For the peculiarity of Socrates, see Tamiolaki 2012: 580–6. For the portrait of Socrates in Xenophon, see now the detailed treatment by Chernyakhovskaya 2014.

The portrait of Cyrus the Great in the *Cyropaedia* is the most thorough and detailed portrait of a leader and has some distinctive features. Unlike Agesilaus' encomium, in which Xenophon devotes a specific section to his virtues, Cyrus' qualities are dispersed throughout the narrative. Moreover, they are not always mentioned explicitly, but the readers often have to surmise them from the context. Furthermore, Cyrus' qualities are often focalized through others: in the *Cyropaedia* we find phrases of the type "they talked about Cyrus being kind, benevolent etc."[61] These phrases reflect a strong oral tradition about Cyrus, but also betray some detachment on behalf of the author. Finally, and more importantly, Cyrus' portrait is not wholly unambiguous. Scholars have highlighted some ambivalent traits: the word ἀρετή (virtue) is rarely used for Cyrus; Cyrus is often depicted as cunning, manipulative, and even deceptive; his relations with his allies and subordinates are asymmetrical, have a strong utilitarian perspective and are based on considerations of profit. Finally, from the moment he captures Babylon, he even acquires some tyrannical traits: he becomes over-cautious about his safety, he is interested in showing off his power, and the measures he undertakes reveal his wish to control everything and everybody.[62]

For the interpretation of Cyrus' portrait and subsequently of the author's intentions in the *Cyropaedia* three lines of approach have been proposed: a) Xenophon's *Cyropaedia* should be viewed as a covert blame of Cyrus and a critique of empire and/or of political life *tout court*. This line of interpretation is followed by scholars who are influenced by Leo Strauss; b) contradictions are only apparent: Xenophon intended to offer a wholly positive portrait of Cyrus; c) the disturbing features of Cyrus' portrait suggest that Xenophon's message is precisely to show that both benevolence and despotism are necessary for the ruling of an empire.[63]

All these approaches have some merits and solve certain issues, while leaving others open. Straussian scholars correctly grasp some problems raised by Cyrus' presentation, but they go too far when they contend that Xenophon wished the *Cyropaedia* to be conceived as a negative portrait of Cyrus. Similarly, attempts to soften contradictions seem strained, since they tend to overlook the contrast between the portrait of Cyrus and the

---

[61] Xen. *Cyr.* 1.2.1, 3.1.41, 6.1.46.
[62] Farber 1979: 499 notes only two contexts for Cyrus' ἀρετή (Xen. *Cyr.* 7.2.24, 8.1.12, 21); Tatum 1989: manipulative Cyrus; Azoulay 2004a: 310–18, Tamiolaki 2010: 289–320: asymmetrical relations; Nadon 2001: 54–60: utilitarian perspective; Breebaart 1983, Gera 1993: 285–99, Nadon 2001: 109–46: tyrannical transformation.
[63] For the first line of approach, see Newell 1981, Nadon 2001, Whidden 2007; the second line of approach is mainly advocated by Due 1989, Gray 2011: 246–90, and with some qualifications by Demont 2003 and Azoulay 2004a: 357–70. For the third line of interpretation, see Tatum 1989, Gera 1993, Danzig 2012, Sandridge 2012.

portraits of other (less ambivalent) leaders, such as, for instance, Agesilaus in the encomium or even Cyrus the Younger in the *Anabasis*. The third line of approach is reconciliatory and represents a "middle road," but it is not fully corroborated by the way Xenophon's narrative is structured. Xenophon does not provide explicit recipes for leadership and, more importantly, he presents his enterprise as a reflection (as the verbs ἐλογιζόμεθα and ἐνενοοῦμεν suggest).

It seems thus more probable that Xenophon *intended* the *Cyropaedia* to be ambivalent and hence more thought-provoking. This interpretation is supported by certain traits that pervade the work throughout and testify to its complex character. Firstly, the *Cyropaedia* contains some overtly ambiguous statements. For example, Xenophon states that the slaves called Cyrus father, "because he took care so that they remain slaves forever, without any complaint" (ὅπως ἀναμφιλόγως ἀεὶ ἀνδράποδα διατελοῖεν). This passage reveals a dubious trait of Cyrus, his tendency to perpetuate the submission of others; for this reason it has been bracketed by some editors. However, this practice finds parallels in other scenes of the work as well.[64] A similarly peculiar attribution of motives can be observed in the case of Persian commoners who followed Cyrus. Xenophon insinuates that their primary motivation was fear.[65] Yet this assertion creates a stark contrast with the inspiring speech of Cyrus that precedes their decision and essentially undermines it, by highlighting motives which are not so noble. These passages are in no case compatible with an idealized picture of Cyrus and his world.

Secondly, Xenophon often allows significant shifts of meanings in the *Cyropaedia*. A notable example concerns the term "tyranny." Tyranny was loaded with negative connotations during the Classical period. The negative nuance is represented in Mandane's speech to the young Cyrus and her worry that her son will acquire the tyrannical (instead of the kingly) *ethos* if he stays in Media. However, Xenophon himself in the proem states that "among those who attempted to exercise tyranny (ὅσοι τυραννεῖν ἐπιχειρήσαντες)" some are more successful than others. In this context, the verb τυραννεῖν does not have negative connotations: Xenophon boldly (though implicitly) flirts with the possibility that some tyrants might indeed be successful. The same goes with the term πλεονεξία (greediness/advantage), which is employed in contexts both positive and negative in the *Cyropaedia*, or the word ἔρως (strong desire), which denotes both the destructive love of Araspas for Panthea and the affection that the followers of Cyrus experience.[66] These oscillations in meaning suggest that Xenophon wished to provoke the reflection of his audience: on

---

64 Xen. *Cyr.* 8.1.44. Cf. Xen. *Cyr.* 7.5.69.
65 Xen. *Cyr.* 2.2.21.
66 Xen. *Cyr.* 1.1.1, 3.1.18: tyranny; Xen. *Cyr.* 1.6.32, 8.5.24: πλεονεξία; Xen. *Cyr.* 5.1.4–7, 5.1.24–5: ἔρως.

the possible (even potential) proximity of the king with the tyrant, on the limits and ambiguities of greediness, on the advantages and disadvantages of desire.

Thirdly, the narrative of the *Cyropaedia* is marked by tensions which cannot be easily reconciled. These do not concern only Cyrus' tyrannical profile. The emotions of those who choose to follow him are also presented as ambivalent: although on a theoretical level the love for the leader is considered the trait of success *par excellence* and is praised, in practice those who are described as loving Cyrus are only the *homotimoi* and Artabazus, his relative who desires to kiss him.[67] These tensions again provoke reflection on the difficulties of achieving virtue or gaining true friendship, when ruling an empire. It is also relevant that we find in the *Cyropaedia* competing perceptions about important issues: Cambyses and Cyrus discuss the nature of leadership, Pheraulas and Sacas converse on the topic of wealth, while Cyrus and Croesus reflect on the theme of happiness.[68] These divergent conceptions suggest that Xenophon is aware of the controversies these issues raise and wishes to present alternative theorizations about them.[69]

Overall, the *Cyropaedia* offers *a dialogic* reflection (and not an authoritative suggestion) about leadership. This is probably due to the fact that Xenophon was caught in a tension. On the one hand, he was strongly preoccupied with the topic of leadership in connection with the ruling of an empire; on the other hand, he wished to praise Cyrus precisely for ruling successfully an empire, but in front of a Greek audience who had no tradition of monarchy and had, on the contrary, constantly experienced the failures of empires. His presentation was thus "contaminated" by his (and his audience's) experiences, expectations, and prejudices. The narrative of the *Cyropaedia* exemplifies the limits of praise of a foreign (political) paradigm; at the same time it displays a high awareness of the complexities of political life in general, in which things are not only black and white. From this perspective, Cyrus' portrait is neither only positive nor only negative; it is a deliberately mixed portrait, inevitably Greek-modeled and Greek-oriented.

As a postscript to the present overview, I would like to make a brief comment on the most perplexing issue about the *Cyropaedia*, the epilogue. The epilogue of the *Cyropaedia* (chapter 8.8) illustrates the decadence of the Persian Empire after Cyrus' death. Its surprisingly sarcastic and aggressive

---

[67] Xen. *Cyr.* 8.1.47: love of the *homotimoi* towards Cyrus; Xen. *Cyr.* 1.4.27–8: Artabazus.

[68] Xen. *Cyr.* 1.6.1–44 (Cambyses and Cyrus about leadership); Xen. *Cyr.* 8.3.32–49 (Pheraulas and Sacas on wealth); Xen. *Cyr.* 7.2.9–29 (Cyrus and Croesus about happiness).

[69] For other episodes which provoke reflection in the *Cyropaedia*, see also Hobden and Tuplin 2012b: 37–9, commenting on the encounter between Cyrus and Cyaxares.

tone, which is not in tune with the rest of the work, has led some scholars to consider it a later addition or even unauthentic. The majority of scholars are currently inclined to accept its authenticity.[70] Interestingly, this section has been utilized to support conflicting interpretations of the work. For scholars who view Cyrus as a negative figure, the epilogue serves as a confirmation of the weaknesses of his paradigm and of his failure to leave a solid legacy to his descendants; conversely, scholars who defend the "ideal Cyrus" interpret the epilogue as a confirmation of his success, which proves that when the ideal leader dies, decline follows.[71] Although these approaches can be more or less convincing, they seem like applying a Procrustean method to the ancient text, in order to make it fit with modern conceptions and theories. In reality, the issue of the epilogue merits a systematic reassessment and this is another enigma that remains to be solved.[72]

Further Reading

The *Cyropaedia* is the only work of Xenophon to which five monographs have been devoted. Due 1989 studies the main themes which pervade this work and stresses the traits that promote a positive image of Cyrus. Gera 1993 focuses on Xenophon's literary debts and the Socratic background of this work, but also stresses its political dimension. This line of interpretation is followed by Sandridge 2012, who adduces more intertextual evidence from literary texts of the fifth century BC. Tatum 1989 insists on the manipulative aspect of Cyrus' character, while Nadon 2001 highlights the ambivalent traits of Cyrus' personality, to support his view that Xenophon wished to paint a negative portrait of the Persian king. Specific topics are discussed in Azoulay 2004a, and 2004b, Johnson 2005b, Pontier 2006, Gray 2010a: 327–453, Tamiolaki 2010: 283–320, and Gray 2011: 246–90. Tuplin 1990, 1996, 2010, and 2013, Sancisi-Weerdenburg 1987, and Kuhrt 2007 deal with the evidence about Persia and discuss the reliability of this

---

[70] The most notable (recent) exception is Hirsch 1985 : 91–7. Cf. also some reservations by Sancisi-Weerdenburg 1987: 127 n. 13.

[71] Gray 2011: 246–63 analyzes these two approaches and views the epilogue as confirmation of Cyrus' praise. See also Dorion 2013b. Gruen 2011: 58–65 also accepts the authenticity of the epilogue; he makes the interesting (though unverifiable) suggestion that Xenophon's severe tone is not sincere, but aims at parodying contemporary criticisms concerning Persia.

[72] This chapter benefited greatly from the valuable suggestions and guidance Michael Flower offered me during the various stages of its preparation. I am also grateful to Tim Rood and Christopher Tuplin for further comments on the revised version. I was able to conduct research and complete this chapter thanks to a fellowship I held at the Center for Hellenic Studies (Washington, DC) in spring semester 2014.

work as a historical source. Important material about Persian issues can be also found in the volumes of *Achaemenid History Workshops*. There is only one recent commentary on the *Cyropaedia*, by Mueller-Goldingen 1995. Another online commentary is being prepared by N. Sandridge (www. cyropaedia.org). A narratological commentary is clearly missing from modern scholarship. Xenophon's intertextual dialogue with contemporary and previous authors also deserves further exploration.

The main interpretive issue raised concerning the *Cyropaedia* is the extent to which its interpretation should be based on the approach of Leo Strauss, according to which Xenophon has a hidden message and writes in a cryptic way, in order to be understood by the elite few. Gray 2011: 7–68 divides readings of Xenophon into Straussian (dark) and "straightforward" (positive) and opts for the latter, but her analysis allows for refinement: scholars who discern a greater subtlety in Xenophon are not necessarily Straussian. I have offered some qualifications and an alternative classification of Xenophontic scholarship in Tamiolaki 2014b. Among the studies mentioned above the only markedly Straussian approach is that of Nadon. The line of interpretation I have outlined in the last section of this chapter takes into account some issues raised by Straussian scholars, but is not Straussian. I believe that there is more to criticize in Leo Strauss than Johnson 2012a would allow us to think, but I agree with Johnson that there is also some benefit to be gained by the study of his method: not only its merits, even if these are few, but also, I would add, its flaws and limitations.

10

JOHN DILLERY

Xenophon: the Small Works

Introduction

The organization of the old OCT five-volume set of the writings of Xenophon tells us a lot. The *Hellenica, Anabasis,* and *Cyropaedia* each get their own volume (I, III, and IV, respectively), while the longer and shorter works with Socrates as their subject make up volume II. The fifth volume is labeled *Opuscula* and contains the *Hiero, Agesilaus, Constitution of the Spartans, Poroi, Hipparchicus, De re equestri,* the *Cynegeticus,* and finally the pseudo Xenophontine *Constitution of the Athenians* (by the so-called "Old Oligarch"). Not only does the OCT collection of Xenophon demonstrate the variety of his work generally, we see also in volume V a significant range of topics in his smaller works specifically.[1] Indeed, the range could be bigger were we to allow in the smaller Socratic texts such as the *Apology, Symposium,* and even the *Oeconomicus* – though at slightly more than sixty-six pages, the last mentioned would count as the longest "short" work of Xenophon by quite a bit, with *Cyn.* coming in second at almost forty.

This quick survey prompts a number of questions: what exactly is a "short" or "minor" work, why and for whom were they written, and why did Xenophon seem to write so many of them, and all of them, as it turns out, in the last phase of his writing career? With the exception of Plato and the orators, the great prose writers before him did not write so many, and so many different types of works. It is tempting to answer my questions with an observation often made of his larger works as well: Xenophon was a restless author who clearly did not limit himself to existing genre boundaries; if he found that there were few (or, in fact, no) antecedents for what he wanted to write, that did not stop him.[2]

---

[1] Cf. Richards 1899: 346–7.

[2] The reflections on the problem of genre invention and "genre mixing" in Nicolai 2004, while focused on Isocrates, are enormously useful; see esp. Nicolai 2004: 33 for passing thoughts on Xenophon. Of greater relevance to this discussion is his enormously important paper Nicolai 2014b.

But this is only a partial explanation I think for the shorter works, and it does not account for why they are concentrated at the end of Xenophon's career. We need to address the issue of what shorter works are.

Some of Xenophon's smaller works have been called "pamphlets" (esp. *Poroi*). Others look more like manuals, or at least adopt the outlook of "how to" works (*Hipp.* and *Eq.*). Still others betray marks of generic affiliation that make them seem familiar, but either belong to what are in fact new literary forms (*Ages.*: encomium and proto-biography), or are in an already attested format but with unusual content (the *Hiero* is a dialogue, but is historical in setting, featuring the late Archaic Sicilian king Hieron I and the poet Simonides; Socrates is nowhere to be seen). All sorts of issues arise when we consider these generic types.

What, for instance, is the purpose of a "pamphlet"? It would seem to be aimed at a clearly defined contemporary audience, would concern a particular set of political circumstances, and would argue for specific measures to address those circumstances.[3] Consider, on the other hand, "manuals." They, by contrast, would seem to be aimed at a wider readership and a timeless one, even if they too betray contemporary concerns. What of works that are said to be apologetic, as is sometimes alleged for *Ages.*? Presumably apologetic works are written close to the attack upon the person concerned, or the circumstances on the basis of which an attack can be anticipated. But crucially, a defense of a deceased person need not be limited in purpose to a defense, but could also have other functions, celebratory and paradigmatic chief among these, and as such, a timeless audience would also be in play. A philosophical dialogue such as *Hiero*, itself set in time anterior to the writer's own by a century or more, and devoted to the successful and unsuccessful tyrant, would presumably be relevant at virtually any period of Greek history, if not always and in every place.

In real terms, then, what we call Xenophon's shorter works and the related matter of how and when we imagine they were read (or heard) expose important assumptions about them. I think it is also worth thinking here about the composition of the shorter works more generally. We must imagine an Athenian audience for at least two of them: *Poroi* urges ways to improve Athenian state finances, and *Hipp.* constructs its world in Athenian spaces. Beginning already in the second half of the fifth century, we can make out both motivations for the writing of short prose works at Athens

[3] Cf. Schöll 1890. Note also the title of his work: *Die Anfänge einer politischen Literatur bei den Griechen* ("The Beginnings of a Political Literature among the Greeks"). Cf. Goldhill 2002: 116.

and evidence of the works themselves.[4] Criticism of the democracy and attempts at establishing what the "ancestral constitution" was (the *patrios politeia*) had given rise to a significant body of pamphlet literature: the ps. Xenophontine *Ath. Pol.* comes to mind here, as do the manifestly politically oriented tracts P. Heid. 182 and Thrasymachus DK 85 B 1.[5] Additionally, the publication of speeches was also common, and for a variety of reasons.[6] The spectacular trial and death of Socrates obviously generated a mass of materials, as had other events connected to the period of the Thirty Tyrants and its aftermath (especially involving the politician Theramenes).[7] Closer in time to the presumed dates of the shorter works (360s–350s) are two distinct sets of texts that also have analogs in Xenophon's corpus of small works: the technical manual,[8] and what we may loosely style "royal literature."

As for manuals, Xenophon's own *Eq.* clearly refers to a like treatise by one Simon (1.1; cf. 1.3 and 11.6). Furthermore, the text *How to Survive under Siege* by Aeneas "the Tactician" is precisely contemporary with Xenophon's activity as a writer of short works, and itself refers to other treatises written by the same author;[9] in terms of genre and readership it has been linked with *Hipp.* by a recent commentator on the text.[10] In any event, a tradition of military experts lecturing at Athens can be traced at least to the visit

---

[4] See esp. Jacoby 1949: 130. While he does cite Stesimbrotus of Thasos as an early pamphlet writer, and hence a non-Athenian, his works were directed against the Athenian *arche*.

[5] On the dating and context of the "Old Oligarch," see esp. Osborne 2004: 13–14, and Marr and Rhodes 2008: 3–6 and 13–16. On P. Heid. 182, Gigante 1957: 68. For Thrasymachus, see e.g. Hansen 1984: 67; while Yunis 1997 disagrees with Hansen, his bibliography on the pamphlet tradition at Athens is enormously useful, Yunis 1997: 58 n. 2, to which should be added Wendland 1910, Wüst 1938, and Jacoby 1949. On the text climate produced by the *patrios politeia* debate, see esp. Finley 1975/1990: 34–59, Ostwald 1986: 367, and cf. Schöll 1890: 14–15. On the related issue of the publication of an approved collection of Athenian law at the end of the fifth century, see esp. Robertson 1990.

[6] See, e.g., Dover 1968: 170; Hansen 1984: 60–8 = 1989: 286–94, and note addendum on 297. Useful still is Adams 1912. Note that Jacoby can claim "that the political speeches of Isocrates are actually pamphlets": Jacoby 1949: 131.

[7] P. Mich. Inv. 5982, the so-called Theramenes Papyrus (Merkelbach and Youtie 1968), together with Lys. 12.69, led Andrewes to posit "a polemical pamphlet in defence of Theramenes" (Andrewes 1970: 37); Lys. 12.77 seems also to suggest the availability of Theramenes' speeches. Many accept Andrewes's suggestion (e.g. Rhodes 1981: 22 with n. 132; cf. 368), others do not (e.g. as Rhodes notes, Sealey 1975; see also the important paper Loftus 2000). For excellent overviews: Engels 1993a and 1993b.

[8] Cf. Vela Tejada 2004.

[9] Whitehead 1990: 8–9 (date: early 350s); from refs. in *How to Survive under Siege* we know Aeneas wrote between two and four other works: Whitehead 1990: 13–16 and 37.

[10] Whitehead 1990: 35–6.

of Dionysodorus referred to by Xenophon (*Mem.* 3.1.1) and (presumably) by Plato (*Euthd.* 273 a–d).[11] On the basis of *Mem.* 4.2.10, in a reported conversation between Socrates and Euthydemus, it appears that handbooks on medicine, architecture, mathematics, astronomy, and *rhapsodia* were all available.[12]

As for "royal literature," I mean the explosion of texts in the fourth century that purported to be letters written to actual monarchs or were other sorts of short works written about them, often encomiastic. Isocrates' several open letters to the Cypriot kings as well as to Philip of Macedon come to mind here; in fact, Speusippus also penned a letter to Philip (*Socr. Ep.* 30),[13] as did Theopompus concerning Hermias of Atarneus (*FGrH* 115 F 250 = Did. *in D.* 5.23–30 Pearson-Stephens).[14] While the authorship of the Platonic epistles is hotly contested, that the majority were at least written in the manner of Plato and in roughly his lifetime is widely accepted;[15] they include several letters to Sicilian dynasts (Dionysius, Dion), as well as one to Philip's predecessor, Perdiccas III, and one to Hermias (and others). A tradition concerning Hermias grew up immediately after his death in 341, and included an epigram and hymn by Aristotle; it was evidently a rich one, featuring both encomia and diatribes by many hands.[16] While the *Hiero* is still something of an outlier, featuring as it does a temporally remote as well as fictitious interaction between the king and Simonides, these texts do provide a parallel to the dialogue insofar as they are in essence records of communications between sage figure and monarch. As for Xenophon's *Ages.*, it is of course routinely paired with Isocrates' own (slightly earlier?) royal encomium, the *Evagoras*.[17]

All this is to say that Xenophon's *opuscula* joined a bustling and ever-increasing crowd of smaller prose works in the later part of the fifth and first half of the fourth century, especially, but not exclusively, centering on Athens.[18] Further, it is important to see that while we can find parallels for almost each of the small works of Xenophon, no one author can

---

[11] Cf. Delatte 1933: 7–17; Whitehead 1990: 34–5.

[12] Cf. Asper 2007: 50 and n. 277.

[13] See Markle 1976: 92–7.

[14] With Flower 1994: 86.

[15] Cf. Irwin 1992: 78–9 n. 4; in general, Guthrie 1978: 399–401. Hackforth 1913: 188 takes a different view (spurious letters much later).

[16] See in general Ford 2011: 9–26; also Wormell 1935; Ostwald and Lynch 1994: 621. On the popularity of the tradition: see esp. Did. *in D.* 4.60–5 Pearson-Stephens.

[17] So, e.g., Breitenbach 1967: 1639; Momigliano 1993: 50.

[18] As will be seen immediately below, there was a tradition of *politeiai* at Sparta in the fourth century. See next note.

rival him for the range of topics he covered with them. It is time to look at the works themselves.

Part 1: Sparta and Kings

Lacedaemonion Politeia *(Constitution of the Spartans)*

It comes as something of a shock I think for those accustomed to suppose that writing about the "ancestral constitution" was something of an Athenian monopoly in the late fifth and fourth centuries that, when Xenophon set down to write his *Lac. Pol.*, at least two and possibly three earlier pamphlet *politeiai* of Sparta were already in existence.[19] According to Ephorus, as preserved in a badly garbled section of Strabo, the Agiad king Pausanias had written one while in exile in the later 390s (*FGrH* 70 F 118 = Str. 8.5.5). According to Aristotle, Thibron had written another (Arist. *Pol.* 1333b18), close to that of Pausanias if not before it, and composed in identical circumstances (if this Thibron is the Spartan general of the same name).[20] Since Aristotle states that Thibron's was but one of a group of such texts, it is perhaps reasonable to suppose that the tradition of Spartan *politeiai* was quite robust by Aristotle's time. Though only one of two non-Spartans to write such a text until Aristotle's time,[21] in other ways Xenophon's authorship is not a surprise. An "insider" at Sparta, Xenophon knows and reports things about Sparta that no other non-Spartan does: his account of the Cinadon incident alone, found at *Hell.* 3.3.4–11, is not only a window into a highly sensitive internal matter at Sparta concerning its underclasses, it also famously contains references to Spartan institutions found no where else.[22] Responsibility for a *Lac. Pol.* seems a reasonable, even logical line on Xenophon's CV.

While it is impossible to date Xenophon's *Lac. Pol.* precisely, many would place the work, as with so many of the other shorter works of Xenophon,

---

[19] See esp. Jacoby 1949: 386 n. 53; Breitenbach 1967: 1747; David 1979; Cartledge 1987: 163; Millender 2001: 124–5; Tober 2010. Millender discusses the notorious speech of Lysander on the Spartan constitution (evidence: Millender 2001: 124 n. 9), which, if it was ever formally written up for broader consumption, would also have also constituted another *politeia* pamphlet.

[20] See recently Millender 2001: 125 n. 14.

[21] The other being Critias, who wrote two, one in prose and one in verse (DK 88 B 32–7 and 6–9, respectively).

[22] References to "lower-grade Spartans" (*hypomeiones*, *Hell.* 3.3.6) and the so-called "Little Assembly" (*mikra ekklesia*, 3.3.8) are unique.

in the 360s.[23] There is no one internal piece of data that locates the treatise in time. However, the general perspective of the work argues for a tract conceived and written after a major challenge to Spartan hegemony. In the notorious chapter 14 Xenophon laments that "the laws of Lycurgus" have not remained "unaltered" or even "undisturbed" (ἀκίνητοι 14.1), that the Spartans no longer conduct themselves in accordance with their requirements, and that as a result the Greeks, who used beg that the Spartans lead them against those who seemed to be doing wrong, were now "encouraging each other to prevent them from ever ruling again" (14.6). Such a sentiment seems to fit best in a period after the battle of Leuctra (371) but before that of Mantinea (362).

Ch. 14 is "notorious" because it is so out of keeping with the rest of the essay, and hence has been viewed by some as inauthentic. Arguments in favor of keeping it in the treatise point to the parallel with *Cyr.* 8.8: there too we find a seemingly unmotivated assertion, very much at odds with the tenor of the rest of the work, that highlights the descent of an ancient society (in this case, Persia) from an ideal past to a compromised present, with wealth and imperialism again serving as the culprits for societal deterioration.[24] In fact, even if not exactly cases of a volte-face in quite the same way as in *Lac. Pol.* 14 and *Cyr.* 8.8, we see in other of Xenophon's work from this same period indications that cherished beliefs about the past and the future were souring for him.[25]

One point that is worth drawing out here is the timing of the *Lac. Pol.*, especially in connection with ch.14. It is argued that the central point of the earlier *politeiai* pamphlets of King Pausanias and Thibron was the claim that the Lycurgan constitution, while excellent in design, was no longer followed or had been irreparably damaged by wrongheaded additions (notably the Ephorate).[26] Xenophon's work could be said to fall precisely into line with this perspective. On the matter of the establishment of the Ephorate, Xenophon is notably ambiguous, suggesting that he had to tread lightly: at 4.3 he seems to assume they were part of the Lycurgan settlement, but at 8.3 he states that it was "likely" (εἰκός) that powerful citizens whose opinion Lycurgus had first won over (cf. 8.1) helped him in setting up the Ephorate (8.3).[27] The earlier treatises, however, all date to the 390s, not the 360s.

---

[23] E.g. Breitenbach 1967: 1751–3; Gray 2007: 42–3 (esp. 43: "[a] date in the 360s BC is probable"). Though note Lipka 2002: 11–12, who takes Leuctra as a *terminus ante quem*, and proposes a date in 395 or 394.

[24] Cf. Dillery 1995: 257–8 n. 35 for further bibliography and discussion. See now esp. Gray 2007: 217–21 for a recent treatment of the problems of *Lac. Pol.* 14.

[25] Cf. Grayson 1975: 34–5; Dillery 1995: 15–16 with notes.

[26] David 1979; Cartledge 1987: 163.

[27] Note Lipka 2002: 23–4 and esp. 170–1 ad 8.3.

The older treatise of Pausanias faulted in particular the imperialist agenda of Lysander; while King Agesilaus famously managed to outmaneuver Lysander, that did not stop him from pursuing a similar policy, one with which Agesilaus became closely associated. Hence, at Sparta the target of a work such as the *Lac. Pol.* would have been unmistakable: the "Hawks," whose chief advocate and champion was indisputably Agesilaus. The genre of Spartan *politeiai* could not but have made the affinities between Lysander's leadership and that of Agesilaus crystal clear.[28]

One final point is worth making about the *Lac. Pol.* here. Xenophon begins his work abruptly as though in the middle of a thought.[29] He suggests that the treatise was the result of a moment of reflection on his part: "now at some point having taken thought ..." (ἀλλ᾽ ἐγὼ ἐννοήσας ποτέ, 1.1). The thought that preoccupied him was the paradox that the most sparsely populated polis became the most powerful and noteworthy in Greece. He characterizes his next step as puzzlement: "I wondered in what possible way did this happen" (ἐθαύμασα ὅτῳ ποτὲ τρόπῳ τοῦτ᾽ ἐγένετο). When he "took notice of the customs" (κατενόησα τὰ ἐπιτηδεύματα) of the Spartans (note again the *nous* concept), he no longer wondered. Xenophon begins several of his other works, longer and shorter, in precisely the same way, and with some of the same language.[30] These opening sentiments create the sense of "occasionality," and thus are especially appropriate for smaller works, written (or creating the impression that they were written) as the immediate response of a thoughtful man to the puzzles of his age. More generally, the framing of all Xenophon's works that begin in this manner suggest a desire on his part to "anatomize" his thought processes – something that I think is unusual in other prose authors, though is not at all unparalleled.

---

[28] Momigliano argued that since much attention is placed on kingship in ch.15, the chapter after 14, and that the focus is on *sunthekai* not *nomoi* there, Xenophon was sparing Agesilaus his negative critique: Momigliano 1936a: 170–3 = 1966: 1.341–5. This seems too elaborate to me: cf. Dillery 1995: 258 n. 35.

[29] Acutely noted already by Richards 1897: 236: "The abrupt X[enophontea]n beginning should be noticed. He likes beginning as though he were continuing."

[30] Consider *Cyr.* 1.1.1 "the thought occurred to me once how many democracies have been brought down ..." (ἔννοια ποθ᾽ ἡμῖν ἐγένετο ὅσαι δημοκρατίαι κατελύθησαν); *Mem.* 1.1.1 "I often wondered with what possible arguments the indicters of Socrates persuaded the Athenians ..." (πολλάκις ἐθαύμασα τίσι ποτὲ λόγοις Ἀθηναίους ἔπεισαν οἱ γραψάμενοι Σωκράτην); *Por.* 1.1–2 is a more complex reconstruction of Xenophon's thinking but results in the same "occasional" reflection (note esp. 1.2: "now to me thinking about what I noted ..." [σκοποῦντι δή μοι ἃ ἐπενόησα]). Cf. Gauthier 1976: 44–5 ad loc. (who compares the language of *Por.* 1.2 with *Lac. Pol.* 1.1); also Gray 2007: 147 ad *Lac. Pol.* 1.1 on ἐθαύμασα, noting the similarity with *Mem.* 1.1.1. Richards 1897: 236 adds the start of the *Smp.*

Agesilaus

This is a good place to think in more detail about Xenophon's encomium of Agesilaus. If ch. 14 of *Lac. Pol.* and the tradition of Spartan *politeiai* encourage us to see that work as critical of the Spartans in general and quite possibly Agesilaus in particular, how can we reconcile the production of this work with Xenophon's composition of an encomium of the same king – a work with very probably a diametrically opposite *Tendenz*? This is precisely the advantage of writing small works. Being as it were freestanding and multiple, they do not have to take account of views expressed by Xenophon elsewhere that may be at odds with what he wants to say on any given present occasion. Indeed, since significant sections of narrative in the *Ages.* are also found (with minor but significant differences) in the *Hell.*, one could say that the problem of the orientation of the *Ages.* relative to that work is even more acute than when we compare it to the *Lac. Pol.*

The *Ages.* is very much a work about retelling: not only does it duplicate important bits from *Hell.*, it tells its own story of Agesilaus twice, or arguably three times, over.[31] Xenophon often seems compelled to rephrase or recast. The retelling of the *Ages.* comes about because of a major structural division that occurs at slightly beyond the midpoint of the work. Having presented the king's life in roughly linear, chronological fashion over the first half (the long chs. 1 and 2), Xenophon shifts gears at the start of ch. 3, at which point he comments serially on the many virtues of Agesilaus, each virtue receiving its own chapter, until he reaches ch. 11, where he wraps up with an epigrammatic revisiting of all the king's virtues in summary form.[32]

Unusually, considering the other short works of Xenophon, we can be pretty sure of the date of the *Ages.*: the text alludes to Agesilaus' death (10.3), which we know occurred in 360, during his participation in the revolt of Tachos in Egypt. The *Ages.* is thought to have appeared shortly after.[33] In the same section where Xenophon mentions Agesilaus' death, he engages in an important "revaluation of terms" regarding what he thinks he has achieved in the work: "but let no one think that, because one who has died is being praised (ἐπαινεῖται), on account of this fact the present work is a 'lament' (θρῆνον); rather, much more, it is a 'laudation' (ἐγκώμιον)." The trope is immediately recognizable. We can compare the famous ode of Simonides on the dead of Thermopylae (*PMG* 531 = Diod. 11.11.6), where

---

[31] Pontier 2010; cf. Luppino Manes 1991: 16–20. For a modern study with multiple retellings of Agesilaus' life, see the splendid volume: Cartledge 1987 (with explanation of his method at viii–ix).

[32] Cf. Breitenbach's schema 1967: 1702.

[33] Breitenbach 1967: 1702.

the poet insists upon the conversion of sorrowful concepts into positive ones that also evoke permanence through time: the "fate" of Leonidas and his men is "renowned," their "doom" "beautiful"; their "tomb" becomes an "altar"; instead of "groaning" there is "memory"; and "pity" for them is transformed into "praise."[34]

Xenophon explains his appropriation of the key terms of laudation of the dead (*threnos, epainos, enkomion*) by collapsing the terms together. His first justification for what he has done is that the words he now uses in praise of Agesilaus were ones the king heard in his lifetime: "inasmuch as he was hearing [these praises] while alive, these ones also now are spoken about him" (10.3), namely, in Xenophon's treatise. This is a crucial and clever move by Xenophon because it allows him to present his praise of Agesilaus as uncontroversial: no apology is needed here because the facts of Agesilaus' life are not in dispute; they were agreed upon already as a matter of record, established during the life of the king by those who witnessed his actions – and not, by implication, the unsupported assertions of a friend and client. But of course 10.3 is precisely special pleading by Xenophon and runs squarely against the view that glorious death helps to erase the bad that men have done (cf. Thuc. 2.42.3).[35] The *Ages.* is in fact apology, but Xenophon is disguising the fact.

The chief ways Xenophon makes his defense of Agesilaus are through a highly selective narrative in the first part of the treatise and removing altogether any substantial historical context in the second. This brings me to address directly the issue of the *Ages.* and its "retellings." As I have already pointed out, externally the *Ages.* retells portions of the *Hell.*; internally, the king's life is viewed diachronically or kinetically in the historical section, and then retold in synchronic form through "snapshots" in the second section on his virtues. Since we can date the *Ages.* fairly precisely to shortly after the king's death in 360, and usually put the final writing up of the second, larger portion of the *Hell.* in the decade following, it seems reasonable to conclude that the *Ages.* was published first and the *Hell.* (as we have it now) later.

---

[34] εὐκλεὴς μὲν ἁ τύχα, καλὸς δ' ὁ πότμος,ǀ βωμὸς δ' ὁ τάφος, πρὸ γόων δὲ μνᾶστις, ὁ δ' οἶκτος ἔπαινος. Parsons 2001: 64 (a "revaluation of terms" is his phrase); also Boedeker 2001: 158–9. Cf. Dillery 1996: 248. In the same volume, Aloni 2001: 98 n. 47 raises a very useful matter in connection with the Plataea Elegy of Simonides, disputing Loraux 1986: 49–50, who seems to imply there that a *threnos* cannot admit any celebratory element. On the question of *threnos, epainos,* and *enkomion,* see esp. Ford 2011: 69–90.

[35] I would further note that the Thucydidean counterexample from the Funeral Oration of Pericles comes from a section that is also concerned with establishing proof for the *eulogia* of the war dead (Thuc. 2.42.1) and is also clearly indebted to the language of eulogy and hymn: see Gomme 1956: 130–1 ad loc.; Kakridis 1961: 64 and Hornblower 1991/2008: 1.308–9 ad Thuc. 2.41.3.

Of course, this does not rule out that Xenophon may have adapted already existing narrative from an unfinished *Hell.* in his composition of the *Ages.*

At the microlevel of word choice and sentence construction, the passages of the *Ages.* that are also found in the *Hell.* tend to have poetic terms where the *Hell.* has prosaic ones, are written with an eye on prose rhythm and the avoidance of hiatus, and demonstrate an even greater attention towards rhetorical figures than is found in the historical work.[36] At the larger level of material included or excluded, practically no references that could reflect badly on Agesilaus are permitted in the *Ages.* Now, there are several places in the *Ages.* where the posture of criticism or doubt is taken, but these have been shown by Elroy Bundy to be merely "foils," opportunities typical of encomia designed in fact to allow for expansion on the excellences of the honorand: "it is possible to state without fear of contradiction that Agesilaus was brave, but he did not perhaps choose the safest course of action" (2.12), and so on.[37] I would argue, though, that something altogether different is going on at *Ages.* 2.21: making explicit reference to Agesilaus' forced repatriations of pro-Spartan exiles on Corinth prior to the King's Peace of 387 and on Phlius in 381, Xenophon can imagine that some may criticize Agesilaus, but that these actions were done out of a sense of "attachment to his friends" (φιλεταιρία). As *Hell.* 5.3.16 famously makes abundantly clear, this was not, or not only, a theoretical objection, for there were "many Spartans" saying precisely this about the Phliasians: that "for the sake of a few men they were incurring the hatred of a city of more than 5,000 citizens." Why permit this puncturing of the encomiastic fabric in this way, so unlike the posturings elsewhere in the treatise of faux-objections so acutely observed by Bundy? *Ages.* 2.21 is categorically different.[38]

We must I think conclude that not only was Xenophon thinking he must engage with such criticisms, thus making the *Ages.* in some sense apologetic (a point most grant), but also at a fundamental level its accounting of Agesilaus' activities was conceived by Xenophon as a riposte to another possible treatment of the king. A competing view is thus acknowledged, making the compartmentalizing of the *Ages.* as "encomium" and therefore as something utterly separate from "history" unsustainable.[39] Although Xenophon is policing the boundary between the two forms, the *Ages.* is not

[36] Note esp. Opitz 1913: 3–35; also Bigalke 1933: 14–15; Henry 1967: 128 (summarizing Opitz's findings).

[37] Bundy 1986: 40 and nn. 14 and 15; he cites, in addition to *Ages.* 2.12, also 2.25, 5.6, and 8.7.

[38] As noted even by Beck 2001: 369 n. 71, otherwise skeptical of my approach. Cf. Cartledge 1987: 262; Dillery 1995: 211.

[39] I am thus in fundamental disagreement with Schepens 2005: 47.

encomium written in a vacuum nor does it completely occlude the historical; indeed, it is to some extent shaped by the historical record insofar as it seems conceived of as a response.

Let me cite a pair of especially illustrative cases of places where the *Ages.* and *Hell.* cover (or seem to cover) the same ground. At *Ages.* 1.38 we are told that the Greeks in Asia not only mourned Agesilaus' departure, they actually went with him voluntarily (ἐθελούσιοι) back to Greece, knowing that they would be fighting men no lesser than they (namely other Greeks and no longer effete Persians). The story is told to emphasize Agesilaus' capacity to generate loyalty among his men (a favorite Xenophontean theme). A glance at the parallel scene in the *Hell.* provides a startlingly different view: "seeing that many of the soldiers were wishing to remain [in Asia] rather than go on an expedition against Greeks," Agesilaus devised a set of incentives to help with his recruitment of troops (*Hell.* 4.2.5 – another favorite subject of Xenophon's). Granted, we see here a similar nod to Agesilaus' leadership abilities, but in the service of getting men reluctant to leave Asia to fight other Greeks! Again, in the same historical context (though from the virtue section of the *Ages.*), when Agesilaus learns of the Spartan victory at Nemea in 394, involving the deaths nearly ten thousand "enemy" but only eight Spartans, the king produces an epigrammatic lament traceable to the sentiments of Gorgias and aligned with the rhetoric of panhellenism: "Alas for you, O Hellas, when the ones now dead were sufficient while alive to defeat in combat all the barbarians!" (*Ages.* 7.5).[40] In the *Hell.* (4.3.2), when given a report of the same battle, Xenophon shows an Agesilaus who is much more ambiguous, calculating whether the news should be brought to the cities in Asia that had contributed troops to his army; and noticeably absent is any Panhellenic lament.

To be sure, we have two different genres in the *Ages.* and *Hell.*, and should not expect them to tell the same stories in the same ways. Furthermore, we do not and can not know how Xenophon thought his writings would interact for subsequent audiences: *pace* the Straussian reader, I do not think we are always authorized to read any given passage of Xenophon against another. But when two works from his pen concern the same man's reactions to the same report of the same event, that is a different matter. I think we are beyond Straussian hair-splitting here. The resulting view need not mean that Xenophon's characterization of Agesilaus was insincere in the *Ages.* But given that the traditional dating of *Ages.* and *Hell.* puts the encomium

---

[40] Compare Gorgias DK 82 B 5b = Philostr. *VS* 1.9.5. Cf. Dillery 1995: 117–18. I acknowledge here that I unintentionally misrepresented the *Hell.* passage, but the larger point I think was and is still valid.

first, that makes the *Hell.*'s version of Agesilaus' life the revision – the final retelling. Such a situation cannot but have made a re-evaluation of the *Ages.* to some extent inevitable.

Hiero

It is time I moved on to the *Hiero.* Though a dialogue, it does not feature Socrates, rather Hieron I of Syracuse and the poet Simonides. I assume this will have been a bold choice on the part of a man who identified himself as a Socratic. To reach back instead in time to a remoter period and to people a dialogue with historical persons of major significance and noto-riety seems a remarkable move. It has been suggested that since the *Hiero* treats a very un-Socratic topic – the happiness of the tyrant – so Socrates is himself absent, just as he is from the similarly un-Socratic *Laws* of Plato.[41] Since Plato is in fact interested in whether the tyrannical man or an actual tyrant can be truly happy, and discusses the matter in dialogues in which Socrates is prominently featured (esp. the *Republic*, e.g. 566d–69c, 578c),[42] this suggestion does not get us very far. Still others have observed that the thought world reflected in the *Hiero* is not really early fifth-century Sicily, but fourth-century Athens, in particular as is felt in ch. 9, and thus aligns the work with the *Poroi.*[43]

Vivienne Gray has drawn our attention to a text that may go a long way towards accounting for, if not fully explaining, Xenophon's choice of Hieron and Simonides as the interlocutors of the dialogue.[44] In [Plato] *Epistle* 2.310e5–311b6, the author states that "wisdom" and "great power" are wont to come together in the same place; they seek each other out, and men enjoy talking about the pair, as well as hearing others discourse about them, both "in private gatherings" and in "poetry." The author then cites particular examples: "such as happens regarding Hieron, when people discuss him and Pausanias the Spartan, they like to bring forward also the companionship of Simonides." Other pairings are then mentioned: Periander and Thales, Pericles and Anaxagoras, Croesus and Solon "as wise men, and Cyrus as dynast." Since we know neither the date nor the authorship of *Ep.* 2, it is possible that its notice of Hieron and Simonides is due to a

---

[41] Hirzel 1895: 1.170–1; cf. Aalders 1953: 213–14.
[42] Indeed, see already Grote 1872: 2.403 n. 3.
[43] Hatzfeld 1946: 57; cf. Aalders 1953: 209 and n. 2: they draw particular notice to *Hier.* 9.4: "whenever we wish choruses to compete, the *archon* puts up the prizes, but it is assigned to *choregoi* to gather them [i.e. the choruses] and to others to instruct and apply 'necessity' to the ones performing anything insufficiently." Cf. Csapo and Slater 1994: 358–9 (IV.300).
[44] Gray 2007: 31.

knowledge of Xenophon's *Hiero*. But if it was not due to such knowledge, then it would show that there was a tradition separate from Xenophon that thought of Simonides and Hieron as a typical sage/ruler pair discussing the nature of happiness and power. At the very least, the epistle shows that the pairing fits neatly into a recognizable ancient tradition.[45] Indeed, in this context it is tempting to venture the guess that Xenophon was inspired by Plato's interest in the Sicilian tyrannies, but sought out an older, historically plausible pairing to discuss contemporary matters of acute interest to him, namely the nature of autocratic power.

It is tempting to think of the *Hiero* as a sort of enacted exchange of advisory epistles, such as one sees in the corpora of Isocrates and others whom I mentioned above. It is illuminating to note that some sixty years or so after the *Hiero* appeared Demetrius of Phalerum wrote a dialogue entitled *Ptolemy* (D.L. 5.81 = *FGrH* 228 T 1).[46] But we are of course still dealing, with this parallel and the epistolary analogues, with contemporary figures. *Hiero* is unusual in this context both because it is a historical pairing and because for the first half of the treatise, the ruler actually has the upper hand, the interlocutor who corrects and speaks from knowledge.

It is important to observe that the literary treatment of the encounter of sage and monarch was not new when Xenophon made it the subject of the *Hiero*; Herodotus had memorably staged the meeting of Solon and Croesus towards the start of his *History*, even featuring a dialogue between them (with Solon doing most of the talking of course). In point of fact, Xenophon does something quite similar to Herodotus, indeed in deliberate imitation of him, in the *Cyr.*, where he has Croesus and Cyrus the Great discuss the post-capture settlement of Sardis and, later, the nature of wealth (*Cyr.* 7.2.9–29 and 8.2.15–23). What is striking about both these passages from the *Cyr.* is that Xenophon has reversed the dynamic of the sage and ruler encounter that we see in Herodotus: the figure in the "driver's seat," the one who gets to dispense most of the wisdom, is the ruler, not the sage, with Cyrus not infrequently speaking words almost identical to ones Herodotus gives to sage figures in his text.[47]

Xenophon pursues a similar line in the first (slightly larger) portion of the dialogue (*Hier.* 1.1–7.13), with Hieron discoursing at length on the nightmare

---

[45] Cf. Gray 2007: 31: "*Hiero* comes from a literary tradition of meetings between the wise and powerful," and follows this up with a translation of the passage from *Ep.* 2.

[46] Hirzel 1895: 1.318 and n. 1.

[47] Cf. Lefèvre 1971/2010; Gray 2007: 32. See also Tatum 1989: 149; Gera 1993: 265–9; Due 1989: 89. I should also point out here that commanders and kings are often given sage-like advice in the *Hell.*, even in dialogue with others (e.g. Agesilaus and Otys in Paphlagonia, *Hell.* 4.1.5–15).

world that autocratic power creates for the strongman (an old topos of course: cf., e.g., Otanes at Hdt. 3.80). The second part (8.1–end) is taken up mostly with Simonides' attempt at showing how the tyrant need not be trapped in a solitary and violent inhumanity if he employs an approach to leadership that one finds in a number of other works of Xenophon: the generation of loyal, willing obedience among the leader's subordinates. Simonides' vision is of a "reformed tyrant."[48] Two points are worth drawing out here. First, that there is a marked division in the work, where it moves from Hieron as lead speaker to Simonides. Similarly, *Ages.* shifts gears too, from narrative to summary of Agesilaus' virtues; and there are strong thematic caesurae also to be felt in *Lac. Pol.* (as we have seen) and *Cyn.* (as we will see).

Second, and perhaps a more important point, the Simonidean treatment of tyranny in the *Hiero*, in which the poet seeks to restore the tyrant from his aporetic despair regarding what he takes to be the built-in and thus permanent shortcomings of autocratic power, constitutes a major bridge to other of Xenophon's works and is also a significant outlining, *avant la lettre*, of Hellenistic kingship. Basically, the tyrant of Simonides' (and Xenophon's) vision is to understand the project of ruling as divided into two parts: "teaching (τὸ διδάσκειν) the people" and (in our modern business parlance) "incentivizing" them to proper and profitable behavior should be the task of the ruler himself (*Hier.* 9.2), whereas he should delegate the coercive aspect of ruling to "others" (9.3). Mercenaries should serve not just as the personal bodyguard of the ruler, they should protect the whole community (10.4); the ruler should even use his own property to benefit the "common good" (11.1). In other words, to some extent there should be an identification of the interests of the ruler and his community; not the vicious predator of his own people (the traditional view of the tyrant), what violence has to be done to them in the name of censure or coercion is to be done by "others." The ruler and his state thus become a single entity, and compete with other states in a grand political athletic competition, with the ruler the main antagonist (see esp. *Hier.* 11.7–9). This vision, to my eyes, new and prescient, for it looks quite like how the Hellenistic rulers thought about themselves and what they were doing.[49]

[48] Cf. Gray 2007: 36 and n. 13, and now the massive treatment of Gaile-Irbe 2011.
[49] Cf. Dillery 2015: 14. Of course precious little remains of political theory regarding Hellenistic kingship, with the exception of the *Letter of Aristeas* (Murray 1967). For an excellent general study: Ma 2003.

Part 2: The Technical Treatises: Cavalry Command, Horsemanship, Hunting

Hipparchicus *(The Cavalry Commander)*

The *Hipp.* was written probably quite late in Xenophon's career, though seemingly before the *Eq.* (cf. *Eq.* 12.14).[50] It aims to instruct the cavalry commander in his duties, but is also an argument in favor of bolstering the cavalry arm of the Athenian military, and in this aspiration similar in spirit to the *Poroi*.[51] The didactic register that was implicit in Simonides' remarks to Hieron ("if you're willing to listen, this is how you should rule") is made explicit in the *Hipp.* A technical work[52] – a "how to" of sorts – it begins very suddenly with an injunction, but not, I think, the sort someone would expect from a military handbook:

> First it is necessary through sacrifice to ask the gods to grant that you think, speak, and do those things on the basis of which you would command in a manner most pleasing to the gods, and most agreeably, with greatest acclaim, and most usefully for yourself, your friends, and your city. (1.1)

The work ends in a similar way, even noting this time that the position Xenophon is promoting will surprise his audience. Anticipating that someone might wonder (θαυμάζει) why it has been often enjoined in the treatise "to work with god" (τὸ σὺν θεῷ πράττειν), Xenophon explains that should such a person take note (κατανοῇ) of the uncertainty of war, he would realize that the only sure proof against this world of heightened contingency is guidance from the divine (9.8–9).[53] Observe that the "noticing" that normally belongs to Xenophon in his programmatic passages is here attributed to another.[54]

If this beginning and end do not seem very "technical," they are morally didactic and are of a piece with Xenophon's views expressed elsewhere, including comments concerning his own actions in the *Anab.* – indeed the language at *Anab.* 5.6.28, where the character Xenophon explains his frequent sacrificing to determine the gods' will, is strikingly similar to *Hipp.* 1.1.[55] Human life in general and warfare in particular are fraught with uncertainty in Xenophon's mind and the advice of the gods is crucial for anyone who seeks to promote his own interests and those of his friends and community in such a world.[56]

---

[50] Breitenbach 1967: 1763: dates it between 366 and 362? Gauthier 1984: 199 = 2010: 135 around 360?

[51] Cf. Gauthier 1984: 199 = 2010: 135.

[52] Cf. Vela Tejada 2004: 141.

[53] Cf. Althoff 2005: 237–8.

[54] See above, n. 30.

[55] Dillery 1995: 183.

[56] Compare, e.g. *Mem.* 1.3.1–4 and 1.4; *Cyr.* 1.6.44–6, *Smp.* 4.48–9, *Ages.* 1.13/*Hell.* 3.4.11. See also Dillery 1995: 225–7.

So rather than seeing this "bookending" of the *Hipp.* as perhaps confounding our expectations of what a technical treatise should say, we should see that the issues of leadership, even highly technical ones and ones that concern smaller commands, are fundamentally the same as those of kings and military leaders of great armies: they are not just practical matters, but are ultimately moral ones in which the gods take acute interest and in which their foreknowledge is of immense use. It is illuminating to consider in this context that the subject matter and tone of the *Hipp.* are virtually duplicated in the *Mem.* in Socrates' discussion with a nameless young man who had recently been chosen to be a hipparch at Athens (*Mem.* 3.3.1ff.).[57]

Three points are worth making about the *Hipp.* First, as with elements of the *Hiero*, the imagined world of the treatise is again Athens – indeed, even more so. So, for instance, at *Hipp.* 7.1 the office of hipparch is assumed as being that "of the Athenians," and at 3.1 the military reviews that he must undertake are referred to as those held "in the Academy, the Lyceum, at Phalerum, and in the Hippodrome."[58] Second, in connection with these processions (*pompai*) in particular, one can see with great clarity the thinking behind the concept of the utility of public display, whereby community aspirations are communicated by its elite members acting in concert under the leadership of a charismatic individual. As we saw in parts of the characterization of the reformed monarch in the *Hiero*, it is hard not to see significant Hellenistic societal features adumbrated in these sections of the *Hipp.* concerning processions.[59]

Finally, there is the tension, already mentioned, between what we may crudely style the "practical" and the "ideal." As with Greek didactic works going back to Hesiod, because a text is written as a work of instruction, that does not necessarily mean that that is the only way it was meant to be read. Indeed, in certain ways it is tempting to view the *Hipp.* as "aspirational,"

[57] See esp. Delatte 1933: 32–46.
[58] Stoll 2010 and 2012. Mention of the "herms" as the starting point for a procession through the Agora (*Hipp.* 3.2) is powerfully confirmed by finds in the Agora that include a number of statue bases, inscriptions, and a horde of lead tokens giving the values of cavalrymen's horses, dating to the mid part of the fourth century: Kroll 1977: 83–84; cf. Bugh 1988: 54–8. I note that Bugh treats the *Hipp.* throughout his book as a documentary source for the realities of cavalry service in Athens. Relatedly, Gauthier goes so far as to assume that Xenophon returned to Athens from his exile on the basis of *Hipp.* 3.2–7 and 9.6 (Gauthier 1984: 199 n. 26 = 2010: 135 n .26), passages that do imply close familiarity with Athens, but do not I think require Xenophon's presence there.
[59] Dillery 2004, following the lead of Walbank 1996 = Walbank 2002: 79–90.

even utopian, rather than by the binary of "practical" or "ideal." In the fourth century, cavalry did not typically carry out major combat functions in Greek armies; they were used instead for the scouting and harassment of the enemy. On the other hand, unusually Athens and a few other areas in the Greek world did employ cavalry units on a considerable scale[60] – indeed Xenophon's own son Gryllus was killed in combat while serving in an Athenian cavalry contingent before the battle of Mantinea in 362.[61] So Xenophon was looking to bolster a military arm at Athens that was most assuredly real. And yet, one still senses that the picture we see in the *Hipp.* of cavalry activity and (still more) of the leadership provided by the ideal hipparch was of a world he desperately wanted to see but that had not yet been (nor would ever be) realized.[62] We shall see the same dynamic in connection with the *Poroi.*

De re equestri *(On Horsemanship)*

Again, as with the *Hipp.*, we jump right in at the start, but the tone is less one of a didactic voice and more one of advice. The Xenophon of the *Eq.* sounds very like the Socratic horse trainer one seems to hear endlessly about in Plato (e.g. *Apology* 20a7, 25b14).

> Since, as it has turned out (διὰ τὸ συμβῆναι) that we have been riding horses for a long time we think that we have become knowledgeable in the art of horsemanship (οἰόμεθα ἔμπειροι ἱππικῆς γεγενῆσθαι), we wish also to make clear to the younger ones of our friends in what way we think they would most correctly deal with horses. (1.1)

The periphrases in the opening line that explain why Xenophon has to write a treatise on *hippike techne* are remarkable: it "has turned out" that he has ridden a lot, and so he "believes" he has become *empeiros* – knowledgeable through experience – in the art of horsemanship. The opening words are not those of an confident narrator laying down a set of "thou shalts," such as

---

[60] Garlan 1994: 681.

[61] D.L. 2.54, Paus. 1.3.4, and 8.11.6; Xenophon famously omits Gryllus' name at *Hell.* 7.5.17 when he tells us that "good men" were among the Athenians who fell on that occasion. Cf. Dillery 1995: 253–4. I note that the painting of Gryllus and Epaminondas by Euphranor in the Stoa Poikile would have been close to the very area associated with the cavalry at Athens.

[62] It is important to observe in this connection, with Kroll 1977: 98 n. 36, that even the apparently nuts and bolts "real" figure Xenophon quotes for the cost of the annual upkeep of the cavalry at Athens (*Hipp.* 1.19: 40 talents) is in fact likely based on an "ideal strength" of 1000 cavalrymen.

we saw at the start of the *Hipp.*, but of an older man of the world who is passing on his wisdom to "the younger ones of his friends."[63]

Note that Xenophon feels he has immediately to go on the defensive, observing that there is already another work on horsemanship before the public: "now it is true that Simon also wrote (συνέγραψε) about horsemanship, the man who also dedicated a bronze horse at the Eleusinion in Athens and on its base had carved [a record of] his own deeds" (*Eq.* 1.1). Simon's work was the first prose treatise on horses,[64] and arguably one of the first technical prose works of any sort. It was not a crowded field, yet Xenophon still apologizes for seeming to duplicate. That is because he is in fact engaging in competitive polemic.[65] If the start of Simon's treatise (which we actually possess) is overtly "intellectual,"[66] even sophistic, giving voice to the authoritative knowledge of an expert (and blowhard) of the type Socrates so relished shooting down,[67] Xenophon's voice seems modest and down-to-earth by contrast. As Hutchinson has observed on the basis of *Eq.* 1.1, "[Xenophon's] treatise is not only practical but searchingly thoughtful."[68] Other than the engagement with Simon and the identification of his dedication at Athens, the setting of the *Eq.*, in contrast with that of the *Hipp.*, could be anywhere in the Greek world.

It is hard to overstate how *Eq.* reads like a work written by a man who has actual, first-hand knowledge of horses (remember: he refers to his knowledge as *empeiria*). It is easily the most "practical" of Xenophon's practical works. "Now of the body first we say it is necessary to examine the feet. For just as there would be no use in a house if the upper parts were exceedingly beautiful, but with the foundations underneath being lacking, so also there would be no use in a war horse, not even if the rest of its features were excellent, and it had poor hooves" (*Eq.* 1.2). We then move on through the rest of the equine body from below in a counter-clockwise direction

---

[63] Cf. Asper 2007: 219.

[64] Hutchinson 2009: 203.

[65] Though elsewhere in the treatise Xenophon endorses Simon's views (*Eq.* 1.3 and 11.6).

[66] Hutchinson 2009: 203. For the fragments of Simon, see Widdra 1964: 39–44; for the start of Simon's treatise, F 1 with Blaß's additions. Might the συνέγραψε of Xenophon's description be deliberately grandiose in the context, carrying the same sort of valence we see at Thuc. 1.1.1?

[67] It is important to note in this connection that Simon may be the figure addressed at Ar. *Eq.* 242. The scholia report that Simon and Panaetius (addressed in 243) were hipparchs, obviously of some note. Modern readers have raised the possibility that this Simon is the author to whom Xenophon refers: e.g. Rodgers 1930: 33–4, Sommerstein 1981: 155 ad loc. Mention of the statue and inscription at the Eleusinion in Xenophon's identification of Simon makes me think of the end point of one of the races in *Hipp.* (3.2).

[68] Hutchinson 2009: 203.

(1.4ff.): shanks, knees, arms, chest, neck, head, withers, loins, haunches, hams, tail, and so on. Then comes the breaking of the colt (*Eq.* 2); the purchase of an already broken horse (3); the stabling of the animal (4); the hiring of a suitably educated groom (5); rubbing down the horse (6); and the riding and training of it (7ff.), including special instructions for the war horse. Modern equestrians point to the profound understanding Xenophon demonstrates in the training of horses; that, remarkably, he seems really to have "understood the way horses learn."[69]

If Xenophon has provided a didactic work that one could actually use, the core aspects of his larger worldview are also present: so, for instance, his devotion to the principle of order ("everything in its place," especially regarding the foundations of things or, in a horse, its footing), and the idea of delegating to a subordinate who is so well trained as to be almost an alter ego of the horse's owner.[70] On the other hand, uniquely for the whole of Xenophon's corpus – if one discounts the troubling allusion to Themistogenes the Syracusan at *Hell.* 3.1.1–2 – *Eq.* may contain a cross-reference to another of his works, namely the *Hipp.* At the very end of the treatise he writes: "Let these things – notes, lessons, and exercises – be written by us for the private person (ἰδιώτῃ); the matters that are proper for a hipparch to know and do, these have been made clear in another *logos*" (*Eq.* 12.14). For an author whom we routinely read against himself in his various works, here would be the one case where he actually authorizes us to do so, but the interpretation of the passage is contested.[71]

Cynegeticus *(On Hunting)*

The *Cyn.* is a definite outlier in Xenophon's corpus of smaller works and a difficult text. It is made up of three distinct parts: an elaborate, mythological preface; an extensive attack upon the sophists at the end; in between, a fairly straightforward practical section concerning hunting. Since it is challenging to make out the unity of the work, and because the preface seems highly ornate and the epilogue poorly attached to the main discussion, earlier scholarship assumed that the *Cyn.* was not an authentic work of Xenophon, or perhaps only the middle section, with the preface and epilogue being later

---

[69] Wyllie 2001: 66–7 (quote from 67).
[70] For the idea of the sure foundation and proper distribution of parts, I think of the image of house-building at *Mem.* 3.1.7; for the capable subordinate, the wife of Ischomachus at *Oec.* 3.15. Dillery 1995: 31–4; also Dillery 2009.
[71] Cf. Wilamowitz 1905: 146–7; Breitenbach 1967: 1764.

JOHN DILLERY

additions.⁷² Vivienne Gray attempted to show in an important article from
1985 that an argument can be made to show that the work is by Xenophon
and is in fact a unity: it is a *parainesis*,⁷³ that is, an "exhortation." There is
much merit to Gray's essay, and I agree with her findings that the *Cyn.* is a
unified work and is a genuine production of Xenophon. My main difficulty
accepting her argument completely is in connection with her description of
the genre of the *Cyn. Parainesis* is not to my mind a *genre*, but a *topic* or
even *mode* of presentation, typically, of speeches: in epic, in oratory, and
in historiography to name just three. One can recognize "parainetic" elements – that is, exhortations – in passages going back to Homer;⁷⁴ self-
standing *paraineseis* are rare indeed.⁷⁵

So what then is the *Cyn.*? In answering this question, it is best to look at
the opening sentences in detail:

> Hunting and dogs are the invention of the gods, of Apollo and Artemis; they
> bestowed it on Cheiron, and thereby honored him, on account of his right-
> eousness. He received it and delighted in the gift and made use of it; and
> his students in the hunt and other good things were Cephalus, Asclepius,
> Meilanion, Nestor ... (*Cyn.* 1.1–2)
>
> τὸ μὲν εὕρημα θεῶν, Ἀπόλλωνος καὶ Ἀρτέμιδος, ἄγραι καὶ κύνες· ἔδοσαν δὲ καὶ
> ἐτίμησαν τούτῳ Χείρωνα διὰ δικαιότητα. ὁ δὲ λαβὼν ἐχάρη τῷ δώρῳ καὶ ἐχρῆτο·
> καὶ ἐγένοντο αὐτῷ μαθηταὶ κυνηγεσίων τε καὶ ἑτέρων καλῶν Κέφαλος, Ἀσκληπιός,
> Μειλανίων, Νέστωρ ...

If many of Xenophon's shorter works begin with little fanfare, suggesting
that the origins of the treatise are found in the author's musings of a particular problem at a particular time (its occasion), the start of the *Cyn.* is
diametrically opposite. The style of the preface has been thought to exhibit
Gorgianic features, or even Asianic ones.⁷⁶ The first words are deliberately,
even artificially deployed so as to form three small *kola*.⁷⁷ The first sentence
subdivides at its main pause (the semicolon) into two limbs of twenty-one
syllables. The phrases detailing the bestowal of the gift of hunting upon
Cheiron and his reception of it are closely paralleled in structure and

⁷² Radermacher 1896/1897; Norden 1909: 431–4; cf. Bigalke 1933: 30–1. See Gray's
account of the earlier scholarly reception of the *Cyn.*: Gray 1985: 156–7. Her findings
are to some extent anticipated by Richards 1898.
⁷³ See esp. Gray 1985: 157, 159, and 172.
⁷⁴ Thus Latacz's noteworthy contribution: Latacz 1977.
⁷⁵ Gray 1985: 159 cites as parallels to the *Cyn.* Isocrates' letters *To Demonicus* and *To
Nicocles.* Cf. Johnstone 1994: 226–7 = 2010: 147. While most assuredly allied to the
Cyn., they are precisely "letters," generically speaking, with strong parainetic elements;
they are not *paraineseis.* See the related problem discussed above by Aloni 2001: n. 34.
⁷⁶ Norden 1909: 379; Gray 1985: 164.
⁷⁷ Norden 1909: 432.

214

serve to isolate the crucial phrase "on account of his righteousness" (διὰ δικαιότητα).[78] These phrases are also highly alliterative, with a strong repetition of δ-terms and χ-terms.[79] Cephalus, whose name means "head," heads Xenophon's list of the famous students of Cheiron.

And then there is the word "invention" (εὕρημα) itself at the start of the treatise and thus its thematic header. While the term is used elsewhere of divine discoveries,[80] it is more normally associated with remedies found or invented by humans or by especially philanthropic deities like Prometheus – solutions to specific human needs or problems.[81] To put it another way, the "first discoverer" of a great benefit or useful art is usually a mortal, not a god.[82] Sometimes, the term is even associated specifically with linguistic sleights of hand and deceptions.[83] At the end of the *Dissoi Logoi* memory is held up as the greatest "discovery" (ἐξεύρημα) for the student of rhetoric (*Dialex.* 9.1, DK 90), and Gorgias, in his *Defense on Behalf of Palamedes*, following an established tradition, has Palamedes point to the many benefactions to mankind he has discovered (εὐεργέτης ... εὑρών, DK 82 B 11a section 30).[84] Indeed, I am sure it is not an accident that Palamedes shows up in Xenophon's list of heroes at the start of the *Cyn.* The word "invention/discovery" (εὕρημα) was an important concept to the sophists,[85] and could be seen almost an identifying marker for them.

Given that the epilogue of the *Cyn.* consists of a blistering attack on the sophists, in which they are identified as a new kind of hunter who hunt young men and the wealthy (13.9: cf. Plato, *Sophist* 223b), it seems clear what Xenophon is attempting in the treatise. While the sophists have written many books on empty and useless topics in order to corrupt the young (note τῶν ματαίων, 13.1), he has shown that he can write in a manner like theirs, but

---

[78] Note how the phrase ἔδοσαν δὲ καὶ ἐτίμησαν τούτῳ Χείρωνα is closely paralleled by ὁ δὲ λαβὼν ἐχάρη τῷ δώρῳ καὶ ἐχρῆτο. They both consist of fourteen syllables and have ending clausulae of identical metrical shape.

[79] δ-terms: ἔδοσαν ... διὰ δικαιότητα ... τῷ δώρῳ. χ-terms: Χείρωνα ... ἐχάρη ... ἐχρῆτο. One could add the τ–alliteration in ἐτίμησαν τούτῳ.

[80] E.g. of drums (*tympana*), the discovery of Dionysus and Mother Rhea/Cybele (Eur. *Ba.* 59, with Dodds 1960: 71 ad loc.). And see P. Oxy. 5194 line 3 with commentary; an echo of the start of the *Cyn.*

[81] E.g. Aeschylus F 181a and Sophocles F 432 line 2. At Dem. 26.26: illnesses cured by the discoveries of doctors. The term can also be used of a "windfall" or "boon," such as we find (significantly) at Xen. *Anab.* 7.3.13.

[82] Cf. Kleingünther 1933: 97–8. Of course in later Euhemerism such a person might become divinized.

[83] See esp. Eur. *Hec.* 250 with Gregory 1999: 76 ad loc.; also Eur. *Hipp.* 716.

[84] Cf. Kleingünther 1933: 80. Note also Palamedes at Xen. *Apol.* 26, *Mem.* 4.2.33.

[85] Cf. Thraede 1962: 169. Note that in the *Lives* of Diogenes Laertius, εὕρημα occurs "with unusually high visibility for the Sophists and others associated with the language arts" (Shalev 2006: 311 and cf. 315–16).

on a truly worthy topic (and one that is traditionally associated with aristocratic youth).[86] Thus his use of "invention" (εὕρημα) at the start can be seen as similar to what Aristophanes does at the end of his personal statement in the second edition of *Clouds*, when he refers in the *parabasis* to his theatrical creations in the language of the very men he is attacking, namely, as *heuremata* (line 561). This posture requires Xenophon to perform his own linguistic high jinks in chapter 13, as when he says somewhat disingenuously that "perhaps (ἴσως) I do not speak cunningly (τοῖς ... ὀνόμασιν οὐ σεσοφισμένως, 13.5),"[87] that is, with the words of the sophists, when clearly he has; or, when he again speculates that some sophist will perhaps (ἴσως) say, in their maddening parrot-like way of gainsaying, that "what is written well and in order has not been written well and in order" (καλῶς καὶ ἑξῆς γεγραμμένα ... οὐ καλῶς οὐδ' ἑξῆς γεγράφθαι, 13.6). This is precisely a sophistic move. It is hard to resist the impression that the *Cyn.* is meant to be seen as a refutation of the sophists and their grand language (μέμφομαι οὖν αὐτοῖς τὰ ... μεγάλα μειζόνως, 13.3), itself written by a "plain man" (13.4: ἰδιώτης), but in sophistic language at key points.[88] It can be viewed then, dare I say, as a serious *paignion* ("game") of sorts (cf. Gorgias, *Helen* 21),[89] complete with mythological play, but on a topic of real importance to him: the moral education of aristocratic youth.[90]

Part 3: The *Poroi* (Ways and Means)

I have saved perhaps the most remarkable of Xenophon's small works for last. Unlike so many of them, but like the *Ages.*, we can date the *Poroi* pretty securely. It is clearly written in the aftermath of the loss of Athenian control of the so-called Second Athenian Confederation, that is, after the Social War of 357–355 (alluded to at *Poroi* 4.40).[91]

It begins with the favorite Xenophontean trope whereby the impression is created that the treatise is an outcome of a moment of reflection by Xenophon (see above). He states that he has always believed (ἀεί ποτε νομίζω)

---

[86] Note Xenophon's own sons at *Anab.* 5.3.10.
[87] The adverb is exceedingly rare.
[88] Cf. Richards 1898: 292: "The writer of the *Cynegeticus* carefully separates himself from the Sophists and modestly professes to be a mere layman in writing (13.4): but a man does not always mean what he says, and he may very well have thought that he could, if he chose, beat them at their own weapons." De Romilly observes that Xenophon can attack the younger sophists with great violence in the *Cyn.* but has no trouble quoting Prodicus on vice and virtue at *Mem.* 2.1.21–34: De Romilly 1992: 27.
[89] Cf. Bona 1974: 33.
[90] I am thus in agreement with Johnstone on the overall aims of the *Cyn.*: Johnstone 1994: 228–9 = 2010: 149–51.
[91] Holzapfel 1882: 242–4; Thiel 1922: viii–xiii; Breitenbach 1967: 1754–5; Gauthier 1976: 4–6. Specific implied dates at *Poroi* 3.7 (post 366 and 361).

that *politeiai* conform to the character of the leading men of their states.[92] However, at Athens this seems not to be the case. Its leading men, while knowing the importance of justice, claim that the poverty of the people has forced the Athenians to be "more unjust towards the cities" (*Poroi* 1.1).[93] While Xenophon was taking note of his thoughts on the matter, it occurred to him that the land of Attica was in fact naturally so endowed as to be able to produce abundant resources (1.2).

The basic point of the *Poroi* is to make the Athenians see that they do not have to resort to hegemonic war and conquest of other states to obtain sufficient resources for their state; that those resources exist already in their land and community. The state would acquire new funds if it found better ways to incorporate its resident alien merchant class (*Poroi* 2), by making Athens a commercial center without peer (3), and, most especially, by working its silver mines more efficiently, chiefly through turning the extraction of ore over to a large corps of publicly owned slaves (4). Some scholars point to the *Poroi* as advancing a plan of economic reform of Athens that was in fact reflected in the policies of Eubulus;[94] still others note that proposals in it anticipate measures that were adopted later in the Hellenistic period (a forward-looking perspective we saw also with *Hiero* and *Hipp.*).[95]

All this may seem like pretty dry stuff, but the language of the treatise is surprisingly allusive and its underlying thinking profoundly radical. In a way similar to the *Cyn.* and its engagement with sophism, Xenophon can be seen in the *Poroi* to subvert the standard language and images of Athenian imperialism by actually deploying them at key points in the interest of an anti-imperialist policy that does not rely on war or coercion to increase the state's resources.[96] Thus at *Poroi* 1.6 Xenophon observes: "one would not unreasonably consider the city to be situated in the middle (ἀμφὶ τὰ μέσα οἰκεῖσθαι τὴν πόλιν) both of Greece and the whole inhabited earth." This thought can be connected to a similar expression in Isocrates' *Panegyricus* (42), where the Piraeus is identified as an *emporion* built "in the middle of Greece" (ἐν μέσῳ τῆς Ἑλλάδος). The idea of the centrality of Athens as a commercial center is found also in Thucydides' Periclean Funeral Oration (Thuc. 2.38.2), the "Old Oligarch" ([Xen.] *Ath. Pol.* 2.7), and Old Comedy

---

[92] Enclitic ποτε in its various meanings is one of Xenophon's favorite terms in opening statements: cf. *Hier.* 1.1, *Lac. Pol.* 1.1, *Cyr.* 1.1.1, *Mem.* 1.1.1, *Oec.* 1.1.

[93] Commentators note that this beginning is very similar to *Cyr.* 8.1.8 and 8.8.5 esp., as well as Isoc. *De Pace* 53: Thiel 1922: 3 and Gauthier 1976: 35 ad loc.

[94] Cf. Boeckh 1886: 1.698–708; Andreades 1933: 1.390; Momigliano 1936b = 1966: 1.481–7; Cawkwell 1963: 63–4 and nn. 89–92. Also Dillery 1993: 1 n. 4 for further bibliography.

[95] Finley 1973: 163–4; Humphreys 1978: 138.

[96] Cf. Dillery 1993, building on the findings of Thiel, Gauthier, and Loraux 1986: 86–7.

(Hermippus, *Phormophoroi* F 63 KA; Ar. *V.* 520). It was clearly an important topos in the Athenian understanding of their *arche*. Similarly, in the next section (1.7), Xenophon encourages his audience to think of Athens as an island, as well as part of the mainland. The idea of Athens as an island is immediately recognizable as another important imperial topos: it appears (famously) in Pericles' first speech in Thucydides (Thuc. 1.143.5), and (again) also in the "Old Oligarch" ([Xen.] *Ath. Pol.* 2.14).[97]

Xenophon deliberately echoes the language of Athenian imperialism, and this in the wake of the city's loss of its second experiment in ruling other maritime states, in order to contrast his new vision of the city's role in the Greek world with the Athenians' older one of a "tyrant city." Athens is to become not just a commercial center, but also one modeled on the Athenian quietist, not "polypragmatist" (an imperial "busybody," *Poroi* 5.3); it will be a cultural center (cf. 5.4),[98] guided by a code of conduct that springs more from the world of elite interpersonal relations than "realist" *Machtpolitik*. It is to be the sort of city that behaves towards other states in a spirit of "nobility," not reciprocity, specifically not demanding what Greeks would normally think is its due – precisely the sort of city that the Phliasian statesman Procles asks the Athenians to be in book 6 of the *Hell.* (6.5.48).[99]

This was a radical recasting of interstate relations. But the vision rests on a still more radical understanding of revenue acquisition. Since the time of Homer, advantage and compensation for loss were thought of in zero-sum terms. To gain more resources, you had to take them from others; if you suffered a loss, you had to recover it from your enemy; you could not make good the loss yourself. Think of the *eris* (strife) between Agamemnon and Achilles at the start of the *Iliad*: the prizes of war have already been divided up, and yet it is wrong for Agamemnon to be without his, and so he must seek a replacement from another lord of the Achaeans. Xenophon took a different view in the *Poroi* and so formulated a concept that was unprecedented. A state can acquire resources without trying to take them from another. As Karl Polanyi so well observed: "[The *Poroi*'s] originality lies in the thought that wealth, power, and security can be the product of peace rather than of war."[100] Or, modifying the words of Xenophon himself in the *Poroi*, war does not pay (*Poroi* 5.11; cf. *Hell.* 6.3.11).[101]

---

97 See Dillery 1993: 3–6 with notes.
98 Dillery 1993: 5–7. See now also Low 2007: 205 n. 73.
99 Dillery 1993: 10 and 1995: 247–8. Cf. Lendon 2006: 94–5; Low 2007: 181–2 with n. 13. See now also Jansen 2007.
100 Polanyi 1977: 196.
101 Cf. Dillery 1993: 10. I would like to thank Michael Flower and Kathryn Morgan for their suggestions.

Further Reading

The shorter works have not received as much attention as they should have. There are notable exceptions. An excellent set of translations and enormously helpful introduction and notes are to be found in the 1997 Penguin edition of Waterfield and Cartledge. Gray's 2007 commentary is also of great help. Critical questions of genre are treated admirably by Nicolai 2004 and 2014b. All of Herbert Richards's essays on the shorter works published in *Classical Review* from the end of the nineteenth century are still worth consulting. Of standard works on Xenophon I have found Higgins 1977 illuminating if also controversial; so also Henry 1967. Important, intelligent, but also highly controversial is Strauss 1948/2000 on the *Hiero*, one of his most important Xenophontine readings, full of insight but also the usual difficulties.

PART III

TECHNIQUES

II

VIVIENNE GRAY

Xenophon's Language and Expression

Language and expression may be a final frontier for Xenophontic studies.[1] They deserve a major study because of the range of his works, but also because his Socratic background gave him a special interest in words and their usage. This can be seen in his engagement in the debate about using commonplace words in beautiful contexts, where humble pots or *chytrai* became a *cause célèbre* of the ordinary word that can achieve beauty.[2] Plato (*Hippias Maior* 288c–d) refers to this debate in Socrates' defense of the "unlettered man" who uses "low words in a high matter" when he names the *chytra* in a disquisition on beauty. Longinus (*On the Sublime* 43.2–6) continues the debate when he criticizes Theopompus for ending a list of the items that the Persian king took with him to Egypt with these same *chytrai* because they ruined the beauty of the rest; he suggests that we use grander circumlocutions for such low words (citing the analogy of the creator god in Xenophon *Memorabilia* 1.4.6, who put the "drains" of our bodies out of sight for fear of spoiling the beauty of the rest). Xenophon himself seems to engage in the debate when he has Ischomachus count *chytrai* among those objects that are not beautiful in themselves but acquire beauty when arranged "with rhythm and good judgment" (*Oeconomicus* 8.19), and more particularly when he makes the lowly *chytra* essential to his high praise of Agesilaus in *Hellenica* 4.5.4. This would mirror his interest in literary theory elsewhere,[3] and foreshadows the richness likely to result from the study of his language.

The explanation of linguistic usage is complex.[4] The same idea can be expressed in different words in different orders, and rhythm, sound, variety,

---

[1] The main book-length study is still Gautier 1911, but more recent chapters in Bakker 1997a and Pontier 2014 address aspects of his usage, even though more general studies have neglected him, e.g. Bers 2010. Norden 1909: 101–3 is very summary.

[2] This debate is explored in Pontier 2014 in the contributions by Pontier on Plato and Gray on Xenophon. That said, the present work is designed to supplement my backlist rather than rehearsing it.

[3] Gray 2011: 44–51, 62–9, 119–32, 187–93, 345–9, beginning with Socrates.

[4] Dover 1997 is an impressive account of the challenges.

personal preference, as well as traditional practice, can all operate at once on the choice. Some choices are dictated by distinct modes of discourse, such as speech and narrative, or by generic requirements. Xenophon shows his sensitivity to generic difference in his rewriting of the same events in his *Agesilaus* and *Hellenica*, the one for epideictic praise, the other for historical narrative.[5] Among the genres that need more linguistic description are works of overt praise, such as *Agesilaus* and the *Constitution of the Lacedaemonians* (which praises Lycurgus for the laws he gave the Spartans). His use of rhetorical figures has been noted in these and other works,[6] but there is room for a more complete description of the language he found appropriate to these works and others in which he uses the praising mode. His technical works on horsemanship, cavalry command, and hunting (*De re equestri, Hipparchicus, Cynegeticus*) need also to be situated within the "rhetorics" of technical discourse;[7] even within non-technical works, such as *Hellenica*, his descriptions of the illnesses of the kings of Sparta (5.3.19, 5.4.58) show his sensitivity to the medical vocabulary and style of Hippocrates. There is a similar need to describe the language of the conversations in his philosophical corpus (the *Hiero* as well as the properly Socratic works) and the exhortatory *Poroi*, his essay on how to improve the Athenian economy. The language of his narrative works has been studied in order to differentiate phases of composition, but there are more literary phenomena to be addressed, such as Xenophon's vividness, which is much admired, but still needs an analysis of the language and expression he uses to create it.[8]

Language and expression involve vocabulary, grammar, and sentence structure. Ancient critics noted Xenophon's use of non-Attic vocabulary, and Gautier thought that he simply soaked up such words in his life abroad as a mercenary and exile and used them almost subconsciously in his writing. Yet Xenophon deliberately recreates Spartan Doric dialect in *Hellenica* 1.1.14 and Syracusan Doric in *Symposium* 9, which suggests a more conscious approach. In this chapter it will become apparent that he uses rare words to enhance their contexts or because unusual subject matter demands them. We need to consider also whether Xenophon's usage is so unusual if compared against the traditions in which he was writing, since it is arguable

---

5 For the relationship see Gautier 1911: 134–5, Buijs 2007, Pontier 2010. But also see Dover 1997: 17–19 on other parallel passages, in a discussion of the relations of form to content.
6 For the influence of rhetoric see e.g. Schacht 1890, Bigalke 1933.
7 See van der Eijk 1997: 77–129; Dover 1997: 112–19 comments on technical vocabulary. The language of *Cynegeticus* has been studied for its authenticity: Gray 1985.
8 Plutarch, *Life of Artaxerxes* 8.1.

that a writer will be more affected by his traditions than by daily speech. His "non-Attic" prepositions, for instance, can be found in Herodotus and Thucydides, who are neither of them models of Attic usage.[9] His philosophical works might mirror the sophists or Plato, who are no models of Attic usage either. Sometimes we must allow him just to relish rare words such as *meiōn* for "less," or to use non-Attic synonyms for variety. The influence of rhythm and sound on his choices also needs attention, as does the very definition of what constitutes a rare word. This latter problem already exercised Aristotle (*Poetics* 1457b–1458a). For us, words count as unusual when appearing for the first time in prose literature, but a harder question is whether his audiences counted, as rare, unique words that build on existing cognates or roots, such as nouns ending in *–is* or *–ēma*.

In grammar, work has started on Xenophon's tenses. It is now insufficient to say that the present tense used in a narrative of the past expresses the action as vivid, and that while the imperfect tense expresses action as still unfolding, the aorist represents it as complete. The focus has switched to tense in context and the idea of backgrounding and foregrounding. This produces the attempt, largely successful, to show that Xenophon uses the present tense in past narrative to delineate the main points in the storyline rather than merely to convey vividness, while the imperfect and aorist render background events.[10] The significance of this is that it shows us where

---

[9] Consider the statistics for the non-Attic *amphi* ("around"), *syn* ("with"), and *hepesthai* ("follow") against their Attic synonyms. Lysias as the Attic model uses only *peri* for "around," prefers *meta* for "with" (only eight *syn*) and *akolouthein* for "follow" (only one *hepesthai*), but Xenophon seems to follow Herodotus and Thucydides. Excluding *meta* in the meaning "after," which is very common in historical writing (it explains almost all uses of *meta* in Thucydides and Herodotus), Thucydides uses the Archaic Attic *xyn* exclusively for "with," *peri* exclusively for "around" and both synonyms for "follow," while Herodotus prefers *syn* to *meta*, *peri* to *amphi* and uses *hepesthai* exclusively. Like Herodotus, Xenophon in *Cyropaedia* prefers *peri* to *amphi* in a ratio of around 3:1, *syn* to *meta* in a ratio of almost 5:1, *hepesthai* to *akolouthein* in a ratio of 7:1. He also uses both synonyms side by side (e.g. follow, 2.4.3, 5.2.37, around, 5.3.25). Herodotus' one use of *amphi* with the preposition, 8.104 (Gautier contests the reading) parallels Xenophon 3.1.8, *amphi tou patros*. Gray 1991: 211–27 observed that synonyms alternate in chunks within *Hellenica* and *Anabasis*. This is also the case in *Cyropaedia*, where *amphi* in the phrase "those around someone" is regular in early books (1.3–4, 3.2–3, 4.1–5, 5.3–4) and appears in later books (7.1–2, 7.5, 8.5), but *peri* also appears and eventually takes over (7.1, 7.5, 8.1–2, 3–4, 8.5, 8.8). Xenophon's *Anabasis* and *Hellenica* reflect the usage of Herodotus too: in *Anabasis syn, peri*, and *hepesthai* dominate. *Hellenica* prefers *syn* and *peri*, but gives the slight edge to *akolouthein*, which concurs with Thucydidean practice.

[10] Sicking and Stork 1997: 147–56. Von Fritz 1949: 197–201 earlier examined this phenomenon at the beginning of *Anabasis*. Buijs 2007 differentiates the use of the imperfect for action within the text, aorist for action outside, the one to be continued, the other not.

the emphasis lies in a storyline, which is not always obvious. Research on Thucydides has distinguished two types of narrative, the diegetic mode reflecting a mainly authorial point of view, in which the aorist marks his voice while the imperfect gives background, and the mimetic mode, in which the imperfect renders the experience of the action while the aorist is used for the authorial point of view. If this is correct, then the aorist shows us where the author invests the narrative with his own interest.[11] My own impression is that Xenophon uses tenses to differentiate sets of actions within passages with some disregard for temporal significance, but even that would help us understand the structuring of his narrative.

What might be said of his syntax and word order? His uses of anaphora and chiasmus have been listed, but not their contribution to contexts, which defines their function. He is not just being "grand" when he uses contrived word orders, because the passages concerned often have no grandeur. Discourse analysis has brought out the distinction between participial constructions and sub-clauses,[12] and that might be worth pursuing, since it could assist our understanding of thought relations between clauses. Functional grammar might be applied.[13] It might also be worth pursuing the contexts in which he uses his idiosyncratic final and object clauses. They confirm his sensitivity to language because they represent a finely honed feeling for the conditionality of purpose or end.[14] There is room also for studying how rhythm dictates his sentence structure even outside his obvious rhetorical tropes.[15]

The paragraphs above suggest how much still needs to be done. The following ones are a kind of praeparatio for a major study. They take whole passages for examination because language is inert without function, and function is the way language serves the context as a whole. The passages chosen represent characteristic types of Xenophontic discourse: battle narrative, love and humor, and philosophical discourse. These invite comment on general narrative habits that contribute to the themes alongside strictly linguistic features, because to separate them is to separate what to Xenophon was a united arsenal of effects. The passages are examined in my own sadly literal translation because more fluent existing translations do not always capture the linguistic features that need to be discussed. Of course it would be better in Greek. But those with Greek can consult their own texts.

---

[11] Bakker 1997b.
[12] Buijs 2005.
[13] For this method see Dik 1995.
[14] Goodwin, *Moods and Tenses*, App. 4–5.
[15] See Dover 1997: 160–82 for the difficulties of assessing prose rhythm.

The ancient critics have left a valuable legacy.[16] They explored Xenophon's vocabulary as a model for imitation or avoidance in rhetoric (where there was a debate; Dionysius of Halicarnassus found it pure but Phrynichus did not).[17] They exemplified for the same purpose his skill in the various styles: Longinus in sublimity (*On Sublimity* 8.1, 28.3), Aelius Aristides (*Rhetorics* 2, e.g. 14, 21, 31) in charm and understatement, which is confirmed in his description by the Suda and DL 2.57 as the Attic bee and the Attic muse. Demetrius (*On Style* 37) added forcefulness to cover the full stylistic range, noting that the different styles were often found in combination. Critics also positioned his language within the canon of historical writers: Dionysius of Halicarnassus (*Letter to Pompey* 4) said that he imitated Herodotus in vocabulary and composition. These critics did not generally pursue the effects of whole passages, however, and even Gautier did not sufficiently illustrate how language serves contexts. So there is ground to explore for those bold enough to take it on. And though a chapter is unlikely to top the hill, it can describe some of its contours.

Battle Narrative

Xenophon's battle descriptions demonstrate surprisingly consistent linguistic features. He often structures them into shorter episodes that may be taken in at a glance; this characterizes the conversations in his philosophical works as well. In my analysis I put phrases for comment in **bold** and number them, using the same number for recurring features. The first three episodes are from the battle of Sardis, the centerpiece of *Cyropaedia*.

The chariot charge of Abradatas against the Egyptian chariots (*Cyr.* 7.1.29–32):

And Abradatas **no longer** delayed, **but** (2) shouting, "**My brave friends, follow me**" (3), he **charges** (1), **not sparing** the horses **but** (2) bloodying them severely with the whip.

There rushed forward with him the other charioteers (4).

And the [Egyptian] chariots fled them instantly, **some** picking up their companions, **some** leaving them behind (5).

Abradatas, racing against them, **smashes into** (1) the opposing line of the Egyptians.

There accompanied him in his attack those stationed nearest (4).

It is clear from many other cases too that there is no line stronger than when it is gathered from friends who fight together; and it was clear here too (5).

For his comrades and table fellows **were accompanying him in his attack** (4).

---

[16] Münscher 1920 reviews ancient allusions to Xenophon's works.
[17] See Bakker 2010: 470–1, 476–80 for these critics.

The other riders, seeing the Egyptians standing firm in a big pack, turned after the fleeing chariots and followed them.

But where those around Abradatas charged in, since the Egyptians could not split ranks because of the resistance on either side of them, **those upright** they were overturning, by striking them with the weight of their horses, and **those fallen** they were crushing, **both them and their weapons**, with horses and wheels (6).

Whatever the scythes touched, everything was being cut forcefully to pieces, both weapons and bodies.

In this **indescribable** confusion (7), with his wheels leaping off, dislodged by the heaps of all kinds of things, Abradatas **falls** (1) from his chariot along with others of those who charged with him, and these, proving themselves good men there, were cut to pieces and perished.

Xenophon's expression serves two themes in this passage: the courage of Abradatas and the loyalty of his comrades.

1) The **present tense** creates drama according to Longinus *On the Sublime* 25, but it also marks the central storyline (Abradatas: he charges, he engages, he falls). Traditional tense analysis might explain the imperfect for the final slaughter as an unfolding action and the aorist for the deaths of Abradatas and his companions as completed action, but some other explanation is needed for why Abradatas' comrades "accompanied him" in the aorist tense in the narrative, but in the authorial comment "were accompanying him" in the imperfect tense (4).
2) To further underline Abradatas' dashing courage, Xenophon opposes **what is done to what is not**. This amplifies the action, giving the negative to show the worth of the positive.
3) Abradatas calls on his comrades' loyalty in his **short speech**, marking the theme of loyalty because it is the only direct speech in the narrative.
4) The repeated short sentences confirm their loyalty, standing out through contrast with the longer sentences around them.
5) Xenophon makes an explicit **authorial comment** on the effect of loyalty.
6) He splits the killing into various **dualities** in order to mark the achievement of Abradatas and his comrades. Demetrius (*On Style* 103) calls this dilogiai "twinning" and says it creates grandeur, but elsewhere vividness.
7) The vocabulary is regular, but the new "indescribable" underlines the extremity of the slaughter in a kind of self-reference (since he has described it, very well too).[18]

---

[18] The word *adiēgētoi* ("indescribable") recurs at *Cyr.* 8.7.22, to create alpha-privative amplification, which is typical of his philosophical discourse (below); but then this part of *Cyropaedia* is a philosophical discourse on the soul.

The battle then turns to the arrival of the main Persian force (7.1.33). The theme is the excellence of the Persians against the superiority of Egyptian weapons.

5) The authorial comment emphasizes the excellence of the weapons: "Their spears strong and long they still have to this day, and their shields shelter their bodies far more than breastplates and wickers, and work with them in pushing by being on their shoulders."

6) Contrasting dualities bring out the excellence of both parties: "The Persians ... beat a retreat, striking and struck ... the Egyptians were struck in their turn."

The final sentence (7.1.35) divides the action into three, the first two elements ("slaughter" and "sound") in chiasmus, with the third action generating another three actions, the first and last also in chiasmus. The effect is to pile up the detail to recreate the vivid aural experience of the battle: "There was a) of men much slaughter, b) much sound of arms and missiles of all sorts, and c) much shouting, d1) of men calling on one another, d2) of men issuing orders, d3) of men to the gods making an appeal."

7) The vocabulary is regular but the largely poetic word for "sound" (*ktupos*) underlines the aural experience of the fighting. At 7.5.28 it is used for synonym enrichment and "k" alliteration.

The focus switches to Cyrus (7.1.36) and how loyalty can save the leader's life; the focus on the excellence of the Egyptians persists.

1) The present tense makes a focus of the actions of Cyrus ("Cyrus is at hand"), his men's fighting ("they strike and kill"), the wounding and rearing of his horse, and his fall ("Some man fallen and trodden down under Cyrus' horse strikes his horse in the belly with his sword. The horse struck rearing (7) shakes Cyrus off") and then his recovery ("One of his attendants leaping from his horse, lifts him up onto his own horse").

5) The authorial comment notes the love of Cyrus that leads to his recovery ("There one would have seen the worth of the leader being loved by those around him").

7) The poetic word (φύρδην) ("Then chaotically did they fight, infantry and cavalry without distinction") underlines the confusion that led to his fall, and the fall itself is made vivid by the poetic word for "rearing" (σφαδᾴζων).

6) The fighting for him after his fall is rendered in the sequence of **opposing dualities without connectives** (called asyndeton), which was noted by Longinus (*On the Sublime* 19.1) ("they **fought, pushed, were pushed, struck**").[19]

New features, but ones that recur elsewhere, include: (9) a complex sentence describing Cyrus' **motivation** ("When he saw the Persians pushed from their lines, he felt anguish, and realizing that he would never more quickly stop the enemy from their forward push than if he were to drive round behind them, telling those with him to follow, he went round behind the lines") and (10) the **anonymous man** strikes the blow and makes the recovery, in the first instance (in the Greek) marked by a sequence of "p" sounds to create further focus.

Hellenica 7.5.15 applies the same devices to celebrate the Athenian cavalry battle in which Xenophon's own son died fighting against a strong enemy.

1) The **present tense** marks their generous action at the beginning, and a *dilogia* (6) underlines their hardship ("Hearing this, the Athenians **go** to their aid, though still without food **themselves and their horses**"). The aorist then becomes the main tense, with only one use of the imperfect for background explanation, perhaps confirming a diegetic mode of presentation in which the author's evaluation is foremost (Bakker 1997b).

5) The **authorial comment** introduces the first part of the fighting, confirming the authorial presence, beginning "Thereupon who would not admire their courage?"

9) This comment includes a long motivation ("Who though seeing the enemy were much more numerous, and though the horsemen had suffered failure at Corinth, of this they made no account, nor of the fact that they were about to fight Thebans and Thessalians who had the reputation of being the best horsemen, but ashamed, lest though present they not benefit their allies, as soon as they saw the enemy, they clashed, mad with desire to recover their ancestral glory").

6) In the actual conflict *dilogiai* abound to emphasize the excellence on both sides ("And of them there died good men, and they killed, it is clear, men of the same sort. Neither side had a weapon so short with which they did not reach one another. And they did not abandon their own dead, but they gave back some of the enemy's under truce").

---

[19] There is another instance after the end of our passage: "he saw the plain full of horses, men, chariots, men fleeing, men pursuing, men winning, men losing."

We see the same features underlining the bravery of Agesilaus in the battle of Coronea (*Hellenica* 4.3.18–19): the **present tense** (1) and the **anonymous man** (10) ("Thereupon some of the allies were already garlanding Agesilaus, when **someone tells** him that the Thebans have cut the Orchomenians to pieces and are in the baggage train"), the **authorial comment** (5), taking in the opposition of **what he did and did not do** (2), as well as the **rare word** for his head-on clash (7) ("And thereupon **it is possible to say** without a doubt that Agesilaus was brave; but he did not choose the safest course (5). Though, by letting those pass who were coming through, it was possible for him to follow them and overpower the ones in the rear, **he did not do this, but** clashed **head on** with the Thebans"). Asyndetic *dilogia* (6) conveys the unrelenting fighting that Agesilaus set off ("they **were pushed, fought, killed, died**").

In the *Anabasis*, the battle of Cunaxa shows the regular features to underline the courageous charge of the Greeks and their complete lack of casualties (1.8.18–20). The **poetic word** (δουπεῖν) (7),[20] reinforced by a new kind of authorial comment that introduces a witness to the description (5, "it is said"), underlines their bravery ("**Some say** that they **thudded** their swords on their shields to frighten the horses"). The **present tense** (1) marks the moment when "the barbarians **bend** and **flee**." The **anonymous man** appears as a potential casualty (10), which the authorial comment (5) then rules out ("**One man** was overtaken, by astonishment, as if on a chariot racetrack. Yet **they said** that not even he was wounded, nor any other of the Greeks was wounded in this battle, except **a man** on the left wing was said to be struck by an arrow." Demetrius (*On Style* 211) already comments on the *dilogia* (6) that further underlines the lack of casualties among the Greeks ("And the chariots were borne along, **some of them through** the enemy themselves, **some of them through** the Greeks, empty of their drivers").

In the same battle Cyrus' drive against his brother (1.8.24–9) is marked by **the short speech** (3), his fall at the hands of the **anonymous man** (10), the **present tense** (1), and the use of "**what is said**" for confirmation of the impact of his drive (5) ("Thereupon Cyrus fearing that [his brother] might get in behind and cut the Greek contingent to pieces, **drives** against him. And falling on them with the 600, he **defeats** those lined up before the king and routed the 6000, and **is said** to have killed with his own hand Artagerses their leader. When the rout occurred, there **scatter** also the 600 of Cyrus, turning to pursuit, except a very few who were left around him, mainly the so-called table fellows. With these, he sees the king and the compact

---

[20] Gemoll 1932 discusses this word.

body around him. And in the moment he **did not endure it, but** (2) saying: "**I see the man**" (3), he **goes** against him and **strikes** him in the chest and **wounds** him through the breastplate, **as says** Ctesias the doctor, and **he says** he treated the wound himself. But as he struck, **someone makes a forceful throw** with a light Persian spear **into** Cyrus' eye. And ... how many of those around the king were dying, **Ctesias tells**; for he was there. Cyrus himself died and the best eight of those around him lay on top of him"). The present is more than usually dominant and creates vividness and focus on the main actions, but more finesse is needed to explain why those on the king's side "were dying" in the imperfect, while Cyrus "died" in the aorist.

In this short analysis of battle narrative, various features of language and expression unite to serve to focus on central themes. A survey of all his battles might not produce such consistency, but those above were chosen at random, and *Cyropaedia* 3.3.59–70 shows again the short speech, the asyndeton, and the authorial comment.

Love and Humor

Ancient critics noted Xenophon's charm in passages about love and beauty and humor, and admired his special trick of blending light and lovely subject matter with serious or dark themes (Demetrius, *On Style* 130). The following is a selection of stories about boys.[21] Their main linguistic feature is economy of expression, and this produces the lifelike writing for which he was famed and which Theopompus destroyed in his rewriting of Xenophon's conversations: *FGH* 107 T 21.

Cyropaedia 1.4.27–8 is a good example of a serious theme being presented in a lighthearted way:

> If it is right to recall a playful story, it is said that when Cyrus left and they separated from one another, his relatives sent him away in the Persian manner by kissing him on the mouth.
>
> For the Persians to this day still do this.
>
> One of the Medes, a very noble sort, for a long time dazed by the beauty of Cyrus, hung behind when he saw his relatives kissing him.
>
> When the others left he went to Cyrus and said, "me alone among your relatives do you not recognize, Cyrus?"
>
> "What," said Cyrus, "are you a relative too?"
>
> "I am," he said.
>
> "So that's why," said Cyrus, "you stare at me. I seem to have seen you doing this a lot.

---

[21] For treatment of this as a stock story: Gray 2011: 203–11.

I always wanted to approach you, he said, but by the gods I was shy."
'There was no need," said Cyrus, "since you are a relative."
And he went and kissed him.
And the Mede, being kissed, asked, "so it's a Persian custom this kissing of kin?"
"It is," he said, "when they see each other after a time or part from each other."
"So it's time," said the Mede, "for another kiss. **For I am going away**, as you see, **right now**."
So Cyrus kissed him again and sent him away and left.
And they had not covered much distance before the Mede turned up again, **his horse all asweat**.
And Cyrus seeing him said, "Have you forgotten something you wanted to say?"
"No, by Zeus," said he, "but I've returned after some time."
And Cyrus said, "some *short* time, by Zeus!"
"**Short?!**" said the Mede. "Don't you know Cyrus," he said, "that **even the blinking of an eye** is a very long time, when I don't see you, in your beauty?"
Thereupon [they say] Cyrus laughed through his former tears, and told him to go in good heart, because he would appear to them again in a very short time, so that he could see him, if he wished, even **without blinking an eye**.

The serious theme is the attraction that Cyrus had for his followers as a leader, which is a major part of his leadership qualities as an adult. The vocabulary is plain except for the **rare word** for "blinking" (ἀσκαρδαμυκτί), which underlines his relative's love for Cyrus and becomes the story's punchline. Xenophon shows again the reluctance of the lover to blink in the presence of his beloved at *Symposium* 4.24, where it finally breaks the stony stare of the lover (as of those who have gazed on the Gorgons); its use by medical writers (Hippocrates, Galen) seems to confirm that this is a pathological condition.[22] The sentences are short, the expression **economical**, using as few words as possible (with ellipses such as "short?"); there are few adjectives. The story combines humor with seriousness even in the motif of the sweating horse, which usually announces a military crisis (*Anab.* 1.8.1 and *Hell.* 4.5.7), but here leads to further kisses. The **authorial comment** has various effects: it brings attention to the custom of kissing that is central to the story; it presents the reader with a charmingly deferential storyteller by "apologizing" for the story; and by insistently presenting the story as **what is said and then what was said in response**, it warrants its truth and creates the vivid impression of a source witnessing the scene.

---

[22] See Gray 2010c on this word (and several others not mentioned in this chapter). Xenophon uses it in another description of the effects of love in *Symposium* 4.24.

Xenophon's variation of the words for "he said" seems to have no rationale, but might repay close consideration.

Hellenica 4.1.39–40 is another scene of farewell. Xenophon blends seriousness with lightness in having the Spartan king Agesilaus serve the Persian boy in affairs of the heart, confirming the mixture of seriousness and lightness he credits to him elsewhere when he says that "he participated in stories about boys, but was serious in promoting everything his friends needed" (*Ages.* 8.1, cf. *Hell.* 5.3.20). The vocabulary is plain but the **poetic form** "enamored" (ἐρασθέντος) in the final sentence underlines the main boy's love for the Athenian boy. The speech is **economical** and elliptical, capturing the haste of the farewell and the impulsivity of the boy in making such an adult gesture towards friendship; the complexity of the last sentence by contrast mirrors Agesilaus' serious service. This lightness is typified by the parenthetical "he had a lovely [spear]."

> After this was said [Agesilaus] ended the talks.
> And Pharnabazus mounted his horse and left, but his son by Parapita, still in his beauty, hanging behind and running up, said,
> "I make you a friend, Agesilaus."
> "I accept."
> "Remember now," he said.
> And quickly he gave his light Persian spear (he had a lovely one) to Agesilaus.
> Receiving it, since Idaeus his secretary had on his horse some reins that were completely lovely, Agesilaus removed them and gave him these in return.
> The boy then leaped on his horse and pursued his father.
> And when in the absence of Pharnabazus, his brother took his province and exiled this son of Parapita, in other ways Agesilaus cared for him, and in particular, because he was enamored of the son of Eualces, an Athenian, [Agesilaus] did everything he could to allow [the son of Eualces], for his sake, to be entered into the stadion race at Olympia, though he was the tallest of the boys.

Anabasis 7.4.7 shows the same features:

> There was one Episthenes of Olynthus, a lover of boys, who seeing a lovely boy in the flower of youth with a shield on the point of being killed, ran to Xenophon and asked him to help the lovely boy.
> And he goes to Seuthes and asks him not to kill the boy and describes the manner of Episthenes and how he gathered a band once, looking to nothing other than if they were lovely, and in their company proved himself a brave man.
> Seuthes asked, "Would you be willing to die, Episthenes, for his sake?"
> He stretched out his neck and said, "Strike if the boy bids and will repay my favour."

And Seuthes asked the boy if he should strike him in his stead.
The boy would not permit it, but begged him to **kill** neither.
Thereupon Episthenes, embracing the boy, said, "Time for you, Seuthes, to
fight me for the boy. I will not let him go."
Laughing, Seuthes let them be.

This combines again the light and dark, love in the midst of battle, the
murderousness of Seuthes turning to laughter, and the serious worth that
Episthenes proves through an act of boyish love. We see again the short
exchanges and the **rare word** for the self-sacrifice in "stretching out"
(ὑπερανατείνας) the neck. The **present tense** marks Xenophon's service to
Episthenes as go-between, perhaps because it is essential to the outcome.
The rare *katakainein* "kill" is used to report the boy's noble plea "to slay
neither," whereas the Attic *apokteinein* is used in Xenophon's own appeal.
Its usage creates a dactylic rhythm that may give his sentiment special
emphasis, though Dover (1997: 160–3) warns that poetic rhythms in prose
can be accidental.

In *Cyropaedia* 2.2.28–31 a heavier humor conveys the serious message
(Demetrius, *On Style* 134 comments on this) that the true friend is defined
by good service rather than good looks. A captain has brought along to
dinner "a **very hairy and ugly man**" (rare words (ὑπέρδασυν, ὑπέραισχρον)
emphasize the lack of looks) and asserts enigmatically that he just loves to
gaze upon him because he gives him such pleasure. It turns out that this
is because the man gives him such service as a friend ("Whenever I called
him night and day, he never made the excuse that he was busy, nor heark-
ened slowly, but always at a run. As many times as I told him to do something, I never saw him do it **unsweatingly**"; the rare adverb (ἀνιδρωτί) – from
Homer (*Il.* 15.228) – humorously emphasizes the epic effort he put into his
service). When the captain is asked whether he kisses his companion in the
Persian style, the ugly man reveals in his unexpected reply that charming
jokes can come even from a man without physical charm: "No, he is not
fond of toil. If he were willing to kiss me, this would take the place of all his
gymnastic exercise."

There are many other examples of charming discourse with these features. Laughter is found in the midst of tears (*Hell.* 7.2.9, 7.1.32), and jokes
in the face of death (2.4, 4.4). Xenophon also finds charm in the hunting
of the hare (*Cyn.* 5.32): "The sight is so delightful that there is no one
who after seeing the hare tracked, found, running, caught, would not forget
whatever he otherwise loved." Xenophon uses the Sapphic idea that the new
sight makes one forget "whatever it is one loves" (fr. 16 L-P); she was the
mistress of charm.

Philosophical Discourse

The philosophical works demonstrate many different modes of discourse. Most are in dialogue, but this often gives way to long speeches, sometimes in reported form; there is forensic argument in defense of Socrates from the author besides. If I had to pick out any one linguistic feature and label it, it would be force through amplification. The economical language of the boys' stories is abandoned even in *Symposium*, though its theme is the pursuit of seriousness through laughter, as when it revisits the unblinking lover (*Smp.* 4.24) or parodies the automatic agreement that we find in representations of Socratic conversational technique (*Smp.* 4.56–9). The amplification takes various forms. One is the kind of sentence structure that creates force with passion, as illustrated in the work on the tribulations of being a tyrant, where Hiero contrasts the peace he had as a private man with the war he now endures as a ruler hated by his subjects (*Hiero* 6):

> I kept company with my peers, delighting in them as they delighted in me, I kept company with myself whenever I desired quiet times, I spent my time in drinking parties, often to the point of forgetting all the distress of the human condition, often to the point where my soul was saturated with songs and delights and dancing, often to the point of putting my desires to sleep and those of my companions. But now I am deprived of those who delight in me because I have slaves as companions rather than friends, I am deprived too of spending time delightfully in their company because I detect no goodwill in them for me. Drink and sleep I avoid like an ambush. To fear the crowd, to fear solitude, to fear lack of guards, to fear those themselves who guard me, and to be unwilling to have unarmed men around me nor to look with delight upon armed ones, how is this not a hard circumstance?

This passage uses groups of three clauses with anaphora, as in the description of the slaughter in the *Cyropaedia* discussed above. The first triple renders the pleasures of different sorts of company, with the third type of company (the drinking party) generating another triple: forgetting pain, filling with pleasure, subduing the desires themselves. A double then spells out the reality: deprivation of the pleasure of company and transformation of the pleasures into an ambush. A second triple then marshals opposites, where no desires are fulfilled because they cancel each other out, climaxing in the rhetorical question. A triple is used of another pleasure, the delights of warfare, at 4.6.[23]

In another kind of amplification designed to achieve forceful exactness in philosophical argument, Xenophon uses other kinds of sentence structures

---

[23] See loc. cit. in Gray 2007.

in repeated clusters, with due regard for variation of vocabulary, as in *Memorabilia* 3.2; here again, ellipse and economy are notably absent.[24]

1. Meeting a man once who had been elected general, he said, **why do you think Homer called** Agamemnon shepherd of the people?
2. **Is it because,** as the shepherd must see to it that the sheep **will be safe and have provisions, and the aim for which they** are fed **will be achieved,** so the general must see to it that the soldiers **are safe and will have provisions, and the aim for which they** go to war **will be achieved?**
3. And **they go to war in order that** they conquer the enemy and become more prosperous?
1. Or **for what reason do you think he praised** Agamemnon thus: Both, good king and mighty spearman?
2. **Is it because** he would be a mighty spearman not if he alone fought against the enemy, but if he was responsible for this for all the army, and a good king not only if he alone should take charge of his own life, but if also being king he was responsible for the prosperity of these?
3. For a **king is elected not in order** to look after himself, but **in order that those electing him** do well?
4. And all **go to war in order** to secure the best life **and they elect generals** for this, in order that they lead them towards it.

This forceful exactness through repetition also marks the report of how Socrates limited scientific learning according to the principle that it be "easy to learn" (*Mem.* 4.7). Here Xenophon repeats over a series of five areas of learning 1) the area, 2) the limit to which it should be learned, 3) the assertion that it is easy to learn, 4) how he deplored learning beyond this limit, 5) how he himself had ability beyond the limit, but 6) discouraged others from going beyond it on the grounds that it sacrificed other more useful areas of learning. The scheme loosens as the examples progress, with a digression on Anaxagoras as one who went beyond the limit and wasted his time. This style appears again in *Lac. Pol.* when he praises Lycurgus' laws, stating time after time: a) the law as it exists in other poleis, b) the different law he passed, c) its motivation, d) how it contributed to Spartan prosperity. A simpler amplification consisting of sequences of rhetorical questions also occurs (sixteen in a row to prove the lawful man happy at *Mem.* 4.4.17). There are sundry examples of this force through repetition also in the defense of Socrates in *Memorabilia* 1, for instance (with litotes) at 1.1.2: "In sacrificing **he was visible, frequently at home, frequently on the**

---

[24] Dover 1997: 131–59 illustrates the importance of variety within patterns, with examples from Xenophon: 139, 154–5.

public altars of the polis, and using divination **he was not invisible,**" and in the denunciation of Critias and Alcibiades (*Mem.* 1.2.24).

There is a high rate of rare words in the philosophical works, due partly to unusual subject matter, but also the tendency towards amplification, where for instance Xenophon imports rare alpha privatives in order to enforce the meaning of the positive by giving the negative notion, or to reinforce a series.[25] Some examples are (rare forms in bold): *Mem.* 4.7.5 wandering ... **unfixed,** πλάνητας ... **ἀσταθμήτους;** *Oec.* 12.18 museless ... mused ἄμουσον ... μουσικούς; *Mem.* 2.1.31 of sight **unseeing** θεάματος **ἀθέατος;** *Mem.* 4.2.20 grammatical ... **ungrammatical** γραμματικός ... **ἀγράμματος;** *Mem.* 2.4.3 untreated ... uninspected **ἀθεράπευτον** ... ἀνεπίσκεπτον; *Mem.* 2.3.4 brothered ... **unbrothered** συναδέλφους ... **ἀναδέλφων;** *Mem.* 3.10.5 sober and thoughtful, proud and **insensitive** καὶ τὸ σωφρονικόν τε καὶ φρόνιμον καὶ ὑβριστικόν τε καὶ **ἀπειρόκαλον;** *Mem.* 4.3.13 untrodden and pure and **deathless** ἀτριβῆ τε καὶ ὑγιᾶ καὶ **ἀγήρατα** (cf. the same vocabulary at *Cyr.* 8.7.22: untrodden and deathless and unerring and indescribable, and at *Ages.* 11.14 ages ... **unageing** γηράσκει ... **ἀγήρατος**). We also find other balanced pairs: *Mem.* 1.4.6 visible ... **hearable** ὁρατά ... **ἀκουστά;** *Mem.* 1.4.4–7 insensate and **unmoving** ἄφρονα καὶ **ἀκίνητα;** *Mem.* 2.1.23 untasting ... unused ἄγευστος ... ἄπειρος. New *dys*-compounds also create amplification: *Mem.* 4.1.3–4 hard to restrain and dissuade δυσκαθέκτους ... δυσαποτρέπτους; *Mem.* 4.2.25 obeying easily or hard εὐπειθής ... δυσπειθής.

This kind of amplification also produces the opposed pairing of nineteen adjectives to describe the qualities needed by the leader (*Mem.* 3.1.6), many of them rare *–ikos* compounds, including "letting go," *proetikon*, to balance "seizing," *harpaga*. More neutrally, *Mem.* 4.2.20 has "writes and reads," "lies and deceives." Amplifications of this kind create grandeur as well as forcefulness in the "Choice of Heracles," which is a version of the lecture of Prodicus that Socrates says used "even grander phrases" than he uses himself.[26] *Symposium* too uses rare words in balance to spell out the spiritual nature of the love of Zeus for Ganymede (8.31): "he was not named for **being pleasant in body** (ἡδυσώματος from comic poetry), but being **pleasant in mind** (ἡδυγνώμων, a unique word) was he honored among the gods."

The example above shows also how the rare word continues to highlight important matters, as it did in other styles of discourse. It happens in other passages where Socrates denounces the carnal lover: *Smp.* 8.23–4, "he follows him round always begging and beseeching for a kiss or some **gross touch** (ψηλαφήματος). If I speak too **torridly** (λαμυρώτερον) do not wonder;

---

[25] Fehling 1969: 235–41 notes such pairings in earlier, often poetic literature.
[26] Gray 2006 studies the language of this piece, focusing on the issue of authenticity.

the wine inspires me and the lust that lives within me goads me on to speak freely against that other lust." *Mem.* 1.2.29–30 uses a rare veterinary image to underscore the denunciation of Critias for such carnality. "He said that he thought Critias was suffering from the swine's disease, in his desire to **rub up against** (προσκνῆσθαι) Euthydemus like a pig rubs against stones." Plutarch uses the word of pigs that rub their testicles against trees and "unman" them (*Aetia Physica* 917d), following Aristotle's indication that this is due to an itching disease of the testicles (*HA* 578b).

In a more uplifting description of the features that make a house beautiful and useful (*Mem.* 3.8.8–10), Xenophon uses *chthamalōtera* for the low-built side of the house that shuts out winter winds ("lofty to the south so the winter sun is not shut out, lowly to the north so the cold winds do not disturb it"). Homer alone uses it before him, and is possibly designed to enhance the need for beauty in the design (*Il.* 13.683, *Od.* 12.101).

Xenophon was of course also bound to use a high rate of rare words in those many sections of his discourse that are technical. One interesting case is the metaphor that uses building terms for how the god "built" men (*Mem.* 1.4.6):

> In addition does it not seem to you that these things are the work of fore-thought, that since sight is weak, he **puts the doors of eyelids** on it (θυρῶσαι), which when it is necessary to use them, open up, but in sleep are closed, and so that not even winds harm it, he implants **eyelashes as a sieve** (ἠθμός), and he **caps** the eyes with a **coping of brows** above (ἀπογεισῶσαι), so that not even sweat from the head harms it? And the ears receive all sounds but are never filled. And the front teeth on all animals are such as to **cut** (τέμνειν), the jaws **to grind smooth** (λεαίνειν) what they receive from them?

The verbs used here seem rare to us because they describe building processes we seldom meet in Greek literature. Perhaps they were in themselves not so rare to the ancient audience, but their metaphorical use might still have struck them as unusual. The processes apply to the basic building materials: stones, brick, wood, clay (*Mem.* 3.1.7). The verbs that describe the eyelids and brows as doors and copings are from carpentry. The word "sieve" for the eyelashes is so rare to us that the meaning is unclear even though the context shows that it serves as a windbreak, presumably restraining the current of air just as in other uses it restrains the current of water.[27] The words comparing the processing of food by the teeth to stone-working include "cutting" as well as the much rarer "grinding smooth."

---

[27] Aristotle *De partibus animalium* 658b continues the image and likens the eyelashes to a fence or curtain in front of an enclosure.

Longinus (*On the Sublime* 32) admired this metaphor ("the anatomy of the human housing is magnificently pictured") but does not specify his reasons for his judgment. That makes Xenophon's imagery yet another subject for fuller investigation, which seems a suitable point on which to end a chapter designed to show how much work is still to be done on Xenophon's language, not only in the areas sketched out above but in others there has been no space to mention even in passing.

Further Reading

There is no truly comprehensive study of Xenophon's language, but Gautier 1911 is a generally accepted starting point and Pontier 2014 devotes a varied volume of papers to the study. Cavenaile 1975 has some interesting insights. Gray 2006, 2010c addresses his use of words, particularly rare words, and Gray 2014 examines how he uses plain style, as well as the more usual grand style, in addressing matters that are humble or grand. Sicking and Stork 1997 show how interesting his use of tenses can be.

12

CHRISTOPHER PELLING

Xenophon's Authorial Voice

Introduction

Let us state it plainly. Xenophon is one of the most interesting and variegated literary personalities of antiquity, someone who can take his place alongside Plutarch and Horace and Cicero. But with Xenophon, even more than those others, that judgment rests on taking all the different works and marveling at how differently the author emerges from each. There is the Xenophon of the *Anabasis*: Colonel Xenophon. There is the Xenophon of *Hellenica*: historian Xenophon. There is the Xenophon of *On Hunting*: country-gentleman Xenophon. There is the Xenophon of *Memorabilia*: reflective, Socratic Xenophon. There is the Xenophon of *Poroi*: hard-nosed economist Xenophon. There is the Xenophon of *Cyropaedia* and *Agesilaus*: hero-worshiper Xenophon, and in the *Cyropaedia* proto-novelist Xenophon to boot. And, fittingly for a prolific writer when prose was still adapting itself to a series of emerging forms, there is the literary experimenter Xenophon, the grandfather of genre after genre. Perhaps there is now the extra Xenophon as well, the Straussian Xenophon,[1] subtly undermining some at least of those stereotypes even as he develops them.

The "personality" that emerges from these self-projections certainly commands fascinated admiration, and invites reconstruction on the basis of his writings. But the subject of this chapter is different, not the global personality that emerges from the combination of all those different Xenophons but the "voices" of the individual works, a matter of constructing the textual narrator – "I-Xenophon" – rather than the flesh-and-blood individual who actually wielded the pen. How far one text makes gestures to others from that same hand is itself a question, as we shall see. But we should start from the principal texts (the shorter works will also appear, but only in passing), and see how each projects a picture of its author.

---

[1] For Straussian readings of Xenophon, see the introduction as well as the chapters by Christesen and Tamiolaki in this volume.

Two points will be recurrent. First, we shall see that the beginnings of most of these major texts tend to convey an impression of their author; middles are often less insistent, but many endings revert to a stronger authorial projection. (This is true of some of the shorter works too, for instance *Apology* and *Symposium*,[2] but not all: *Agesilaus*, *Poroi*, and *Lac. Pol.* have a strong first-person presence throughout, *Hiero* very little.) Secondly, analysis of the "authorial voice" usually implies a construction of a reader as well as a writer, sometimes with an explicit "you" (as often in the didactic *Hipparchicus*) but usually in more subtle ways. This is not a game for one but for two, and we are talking not just of constructing a writer but also of building a writer-reader dynamic. A writer is always a mouth in search of an ear.

Cyropaedia

On one occasion we fell to thinking about how many democracies had been overthrown by those who preferred some other form of government, and how many monarchies and how many oligarchies had been destroyed by the ordinary people, and how many men who had tried to become tyrants had either been totally overthrown or, if they survived in power for any time at all, had won admiration for their wisdom and their good fortune. (*Cyr.* 1.1.1)

Thus the *Cyropaedia* begins. Who are these "we"? Is it even a genuine plural at all, or is it just a case of a "writerly" plural-for-singular of the sort that we find in many early genres (and as we will find soon enough in this work, with "this is what we have to relate" and "we will recount the doings of Cyrus" at 1.2.16, then in many later cases)? More about "us" emerges as we go on in the proem. "We" know of many masters who have trouble with their servants, however many or few they may be (1.1.1); "we" reflected on how herdsmen manage their flocks more successfully than leaders manage their fellow humans (1.1.2); and then "we" remembered the case of Cyrus the Great and his massive empire, many accepting his rule willingly (1.1.3), some doing so through fear (1.1.5).

Such a man, we thought, deserves our admiration; and so we pondered who he was by birth, what sort of man by nature, and what sort of education he had had to make him so supereminent as a ruler. We will try to relate what we discovered and what we think we could perceive about the man. (1.1.6)

---

[2] At least this is true of the beginning, where Xenophon claims to have "been present" himself at an event datable to 422 BC, too early for this to be literally true.

So "we" are quite well informed about the constitutional history of various states, but not so well informed that we could relate the tale of Cyrus without further investigation; we are interested in leadership, we know it is difficult, and we admire those who carry it off. We are certainly not appalled by the notion that even an absolute ruler might have lessons to teach us through his style, nor that, like Socrates and Thrasymachus in *Republic* 1 (343b, 345d), we might find purchase in an analogy between leadership and herdsmanship, and in a less caring sense than in the old Homeric "shepherd of the people."[3] There is certainly no idealization of popular wisdom along the lines of Thucydides' Athenagoras (6.36–40); it is the qualities of the men who lead that matter. "We" also assume that education should be a prime target for our investigation; and we will include what "we think we could perceive about the man," language that suggests a process of inference as well as of straightforward factual discovery – a point not without importance to the "truth-value" of the work.[4]

Are "we" genuinely plural, or just the writer? (The opening of *Poroi*, otherwise rather similar, has "I" throughout.) At the beginning it may sound more plural, the topic of a reflective conversation among like-minded gentlemen; by the end, the research sounds more a matter for the single investigator, and the "relating" even more so. But those initial suggestions of plurality may still insinuate the notion that the investigation is of interest to more than the single writer (rather as the recurrent "we praise" and "we blame" in *On Horsemanship* leaves some impression of "we experts" even when closely juxtaposed with a writerly "we," 10.5, 12.12–13). He may not be the only one who can extend intrigued admiration even to the exotic, feared, and distant Persian court.

Most of the *Cyropaedia* is narrative of what happened, or what Xenophon affects to have happened, in a reasonably distant past; but there is also modulation between "then" and "now," keeping an eye on the present day of writer and of the first audience. There is some "now" even in the way that Cyrus is introduced: "he is said ..." to have been son of King Cambyses; "it is agreed" that his mother was Mandane; he is "spoken and sung about even today" (1.2.1).[5] Then the "now" becomes stronger, as the initial description of Cyrus' education is put in terms of current Persian practice in 1.2. That is

---

[3] "The prologue shows signs of becoming an introduction to a handbook on human husbandry," Tatum 1989: 61–2; cf. Brock 2004: 247, 250–1. The gentler implications of the Homeric use are discussed by Xenophon himself at *Mem.* 3.2.
[4] Due 1989: 30.
[5] Gray 2004c: 394.

also contrasted with what goes on "here," placing readers as well as writer as distinctively Greek[6]:

> In promoting the common good, Persian educational customs seem to start from a different point from that of most of the cities here. For most cities allow people to educate their own children in any way they like and the older people to live any way they please, and then tell them not to steal or to rob, not to force their way into any house, not to strike anyone unjustly, not to commit adultery, not to disobey anyone in authority, and everything else along similar lines. If anyone breaks any of these rules, then they punish him. The Persian customs by contrast are preventative: their concern is to ensure that citizens will not be the sort of people in the first place to feel any desire for anything bad or shaming ... (1.2.2)

And so it goes on, again conveying the impression of a writer who is prepared to admire that different approach, and of readers "here" who are prepared to listen. There is also an individual note in some of the values:

> The students also hold trials of one another on the charge that leads people to feel most mutual hatred but is most rarely the subject of lawsuits – ingratitude: and when they find someone who was in a position to repay a favor and did not do so, they impose a harsh punishment. (1.2.7)

So again a hint of what happens (or in this case does not happen) in the world that the reader knows, though this time the "here" is not made explicit.

"Throughout most of the *Cyropaedia* there is little doubt that Cyrus is meant to be an ideal figure, a successful ruler whose model conduct is well worth emulating."[7] This is not the place to debate the case for ironic or subversive readings,[8] but it can at least be said that such interpretations have to penetrate below the narrative surface: the narrative provides no explicit prompt to suggest that the writer himself feels reservations. Still, once or twice one can also understand why others might have taken a different view. There are hints in book 1, for instance, that young Cyrus' precocious questioning at Astyages' court might have been tiresome, acknowledging that perhaps he *was* a little mouthy (πολυλογώτερος, 1.4.3). It is genuinely unclear, too, whether he was right in judging that a small boy with a big coat should give it up to a big boy with a small coat.[9] His mentor thinks

---

[6] A little later there is a reference to "our" education (παρ' ἡμῖν, 1.2.6), which is usually taken as "Athenian" (as in a similar "with us" at *Hiero* 9.4): but at 1.2.2 "most of the cities" clearly points to something more general about Greek practice, and Due 1989: 104–5 and n. 54 is right to think that at 1.2.6 too the perspective is broader.

[7] Gera 1993: 280.

[8] See Tamiolaki in this volume. For discussion and rejection of such readings see esp. Due 1989: 207–29.

[9] For recent discussion see Gera 1993: 74–5; Nadon 2001: 47–50; Danzig 2009; Field 2012: 726 and n. 5.

that the decision was unjust, and punishes Cyrus for it (1.3.16–17). But even the precocity is a sign of great things to come, and the decision on the coats is hardly to Cyrus' discredit. It is no surprise, after all, if even this most talented of young men still has something to learn.

The modulation between "then" and "now" also recurs: many phrases like ἔτι καὶ νῦν ("still even now") point to customs that survive "even now," again underlining the lasting importance of Cyrus' achievement. There is the occasional use of the first person as well, almost always of a "writerly" kind – "I (or "we") will relate ..." or "as I said earlier" – but on a few occasions to express an approving judgment, always marking moments of some importance.[10] But for most of the work these "zoomings"[11] to the writer's or audience's own day are quite sparing. The narrative simply moves forward in the "then" mode, drawing the audience into those distant times and places and retaining their attention through its vividness.

As the narrative reaches its later stages, those ἔτι καὶ νῦνs become more frequent; that may just reflect Cyrus' increasing power, creating even more ability to make lasting reforms, but the zooming also goes with an increasing focus on the writer-reader dynamic. From 7.5 onwards the all-conquering Cyrus decides to cloak himself in a greater veil of inaccessibility and to adopt more Median and less Persian ways. Readers have often found this drift jarring after so much emphasis on his earlier restraint. Several shifts, sometimes gentle ones, in the narrative technique may suggest that such a readerly response is assumed, and even that a reader is constructed who is expected to be resistant, feeling the debatability of the new policy's wisdom. The writer defends – but the need for defensiveness is acknowledged, and there is a new sense of dialogue.

Grammatical first persons duly become more frequent, including a new emphasis on that process of interpretative inference that the proem had suggested:

> We seem to learn (καταμαθεῖν) of Cyrus that he thought that rulers should differ from their subjects not merely by being better than them, but also thought that he ought to bewitch them. At least, he decided to wear Median dress himself and persuaded his associates to wear it too ... (8.1.40)

---

[10] Due 1989: 31–2; Gray 2004c: 392–3.

[11] I adopt here the terminology applied illuminatingly to several aspects of Greek culture by Christiane Sourvinou-Inwood, e.g. 1989 on *Antigone*, explaining the term at 136 ("'*zooming-devices*', which had the effect of bringing the world nearer, pushing the audience into relating their experiences and assumptions directly to the play"), and more generally 2006: 296–302. Both types of zooming mentioned here, the ἔτι καὶ νῦνs and the writerly first persons, have historiographic precedents in Herodotus and Thucydides.

"To bewitch" (καταγοητεύειν): mystification is becoming the order of the day, and it is to make the elite "harder to disrespect" (δυσκαταφρονητοτέρους, 8.1.42). Then a clutch of rhetorical questions address the Persian king's habit of generous giving:

> For who has friends who are more conspicuously wealthy than the Persian king? Who gives his companions finer outfits to wear than the King? Whose gifts are so readily recognized as some of the King's, bracelets and necklaces and horses with golden bridles? (8.2.8)

By now the impression is of a reader who needs to be persuaded, not just told. That reader may be coming with false assumptions, too: "if anyone thinks that there is one chosen King's Eye, he is mistaken," for "we have learned" better – κατεμάθομεν again. Nor is it difficult to sense some defensiveness, this time in a direction that would seem to go against Xenophon's usual praise of leadership based on willing followers:

> People are everywhere afraid about saying things that go against the King, as if he were himself listening, or do such things, as if he were himself present. No one would even say anything negative about Cyrus to anyone else, but each person would behave as if everyone present was the ears and eyes of the king. I do not know how one could explain this attitude towards him unless one says that he wanted his benefits to others to be big ones in return for small. (8.2.12)

The wording of that last sentence is crabbed, and there may be some extra nuances. The word for "explain" (αἰτιάσαιτο) can also carry a sense of "find to blame," leaving it open whether the critics or Cyrus might be blameworthy; and does "in return for small" mean "big benefits that outweigh the small harms or "big benefits that Cyrus conferred in return for the small benefits that he received"? Either way, it is made clear that not all Cyrus' subjects were as enthusiastic as the narrator has been, and "what one could find to blame" draws readers in too to try their own speculative interpretations.

That sense of writer-reader engagement is not wholly new: when Gadatas' force was in grave danger, they suddenly see Cyrus approaching with his army, and "one must imagine them rushing up to the new arrivals with joy, like voyagers reaching harbor after a storm" (5.4.6). But it has become much stronger. Several instances of "it is not surprising" (οὐ θαυμαστόν, 8.2.5, 13, 14; 8.4.6) deflect but also assume the "surprise" that a reader might feel with a lesser mortal. Another first person introduces the grandeur of Cyrus' royal progress as he leaves the palace, and again one senses some defensiveness: "The majesty of this very progress seems to us to be one of his techniques for protecting his rule from disrespect" (8.3.1). That "majesty," σεμνότης, strikes an important note, as it is the elaborate Median costume of his entourage that is stressed: "and that was the first time that Persians put on Median dress." The narrative still takes Cyrus' side (8.3.4); but even if I-Xenophon approves, the need for explanations also assumes a reader who is uneasy. Not for the only time, there is a strange prefiguring of events a generation or so later than Xenophon, when Alexander's adoption of Median dress and customs went down so badly with Greeks. Here it is Xenophon's Greek readership that may feel similar reservations.

In the text as we have it,[12] that readerly unease culminates, strikingly, with the denouncing of the degenerate Persia of today (8.8). Hitherto the ἔτι καὶ νῦν stressed continuities from those earlier glory days; the "now"s of this final appendix stress differences. How well this sits with the earlier narratorial persona is a good question.[13] Certainly, the tune seems rather different here from that idealized picture of contemporary Persian education in 1.2, and that can only partly be explained by the difference between "Persian" in 1.2 and the "Median" emphasis of book 8, for it is made clear that the Persians themselves have generally adopted those Median ways (cf. esp. 8.8.15 and then 8.8.27, quoted below). Still, this stress on degeneration does not come wholly out of the blue[14] (any more than the negative ch. 14 of *Lacedaemonion Politeia* is wholly unprepared: Humble 2004a). Cyrus' dying speech carried clear hints of the fraternal squabbling among his sons that will follow: sharp as ever, the old man knew what there was to fear (8.7.14–17), and the reader is clearly assumed to know, from Herodotus or elsewhere, that young Cambyses and his brother have trouble ahead. Plato's response to *Cyropaedia* in the *Laws* (694a–5b) can indeed be seen as accepting an invitation that Xenophon's own text offers, whether or not the reader would also follow Plato's individual train of thought there – that Cyrus had only himself to blame if he did not give his sons a proper ... *education!*[15]

---

[12] See Tamiolaki in this volumeon the authenticity of 8.8.

[13] Cf. Hirsch 1985: 92–5 for a vigorous attack on these "inconsistencies"; *contra*, Due 1989: 37–8, and, for a particularly insightful treatment of "the Medo-Persian balance" that the *Cyropaedia* may eventually commend, Azoulay 2004b. Note also Tamiolaki in this volume.

[14] Gera 1993: ch. 5 has a sensitive discussion of this growing unease in the later books; Gray 2004d: 394 similarly thinks that it "underestimates the narratees" to suppose that the epilogue comes as a shocking surprise. Delebecque 1957: 406–7 identifies some other trails in the earlier narrative that lead to 8.8.

[15] "Xenophon had given Plato all the opening he needed," Tatum 1989: 231; cf. Due 1989: 21–2. In contrast Gera 1993: 125 argued that Cyrus' words "virtually refute in advance" Plato's criticisms.

That increased sense of writer-reader dialogue also continues. The turn to the present is immediately marked by a first person (8.8.1), the first of many in this chapter: "that I am telling the truth I shall now demonstrate, starting with the gods. For I know" that earlier the king and the associates would keep their oaths ... Some specific contemporary misdeeds are adduced as proof of the decline, beginning with the episode that Xenophon recounts – had probably already recounted[16] – in the *Anabasis* where the generals were lured to Tissaphernes' camp and sent on to their deaths (8.8.3, cf. *Anab.* 2.5). A rhetorical question keeps the reader engaged: "when it comes to warfare, how can they *not* be expected to be weaker in every respect than they once were?" (8.8.20). And the work ends with a vigorous challenge to the reader:

> I think, then, that the task I set myself is now complete. My claim is that the Persians and their associates have been shown to have become more irreligious to the gods, more impious to their kinsmen, more unjust to others, and more cowardly with regard to warfare than they once were. If anyone takes the opposite view, examination of the facts about the Persians will be found to bear out what I say. (8.8.27)

In most of book 8, the hints of a sceptical, cross-grained reader have pointed to one more critical of Cyrus than the narrator has been; here the cross-graining points in a different direction, to one who is less hard on contemporary Persia than I-Xenophon himself. But this time it is more likely that this construction of a hostile reader is an empty gesture. I-Xenophon's contempt for Persian degeneracy and unmanliness is more likely to chime with his audience's prejudices than his defense of Cyrus' authoritative remoteness.[17]

How much does the reader know or care about Xenophon himself by the end of all this, especially now that those first persons have intruded the writer's presence more forcefully? The only explicit indications of the author's life were those in the proem, and they were generic rather than specific; most of the work could have been written by anyone with some knowledge of the Persian world as it is "even now." Even hints that the author is a military man are rare (one perhaps at 7.1.30, "it has become clear on many other

[16] Not that the dates of the works are at all secure.
[17] As Gruen 2011: 64–5 rightly says. But Gruen reads 8.8 as a caricature of such dismissiveness, one that the canny reader will reject as ridiculously overstated. If this was Xenophon's strategy, then he was playing a dangerous game: sophisticated irony is seldom more likely to misfire than when it parodies its audience's strong views, especially when doing so in ways which (as here the history of scholarly bemusement makes clear) are very easy to miss.

occasions too that a phalanx is at its strongest when composed of allies on good terms with one another ...")[18] and if Xenophon draws on his own experience during the long march he gives only the barest hints of it. There may be occasions when the reader is prompted to remember Socrates and Athens, and plot Persian experience against that Greek paradigm (especially 3.1.38–40);[19] there are certainly times when the story may seem to prefigure the younger Cyrus.[20] Knowledgeable readers might recall that the author was himself a follower of both the philosopher and the prince, just as they might when *Oeconomicus* discusses the merits of the younger Cyrus (4.18–25); but not much is lost if they do not.

What, though, of this last chapter? Is it mere coincidence that his first contemporary example should be one that touched his own experience so closely? Do the audience remember that he, of all people, should know, as he has fought these Persian foes? And if so, do they wonder what inferences he might want them to draw? Panhellenism was after all a flavor of the period; Isocrates was probably already arguing for a Panhellenic crusade against that ancestral Persian foe.[21] It was an atmosphere that Philip and then Alexander would know how to play to. Is it one that Xenophon too is encouraging, as some have thought?[22] Is the inference that the Persians are an easy target now, even if they had not been a century and more earlier? That Greeks should not be doing their fighting for the Persians as mercenaries, but against them? That question is left hanging in the air; but that increasingly dialogic tone encourages an audience to carry on wondering. Maybe the reader-writer dynamic has ended in an odd place, where the admiration for Persia has given way to an aggressively bellicose Hellenism; but the moral is left for the reader to draw, and the writerly persona ends as an enigmatic one.

---

[18] For further possible cases cf. Due 1989: 109–14.

[19] Cf. Gera 1993: ch. 2.

[20] Gera 1993: 11, 124–5, 240–1; Flower 2012: 51.

[21] Esp. Isoc. 4 (*Panegyricus*, 380 BC) 184. On Panhellenism in the fourth century see esp. Mitchell 2007 and Flower 2012: 169–88, though Flower, like Rood 2004a, is sceptical of such readings of *Anabasis*. In contrast Dillery 1995 finds a consistent strand of nuanced Panhellenism throughout Xenophon's works.

[22] Notably Prinz 1911 and Luccioni 1947a: 232 ("La *Cyropédie* est comme le manuel du futur conquérant de l'Asie"); *contra*, Due 1989: 23–4, 162. In a thoughtful discussion Carlier 1978/2010 eventually decides that the reader might conclude that conquest was practicable but undesirably disruptive, for only an absolute monarch could carry it through. Still, it is hard to think that all readers, once encouraged into this train of thought, would reach exactly that nuanced conclusion.

Memorabilia

Like *Cyropaedia*, the *Memorabilia* begins with a strong first person, this time unambiguously "I" rather than "we":

> I have often wondered what could possibly be the arguments that Socrates' accusers used to persuade the city that he deserved to die. The charge was as follows: "Socrates' crime is that he fails to believe in the gods recognized by the city and that he is introducing new divinities; it is also that he corrupts the young." (1.1.1)

Then comes a flurry of rhetorical questions:

> Whatever proof did they use to demonstrate his failure to believe in the gods that the city recognized? ... Who would not agree that he did not want to appear foolish or boastful to his companions? ... In whom would anyone place more trust than in a god? And if he trusted the gods how could it be that he failed to believe in them? (1.1.2, 5)

These are a particular sort of rhetorical question, though: not ones like those towards the end of *Cyropaedia*, implying a resistant reader; more ones that convey the writer's indignation, and if anything imply a reader who will share that perplexity. The tone does become calmer, but both the rhetorical questioning – one can understand jurors getting wrong things that were not known, but "is it not amazing that they did not recall matters that everyone knew?," 1.1.16 – and the grammatical first person come back to round off the argument:

> So I wonder (θαυμάζω, the same word as in the first sentence) how the Athenians could ever have been persuaded that Socrates had unsound views about the gods, this man who never said or did anything impious about the gods but said and did those things which would make one be, and be seen to be, the most pious human alive. (1.1.20)

Similar rhetorical questions and first persons then mark off subsections in the argument of 1.2 – we see that too in works like *Agesilaus* and *Lac. Pol.* where the authorial voice is prominent – and here they also build a picture of I-Xenophon as someone very different from the accusers.

> How could a man like that corrupt the young? Unless of course practicing virtue is a form of corruption. And then – by Heaven – the accuser claimed that he made his companions despise the established laws ... I by contrast think that people who practice wisdom and believe they will be able to teach citizens useful lessons are the least likely to employ violence ... (1.2.9–10)

And so on, with insistent contrasts of "the accuser" (or a "someone" who "might say") and an "I" who recurrently knows better; "them" and "us," or at least "them" and "me."

Where does this better knowledge come from? The picture of that too fills out in 1.2, and with it the presentation of this "I." Sometimes he cites others' reports: look what Socrates is claimed to have said about Critias' infatuation with Euthydemus before many witnesses, including Euthydemus himself (1.2.30). Sometimes it is life experience: "I" have seen enough people led astray by drink or sex to know that acquired prudence sometimes does not last (1.2.22). But there are indications too of personal encounters:[23] "I never heard Socrates say anything like that myself, nor did I gather from anyone else that they had heard any such thing" (1.2.32); "I know that he did say that about fathers and other relatives ..." (1.2.53). That leaves open the possibility that other "I knows" are based on personal knowledge, not just report:

> I know that that pair too (Critias and Alcibiades) were sensible for as long as they were with Socrates, not because they had any fear that they might be fined or struck by Socrates but because they thought at that time that this was the best way to behave. (1.2.18)

These briefer cases provide the setting for the more elaborate versions of encounters, including reported conversation: the exchange of Socrates with Critias and Charicles about exactly what conversations he was allowed to have with "the young" (1.2.33–8), or that of the young and precocious Alcibiades with his guardian Pericles (1.2.40–6). Those clearly do not rest on first-hand knowledge ("it is said," 1.2.40), and any reader who wondered about the circumstantial detail would have few doubts that the narrator had elaborated what he had heard. In that way they presage the manner of the rest of the work. But their insertion into this setting where those "I knows" have been building the narrator's authority also suggests more authenticity than that "what we discovered and what we think we could perceive about the man" in *Cyropaedia*, and that continues in the transition into the main narrative:

> As for the ways that he seemed to me to give benefit to those around him, partly by showing in his actions what sort of person he was, partly by his conversation – I will now describe as many of these as I can remember. (1.3.1)

---

[23] This need not imply that all these claims are historically accurate: Waterfield 2004: 87 and Patzer 1999/2010: 232–3 indeed took such passages in *Mem.* and elsewhere as markers of literary fiction, along the lines of the *Lügensignale* ("pointers to lying") that Fehling found in Herodotus' claims to autopsy (Fehling 1979: esp. 120–1). That seems to me to go too far (as does Fehling), even though a similar claim at the beginning of *Apology* is demonstrably false (n. 1); but my subject here is anyway literary presentation, not historical truth.

By now we know that "I-Xenophon" knew Socrates, took part in discussions, and has many memories. What may come as a surprise, though less so if (a big "if") he had already written the *Anabasis*, is the introduction of a third-person "he-Xenophon" as well: but he comes in soon enough (1.3.8–15). Socrates had heard from Crito that Critobulus had kissed the beautiful son of Alcibiades (so already the story has a crowded stage), and asked Xenophon whether he thought Critobulus a prudent man rather than a risk-taker… And the story goes on, with Socrates dwelling on the dangers of lust for the beautiful, with a kiss being as dangerous as the bite of a venomous spider. He-Xenophon admits that he'd have quite liked such a kiss himself, so is given some personality; that adds something as well, indicating that this is not just about Critobulus (even though his taste for a pretty boy crops up elsewhere, 2.6.30–3) but that others too might easily have been the risk-taking men of lust.

Still, any interlocutor making the same confession could have added that much. Why "he-Xenophon" in particular? This is the only time in the entire work that he appears, and it is unlikely to be coincidence that it comes so early. He may, of course, simply be there because it is true and he played exactly the role that he describes, but if we take it just as a story, he-Xenophon's role is unnecessary: it could have been filled by Crito, for instance. At least for those who appreciated that the narrator and "Xenophon" are one and the same – and admittedly there is no phrasing like "Thucydides son of Olorus, who wrote this history" (Thuc. 4.104.4) to give a pointer – the effect is presumably one of building the text's authority still further. This conversation can be taken as programmatic, an example of all the others that he-Xenophon witnessed and I-Xenophon will relate. But it is also an example of something more, for he-Xenophon was clearly chastened and learned from it, in the words of that transitional rubric, "what sort of person" Socrates was and how that model could give him benefit. He may be gesturing towards his own life, not just Socrates', as a witness for the defense: his own sexual behavior in later life, and perhaps Critobulus' too, had been reputable enough to stand muster (which need not mean total homosexual abstinence[24]), and they have Socrates' teaching to thank for it.

He-Xenophon then disappears from the work; even I-Xenophon mutes his voice for most of books 2 and 3, with a diminishing use even of that bookending "I" (only three cases in book 3). Perhaps the warmth of personal admiration no longer needs the explicit first persons, especially at the strong opening of the final book:

[24] Cf. Hindley 1999.

In this way, then, Socrates brought benefit in everything he did and in every way, so that anyone considering it with even the slightest perception would see that nothing could be more beneficial than keeping Socrates' company, spending the day with him in any way and in any matter that they could. (4.1.1)

And that book goes on to dwell on the impact that Socrates had on those around him, especially well-born youths with political aspirations, men like Euthydemus (4.2–3), men indeed like Critias and Alcibiades: that too no longer needs to be explicit, but those terms of the accusation lurk particularly in the background of this final book.

The personal tone comes back more explicitly as well, not just with a recurrence of those initial and concluding "I"s (five such beginnings in the book and one conclusion, "He won over his audience more than anyone else I know," 4.6.15), but more pointedly: "I was there myself when he had the following conversation with Euthydemus" (4.3.2, cf. 4.4.5, 4.5.2, 4.8.3). As the work nears its end, there is a stronger awareness too of a possible adversary:

> If there is anyone who has in mind his death sentence on the grounds that he said that the divine told him what he should and shouldn't do and thinks that he has been shown to be lying about the heavenly power, this is what they should bear in mind: ... (4.8.1)

And the narrator takes again to rhetorical questions, a technique that has been left aside since the early chapters of book 1 – perhaps because there have been questions enough, those put in the stories by Socrates himself. But now:

> How could one have a finer death than this? How could any death be finer than the finest way to die? How could any death be happier than the finest? How could any be dearer to the gods than the happiest? (4.8.3)

The personal and adversarial note culminates in the final paragraph:

> As for my own view of this man who was as I have portrayed him: I thought him so pious a man as to do nothing without the gods' will, so just as to avoid harming anyone even in the slightest degree but to give the greatest possible help to those who kept his company, so self-controlled as never to choose the more pleasurable over the better course, so wise as never to go astray in discriminating the better from the worse or to need anyone else to help him as his own abilities were sufficient to judge, so lucid as to be able to define and convey such insights and able also to evaluate others, show them where they were going wrong, and spur them on to virtue and to honorable conduct. That was the sort of man I thought him, with the qualities to make him the best and most blessed man alive. And if anyone takes a different view, let them compare other peoples' character, and make their choice. (4.8.11)

We have seen that note of final challenge before, but here it is rather different. There is no hint here of a really resistant reader as there had been in *Cyropaedia*, any more than towards the end of *Agesilaus*, "if anyone doesn't believe me, let them take a look at the man's house ...," 8.4 (contrast *Poroi* 4.18–32, where there is a genuine sense of potential skepticism); no hint either of a challenge to a potential historian-follower, as we shall see in *Hellenica*. Instead, there has been that recurrent and gathering hint of a different party – those accusers, so very different from I-Xenophon or, by now, from his implied readers who have the "perception" that he invoked at 4.1.1. And "benefit," "help," "spur them on": those keynotes have kept recurring, and form Xenophon's riposte to those accusers who thought his influence on others was pernicious. The case has been made, and the glove defiantly thrown down.

Hellenica

"After these things ...": thus Xenophon begins, almost but not quite continuing Thucydides' truncated end;[25] rather as Thucydides' *pentekontaetia* began almost but not quite where Herodotus finished. In each case the suture comes in the region of the Hellespont, itself a bridging- and dividing-point between two worlds. No formal proem here, not even any grammatical first or second persons, but still an implied point about both author and reader. Xenophon aspires to be the new Thucydides; the idea of a serial canon is taking shape, with a sequence of writers each in turn claiming to be the authoritative narrator for the newest period of history.[26] So this, in a different way again, is a further case where the authorial presence is strongly felt as the work opens. And it is a construction of reader too, just as any hints of Herodotus in *Cyropaedia* or of Plato in the Socratic works assume a reader familiar with those texts. Here the allusiveness similarly implies a reader who knows enough about Thucydides to catch the point, perhaps including Thucydides' own relation to Herodotus, just as various passages later in the work construct a reader who has expectations of what will appear in a historical narrative and (so I-Xenophon affects[27]) finds them dashed or expanded: Theramenes' dying joke at Critias' expense may seem "not worth mentioning," but I-Xenophon finds it "admirable" (2.3.56); big cities get all the attention, but little ones like Phlius deserve it too (7.2.1).

---

[25] Marincola 1997: 237–8 and n. 107; Gomme, Andrewes, and Dover 1981: 439–40. On the subtle and allusive texture of Xenophon's "continuation" see esp. Rood 2004b, and now Pitcher forthcoming.

[26] On this see Marincola 1997: 237–41 and 289–92.

[27] Though in fact such material is not so unconventional as all that: the similarity to Herodotus is stressed by Gray 1989: e.g. 28.

It is notable, indeed, that these projections of a strong I-Xenophon come precisely at points where he is redirecting the nature of the historiographic enterprise.[28] This, indeed, is to be something big.

If, too, the narrative texture changes, moving after the end of the Peloponnesian War to something perceptibly less Thucydidean,[29] that may be a point about the historian growing more confident in projecting his own voice,[30] or (more interestingly) responding with interpretative and literary sensitivity to the changing nature of history itself, with its complex and interlocking movements no longer so suited to telling in terms of two power blocks and clashing ideologies. The expanded Corcyra sequence at 6.2.6–39, with several strong Thucydidean echoes, makes a fascinating test case, exploring how much has changed since the Peloponnesian War, e.g. the character of naval warfare now that Athens is no longer dominant at sea, and how much has not or has got worse, e.g. the boorishly brutal Spartan leadership style at §19. For the sophisticated ear that such allusiveness implies, narrative manner, however superficially impersonal, is never as impersonal as all that.

"However superficially impersonal ...": but how impersonal *is* the narrative? He-Xenophon is not even allowed the miserly single appearance he had in *Memorabilia*: when the opportunity offers the text simply has "the one who was in charge of the Cyreans" (3.2.7, if we assume that this still is Xenophon[31]); and the author of a monograph on the Ten Thousand is, mysteriously, "Themistogenes of Syracuse" (3.1.2, below, p. 260). As for I-Xenophon, the various markers we have seen already in *Cyropaedia* and *Memorabilia*, grammatical first persons or rhetorical questions or references to "even now," are fairly rare.[32] When they do come, they tend to cluster at times when moral judgment is hard to resist, for instance in the last quarter of book 2 with the Theramenes trial and the dark days of the Thirty (2.3.56, 2.4.27, 2.4.43). Enthusiasm for individuals can particularly excite such interventions: it is no coincidence that some comments on Agesilaus show those authorial markers, overlapping in style as well as content with the parallel passages in the encomium (3.4.16–8 and *Ages.* 1.25–8; 4.3.19–23 and *Ages.* 2.12–16). Teleutias is another who excites that sort of explicit personal enthusiasm (5.1.3–4, 5.1.19, 5.3.7); Phoebidas equally explicit disapproval

---

[28] I owe this point to John Marincola.
[29] "A progression suggestive of a stronger Thucydidean *color* at the start," Moles 1992: 283. Cf. Marincola 1999: 310–11 and Luraghi in this volume.
[30] "The author was beginning to fashion a new style, a new manner of treating history," whereas earlier he "was still feeling his way as a historian," Badian 2004: 46–7.
[31] As there is good reason to believe: Dillery 1995: 271 n. 29.
[32] Gray 2003: 119 = 2010: 566 and 2004a.

(5.2.28); and we shall see a mix of both for Iphicrates (below).[33] The implied praise or blame can be collective as well as individual: the Spartan response to the news of Leuctra draws the reader into visualization in a way that we saw in *Cyropaedia* (see p. 246):

> The next day it was possible to see the relatives of the dead in public looking sleek and radiant, but you would not have seen many of those whose menfolk had been reported alive, and those were looking grim and depressed. (6.4.16)

There are strong narratorial judgments too, often concerning the gods.

> The god then granted them an achievement such as they could never even have prayed for. To hand over to them a mass of enemy who were frightened, terrified, unarmed, with no one ready to fight and everyone performing every service to produce destruction – how could anyone fail to regard that as divine? (4.4.12)

Such passages sometimes nestle next to those apparently routine "writerly" first persons, a mannerism that we can also see in Tacitus:[34]

> There are many other instances one could quote, both Greek and barbarian, to show that the gods do not overlook those who are impious or do unholy things: now I will tell the tale. The Spartans who swore that they would respect the cities' autonomy but then occupied the Theban acropolis were punished by the very people they had wronged, when no one had ever defeated them before; and the local citizens who had brought them to the acropolis and wanted to enslave the city to the Spartans in order to get tyrannical power for themselves had their rule destroyed. A mere seven of the exiles were enough to bring this about. I will tell how it happened. (5.4.1)

There is certainly a clear personal voice there, projecting an author who himself cares about human morality, just as the gods care.

Such judgments are more frequent in *Hellenica* than in the other major works, but we can again here see a noticeable shift of manner as the narrative goes on, with the personal voice sounding louder. We can see this even in that Corcyra sequence, rich though it is with memories of Thucydides:

> I know that such training and precautious are common practice when people are expecting a naval battle. But I do commend the way that, at a time when he would soon have to arrive at the place where he expected to fight the enemy fleet, Iphicrates still found a way of ensuring that the voyage would not make

---

[33] The case of Iphicrates is discussed by Dillery 1995: 169–71, and those of both Teleutias and Iphicrates by Gray 2004b: 138–41.

[34] Pelling 2009: 152–4. Gray 2003: 115 = 2010: 560 notes that source citations also often feature alongside such "first person interventions": those are a further way in which the text can draw attention to the narratorial process of sifting and writing.

his men unskilled in what they would have to do in combat, and of doing so without delaying his arrival. (6.2.32, cf. 39)

And a bookending further first person, this time with a rhetorical question as well, rounds off the book, this time in criticism:

> I have no criticism for any fine generalship of Iphicrates on other occasions, but I find all his actions at that time to be either pointless or inexpedient. [They included sending an over-large scouting contingent.] Yet a small group can see things just as well as a big one, but if withdrawal is necessary the smaller numbers find it much easier to find an easy route and to get away quickly. As for sending a large number that is still inferior to that of the enemy – how can that not be extreme foolishness? (6.5.51–2)

That is a case too where a reader who knows of Xenophon's own military career may get an extra frisson: the narrator speaks from experience of those dangerous days when so much scouting was necessary if the Ten Thousand were to escape. But even without that knowledge the comment builds the persona of an author who knows his way around the world of marches and battlefields.

This increased sense of an author continues, and again with a particular interest in dispensing praise and blame. The small state of Phlius gets a specially good press, as we saw (7.2.1, p. 254), and then there is praise for the Eleans too (7.4.32); but it is in the run-up to the battle of Mantinea that the personal touches become particularly strong.[35] The reader is left in no doubt about the moral questionability of Theban behavior (7.4.36–40), and the Peloponnesian indignation is easy to understand, voiced in a series of rhetorical questions of their own (7.5.3). Then the author's own voice takes over, with that characteristic mix of grammatical first persons and, separately but nearby, strong projections of an authorial verdict:

> I would not myself say that Epaminondas' command went well – but, as far as forethought and daring are concerned, the man seems to me to have left nothing undone. (7.5.8)
>
> Then who could fail to admire the valor of the Athenians? They had seen that they were vastly outnumbered and had suffered a cavalry reverse in Corinth, but took no thought for that, nor for the fact that they were about to fight the Thebans and the Thessalians with their reputation for consummate horsemanship; instead they felt shame at the notion of failing to help their allies when they were on the spot, and joined battle as soon as they caught sight of the enemy, in love with the thought of preserving the glory they had inherited from their fathers. (7.5.16)

---

[35] Cf. Gray 1989: 170–5, 179–80.

"In love with"? Strong language, indeed: this is *erōs* – very likely an echo of Pericles' idealization of the Athenian hoplite in Thucydides' version of his Funeral Oration (2.43.1). Not all the old qualities are dead, then. There is old-fashioned virtue too in Epaminondas himself, knowing his responsibility for the predicament and that the time had come for glorious victory or glorious death, but taking care of his men first (7.5.19).

Yet there is one final paradox and again the divine plays a part. It was "the god" who determined that both sides behaved similarly, giving and taking back the dead under flags of truce, both claiming victory but neither with any greater territory nor power than before. "There followed even greater indecisiveness and confusion in Greece than before. Let that be the end of my tale: what followed will perhaps be the concern of someone else (7.5.27). "What followed" (τὰ δὲ μετὰ ταῦτα) echoes the "after these things" (μετὰ δὲ ταῦτα) with which the work began, and the echo is another gesture towards that serial canon. Herodotus, Thucydides, now Xenophon, and then: who? We have seen the other works raising a challenge at the end; this is in some ways the most startling, as the challenging finger could point to – you, the reader and maybe the next writer, sucked in more and more to engagement as the story has reached that climax.

Still, what a climax! Not the decisive encounter to which the narrative rhythm of book 7 may have seemed to be building: just indecisiveness and confusion. Yet, here as in the *Cyropaedia*, on a broader view a surprising ending might not after all be so unprepared. We saw how that clean-cut Thucydidean summer-and-winter, one-power-block-against-another structure has fallen away, as smaller states have come into the limelight and as old alliances have been reassessed and realigned:[36] so there has been a degree of confusion and indecisiveness already, at least compared with those old days and that older author. Is there an intimation here too of a broader insight, at least an embryonic one, into historiography itself – that a story can only be told when one can see what sort of story it is, when one can see how it is shaping? That the time has not come yet to find that shape, and may not come in time for Xenophon himself to tell the tale?[37]

Perhaps. If so, he was not wrong. It would take a generation, and the decisiveness would come from Macedon.

---

[36] Though, as Simon Hornblower reminds me, Thucydides' book 5 shows some of the same features. Closer analysis of the similarities between that book and the later parts of *Hellenica* might well be rewarding.

[37] So, tentatively, Pelling 1999: 327–8, 350 and cf. Grethlein 2013: 53; *contra*, Rood 2004b: 350 n. 27 (and cf. below, p. 269); Dillery 1995: 11, 20–7 has something in common with both my view and Rood's.

Anabasis

In comparison with *Hellenica*, Xenophon's voice in *Anabasis* is either remarkably muted or remarkably loud. All depends on whether we include he-Xenophon, the third-person leader who dominates the narrative of books 3–7, along with I-Xenophon, the narrator of the text. He-Xenophon has quite a lot to say for himself: over 20 percent of books 3–7 is taken up with his formal speeches, and there is a fair amount of dialogue and indirect speech as well. There is a lot to say about this he-Xenophon as the text portrays him: is he always right, as many have thought?[38] Or is he someone who is portrayed as feeling his way, making early mistakes that may be understandable and even creditable but finding a surer path as his experience increases[39] – someone more like the older Cyrus of *Cyropaedia*, perhaps, whose first steps were also not impeccable? Those are good questions.

Still, it is I-Xenophon that is the subject of this chapter, and in *Anabasis* he is subdued. There are still some writerly "I"s; there are still one or two expressions of the author's personal views, especially where the younger Cyrus is concerned – "so I think, based on what I hear, that no one has ever been more loved by either Greeks or barbarians," 1.9.28. Nor are we left in doubt about the qualities of the generals who meet their unfortunate end at Tissaphernes' hands, the intimidating Cleitarchus, the amiable Proxenus, and the detestable Menon (2.6). But these cluster in the first two books, especially in the context of the battle of Cunaxa;[40] afterwards, I-Xenophon sinks into silence. We can continue to infer that the story is told by an eyewitness (as when the wine needed diluting "but was then very pleasant," 4.5.27), but no more. There is an obvious explanation, for this disappearance coincides with the emergence of he-Xenophon, and the voice of the one Xenophon drowns out the other. That too is presumably the explanation for why there are so few of those strong moralizing verdicts that were such a feature of *Hellenica*. He-Xenophon is by now the one to tell people how things ought to be, and I-Xenophon discreetly leaves the stage to him.

Still, he-Xenophon cannot be left out of it completely, as of course I-Xenophon and he-Xenophon work together.[41] The analysis of the three

---

[38] E.g. Cawkwell 2004: 60, "he seems never to make a mistake … The Xenophon of the *Anabasis* always was right and righteous"; Flower 2012: 78.

[39] Thus Rood 2006: 53, 57–61; Pelling 2013: 65–6.

[40] 1.2.5, 1.9.22, 1.9.24, 1.9.28, 2.3.1, and 2.6.6. The same is true of source citations, including anonymous cases such as "it is said," which themselves convey an impression of an author weighing and manipulating the material: Gray 2003: 115 = 2010: 560; Grethlein 2013: 86–90; Pelling 2013: 43 n. 17.

[41] Cf esp. Grethlein 2012.

generals' strengths and weaknesses shows what is needed to fill the leadership vacuum at the beginning of book 3: enter he-Xenophon, and we are given a template against which to evaluate him. After the Ten Thousand had finally reached the sea, he-Xenophon is clearly attracted by the notion of founding a colony; I-Xenophon's praise of the setting at Calpe Harbor, "large enough to accommodate 10,000 people" (6.4.3), tells its own supporting tale. Earlier in the story too, Rood (2014) has shown how I-Xenophon's narrative treatment of space is molded to accentuate he-Xenophon's grasp of terrain, as he finds the right tactic to escape one predicament after another.

Yet the question exactly *how* the two Xenophons combine, the author and the general, raises the further issue whether readers would always have realized, as we do today, that they are one and the same person. Famously, the *Hellenica* seems to attribute what is pretty clearly the *Anabasis* to a certain "Themistogenes of Syracuse" (3.1.2): so was the work originally published pseudonymously? Some dismiss the idea, or at least regard any pseudonymity as a pretence that was always transparent,[42] others regard it as at least a possibility, while recognizing that we just do not know enough about contemporary book production and circulation to be sure how this would or could actually work. That is my own position, and I have mused elsewhere on how much difference it might make to one's response if one did or did not know that "Xenophon" was the author (Pelling 2013). If one did not know, then I-Xenophon's obvious approval of he-Xenophon's leadership skills might carry more weight: that was, at least partly, how Plutarch took the point of the "Themistogenes" pretence (*On the Glory of the Athenians* 345e). If one did know, then the insight he-Xenophon shows on campaign might make one more ready to acknowledge I-Xenophon's narrative knowledgability too, when for instance analyzing the difficulties or dilemmas faced on the march. He should know, after all, as he was there.

Maybe, indeed, some did not know the author's identity and some did, with the relative proportion changing over the decades until, a century or so later, the latter group finally numbered 100 percent.

Conclusion

This chapter began by distinguishing the search for Xenophon's "authorial voice" from the more global reconstruction of his personality: the one is a

---

[42] Thus, most recently, Flower 2012: 53–7.

matter of texts, the other of the flesh-and-blood author who wrote them, and in *Anabasis* in particular we have found the distinction between the textual I-Xenophon and the character he-Xenophon an important one. Yet even there we found the distinction eventually a hard one to maintain, for how else do we build our picture of the personality – the "implied author' – except by reading those texts? Grammatical first persons, as we have seen, are by no means the only way of making one's personal voice heard. A glance at *On Hunting* can show that, a work that is sparing in first persons until its last few pages, but one that still superbly conveys the writer's enthusiasm through, for instance, the hunter's direct speech – "Hey dogs! Well done, dogs! Clever dogs!" "Back here, dogs! Back here!" (6.17, 20, with more shouting in between). An author's explicit and implicit moral verdicts, likes and dislikes, favored themes and characterizing strokes, even reticences all convey a singular character behind them, pious, conservative, but willing to play with radical ideas, more practical and less metaphysically inclined than Plato, liking to find a sense of humor as well as irony in Socrates, fascinated by education, an admirer of strong but humane leadership, a man of action on campaign but a contented family man at Scillus, so very happy when he can combine the two by taking his sons and his friends hunting (*Anab.* 5.3.10). His concern with friendship and with personal relations is as clear when he picks out what he admires about Agesilaus and Socrates as when he talks of the evils of ingratitude in *Cyropaedia*.

Still, that textual analysis of authorial voice has explored one particular way in which this implied author is built; and not just a writer but an audience too, with a reader to talk to or a third party to persuade. This, then, is an I-Xenophon who delights in personal interaction and convivial dialogue on topics of passionate concern. And I dare say that the real Xenophon, not just the "implied" one, was very much the same.[43]

Further Reading

There are many incidental comments on authorial voice and personality in the standard critical works, particularly in Due 1989: focused discussion is less frequent, but has figured in important contributions of Gray, beginning with her 1989 book and continuing in separate articles and chapters (Gray 2003, 2004b–d). More recently there have been narratologically

[43] Many thanks to John Marincola, Simon Hornblower, Tim Rood, and the editor for very helpful remarks on an earlier draft.

sophisticated contributions by Rood, especially 2004a, and Flower 2012. The relationship of *Hellenica* to Thucydides is now well handled by Pitcher (forthcoming). I discussed the interaction of I-Xenophon and he-Xenophon in the *Anabasis* in Pelling 2013, and now Rood 2015b gives a subtle analysis of Xenophon's self-presentation in the crisis of *Anab.* 3.1–2.

13

TIM ROOD

Xenophon's Narrative Style

> In my opinion, the modesty of Xenophon adds a redoubled lustre to
> his merit. I find it impossible to contemplate, with a mind at ease, the
> fate of the ten thousand Greeks who followed the young Cyrus into
> the heart of Asia, until I perceive them returned to their own country.
> After having felt more anxiety than their Generals, I, at length, become
> a participator in their joy when they discover and hail that fortunate
> ocean which is to transport them into Greece.
>
> Abbé de Mably, *Two Dialogues Concerning the Writing of History*[1]

Xenophon's narrative style is remarkable for three qualities in particular. One of these qualities is hard to convey in a single word, but Mably
describes its effect admirably in his account of the emotions aroused by the
famous account of the Ten Thousand's sight of the sea in *Anabasis* – the
idea of the reader as *participant*, drawn in to the world of the narrative,
often through an overt appeal to the senses. This quality – we might call
it *immediacy* – is nonetheless frequently in tension with a strong sense of
narratorial control and artifice. And this tension between immediacy and
mediation itself is an important component of the second of Xenophon's
qualities – which we may term *inscrutability*. Particularly in their narrative
sections, his writings can often seem simple, charming, perhaps even naive.
But this superficial impression of naivety is deceptive. Xenophon entices his
readers with the charm of his narrative style, and yet there often remains
a lingering sense of uncertainty over the tone of particular scenes. And
this uncertainty becomes particularly provocative when these scenes have
a strong ethical and political charge. The third quality is much commented
on and easiest to label. It is Xenophon's *variety* – a variety seen not just in
the different genres in which he wrote but also in his handling of narrative
within genres.

---

[1] Mably 1783: 283.

This chapter will explore these qualities of Xenophon's narrative style across the full range of his works. It will focus above all on the three main historiographical works, offering a broad stylistic overview while looking at each in relation to one of the qualities outlined above: the shifting styles of *Hellenica* (variety), the tonal complexities of *Cyropaedia* (inscrutability), and the use of narrative perspective in *Anabasis* (immediacy). It will start, however, by looking at the narrative element in Xenophon's non-historiographical works – the Socratic dialogues and speeches as well as non-Socratic works such as *Hiero*, *Constitution of the Spartans*, and *Agesilaus*. My analysis will necessarily be highly selective, but despite this selectivity the breadth of coverage will help to reveal patterns of stylistic similarity and difference across the various works – and ultimately perhaps something of Xenophon's thoughts on the uses of narrative itself.

The Non-Historiographical Works: Narrative Modes

Many of Xenophon's non-historiographical works are formally narratives, but the narrative element is often so exiguous that it seems hard to speak of a narrative style at all. *Hiero*, for instance, starts with the bare statement that "Simonides the poet once paid a visit to Hiero the tyrant" (1.1); the two men proceed to hold a conversation which is reported without any closing frame. Even at this minimal level, however, the narrative style is not without effect. The simple opening sentence hints at the traditional nature of the scene that will follow – wise poet meets ruler.[2] At the same time, the bare account of the conversation that follows leaves it to readers to work though the two speakers' motivation. Even in the case of a short dialogue such as *Hiero*, the combination of narrative simplicity and reticence has opened up strikingly variant readings of what Simonides is hoping to achieve and to what extent Hiero is really swayed by his arguments.[3]

The narrative element in *Constitution of the Spartans* is similarly exiguous, but again not without a distinctive effect. Though there are some generalizing descriptions of Spartan institutions in this work, Xenophon for the most part reports by means of brief narrative sentences a series of measures that Lycurgus introduced to ensure that Sparta was different from other Greek cities (e.g. 7.1–2: "In other cities people all make as much money as they can ... But at Sparta Lycurgus forbade free men from having anything to do with money-making"). The repetitive narrative mode underlines the uniqueness of Sparta – and yet ultimately it proves deceptive: a remarkable

[2] Gray 1986.
[3] Contrast Strauss 1948 and Gray 2007: 211–13.

twist near the end of the work brings out that Lycurgus' laws are no longer obeyed by the present-day Spartans (14). The gap that emerges between the simple and upbeat way in which Lycurgus' measures are initially described and the blunt revelation of their long-term inefficacy is another sign of Xenophon's inscrutability.

Aspects of the Spartan character are handled in a notably different style in *Agesilaus*, an encomium of the Spartan king Agesilaus. While *Constitution of the Spartans* leads off from a series of reforms, *Agesilaus* starts with an account of deeds (ἔργα) that professes to display Agesilaus' character (1–2) before subordinating narrative to broader categories such as patriotism, financial probity, courage in battle, and sexual self-control that not only illustrate "the virtue in his soul" (3.1) but also provide an explanatory frame for the preceding narrative of his deeds. *Agesilaus* can also be fruitfully read against *Hellenica*, where Agesilaus' exploits are presented as part of a continuous narrative of Greek history, often in more or less the same words, but with a number of notable differences. Focusing on these differences shows up the encomiastic purpose of *Agesilaus* while leaving a residue of uncertainty about the relation between literary ideal and Spartan reality.

The stylistic contrast between the historiographical and the encomiastic genres is weakened by the fact that Xenophon's historiographical works show a similar concern for moral exempla. At times indeed Xenophon adopts in these works a method of presentation very similar to that found in *Agesilaus*. In *Anabasis*, the obituaries of the younger Cyrus and of Clearchus (1.9, 2.6.1–15) both subordinate narrative of actions to explication of the qualities of character suggested by those actions. A similar technique appears in the closing sections of *Cyropaedia* when Xenophon describes the elder Cyrus' institution of a royal court at Babylon (e.g. 8.2.1, 7).

The sense of narrative variety that we have already observed becomes greater still if we turn to Xenophon's Socratic works. These works are all formally narratives, even if, like *Hiero*, they are dominated by conversation and speech. But here too there is much variety: *Memorabilia* and *Oeconomicus* include accounts of Socrates conversing with a single interlocutor; *Apology* frames a selective report of Socrates' two defense speeches in his trial with a brief account of his behavior and conversations immediately before and after the trial; while *Symposium*, a broadly linear account of a single dinner party involving Socrates and some friends, includes Socratic conversation, but has a stronger focus on rhetorical exposition and display and on painting an attractive picture of a Socratic milieu.

In the cases of *Memorabilia* and *Oeconomicus*, the variety of Xenophon's narrative style is enhanced by the complexity of the works' structures. *Memorabilia* starts from the narrator's astonishment at how the Athenians were persuaded to put Socrates to death. It then reports many different conversations involving Socrates. Sometimes the narrator describes in detail a single conversation with one individual, often named but sometimes anonymous; sometimes he dwells on a series of such encounters with a particular individual; while at other times he reports in brief and in rapid succession a number of meetings with unnamed characters. As in *Agesilaus*, sections of the work tend to be grouped by topic (e.g. 4.4.1: "he did not use to conceal his own judgement about what is just, but would display it in action"), while particularly in the later stages of the work the narrator tends overtly to mark a scene as paradigmatic (e.g. 4.3.18: "by saying and himself doing such things he tried to instill more piety and prudence in his companions"). The overtly paradigmatic narrative style reinforces the effect of the different ways of presenting conversations: the varying narrative modes amount to a powerful rhetorical defense of Socrates against the charges that the Athenians brought against him.[4]

Whereas *Memorabilia* shows variety in the narrative organization of numerous different conversations, *Oeconomicus* stands out for the complexity with which a single conversation is narrated. The opening sentence announces the theme ("I heard him once discuss estate management also in the following manner," 1.1) while hinting that the narrative is motivated by a desire to show off the breadth of Socrates' interests and to preserve the memory of his wisdom. Together with the word "also," the fact that Socrates is not named in the opening sentence may hint that the work is to be read as a sort of continuation of *Memorabilia* (equally Xenophon could be naturalizing the narrative by hurrying *in medias res*). The narrator then describes a conversation between Socrates and Critobulus that includes a long account by Socrates himself of a conversation he had once had with an estate owner named Ischomachus (7–21); and part of this (secondary) conversation consists of a report by Ischomachus of a (tertiary) conversation with his wife. Some of these embedded conversations themselves feature narratives, notably Socrates' report of a meeting of the Spartan general Lysander and the younger Cyrus (4.20–4).

While the stylistic methods used to introduce the embedded sections of *Oeconomicus* are not complex, the work as a whole does suggest a striving on Xenophon's part to experiment with narrative structure, perhaps as part of an ongoing competition with Plato's experiments in the dialogue form. And even if the narrative style is straightforward, the embedding of accounts of different conversations does produce complexity by raising questions about the power relations between the speakers and by prompting

4 See Gray 1998.

comparison between the types of managerial control treated in the different conversations. Particularly provocative are comparisons between the Persian king's handling of his vast empire by means of military and civil subordinates and the seemingly similar joint action of husband and wife in running an estate – or at least the way that joint action is presented to the wife by the (possibly self-interested) husband.

The non-historiographical narrative works we have surveyed have provided plenty of evidence for two of the key qualities of Xenophontic narrative noted at the start of this chapter. They show narrative variety while their affected simplicity raises puzzles of tone and motivation for the careful reader. If we have not yet seen much sign of participation, that absence is largely because the key participatory aspect of the Socratic works lies not in the narrative component but in the way the dialogue form allows readers directly to assess the competing arguments. But we may close this section by glancing at two scenes where Xenophon does draw readers in, either through an implied observer or by evoking the perspective of participants.

The first example, from *Agesilaus*, presents a strongly visual picture of Agesilaus' military preparations at Ephesus:

> It was possible to see the gymnasia full of men training, the racecourse full of cavalrymen riding, and javelineers and archers shooting at the target. In fact he made the whole city in which he was based worth seeing. For the market was full of all sorts of weapons and horses for sale, and the bronzesmiths, carpenters, ironworkers, cobblers, and painters were all preparing military gear, so that you might really have thought that the city was a workshop of war.[5] (1.25–6)

This passage shows a typical Xenophontic use of parataxis – the stringing along of one clause after another, without subordination. The effect is to give a sense of bustling energy as the narrator moves from scene to scene. The participatory element here differs from the emotional engagement felt by Mably in reading of the Greeks' escape from Asia. The visual element in the narrative inspires admiration and emulation – just as Xenophon's vivid rendering inspired imitation (the phrase "workshop of war" was picked up later in antiquity (Plb. 10.20.7, Plut. *Marc.* 21.3, Athen. 10.421bc)).

My second passage comes at the end of *Symposium*. The work ends with a scene in which dancers play the roles of Dionysus and Ariadne so skillfully that the onlookers feel as if they are watching a real demonstration of

---

[5] The imaginary second-person observer is omitted in the otherwise very similar parallel narrative in *Hellenica* (3.4.17–18).

affection rather than a mere show. Here the link between visuality and emulation works in spectacular fashion:

> they did not look like people who had been taught their gestures but like people allowed to do what they had long been desiring. Finally when the diners saw them embracing each other and departing as if for bed, those who were unmarried swore they would get married, and those who were married got on their horses and drove off to be with their wives. (9.6–7)

This passage offers instances of two more stylistic techniques common in Xenophon: negative-positive contrast ("not ... but ...") and antithetical balance ("those who were unmarried ... those who were married ..."). Both techniques contribute strongly to narrative clarity. Yet sometimes Xenophon's neatly balancing clauses may be felt to undermine themselves by their very neatness. Given the sexual opportunities on offer at symposia, perhaps Xenophon is constructing through stylistic means an ideal of sexual moderation that those same stylistic means hint is too good to be true.[6]

The stylistic effects and experiments we have noted so far are also on display, as we shall see, in the long historiographical works *Hellenica*, *Cyropaedia*, and *Anabasis*. At the same time, these works provide a number of more precise cross-echoes of elements found in the Socratic works. Thus an equally careful staging of conversational scenes can be seen, for instance, in the account in *Anabasis* of Orontas' trial in Cyrus' tent, relayed to the other Greeks by Clearchus (1.6); or in the orientalizing setting for the meeting of Agesilaus and Pharnabazus in *Hellenica* (4.1.30–9); or again in the numerous conversational scenes (some with quasi-Socratic question-and-answer) in *Cyropaedia*. Similarly *Anabasis* and *Cyropaedia* feature long accounts of symposia that have the same charm as *Symposium*, with the scenes in *Anabasis* in particular showing fine observation of local customs.[7] These fertile cross-echoes suggest that internal variety within the historiographical works can still contribute to the sense of an overall cohesiveness in the Xenophontic corpus as a whole. It is time now to explore them in more detail in their own right.

Hellenica: Variety

Hellenica enters straight onto a linear narrative without a proem explaining Xenophon's aims:

> After this, not many days later, Thymochares came from Athens with a few ships; and the Spartans and the Athenians at once fought another naval battle,

---

[6] Hobden 2013: 220–2 discusses the relation of the ending of *Symposium* to the rest of the dialogue.

[7] Gera 1993: 132–91.

and the Spartans were victorious, with Agesandridas as leader. Soon after this, Dorieus, the son of Diagoras, sailed from Rhodes to the Hellespont at the beginning of the winter with fourteen ships, arriving at daybreak. When the Athenians' scout saw him, he signaled to the generals, and they set sail against him with twenty ships. Fleeing from these towards the shore, Dorieus, as soon as he started getting into open sea, tried to beach his triremes near Rhoeteum. And when the Athenians came near, they fought from ships and land until the Athenians sailed away to Madytus to the rest of their fleet, after accomplishing nothing. (1.1.1–3)

Any bafflement the reader feels from the lack of a proem is strengthened by the style of the opening section. There is little sense of a guiding narrative strand in this passage or in the immediately ensuing sections. Unlike *Anabasis* and *Cyropaedia*, both of which maintain a fairly tight spatial orientation, the narrative moves rapidly from place to place and from one military unit to another, with scarcely any expositional material. A clear interpretative framework is nonetheless provided by the fact that *Hellenica* starts where Thucydides' unfinished *History* left off. Thucydides' work had begun to adopt a different style of narrative in its closing stages to bring out how the Peloponnesian War moved after Athens's defeat in Sicily from being an uneven contest between a land and a sea power to a more equal contest at sea. The sense of swift movement and fragmented warfare at the start of *Hellenica* may owe something to imitation of the final section of Thucydides' narrative.[8]

The idea that Xenophon aimed in *Hellenica* at a narrative style that in some sense replicates the confusion of warfare receives some support from the very end of the work, where Xenophon treats the indecisive battle of Mantinea. On the one hand he looks ahead to his work's own possible continuation by another historian, suggesting that the narrative style adopted in the work is governed by a sense of the past as continuum rather than by a strong emplotment of events into discrete historical periods with their own unity. At the same time, the unprecedented "confusion and disorder" (7.5.27) marked by that final battle itself seems to be but the culmination of the disorder that has plagued Greece throughout the narrative.

Any attempt to pin down the narrative style of *Hellenica* as paradoxically ordered by disorder must still try to explain exactly why the narrator adopts the different styles that appear throughout the course of the work. Within *Hellenica* there are three notable shifts: the narrative's temporal framework becomes looser; it is increasingly dominated by more extensive and clearly demarcated narrative episodes; and the narratorial voice becomes more

---

[8] For the way *Hellenica* builds on Thucydides' narrative see Rood 2004b.

overt. These shifts are perhaps all to be explained by the increasingly overt ethical concern shown as this work progresses.

We shall concentrate here on the shifting narratorial voice of *Hellenica*. Narratorial variety is not itself unique to this work: there is a contrary move in *Anabasis*, for instance, where there is a greater accumulation of overt narratorial interventions in the first two books, above all in the account of the battle of Cunaxa and in the obituaries for Cyrus and the murdered Greek generals, and a much less intrusive narratorial presence subsequently. But in *Hellenica* the shift is more gradual and the range of narratorial registers wider.

The shift in *Hellenica* towards more overt narratorial guidance can first be observed after the end of the Peloponnesian War, in the account of the rule of the Thirty Tyrants at Athens. One of their victims is the politician Theramenes: "When he was compelled to die by drinking hemlock, they said that he cast out the dregs like someone playing *kottabos*, and exclaimed: 'Let this be for beautiful Critias.' Now I am not unaware that these remarks are not worth mentioning, but I judge it admirable in the man that even when death was at hand, neither his presence of mind nor his playfulness left his soul" (2.3.56). This strong narratorial intrusion forms a climax to a long political narrative, with lengthy speeches by Critias and Theramenes as well as a nicely sinister account of Critias' underhand use of force. The anecdotal conclusion is appropriately mediated through contemporary reports ("they said ...") – not so much a sign of uncertainty about whether the incident actually happened as a means of indicating both its contemporary resonance and its long-term paradigmatic value.[9]

The Theramenes scene illustrates another narratorial element that becomes increasingly prominent in *Hellenica* – the use of comparisons (here directly expressed through the verb, ἀποκοτταβίσαντα, "like someone playing *kottabos*"). Often these comparisons feature animals: in a battle, Greeks are shot down "as if shut up in a pen" (3.2.4); a house is surrounded on all sides "like a leader of bees by his swarm" (3.2.28); horsemen cling to walls "like bats" (4.7.6); and a city comes close to being captured "like a nest entirely empty of defenders" (7.5.10). Elsewhere the narrator introduces comparisons with nomads (4.1.25), a pentathlete (4.7.5), and the ramming action of a trireme (7.5.23). Xenophon also allows a similar license in his speakers: Pharnabazus complains that he is reduced to living "like beasts" (4.1.33), while another speaker draws analogies between crushing Sparta and destroying wasps' nests or crossing rivers (4.2.12–13). Such analogies

[9] Cf. Gray 2004b: 132–3, though she sees such source citations primarily as authenticating devices.

are by no means restricted to *Hellenica* (compare, e.g., the analogy between an army and a chorus at *Cyr.* 3.3.70); they stand indeed as a small-scale narrative instantiation of the Socratic tendency to draw comparisons between different areas of life.

A pointed example of the more prominent narratorial voice in *Hellenica* comes at the end of the account of the siege of Mantinea after the King's Peace. In apparent breach of the terms of that peace, the Spartans attack Mantinea for uniting several villages in a walled city. They proceed to dam a river that flows through the city, causing a flood that forces the inhabitants to surrender: "This is how things turned out at Mantinea, with people made wiser in this point at least – not to let a river run through one's walls" (5.2.7). This sentence starts with what looks like the sort of understated closure familiar from Thucydides (e.g. 4.41.4: "This is what happened concerning Pylos"). The run-on ("with people made wiser …") then provides an unexpectedly sardonic twist. Xenophon alludes to the idea that history can provide examples, yet the example he provides has a high degree of specificity. The disadvantages of a river running through a city are also shown in Herodotus' account of the elder Cyrus' capture of Babylon, though here drainage rather than flooding is used (1.190–1). The narrator in *Hellenica* implies that the lesson should not have needed to be learnt – and perhaps that more difficult lessons may be harder to extract from the past. It soon emerges that this is one of a number of Spartan successes that give the appearance that their rule has been safely established (5.3.27) – an appearance that is immediately shown to be deceptive.

The changing narrative style in *Hellenica* may itself be related to the fact that the work moves from focusing on the defeat of Athens to explaining the failure of the Spartans to capitalize on their victory. Xenophon adopts a strongly political register in his analysis of Athenian political failings in the closing years of the Peloponnesian War, notably in his full accounts of the conflicting perceptions of Alcibiades on his return to Athens (1.4.11–20) and of the Arginusae trial (1.7). In these passages, his narratorial role is more covert and Thucydidean. When he turns to Sparta's downfall, by contrast, he adopts a different explanatory mode:

> There are many other events, both Greek and barbarian, that one could mention to show that the gods do not pay no attention to the impious or to those who do wicked things. But for now I will tell of the matters at hand. The Spartans – who had sworn to leave the cities autonomous – after seizing the acropolis at Thebes were punished by the very men, alone, who had been wronged, though before then they had never been conquered by anyone … How this happened I will now narrate. (5.4.1)

Following a vivid account in storytelling mode (5.4.2: "There was a certain Phillidas ...") of the seizure of the Cadmea (the acropolis of Thebes), Xenophon proceeds in the closing sections of Hellenica to offer a selective series of detailed accounts of how Greek cities (notably the small and loyal city of Phlius) fare amidst the collapse of the Spartan order. The failings of the Spartans make such praiseworthy behavior both harder to achieve and worth dwelling on.

Cyropaedia: Tone

Unlike Hellenica, Cyropaedia starts by openly framing a question. The narrator has observed the problem of political instability (reflected above all in changes of constitution) and the similar problem of disobedience in the household. He contrasts the human and animal realms, and holds up the elder Cyrus as a paradigm to show that rule over humans need not be different from rule over animals if it is done with proper knowledge. A summary of Cyrus' conquests and the means of his continuing rule leads to a promise that the narrator will answer the questions "who he was in birth, what sort of nature he possessed, and in what sort of education he was trained, that he excelled so much in ruling people" (1.1.6).

The clarity of the work's goal is belied by the difficulty of assessing the texture of the narrative. The account of Cyrus' rise is strongly scenic: the narrator dwells particularly on scenes of personal interaction about the art of leadership and on a small number of military and political encounters in which the precepts Cyrus has learnt are put to the test. The narrative differs strongly from the other historiographical works in its handling of space and time.[10] Marches, for instance, are described briefly, with no attention to specificities of route. At one point, a long conversation is described between Cyrus and his father as he sets out on his first expedition (1.6); at its end, it is revealed that what had initially been presented as an account of a single conversation in fact blends together all their conversations on the way to the frontier (2.1). By contrast with this lack of attention to particulars, there is a much greater focus on how Cyrus approaches universal features of warfare (e.g. making camp, march orders). All these features are in line with the narrative's overtly paradigmatic goal. But the narrative can seem languid at times and also rather too distant from reality. Perhaps it is too paradigmatic for its own good.

The narrative is also marked by some gratuitous oddities, notably in the naming of characters. In the case of a number of prominent characters,

---

[10] Stadter 1991/2010.

there is a significant and unmotivated gap between introduction and naming. This technique is adopted in the cases of Cyrus' uncle Cyaxares (1.3.12, 1.4.9); Araspas, the recipient of Cyrus' robe (1.4.26, 5.1.12); Panthea, a captive from Susa, who is first "said to be the most beautiful woman in Asia" (4.6.11), then identified as Abradatas' wife (5.1.2), and finally named at 6.1.41; and again Artabazus, the supposed kinsman of Cyrus who tries to steal kisses from him (1.4.27), who is mentioned twice as "the man who once said he was Cyrus' kinsman" (4.1.22, 5.1.24) before reappearing as "Artabazus the man who once said he was Cyrus' kinsman" (6.1.9) – an introduction which leaves it unclear whether he is the same as the Artabazus who has been mentioned in the meantime at 5.3.38.

Quirky character introductions seem to be a stylistic trait of Xenophon. Xenophon as historical agent may be concealed behind "the leader of the Cyreans" at *Hell.* 3.2.7 and "one of Agesilaus' companions" at *Agesilaus* 5.4–6. In *Anabasis*, the character Xenophon receives a formal introduction after the arrest of the generals (3.1.4: "There was in the army a man called Xenophon, an Athenian"), even though he has already appeared several times earlier (1.8.15–17, 2.4.15, 2.5.37–41). Robust contributions have also earlier been made by a philosophical Athenian, Theopompus (2.1.12), and by an anonymous "young man" (2.4.19) – two figures sometimes read as ciphers for Xenophon. Whatever the case with these two characters, the narrator's aim seems to be to delay the most detailed exposition of how Xenophon came to serve with Cyrus until his decisive intervention.

The instances of delayed naming in *Cyropaedia* are harder to explain. In the case of Panthea, the delayed naming highlights the increasing weight that is attached to her romantic story. Xenophon may also be suggesting something about Cyrus' approach to his subordinates: he seems to use them according to his own needs – and the narrator imitates his character through his own art of naming.[11] The play with names can also be seen as a sign of a rather arch narrative self-consciousness, increasing the strange dissonance in *Cyropaedia* between hard-headed political analysis and a sense of detachment in space and time from the Greek world known to Xenophon and his readers.

The stylization in *Cyropaedia* is particularly marked in the story of Panthea and Abradatas. It peaks at key moments: Abradatas' departure for war, when Panthea kisses his chariot box – "and the people, though the sight of Abradatas and his chariot was beautiful, were unable to see him until Panthea had gone" (6.4.10–11); Cyrus' lament for the dead Abradatas – when he "clasped him by the hand, and the hand of the dead man came

---

[11] Cf. Tatum 1989: 164–5, 175–7.

away with his own," and "the wife lamented; but taking the hand from Cyrus, she kissed it and fitted it back on as best she could" (7.3.8–9); or finally Panthea's suicide, when Cyrus seems strangely obtuse in response to her hints as to the course she plans to take (7.3.13: "'Cyrus,' Panthea said, 'do not be afraid; I shall not hide from you who it is I want to go to'"). The high style emphasizes how this Cyrus was able to attract loyal followers. And having lost two virtuous figures, he knows how to do the right thing: "when Cyrus approached the scene of suffering he marveled at the woman, and after lamenting for her he departed. He also took care that they should receive all due honors, and the memorial built was very large, as they say" (7.3.16). That final qualification ("as they say") could be read as authenticating a detail that might seem extraordinary.[12] But it seems better to take it as yet another sign of the work's cryptic tone. It underlines the fact that the Cyrus of *Cyropaedia* could hardly have done anything else.

Anabasis: Perspective

Anabasis resembles *Cyropaedia* in that it begins in a Persian royal setting, and *Hellenica* in that it has no formal proem: "Darius and Parysatis had two sons, the elder Artaxerxes, the younger Cyrus ..." (1.1.1). This opening sentence nonetheless encapsulates a key part of the plot: the opposition of elder and younger brothers is central to the opening stages of the work – rather as the *Iliad*'s proem, in opposing Agamemnon "king of men" to "godly" Achilles (1.7), encapsulates the underlying cause of their quarrel. The difference is that the *Iliad* overtly sets up the quarrel of the two men as the root cause of its basic theme, the wrath of Achilles. In *Anabasis*, by contrast, there is no such narratorial control. And, as in *Hellenica*, any initial uncertainty we may feel about the goal of the work is compounded by its change of focus as it progresses and by the ultimate lack of resolution.

The opening statement of the birth of the two brothers leads at once to their mutual suspicions at the time of their father's illness and death. The work then slowly shifts from focusing on the ambitions of the younger Cyrus to the fate of his army of Greek mercenaries; it ends with that army setting off to serve a new master. Within this overarching framework there is a good deal of narrative disparity. Memorable episodes such as accounts of dinner parties among the Paphlagonians and at Seuthes' court are interspersed with the successive stages in the army's journey. Unlike in *Cyropaedia*, moreover, these successive stages are described in detail, initially in list form ("Thence he marched two stages, ten parasangs ... Thence he marched one stage, five

---

[12] Gray 2004d: 395.

parasangs," 1.4.1, 4), but later with much more flexibility, matching the more varied conditions faced by the Greeks in their march back.[13]

The *Anabasis* is also notably rich in speeches, but these speeches are distributed very unevenly. There is a strong concentration in three places: the start of book 3, when Xenophon inspires two groups of officers, and then the whole Greek army, into action; the end of book 5, when Xenophon, forced to defend his earlier leadership during the retreat to the sea, issues a warning against disorder; and book 7, when Xenophon makes two long speeches, firstly defending his own behavior in front of the army (7.6.11–38), and secondly lecturing the Thracian despot Seuthes on the importance of keeping trust (7.7.21–47). These speeches illustrate both the "intimate relationship with Xenophon's personal experiences" and the "taste for didactic discourse" that Tuplin sees as "the clearest common features" of Xenophon's works as a whole.[14] The speeches of the character Xenophon in particular may offer hints, through their stress on the importance of paradigmatic leadership, of how to interpret the narrative as a whole.

We shall focus here on the treatment of narrative perspective in *Anabasis*. The sense of participation Mably felt is conveyed above all by the famous passage to which he alludes – the account of the Ten Thousand's sight of the Black Sea after their long struggles through Kurdistan and Armenia:

> When the men in front reached the top of the mountain, there was much shouting ... As the shout kept on becoming louder and closer, and the successive ranks moving forward kept on running to the men ahead who kept on shouting, and the shout was becoming much louder the more men there were, it seemed then to Xenophon that this was something of great importance. Mounting his horse, and taking Lycius and the cavalrymen with him, he rode up to give help, and soon they heard the soldiers shouting "The Sea! The Sea!" (4.7.21–4)

The shout is described as it is heard from the rear, and the simple repetition of the shout "The Sea! The Sea!" (*thalatta, thalatta*) forms a suitable climax to the growing sense of excitement in the preceding clauses. Through much of the rest of the account, too, the narrator sticks to the same perspective, leaving readers in much the same state of knowledge about the actions of the Persians or about the dangers that lie ahead as the army had at the time.

It would be a mistake nonetheless to suppose that the same use of perspective found in the account of the first sight of the sea runs throughout the narrative. Xenophon never shifts the spatial focus to the enemy camp, but he does include reports of Persian thoughts, often to highlight how the

---

[13] Rood 2010b.
[14] Tuplin 2012: 1581.

Greeks outwit them (e.g. 3.4.2). And variations of perspective are handled with particular skill in the account of the march upcountry. At the start, Cyrus' ambitions to overthrow his brother are revealed before the Greek mercenaries have learnt of them. The narrator also makes effective use of non-Greek perspectives. A good example occurs in the detailed account of a parade early in the march:

> Cyrus issued orders for the soldiers to level their weapons and for the whole phalanx to advance. The generals then gave these instructions to the soldiers, and when the signal was given they leveled weapons and charged. The soldiers then started advancing more quickly and with a shout they spontaneously started running towards their tents. The barbarians were very afraid, and the Cilician woman fled in her carriage, and the people in the market left their goods and fled; and the Greeks reached their tents laughing. The Cilician queen after seeing the brilliance and discipline of the army was full of admiration, and Cyrus was delighted at how the barbarians were afraid of the Greeks. (1.2.17–18)

The narrator describes Cyrus observing the Greeks, but the goal is not primarily to allow readers to share in Cyrus' emotions as he sets out on his march. The description of a would-be king viewing his army evokes Herodotus' portrait of Xerxes (7.44, 7.212.1, 8.86, 8.88.2);[15] and Cyrus' delight (ἥσθη) at the sight of the troops also draws on conventional Greek characterizations of oriental despots. His delight is ironic: he is prematurely adopting a royal gaze.

Perceptions are again used to undermine Cyrus' aura of authority when the army arrives at the Euphrates. As the soldiers cross, none of them gets wet above the chest, and the locals claim that "the river had never been fordable": "it seemed clear that the river had yielded before Cyrus since he was destined to be king" (1.4.18). Here again the narrator presents the perspective of participants, though it is unclear whether the perception is that of the army, the locals, or both. At any rate, here too the effect is to foreshadow Cyrus' failure. A similar foreboding of failure is created by the use of perspective in the run-up to Cunaxa. As Cyrus continues his march down the Euphrates, he becomes careless, convinced his brother will not oppose him. Finally he is caught by surprise by an enemy he had hoped to catch unprepared.

These ironic notes are strengthened when Xenophon describes the Greek hoplites in operation during the battle of Cunaxa. Xenophon connects his account by verbal and thematic repetition with earlier scenes: first he describes how Cyrus is "pleased" (1.8.21: ἡδόμενος) when he sees that the

[15] Cf. Grethlein 2013: 58, though he lays too much stress on the experiential aspect.

Greeks have put the Persians opposite them to flight, echoing his response to the sight of the Greek troops on parade; then he reports that Cyrus' entourage even started "doing homage to him as king," echoing the perception that the Euphrates had humbled itself before the future king. But Cyrus' pleasure at the Greeks' charge is misguided: they had refused his initial order to charge across the battlefield directly against the king. Cyrus was basing his strategy on the shock effect of Greek hoplites seen in the parade scene; those hoplites are not at hand to support him as he leads his own doomed charge against his brother, shouting "I see the man!" (1.8.26). At this climactic moment the foregrounding of the visual brings out that Cyrus is making a spectacle of himself.

Endings

"Socrates and those of the others who had remained behind went off with Callias to join Lycon and his son for a walk. This was the end of the banquet held at that time." (*Smp.* 9.7)

"Thibron arrived and ... started waging war on Tissaphernes and Pharnabazus." (*Anab.* 7.8.24)

"Let it be written by me up to this point; events after this will perhaps be a concern to someone else." (*Hell.* 7.5.27)

This survey has aimed to suggest something of Xenophon's skill in the construction of his narratives. The qualities of his narrative that we have picked out – variety, inscrutability, and immediacy – could of course be supplemented by others. Even in this chapter we have seen signs of how his stylistic registers are sensitive to the different spatial and temporal contexts of his narratives, and signs too of his awareness of the ethical implications of narrative – of questions of which actions deserve to be remembered and imitated. A fuller analysis could also do more justice to the careful way he builds up individual scenes. But it may at least be appropriate to end here with the observation that Xenophon – whether telling the story of a single erotically charged party, of a two-year expedition, or of events in Greece over some fifty years – himself closes by suggesting that the story he has told is always part of a larger whole.

Further Reading

General books on Xenophon with much to say on narrative style include Higgins 1977, Dillery 1995 (on *Hell.* and *Anab.*), and Gray 2011 (on topics such as authorial evaluations, narrative patterns, and adaptation of predecessors). Narrative style is also discussed in broader studies of particular works, in particular Gray 1989 and Tuplin 1993 on *Hellenica*; Tatum 1989 and Gera 1993 on *Cyropaedia*; Flower 2012 on *Anabasis*. For narratological approaches see Gray 2004b–d (the narrator), Rood 2007 (time), 2012b (space); also Pelling 2013 on the narrative persona and Tsagalis 2009 on naming in *Anabasis*. Visual elements are analysed in several studies by Harman (e.g. 2013 on *Anabasis*).

14

EMILY BARAGWANATH

The Character and Function
of Speeches in Xenophon

That speeches are prevalent in the ancient historians reflects the crucial importance of rhetoric in the real life of the ancient Greek city states. They are particularly important to Xenophon, in whose works we find even more examples than in his literary predecessors outside of Homer. Diverse in kind and effect, they inject variety, since a speaker other than the narrator is given a voice, and they captivate readers not only intellectually but also emotionally; for the Greek orator Dio Chrysostom the speeches of *Anabasis*, "amidst such deeds of valor," moved him to weep (18.16).

I first address the theory behind Xenophon's use of speeches, so far as he offers us a glimpse of it (the first two sections below), and then review the functions of speeches across his literary oeuvre (the third section). We shall see that Xenophon is remarkably creative in employing speeches, even as he finds inspiration both poetic and historiographical.

His speeches take many forms. They include mere references to a speech act; informal dialogues, like those of his Socratic works; conversations that embed longer, continuous speeches; and lengthy formal speeches to larger audiences (and yet even these are usually interrupted by insertions of *ephe*, "he said," which inject liveliness and recall the performance occasion). Direct and indirect (reported) modes are closely intertwined: often a speech is recorded in indirect discourse, with direct being saved for the forceful culmination and closure; a short indirect speech may be followed by a long directly reported speech; or direct speech by one speaker and indirect by another will alternate over the course of an exchange. Direct is especially useful for rhetorically intense moments, an impression of dramatic vividness, characterization of the speaker, and to highlight crucial themes. Indirect may focus reader attention on content more than style, usefully summarize (e.g. *Hell.* 6.5.33), forestall the deceleration of a dramatic narrative, presage the failure of a speech, or suggest that a speaker is of secondary importance or wrong (as in the case of Apollonides' craven counsel that the Greeks cooperate with the Great King (3.1.26), sandwiched between and interrupted by the character Xenophon's direct speech).[1] In its narrative functions it tends to be more versatile than direct speech, for it fits into the narrative without creating a pause in the action.[2]

I focus on the long, continuous, direct speeches that dramatically punctuate most of Xenophon's works. But these represent just one point on a much broader spectrum, a rich topic that invites further work.

Selectivity and Truthfulness

Though speeches in Xenophon are prolific, his approach to them is marked by extreme selectivity. He selects which speeches to describe, what parts of a speech to include and at what length, and how to arrange them in his narrative.

We find a perspective on selectivity in relation to speeches at the beginning of his *Apology*:

> Others too have already written about this [Socrates' defense speech and the last stages of his trial], and all have captured his big talking (*megalegoria*). From this it is clear that the speech Socrates gave really was like that. But that he already considered death preferable to life for himself, this they have not made clear; so that they make his big talking seem rather stupid. (*Apol.* 1)

What others have written has, then, established the character of Socrates' speech. Xenophon addresses a problem of a higher order, the *attitude* that gave rise to this lofty tone in addressing the jury at his trial. Rather than focusing on conveying what the speech was really like, he will recount what fulfills his argumentative purpose and helps readers understand an important truth: that the character of the philosopher's speech directly reflected his prior decision.

Anabasis 5.8.26 brings out how selectivity may be ethically charged. The character Xenophon observes that his audience of Greek soldiers remember and talk about occasions on which he has incurred their *ill*-will, but fail to remember the positive things – and yet "surely it is more honorable and just, more pious and gracious to remember good deeds than bad" (5.8.25–6). What we choose to remember and talk about therefore reflects on our character; one should promote the positive and elide the more negative dimensions of the truth – even if the writer Xenophon's own omissions and inclusions are *not* always in the direction of remembering the good; one might point to the shameful speech of Pelopidas to the Persian king included in indirect discourse at *Hellenica* 7.1.34.

---

[1] Cf. Grethlein 2012: 28, Tuplin 2014a: 86.
[2] Foster 2012: 339.

Even in the historical works, Xenophon never claims to be reporting "what was actually said,"[3] and it is unlikely that his audience expected it either. They expected *more*: more interesting and significant was the deeper meaning the speeches enabled the reader to grasp. *We* expect speeches in news reports or modern historical works to be transcripts of what was actually said, which is something modern technology allows, but the model for Xenophon and his historiographical predecessors was Homer. Thucydides is unusual in worrying explicitly about the problem (1.22.1, cf. also Polybius, 2.56.10, 12.25a, 36.1.7), and yet even he, in his reference to including in his reports of speeches *ta deonta* (what a speaker *ought* to have said),[4] allows plenty of room for subjectivity and creative reconstruction. The only place where Herodotus emphasizes the literal truth of characters' speech occurs after the patently fictional speeches of the Persian constitutional debate (3.80–2) – speeches that could not possibly have been spoken in that form, though they convey important higher truths, not least that Persians were *capable* of entertaining such ideas.[5] Xenophon's readers, like Herodotus', probably understood speeches to be an area that invited some degree of free composition on the author's part. In fact it is in the most disingenuous of speeches in *Hellenica* and *Anabasis* where we find the strongest claims to be telling the truth (*alethe legein*), as when the Thebans petition the Athenians with offers of empire (3.5.8–15, and below).

Cyropaedia (2.2.11–16) highlights the beneficial potential of material in speeches that is *pseudos* – lying or fictional (cf. *pseudontai*, 2.2.11). One of Cyrus' captains has told a tall story about the extraordinary obedience of his men: how he once instructed his soldiers that they must always advance as a unit, each one taking care to "follow the man in front." A rider was about to set off for Persia, so the captain had ordered his lieutenant to run and fetch a letter for the man to take with him; with the upshot that the entire company of soldiers "followed the man in front," and the letter was given a military escort (2.2.7–10). An earnest captain points out that the teller of the tale has not told "the truth." He has however made the men laugh, and Cyrus' response indicates that untruth need not matter if one's intentions are good. Here then is a positive judgment about the effect on

---

[3] Just occasionally, he does draw attention to the problem of how the narrator knows the actual words spoken, as in the trial of Orontas in *Anabasis* (1.6.1–11): but this is a special case, where the detail that Clearchus reported the speeches from this trial held in closed Persian quarters (1.6.5) explains the otherwise unusual narratorial access to events to which the Greek mercenaries were not party; and it adds to the atmosphere of mystery.

[4] Pelling 2000: 114–21 helpfully reviews the possible meanings of this highly contested phrase.

[5] Cf. Moles 1993: 118–20.

listeners of fictionality in relation to speech; Reichel has even suggested that Xenophon is specifically contesting Plato's derogatory views on fiction.[6]

Speeches always constitute a site of subjectivity, as this is a moment where a character other than the author is given voice. Harnessing this inherent subjectivity, Xenophon exploits direct speech for its ability to express distinctly subjective perspectives, for example in introducing new historical developments. The threat of Olynthus is presented through the direct speech of an ambassador from northern Greece who has come to Sparta to inform Spartans and their allies about a new power emerging in his local Chersonese (*Hell.* 5.2.12). Readers are at this point as unaware as the Spartans are of this new "great danger" (*pragma mega*). Similarly the speech of Polydamas of Pharsalus (in Thessaly) to the Spartan assembly (*Hell.* 6.1.1–3) is a gripping introduction of Jason of Pherae. Polydamas both quotes at length Jason's words and offers his own analysis of the threat that Jason represents. The Spartans decide that they cannot send an adequately large force, so the speech does not change what happens next; but readers have been given a thrilling glimpse of Jason's power, and wait on tenterhooks to learn more. The information conveyed in such speeches is both authorized as local knowledge (the account derives from a witness who should know), *and* acknowledged as subjective. The effect on readers is dramatic and experiential, for they are set in the shoes of the internal audience listening; the past is made present. The technique can heighten the emotional conviction of an episode, as in Araspas' introduction of the beautiful Panthea (*Cyr.* 5.1.4ff.): in his charming, detailed description we get the sense that he has already fallen for her; his emotions infuse the account, and engage ours, as well. One of the catalogues of Cyrus the Elder's troops is reported through a speech by Cyrus himself (*Cyr.* 5.3.34–45). The distinctive perspective of a brilliant commander thereby grants readers access not just to the facts of the array, but also to the rationale behind each positioning of men. This novel and effective use of direct speech, reminiscent of Homer's *teichoscopia* (the "viewing from the walls," where Helen stands upon the walls of Troy and points out Achaean heroes in the plain below: *Iliad* 3.121–244), makes the catalogue come alive.

Words and Actions

Logoi (words, speeches; singular *logos*) are in an important sense "historical": they are themselves *erga* (events or actions; singular *ergon*); and, whatever the relationship to reality of their contents, they can affect ensuing

[6] Reichel 1995/2010: 437.

events, shaping reality for example through decisions made in an assembly or court of law. The efficacy of *logos* in shaping reality is powerfully expounded in a triad of speeches by the character Xenophon that marks the crucial turning point of the *Anabasis* (3.1.13–45). Here Xenophon steps forward to lead the mercenaries, and through his speeches transforms his own and his audience's attitude from one of listlessness and depression (cf. 3.1.2–3) to keenness to fight on and march home.[7] Within one of these speeches Xenophon notes its power to "turn around mindsets" (3.1.41). Since it is psychological disposition more than strength or numbers that in Xenophon's opinion wins wars (cf. *Anab.* 3.1.42), speech can be crucial in shaping military outcomes.

So speech is itself an *ergon*: but frequently it is figured in Greek and Xenophontic thought as separate from and even in an antithetical relationship to *erga*. Central to the structure of Xenophon's *Symposium*, for example, is the competition between words and deeds: Socrates invites the symposiasts to deliver speeches in a bid to prove as skilled at entertaining and enlightening one another as are the performers of *erga* – the girl acrobat, the *silent* mime artists, and so on. *Logoi* at times lose the contest with *erga*. Thus Cyrus the Elder belittles the value of traditional battle exhortations (*Cyr.* 3.3.49): no speech in a day could make virtuous those who are not (3.3.50). Urging him to fight gallantly for Cyrus, Panthea tells her husband that she has valued him more than her own life, and asks (6.4.5–6): "but why should I catalogue this? For I think that my *deeds* are more persuasive to you than any *words* I could now say" – though her words have already played their part in his persuasion, and that is a familiar paradox. *Logoi* can be acknowledged as valuable and yet less so than *erga*: in Xenophon's speech to the Thracian prince Seuthes (*Anabasis* 7.7.43) words come *after* deeds in the hierarchy of means available for reading another person's character. But at times *logoi* are regarded as being as powerful as force: Cyrus the Elder observes that making people agree in words is *equivalent* to conquest in war (*Cyr.* 5.5.45–6).[8]

The problem of *logos* in its relation to *ergon* in fact hovers over Xenophon's entire literary output, in parallel to its crucial presence at a defining event of Xenophon's life, the trial of his teacher Socrates. The beginning of Xenophon's *Apology* sets up assumptions about the potential identity of *logoi* and *erga* in Socrates' conviction that his life spent practising virtuous deeds has trained him for his defense *logos* (*Apol.* 3) – only for the

---

[7] Lendle 1995 ad 3.1.13/14–45/46, Flower 2012: 126–30.
[8] There is slight irony or qualification as Cyrus continues, for it is the *erga* of those persuaded, not their persuaders' *logoi*, that will count in proving that persuasion has occurred: 5.5.47.

trial itself to overturn those assumptions, serving as proof of how far *logoi* can *misrepresent erga* (in the sense not just of action but of reality). In the teeth of reality, the prosecutors convince the jurors that Socrates is a force of corruption and deserves capital punishment.

At times the relationship of *logoi* and *erga* is smooth, with *logoi* directly illuminating the *erga* described in the narrative, analyzing them, and illuminating the motives that lie behind them. Thus in *Hellenica* the *logoi* of the sub-satrap Mania match her *erga* (3.1.11–13), as do the commander Teleutias' (*Hell.* 5.1.14ff.), and that is a major reason why his speeches *are* effective: words and reality coincide, for as Xenophon the character observes in *Anabasis*, speeches can be as powerful as force (*bia*), but only so far as the person delivering them is trustworthy (*Anab.* 7.7.24). At least as often, *logoi* are deceptive (see below).

The differing inflections of the expression of this relationship in part map on to a difference in genre. The fictional *Cyropaedia* presents the most tranquil relationship of *logoi* and *erga* in how (until the final books) Cyrus' words express his thoughts, and translate directly into action. In this didactic work *logoi* offer instructions, explanations, and clarifications that draw out lessons from the *erga*. The commander employs speeches to make explicit the lessons to be learned, as where he reflects on the type of past behavior that has led to recent success, and urges his men to keep it up in future (3.3.6ff.). Cyrus' speeches also *generate* future reality on the many occasions where speeches offer a rationale for and then enact new Persian customs (for example, the custom of cavalry use), which the narrator then affirms are "still now' functioning.

Similarly, speeches in this work usually do *not* present antithetical perspectives. Instead they lend emphasis to a single one, that of Cyrus,[9] thereby dramatizing the degree to which this great king inspires consensus. Take for example the triad of speeches (2.3.1ff.) that highlight the principle of reward according to merit. Two individuals deliver speeches responding to Cyrus' question about whether it would lead to better performance if everyone received the same prizes, or if the brave received more. One respondent is a commoner who would be sidelined by a system that awarded prizes in accordance with social status, the other, a man who is less physically able, who would be disadvantaged by a meritocratic system. But they take the same line (2.3.16) – that prizes should be awarded according to merit. Where we *do* hear alternative voices in *Cyropaedia*, the usual upshot – when the other party caves in – is to highlight the superiority of Cyrus' view.

---

[9] Cf. Gera 1993: 282–4.

And yet even in this work speeches do occasionally promote genuinely alternative perspectives. Panthea's disenchanted viewpoint is revealed in a direct speech to Cyrus after the loss of her husband fighting for him (7.3.10). Her regret at her decision to befriend Cyrus (which is the ultimate cause of her husband's death) represents a regret at having been compelled to choose between a utilitarian, contractual sort of *philia* (friendship), such as that which characterizes her relationship with Cyrus, and *philia* accompanied by deep affection (such as that shared with her husband); her criticism thus hits at the heart of the entire system, including the code of honor on which it depends. Like Cyaxares',[10] her harrowing reproach turns *Cyropaedia* into a far more polyphonous text, and one wide-eyed to the challenge of translating ideals into reality. In this way Xenophon exposes some of the most problematic features of Cyrus' leadership code and the qualified nature of the reciprocity that exists between leader and led.

Cyrus' complete frankness in speech is conveyed nicely at *Cyr.* 4.5.26, where he instructs his messenger "to say (*legein*) to the Persians what has been set forth in the foregoing *logos*" (here in the sense of Xenophon's narrative): the contents of the message are thus to replicate the historian's narration of deeds! Only in this fictional work could *logoi* be identical in this way with *erga* (events as described by the narrative).[11] Socrates perhaps comes closest to Cyrus the Elder, since his own *erga* match his words, only more so: after recounting Socrates' speech in *Memorabilia* about *enkrateia* (self-control) (1.5), Xenophon comments: "Socrates however showed himself even more self-controlled in deeds (*erga*) than in words (*logoi*)," and goes on to describe his physical self-control (1.5.6).

So, in the *Cyropaedia*, speeches largely explain what has happened and what will happen, theory matches practice – unlike in the historiographical works, where speeches more often stand in a complicated relationship to *erga*. Yet even in the latter, the equivalence of words and deeds remains an ideal to aspire to: the Spartan general Cheirisophus praises Xenophon (in the tradition of Homeric heroes) for how his words match his deeds (*Anab.* 3.1.45). But more often, words fail to reflect a speaker's thoughts, or else thoroughly misrepresent them; they serve as covers for or justifications of deeds, and present a distorted view of reality. Thus while the words of the Persian satrap Tissaphernes in *Anabasis seem* to match perfectly his friendly deeds (his hospitality towards the Greek commander Clearchus), and imply

---

[10] *Cyr.* 5.5.8–9, 25–34, Sandridge 2012: 90–3.
[11] For the same reason Cyrus' direct speeches in this work come very close in effect to the reports of his *thoughts*: see e.g. *Cyr.* 7.5.60. Since they lack a rhetorical dimension – an outside audience – reports of thoughts would normally be expected to read rather differently from reports of speech.

motives on his part that the Greeks find entirely credible (including the idea that he is driven to befriend them by the prospect of increasing his power, 2.5.23[12]), *in fact* this is part of a plan to deceive the Greeks and execute their leaders (*Anab.* 2.3.17–2.6.1).

As well as failing to *express* reality, words at times fail to *shape* it; instead they spotlight the human inability to control the effects of contingency and to shape the future. In this way the disingenuous speech of the Thebans in *Hellenica* asking the Athenians for help fighting Sparta in 395 BC[13] has a strangely oblique relationship to the ensuing *erga*: it does *not* motivate the action – the Athenians are already chafing at the bit for war (3.5.2), even without the Persian money that has been given to the other parties – and the assistance they go on to offer makes negligible difference to the subsequent campaign. The speech is therefore superfluous in terms of shaping action. And far from presenting a valid analysis of the situation, its bad (inconsistent and irresponsible) arguments gloss over the truth and facilitate decisions that are morally and ethically problematic. If the Thebans' arguments effect any change in the Athenians' intellectual stance, what persuades is not their cogency, but their appeal to Athenian self-interest (the possibility of regaining their empire of old).

The Functions of Speeches

Xenophon employs speeches across the various genres of his literary oeuvre to lay out a meaningful construction of events (or in the case of historiographical works a *re*construction of events), and to assist readers to engage with that (re)construction.[14] This assistance may be a matter of bolstering the narrative's intelligibility, whether by revealing characters and motivations, and the abilities or lack thereof of those responsible for shaping policy or strategy; by exposing economic and other explanatory factors; by dramatizing events, enabling readers to see the past more clearly and even *experience* it, as if they were present; by highlighting decisive moments; and by signposting the narrative's structure. The speeches may also assist readers to discern deeper meanings. Indeed one of their key functions, as we shall see, seems to be to open up space for reflection on key issues and problems, especially in relation to personal and international relations and leadership. The speeches help Xenophon not only to present ideals and philosophical

---

[12] Cp. Braun 2004: 107.
[13] *Hell.* 3.5, mentioned above; Rood 2012a: 80–4, Schepens 2012: 228–31.
[14] Cf. Wiater 2010 for a functionalist analysis of Polybius' speeches.

truths, but also to engage with the problem of how to translate those ideals into reality.

But let us look more closely at some of these functions. Xenophon is a subtle writer who favors implication. In the near-absence of explicit authorial evaluation and commentary, the speeches serve as crucial interpretative guides. The long, direct speeches that stand out from the narrative are especially effective in emphasizing key moments. In this way the four "pure" speeches of the *Memorabilia* hone in on and crystallize four of its most crucial topics: self-control (1.5), how to seem good by being good (1.7), friendship (2.4), and the ability to make followers happy as the characteristic virtue of a good leader (3.2). The pause generated by direct speeches punctuates the narrative, slowing it down and inviting readers to pay closer attention and enter into a more reflective mode of engagement. Clusters of speeches generate meaning and guide interpretation through their mutual responses, for example in the remarkable triads of Peloponnesian and Athenian speeches in *Hellenica* (6.3.4–17 and 6.5.33–48[15]). Speeches also generate meaning in combination with the surrounding narrative. In this way Euryptolemus' in *Hellenica* (see below), with the hope it raises that Athenians will act justly, works with the narrative that follows to highlight the pattern that imbues the broader text of hope followed by disappointment (seen for example in the frustrated hopes on the part of those dismantling Athens's walls at the close of the Peloponnesian War that they will now be free, 2.2.23, and on the part of observers that there will be a clear winner after the battle of Mantinea, 7.5.26–7).

Another crucial function is to illuminate the characters and motivations of states and individuals, often as they make decisions. A speaker may describe another's character, as where Gobryas describes the despicable son of the Assyrian king (*Cyr.* 4.6.2–7). How a speaker speaks may also characterize himself, as in the case of Xenophon's speeches in *Anabasis* 3 (see also Pharnabazus' below). Since an orator speaks with a view to persuading a particular audience, his speech may also characterize that audience. Thus in Euryptolemus' speech to the Athenians on the occasion of the Arginusae trial, his repeated appeals to the Athenians' desire to do "whatever they want" (*Hell.* 1.7.19, 1.7.22, 1.7.23, 1.7.26) and their desire for money build up a picture of them as greedy and tyrannical. The modalities of speech in *Anabasis* 5 contribute to the broader characterization of Greeks and *barbaroi* (non-Greeks): the simplicity and rhetorical frankness of Xenophon's communication with the foreign Mossynoecians (5.4.5–7) contrasts starkly with the rhetorical sophistication, at times disingenuousness, used in the

---

[15] See below, and Dillery 1995: 243–9.

surrounding narrative by and with Greeks. Thus Xenophon must employ elaborate rhetoric himself in unmasking the insincere arguments of the representative of Greek Sinope, a man with a reputation as a clever (*deinos*) speaker (*Anab.* 5.5.7), and in countering his soldiers' accusations that he desires to lead them eastwards rather than home to Greece (5.7.5–11). In contrast to some Greek communities encountered, the Mossynoecians remain true to their oaths (5.4.10–11).

An audience's response can also contribute to characterization, for example the Spartans' to an Athenian request for peace at *Hellenica* 6.3. No response is recorded to the Athenians' first speech, silence is the response to the second, and after the third, Xenophon reports merely a brief, global response to the three speeches taken together: "Since they judged these men to have spoken well, the Lacedaimonians voted to accept the peace" (6.3.18). By contrast the Athenians are characterized as analytical and critical receivers of speeches. Thus in responding to a Spartan and allied request for assistance the Athenians "did not altogether accept" the Spartan speakers' arguments (6.5.33–5), and Xenophon gives a sense of their weighing different aspects of the argument and debating heatedly about its moral import (6.5.35–7). The lack of reasoned debate and dissent on the Spartan side opens a wider line of explanation, inviting readers to reflect back on episodes where the absence of critical engagement and argument enabled troubling outcomes.[16] On the Athenian side the problem is rather that of yielding too easily to clever arguments, and the volatility of decision-making.[17] In this way Xenophon's careful description of responses to speeches not only characterizes but also brings out the explanatory value of Athenian and Spartan public deliberation.

The long speeches that are quite frequent in a work's closing stages at times engage with the broadest issues of the human condition and set forth ideals and possibilities, reminding readers that the work does *more* than just recount particulars. Cyrus' major speech after taking Babylon and establishing himself as king, urging his mercenaries to the pursuit of virtue (*Cyr.* 7.5.72–86), thus deals with the human condition and the problem of change. Looking to the future, Cyrus advises the men to avoid laziness and luxury. *Becoming* good men does not suffice for *remaining so*, unless one is attentive to this through to the end. Virtue must be practised, or it turns towards vice; the greatest challenge is to *preserve* an empire: you can gain one with daring, but to preserve it you need moderation, self-control, and

---

[16] E.g. the lack of voices raised to test Agesilaus' proposal not to condemn the man responsible for seizing the Theban Cadmeia, 5.2.32; the failure to pay heed to the wise adviser Prothous before Leuctra, 6.4.2.

[17] Cf. Rood 2004a: 378–9.

attention. As the holder of an empire it is your continuing display of virtue that gives you your claim to continue ruling. And so through Cyrus' direct speech, Xenophon addresses problems presented by the future, returning to the guiding notion of moral worth.

There are resonances here of both Herodotus' wise advisor Solon[18] and the *wise* Cyrus who appears in the final paragraph of the *Histories* (9.122), where Herodotus raised the same problem or paradox: that having gained an empire, you risk becoming less capable in war (9.122). But Xenophon defines virtue more broadly. Then at *Cyr.* 7.5.80 the speech offers a different take on Herodotus' Cyrus' display of *toil* followed by *feasting* (Hdt. 1.126). Herodotus' Cyrus directed the Persians first to clear a large thorny tract of land, and then to enjoy a great banquet, finally posing the question of which of those activities they preferred; thus he inspired them to revolt against Median rule. Surely inviting readers to think back to that moment in Herodotus, Xenophon's Cyrus says: "if anyone is thinking about" the point of achieving what one wanted if one must still endure hunger and thirst, he should bear in mind that good things bring more pleasure to the extent that one has toiled for them in advance. However delightful in themselves, things give pleasure only if needed, and so one can enjoy any sort of food if it satisfies a need. The transformation that is to occur does not depend on outside conditions; it is purely psychological. Thus at this moment of imperial transition, from Median to Persian rule, the Herodotean references intensify the problem of change over time, and define a different sort of Cyrus and a different sort of Persian virtue – at the same time spotlighting Xenophon's more philosophical approach.

Near the end of the *Hellenica*, the two long speeches of the wise advisor Procles of Phlius, in which he urges the Athenians in 370 BC to assist Sparta against Thebes and to forge a complementary alliance (Sparta leading on land, Athens on sea), have strong intertextual connections with both Herodotus and Thucydides.[19] His first speech (*Hell.* 6.5.38–48) combines expediency and ethics through the argument that friendship is the most expedient commodity, thereby updating the arguments of Thucydidean speakers who fail to achieve such a combination. His second speech (*Hell.* 7.1.2–11) contains several echoes of Herodotus' Solon, but shifts the focus from the individual's good to the city's, defining happiness as enduring friendships with other cities (developing on the level of cities Herodotus' Solon's views on the impossibility of self-sufficiency). In this way Procles' speeches – near the end of the work – help crystallize for readers the distinctive character of

---

[18] Cf. Lefèvre 1971/2010, Gera 1993: 119–22 on Herodotean echoes in 8.7.
[19] Baragwanath 2012a.

Xenophon's contribution, authorizing the novel ethical and moral focus of his historiography.

In all these cases we see with particular clarity how the perspective of Xenophontic speeches on historical reality is always a double one.[20] The speeches look through the eyes of a character, but they are *also* mediated by a narrator with a wider picture: with knowledge of what will come later, and knowledge of the literary tradition as well. The direct speeches quite often also point to truths about the potential utility of history and of narrative. Thus in the deathbed speech of Cyrus he advertises the value of history: if he hasn't taught his sons adequately how they should behave towards each other, then "you must learn it from previous events, for this is the best source of instruction' (*Cyr.* 8.7.24). The problem with his sons – under whom Cyrus' order collapses – appears to be that they did not read enough history![21] The historical *exempla* found in the speeches of *Hellenica* are likewise suggestive for history's potential to teach us about the present and future (Marincola 2010).

Finally, we shall look at some examples that further illuminate the role of direct speeches in tandem with the narrative to bring out higher truths, especially relating to character and relationships.

Euryptolemus to the Athenians

The first extended direct speech of *Hellenica* (1.7.16–33) occurs in the account of the aftermath of Athens's victory in the sea battle off the Arginusae islands (406 BC). Euryptolemus is defending the Athenian generals who face prosecution and a death sentence after a storm prevented their rescue of sailors from triremes that had been disabled or sunk.[22] The speech contributes little to our grasp of the immediate situation and makes no difference to the short-term outcome of events; but it is highly effective in other ways, especially in highlighting the significance of the Athenians' actions in the immediate and longer term.

Euryptolemus' observation that if the Athenians follow his advice and try the generals in accordance with the law, "you will not be fighting on the side of the Spartans" (1.7.25) is prescient for the immediate future: his warning that the Athenians will regret their decision (1.7.27) is soon answered in the narrative describing their regret (1.7.35). He explicitly guards against the possibility of their later charging that they have been deceived (1.7.19);

---

[20] Cf. Schmitz 2010: 48 on Thucydides.
[21] Cf. Callistratus' speech, *Cyr.* 6.3.11: history has now taught us that seeking selfish advantage is not profitable.
[22] Gray 1989: 83–91, Krentz 1989 ad. 1.7.16–33.

in the aftermath, they make exactly this charge (1.7.35). The speech characterizes Euryptolemus as a pious and wise advisor, the Athenians as rash and unthinking. Its long, reflective character highlights through contrast the hastiness of the Athenians' vote and execution of the generals. The speech also casts a longer shadow, in its characterization of the Athenians in their problematic relationship with their leaders – a characterization that begins to explain how they will go on to treat Alcibiades.[23] It is by treating in this way leaders upon whose talent they depend that the Athenians will lose the Peloponnesian War.

But the speech also looks beyond the Peloponnesian War to the trial of Socrates, with its failure to uncover the truth and deliver justice. The mention of Socrates in the preceding narrative – the only reference to him in *Hellenica* (1.7.15) – plants this train of thought in readers' minds, as does Euryptolemus' argument that the generals have come into harm's way *because of* their *philanthropia* (kind-heartedness, humanity, 1.7.18). Euryptolemus urges the Athenians to act justly and righteously, in a way that will allow them to learn the truth and avoid sinning against the gods and themselves (1.7.19). Shortly afterwards the mask comes fully off, his words seeming directly to address Xenophon's (Athenian) *readers*:

> Yes, but possibly you would be putting to death some one who is not guilty; and repentance afterwards – remember how painful and unhelpful it always is (ἀναμνήσθητε ὡς ἀλγεινὸν καὶ ἀνωφελὲς ἤδη ἐστί), and especially when one's mistake has brought about a man's death. (1.7.27)

"Unhelpful" (ἀνωφελές) here is eye-catching, since "helpful" is a term in Xenophon that is particularly associated with Socrates. The notion that it would be far more just to honor the victors at Arginusae with garlands than to punish them with death (1.7.33) recalls a feature of Socrates' trial as described by Plato (Socrates' remark that he – rather than victorious athletes (who would be garlanded) – deserved to be honored with free meals in the Prytaneum: *Apol.* 36d–e).

The speech reaches towards higher truths, in the form of ideals and counterfactual possibilities relating to the Athenians' character. Xenophon isolates and draws attention to a key moment when the Athenians might have chosen a different course, lived up to Euryptolemus' aspirational rhetoric, and so carved out a different character and future path for themselves: a moment when the Assembly might have made proper use of their wise advisor, and challenged the problematic recommendation that emanated from the Boule, rather than follow a course that would lead to further injustice, defeat, and

---

[23] Cf. Rood 2004a: 369–71.

literal tyranny at Athens (in the form of the Thirty Tyrants), and finally the supreme injustice of Socrates' execution. The speech finds a response at the other end of the work (at the end of book 6) when the Athenians show their potential to live up to a higher ideal, *persuaded* by the intelligent and virtuous words of a wise advisor, in that case Procles of Phlius (see above).

Pharnabazus and Agesilaus

The Spartan king Agesilaus and the Persian satrap Pharnabazus meet in Daskylium and exchange speeches shortly after Agesilaus' plundering of Pharnabazus' territory (395 BC; *Hellenica* 4.1.29–40).[24] The setting is significant. Spatially, Pharnabazus' satrapy lies on the threshold between Greece and Asia. Temporally, the encounter occurs just before Agesilaus is obliged to return to Greece and make war there against Greeks. So the speeches unfold in a liminal space and at a transitional moment, a very effective backdrop for the contest they stage between Greek and Persian perspectives on friendship and honor. Pharnabazus is led to the agreed-upon spot, where Agesilaus and his thirty Spartans are lying on the ground in the grass waiting. Pharnabazus arrives wearing expensive clothes and his attendants spread out rugs for him to sit on, but upon seeing the simplicity of Agesilaus he is ashamed to indulge in luxury; so he too "lay down on the ground just as he was" (4.1.30).

The theme of the speeches is identified as friendship (cf. *peri philias*, 4.1.29), on which each speaker sets forth a contrasting perspective. Pharnabazus begins, as he is the older, and sets out his complaint, reminding the Spartans of his aid during the war; Agesilaus responds; and then the exchange continues, until the meeting breaks up (*Hell.* 4.1.34–9). The background information informs our sense of the authority of each speaker to address the theme. The broker of the meeting has been Pharnabazus' guest friend "for a long time," whereas only more recently has he become a friend of Agesilaus (4.1.29). And so Pharnabazus is characterized as one who knows how to conduct friendships that last over time; and the characterization has been endorsed by the earlier narrative, for in his dealings with Mania Pharnabazus proved a very good friend indeed (and his remark that he would prefer to avenge her than to live (3.1.15) contrasts with the highly qualified notions about friendship here expressed by Agesilaus). Pharnabazus again proves a loyal friend in refusing the temptation of Agesilaus' offer of alliance, wealth, and freedom, and remaining loyal to the Great King for as long as the king reciprocates (4.1.37).

[24] Gray 1989: 52–8, Krentz 1995 ad loc.

Pharnabazus' constancy of friendship in both words and deeds feeds into Xenophon's wider exploration of factors that work against *tarache*, confusion (in this case the confusion evident on the Greek side of changing alliances and friendships): we see how friendship has the capacity to supply constancy and order. This constancy of Pharnabazus' friendship challenges Greek notions of *barbaroi* as treacherous and changeable, notions that Pharnabazus explicitly addresses in remarking that *he* can *not* be accused of double-dealing: he is *not* another Tissaphernes. His speech uncovers a Spartan failure to be a proper friend and to return *charis* (favor, kindness), and highlights the disquieting ease with which Greek wars begin. Challenging the idea that friendship represents constancy is the picture of friendship set out by Agesilaus: the idea that "by necessity" all sorts of close relationships, including those between guest friends, mean nothing if one is at war.

The carefully described preliminaries expose an irony: for the embarrassment of Pharnabazus about the fancy carpets leads to far more profound embarrassment of the Spartans about their *moral* failing: their failure to reciprocate friendship. The rugs, by contrast, are not external indications of inner character or morality at all; Pharnabazus proves a man of virtue and honor. The shame and silence with which the Spartans respond to Pharnabazus gives the impression that they have been made to reflect. Readers might be prompted to reflect too, whether back on the preceding narrative through a different lens (on Pharnabazus' role in book 1, helping Sparta, fighting on horseback in the sea, which he explicitly recalls in this speech), or on a literary resonance, the encounter of Glaucus and Diomedes in the *Iliad*. Those heroes managed to respect their family's old ties of *xenia* (guest friendship); Pharnabazus, through his similar conduct, proves a more heroic and truer friend than the Spartan king.

Beyond characterizing Pharnabazus, offering a powerful alternative perspective on friendship that comes from the lips of one with authority, and contesting ethnic stereotypes, the speech *also* helps explain the particular event, by showing why Pharnabazus does not ally with Agesilaus. In honing in on friendship these speeches address a key ethical but also explanatory concept, since friendship and alliances are for Xenophon forces that can trump other factors, for example transforming a weak party into a strong one. Friendship – along with the ethical underpinning that true friendship requires – is indeed in Xenophon's conception one of the few things that can hold out hope of stability in the turbulent world of the fourth century.

Xenophon to the Greek Mercenaries

After the Spartans take over leadership of the Greek mercenary force (*Anab.* 7.6.6), offering pay and resolving their predicament, the soldiers immediately denounce Xenophon (7.6.8). They accuse him of pocketing Seuthes' money without paying them, and propose that a fair wage would be to see him stoned to death (7.6.9–10). Xenophon then delivers a long speech of defense and justification (7.6.11–38) recapitulating the past narrative, highlighting his best efforts to help the mercenaries and the injustice of their treatment of *him*. He emphasizes the problem of change in human relationships, and a crucial difficulty: that however good a friend you may be, you may not be rewarded with gratitude: "Well, now, a human being must expect anything and everything, seeing that I now find myself blamed by you in a matter in which I am conscious of having shown the greatest zeal on your behalf" (7.6.11).

His comment that the Greek mercenaries now have *euporia* ("ease, solution of difficulties," 7.6.37) rounds off a key motif – *aporia* ("difficulties") – of the preceding narrative.[25] The speech also crystallizes the explanatory and structural theme of failed expectations and broken promises (which has pervaded the narrative ever since the hopes flamed by Cyrus the Younger in book 1). Associated with this is the theme of memory, and how memories, like promises, frequently do not stand the test of time. At the end of the speech Xenophon ironically addresses his audience as "the best rememberers of all" (7.6.38).

The speech sets forth an ideal: Xenophon's expectation that the Greeks would be grateful for his efforts on their behalf, which parallels his expectation (expressed in the same speech) that the more he helped Seuthes, the more he would be his friend once he was in a position of power (7.6.20): both of which expectations are frustrated in reality. This represents a major obstacle to the potential for friendship to serve as insurance against contingency. Here as elsewhere we find Xenophon using speech as a means not to gloss over challenges to his treasured ideals, but to expose and confront them.

Athenians to the Spartans

Nervous of the intentions of their ally Thebes after her expulsion of the Plataeans from Boeotia and her campaigns against the Phocians (*Hell.* 6.3.1–2), the Athenians send ambassadors to Thebes and then Sparta to petition for peace (371 BC). Xenophon sets out in direct discourse the three

---

[25] For this motif see Purves 2010: 177–9.

speeches that the ambassadors deliver at Sparta (*Hell.* 6.3.2–17). These supply little in the way of political or military arguments to explain reasons for peace at this time; and shortly after the peace negotiation, Sparta and Thebes slide into war, with the battle of Leutra the upshot. But the petition gives Xenophon an opportunity: for the speeches together explore the problem of how to develop and sustain friendships. In the first speech, Callias touches on the theme of friendship between individuals, and between individuals and the state. His family has long-standing ties of guest friendship with Sparta (6.3.4), so he speaks as one who knows how to sustain such relationships over time. The example from myth of a favor done by Athenian individuals to Spartan friends highlights just how long such relationships should endure. The second speaker, Autocles, turns to interstate friendships and the need for frankness in these (6.3.7), in a startlingly frank speech charging that the Spartans' claim to value Greek independence is belied by their actions. The third speech, Callistratus', returns to the subject of relationships over time: "I see," he says, "that no mortal continues through to the end without making mistakes"; but that does not mean that one should not have relationships with people who have made mistakes. Instead one should recognize that mistakes present an opportunity, for those who make mistakes become easier to deal with.

The triad of speeches sets out a temporal movement, from mythical past to present and into the future. Along the way, challenges are acknowledged (especially in Autolycus' speech), but the possibility of a better future is then aired. In this way speeches can open up possibilities for reconciling ideals and reality. Three speeches working together in this way find no parallel in earlier historiography; their closest model is the embassy scene to Achilles in *Iliad* 9 (where the three speeches also concern friendship).

Conclusion

Why speeches? One advantage of the narration of *words* over the narration of *deeds* was perhaps how they are especially conducive to opening up space for reflection – because direct speeches place readers in a position alongside the internal audience, as receivers and judges, and Greek readers were highly *au fait* with this role of judger of speeches. The description of *responses* to speeches underlines this potential for independent reactions and critical responses, and trains readers to respond in a similar way.

The philosophical element of Xenophon's speeches owes much to Herodotus, who was never one to refrain from creative construction of speeches where it helped readers grasp a higher truth; the factually impossible meeting at the Lydian court of the wise Athenian lawgiver Solon and

King Croesus (Hdt. 1.30–3) is recalled by several Xenophontic speeches. Thucydides, with his use of speeches to analyze abstract concepts, is another source of inspiration. Homer supplies a model for Xenophon's internal monologue in *Anabasis* (the first of the crucial triad of speeches that turns around his own and then the army's psychological state) and for three speeches that make the *same* overall point. Xenophon's own experiments with Socratic dialogue perhaps influenced the eclectic forms of speech of the historical and pseudo-historical works (such as the *Cyropaedia*). There are affinities also with tragedy's messenger speeches and choral odes. The odes' content may relate only obliquely to the events on stage, but opens up avenues of reflection, draws attention to motifs that run through a play, and reaches towards deeper meanings.

Xenophon in recounting speeches was thus not playing "things exactly as they are," in the words of Wallace Stevens' poem "The Man with the Blue Guitar," or as demonstrated by the painting that inspired it, *The Old Guitarist* by Picasso. Instead of seeking exactly to reproduce reality, the speeches reach beyond immediate contexts and open up broader perspectives, explanations, and truths; and the creative means by which Xenophon achieves this objective highlight his status as creator, *poietes*, whether in the realm of fiction or history. And as "The Man with the Blue Guitar" was on one level a statement about the value of poetry, so too the speeches across Xenophon's works have a strong metaliterary function, reminding us of the value of the very works in which they appear.[26]

Further Reading

Scardino 2007: 1–26 reviews approaches from antiquity to the present to the function of speeches in ancient Greek histories, demonstrating how the nineteenth- to twentieth-century emphasis on the question of authenticity (for which see, e.g. Fornara 1983: 142–68) has given way to approaches informed by narratology and reader-response theories. The functions of direct versus indirect speech and the degree to which they are equivalent exegetical tools remains contested: see Scardino 2012 (with reference to Herodotus and Thucydides), Foster 2012 for a review of recent scholarship. For speeches

[26] For their suggestions and insights at various stages I would like to thank the extremely helpful members of the departments of Classics at St. Andrews, Newcastle, and Manchester, the audience at ASCS 2016 in Melbourne, and also Antonis Tsakmakis, Melissa Mueller, Luuk Huitink, Jonas Grethlein, David Baragwanath, Melina Tamiolaki, and Michael Flower. The chapter was written in the ideal environment of the Seminar für Klassische Philologie, Universität Heidelberg, supported by an Alexander von Humboldt fellowship.

in Greek historiography, often with great relevance to Xenophon as well, see Pelling 2006 (on Herodotus), Marincola 2007b, Scardino 2007: 1–59, Pitcher 2009: 103–11, Pausch 2010: 3–8, and the remainder of the collected papers in Pausch 2010. For the speeches of Xenophon's *Hellenica* see Gray 1989: 79–140 (underscoring the moral and characterizing function), Marincola 2010 (examining intertextuality and *exempla*), Rood 2012a, Baragwanath 2012a, Tamiolaki 2014a; of *Anabasis*: Rood 2004a, 2006, Grethlein 2012: 27–30, 2013: 64–9 (emphasizing the power of speech to make the past present), Tuplin 2014a (including an inventory of all instances in *Anabasis* of direct and indirect discourse); of *Cyropaedia*: Gera 1993: *s.v.* "Speeches," Nicolai 2014a; of *Symposium*: Hobden 2005. The importance of rhetoric in Xenophon's Socratic works: Dorion 2014. Pontier 2014 examines rhetoric in Xenophon.

PART IV

MAJOR SUBJECTS

15

MICHAEL A. FLOWER

Xenophon as a Historian

What Kind of "History" Is This?

"History books that do not lie are all very dull" ("Les livres d'histoire qui ne mentent pas sont tous fort maussades"), observes the protagonist in Anatole France's novel *Le Crime de Sylvestre Bonnard* (1881). A reader who comes to the "history books" of Xenophon with an interest in learning about the events of the first half of the fourth century BC will certainly not find them dull.[1] But this reader will also want to know certain things about the nature of these works. First of all, when Xenophon's narrative is contradicted by other extant sources, whose account should one prefer? Which account, in other words, is more truthful, in the narrow sense of corresponding more closely to "what actually happened" in the past? Secondly, this reader will wonder why Xenophon has chosen not to discuss some of the most important developments of the period in question. Do these omissions make him a "bad" historian?

In this chapter I want to evaluate Xenophon's *Hellenica* (a history of Greece between 411 and 362) as a narrative of historical events. This is not nearly as straightforward a matter as one might expect. The traditional way in which one evaluates a work of history is in terms of its factual accuracy and the cogency of its interpretations. But being a "good" historian is not exclusively a function of "getting the facts right" and of explaining them persuasively. The most admired and enduring historical narratives, both ancient and modern, are those that conjure up the past in the reader's imagination, creating the illusion that events are being witnessed in the mind's eye just as they had happened. Ancient critics called this aspect of historical narrative *enargeia* or "vividness."[2]

Facts alone constitute a chronicle, not a narrative.[3] To create a historical narrative one must also arrange the "facts" into a story with a plot,

---

[1] All dates are BC.
[2] See Walker 1993.
[3] White 1980.

characters, and themes, and one must do so in such a way that this particular story is a memorable one.[4] Of course, as soon as one does this, to a greater or lesser degree, one begins to fictionalize, and that can come close to what Anatole France considered "telling lies." For these reasons the literary qualities of the *Hellenica* and *Anabasis* are not really separable from their evidentiary value when it comes to evaluating their effectiveness as works of narrative history. To be sure, in places Xenophon displays a chronological laxness that is difficult to excuse on artistic grounds, but that will not be my concern in this chapter.[5]

As a literary artist, Xenophon is capable of reaching the dramatic heights of Herodotus and Thucydides. The whole first book of his *Anabasis* is calculated to create suspense leading up to the battle of Cunaxa near Babylon in 401, which is the book's climax. His account (3.1.11–15) of how he subsequently was prompted by a heaven-sent dream to rouse the dejected army contains the only internal dialogue in extant Greek historical writing. Likewise, the tragic love story of Abradatas and Panthea in the *Cyropaedia*, culminating in his death in battle and her suicide (7.3), anticipated the story pattern of the Hellenistic novel, and is justly famous for its pathos. In the *Hellenica* (2.2.3–4) the reaction of the Athenians to the news of the annihilation of their navy at Aegospotami in 405 vividly captures, in just a few succinct phrases, their grief and despair. The meeting of the Persian satrap Pharnabazus and King Agesilaus of Sparta (*Hell.* 4.1.29–41), in which the Persian shames the Greek, has been much admired since antiquity. Even the brief historical overview of the honoree's career in the encomium *Agesilaus* contains some remarkable scenes, not least of all the description of the battlefield of Coronea, with "the earth stained purple with blood" (*Ages.* 2.14).

To us moderns it seems obvious that Xenophon's two works of "history" are his *Anabasis* and *Hellenica*. Yet it cannot be taken for granted that the *Cyropaedia* (*The Education of Cyrus*) should not be added to this list. Although it is now generally considered to be a work of fiction (a faux-biographical philosophical romance), the *Cyropaedia* is the only one of Xenophon's historical works that contains a preface ("We will try to relate what we have learned from inquiry and what we think we have perceived about him," 1.1.6). Moreover, as Melina Tamiolaki argues in her chapter, "despite the undeniable blending of different genres, Xenophon intended the *Cyropaedia* to be conceived *more* as historiography (albeit of a peculiar sort)."

---

[4] White 1978 is a fundamental statement of this point.
[5] To take an egregious example, Xenophon's synchronization (*Hell.* 3.2.21) of Sparta's war against Elis (probably 402–400) with Dercylidas' campaign in Asia Minor (probably 399–397) is most likely incorrect.

Ancient readers themselves seem to have been divided as to what kind of work it is: history or fiction. The critic Dionysius of Halicarnassus (*Letter to Pompeius* 4) counts the *Cyropaedia* among Xenophon's other historical works (*Anabasis* and *Hellenica*); whereas Cicero considered it a philosophical fiction (*Letter to His Brother Quintus* 1.1.23): "The famous Cyrus was portrayed by Xenophon not in accordance with fidelity to history, but as a model of just rule." We cannot know for certain how Xenophon *intended* it to be perceived. But the arresting differences with all other extant versions of Cyrus' career, the languid preachiness of its many speeches and dialogues, the imbedded novellas, the overwrought battle scenes, and the surprisingly thin veneer of Persian decor (in conjunction with the similarities between Spartan and Persian institutions) might well have alerted ancient readers that Xenophon was playing, for didactic and ethical purposes, with their generic expectations of what a properly historical narrative consisted of.[6] The very length of the extended conversations in the *Cyropaedia* (so different from the concentrated economy of those in the *Hellenica* and *Anabasis*) may be an intentional marker of their fictiveness. Moreover, the great distance in time would have suggested to readers that not everything was to be accepted as "history."[7]

Despite some modern attempts to demonstrate otherwise, the *Hellenica* and *Anabasis* were intended to be, and were perceived by the ancients as being, attempts at historical narrative. What kind of attempts is another question, and one not easily answered. I have elsewhere suggested that the *Anabasis* is an example of what we now call microhistory (which treats an isolated event in great detail) and the *Hellenica* of macrohistory (which provides a grand narrative).[8] In the form that Xenophon wrote them, the two-year (401–399) story of Cyrus the Younger's expedition and the subsequent travails of the Ten Thousand Greek mercenaries whom he hired, could not be structured as a part of Xenophon's forty-nine-year history of Greece without creating an immensely awkward digression, since both works are roughly of the same length. Yet as an explanatory lens that only gets us so far. I will now proceed to make some general observations about Xenophon's historical methods and interests, and then turn to some case studies where his version of events can be compared to other accounts. I will end with a discussion of his notion of historical causation.

---

[6] See Tuplin 1996, Azoulay 2007a, and Stadter 1991/2010.
[7] Ephorus of Cyme, a historian writing at the end of the fourth century, observed that those who give highly detailed accounts of past events are considered to be highly untrustworthy (*FGrHist* 70, F9).
[8] Flower 2012: 47–8.

Xenophon does not employ prefaces either in the *Hellenica* or the *Anabasis*, and here the contrast with Herodotus and Thucydides is striking. They tell us what they were writing about, why they wrote it, and, later on, they discuss their methods (although of the two Thucydides is much more explicit about his methods and Herodotus about his sources).[9] Xenophon does none of this. At most we can infer that the *Hellenica* (or at least the first part of it) was intended to be a continuation of Thucydides because it begins roughly where Thucydides' history ends, with the simple words "And after these things." The *Anabasis* begins in story mode (the "once upon a time" technique): "Darius and Parsyatis had two sons."

It is possible, however, to say something about his methods and motives by piecing together isolated statements from his different works. From these it seems fairly certain that Xenophon, like Thucydides (1.22), considered the study of the past to be something that individuals can learn from, and that history, like philosophy, has an educational value. Yet even though moral and political didacticism, on the surface at least, seems to be one of his driving concerns, a great deal of interpretative space is left for readers to draw their own lessons. Is imperialism ever advantageous to a state? What is the best way of organizing a community? Could the Greeks ever be expected to join in common cause, either to establish peace amongst themselves or to attack the Persian Empire? What was the primary reason for the defeat of Athens in the Peloponnesian War or for the collapse of the Spartan hegemony? The answers are never made explicit, even if there are some signposts along the way. Ultimately, it is up to readers to provide answers based on how they understand Xenophon's narrative. Xenophon is clearest when it comes to the specific qualities that constitute good leadership (most explicitly in his catalogue of Agesilaus' virtues in the encomium), but even here one has to piece together the lessons for oneself.

Xenophon is notoriously reticent about his sources of information. He even employs an anonymous third-person narrator, so that the innocent reader would never guess that the character Xenophon, who takes center stage from book 3 of the *Anabasis* to its end, is the same person as the work's author/narrator. It is often asserted that Xenophon's alleged errors and random emphases in the *Hellenica* are due to an overreliance on the testimony of friends and acquaintances (whose information was partial and sometimes misleading) and to a tendency to focus on those events in which he personally had participated. This argument is entirely circular, since vividness of narration is no more dependent upon eyewitness testimony than it is in a modern novel, as a comparison between scenes in the *Cyropaedia*

---

[9] Thuc. 1.22; 5.26.5; Hdt. 2.99, 7.152.

and *Hellenica* can easily demonstrate. It is best to begin with the premise that Xenophon's narrative choices are not haphazard, but are a function of his historical and literary project. So, for instance, he refers to the Spartan establishment of narrow juntas (the notorious oligarchies either of thirty or ten men) in allied cities both in his narrative and in speeches, but he only discusses one of them in any detail, the Thirty at Athens.[10] This is equivalent to Thucydides discussing only one of the many civil wars that broke out throughout Greece during the Peloponnesian War, that on the island of Corcyra (3.69–85). Likewise, although a funeral oration was delivered in Athens each year for that year's collective war dead, Thucydides (2.34–46) only relates one such speech, that delivered by Pericles at the end of the first year of fighting.

A Biased and Partial Account?

Although all historians, both ancient and modern, cannot record everything that they know about, Xenophon chose not to discuss three of the most important developments of the period covered in his *Hellenica*. These major omissions are the creation of the Arcadian League and the foundation of the federal capital of Megalopolis in around 370, the refoundation of Messene with the concomitant liberation of the Messenian helots in 369, and the formal establishment of the second Athenian naval confederacy in 378.[11] What all three events have in common is that they were detrimental to Spartan interests, and that has naturally given rise to the modern explanation that Xenophon's silence must be due to pro-Spartan bias. Now one cannot claim that these were unimportant events in the history of Greece. It would not be quite right, however, to say that Xenophon has completely omitted these events, since he does refer to them obliquely.[12] He is not trying to conceal their existence from posterity, but rather assumes that his readers know about them. And yet would not those informed readers wonder why Xenophon has not discussed events of such importance? That depends on what they expected a work such as this to contain (that is, what their generic expectations were) and on how much leeway they were willing to grant

---

[10] Dillery 1995: 138–63 shows how the Thirty serve a paradigmatic function as models of tyrannical behavior.

[11] Various explanations for these and other omissions have been given: Cawkwell 1979 (and his many followers) attributes them to his pro-Spartan, anti-Theban bias; whereas for Pownall 2004 they are primarily a result of his emphasis on using lessons from the past for moral instruction. Tuplin 1993 sees the *Hellenica* as a cross between historical narrative and political pamphlet, an accommodation that permitted Xenophon to omit certain subjects.

[12] Second Athenian confederacy 6.3.19; Megalopolis 7.5.5; Messene 7.1.27, 36; 7.4.9.

an author in determining what was relevant to the topic at hand. It is very doubtful that their expectations and requirements were the same as ours.

Despite what most modern historians think that he should have discussed, these aspects of the past were not the ones that he chose to place under the "floodlight" of historical analysis.[13] Xenophon was not, after all, writing for modern readers who need to know certain other things in order to understand the full implications of the things that he does tell us. He was writing for contemporary readers who knew the basic outline of events well enough. He could not have foreseen that modern readers would need to rely on much later authors to supplement his account (principally Cornelius Nepos, Diodorus Siculus, Plutarch, and Pausanias, ranging in date from the first century BC to the second century AD). There is always a tension between comprehensiveness and selectivity in historical narrative, whether ancient or modern. Even Thucydides has some significant omissions and distortions in his history of the Peloponnesian War, though that has not diminished his reputation as the greatest historian of antiquity.[14] Xenophon has been picked out for special censure because his narrative in the *Hellenica* can be checked against other sources to an extent that the narratives of Herodotus and Thucydides cannot.

The focus of so much of modern scholarship on explaining such omissions has resulted in two schools of thought. One emphasizes Xenophon's alleged personal biases (admiration for Agesilaus, hatred of Thebes, attachment to Panhellenism) as being responsible for his omitting anything or anyone that he must have found too unpalatable to mention. All historical accounts suffer from some degree of bias. This is because historians select, arrange, and inflect their material in such a way as to promote a particular view of how and why things happened in the way that they did. Bias becomes a serious problem only when it is so severe and of such a nature that it results in a distortion of the historical record that is tantamount to disinformation. Now it is actually very difficult to prove that Xenophon

---

[13] As Ankersmit 2010: 44 expresses it: "in the context of historical representation an element of individuality or of particularity is involved as well – and that has its origin in the uniqueness of each historical representation proposing the delineation of a certain aspect of the past. Such proposals function as a kind of floodlight that may lighten, so to say, aspects of the past, while others, deemed to be less relevant, are left in the dark. And each proposal will do this in a different way."

[14] No reader could infer from his history that a peace between Athens and Persia, the so-called Peace of Callias, had been concluded in the mid-fifth century or renewed with Darius II in 425 (see Cawkwell 1997). And his failure to give a precise date and context for the Athenian decree against Megara has caused insuperable problems for modern historians. But there are other serious omissions (and distortions) as well: see Badian 1993 (on the outbreak of the Peloponnesian War) and H. Flower 1992 (on the Pylos debate).

ever says something that is untrue.[15] It is another matter whether any of his omissions are purposefully misleading.[16]

Another approach has been to emphasize what Xenophon was seemingly most interested in: which was not so much traditional historical narrative of the kind found in Thucydides, but presenting paradigms of successful leaders and admirable behavior with a view towards the moral instruction of his readers. It is certainly true that themes appear in the *Hellenica* and *Anabasis* that run through his entire corpus, most conspicuously the delineation of the qualities that comprise effective leadership over willing followers or the value of loyalty to one's friends and allies.[17] And the narrator himself admits that some of the digressions on these themes might seem out of place in a historical narrative.[18]

Both of these modern interpretative approaches, while containing some explanatory value, tend unjustly to minimize the extent to which Xenophon is actually good at narrating and explaining the important historical trends of his time in terms that his contemporary audience would have found convincing. That is, he explains events both in terms of Thucydidean Realpolitik and in terms of a Herodotean dual causality in which impiety and hubris lead to a fall. The single most pervasive theme in the *Hellenica* (obvious to the reader if never stated by the author) is the rise and fall of the Spartan hegemony. The focus on that theme may not account for all of the omissions, and one can hardly deny that the establishment of a free Messenia is integral to the story of Sparta's decline in the fourth century. Yet it does go a long way towards explaining the inclusion of events in which Spartans were directly involved and the exclusion of those (including developments affecting the fortunes of Athens and Thebes) in which they were not.

It is all too easy, and tempting, to jump to the conclusion that all of Xenophon's silences and alleged errors must be explained by his strong personal biases. Anti-Theban bias indeed seems to be the most obvious explanation of why he gives such a highly jejune account of the two most prominent and famous Theban leaders of the fourth century: Pelopidas and Epaminondas. Xenophon himself may have believed the gods to be primarily responsible for the rise of Theban power and the collapse of the Spartan

---

[15] See Tuplin 1993: 12 and Thomas 2009a: lxiii. The same holds true for the *Anabasis*: see Flower 2012: 60–80.

[16] For Lévy 1990 the apparent naiveté of Xenophon's narrative masks an artful deformation of the historical record.

[17] For the *Hellenica* note the following. Good leadership: Teleutias (Spartan), 5.1.3–4; Jason of Pherae, 6.1.4–19; Iphicrates (Athenian), 6.2–13–14, 27–39; Epaminondas (Theban), 7.5.18–25. Loyalty of Phliasians to Sparta, 7.2.1–4. Bad leadership: Iphicrates 6.5.51–2.

[18] *Hell.* 5.1.4 and 7.2.1, on which see Gray 2003.

hegemony (see below); but his contemporaries would have considered these two Thebans to be the primary human agents behind those developments. Pelopidas (in his sole appearance) is revealed as ready to fawn upon the king of Persia in order to gain power over other Greeks (*Hell.* 7.1.34). On the other hand, Xenophon's treatment of Epaminondas is not quite that simple. Epaminondas is depicted as seeking to prevent the banishment of the Achaean aristocracy (7.1.41–3) and, in an authorial intervention, he is given high praise for the way he prepared and arrayed his army for the battle of Mantinea in 362 (*Hell.* 7.5.18–25). Yes, a great deal more could have been said about Epaminondas, but what is said is surprising if his omissions were entirely motivated by hatred of Thebes. Xenophon's treatment of Thebes can be dismissive and even sarcastic (*Hell.* 7.5.12); but perhaps, at the same time, he did not see Thebes or its leaders as the primary reason for the fall of Sparta, being more interested in Sparta's own errors and internal weaknesses.

Xenophon on Agesilaus

One accusation often leveled against Xenophon is that he suppresses material detrimental to his "hero" Agesilaus, whom in his encomium he calls "a perfectly good man." It is indeed striking that Plutarch (*Ages.* 28), who drew on other fourth-century historians who are now lost (see below), relates some sensational examples of Agesilaus' hatred of Thebes and its fatal consequences for Sparta that are not to be found in the corresponding episodes in Xenophon (*Hell.* 6.3.18–4.3). These include Agesilaus' personal confrontation with Epaminondas in 371 during a peace conference at Sparta and his decisive intervention in the subsequent Spartan decision to declare war on Thebes. Those two actions led directly to the crushing defeat of a Spartan army by Thebes at the battle of Leuctra in the very same year.

It is curious, however, that Xenophon has not suppressed two incidents that make Agesilaus look cynically self-interested. In 382 he intervened on behalf of Phoebidas' illegal seizure of the Theban acropolis in violation of the King's Peace by asserting that the main consideration should be whether Phoebidas' actions were "good or bad" for Sparta (*Hell.* 5.2.32). A few years later in 378, he intervened, this time for personal reasons, on behalf of Sphodrias, who was on trial for attempting to seize the Piraeus in peacetime (*Hell.* 5.4.20–34). Xenophon's narrative makes it clear that both of these Spartan commanders had acted without orders, that most Spartans were displeased with what they had done, and that Agesilaus' personal intervention was both decisive in securing their acquittal and disastrous in its consequences for Spartan hegemony in Greece. Since the immediate consequence of Sphodrias' acquittal was war with Athens (5.4.34), this would have been the appropriate place for Xenophon to mention the concurrent foundation of the second Athenian confederacy.[19] To the chagrin of modern scholars, he lets the opportunity pass. I think that this is not just a case of Xenophon taking knowledge of the new Athenian alliance for granted; he was simply not interested in describing institutional structures.[20] Similarly, he does not list the specific provisions of the King's Peace (which modern historians have worked hard to infer), but merely records the Persian king's rescript (*Hell.* 5.1.30–1).

Although Xenophon sometimes relates incidents that are not to Agesilaus' credit, there is never any hint that he was unworthy to be a Spartan king. It would have been easy enough to insinuate doubt about Agesilaus' credentials, had he chosen to do so. This brings us to a seemingly minor, but all too telling, omission in Xenophon's account of the succession debate after the death of King Agis around 400 BC. Xenophon presents a very vivid direct exchange, partially in the Spartan Doric dialect (e.g. "Poteidan" for "Poseidon"), between the two contenders: Agis' brother Agesilaus and Agis' son Leotychides (*Hell.* 3.3.1–4):

> Leotychides said, "Well, the law, Agesilaus, directs not that the brother of the king become king but rather his son. If there should not happen to be a son, then the brother would be king."
>
> "It would be necessary for me to become king."
>
> "How, when I am alive?"
>
> "Because the person whom you call your father said that you were not his son."
>
> "But my mother, who knows far better than him, even now still says that I am."
>
> "Well, Poteidan gave testimony that you are very much mistaken, when by an earthquake he drove your father out of the bedchamber and out into the open. And time, which is said to be the truest witness, testified in his support in this matter; for, as you know, you were born in the tenth month from the time when he fled[21] and appeared in the bedchamber."
>
> They were saying such things.

This is an example of what modern literary critics call "free direct speech." By omitting the introductory words "he said/he replied," Xenophon creates

---

[19] I follow those scholars who place the foundation after Sphodrias' raid on the Piraeus rather than before it (as in Diod. 15.28–9). See Rhodes and Osborne 2003: 98–100.

[20] Jehne 2004, however, suggests that Xenophon avoids discussing the second Athenian confederacy in order to draw his reader's attention to the omission and is thereby playing with their expectations.

[21] I am here accepting the emendation ἔφυγε for ἔφυσε.

the illusion that the characters are speaking in our presence without the narrator as an intermediary. Why does he do this? Is it for the purely aesthetic goal of making the scene come alive before the reader's very eyes? Or is vividness a strategy of concealment, for erasing something that he did not wish his readers to know? In Xenophon's version, Agesilaus gives the decisive argument: Agis himself had claimed that Leotychides was not his son. Two later sources, however, claim that Agis, while on his deathbed and in the presence of many witnesses, acknowledged the legitimacy of Leotychides (Pausanias 8.7–10; Plutarch, *Ages.* 3; *Alcib.* 23; *Lys.* 22).

It is hard to escape the conclusion that Xenophon has suppressed this detail because including it would have undermined Agesilaus' claim to the throne and supported those who referred an oracle warning against a "lame kingship" to Agesilaus (who was physically lame) rather than to Leotychides (who was metaphorically lame). In the aftermath of Leuctra most Spartans, according to Plutarch, felt regret at having chosen him over Leotychides in contravention of the oracle.[22] Xenophon, however, has artfully shaped his own account in such a way as to make Agesilaus appear the indisputably correct choice.

The Thirty at Athens

The strengths and weaknesses of Xenophon's historical method are well brought out in his account of the Thirty oligarchs (later known as the "Thirty Tyrants") who ruled Athens for roughly eight months (summer 404 to spring 403) after the end of the Peloponnesian War. This is the longest and most detailed account of any single episode in the *Hellenica*, covering a single year in twenty pages of the Oxford Classical Text (2.3.11–2.4.43).[23] Even so, it is beyond doubt that Xenophon has simplified events in order to present an account that focuses on the Thirty's escalating use of violence and terror to achieve their ends.[24] At the same time, the story of their rise and fall has a very novelistic quality to it: extraneous details are omitted and the narrative focuses on three characters: the brutal and extreme Critias, the moderate oligarch Theramenes, and the exiled democratic leader Thrasybulus. The trial and execution of Theramenes by the Thirty is one of the finest set pieces in Greek prose literature (replete with speeches, dialogue, anecdotes, and dramatic action).

---

[22] *Ages.* 30.1. Xenophon records the debate over the oracle, but unlike Plutarch (*Ages.* 3.3–5) he does not provide a text of it.

[23] Dillery 1995: 139, 146.

[24] Other sources contain details omitted by Xenophon: Aristotle, *Ath. Pol.* 34–41; Lysias, speeches 12 and 13; Diod. 14.3–6, 32–3.

Now there is nothing remiss in the way that Xenophon emplots the story of the Thirty in terms of the progression of violence (and in this respect it resembles Simon Schama's emplotment of the French Revolution).[25] What is disturbing to the modern historian is the possibility (and for some the *probability*) that he not only has omitted a great deal of information, but even has rearranged the sequence of events in order to bolster his trajectory of violence followed by resistance followed by even severer violence.[26] For instance, Xenophon places the main events in this order: arrival of Spartan garrison (summoned by the Thirty), escalation of violence, execution of Theramenes, Thrasybulus seizes Phyle (a fort in the Attic countryside). Aristotle, in his *Constitution of the Athenians*, inverts this sequence: Thrasybulus seizes Phyle, execution of Theramenes, escalation of violence, arrival of Spartan garrison.[27] The former scheme emphasizes the Thirty's initial brutality; the latter makes that brutality a reaction to external opposition.[28] Scholars will continue to argue over which chronology is correct; nevertheless, one temporal displacement does seem certain.

According to Aristotle, the deposing of the Thirty in 403 was accompanied by a reconciliation and an amnesty.[29] Xenophon indeed places the initial reconciliation in this context (*Hell.* 2.4.38), but he mentions an amnesty only after the subsequent reconciliation with those oligarchs who had taken refuge in Eleusis. In other words, he has transferred the initial implementation of the amnesty to the time of its extension. In 401 the democrats from the city were reconciled with the oligarchs residing in Eleusis and then (*Hell.* 2.4.43), "They swore oaths that they would not remember past wrongs, and still even now they live together as citizens and the people abide by their oaths." Xenophon's displacement of the amnesty to the very last sentence of the story of the Thirty has a purely literary function, allowing him to end his account of this brutal episode in Athenian history on a positive note. To most of us this type of chronological rearrangement may be acceptable in a historical novel, but it is completely inadmissible in a modern work purporting to be narrative history.

The *Hellenica Oxyrhynchia* versus Xenophon

This brings us to the most controversial and difficult question of all, the relative reliability of Xenophon's narrative and that of the papyrus fragments

---

[25] *Citizens: A Chronicle of the French Revolution* (London, 1989).
[26] For lists of his omissions, see Tuplin 1993: 43 n. 1 and Krentz 1995: 122.
[27] See Table 2 in Wolpert 2002: 17.
[28] Wolpert 2002: 15–24; Shear 2011: 180–5.
[29] *Ath. Pol.* 39.

of a highly detailed account of the period from 411 to 394 (or perhaps to 386) of unknown authorship. The work is called, for convenience, the *Hellenica Oxyrhynchia* because the papyri were discovered at Oxyrhynchus in Egypt (the first papyrus was published in 1908 and two others in 1949 and 1976).[30] The fragments comprise a total of about 1200 lines, or roughly twenty pages of modern text, although there are many gaps.

It is generally assumed the author must be someone who is already known to us, since the fragments come from three different papyrus copies of the same text (thus showing the work's popularity, at least in second-century AD Egypt). But stylistic grounds, in my opinion, rule out the two most distinguished candidates, Theopompus of Chios and Ephorus of Cyme, both of whom produced substantial, but no longer extant, accounts of fourth-century history.[31] Theopompus' *Hellenica* covered events between 411 and 394 (and was at least three and a half times longer than Xenophon's);[32] whereas Ephorus wrote a universal history of Greece from earliest times to 341.[33] That only leaves the Athenian Cratippus and Daemachus of Plataea, about whom we know exceedingly little, as possible candidates.[34] So the historical value of these fragments must be judged on their own terms and without recourse to the reputation in antiquity of their author. Whoever this author was, we do not know whether he published before or after Xenophon (if Cratippus before; if Theopompus or Ephorus after). In some places their accounts are not mutually exclusive; but in other places their versions cannot be reconciled.

The main issue at stake is whether this historian not only gave a considerably more detailed version of events than did Xenophon, but also a much more accurate one (the majority view). It is possible that he was more thorough and careful in his use of sources (oral and written); but, if he wrote after Xenophon, it is also possible that his primary method was systematically to expand Xenophon's narrative through free invention and the employment of stock scenes.[35] Given the current state of the evidence, it is not possible

---

[30] See McKechnie and Kern 1988: 3–7.

[31] See Flower 1994: 27–8. A comparison of the fragments of the *Hellenica Oxyrhynchia* with two verbatim quotations from Theopompus' *Hellenica* should make this obvious: *FGrHist* 115 F 20 and F 22 (= Athen. 543b–c and 675b–c).

[32] Flower 1994: 159–60.

[33] The account of Greek history in books 11–16 of the universal history of Diodorus Siculus (first century BC) is very similar, but not identical, to some fragments of the *Hellenica Oxyrhynchia*. It has long been assumed that Ephorus himself, who seems to have been Diodorus' main source for this part of his history, made substantial use of the *Hellenica Oxyrhynchia*. It is possible, of course, that Diodorus consulted the *Hellenica Oxyrhynchia* directly.

[34] On Cratippus, see Plut. *De glor. Athen.* 345C–E and Dion. Hal. *de Thuc.* 16. See further Luraghi in this volume.

[35] So Bleckmann 2006 in a highly controversial study.

to settle this issue definitively. Nonetheless, we must resist the temptation *a priori* to equate narrative detail with factual accuracy (as so many modern historians have done). Some of his modern admirers have judged the author of the *Hellenica Oxyrhynchia* to be not only a self-conscious imitator of Thucydides, but in some respects "even superior to his exemplar."[36] In what follows, I am going to compare Xenophon's version of the battle of Sardis (395 BC) and of the subsequent outbreak of the Corinthian War with the much fuller, and conspicuously different, account of these events in the *Hellenica Oxyrhynchia*.[37]

The Battle of Sardis

The battle of Sardis was the high-water mark of Agesilaus' unsuccessful attempt in 396–395 to liberate the Greeks of Asia Minor from Persian rule. In Xenophon's account (*Hell.* 3.4.20–6), Agesilaus marches from Ephesus towards Sardis for three days without an enemy in sight. On the fourth day he defeats the Persian cavalry and captures the enemy camp, which results in the replacement of the Persian satrap Tissaphernes (who was in Sardis at the time of the battle) by Tithraustes. He then makes a truce with Tithraustes and leads his army up north to Phrygia. In the *Hellenica Oxyrhynchia*, by contrast, during the lead up to the battle Tissaphernes in person follows, and continually harasses, the Greek army with his infantry and cavalry. Agesilaus sets an ambush and then attacks and routs the enemy army, both cavalry and infantry, killing six hundred of them and capturing their camp (Chambers F 14–15 = McKechnie and Kern F 11–12).

How can one explain these differences? Given that Xenophon was surely present on the campaign, probably as a member of Agesilaus' staff, it seems extraordinarily unlikely that he unwittingly could have given so erroneous an account of the major battle. And it is difficult to imagine any rational motive for his purposefully suppressing the extent of the Greek victory, since he later emphasizes that the outbreak of the Corinthian War dashed Agesilaus' hopes for greater successes still to come (*Hell.* 4.1.41–2.4).[38] So too it is highly implausible that the two historians are in fact describing two different battles that took place in the vicinity of Sardis.[39] Furthermore, the

---

[36] Cartledge 1987: 66.
[37] The bibliography is vast on both topics, so references to modern scholarship will be selective. On the battle of Sardis, scholarship is divided: for example, Bruce 1967: 150–6 and Cartledge 1987: 215–17 argue against Xenophon's version; Anderson 1974b, Gray 1979, and Wylie 1992 in favor.
[38] But for different views, see Gray 1979 and Dillery 1995: 109–19.
[39] Most recently argued by Thomas 2009a: xxxix–xl.

author of the *Hellenica Oxyrhynchia* seems to have had a penchant for narrating ambushes (where they are missing in Xenophon's account of the same events), and that leads one to suspect that he routinely inserted an ambush as a stock narrative device.[40]

However that may be, their differing descriptions of the aftermath of the battle are, if anything, even more remarkable. In the *Hellenica Oxyrhynchia*, Agesilaus ravages the area around Sardis for three days, then marches inland with Tissaphernes' army following at a safe distance. Agesilaus advances inland as far as the Maeander River, but unfavorable sacrifices prevent him from crossing and proceeding even further inland against Celaenae in Phrygia. Xenophon, on the other hand, gives the impression that Agesilaus made a treaty with Tithraustes immediately after the battle and forthwith headed up north to the satrapy of Pharnabazus.

Has the author of the *Hellenica Oxyrhynchia* invented this aborted push into the interior of Asia Minor or has Xenophon purposefully omitted it? The answer, I think, has less to do with Xenophon's biases or failing memory than with his artistic concerns. The whole of Agesilaus' reign up to this point has been presented as a series of loosely connected tableaux, and that is in keeping with his general preference for an episodic manner of narration. If one turns to the account of this same event in his *Agesilaus* (1.28–33), it is apparent that Xenophon knows more than he is telling. For we are here told that after the battle Agesilaus advanced on Sardis and burned and pillaged its suburbs. This is omitted in the *Hellenica*, and it cannot be for any other reason than narrative economy. This leads me to believe that in this case at least the *Hellenica Oxyrhynchia* is reporting things that did happen, but that Xenophon prefers not to narrate actions that had negligible consequences or little in the way of thematic value. On my reading Xenophon is not covering up a failure, but simply moving from one episode to another. His focus on vivid tableaux also explains why he forgoes the highly detailed itinerary that characterizes the *Hellenica Oxyrhynchia*'s entire account of Agesilaus' campaign in Asia. If historical narrative can be considered a verbal picture of past events, Xenophon prefers to paint with broad strokes.

The Outbreak of the Corinthian War

The outbreak of major wars can be extremely difficult to explain. Modern scholarship has not come to any consensus about the reasons for the outbreak of the Peloponnesian War, despite the fact that Thucydides devotes the first book of his history to that very question. So it should come as no

---

[40] See Gray 1979, who argues for such inventions of detail.

great surprise that Xenophon and the *Hellenica Oxyrhynchia* give different accounts of the outbreak of the Corinthian War or that the opinion of modern scholarship is divided between them.[41] If one looks only at the narrative section, Xenophon appears to give a very simple explanation (*Hell.* 3.5.1–7). After the battle of Sardis, Tithraustes, fearing the intentions of Agesilaus, sent Timocrates of Rhodes to distribute gold to the leading men in Thebes, Corinth, and Argos on condition that they stir up a war against the Spartans. This achieved the desired results (*Hell.* 3.5.2):

> Although the Athenians did not take a share of the gold, they were nevertheless eager for war, believing that it was their prerogative to rule. But those who had accepted the money into their own cities began to slander the Spartans. When they had induced their own cities to hate them, they then attempted to form an alliance of the greatest cities.

Taken at face value, this passage seems to imply that Persian gold was the necessary and sufficient cause of the war. As a preliminary observation, such a reading is undercut by Xenophon's later distinction between two groups of Corinthians who were opposed to making peace with Sparta in 392 (*Hell.* 4.4.2): "those who possessed a share of the Persian king's money and those who were most responsible for the outbreak of the war."[42] As we shall see in a moment, there is more to Xenophon's analysis than a simpleminded focus on the influence of Persian gold on Greek statesmen.

The *Hellenica Oxyrhynchia* allegedly gives a much more sophisticated and nuanced explanation by claiming that the gold was not as significant a factor as the fact that the leading men in Athens, Thebes, Corinth, and Argos had long hated the Spartans. He is usually credited with the insight that the Greek cities were for a long time ill disposed to Sparta; but that is an overinterpretation of what he actually says. The key fragments make it clear that he is only referring to the anti-Spartan faction in these cities, not to the citizenry as a whole (F 10 and 21 Chambers = McKechnie and Kern F 7 and 18).

> And yet some say that the money from him [Timocrates] was the cause of joint action by these men [the Athenians Epicrates and Cephalus] and those in Boeotia and those in the other cities that were mentioned previously. But they do not know that all had for a long time been ill disposed to the Spartans and

---

[41] Schepens 2012 is a recent and extremely thorough condemnation of Xenophon's account, arguing that Xenophon is a willing cipher for Spartan propaganda. Buckler 2004 and Rung 2004 are attempts to defend it.

[42] The translation of this sentence is controversial (see Schepens 2012: 221 n. 26), since some scholars refuse to believe that Xenophon could have intended to refer to two distinct groups of Corinthians. My translation represents what the Greek actually says.

were looking for a way to involve their cities in war. For the Argives and <the leading men of the>[43] Boeotians hated the Spartans because they were treating as friends their opponents among the citizens; whereas those in Athens who hated them desired to turn the Athenians from tranquility and peace and lead them towards war and external entanglements in order that it might be possible for them to obtain money from the common treasury. Those of the Corinthians who were seeking to change the present state of affairs, like the Argives and Boeotians, were ill disposed towards the Spartans, but Timolaus alone was opposed to them on private grounds (F 10.2–3).

It was for these reasons much more than on account of Pharnabazus and the gold that those in the aforementioned cities had been incited to hate the Spartans (F 10.5).

The supporters of Androcleides and Ismenias [at Thebes] were eager to involve the people in war against the Spartans, wishing to put an end to their empire so that they themselves would not be destroyed by them [the Spartans] on account of the pro-Spartan party [at Thebes]. They believed that they would achieve this easily, supposing that the king would provide the money that his messenger was promising, and that the Corinthians, Argives, and Athenians would take part in the war; for these, being enemies of the Spartans, would secure for them the assistance of their respective citizens (F 21.1).

All three extracts make it clear that it is not the cities as collective entities that hate the Spartans, but the anti-Spartan political factions in those cities, who fear destruction at the hands of their pro-Spartan political opponents. Even the final sentence of F 21.1 must be referring to anti-Spartan groups among the Corinthians, Argives, and Athenians, because it would make no sense for the citizenry as a whole to "secure the assistance" of themselves. Athens is the only exception to this pattern, since the pro-war faction there was principally motivated by the hope of personal enrichment from public funds. I find this to be a narrowly focused explanation.[44]

At the same time, there has been a general tendency to underestimate the level of sophistication in Xenophon's account.[45] This is because the main narrative gives only the motives of the Athenians (that they wanted to regain their empire) and of the Spartans (that they desired to put an end to Theban insolence and disobedience). The motives of other Greeks are brought out in the speech of the Theban ambassadors at Athens, who persuade the Athenians to assist them against Sparta (3.5.8–15). It should not strike us as anomalous that Xenophon would employ a speech delivered by

---

[43] The text of the papyrus is uncertain here, but "the leading men of the" seems to me the most likely restoration.

[44] As well pointed out by Bruce 1967: 60–1, 116–17. Lendon 1989, however, finds it persuasive.

[45] Tuplin 1993: 43–64, however, gives a highly nuanced and very detailed close reading.

Thebans, who are generally depicted unfavorably in the *Hellenica*, to deliver the fundamental critique, at a pivotal moment in history, of Sparta's fraught relationship with her allies.[46] Xenophon uses much the same technique before the decisive battle of Leuctra (371), when during a peace conference at Sparta the Athenian Autocles denounces Sparta's cynically self-interested violations of Greek autonomy (6.3.7–9). To be sure, speeches have specific rhetorical purposes and speakers may include exaggerated claims; at the same time, however, speeches can serve to focalize events from a distinctive point of view.

The reader could easily have inferred from the previous narrative that the Eleans could not have been pleased with their post-Peloponnesian War treatment at the hands of Sparta (*Hell.* 3.2.23: the Spartans "decided to make them prudent"), but in the Theban speech their resentment, as well as that of Sparta's other allies, is made explicit (*Hell.* 3.5.12):

> Who is left that is still well disposed towards them? Have not the Argives always been hostile to them? And now the Eleans, who have been deprived of much land and many cities, have become their enemies too. What are we to say about the Corinthians, Arcadians, and Achaeans? In the war against you [the Peloponnesian War], in response to the Spartans' persistent entreaties, they had a share of all the toils and dangers and expenditures. But when the Spartans had accomplished what they wanted, what empire, or honor, or money did they ever share with them? Rather, they think that it is appropriate to establish helots [Spartan serfs] as governors, and, ever since their success, they have shown themselves to be despots over their allies, even though these allies are free men.

In this way the Theban speech explains the consequence of Spartan behavior. And although the Thebans may exaggerate the benefits that await the Athenians by entering into this alliance with them ("you will become the greatest power ever," 3.5.14), it does not follow that they have also exaggerated the degree of alienation amongst Sparta's allies. If Xenophon intended to endorse a Spartan version of these events (that put the sole cause of the war on Persian bribery) and included the speech of the Thebans merely as an example of unjust defamation of Sparta, his plan has backfired.

The author of the *Hellenica Oxyrhynchia*, by contrast, focuses on personal motives and rivalries between various political factions in the Greek cities. At least in what survives of his work, he fails to discuss why, as a matter of foreign policy, these cities might have wanted to free themselves

---

[46] Here again opinions are sharply divided: Gray: 1989: 107–12; Riedinger 1991: 153, and Schepens 2012: 228–31 argue that Xenophon could not have intended the speech to be read in this way, whereas Tuplin 1993: 62–3 and Krentz 1995: 195 maintain that he did.

from Spartan control once the danger of Athenian imperialism had passed. He does not seem to realize that there was more to foreign policy than merely eliminating one's domestic political opponents who happened to have Spartan support. In other words, there is something overly simplistic in the *Hellenica Oxyrhynchia*'s analysis, even if the presence of pro- and anti-Spartan factions in various poleis was a common feature of Greek politics.

This is not to say that we should prefer Xenophon's account in all of its details, and it is extraordinarily difficult to choose between them when they disagree on particulars. For instance, in the *Hellenica Oxyrhynchia* (F 10.5) it is Pharnabazus, rather than Tithraustes, who sends Timocrates to Greece with the gold (probably in 397 or 396, and not, as Xenophon has it, in 395). And the Corinthian War actually starts when Theban statesmen persuade the Phocians ("Locrians" in Xenophon) to invade disputed border land in western (Xenophon says "eastern") Locris (F 21). The suspicion that the author has systematically reversed Xenophon's narrative, in order to make his own seem more authoritative, is not completely unfounded.[47] On the other hand, Xenophon may well be mistaken about which satrap dispatched Timocrates to Greece.[48]

Why Things Happen

Let us now turn from how Xenophon analyzes specific events (the outbreak of a war or a battle) to how he explains a historical process (the collapse of an hegemony). In a very famous and often discussed passage of his *Hellenica* (*Hell.* 5.4.1), Xenophon gives a theological explanation for the failure of the Spartan hegemony in the early fourth century B C.[49] He begins by highlighting the totality of Sparta's successes since the conclusion of the King's Peace in 387/6 (5.3.27):

> Given that events had turned out so successfully for the Spartans that the Thebans and the other Boeotians were completely under their power, the Corinthians had become especially loyal, the Argives had been humbled because their excuse of the sacred months was no longer of any help to them, the Athenians isolated, and those of their allies who had been ill disposed to them had been punished, it seemed to them that their empire was now completely well and safely established.

---

[47] See Bleckmann 2006. Buckler 2004 makes a strong case that Xenophon's account is the more reliable.

[48] Rung 2004 argues that their accounts of Timocrates' mission are actually complementary.

[49] So Dillery 1995: 179–94, 221–37; *contra* Bowden 2004. On religion in Xenophon, see also Anderson 1974b: 34–40; Parker 2004; Flower 2012: 203–16.

This long sentence, the last clause of which emphasizes Spartan self-satisfaction with the state of their empire, forms a jarring juxtaposition with the authorial intervention that immediately follows (*Hell.* 5.4.1):

> Now one might be able to mention many other examples, both Greek and barbarian, where the gods do not overlook those who are impious or who do unholy things. But at present I shall speak of the example that lies before us. Even though the Spartans swore that they would permit the cities to be autonomous, they occupied the acropolis in Thebes and were punished by the very men who had been wronged, although they had not previously been conquered by anyone. And as for those Theban citizens who had brought them into the acropolis and who wished their city to be a slave to the Spartans so that they themselves could be tyrants, it took only seven of the Theban exiles to put an end to their government. I shall narrate how this came about.

The logical connection between these two passages is implicit. The reader needs to infer that the pride implied in their confidence ("their empire seemed well and safely established") led to the hubristic act of seizing the acropolis of Thebes, for which the Spartans were subsequently punished. The theme of pride leading to a fall is very familiar to both ancient and modern readers. Nonetheless, it is easy enough to misconstrue what Xenophon is saying, and not saying, in this passage. He is not saying that the gods alone, acting outside of human agency, punished the Spartans. But rather, like Herodotus, he explains events on two levels, the divine and the human.[50] He then goes on to narrate in essentially human terms how the Spartans were punished for their transgressive acts against the Thebans.

It is only much later in the narrative that Xenophon again refers to the influence of divine intervention (*Hell.* 6.4.2–3).[51] In 371, after a general peace treaty had once again been signed by all of the mainland Greek cities except Thebes, the Spartans were debating whether to order King Cleombrotus to attack Thebes immediately. A Spartan by the name of Prothous advised the Spartan assembly to disband their army in accordance with their oaths, and then to assemble another army if someone was not permitting the cities to be autonomous, "for he said that in this way he thought that the gods would be most well disposed towards them and the cities least annoyed." Xenophon indicates that this was sound advice (that would indeed have been pleasing to the gods), but it was rejected. How does he explain the rejection? He writes (6.4.3), "When the assembly heard these things, they thought that he was speaking nonsense. For already, it seems, the divinity (*to daimonion*) was leading them on. They ordered Cleombrotus not to disband

---

[50] See especially Gould 1989: 70–1.
[51] Tuplin 1993: 134 is excellent on this passage.

his army, but immediately to lead it against the Thebans, unless they allowed the cities to be autonomous."

Xenophon does not need to make it explicit where the divinity was leading the Spartans, because it was absolutely obvious. The divine power, punishing them for the seizure of the Theban acropolis in peacetime, was leading them to the catastrophic annihilation of their army at Leuctra. This is a nice example of the kind of reciprocity so attractive to Herodotus and so imbedded in Greek thought at all levels of experience. Yet at the same time, in his account of the battle, Xenophon seems to be thinking in terms of "divine displeasure working through chance and good Theban tactical planning."[52] It was not only divine intervention that destroyed the Spartan army at Leuctra (four hundred of the seven hundred Spartan citizens involved were killed: *Hell.* 6.4.15) and brought down their hegemony, but there were also purely human factors at play.

The role of divine agency comes out again in Xenophon's narration of Epaminondas' final invasion of the Peloponnese in 362. We are told that he would have captured Sparta itself "had not a Cretan, by a certain divine allotment (*theiai tini moirai*), come and reported to Agesilaus that the enemy was approaching" (7.5.10). Subsequently, less than a hundred Spartans, led by the king's son Archidamus, beat off the Theban attack despite the fact that the enemy held the higher ground. To explain this, Xenophon resorts to a type of double determination (7.5.12–13). "As for what happened next, it is possible to hold the deity (*to theion*) responsible, or it is possible to say that no one can withstand desperate men." But then Archidamus made a tactical error and pushed the pursuit too far. Again, a double determination comes into play. "When those from within the city [the Spartans], exalting in their victory, pursued beyond what was fitting, they in turn were killed. For it had been determined by the deity (here again, *to theion*), as it seems, up to what point victory had been granted them." Finally, the *Hellenica* ends (7.5.26–7) with another, even more emphatic, reference to the will of "god," here more explicitly *ho theos*. Although everyone was expecting the battle of Mantinea decisively to settle the balance of power in mainland Greece, "the god so made it" that the battle was a complete stalemate and neither side gained an advantage over the other.

In all of these passages Xenophon sees a divine power at work. The most obvious interpretation is that some divine force, some god who could not be identified, had set limits on both Theban and Spartan success. I cannot disprove conclusively that Xenophon, for lack of a better explanatory vocabulary, is simply invoking a randomized chance or employing a commonplace

---

[52] Tuplin 1993: 138.

façon de parler. Yet that would be out of keeping with his view of the gods that runs throughout his entire corpus: that they are mindful of human actions, that they communicate with mortals through signs, and that they are willing to punish the impious and assist the just. As Xenophon emphasizes repeatedly, the gods favor those who attend to them (through prayer and sacrifice) in good fortune as well as in bad and who do not pray for things that are unlawful (*Cyr*.1.6.3–6 is a paradigmatic statement of his views).[53]

In any case, it is extremely important to realize that "the hand of god" was not Xenophon's only explanation for Sparta's demise any more than Herodotus saw divine retribution for the "crime" of Gyges as the only explanation for Croesus' fall from power.[54] Xenophon was quite aware of the weaknesses, both internal and external, that led to Sparta's defeat at Leuctra. These are well summed up by the speech of the Thebans at Athens (3.5.12–15), who point out the Spartans' ill treatment of their allies, their selfish greed for dominion, and their small numbers.[55] So too the Athenian ambassador Autocles highlights the greed and high-handedness of the Spartans in his speech at the peace conference before Leuctra (6.3.7–9). Their unjust treatment of the Thebans in particular is stressed both in Autocles' stern speech and in the much more conciliatory one delivered immediately afterwards by his fellow Athenian Callistratus (6.3.7–9).

All three speeches (that of the Thebans in 395 as well as those of the two Athenians in 371) use the same loaded verb (*pleonektein*, "selfishly to grasp at more than one's fair share") to characterize Sparta's self-seeking pursuit of power at the expense of her allies. Furthermore, Sparta's major internal weakness, the dearth of full citizens and the hostility of the subordinate classes, is vividly revealed, not in authorial analysis, but indirectly in the reported account of the conspiracy of Cinadon in 400 (*Hell*. 3.3.4–11). A modern historian would have said directly what Xenophon puts into the mouth of Cinadon (*Hell*. 3.3.6): "Whenever any mention is made of the Spartans, there is no one who is able to conceal that he would gladly eat them raw."

I am not the first to point out that Xenophon's way of writing history is not the same as that of modern historiography, at least as it has been practiced since the nineteenth century. But that observation, easy as it is, should

---

[53] See further Flower 2016.

[54] Cawkwell 1979: 45 says of the *Hellenica*: "The hand of God is an explanation that dulls the quest for truth, but it is the explanation to which Xenophon, so unlike Thucydides, readily had recourse."

[55] Riedinger 1991: 126–8, 131 argues that Xenophon places the beginnings of Sparta's decline well after the King's Peace, which seems to me to be incorrect.

not then be conflated with the comfortable assumption that his way is inferior to ours as a means of conveying a cogent and persuasive analysis of events. The *Hellenica* may contain lessons pertinent to leadership, examples of loyalty, wonderfully told stories, and vivid tableaux. It may have been written in old age and it may reflect Xenophon's personal experience of epoch-making events. And it may contain omissions that strike us as perplexingly idiosyncratic. Nonetheless, it is a work of history that constructs a plausible and compelling narrative of events and it was conceived as such by all of those Greek and Roman critics who included Xenophon among the canon of great historians.

Further Reading

Historians and literary critics have long been divided over the essential nature of Xenophon's *Hellenica*. Cawkwell 1979 considers it bad history in the sense of essentially being the poorly researched and highly partial memoirs of a forgetful old man (a similar line is taken by Thomas 2009a). Riedinger 1991 views Xenophon as deforming the genre of history, whereas Gray 1989 and Pownall 2004 reveal how Xenophon shapes his narrative in order to provide moral instruction. Tuplin 1993 provides a close reading of the *Hellenica*, arguing that it provides a subtle critique of empire, both Athenian and Spartan. Dillery 1995 focuses on themes of leadership, utopianism, and Panhellenism in both the *Hellenica* and *Anabasis*. A recent book-length study of the *Anabasis* is Flower 2012. The most authoritative edition of the *Hellenica Oxyrhynchia* is Chambers 1993. There is a Greek text with facing English translation and useful commentary by McKechnie and Kern 1988. Good modern studies of the historical period are Cartledge 1987 and Jehne 1994.

16

RICHARD FERNANDO BUXTON

Xenophon on Leadership: Commanders as Friends

In a remarkable sequence from the *Hellenica* set during Xenophon's brisk account of naval actions in the Corinthian War, the author slows down his otherwise summary narrative to provide a picturesque description of the farewell given to the Spartan admiral Teleutias by his men. At the end of a successful tour, Xenophon records how the rank and file crowned Teleutias with a wreath, jostled to shake his hand, and tossed garlands into the sea as he sailed off for home. Almost sheepishly, the author confesses:

> Certainly, I know that here I am describing nothing considered worthy of mention; not outlays of money, not any dangerous action, not clever maneuvers. But, by Zeus, this seems to me a worthy thing for a man to consider: what exactly it was that Teleutias had done to dispose the men he commanded to act in such a way. For a man this truly is an accomplishment most worthy of mention, more than lots of money and dangers overcome. (*Hell.* 5.1.4)

Xenophon's self-reflexive remarks provide an excellent starting point for examining the outsize importance of leadership in his works. First, they make clear the author's deep interest in exploring what makes an effective commander, and his intention to use literature as a means to teach his audience about this ability. Second, these remarks show that Xenophon is willing to pursue the topic even when it leads him beyond what he thinks a typical reader might consider strictly relevant subject matter.[1] Finally, they reveal that at the core of Xenophon's conception of the model commander is the leader's ability to elicit genuine affection from his subordinates. This emphasis suggests that leadership for the author is about more than just battlefield strategy and, instead, carries lessons for management beyond the narrow confines of warfare. It also anchors leadership in a cooperative basis that closely resembles friendship. It is the ability to command willing

---

[1] Pownall 2004: 76–83, Tuplin 1993: 36–41, and Rahn 1971; cf. Gray 2003: 112–14, who sees the apologetic tone as a rhetorical pretense employed to draw attention to the leadership theme that Xenophon wishes to emphasize.

followers, in fact, which Xenophon here esteems even above any actual accomplishments.

At one level, Xenophon's fascination with military leadership is unsurprising. Xenophon was himself a celebrated general and his role in leading the Ten Thousand out of Mesopotamia earned him admiration throughout antiquity from such figures as Alexander the Great (Arr. *Anab.* 2.7.8–9). His friend and patron, the Spartan king Agesilaus, was also a leading military figure of the early fourth century (Plut. *Ages.* 10.5). Moreover, much of what Xenophon wrote about inevitably involved warfare. Nevertheless, the figure of the model general holds a position of striking prominence in Xenophon's writings. Even a casual reader will notice the author's tendency to interrupt war narratives to provide detailed profiles of battlefield leaders. Tellingly, all of these figures exhibit a remarkably consistent set of attributes, the most important of which, as with Teleutias, is the ability to command willing followers.

Xenophon is not, therefore, so much interested in surveying a range of successful leadership styles as he is in advocating a single set model. Throughout his oeuvre, this model leader and his stock virtues continuously elicit direct praise from both the author and figures like Socrates whom Xenophon has clearly designated as authoritative.[2] Further, the paradigmatic commander is ubiquitous, prominent even in those works least related to the battlefield and appearing in both male and female forms. A telling example is the *Oeconomicus* (discussed below), a Socratic dialogue about managing an agricultural estate in peacetime, which repeatedly posits that successful large-scale farming involves a form of management analogous to generalship (*Oec.* 5.15–16, 20.6, 21.2 and 4). Nevertheless, since armies are the most frequent context for Xenophon's discussions of leadership, I will for convenience generally speak of a "commander and his men." Paradoxically, then, the great variety of genres in which Xenophon writes coexists with his incessant advocacy of a single approach to leadership.

This chapter will begin by looking at three of Xenophon's most theoretical discussions of the model commander, each taken from a different genre, in order to draw out the major – and consistent – characteristics of the figure. Next, it will examine the pragmatic logic animating Xenophon's approach to leadership and how, beyond the battlefield, he saw his method as applicable to all spheres of human relations; even providing, with slight modifications, a paradigm for a virtuous form of friendship. The chapter

---

[2] Gray 2011: 8–9. Conversely, those whom Xenophon explicitly condemns as bad leaders are invariably shown to lack one or more of the qualities demanded by his paradigm.

will also consider the sources that influenced Xenophon's model and what limitations he assigns it.

The Characteristics of Xenophon's Model Leader

In the sixth chapter of the *Hipparchicus*, a treatise advocating specific reforms that Athenian commanders should undertake to improve the city's cavalry, Xenophon pulls back to consider more broadly the conditions required for any successful exercise of military leadership. The author begins by comparing the commander to a craftsman, who to realize his vision must employ materials that will bend themselves to his wishes. The military leader's materials are his men, and making them malleable to his designs requires two things above all else: "that they feel friendly (*philikōs*) towards the commander and that they consider him wiser (*phronimōteron*) than themselves as regards engagements with the enemy" (*Hipp.* 6.1).[3] The former, he goes on to say, involves the commander treating his men with benevolence – literally behaving towards them *philophronōs*, or "friendly mindedly" – and the latter depends on his successful demonstration of foresight (*pronoōn*, "thinking ahead") in all matters relating to the army's well-being (6.2). For Xenophon, the leader who can convince his followers that he possesses these two qualities will gain their goodwill and active support (6.6). This is presumably because the commander's eagerness to put his superior strategic competence at the service of the army's collective interest offers its members the best opportunity for both survival and victory.

The areas in which the commander must display foresight are legion (6.2–3 and 6): observing proper worship of the gods to avoid incurring their displeasure, the securing of reliable provisions, establishing safe routes of retreat, posting adequate guards around camp, and, of course, outmaneuvering the enemy in battle. He must also foster good relations through sharing out any fruits of success with his men and, of particular importance, make a consistent display of superior effort, since a leader who works even harder at the tasks he assigns his men than they do inspires respect and reciprocal effort (6.4). Ironically, therefore, in order to make his men pliable material for his own goals, the commander must convince them that he is the one who is working hardest and smartest for their interests.

At *Cyropaedia* 1.6 one finds an expanded but identical model placed in the mouths of Xenophon's Cyrus the Great and his father Cambyses.[4]

---

[3] The Greek stem *phil-* denotes affectionate feeling for another and forms the basis for words related to friendship.

[4] As recognized by Wood 1964: 48–9, who goes on, as I shall, to juxtapose the two passages with material from *Memorabilia*.

Although the *Cyropaedia* as a whole is an examination of the exemplary leadership of the fictionalized Cyrus, this sequence, in which the pair discuss the requirements of effective military command on the eve of Cyrus' first campaign, is the work's most theoretical investigation of the topic.[5] Father and son begin by agreeing that it is necessary to court divine favor and respect omens, seeking help from the gods for what is beyond human control (*Cyr.* 1.6.1–6). Cyrus then suggests that a good leader must outstrip his men in both exercising foresight (*pronoein*) and working hard. The former certainly involves battlefield tactics, but, as Cambyses is careful to stress, securing reliable provisions and keeping the troops in shape between battles is just as important (7–11). This prompts Cyrus to recall how his father had criticized his son's military tutors for teaching only tactics, instead of also covering the management and exercise of an army off the battlefield and, of even greater importance, how to inspire its enthusiasm and obedience (12–14).[6]

Cyrus suggests that proper obedience can be obtained through using praise and punishment to incentivize good behavior, for example through holding frequent athletic competitions with prizes that motivate soldiers to keep in shape (15–20).[7] Although Cambyses acknowledges the importance of such incentives, he adds that "obedience willingly given" (*to hekontas peithesthai*) is of even greater use. He then links this idea back to the two main criteria of leadership outlined by his son: foresight and hard work. Beginning with the former, Cambyses argues that "men very gladly obey whomever they consider to be more knowledgeable (*phronimōteron*) than themselves about what is advantageous for themselves," just as a patient entrusts himself to the expertise of his doctor (21). Cyrus adds that affection is also won from subordinates the same way that it is won from friends (*philoi*): through clearly appearing to work on their behalf. Cambyses agrees and, continuing on to his son's other main criterion, emphasizes that visible

---

[5] So Danzig 2012: 508 calls Cambyses "one of the most authoritative voices in *Cyropaedia*"; cf. Gray 1979: 198 n. 5, and Gera 1993: 50.

[6] Cambyses does devote much of the last third of his discussion with Cyrus to actual tactics (26–40), advocating stratagems that employ deception to catch the enemy off guard, either through ambush or lulling it into a false sense of overconfidence. Such ruses minimize the risk faced by the attacking army, thereby (presumably) demonstrating the benevolent foresight for the well-being of followers that defines the Xenophontic leader. Xenophon praises commanders throughout his works who employ similar stratagems; see Breitenbach 1950: 58–60.

[7] Promoting military training by establishing competitive athletic events that promise prizes and prestige is a favorite device of Xenophon's commanders, particularly Agesilaus; see Krentz 1995: 188.

displays of hard work by the commander are the most effective way to create this image as a selfless benefactor (24–5).

As in *Hipparchicus* 6, the ideal leader of *Cyropaedia* gains willing obedience through displaying superior foresight and effort in caring – as a friend would – for the army's interests, starting with a baseline concern for securing provisions and divine favor. However, the stress both in this passage and in other parts of the *Cyropaedia* on *appearing* to be a tireless champion of one's followers has troubled some critics. They have read this as leaving open the possibility of using one's troops cynically, the image of benevolence merely a public-relations façade masking a one-sided exploitation of underlings.[8] But Cambyses is careful to point out that appearances will get a leader only so far, and that he must also truly be the helpful figure he advertises if his men are, in the long run, to continue serving him with enthusiasm (22–3).[9] As he tells Cyrus, "there is no shorter road to being esteemed as knowledgeable (*phronimos*) in your chosen field than to be knowledgeable about it" (22); time exposes all false pretenses, alienating support for those hiding behind them.[10] The emphasis on appearances, then, is better understood as drawing attention to an additional and performative dimension of model leadership: the commander's need to create a sufficient level of awareness about his efforts on behalf of the army. Unadvertised virtue does not harm one's followers, but it also does not inspire them to become willing partners.

The importance of genuine benevolence in a leader also appears in Xenophon's Socratic works. In *Memorabilia* 3.2 the author stages a conversation between Socrates and a newly elected Athenian general about how the epithets that Homer uses to describe Agamemnon, the commander in chief of the legendary Greek army at Troy, highlight key leadership qualities.[11] Socrates cleverly reinterprets the hero's characterization as "both a good king and a strong spear bearer" (Hom. *IL.* 3.179) as signaling not two separate qualities, but an interdependent pair. He begins by claiming that a king's legitimacy rests ultimately upon his ability to provide prosperity (*eudaimonia*) for his community and not just himself, "for a king is chosen not so that he may take

---

[8] Nadon 2001, esp. 164–78; Gera 1993: 294–6; and Tatum 1989. *Hipparchicus* also stresses how the leader must *appear* to demonstrate foresight (*pronoōn phainētai*, 6.2).

[9] Gray 2011: 46, 100–4, and 265–7; Danzig 2012; Sandridge 2012: 21–43. Nadon 2001: 171 finds the idea hopelessly naïve, but that does not mean Xenophon was not convinced of it.

[10] Socrates makes the same point using the exact same imagery at *Mem.* 1.7 and 2.6.37–9 (discussed below).

[11] For the frequent use during the Classical period of Homer's characters as behavioral paradigms, often through selective and dubiously interpreted citation, see Hunter 2004: 246–9; cf., e.g., Plato's Socrates at *Smp.* 174b–c and Xenophon's Niceratus at *Smp.* 4.5–9.

good care of himself, but so that those who chose him may also, on account of him, fare well" (*Mem.* 3.2.3). On the battlefield this is done not just through the personal valor and superior effort that the tag "strong spear bearer" immediately suggests, but also by training his entire army to become strong spear bearers on its own behalf. As in *Cyropaedia*, superior knowledge, visible effort, and incessant training undergird the leader's achievement of goals benefiting himself and his men. Xenophon closes the scene by noting how Socrates had seen that the essential quality of any leader was "making those whom he leads prosperous (*eudaimonas*)" (3.2.4), precisely the capacity in *Hipparchicus* that a commander's men must believe him to possess if they are to provide the willing obedience that makes them useful to him.

The Practical Advantages of Benevolent Leadership and its Universal Scope

The leadership theory that Xenophon puts forth in his didactic, idealizing, and philosophical works informs the many evaluative profiles of commanders scattered throughout the author's contributions to historiography, as seen already in the case of Teleutias. Accordingly, the leader's tireless devotion to promoting the interests of his followers – and thereby winning their willing obedience – provides the central motif for what is perhaps the best known of these digressive sketches: the laudatory obituary at *Anabasis* 1.9 of Cyrus the Younger, the Persian prince whose unsuccessful coup against his brother's throne was the mission for which the Ten Thousand were initially recruited and marched to Mesopotamia. Xenophon's portrait dwells on many familiar elements of his theory but expands their application from the military sphere to the political, mirroring Socrates' redefinition of the leader's purpose from achieving the particular goal of battlefield victory to the more general state of communal *eudaimonia*. The obituary, moreover, provides an excellent window into what Xenophon saw as the practical benefits recommending his approach, despite the constant effort on behalf of others that it requires of a leader.

Cyrus the Younger: a Practical Gentleman

After treating Cyrus' youth (*Anab.* 1.9.2–6), Xenophon turns to the prince's career as a provincial governor in Asia Minor. Cyrus won the loyalty of Persia's subjects and allies in the region through keeping his word in all diplomatic matters, creating a predictable and safe environment that encouraged still others to put themselves under his protection (7–8). Here one

328

finds in political relations the same premium that Xenophon places on subordinates trusting in the good faith of their battlefield commander. Also transposed into the political realm is the need for the leader to outdo his followers in effort, since the author repeatedly praises how Cyrus strove with reciprocal kindness to best anyone who had benefited him (6, 9–12, 20–8). Accordingly, the prince rewarded local potentates who increased the taxable yield of their estates (19) and made many of the Persian nobility his loyal friends (*philoi*) through working even harder to realize their goals than they had in helping him achieve his (21).[12]

In military matters Cyrus attracted quality mercenaries by the generous distribution of spoils – just as *Hipparchicus* 6 recommends – and kept these men effective and well behaved through rewarding bravery and proper conduct (14–18). Unsurprisingly, there is an emphasis throughout on the visible display of such practices for the purpose of influencing followers: Cyrus dispenses promotions and rewards specifically "so that good men appeared as the most prosperous (*eudaimonestatous*)" (15), incentivizing similar behavior from others.

Xenophon's obituary closes with his observation that it was the scrupulous generosity of Cyrus towards those contributing to the prosperity of his kingdom that explains why so many voluntarily joined his revolt and elected to die at his side during the battle of Cunaxa (29–31). The author's focus on this ultimate display of willing obedience illustrates succinctly what he saw as the decidedly pragmatic advantage of his leadership model, namely the unmatchable degree to which it inspires the steadfast devotion and hard work of followers.[13] True, the collaborative nature of Xenophontic leadership limits the leader's capacity for arbitrary action: he cannot, like the tyrant, coerce his subordinates into serving his personal interests exclusively. But the reward for accepting such limitations is a force that is more loyal and one willing to train for optimal performance. In turn, this maximizes the probability of success in the narrower field of ventures involving the mutual prosperity of leader and led, even if, in the case of Cyrus at Cunaxa, this does not ultimately guarantee victory.[14]

The negative complement to Cyrus' ease in winning unwavering followers for his revolt through generosity is the constant risk of defection

---

[12] Cf. the discussion of wealth's political uses in *Cyr.* 8.2.15–23.

[13] For Xenophon's practical idealism, see Wood 1964: 60–5 and Lendon 2006; by contrast Schorn 2012: 700–1 overstates the selflessness of the Xenophontic leader.

[14] Tamiolaki 2012: 569–70 stresses the lack of any simple correlation for Xenophon between virtuous leadership and success, even if the former actively increases the odds of the latter. Cyrus' death in combat, therefore, does not subtract from his value to the author as a paradigmatic leader.

or rebellion for those leaders who do not practice such benevolence. Thus a major theme of the author's philosophical dialogue *Hiero* is the tyrant's incessant fear of his subjects and the manner in which despotic power inexorably alienates them.[15] In contrast, a leader like Cyrus the Great can confidently claim that "by making men wealthy and doing them favors, I get from them loyalty and friendship (*philian*), and from these I reap security" (*Cyr.* 8.2.22). Far from an exercise in altruism, Xenophontic leadership creates the most effective and lasting basis for wielding power over others.[16]

Leaders as Managers

At first glance Xenophon's conflation of political and military leadership is unremarkable in the context of both Persia's military monarchy and the constantly warring poleis of Greece. However, the obituary of Cyrus makes clear not only that the prince combined political and military leadership, but also that his tools and approach for success in both spheres were identical. Xenophon's paradigm, in other words, concerns the stable and successful management of human communities in general, whether armies at war or polities at peace, even if the author's choice of genres tends to foreground battlefield commanders.

Xenophon makes the universal scope of his management model the explicit subject of *Memorabilia* 3.4.[17] Here Socrates argues that Antisthenes, the head of a profitable agricultural estate who is seeking election as a general, is fully qualified by virtue of his experience to serve in this military post, despite lacking a distinguished combat record. In Socrates' telling, Antisthenes' success in estate management (*oikonomia*) has resulted from a capacity to motivate his workers (presumably slaves) towards achieving set goals through using a catalog of Xenophon's standard leadership practices: inspiring willing obedience, using rewards and punishments to incentivize better performance, and displaying tireless dedication (3.4.8–9). Moreover, Antisthenes has already proven the transferability of his management skills with his success as a *chorēgos* (3), a form of public service expected of wealthy Athenians that involved organizing and funding one of several choruses which competed at public festivals. As will be true with the

---

[15] Compare the way that Xenophon sees Sparta's increasingly autocratic treatment of its allies as driving them to unite against it (*Lac. Pol.* 14.5–6), which shows the author interpreting interstate relations between a hegemonic power and its dependents through the lens of his interpersonal theory of leadership.

[16] Gray 2011: 315–17 ("the leader's security is Xenophon's major concern").

[17] See Gray 2011: 20–4 and Wood 1964: 49–50 for discussion.

army, Antisthenes did not have any technical knowledge of music or dance, but being an effective manager he knew how to select qualified subordinates and inspire them with his own zeal for victory (4–5). For Socrates, therefore:

> Whatever someone oversees, if he both has knowledge of what things are necessary for it and is able to furnish these, he would be a good overseer, whether he should be overseeing a chorus or an estate or a polis or an army. (6)

Just as the battlefield commander in *Hipparchicus* 6 has to have a superior foresight about how to achieve victory against the enemy, the *chorēgus* must know best how to win his own contest. In each case this involves clearly understanding the goal of a communal undertaking, and then selecting, coordinating, and motivating those subordinates most capable of achieving this.[18]

The *Oeconomicus*, an entire dialogue dedicated to the art of running an agricultural estate, further stresses the transferability of the author's leadership model to all situations involving the management of others. In this work another successful farmer, Ischomachus, tells Socrates that he believes there is a "ruling principle common to all affairs: agricultural, political, estate management, and military" (*Oec.* 21.2), and that in all of these areas this principle centers on "ruling over men who wish it" (21.12).[19] Thus Ischomachus, like Antisthenes, inspires his field slaves towards excellence in the typical fashion of a Xenophontic leader, and he even delegates oversight of subsidiary operations to slave foremen whom he has taught to emulate his style of leadership (12.3–14.10).[20]

In the domestic sphere, Ischomachus relies on his wife's management of female slaves involved in the processing of raw materials from field and stable into useful products such as meals, preserves, and clothing (7.35–6). In a telling passage for just how universal Xenophon considered his model to be, Ischomachus fondly recalls what occurred when he first informed his wife (whom he never names) that her supervisory responsibilities would include caring for any slave who became sick; a task that he assumed she would find distasteful. Instead, his wife replied that this would in fact be a

---

[18] Johnstone 1994: 229–35.
[19] Whether Ischomachus is a reliable mouthpiece for Xenophon's views is a contested point; see Danzig 2003 and Strauss 1970. But on questions of leadership he exactly mirrors the attitudes of the author, Socrates, and other authoritative figures, especially Cambyses at *Cyr.* 1.6.13; see Gray 2011: 351–60.
[20] Although the notion of a collaborative relationship between master and slave is disingenuous at best, Xenophon at least argues for the greater productivity of slaves who are treated kindly rather than by force, and he does not believe that servile status precludes a faculty for leadership; see Baragwanath 2012b: 646–52.

pleasure, since "those who are well cared for will feel gratitude and be more loyal than before" (7.37). Amazed by her appreciation for the value of cultivating enthusiastic subordinates, Ischomachus replied:

> O wife, also in the case of a hive's leader, on account of some foresightful acts (*pronoias*) such as these, the bees are disposed to act in such a way towards her that, whenever she abandons it, none of the bees considers staying behind, but all follow her. (7.38)

For Ischomachus the utility of leadership based on willing obedience does not just transcend situations, social categories, and sexes; it even cuts across species, forming a sort of natural principle. Xenophon underscores this universality by reusing this analogy of the Greek Ischomachus in *Cyropaedia* for a character's description of how men follow the Persian Cyrus as bees "willingly obey" (*hekousai peithontai*) their queen (5.1.24). Indeed, the scene's imagery of an enthusiastic retinue attending its commander's departure and its language about how followers are "disposed to act in such a way" (*houtō diatithesthai*) towards a good leader is identical to that seen at the start of this chapter in the tableau of Teleutias' farewell.

The Role of Friendship and its Nature

As noted, Xenophon uses terms derived from friendship (*philia*) throughout his discussions of model leaders to characterize the proper attitude of both managers to subordinates and subordinates to managers. Despite the hierarchical difference between the two parties, Xenophon's analogy is apt, since the effectiveness of his paradigm depends on a bond of reciprocal goodwill – rather than forced subordination – motivating each side to help the other. Although the leader makes the more significant contribution, he cannot, like the sculptor in *Hipparchicus* 6, achieve his goals without appropriate materials in the form of the labor and technical skills of his followers. Their relationship, therefore, although unequal, is still fundamentally one organized around the willing exchange of favors that are geared to promote mutual success by pooling resources. Such voluntary reciprocity forms the core of popular Greek conceptions of friendship, which were rooted in a widely attested expectation that individuals "help friends and harm enemies" (Pl. *Resp.* 332d).[21]

A friendly leader, however, should not be confused with a permissive one, since Xenophon acknowledges the commander's need to use coercive punishments to mold the behavior of recalcitrant subordinates. Punishments,

---

[21] See Mitchell 1997: 1–21; Konstan 1997; and, still essential, Finley 1977.

however, are a last resort after persuasion and rewards have failed, and their purpose is the same as these other devices: to foster practices that will make men better instruments for the achievement of common goals which facilitate their greater long-term flourishing.[22] The leader is thus friendly towards his followers in the sense of being an enthusiastic champion of their overarching interests. But this is very different from simple indulgence, which Xenophon abhors as undermining the discipline conducive to success. Accordingly, the author censures Proxenus, one of the original commanders of the Ten Thousand, for pairing generosity with insufficient discipline, since this left him an object of contempt open to manipulation by subordinates willing to take advantage of his good nature for private ends (*Anab.* 2.6.19–20).

If Xenophon's leader and follower are thought of as being friendly, in the case of Cyrus the Younger we have seen that the author refers to the prince's allies both within and beyond the Persian court as his actual friends. Alliance, both in war and peacetime, turns out to be another kind of relationship in Xenophon that is best cemented by the benevolent pursuit of mutual goals. But unlike in rigidly hierarchical organizations such as an army, all the parties involved here, being either rulers of their own communities or powerful figures within the Persian aristocracy, are nominal peers. In styling these men as friends, Xenophon is operating from another commonplace of ancient thinking: that friendship arises most easily between social equals and reaches its fullest expression among elite male peers, since these affluent individuals have the most resources and occasions for providing each other with reciprocal favors.[23]

Elite male friendships, since they involve the main political actors within ancient communities, necessarily possess a public dimension and, as in the case of Cyrus, fuse the realm of personal affection with professional networking undertaken to forward complex sociopolitical ends. Thus in *Memorabilia* 2.4, a dialogue where Socrates argues that friendship is the greatest of all possessions, he automatically envisions it as a mutually beneficial partnership between aristocratic peers in a polis, undertaken for both personal and political gain: "For the good friend takes up any deficiency of his friend in the arranging of the latter's personal and public affairs" (*Mem.* 2.4.6). Among status equals an ideal of benevolent leadership is replaced with one of benevolent partnership. Unchanged, however, is the pragmatic

---

[22] Gray 2011: 72, 123–4, and 278.
[23] Mitchell 1997: 6. These assumptions, for instance, are the starting point from which Aristotle sets out his more expansive vision of *philia* in the eighth book of *Nicomachean Ethics*, where he famously notes "it is said that friendship is equality" (Arist. *Eth. Nic.* 1157b36).

motivation for pursuing friendly relations as the most dependable manner in which to catalyze group resources towards shared goals and create security for oneself.[24] It is for this reason that Cyrus the Great can, as seen, claim that the vital affection of subordinates is won through the same attention to their well-being as with friends.[25]

Xenophon's Socrates, however, is clear in a subsequent dialogue on friendship, *Memorabilia* 2.6, that good friends must, like good leaders, actually be the useful partners that they claim to be, if they are to inspire loyalty from their allies and see friendships endure over time (2.6.37–9). For Socrates, this requires that the ideal friend must be, in addition to generous and reciprocal, a master of his own emotions and desires (*enkratēs*, 2.6.5), a quality attributed elsewhere in Xenophon's works to model leaders such as Cyrus the Great (*Cyr.* 8.1.32–7) and Agesilaus (*Ages.* 4.3, 5.4 and 10.2). It is this quality that lets both leader and friend prevent the temptation of more immediate gratifications or the influence of strong passions from distracting either from the hard work of achieving larger long-term goals, which is in turn the key to inspiring a corresponding degree of effort from friends and followers.[26]

Xenophon's Model: Sources and Limits

Xenophon's thinking on leadership reflects a complex combination of traditional elements, personal influences, and his own experience of command.[27] Just as the author's vision of friendship unfolds within orthodox parameters, his ideal general incorporates many common-sense qualities that mainstream Greek thought had endorsed as far back as Homer's *Iliad*. There, for instance, anticipating a hallmark of the Xenophontic model, the warrior Achilles upbraids Agamemnon for not setting a personal example of bravery equal to the efforts of his men (Hom. *Il.* 1.225–31). Nevertheless, the priority that Xenophon places on the cultivation of willing obedience through

---

[24] The resources of friends are a form of insurance against hard times (*Mem.* 2.4.6 [cont.]; cf. 2.6.25), and the benevolent treatment of friends is the best way to guarantee access to these in case of need (cf. *Cyr.* 8.2.22, quoted above).

[25] In a similar vein, Ischomachus envisions himself and his wife as partnering in their separate management of his estate's outdoor and domestic spheres to promote its overall flourishing above and beyond their individual capacities (*Oec.* 7.39–40).

[26] See *Cyr.* 1.5.9, Schorn 2012: 699–700, Morrison 2008, and Due 1989: 170–81.

[27] Dillery 1995: 5–6 argues that Socrates, Cyrus the Younger, and Agesilaus were the key figures in shaping Xenophon's thought. Wood 1964: 59–60 posits a leadership model informed by a combination of first-hand command experience and Socratic influence. Breitenbach 1950: 144 sees a Socratic interest in psychology filtered through a traditionalist mindset.

adapting benevolent reciprocity from elite friendships to the world of commander and subordinate represents a decidedly novel contribution. Perhaps his leadership of the Ten Thousand, a fractious army of mercenaries drawn from throughout Greece, had early focused the author's thinking around the problem of how to inspire a unifying sense of devotion. Unlike with the typical citizen militia of a Greek polis, these men lacked ties of common citizenship to bind them together and possessed greater latitude to abandon an unsatisfactory general.[28]

At the same time, however, Xenophon's emphasis on the practical advantages of moral behavior and his inclination to see universal principles of management manifested across multiple particulars cannot help but suggest the influence of Socrates, which antedates that of the Ten Thousand. But, adding further layers of complexity, the author's professed admiration for the generalship of his patron Agesilaus also positions the Spartan king as a key reference point, while the vision of friendship that is outlined by Xenophon's Socrates finds its fullest expression only with Cyrus the Younger. Ultimately, all arguments about the priority of any individual influence on Xenophon's leadership paradigm risk circular reasoning, since the figures most liable to have molded his thinking are also among those that the author later depicted as most fully embodying or espousing his leadership ideal; a complexity emblematized by Xenophon's status as both author and protagonist of *Anabasis*.[29]

Despite the monolithic nature of Xenophon's leadership model and the challenges that this poses for understanding its development, the author shows a great sensitivity in exploring the many difficulties for realizing this ideal in a world of imperfect individuals and uncontrollable circumstances.[30] The once-model Teleutias, for example, resurfaces in the *Hellenica* as an object of censure during a term as field commander in Sparta's war against the polis Olynthus (*Hell.* 5.3.3–6). Provoked by a cavalry raid, a quick temper leads him to commit his entire force to a pursuit that leads it dangerously close to Olynthus' walls. This allows the enemy to storm out and catch the Spartans off guard, killing Teleutias in the process. His experience is once again something that Xenophon believes "men can learn from" (5.3.7), but is now a negative lesson reinforcing the need for emotional self-mastery,

---

[28] The final three books of *Anabasis*, set after the remnants of the Ten Thousand escape immediate danger and arrive in Pontus, coincide with the longest stretches of Xenophon's sole command. Tellingly, a focus throughout them is on Xenophon's constant need to keep the army from splintering into separate forces along Greek ethnic lines. See Buxton 2016.

[29] Gera 1993: 26–7.

[30] See n. 14 and, on *Cyropaedia*, Sandridge 2012: 79–118.

which implicitly draws attention to the difficulty of sustaining the draining effort required of model leaders.

Meanwhile, there is the case of the great Theban general Epaminondas, whom Xenophon concedes does everything a model commander should to secure victory during his Peloponnesian campaign of 362 (7.5.8). Nevertheless, Epaminondas is foiled in his attempt to storm an undefended Sparta when, "by some divine providence," a chance passerby is able to alert nearby Spartan forces just in time (7.5.10).[31] We have seen Xenophon's insistence that a leader must do everything in his power to try to win the favor of the divine powers that Greeks envisioned as overseeing all those factors beyond the individual's control. Ultimately, however, as with Cyrus the Younger, no amount of preparation can predetermine success.

Most difficult of all, leaders must often cultivate multiple audiences simultaneously, whose willing obedience may depend on the pursuit of conflicting projects. Thus the Thessalian potentate Jason of Pherae masters the tricks of Xenophontic leadership in order to create an unswervingly loyal army of mercenaries that transform him into a regional powerbroker (6.1.4–6). But this very success leads Jason's neighbors to become unwilling and resentful allies who view him as a tyrant and gleefully provide shelter to his eventual assassins (6.4.31–2). If Xenophon's writings are a vehicle for advocating his theory of management, an important element of his didactic project is to foster a realistic sense among his readers for the challenges involved in realizing this ideal within the complex word of actual practice.

Further Reading

Gray 2011 is the most comprehensive treatment of Xenophon's leadership theory, outlining its core tenants and discussing its appearances across his entire corpus. She dedicates a chapter to the relationship between Xenophon's theory of leadership and his vision of friendship. Due 1989: 147–206 and Wood 1964 remain excellent primers, the former focusing on *Cyropaedia* and the latter highlighting the influence of Xenophon's military background on his model. Lendon 2006 looks at Xenophontic leadership in the realm of interstate relations and does an excellent job placing the author's thought in its contemporary context. Tamiolaki 2012 is a probing analysis of the different ways that Xenophon portrays leaders as falling short of his own ideal. Hutchison 2000 mines Xenophon's works for what they reveal about the

---

[31] Sterling 2004: 458–60.

practice of ancient generalship. Several publications that treat leadership in specific works are Sandridge 2012 and Danzig 2012 on *Cyropaedia*; Schorn 2012 on *Poroi*; and Anderson 1974a: 120–33 on the character Xenophon as a model leader in *Anabasis*. Important studies outside of English are Breitenbach 1950: 47–104 covering the *Hellenica*, Azoulay 2004a on the *Cyropaedia*, and Schorn 2008 on both the Socratic works and *Hiero*.

17

CHRISTOPHER TUPLIN

Xenophon and Athens

Xenophon is famous as an exile from Athens and an uncomplicated admirer of Sparta. The former description is incontestable, the latter wrong, and any imputation that Xenophon's Athenian identity is insignificant deeply misleading.

As resources for Xenophon's relationship with Athens we have the facts of his life and the contents of his writings. But the two categories are not wholly distinguishable, neither is plain sailing, and both involve subjective responses to elusive data. Nor is it only Xenophon's life and writings that are salient: there are significant questions about his interaction with other players in the intellectual life of late Classical Athens.

Some Biographical Issues

There are some straightforward elements in Xenophon's Athenian biography. He was born and educated there. He presumably fought for the city, certainly associated with Socrates, and left in 401 in defiance of Socrates' warning (*Anab*.3.1.4–10). He subsequently dedicated Cyrean booty in the Athenian treasury in Delphi (5.3.5) but was exiled and settled in the Peloponnese. Nonetheless he had an Athenian wife,[1] and his sons fought in the Athenian cavalry at Mantinea.

There are also contested issues, notably the date, cause, and length of his exile. My view is that he was exiled in 395/4, a victim of the outbreak of the Corinthian War.[2] His past association with Cyrus and his present association with Sparta were both open to criticism, but the latter was the primary complaint, and, since he fought fellow-Athenians at Coronea, punishment was not simply inappropriate. (Evasive treatment of the topic in *Anabasis* is a tacit acknowledgement of this.) It became easier to take that

---

[1] Badian 2004: 42.
[2] Tuplin 1987. Other views: Green 1994; Flower 2012: 36.

view (and to admit that the Athenian perception of Socrates was understandable: see below) when his exile was eventually reversed. His status must have been resolved by 362: one cannot otherwise imagine his sons Gryllus and Diodotus fighting for Athens at Mantinea, whether or not they were formally affected by their father's exile. And, although a resolution by pardon or penalty-waiver presupposes an individual of high status – the analogies are people like Alcibiades or the surviving Arginusae generals – we can legitimately judge Xenophon sufficiently high-profile to have benefited from the change in Atheno-Spartan relations in 370/69. His conviction already reflected a high profile (commander of an extraordinary mercenary force), and the years in Scillus had not wiped this out. Someone who creates a simulacrum of the Ephesian Artemisium in the Triphylian countryside is not of retiring disposition; and the post-Leuctra Elean overthrow of the Triphylian state found in him a victim whose fate will have attracted interest.[3] The existence and apologetic color of *Anabasis* betoken someone who was in the public eye.[4]

Whether Xenophon returned permanently to Athens is debatable. Absence of circumstantial data in the biographical tradition suggests not, and the greater "distance" in *Hipparchicus* as against *Poroi* (see below) does not require an intervening homecoming. Something that probably does belong between those two works is the death of Gryllus at Mantinea and the eulogies written in part as a tribute to his father (Diog. Laert. 2.55), which both confirm Xenophon's continuing prominence and raise issues about his relationship to the contemporary Athenian literary and intellectual environment. I return to that later (see below), but first I examine Xenophon's literary oeuvre.

Athens in Xenophon's Oeuvre

Xenophon never names himself or his city at the start of a work, and (*Anabasis* aside) only once names himself anywhere.[5] (But this *is* in the first chapter of the main body of *Memorabilia*, and may count as a somewhat self-deprecating "signature.") The authorial *ego* is anonymous and largely stateless. There are first-person plurals in *Poroi* that make the author Athenian, but none in *Hipparchicus*. The *ego* of *Constitution of the Spartans, On Horsemanship, Agesilaus, Cynegeticus, Cyropaedia,* and *Hellenica* is not identified as Xenophon of Athens (*Hiero* lacks authorial interventions),

---

[3] Tuplin 2004c.
[4] Flower 2012: 142.
[5] *Mem.* 1.3.9f

and that of *Anabasis* was perhaps identified as Themistogenes of Syracuse (*Hell.* 3.1.1) – a transparent disguise.[6] The phenomenon is a side-effect of exile: Thucydides still called himself "Athenian" and an Athenian exile was more an Athenian than anything else (unless he acquired another citizenship), but Xenophon's is an understandable alternative response. Formally he claims no authority (and acknowledges no bias) based upon birthplace: there is implicit critical distance from any city state as such.

The actual presence/impact of Athens varies considerably. Athens is entirely absent from *Constitution of the Spartans* and *Hiero* – unless discussion of Sparta inevitably evokes Athens[7] or Simonides is an ersatz Socrates. There was no way Socrates could converse with a real tyrant (he rarely left Athens and Athens had no real tyrants in his time), but Xenophon's interest in leadership is not so intrinsically Socratic that every example evokes Socrates, even if there is a consistent underlying value system;[8] nor did *Xenophon* need to come at Sparta from an Athenian angle: the text contrasts Sparta with *Greece*, and we can take this at face value.

Hiero and *Constitution of the Spartans* are non-Socratic exercises in discussing leadership through a problematic historical context. That goes also for *Cyropaedia*, but here we *do* get an Athenian, indeed Socratic, element in the good teacher executed by the Armenian king for corrupting his son Tigranes (3.1.14, 38–40). Xenophon describes the man as a "sophist" – not a term he would use of Socrates, even if not intrinsically pejorative (see below) – but Socratic overtones are unmistakable; and they become startling when Cyrus says that Tigranes should forgive his father. Is that what Xenophon thought about Socrates' execution? Many scholars see a sign of rapprochement with Athens; another view (not incompatible) is that the episode reminds us that the dialogue-rich world of *Cyropaedia* is not that of Socrates.[9] Either way Athens momentarily intrudes into a depiction of Persian leadership.

Less startling minimal Athenian intrusions occur in *Horsemanship* – which mentions *Hipparchicus* (12.14) and repeats some of its injunctions (6.12, 11.10, 11.13) – and *Agesilaus*, whose hero cured the political unrest caused by Athenian imperial failure (1.37) and faced an army at Coronea that included Athenians (2.6). Other contacts between Agesilaus and Athens visible in *Hellenica* (e.g. 4.5.7–18, 5.4.20–33), are understandably missing in an encomiastic context. Hare-hunting in *Cynegeticus* is geographically non-specific, and the same is true of the sophists denounced at the work's

---

[6] Flower 2012: 53–5.
[7] Kroeker 2009: 202–5.
[8] Schorn 2008.
[9] Gera 1993: 24; Mueller-Goldingen 1995: 161; Azoulay 2004a: 354; Atak (forthcoming).

end, though they could hardly *not* have an Athenian component, and the politicians who steal public property (13.10–11) are an Athenian stereotype (*Anab.* 4.6.16). In the list of mythological hunters (1.5–17) the extravagant praise of Menestheus (1.12), the unusual statement that Theseus is "even now admired for extending the borders of his fatherland" (1.10), and the observation that Telamon's Athenian wife came from "the greatest city" (1.9; cf. Diod. 4.72) are the mark of an Athenian author.

With *Anabasis* we reach a much more substantial work, and a more substantial Athenian component.

Eleven individuals with Athenian connections are mentioned. Eight appear just once,[10] two play a slightly more substantial role,[11] and the eleventh is Xenophon, who dominates books 3–7 and envisages honor in his native city from becoming the Cyreans' commander in chief (6.1.20). The narrative is framed by his departure from Athens and his failure to return: the Socrates story in 3.1.5–8 anticipates his exile, as do later passages (5.3.7, 7.7.57), one near the end; and even nearer the end we encounter an enigmatic story (7.8.4) in which Xenophon meets the omen-interpreter Euclides of Phlius, who deploys information from his Athenian past to benefit Xenophon and gives advice based on mantic intervention, thus closing a circle that starts with Socrates and Delphi.

In between Xenophon's Athenian quality comes out passingly in an allusion to Marathon (3.2.11) – the sacrifices to Artemis add a peculiarly Athenian twist – and more substantially in two contexts.

1. An unresolved comparison of Spartan and Athenian education occurs in 4.6.14–16: Xenophon is not really being critical of Sparta but Cheirisophus employs anti-democratic rhetoric, and is unduly waspish in response to well-intentioned banter. Later the issue of who should be commander in chief evokes talk of Sparta's victory in the Peloponnesian War (6.1.27). That comparison recurs in 7.1.27 (stressing the erstwhile extent of Athenian power) and provides an undercurrent throughout Xenophon's dealings with Spartans in books 6–7. All things considered we learn more about Spartans *qua* Spartans in *Anabasis* than we do about Athenians *qua* Athenians.

2. Seuthes professes to like Athenians and alludes to a "family relationship" (7.2.31, 3.39), and offers Xenophon fortresses:[12] Heraclides (7.3.19) notes that other Athenians have received such benefactions, and we certainly think of Alcibiades. Xenophon's eventual refusal of the offer mitigates the awkwardness, but cannot eliminate it: the author of *Anabasis*

---

[10] See 2.1.8, 4.2.13–17, 8.4, 5.6.14, 6.5.7, 7.3.28, 8.4.
[11] Lycius: 3.3.20, 4.3.22, 25, 4.7.24; Lane Fox 2004: 11. Polycrates (Xenophon's trusted subordinate): 4.5.24, 5.1.16, 7.2.17, 29–30, 6.41.
[12] 7.2.25, 37–8, 5.8, 6.34, 43, 7.50.

has deliberately allowed the analogy to surface, assisted by the fact that Xenophon and Alcibiades also shared the experience of exile and return, association with Sparta during that exile (underlined in Xenophon's case by the Scillus interlude: 5.3.7–13), and a youthful link with Socrates. We may doubt that Xenophon gloried in assimilation to Alcibiades. But Xenophon the *Anabasis* character is not quite identical with Xenophon the author. The character's momentary, if unfulfilled (indeed rejected), aspirations to personal power (5.6.15–17, 6.1.20, 7.1.21) – another Alcibiadean characteristic – show the danger to which even someone good at leadership is exposed. And someone who gets exiled by his city has not done *everything* right. Xenophon's paradigmatic pedagogy is rarely black and white.

The peculiar nature of *Anabasis* means that Athens is both everywhere (through Xenophon the Athenian) and still hardly present. *Hellenica* presents a different case.

Athenian presence in the text, when not merely transient, can be undeveloped.[13] Even when there are major narrative threads with an Athenian component,[14] they are only partially Athenian: the major focus is apt to be Spartan or Theban. In most of book 7 Athens makes only incidental (often unimpressive) appearances and the most successful Athenian leader, Chares, commands mercenaries and is not identified as Athenian. Athens does play a role in the final episode of *Hellenica*: Epaminondas' unsuccessful attempt to intercept the Athenians delays his campaign in Arcadia and Laconia (7.5.6–7); Athenian cavalrymen save Mantinea (7.5.15–17); and the Athenians are the only anti-Theban contingent name-checked in the final battle. Here the cavalry action sticks out – and the motive is certainly personal (Gryllus' death).

So, *Hellenica* is not quantitatively Athenocentric history: only 33 percent of the text describes events involving Athenians, whereas for Sparta the figure is 75 percent. But, Sparta aside, there is no state in which it is more interested than Athens, and one certainly needs to assess its representation qualitatively.

Xenophon can report unfamiliar institutional or historical data, and the fact that the number of named Athenians and Spartans is almost identical is striking, given the unequal space devoted to the cities. Still, there are no

---

[13] Nemea (4.2.16–23), Corinthian war (4.4.3, 9, 15–16, 5.3, 13–19), Boeotian War (5.4.34, 54, 59), Leuctra (6.4.19), peace of 371/0 (6.5.1–3).

[14] Alcibiades' later career (1.1.1–1.5.17), Arginusae (1.6.1–1.7.35), Athens's defeat (2.1.1–3.10), the Thirty and the civil war (2.3.11–2.4.43), the Theban alliance and Haliartus (3.5.1–25), the sea war of 394–386 (4.8.6–16, 25–39, 5.1.1–36), the liberation of Thebes in 379/8 (5.4.2,9–11, 19, 20–4, 34), Corcyra and the peace of 375 (5.4.60–6; 6.2.1–39), the peace of 372/1 (6.3.1–20), and the Spartan-Athenian alliance of 370/69 (6.5.1–3, 33–52, 7.1.1–15).

exact parallels, especially post–404, to the privileged insights of the Cinadon or Sphodrias narratives: the imaginative engagement with Athenian politics in 6.3.3–17 is not quite the same. So qualitative assessment is more a matter of judging the impression the reader gets of the Athenian state and its historical behavior.

I discuss Xenophon's view of Athens as democratic state below. What about Athens as imperial state? *Hellenica* disapproves of imperialism in general.[15] But are there any distinctions?

5.4.1 provides an explicit framework for negative judgment of Sparta at the apogee of her power. The case of Thebes is less immediately clear: Thebans are represented – perhaps rightly – as stumbling unwillingly towards anything more than domination of Boeotia. But Thebes's wish to rule Greece is assumed by Procles (6.5.38–9) and the link between Theban hegemony and historical medism (7.1.33) provides a general framework for critical assessment of Thebes's activities.

For Athens recovery of empire is a framework in 395. Given Athenian expectation of punishment for past imperial crimes (2.2.3), this is not an attractive framework either. But is it the whole story? Athenian aspirations were terminated by the King's Peace and the later story is marked by Xenophon's near silence about the second Athenian confederacy, a silence characterized by a failure to describe its formation, a near-total absence of formal reference to its existence, and a narrative of Athenian activity in 378–362 that either suggests that Athens had no allies or directs attention away from the benefits she derived from them.

This is arguably the oddest silence in *Hellenica* and distinguishes treatment of Athenian imperialism from other sorts. Whether this is a species of *apologia* or simply the suppression of an embarrassment (not entirely distinct possibilities), it feels as though Athens is treated differently because the author is Athenian.

A negative attitude to what became of the confederacy is clear in *Poroi*, a work whose agenda is the transformation of Athens's relationship with other Greeks. This is Xenophon's last work and his most concentratedly and overtly Athenian one, strongly characterized by first-person plurals that associate author and fellow-citizens. (He also occasionally addresses them in the second person – a mixture proper to Assembly speeches.) Some read the work as moral philosophy masquerading as practical political advice (Schorn 2012), but that makes little difference here, both because the external appearance remains Athenian and because (although moral philosophy may have wider applicability) there is no reason to imagine its intended audience not including Athenians: indeed the work's form identifies them as a privileged audience. Xenophon ends his writing career firmly re-embedded in the city that had once rejected him.

Poroi was not his first engagement with a specific Athenian problem. That honor belongs to Hipparchicus. This is less overtly Athenian. Unlike Poroi it does not open with a reference to Athens, and the word "Athenian" appears rarely (1.26, 7.1–4). But an Athenian setting is underlined by references to Athenian locations (3.1–14); and these passages together guarantee that the one thousand-strong cavalry, ten tribes, tribal- ommanders, Council, displays, and sacred processions encountered elsewhere are also Athenian. Association of tribal commanders and the law (1.23) shows in turn that other references to legal requirements have Athenian law in mind. Athens is the state that spends 40 talents a year on cavalry (1.19), should hire foreign cavalrymen (9.3–6), and be advised that cavalry are better when accompanied by infantry (5.13). In short, there is no reason to doubt that this is a work conceived from the outset as about Athenian cavalry, not a generic work adapted for an Athenian context. It is true that the work is not addressed to the Athenians or even to the hipparchs as a pair. (The absence of advice about how they should cooperate is striking, especially as there is advice about cooperation with tribal commanders and orators: 1.8.) Instead we hear about what the hipparch (singular) should do, and direct instructions are couched either in the second-person singular or in a grammatically impersonal form, the latter method being used exclusively in chapters 6–9. Nonetheless, it would be odd to deny that the circumstances of creation had a real Athenian impetus: it makes no sense to see it as driven by the desire, for example, to explain the current weaknesses of Athenian cavalry to outsiders. At the same time it is formulated as an outsider's observations: although the author often speaks in the first-person singular, he never identifies with the Athenians by using the first-person plural. There is a clear contrast with Poroi, where Xenophon is conceptually in Athens in a way that is not true in Hipparchicus. This is not a necessary concomitant of the decision to formulate Hipparchicus as advice to an individual: Xenophon could have done that from within a shared politico-military community. So he has chosen to keep a certain distance – and does so even when discussing Boeotia (7.1–15), a topic of personal importance, judging by Memorabilia 3.5.2–6, 25. It is tempting to regard this as the conscious or unconscious result of a continuing degree of emotional and/or physical distance from Athens.

There is a different issue of distance in the final part of the oeuvre. Poroi and Hipparchicus engage with Athens to amend Athenian institutions. The Socratic works address their readers through a sort of Athenian history – a fictive version of a fifth-century past wherein intellectual and moral principles are presented through a figure who is both quintessentially Athenian and unique, and in an environment both distanced from the here and now and yet colored by it.

In undertaking such an enterprise Xenophon is not doing something radically different from things he does elsewhere. Not only are his Socratic roots fundamental for his entire literary and intellectual activity,[16] but the inspection of things that matter through an apparently unpromising historical lens is characteristic. If one can inspect leadership through Persian kingship or Syracusan tyranny even though no reader is going to (admit to wanting to) be a tyrant or a Persian king, then one can inspect leadership and other important topics through the later fifth-century world of Socrates and his mostly upper-class associates: it does not matter that no reader is going to (admit to wanting to) be either Socrates (a *non pareil* and too ascetic for any sensible person to imitate) or any of his companions, who inhabited a fractured and irrecoverable world and often prospered less than their apparently privileged circumstances might have led one to expect.

The Socratic works are Xenophon's most extensive Athenian products: they far exceed *Poroi* and *Hipparchicus* in length and Socrates impregnates them with an Athenian presence from start to finish. Non-Athenians are not wholly absent; but across the corpus only four non-Athenians participate in dialogues and fewer than twenty other non-Athenians are mentioned, so the non-Athenian world is largely represented by more or less passing allusions to places or institutions. (The Persian and Phoenician element in the otherwise very Athenian *Oeconomicus* stick out here.) But such things are more than matched by the Athenian decor – topographical, material, institutional, cultural – that defines the environment within which Socrates operates. Although the location and occasion of episodes are rarely well individuated, we are always conscious of being physically and conceptually in Athens. This is where Xenophon the Athenian author really comes into his own. But he does so in an invented and peculiar version of reality; and that this happens is a tribute not only to Socratic exceptionality but to the fact that others responded to that exceptionality in comparable fashions. Interaction with other literary or intellectual products is not absent elsewhere in the oeuvre but it is peculiarly fundamental in the Socratic material because the entire genre is interactive. Although not all Socratic writers were Athenians and other literary antecedents play a role in some of Xenophon's Socratic works,[17] the Socratic enterprise is fundamentally Athenian – particularly when, as with Xenophon, the author *is* Athenian.

[16] Hobden and Tuplin 2012b: 20–39.
[17] Gray 1998: 105–22, 159–77.

One aspect of this is the ironic interplay between Socratic text and Athenian reality. *Symposium* assembles an associate (Charmides) and victims of the Thirty (Autolycus, Niceratus), has Socrates praised by his eventual accuser Lycon (9.1), and presents a Syracusan who can use a dancing girl to teach Athenians how to face swords (2.12). *Oeconomicus* offers the domestic and economic orderliness of a man notorious for marital disorder and financial profligacy.[18] *Memorabilia* includes an exhortation to Charmides to practice democratic politics (3.7) and a discussion with the younger Pericles about the restoration of Athenian greatness (3.5), neither of which can be read without consciousness of the two men's eventual fate. (The former was killed while fighting for the Thirty against democratic exiles, the latter executed for dereliction of duty after his victory at Arginusae.) The Pericles chapter is peculiarly striking. Socrates seeks to convince the sceptical Pericles that his election as general bodes well for improved Athenian military efficiency in a context in which Boeotia is the principal enemy and there are lessons to be learned from Spartan values. In the real world the principal enemy was Sparta, Pericles was one of those who won a spectacular victory at Arginusae (improved Athenian military efficiency indeed) – and was executed by the *demos* for failing to rescue shipwrecked sailors. *Oeconomicus* plainly resembles *Hiero* and *Cyropaedia*, in investigating leadership through a problematic case,[19] and *Memorabilia* 3.5 does something similar, especially when seen in the wider context of 3.1–7 (see below). Xenophon believed in the paradigmatic value of history, but, suspicious of simplistic ideas about learning from the past, he also had a penchant for disconcerting his readers with unexpected versions of history. This arguably came from his Socratic background: he is not the only Socratic writer who engages in fictive (even impossible) history, for the good reason that the entire Socratic literary enterprise was an exercise in fictive history.

Xenophon the Athenian

Having surveyed Xenophon's oeuvre and broached the issue of his relationship to one strand of Athenian intellectual endeavor, I turn more directly to his place in and view of fourth-century Athens.

When Gryllus died, eulogies were written "in part as a favor to his father." Not long afterwards Aristotle wrote a work attacking the Isocratean view of rhetoric.[20] That he entitled it *Gryllus* is eloquent testimony to the

---

[18] Nails 2002: 176–8. But for a different view, see Hobden in this volume.
[19] Azoulay 2004a: 441; Kronenberg 2009; Danzig 2010: 239–63; Tuplin forthcoming b.
[20] Diog. Laert. 2.55, Quint. 2.17.4.

prominence of the encomiastic outburst occasioned by the young man's death, and specifically to the status of Isocrates' contribution; this is underlined by Cephisodorus' subsequent response to *Gryllus* from the Isocratean camp.[21] Some believe that Isocrates' *Antidosis* was also a response to Aristotle and, if so, its Socratic overtones give an additional twist.[22] More was involved than just an argument about rhetoric: at stake were the proper nature and goal of education – and in this the Academy could not claim a monopoly on the iconic figure of Socrates. That brings us back to Xenophon, who had his own moral and intellectual investment in the Socratic tradition.[23] As a Socratic writer Xenophon already had an indirect connection with the Academy. The Gryllus affair exposed his potential for contact with the Isocratean alternative.

Xenophon, of course, occupied his own place, distinct from both Isocrates and the Academy – and the wider Socratic environment. Socratic writers could be standoffish. Antisthenes figures in Xenophon but not vice versa; Xenophon figured in Aeschines (rather prominently: Cic. *de inv.* 1.51–2), but not vice versa, though Aspasia the matchmaker (*Mem.* 2.6.36) might be a covert allusion to Aeschines' text. Plato appears in *Memorabilia* once (3.6.1: Socrates was well disposed to Glaucon for the sake of Charmides – future associate of the Thirty – and Plato), but Xenophon is never encountered in Plato. But there are signs of interaction between their writings (*Laws, Alcibiades, Statesman,* and *Cyropaedia*; the two *Symposium*s; *Hellenica, Critias,* and *Seventh Letter; Charmides* and *Memorabilia* 3.7; *Meno* and *Anabasis* 2.6.21–9),[24] and, although the two men were dissimilar in intellectual profile (Plato being more dialectically pertinacious, more poetically fantastical, and less interested in the real world) and disagreed on fundamental things such as the teachability of virtue or the possible existence of good leaders,[25] the relationship was not necessarily one of outright hostility.

But Isocrates would perhaps have been a more congenial character from Xenophon's perspective. There are certainly points of literary convergence: *Cynegeticus* has been called an Isocratean *parainesis* (exhortation), *Agesilaus* follows the lead of Isocrates' *Evagoras* (albeit in a different form), both authors inspect principles of leadership through autocrats (though Xenophontic examples are more complex than Isocrates' Cypriot orations),[26] and they had a shared interest in Prodicus' *Heracles*.[27] At the same time,

[21] Weissenberger 2003.
[22] Nightingale 1995: 28–9, 42, 43; Too 2008: 24; Murphy 2013: 343, 348.
[23] Waterfield 2004.
[24] Danzig 2005, 2013, 2014b, Atak (forthcoming), Tuplin forthcoming.
[25] Dorion forthcoming.
[26] Gray 2000: 149.
[27] Murphy 2013: 327–8; Wolfsdorf 2008.

although they agreed about city-state imperialism, they do not sing from identical songsheets in the mid-350s,[28] and Xenophon was no Isocratean Panhellenist. Isocrates in turn probably regarded *Hellenica* as stylistically beneath history writing's proper aspirations[29] and might have preferred Thucydides – an Athenian historiographical model that Xenophon deliberately abandoned. They also differed somewhat in the categorization of intellectual opponents. Isocrates sometimes treats sophists and philosophers as overlapping (not necessarily qualitatively discrepant) groups – though elsewhere sophists are deviant practitioners of philosophy and "sophist" is more likely to appear in already negative contexts. Xenophon also treats "sophist" both as intrinsically evil and intrinsically neutral;[30] but "I will not call them philosophers" (*Cyn.* 13.6) asserts a firmness of distinction that Isocrates does not always maintain. The sophists whom Xenophon criticizes in *Cynegeticus* are certainly not people Isocrates would not criticize. But Isocrates (13.1–10, 19–20) has a more complex set of targets – both modern sophists (teachers of eristics; teachers of political discourse) and the sophists of the past – and (probably) a greater animus against the Academy (if only because there was a more straightforward issue of professional rivalry), while Xenophon's alternative educational program in *Cynegeticus* (hunting as training in truth: 12.7) is not immediately relevant to Isocrates, and his general pedagogic posture is not quite that of Isocratean "philosophy." Xenophon certainly knew the practical value of rhetoric (embedded in *Anabasis* and *Cyropaedia*, and spelled out in *Memorabilia* 3.3.11), and he and Isocrates might agree (against Plato) that there was no fundamental distinction between dialectic and rhetoric;[31] but the Isocratean view that dialectic or eristics are at best a resource for private training of the mind would have left him ill at ease with the aspiration to be "best in character, leadership and dialectic" (*Mem.* 4.5.12–4.6.1); and the primary goals of Xenophontic education are moral virtue and both being and being seen to be better than one's subordinates, not becoming skillful at "using language in a public context such that an individual can function for the good of society"[32] or expressing cogently reasoned conjectures about the future (Isocrates 15.271). Crudely, Isocrates was a man of words, while Xenophon remained at heart a man of action.

---

[28] Bodei Giglioni 1970: xxi–xxviii; Näf 1997.
[29] Marincola 2014: 46.
[30] Evil: *Cyn.* 13.8, *Mem.* 1.6.13. Neutral: 4.2.1, *Por.* 5.4. Good context: *Cyr.* 3.1.14, 38–40. Bad context: 6.1.41, *Mem.* 1.1.11, 1.6.1, *Cyn.* 13 *passim*.
[31] Dorion 2014.
[32] Too 2008: 23.

One thing Xenophon, Plato, and Isocrates do have in common is the perception that they were hostile to the democratic ideology prevalent in their lifetime, and this brings us to what many will see as the most important question: what was Xenophon's attitude to his native city?

The Athenians exiled him: he must have felt pretty negative at times. On the other hand, he may have recognized that there was justification in his treatment, there was clearly an eventual rapprochement, and *Hipparchicus* and *Poroi* show concern for the city's well-being. So, indeed, does his sons' service in the Athenian cavalry, for no one supposes they acted in defiance of his wishes. But this only scratches the surface. Concern for the city does not entail approval of all its ways – and the two treatises do call for change. How far did Xenophon actually think that much more profound changes would be necessary to make Athens a city of which he could really approve?

In strictly biographical terms it is hard to get much handle on this. Judging from *Anabasis* (which muddies the bounds between biographical data and literary construction) he was capable of flourishing in an assembly-based community. But assemblies are not a preserve of democracies, and the army held none between the Zab and the Black Sea, so was not a doctrinairely assembly-based, let alone democratic, body. (Since they were all soldiers, their assembly also evaded the criticism of lack of expertise addressed at democratic assemblies.) Seuthes saw Xenophon as "soldier-lover" and Heraclides assented to a Spartan suggestion that he was a demagogue (7.6.4). Xenophon would probably have accepted the former term, but what about "demagogue"? That is an oligarch's term of abuse (*Hell.* 2.3.27, 5.2.7), and the reader of *Anabasis* should not take it at face value. But did Xenophon imagine himself as embodying a more acceptable version of democratic leadership? The soldier-lover who does not benefit himself personally as much as he might could certainly fit the bill: talk of love is specifically resonant of some democratic rhetoric. But perhaps he is simply inviting us to see him as a good leader. Still, the principles of good leadership are theoretically applicable in all environments. Nothing about Xenophon's views requires him to deny there could be good leaders in a democracy; and it has even been claimed that he developed a literary style that reveals sympathy for the *demos*[33] – another (putative) biographical fact on the margin between actual life and the literary construction thereof.

The truth is that we can only assess Xenophon's attitude to the Athenian state and/or its characteristic democratic ideology by assessing the impression of these things his writings seem calculated to create.

[33] Gray 2014.

Hellenica offered Xenophon the most extensive opportunity to reflect on differing political structures and convey an opinion about them. Full discussion of his response is impossible here. Instead I make two observations.

(1) The institutional characteristics of most city states that figure in *Hellenica* are a matter of relatively little interest to Xenophon – startlingly so in several cases. The heroism of Phlius is a matter of loyalty and valor, not a particular political organization (7.2.1–23). The judgment and personal probity of Polydamas matter more than the constitution of Pharsalus (6.2.1–19). Xenophon's treatment of Corinth (4.4.1–13) and Olynthus (5.2.11–19) ignores the chance of explicitly linking democratic ideology with sacrilege or regional imperialism. The democratic character of post-379/8 Thebes is soft-pedaled and plays no serious role in Xenophon's negative depiction of the new would-be hegemonic state. Political turmoil in Anatolian city states (restored to "ancestral constitutions" by the ephors) is simply the background for a power struggle between Agesilaus and Lysander (3.4.7–10): there is no precision about constitutions and even less explanation of Agesilaus' resolution of the problems than in *Agesilaus* 1.38.

(2) Athens and Sparta do get more attention. The Spartan system involves a distinctive mix of kings (who engage in political manoeuvring), ephors (plainly important), and assemblies. It is not explicitly labeled in constitutional terms, but its non-democratic color is clear from the character of pro-Spartan groups elsewhere; and its behavior is not always unimpeachable. Spartan laws are circumvented (*Hell.* 2.1.7), justice can take a strange – and explicitly criticized – form (5.4.24–33), and the city's political vulnerability is underlined by the Cinadon story (3.3.4–11). At Athens (except under the Thirty) we are definitely dealing with democracy.[34] In the Arginusae trial (1.7.1–35) motivation mostly lacks ideological character and is sometimes a matter of self-preservation; but the Athenians' view that legal procedure (richly present in the story) matters little compared with their right to do as they wish is worrying (1.7.12). There may have been understandable reasons for hostility to the generals,[35] the whole story may have a knife-edge quality, and we see a system that is derailed in a particular case (something the *demos* eventually acknowledges) rather than intrinsically ill-formed. But it is not a pretty sight. But neither is Critian oligarchy. The civil war narrative only dwells on ideological issues at the end (conflict between the *demos* and the rich: 2.4.40) and the eventual settlement is more a factional deal than

[34] One mark of this is a greater than average tendency to refer to Athenians *voting* to do such-and-such a thing: 1.2.1, 1.5.18, 1.6.24, 1.7.7–35, 2.2.15, 2.3.45, 51, 2.4.9, 23, 3.5.16, 5.1.5, 6.2.11, 6.3.2, 6.5.49, 7.1.14. In other states: 5.2.10, 15, 19, 5.3.21, 6.3.18, 6.5.3.
[35] Gish 2012.

the restoration of concord (2.4.43, 3.5.9). But thereafter, apart from the despatch of cavalry to Anatolia (3.1.4), there is little sign of internal ideological divisions – there are different views about Boeotia (5.4.19, 34, 7.1.38), but even the individuated figures of Callias, Autocles, and Callistratus (6.3.3–17) are not explicitly represented in factional or ideological terms, and praise of Iphicrates' cooperation with the hostile politician Callistratus and the excellent general Chabrias (6.2.39) evokes natural political rivalry without further explicit overtones or any suggestion that democracy is peculiarly open to criticism.

So, if we ask how interested Xenophon's longest study of Greek historical relations is in the constitutional and/or ideological categorization of states and what is its author's attitude to the various possibilities, the answers are (i) not very and (ii) unforthcoming or ambivalent. And, even in the cases of Athens and Sparta (where there is more interest), the work does not convey an overall preference for the political culture of one over the other. This is in line with criticism of Sparta in *Constitution of the Spartans* and with Socratic passages that juxtapose Athens and Sparta (*Smp.* 8.38–9, *Mem.* 3.5.14–16): Socrates does not think that states should stop being like themselves and become like Sparta instead, and there is no reason to imagine Xenophon took a different view. (Nor, of course, did he think they should simply become like Athens either.)

I return to Socratic writings shortly. Some other non-Socratic parts of the oeuvre have little to say of Athens and cannot help much here. *Cyropaedia* involves the empowerment of the lower class, embodied in the figure of Pheraulas but affecting a much larger group. But this still all happens in the context of autocratic sociopolitical organizations, and common people do not as a class become part of the honor elite. The very fact that *Cyropaedia* (like *Hiero*) deals with autocracy will strike some as a demonstration of Xenophon's disconnection from the world of the democratic city – and, perhaps, preference for the monarchic republicanism of the Persia of *Cyropaedia* 1. But, inasmuch as *that* polity is quasi-Spartan, what is said above about Xenophon's attitude to Sparta should be kept in mind. And what *Cyropaedia* or *Hiero* really show is the extent to which Xenophon is interested in leadership, not constitutions. That is the same as the message of *Anabasis* (see above) and is also relevant to what we found in *Hellenica*.

Some historians find a clearer critical stance towards democratic Athens in *Hipparchicus* and *Poroi*, seeing both as supportive of the elite.[36] In *Hipparchicus* there *is* apprehension about the Council taking wrong decisions (1.8) and the cavalry lacking influence (3.5), and perceived hostility

36 Pownall 2012.

to cavalry may explain recruitment difficulties (1.9–12); but Xenophon soft-pedals these issues, and simply wishes the cavalry to play a satisfactory civic role by realizing an ambition for technical excellence. Political ideology plays no obvious role; cavalry *is* a way that the upper classes can help the city (and therefore the democratic city) but Xenophon is not suggesting that this should earn the upper classes political advantages inconsistent with the principles of the democratic constitution.

Poroi does seek to release the rich from the expense of war (6.1), but it does not envisage the immediate abolition of property taxation, merely its redirection (3.6–10), and the aim is that the *demos* will be well provided with maintenance (*trophê*) and the poverty of the masses cured. Some problematize this by suggesting that the masses will be disempowered and that a (democratic) principle of state pay risks substitution by a demeaning and patronizing maintenance.[37] But distribution of resources is not undemocratic – theoric payments were the glue of democracy (Demades fr.36 de Falco) because they kept rich and poor together:[38] in those terms Xenophon's proposals are pro-democracy. It also has been claimed that the promise that (with universal maintenance) the city will become more obedient, more disciplined, and more warlike (4.51) envisages a depoliticized society of docile subjects beneath an elite of priests, council, magistrates, and cavalry getting "ancestral" payments (6.1) – actual state pay – to perform civic functions. This claim too strikes me as misleading. State pay is only mentioned at 2.2, where the point is that metics provide public service without having to be given it. Otherwise everything is collapsed into maintenance, and the effect is arguably to assimilate all classes. And, if some people receiving maintenance perform useful tasks (4.52: ephebes), may we not assume that all recipients might sometimes be obligated to do something useful? The omission of the Assembly and law-courts from the list of beneficiaries whose ancestral rights are to be guaranteed (6.1) is probably due to the fact that ecclesiastic and dicastic pay had been well protected in hard times, not to a reactionary prejudice against such payments. The premise of *Poroi* is, of course, that democratic leaders espouse policies that result in other Greeks being treated unjustly. That is a more serious complaint than that the cavalry force is substandard and – unlike the latter, which is partly to the discredit of the elite (*Mem.* 3.5.19) – it is a complaint aimed at the democratic establishment. But Xenophon's solution is economic intervention, not constitutional change. Moreover, although his advice in *Hipparchicus* cannot be seen to have had much impact,[39] the situation is

[37] Azoulay 2004a: 222–5.
[38] Badian 1995: 101.
[39] Bugh 1988: 155; Spence 1993: 223–4.

different with *Poroi*, for there are signs that his opinions were shared by those who currently exerted real political influence in the city.[40]

It remains to consider the Socratic aspect.[41] What does it say about Xenophon's attitude that he turned a fellow victim of the Athenian judicial system into a moral and intellectual paradigm? After all, it is widely assumed that Socrates' real sin in Athenian eyes was hostility to democracy.

The claim that Xenophon's Socrates was "a man of the people and philanthropic" (1.2.60) does not settle the issue, since this is more about his refusal of payment than about political ideology and the claim to philanthropy might even be regarded as suspect.[42] But he lives in a democratic state, never claims it was improperly constituted and, as a legal positivist,[43] accepts its authority. His autarky is not inconsistent with state service (1.6.10). His belief that people incapable of being useful to army or city and of assisting the *demos* when necessary should be made to reform (especially if they are confrontational and even if they are rich: 1.2.59) and his professed desire to empower others to do politics (1.6.15, *Smp.* 8.37–43) – even to be seen as a teacher of politics (*Mem.* 1.2.17, 4.2.2–7) – arguably represent an aspiration to contribute to the democratic state. (This is also implicit in *Memorabilia* 3.1–7.) The suggestion that some pupils, such as Alcibiades or Critias, were taught to subvert the democratic state is, of course, rejected. Discussion of that issue does momentarily create the impression that a desire to "lead the city" means one is out of sympathy with Socrates (1.2.39), but this is misleading. Glaucon's comparable desire (3.6.1) is only inappropriate because of his incompetence (even the disconcerting reference to Themistocles in 3.6.2 mocks Glaucon, not the aspiration to be a democratic leader) and 4.2.2 describes city leadership as "the greatest of things." (That comes at the start of four chapters in which Socrates shows another young man, Euthydemus, how much he does not understand and reinforces the idea that moral virtues must underlie political skills and action.) It is true that 1.2.48 declares that proper associates came to Socrates not to become politicians or courtroom speakers but to become *kaloikagathoi* and therefore be able to relate properly to household, friends, city, and citizens. But it is Xenophon's understanding that this fundamental moral achievement could in a particular case underpin the use of skill in political or forensic rhetoric as a means to leadership in a democratic city.

---

[40] Cawkwell 1963: 61–6; Gauthier 1976: 223–31; Burke 1984: 113–15; Oliver 2011.
[41] Dobski 2009, Gray 2004a, Kroeker 2009, Pownall 2012, Seager 2001, Waterfield 2004: 104–7, Waterfield 2012.
[42] Azoulay 2004a: 318–26, Christ 2013.
[43] *Memorabilia* 4.4.1–25, 6.5–6. Dorion forthcoming.

That said, there are negative indicators to be considered. One is the very fact that the moral underpinning for civic life is described as *kalokagathia* (the quality of a gentleman of good character and taste). This is a distinctively Athenian concept,[44] but its real-world associations are socially elite and not naturally compatible with democratic ideology. Moreover the world in which Xenophon's Socrates moves is generally the one of that very social elite. Socrates may be a man of the people, but he does not characteristically talk to the ordinary man in the street – or the ordinary woman: for Theodote (*Mem.* 3.11) is precisely *not* a common prostitute. He is not, it is true, simply engaged in reinforcing the real-world values of Athenian *kaloikagathoi*. But, even if Xenophon is trying to reinvent *kalokagathia* as a civic virtue rather than one peculiar to a particular class,[45] the decision to include it in the philosophic substrate of his Socrates[46] shows that he is comfortable with the risk that his hero will be seen as non-democratic.

But one passage, *Memorabilia* 2.6.22–7, has been seen as going further – as amounting to a proposal for *kaloikagathoi* to establish oligarchy. The starting point is that the moral qualities of *kaloikagathoi* enable them to behave cooperatively. That will be relevant to "political honors"; for in politics (unlike athletics) people are allowed to cooperate. This need not be sinister, but what perhaps gives the passage a slightly dark quality is the contrast it draws between (a) those who want to be honored and to hold office so that they can steal money, treat people violently, and indulge in pleasure and (b) those who want to be honored in the city so they do not suffer injustice and can help their friends in a just fashion and who, in office, try to do their fatherland some good. This alludes to a stereotype about bad politicians in Athens (*Anab.* 4.6.16, *Cyn.* 13.11) and evokes the idea that *kaloikagathoi* risk mistreatment by the democratic state. So what could have been a simple moralizing proposition about good people getting on with one another takes on a partisan edge. Any implicit suggestion in the contrast with athletic games that *kaloikagathoi* will collude to "win all the prizes" sounds disturbing too. At the same time, no political analogy for that achievement is articulated: all that is said is that in politics no one stops anyone joining others to help the city and that it is advantageous to do politics with the best friends and have such people as coworkers not competitors. We are at liberty to identify "all the prizes" as the maximum number of opportunities to benefit the city. The passage is not inconsistent with constitutionally proper and non-subversive engagement in democratic politics; but it exemplifies

---

[44] *pace* Bourriot 1996. See Davies 2013.
[45] Roscalla 2004.
[46] Waterfield 2004: 110.

again a certain insouciance about the way in which Socrates is presented. Xenophon is not striving to make compromises between his vision of morally informed political action and democratic sensitivities.

There are other examples of this. Xenophon cites the complaint that Socrates taught that it was stupid to choose people by lot (*Mem.* 1.2.9) – and then does not answer the accusation but gets sidetracked into a different one about incitement to violence. Socrates evidently *did* disapprove of lot. And the reason is clear in 3.9.10: only those who know how to rule are real rulers, not those who have scepters or who are elected by random people or alloted or gain power by force or deception. So allotment is not necessarily worse than other mechanisms – but it is not better either. In the real world you have to tolerate it (disapproval is no excuse for violence), and there may be mitigations: informed rule is easier in narrowly focused settings and can be paradoxical (women spinners ruling men, *Mem.* 3.9.10; Ischomachus' wife, *Oec.* 7–11); *dokimasia* (post-selection vetting) may protect against bad allotments; the problem with alloted officials is perhaps that they are not best qualified to ensure that people obey laws.[47] But none of this is explicit or quite eliminates the impact of Xenophon's failure to deny Socrates' hostility at the outset. That failure is doubtless a tribute to historical accuracy but also another example of insouciance.

Three passages dealing with the contrast between knowledge of trades and knowledge of higher values do entail that an Assembly containing all sorts of people (including tradesmen) must contain some who are not qualified to judge according to proper moral or intellectual values (*Mem.* 1.2.37, 4.2.22, 4.5–6). That inference is not spelled out, but in 3.7.5–6 we find something similar: here the Assembly contains fullers, cobblers, carpenters, smiths, farmers, merchants, and market traders – people characterized as "very foolish and very weak." This is both a more extreme claim than is entailed in the other passages about tradesmen (which do not accuse them of extreme stupidity or feebleness) and a less extreme claim because the weakness of fullers and others is that they have never paid heed to politics, not that they do not know about justice or what is *kalonkagathon*. Perhaps we should not make too much of these distinctions (4.2.22 does call tradesmen "slavish"; and for Socrates politics properly conceived includes broader moral understanding), but we should note that 3.7.5–6 inhabits a particular rhetorical context. In questioning Charmides' unwillingness to address the Assembly, Socrates exaggerates both the foolishness of ordinary Assembly members and the cleverness of the politicians among whom Charmides feels at home – and echoes the terms in which someone like Charmides might actually see the Assembly. We should not forget that, although Arginusae showed the Assembly in a bad light (*Mem.* 4.1.2, *Hell.* 1.7.1–35), Socrates accepts that it *can* follow wise advice when legislating (*Ap.* 20), expose incompetent speakers to deserved derision (*Mem.* 3.6.1), and elect appropriate generals (3.4.1–12). And Socrates is right that, in a democratic state, a political mover and shaker must engage with the Assembly: Charmides' attitude is wrong and (in retrospect) sinister. But, again, Socrates' way of arguing the point makes no concessions.

Allotment and the citizen Assembly are objective constitutional features. Other passages evoke criticism of the way institutions actually operate. Two are relatively unimportant (*Smp.* 5.9, *Mem.* 4.4.4), though the latter does charmingly imply that Socrates was *so* law-abiding he even refused to break laws that did not exist. More interesting are broader suggestions of institutionalized hostility to the rich. This is expressed most fully by Charmides in *Symposium* 4.30–4, a bravura contrast between the disadvantages of wealth in democratic Athens and the empowering freedom that comes from impoverishment. But the critical effect is substantially undermined by his ready admission that, given the chance to be rich again, he would probably take it. Are things different in any of the other passages in which elements of Charmides' denunciation recur?

I think not. Socrates' description of Critobulus' predicament over liturgies (*Oec.* 2.6–8) simply (and good-humoredly) echoes the negative terms that Critobulus might use in order to make the paradoxical claim Socrates is the richer of the two. Ischomachus and Crito complain of sycophancy but each has found a solution, Ischomachus in private practice of skills that allow him to resist (*Oec.* 11.21–5), Crito in a relationship with someone (Archedemus) who can defend him (*Mem.* 2.9.1–8). Each uses the weapons of democratic society against a problem created by democratic society. There *are* oddities here: Ischomachus is sometimes convicted before the court of his wife because he cannot make the weaker argument appear the stronger; and the picture of Archedemus as a poor but honest client sits ill with the little else that we know about him.[48] Such are the ironies of the strange version of fifth-century Athens seen in Socratic literature. But the underlying message is that, confronted with a problem, you should address it, not simply complain. This matches the message to Charmides (you must engage with the system) and the message of *Memorabilia* 1.2.9 (disapproval of allotment is no excuse for violence).

A similar thing recurs in some analogies for the comparison of democracy and tyranny encountered in *Symposium* 4.32. In *Memorabilia*

---

[48] Nails 2002: 41–2.

2.1.8 and *Symposium* 4.45 Socrates' response to people drawing that comparison is that they should just live with it: Aristippus' systematic self-deracination is rejected (dissociation from the city state is neither realistic nor proper) and Callias is told to engage in (democratic) politics. In *Memorabilia* 4.2.39, by contrast, an association of tyrant and pauper represents a dialectic impasse whence Euthydemus departs dejected. It is doubtless true that tyrants are driven to crime by (perceived) poverty, and readers of *Poroi* discover that democratic leaders pose as victims of the same phenomenon. But the present passage is more interested in paradox than critique of democracy. But the most interesting salient passage is undoubtedly the dialogue between Pericles and Alcibiades about law in *Memorabilia* 1.2.40–6 – salient because of its suggestion that the masses impose "law" on property owners by power rather than persuasion, and interesting – indeed captivating (it is one of Xenophon's deftest literary creations) – because of the spectacle of the iconic democratic leader worsted and lightly mocked by the clever upstart.

What matters is whether Alcibiades' view of law as a violent imposition upon the rich is seen as valid. Fine scholars have answered in the affirmative.[49] But it seems clear to me that Xenophon could never have put this vignette where he does (a defense of Socrates against criticism engendered by his association with Critias and Alcibiades) with the intention that Alcibiades' view be thought acceptable. Even if it is theoretically possible that Xenophon's Socrates agreed with Alcibiades, that theoretical possibility remains unarticulated elsewhere, and it would ruin Xenophon's defense of Socrates for Alcibiades to be articulating it on Socrates' behalf here – or indeed on Xenophon's behalf. Because the purpose of *Memorabilia* 1.2.12–47 is to preserve Socrates from guilt by association with Alcibiades, the Pericles conversation must illustrate Alcibiades' dissociation from him; and it *can* do so, both because Alcibiades (it is suggested) was using commonplace and long-established "sophistic" reasoning (not something learned from Socrates) and because 1.2.47 explicitly makes the story exemplify the belief of Critias and Alcibiades that they were "better than the politicians" – the belief that resulted in their leaving Socrates and engaging in politics (their ultimate aim from the outset). Alcibiades' youth ("not yet twenty") signifies not that he has not yet started associating with Socrates[50] but that his dissociation set in very early.

In short, elite complaints about the democratic environment were natural in the fictive historical environment of Socratic literature, but Xenophon's

---

[49] Danzig 2014c. Contrast Sanders 2011, Dorion 2000: clx–clxix.
[50] *pace* Sanders 2011: 351–5.

Socrates does not endorse them. But it must be conceded (and it applies to the Pericles-Alcibiades dialogue too because of its literary elegance) that Xenophon does not hide the criticisms and that Socrates' way of not endorsing them does not amount to trenchant refutation.

In his use of Socrates, then, Xenophon articulates a moral-political posture that can coexist with democracy. And in *Memorabilia* 3.1–7 he provides an unusually rich treatment of the qualities required for political leadership in an institutionally Athenian context. Throughout there is a presumption that the system can work well if people of appropriate quality serve it. But there is also a recognition that some who aspire to do so fail to grasp what is required or (as with the younger Pericles) are unconvinced of their capacity to make a beneficial impact. That Socrates is optimistic and the son of the great Pericles pessimistic is a sobering spectacle; and what we know of his fate (and that of Charmides, the subject of 3.7) does not make it less sobering. The provocative association of Funeral Oration clichés with recommendation of the Spartan model, the observation that ordinary Athenians and the Areopagus are more disciplined than the hoplites and cavalry, and the eventual assimilation of Athenians to Mysians or Pisidians enhance the sense of dislocation. The message of *Memorabilia* 3.1–7 is that Athens has potential, but its realization is elusive. Here, too, the democratic setting is a given, but it is not promoted as a good in itself or an answer by itself; and that pretty much goes for Xenophon's attitude throughout the oeuvre.

Conclusion

Xenophon's expatriate experiences are an important part of the mix – they gave critical distance and enabled unconventional views.[51] But he remained a loyal Athenian – the judgment of a modern historian not noted for swallowing ancient imposture[52] – and, whatever conclusions we might reach about the practical impact of Xenophon's ideas on cavalry command or economics or about his interactions with Academics, sophists, and Isocrateans, it is certain that he made a substantial contribution to the perception of Athens as the intellectual centre of Classical and post-Classical Greece.

---

[51] Greater interest in personal leadership than constitutional systems (Azoulay 2004a: 435); unconventional attitudes to women (Azoulay 2007b), slavery (Jansen 2012: 734), and status distinctions in general (*ibid.* 754).
[52] Badian 2004: 33.

Further Reading

Xenophon's Athenian identity, rarely addressed as such, may be pursued indirectly in many publications. *General*: Higgins 1977, Gray 1989, Tuplin 1993, Dillery 1995, Tuplin 2004a, Azoulay 2004a, Gish and Ambler 2009, Gray 2010a, Gray 2011, Hobden and Tuplin 2012a, Pontier 2014. *Socratic works*: Gray 1998, Huss 1999b, Dorion 2000, Danzig 2010, Danzig and Alon (forthcoming). *Poroi*: Gauthier 1984/2010, Jansen 2012. *Hipparchicus*: Petrocelli 2001, Dillery 2004.

18

KOSTAS VLASSOPOULOS

Xenophon on Persia

Persia looms large in Xenophon's biography. In 401 BC the young Athenian Xenophon took the momentous decision to leave his country, recently restored to a democratic regime, and accept the invitation of his Boeotian friend Proxenus, who was recruiting mercenaries for the Persian prince Cyrus, then overlord of the Persian provinces of western Asia Minor. The result was Xenophon's participation in Cyrus' expedition to overthrow his brother, Artaxerxes II, and claim the throne. The expedition proved ultimately a failure in the Mesopotamian battlefield of Cunaxa, and Xenophon and the Ten Thousand Greeks who had accompanied Cyrus found themselves encircled by the victorious Persian forces; despite overwhelming odds, they managed to escape the Persian attacks into mountainous eastern Asia Minor and reach the Black Sea, from which they ultimately returned to the Aegean. After various travails, they ended up enlisting as part of a Spartan expeditionary force in Asia Minor, battling against the satraps of Artaxerxes II, and ultimately returning to mainland Greece, where Xenophon fought with the Spartans against a Persian-backed Greek alliance that included Athens. Accordingly, Xenophon spent years of his life fighting with and against Persians and traversed a significant part of the huge Persian Empire.[1]

But Persia plays an equally important part in Xenophon's oeuvre; Persia is the dominant theme in the *Anabasis* and the *Cyropaedia*; it plays a major role in the *Hellenica* and *Agesilaus* and has a considerable presence in the *Memorabilia* and the *Oeconomicus*; it is thus only in the minor treatises that Persia plays a negligible role. Given this importance, discussion has traditionally focused on the twin topics of how trustworthy is Xenophon as a source for the history of Persia and on Xenophon's attitude towards Persia. Scholarly attitudes range from those that consider the *Cyropaedia* as an Orientalist fantasy with little connection to "real" Persia, to those who accept Xenophon as an accurate source on Persian affairs; and from those

[1] Lane Fox 2004; Tuplin 2007b.

360

that see his works shaped by a Panhellenist perspective to those who argue that Xenophon presents a largely positive image of Persia and Persians.[2] While important, these questions can only be answered within a wider framework from that usually adopted.

We need first to divest ourselves from adherence to a simplistic distinction between Greeks and Persians. In order to understand the diverse encounters and interactions between Greeks and Persians that are represented in Xenophon's works, we need to situate them within four parallel but interconnected worlds: the world of networks; the world of *apoikiai* (colonies); the Panhellenic world; and the world of empires.[3] The world of networks moved people, goods, ideas, and technologies across the Mediterranean and beyond.[4] Xenophon rarely comments explicitly on the processes of this world, but his works contain numerous vignettes. As regards the mobility of merchants and sailors, we come across the Syracusan Herodas, who sails to Phoenicia with a ship owner, observes the Phoenician warships prepared for the Persian counterattack in the Aegean, and reports it to the Spartan authorities,[5] or the immense Phoenician ship that arrives in Piraeus and whose meticulous organization so impresses Socrates, who engages in conversation with the Phoenician sailors.[6] The mobility of goods is represented by Persian items like the drinking cups of Pharnabazus captured by the Spartan army,[7] the camels that Agesilaus captures from the Persians at Sardis and brings to Greece (396/5 BC)[8], the Persian clothes and golden coins (darics) that the Greek army gives to a guide in western Anatolia,[9] or the Persian drinking cups and carpets that a Greek general donates to the Thracian prince Seuthes.[10] Less important for our subject here is the second world of *apoikiai*, which perennially hovered between the tendency to create frontier societies through interaction between Greeks and various non-Greeks, and the tendency to create communities which stressed their Greek identity.[11] We come across the mixed Graeco-Carian communities attacked by Lysander,[12] the relationship between Trapezus and Cerasus and their

---

[2] Momigliano 1975: 132–7; Hirsch 1985: 61–97; Gera 1993: 13–22; Georges 1994: 207–43; Tuplin 1996; Sancisi-Weerdenburg 1985/2010; Gruen 2011: 53–65.
[3] For such an approach, see Vlassopoulos 2013a: 11–19.
[4] Vlassopoulos 2013a: 85–94.
[5] *Hellenica* 3.4.1.
[6] *Oeconomicus* 8.11.
[7] *Hellenica* 4.1.24.
[8] *Hellenica* 3.4.24.
[9] *Anabasis* 4.7.27.
[10] *Anabasis* 7.3.18.
[11] Vlassopoulos 2013a: 102–28.
[12] *Hellenica* 2.1.15.

neighboring non-Greek communities,[13] or between Greek *apoikiai* in the Black Sea and Thrace and Paphlagonian and Thracian kings, respectively.[14]

The Panhellenic world was characterized by a number of peculiarities.[15] Greek-speaking communities were scattered all over the Mediterranean, and they never achieved political, economic, or social unity; even their cultural unity was not centered on a dominant institution. Because it lacked a center, the Panhellenic world could exist only through a combination of various discordant elements.[16] Until the Persian Wars, the Panhellenic world consisted of diverse communities whose unity was maintained by a literature based on Panhellenic myth and written in shared literary dialects, and by Panhellenic shrines and festivals. The Panhellenic community existed in the distant past, when heroes from all over Greece had joined together on expeditions like that against Troy, and in a separate present, when Greeks joined together to worship the gods and participate in games. By linking the heroic past with the present, the Persian Wars had brought into existence a third level of the Panhellenic world, as a political community united into a common purpose: the fight against a common enemy. The memory of the Persian Wars is unsurprisingly significant in Xenophon's oeuvre: it is, for example, employed in Xenophon's speech to the Ten Thousand to raise their spirits.[17] Agesilaus' campaign in support of the Greek poleis in Asia Minor employs the mythical past as a means of giving meaning to the present: Agesilaus' wish to sacrifice at Aulis before embarking for Asia, in imitation of Agamemnon, was intended to assimilate the Persians to the Trojans and portray the campaign within a series of glorious struggles between the Greeks and their enemies.[18] Xenophon portrays Agesilaus' aims as protecting the Greeks of Asia Minor, avenging the Persian crimes of the Persian Wars, and subduing Asia.[19]

The problem was that this Panhellenic community was a project and not a given; the Greek world lacked a center and was perennially ravaged by hostilities among its members. As at Troy under Agamemnon, or during the Persian Wars under Sparta, its unity and common action were impossible without a leader. Given the ambitions of Greek states, it was always possible to exploit the Panhellenic project as a means of achieving hegemony over the Greek world; equally, every Panhellenic project was likely

---

[13] *Anabasis* 5.2.2; 5.4.1.
[14] *Anabasis* 5.6.11; 7.4.1.
[15] Vlassopoulos 2013a: 34–41.
[16] Malkin 2011: 3–15.
[17] *Anabasis* 3.2.11–3; Dillery 1995: 41–98.
[18] *Hellenica* 3.4.3–4.
[19] *Agesilaus* 1.7–8.

to face opposition from other Greek states.[20] This inherent disunity finds copious references in Xenophon's work: a characteristic example takes place when the Ten Thousand reach Cotyora, and each ethnic contingent in the Greek army performs their own religious procession.[21] This inherent disunity allowed Persia to play a fundamental role in Greek politics: the chronic conflicts between Greek polities and their limited resources created an opening in which Greek polities sought Persian military and financial resources in order to overcome their opponents and ensure their hegemony. The King's Peace of 387/6 BC defined the role of Persia as arbitrator of Greek affairs for the next half century.[22] This continuous Persian intervention in Greek affairs is amply documented by Xenophon: Pharnabazus sending Timocrates of Rhodes to bribe Greek politicians into creating an anti-Spartan alliance;[23] Philiscus of Abydus convening a conference of Greek states at the Panhellenic center of Delphi to negotiate peace in terms favorable to his employer, the satrap Ariobarzanes;[24] or the embassies of Greek polities at the court at Susa, vying with each other to secure Persian support for their own projects.[25]

The world of empires presented a different arena of interactions between Greeks and Persians.[26] The military confrontations, the diplomatic negotiations, and the political interventions between these empires and the Greeks shaped Greek history in important ways. Xenophon's oeuvre allows us to observe a series of complex political-military triangulations between Greeks, Persians, and other non-Greeks.[27] We come across Greek polities supporting rebel Persians, like the Spartan support for Cyrus the Younger,[28] or Agesilaus' fighting alongside the rebel satrap Ariobarzanes against loyal Persian forces;[29] Greek states allying with non-Greek polities who had rebelled from Persia, like Agesilaus' support for the rebel province of Egypt;[30] rebel Persians allying with non-Greek and Greek polities, like Agesilaus' brokerage of a marriage alliance between the Persian rebel Spithridates and the Paphlagonian king Otys.[31]

---

[20] Mitchell 2007: 77–104, 169–94.
[21] *Anabasis* 5.5.5.
[22] *Hellenica* 5.1.31.
[23] *Hellenica* 3.5.1.
[24] *Hellenica* 7.1.27.
[25] *Hellenica* 7.1.33–7.
[26] Vlassopoulos 2013a: 41–52.
[27] Cartledge 1987: 324–30.
[28] *Hellenica* 3.1.1–2.
[29] *Agesilaus* 2.26.
[30] *Agesilaus* 2.28.
[31] *Hellenica* 4.1.3.

But equally important were the enormous manpower needs of these empires: thousands of Greeks and non-Greeks entered the service of these empires in one capacity or another. The majority were of course Greek mercenaries serving Persian kings and satraps. The *Anabasis* is a book devoted to these people, their stories, and motives: Xenophon argues that the promise of his friend Proxenus to introduce him to Cyrus, whose friendship would prove more important than Xenophon's country, was his main motive for joining the campaign.[32] Xenophon presents an impressive panorama of other Greeks employed by the Persians: the doctor Ctesias of Cnidus, who was physician of Artaxerxes II and took care of his wound at the battle of Cunaxa;[33] the military expert Phalinus, serving with the Persian satrap Tissaphernes;[34] the Greek-speaking secretary who translates to the Great King the comments uttered by Leon the Athenian in the king's presence;[35] the wise men that are carried off as slaves to the king's court;[36] or the Greek concubines in Persian courts, like the Milesian and Phocaean concubines of Cyrus the Younger.[37]

We also come across a number of Greeks ruling communities in the western coast of Asia Minor as vassals of Persia. Xenophon presents in detail the case of Mania, the wife of Zenis of Dardanus; when Zenis died, she managed to convince the Persian satrap Pharnabazus to allow her to succeed her husband as ruler of Aeolis. Xenophon describes how she collected taxes from the Greek cities, sent tribute and gifts to Pharnabazus, and hired mercenaries to attack Greek cities and participate in Pharnabazus' campaigns.[38] Another example concerns Hellas, whom Xenophon met at Pergamum, who was the scion of an Eretrian family who had sided with the Persians in the Persian Wars and had been given four cities to rule in the Troad as a gift.[39] But we also get glimpses of the non-Greek imperial diaspora serving the Persian Empire. Many Persians and other Iranians migrated and settled in Asia Minor, along with other ethnic groups;[40] Xenophon mentions Egyptian settlers in Aeolic Larissa and Cyme,[41] but the most characteristic example is the Persian noble Asidates, who lived in a fortified residence along with his

---

[32] *Anabasis* 3.1.4.
[33] *Anabasis* 1.8.27.
[34] *Anabasis* 2.1.7.
[35] *Hellenica* 7.1.37.
[36] *Memorabilia* 4.2.34.
[37] *Anabasis* 1.10.3.
[38] *Hellenica* 3.1.10–14.
[39] *Anabasis* 7.8.8; *Hellenica* 3.1.6.
[40] Sekunda 1988.
[41] *Cyropaedia* 7.1.45.

family and hundreds of slaves near Pergamon in Asia Minor, alongside other Persians, Syrian infantrymen, and Hyrcanian cavalrymen.[42]

These four parallel worlds engendered a range of interactions and encounters between Greeks and Persians; these were based on practices of intercultural communication for which Xenophon's works provide ample documentation.[43] We come across translators mastering two or more languages, who mediate between Greeks and Persians, such as the Carian Pigres who acted as translator for Cyrus the Younger,[44] the Persian Pategyas, who announces to the soldiers in both Greek and Persian the coming of the king's army,[45] or the translator in the army of the Ten Thousand who mediated between the Greeks and the Armenians in Persian.[46] Intercultural communication was also fostered by ritualized practices, like that of guest friendship (*xenia*).[47] Xenophon mentions various guest friendships between Greeks and Persians: between the satrap Ariobarzanes and the Spartan Antalcidas,[48] or that between the Thessalian Meno and Ariaeus.[49] Finally, we should emphasize the significance of cults and the participation in rituals and festivals. The cult of Artemis of Ephesus, whose chief priest bore the Persian name Megabyzus,[50] was popular among Greeks and Persians, as well as the neighboring Lydians.[51] Xenophon's attachment to Ephesian Artemis is immortalized in his description of the sanctuary and temple he dedicated to the deity in his retirement at Scillus;[52] but equally significant is the attachment of Persian grandees, as seen in Tissaphernes' rally to protect Ephesian Artemis from Athenian depredations.[53]

We have examined above the diverse interactions and encounters in the four parallel worlds and the practices of intercultural communication. One of their major results is the generation and circulation of ethnographic observation and knowledge; the casual employment of this ethnographic knowledge in Xenophon's oeuvre is truly striking. The Xenophontic Socrates casually employs the Persian Empire and its king as an example: the need for the master to personally supervise his dependents is illustrated with a story

---

[42] *Anabasis* 7.8.8–24.
[43] Vlassopoulos 2013a: 129–60.
[44] *Anabasis* 1.2.17.
[45] *Anabasis* 1.8.1.
[46] *Anabasis* 4.5.34.
[47] Mitchell 1997: 111–34.
[48] *Hellenica* 5.1.28.
[49] *Anabasis* 2.1.6.
[50] *Anabasis* 5.3.6.
[51] *Anabasis* 1.1.6.
[52] *Anabasis* 5.3.4–13; Tuplin 2004c.
[53] *Hellenica* 1.2.6.

about how the king sought advice to properly fatten his horse;[54] the argument that the rulers live a pleasanter life than the ruled is illustrated through the example of Persian rule over Syrians, Lydians, and Phrygians;[55] the protection afforded by high mountains and narrow passes is illustrated by the example of how the mountainous Mysians and Pisidians attack unharmed the king's land.[56] An equally illuminating example is a conversation between Polydamas of Pharsalos and the Thessalian tyrant Jason. In an attempt to convince Polydamas to ally with him, Jason tries to impress him with the size of his resources by claiming that the resources he would command from the Thessalians and their mainland subjects would be far superior to those Athens draws from its naval empire; Jason supports his claim by arguing that the immense wealth of the Persian king is drawn from mainland communities, rather than islanders. If this image of Persian wealth is used to support Jason's plans, in the very next sentence he argues that it is easy to subdue the Persian Empire due to its weakness, and uses the example of the successful campaigns of the Ten Thousand and Agesilaus to illustrate it.[57]

Equally important is the incorporation of the ethnographic knowledge within stories which allude to or focus on the context of interactions and encounters within which the knowledge is generated. One such illustration is Xenophon's description of the report of the Arcadian ambassador to the Persian court made to the Arcadian assembly. In order to justify his policy of rejecting siding with Persia, the ambassador finds it useful to employ ethnographic evidence in order to argue that the king lacks sufficient military forces and wealth: the king is presented as having many bakers, cooks, and wine pourers but hardly any soldiers. But equally important is to respond to the audience's ethnographic knowledge, by claiming that the king's golden plane tree, a famous example of the king's wealth, was so small it could hardly provide shade for a grasshopper: clearly, the king's wealth was not as extensive as imagined.[58] An equally characteristic example appears in the context of a discussion between Socrates and Critobulus on ideal household management. Trying to convince Critobulus about the significance of agriculture, Socrates narrates a story about a meeting in Sardis between the Spartan commander Lysander and Cyrus the Younger; impressed with the beauty of the trees in Cyrus' *paradeisos*, Lysander is surprised when Cyrus reveals that he has planted them himself, because of Cyrus' fine and luxurious clothes and ornaments.[59]

[54] *Oeconomicus* 12.20.
[55] *Memorabilia* 2.1.10.
[56] *Memorabilia* 3.5.26.
[57] *Hellenica* 6.1.12.
[58] *Hellenica* 7.1.38.
[59] *Oeconomicus* 4.20–5.

If even a luxurious Persian prince pays attention to agriculture, Socrates argues, its significance should be obvious to everybody.

These examples of casual employment are indications of a wider phenomenon: the textualization of intercultural encounters in Greek literature and its deep impact on Greek culture.[60] We have no reason to doubt that ethnographic practice by everyday people was a common occurrence among most communities in the wider Mediterranean and Near Eastern world. There should be no doubt that Persians, Thracians, Carians, or Babylonians participated in intercultural communication and reflected on it as much as the Greeks. This was a primarily oral universe in which countless stories, customs, information, and ideas endlessly circulated. The Greek peculiarity was the textualization of this oral universe through the development of literary genres which were based on the encounters and interactions of the four parallel worlds and the processes of intercultural communication.

Perhaps the quintessential example of this textualization of intercultural encounters is one of Xenophon's most famous works: the *Anabasis* is the textualization of the intercultural encounters between a force of primarily Greek mercenaries, the Persian Empire, and various other Greek and non-Greek communities and individuals. It gives an account of the everyday experiences of the Greek mercenaries on the march; it includes accounts of battles, marches, ambushes, and looting against and with non-Greeks, diplomatic negotiations, drinking, eating, and dancing with non-Greeks, as well as ethnographic observations on the foreign landscapes and the customs of the people encountered.[61] But the *Anabasis* is not merely a piece of reportage; Xenophon liked to experiment by incorporating within one work elements from different genres, and the *Anabasis* combines historiography, ethnography, and military treatise.[62] The *Anabasis* is Xenophon's exploration of what it means to be a leader of men; it reworks the interactions in the four parallel worlds into a concrete illustration of the qualities needed in ruling soldiers, motivating comrades, persuading audiences, taking the initiative, creating and maintaining friendships, conducting diplomacy, and surviving in extreme circumstances.

The textualization of intercultural encounters is also manifest in Xenophon's other great Persian-related work, the *Cyropaedia*.[63] This is a work which examines the education of an individual in the art of ruling through a narrative of the life of Cyrus the Great, the creator of the Persian Empire. The *Cyropaedia* mixes together historiography, biography,

---

[60] Vlassopoulos 2013a: 179–86.
[61] Briant 1995; Lendle 1995; Lane Fox 2004; Lee 2007.
[62] Flower 2012.
[63] Due 1989; Tatum 1989; Gera 1993; Gray 2011.

ethnography, political utopia, philosophical dialogue, technical writing, and novella. There are good reasons to believe that, as Xenophon explicitly claims, various Persian stories and songs about Cyrus have been reworked and reframed within the structure and aims of the work.[64] Particularly interesting is a series of novellas which Xenophon craftily interspersed through the main narrative of the story, the tragic love story of Pantheia and Abradatas being the most famous of them. Novellas concerning court or love stories were particularly prominent in the eastern Mediterranean and beyond, but hardly developed in Greek culture, where the dominant role of myth had incorporated novelistic elements within mythical narratives; Xenophon reworks them into an exploration of the relationship between politics, education, and morality.[65]

This textualization of intercultural encounters can be seen through two different spectra: one according to content, and one according to perspective.[66] The spectrum of content can range from stories that take as their subject issues that focus either on the differences between Greeks and Persians (polarity), or on common, shared, or universal values and ideas (universality). As regards perspective, stories can be seen from either a Greek perspective (*interpretatio graeca*) or from a Persian perspective (*interpretatio persica*). In other words, stories can either try to translate the customs, values, and history of one community in terms understandable by another (i.e. the Greeks in the case of Xenophon), or explain them in terms native to the community from which the stories originate (the Persians).

It is easy to find stories in Xenophon that stress polarity. An illuminating example is the story of Agesilaus' decision to expose naked the Persians who were captured in the course of his expedition in Asia Minor before selling them as slaves. The white skin of the exposed Persians was perceived by Agesilaus' Greek soldiers as evidence of the effeminate luxury of people unaccustomed to toil and convinced them that fighting against the Persians would be an easy task.[67] On the other hand, the Persians can be depicted as fundamentally similar, adhering to the same codes of conduct that Greeks appreciated, or even surpassing them in that respect. Xenophon's eulogy of Cyrus the Younger is a revealing example of how a Persian prince can be presented as an ideal version of a Greek gentleman. Xenophon places a great deal of emphasis on the various ways in which Cyrus cultivated the friendship of his associates and inferiors: his reputation for trustworthiness, his repayment of favors, his honoring of people for their acts or character,

[64] Tuplin 1996.
[65] Gera 1993: 192–279.
[66] For a similar approach to Herodotus, see Vlassopoulos 2013b.
[67] *Hellenica* 3.4.19.

his taking care of his friends, his generosity.[68] It is hardly accidental that these same aspects feature so prominently in the various pieces of advice given by Socrates to his Athenian interlocutors about how to create and maintain relationships of friendship, as presented in the *Memorabilia*.[69]

As regards perspective, Xenophon commonly chooses to present and interpret Persia from a Greek point of view.[70] This is best reflected in *Cyropaedia*'s description of Persian society before Cyrus' rise to power and his creation of an imperial polity. Although Xenophon points out a number of peculiar Persian institutions and practices, they are presented within an overall framework in which Persian society is effectively assimilated to that of a Greek polis. Peculiar Persian institutions like the Persian state-organized educational system, the dissociation between politics and economic activities, the division of Persians into mass and elite, are represented in a thoroughly Greek framework;[71] but although Greek polities like Sparta provide analogies that make the early Persian society of the *Cyropaedia* comprehensible to a Greek audience, overall Xenophon is careful to avoid any direct conflation between Sparta and Persia.[72]

Xenophon is equally capable of presenting things from the Persian point of view. A characteristic example is the episode between Agesilaus and Megabates, the son of the Persian grandee Spithridates, who had seceded from the Persian side to Agesilaus. Xenophon explains how Megabates attempts to kiss Agesilaus on the lips, following the Persian custom in which a kiss is a sign of honor; but Agesilaus interprets it as a sign of sexual advance and resists it out of moderation.[73] Another example is Tissaphernes' cunning employment of Persian ethnography in his reply to the offer of the Greek generals to use the Ten Thousand in future Persian campaigns; while only the king might wear the tiara upright on his head, with the support of the Ten Thousand someone else might so wear the crown that is in his heart. Tissaphernes' statement may have deceived Clearchus into believing that Tissaphernes would attempt to seize the throne and thus make Clearchus think that he would accept the Greek offer.[74]

More generally, Xenophon can choose whether his depictions of Persians are ethnographically informed and colored in detail, whether they are based on a few general clichés, or whether Persians are depicted without

---

[68] *Anabasis* 1.9.7–28.
[69] Gray 2011: 7–25.
[70] Sancisi-Weerdenburg 1985/2010: 450–1.
[71] *Cyropaedia* 1.2; Tuplin 1996:135–44.
[72] Tuplin 1994.
[73] *Agesilaus* 5.4; Pontier 2012.
[74] *Anabasis* 2.5.22–3; Tuplin 2007c.

any ethnographic coloring and as basically similar to any other people, or more specifically the Greeks.[75] There is abundant ethnographic detail when Xenophon chooses to provide it: an excellent example is the scene in which the judges vote to condemn the accused Persian Orontas by successively seizing his belt, while those Persians who used to pay homage to Orontas continue to do so as he is led to his death.[76] Xenophon here chooses to capture both a specific Persian ritual and the importance of paying proper respect to grandees in Persian society.[77] On the other hand, the ethnographic detail in Xenophon's depiction of Persian society in the *Cyropaedia* is very severely limited, even in comparison with other Greek accounts of Persian society.[78] Despite the significant differences between Greek and Persian religion, Xenophon chooses to elide them: Artabazus' swearing by the name of Mithras is one among a tiny number of occasions of ethnographic detail.[79] The obvious conclusion is that we need to credit Xenophon with sufficient sophistication in his decisions how to depict Persians; his Persian depictions largely depend on the context and the aims that they serve.

Xenophon is equally able to present diverse positions within the two spectra of content and perspective. The image of the Persian king that can be found in Xenophontic texts can range very widely. On the one hand, we can find the image presented in the *Oeconomicus*, where the king is a model ruler who takes a series of concerted measures both to ensure that his subordinates take proper care of military issues as well as for the advancement of agriculture.[80] On the other hand, the image is completely reversed in Xenophon's comparison between the Spartan king Agesilaus and the Persian king; the Great King is described as unapproachable, avoiding toil and living in laziness and luxury, in stark contrast to Agesilaus who lives simply.[81] In between, one can find *Cyropaedia*'s image of Persian kingship devised by Cyrus in the aftermath of his creation of the Persian Empire.[82] Many elements used by Greek authors to castigate the Persian king are here reinterpreted and valued as means towards achieving the loyalty and obedience of the king's subjects: the lack of approachability becomes the means of honoring the king's friends who act as intercessors;[83] ostentatious eating becomes

---

[75] Tuplin 2010.
[76] *Anabasis* 1.6.10.
[77] Herodotus 1.134; Briant 2002: 334–6.
[78] Tuplin 1990.
[79] *Cyropaedia* 7.5.54.
[80] *Oecomonicus* 4.1–17; Briant 2002: 232–40.
[81] *Agesilaus* 9.
[82] Breebaart 1983; Azoulay 2004b; Danzig 2012.
[83] 7.5.45.

a mean of honoring friends with food portions;[84] luxurious clothing and make-up are seen as essential elements for creating imperial majesty;[85] while the employment of eunuchs is reinterpreted as a wise employment of trusted servants.[86]

Finally, all these positions can be combined, or reinterpreted, in an ironic way. If the distinction between Greek freedom and Persian despotism is indicative of the polarity end of the content spectrum, the presentation of the Persian prince Cyrus giving a speech to the Greek mercenary leaders in which he extolls and envies Greek freedom unsettles polarity: are we meant to see Cyrus cleverly manipulating the sensibilities of his Greek audience, or should we see Cyrus as an example of how a great Persian prince could overcome the dividing lines of polarity?[87] Equally interesting is the episode of the meeting between Agesilaus and the Persian satrap Pharnabazus. The episode starts with a scene in which the Spartan simplicity of Agesilaus' entourage, who sit on the ground, is contrasted with the effeminate luxury of the Persian embassy of Pharnabazus, who is about to sit on soft rugs. Xenophon describes how Pharnabazus notices the difference and chooses to accommodate to the Greek custom, by stopping his servants from setting the rugs and by sitting on the ground.[88] The episode continues with a debate on the common link of guest friendship. Pharnabazus complains that the Spartans and Agesilaus have attacked his lands, despite the fact that they had been friends ever since the time they were fighting together against the Athenians; to which Agesilaus responds that in the Greek world bonds of guest friendship between people belonging to different poleis do not stop them from fighting against each other when their communities are at war. This debate on ethnographic difference is followed by the description of the ritual that establishes a new guest friendship between Agesilaus and Pharnabazus' son through the exchange of gifts, and how the relationship lasted for a long time.[89]

The result of this skillful complexity is that Xenophon is able to present and employ Persia in the most diverse ways, depending on his aim and context. It is possible to present the Persians as the polar opposite of everything the Greeks valued as important; but it is equally possible to employ Persian alterity as a positive model of emulation for various aspects of Greek society that Xenophon considers inferior. It is also possible to present Persians at

---

[84] 8.2.2–4.
[85] 8.1.40–1.
[86] 7.5.59–65; Azoulay 2004c.
[87] *Anabasis* 1.7.3.
[88] Tuplin 2010: 201.
[89] *Hellenica* 4.1.30–40.

any point of the spectrum between completely alien and totally assimilated; and, in fact, one of the most fascinating aspects of Xenophon's approach is the way he employs various techniques for keeping the Persians both alien and similar, both appreciated and despised.

The *Cyropaedia* is a remarkable example of these techniques, which has often baffled readers with its complexity.[90] The Persian Empire presented the Greeks with a series of problems of how to fit it within their discursive frameworks. Persia was a mountainous and harsh country, which, according to a standard topos of Greek anthropology, should produce stout and brave warriors.[91] The Persian Empire was unfathomable in size and, despite a series of revolts and secessions, lasted without any serious challenge for over two hundred years; countless Greeks and other non-Persians served and benefited from it. On the other hand, the Persian political system could be seen as Oriental despotism, while the Persian lifestyle could be described in terms of luxury and effeminacy. The paradox inherent in these contradictory depictions of Persians becomes visible in Xenophon's admiring description of how Cyrus the Younger's Persian associates, while dressed in fine robes, drop to the mudded ground to dislodge some trapped wagons.[92]

How to combine the irreconcilable images of a mountainous land of brave warriors with that of an effeminate luxurious society? How to combine admiration for the creation and maintenance of such a great empire with contempt for its political structure?[93] Xenophon solves the problem by creating a disjuncture between an early Persia largely presented as a virtuous Greek polis and a Media shaped by despotism and luxurious effeminacy. Cyrus the Great's imperial polity combines elements from both models, by using the court rituals and luxurious practices of Media in order to control Cyrus' subjects and make them obedient, and by maintaining the moral rectitude of early Persia in order to put Median luxury and court ritual to proper use. Equally, the presentation of Cyrus as an admirable empire creator can be squared with contemporary negative Greek reactions to Persia by creating a temporal disjuncture between Persia of Cyrus' time, a middle horizon in which Cyrus' reforms are still present "up to the present time," proving their success and durability, and the contemporary Persia, as described in the acerbic epilogue (8.8) to the *Cyropaedia*, in which Cyrus' system has been perverted or abandoned.[94]

[90] Due 1989: 16–22; Tatum 1989: 215–39; Johnson 2005b.
[91] Herodotus 9.122.
[92] *Anabasis* 1.5.8.
[93] Tuplin 2013.
[94] Gray 2011: 246–63.

Let us finally explore the major contexts in which Persia figures in the words of Xenophon: we shall focus on three major quests of Greek political, moral, and philosophical discourses.[95] A first quest concerns identity and morality. We have commented above how the discourse of the Panhellenic community was one among the various levels of the Panhellenic world. In that respect, opposition to Persia provided a pole that could unify the disparate poleis and their divergent strategies. Even more, polarity could create an image of Barbarian Other that could serve as a mirror for defining Greek identity.[96] We have seen above how the exposed bodies of Persian captives illustrate the polarity between Persian effeminacy and Greek virility, as well as the lists of negative depictions of Persians as luxurious, effeminate, and corrupted in the *Agesilaus* and the *Cyropaedia*. So too the polarity between Greek freedom and Persian despotism is continuously employed across a range of works. The Persians are mere slaves to a single despot, and this is why the Ten Thousand come across Persian troops that are urged into battle under the lash.[97] The theme is also employed in the case of the Persian custom of prostration (*proskynesis*) in front of the king; in his exhortation to the Greek troops, Xenophon exalts Greek freedom, which can be seen in the fact that Greeks only prostrate themselves in front of the gods, rather than to a human despot.[98] The same theme is presented in the contemptuous way in which Cyrus treats the Spartan general Callicratidas, who bemoans the fact that Greeks fight against each other and have to toady to the barbarians to find the financial means to do so.[99]

But we also need to pay attention to the context within which this discourse is employed. The *Agesilaus* is undoubtedly Xenophon's text with the most explicit Panhellenic message; and given the recurrent derogatory depictions of Persians in this work, readers might wonder how the anti-Persian views expressed here might fit in with the other depictions of Persians in a very different light. But we need to remember that the *Agesilaus* is an encomium, and the anti-Persian rhetoric serves the aim of focusing attention away from the uncomfortable fact that Agesilaus, as enforcer of the King's Peace for fifteen years, could legitimately be criticized for having betrayed the Greeks of Asia Minor to the Persians and for loyally collaborating with Persian aims.[100] The discourse of Panhellenic identity could be employed to serve certain purposes; but it could be conveniently set aside when other purposes were at the forefront.

---

[95] Vlassopoulos 2013a: 190–206.
[96] Hartog 1988; Hall 1989.
[97] *Anabasis* 3.4.25.
[98] *Anabasis* 3.2.13; Briant 2002: 222–3.
[99] *Hellenica* 1.6.6–7.
[100] Hirsch 1985: 39–60.

A second key quest is the role of law and institutions in shaping the body politic in the best possible or ideal manner. Xenophon is capable of using Persian alterity as a positive model of emulation for his Greek audience. The Persian Empire and its institutions could provide food for thought and practices to be imitated and adapted. Most Greek poleis had no system of public education and left it to individual citizens how to raise their children. For Greek thinkers, the proper organization of the civic body depended on the proper education of its future citizens: accordingly, a system of public education like that of Persia could be used as a model for the ideal state. Xenophon's description of Persian education places its emphasis on physical training to inculcate endurance and the teaching of moral values like justice and self-control.[101] Another important aspect concerns the aims of the legal system. While the laws of the Greek poleis aimed merely to punish those violating the rules, and were thus merely reactive, Persian laws were proactive: they aimed to create citizens whose character would make them refrain from bad acts.[102] Accordingly, Persian laws aimed to reward those actions of their citizens that were meritorious and praiseworthy.[103]

This leads us to a third major quest, which is particularly prominent in the various works of Xenophon: that of the nature and conduct of interpersonal relationships in their various guises (relationships between rulers and ruled, relationships within the household, relationships between friends). The image of the Persian king plays a major role in Xenophon's thinking about these relationships. The first thing to note is the way in which specific Persians can function as role models. This is already evident in the eulogy of Cyrus the Younger in the *Anabasis*, which places great stress on his success in courting allies and friends and maintaining their loyalty and his success in maintaining peace and order in his domains. It becomes the major theme of the *Cyropaedia*: given the obvious difficulties of governing human beings, the career of Cyrus the Great, who created and ruled an immense empire, bequeathed it to his descendants, and was loved by his multinational subjects, becomes an excellent opportunity for exploring the aspects that make ruling over humans possible.[104] In exploring this theme, Xenophon employs various elements. On the one hand, he approaches Persians as exemplifying to a greater extent values and ideals that were inherent in Greek society. Helping friends and harming enemies was a Greek cliché, and Persian kings possessed means beyond the reach of any Greek for benefiting their friends

---

[101] *Cyropaedia* 1.2; Tuplin 1996: 69–95.
[102] *Cyropaedia* 1.2.3.
[103] *Oeconomicus* 14.6–7.
[104] I.I.

and honoring their benefactors.[105] Xenophon emphasizes the way in which Cyrus employed his immense wealth in order to benefit his friends, and the way that he could count on the wealth of his friends.[106] On the other hand, as we have already seen above, Xenophon explores how elements of Persian alterity (lack of approachability, luxurious clothing, eunuchs) could be usefully employed by the ideal ruler to create and maintain relationships.[107] Particularly interesting in this regard is how Xenophon uses Cyrus as a model to think through the similarities and differences between voluntary and involuntary submission of different groups and subjects.[108]

In conclusion: we need to appreciate the complex interactions between Greeks and Persians in the four parallel worlds, which are so visibly depicted in Xenophon's oeuvre, in order to understand the diverse ways in which Persian images are employed by Xenophon. This diversity of images is not peculiar to Xenophon's works, but is one manifestation of how a complex barbarian repertoire is employed across the whole of Greek literature and art in its longue durée. But there is no doubt that the skill with which Xenophon chooses to depict Persians at any point of the spectra of content and perspective testifies to his often unappreciated originality and ingenuity.

Further Reading

Briant 2002 is the best current introduction to the Persian Empire, while Vlassopoulos 2013a explores the manifold interactions between Persia and the Greek world. Hirsch 1985 provides the best book-length discussion of Persia in Xenophon's writings. Briant 1995 and Lane Fox 2004 are excellent collections discussing the Persian entanglements of the *Anabasis*, while Gera 1993 and Gray 2011 do the same for the *Cyropaedia*. Christopher Tuplin's many essays are essential reading for anyone interested in this topic: Tuplin 1990, 1996, and 2013 are the most important.

---

[105] Briant 2002: 302–15.
[106] *Cyropaedia* 8.2.7–23.
[107] Gray 2011: 276–82.
[108] Tamiolaki 2010: 289–369.

19

PAUL CHRISTESEN

Xenophon's Views on Sparta

Introduction: Interpreting Xenophon's Views on Sparta

Xenophon's affection for Sparta ran so deep that he was willing to introduce deliberate distortions into his writings in order to present Sparta and its leaders in a favorable light. Xenophon's ostensible praise for Sparta masks a deep-seated dislike for Sparta and its leaders.

Both of these opinions have been voiced in the modern scholarship on Xenophon's writings. It may seem odd that there could be such fundamental disagreement about the views of an author who wrote at length about Sparta and whose corpus of work survives in its entirety. However, as we shall see, Xenophon's writings present significant interpretive challenges.

Some facets of Xenophon's relationship with Sparta are reasonably clear. Around 400 BC Xenophon, who was born and raised in Athens, joined a group of mercenary soldiers assembled by Cyrus the Younger, a pretender to the throne of Persia. Those soldiers subsequently entered Spartan employ and fought in a series of campaigns against the Persians in Asia Minor. Xenophon occupied important positions of command during that period and seems to have seen much of Agesilaus, the Spartan king who was in control of Spartan forces in Asia Minor. When Agesilaus and his forces were recalled to Greece in 394, Xenophon accompanied him. At some point (the timing remains unclear), Xenophon was exiled from Athens, possibly because of his service in a Spartan-led army. Upon his return to Greece, Xenophon took up residence on an estate at a place called Scillus in the northwestern Peloponnese; this was almost certainly made possible by the good graces of the Spartans, who had taken control of the area from the Eleans. Xenophon remained there until 371, when the Eleans, in the wake of the Spartans' crushing defeat at the battle of Leuctra, regained control of Scillus. Xenophon thus had good reason to be grateful to Sparta, and, at least while at Scillus, may have been reluctant to criticize Sparta openly.[1]

---

[1] On Xenophon's biography and the sources for his life, see Lee's chapter in this volume.

I am grateful to Paul Cartledge and Michael Flower, who provided invaluable comments

376

Sparta was certainly much on Xenophon's mind. He composed two works that focus solely on Sparta and Spartans: the *Lacedaimonion Politeia* (*Constitution of the Spartans*) and the *Agesilaus* (a posthumous encomium for the Spartan king). In addition, Sparta and Spartans figure prominently in Xenophon's other work. For example, much of the *Hellenica*, a historical account covering the years 411–362, directly involves Sparta and Spartans. Sparta is also discussed in non-historical works such as the *Memorabilia* and *Oeconomicus*, where the subject matter made examination of Sparta entirely a matter of authorial choice. There is, moreover, good reason to believe that Sparta is an unmentioned but important referent in other works of Xenophon, such as the *Cyropaedia*, a fictional account of the life of Cyrus the Great.[2]

Once we move beyond the basic statements that Xenophon had a long and close relationship with and wrote at length about Sparta, we encounter a great deal of uncertainty. One source of uncertainty is the frustrating lack of clarity about the chronology of Xenophon's writings. Xenophon offers relatively few unambiguous indications of what was written when, and it is likely that some of his works were written in sections that were produced at different points in time.[3] This, as we shall see, has significant interpretive ramifications.

Another source of difficulties is that Xenophon offers contradictory views on Sparta, even within individual works. A paradigmatic instance can be found in the *Lacedaimonion Politeia*, in which Xenophon explores the reasons why Sparta had become "the most powerful and famous city in Greece" (1.1). He discusses a number of laws and customs introduced by the semi-legendary Spartan lawgiver Lycurgus and shows every sign of approving of most if not all of them. However, just before the end of the treatise, his tone suddenly changes:

> If someone should ask me whether the laws of Lycurgus seem to me to remain still even now unchanged, by Zeus, I could not say this with confidence any more. For I know that previously the Spartans preferred to live together at home with modest possessions rather than be corrupted through being flattered while serving as harmosts in the cities.[4] I also know that formerly they

on earlier drafts, and to Edward Henderson and Chad Wilson for their editorial assistance. Responsibility for the views expressed here and for any errors or omissions is solely my own.

[2] On the complicated question of the relationship between the real-life Spartan state and the Persia described in the *Cyropaedia*, see Azoulay 2007a and the bibliography cited therein, as well as Tuplin 1994. For studies of the individual works in the Xenophontic corpus, see the essays in Part II of this volume.

[3] Humble 1997: 22–45.

[4] After the Spartans defeated Athens in the Peloponnesian War, they controlled an extensive empire and placed governors (called harmosts) in many cities under their rule.

feared appearing to be in possession of gold, whereas now there are some who even take pride in possessing it. I know also that formerly foreigners were expelled from Sparta, and it was not permitted to live abroad, so that the citizens would not be immersed in self-indulgence by foreigners. I know that now, by contrast, those who are by reputation the leading men in Sparta are eager to never cease serving as harmosts abroad. And there was a time when they took care to be worthy of serving as leaders, but now they concern them-selves much more with ruling than being worthy of ruling. Therefore, whereas Greeks used to go to Sparta to ask the Spartans to lead them against those whom they thought were acting unjustly, now many call on each other to help prevent the Spartans from exercising power again. There is, to be sure, no need to be amazed that the Spartans are objects of reproach, since they manifestly obey neither the gods nor the laws of Lycurgus. (14.1–7)

Given the laudatory tone of the remainder of the treatise, it is by no means obvious what to make of this passage.

Over the course of time, three basic interpretations of Xenophon's views on Sparta have come into being. Before discussing those interpretations an important caveat is called for: what follows is a rapid and necessarily simpli-fied description of a voluminous and complex body of scholarship; the work of each scholar is unique and rarely corresponds precisely to any of the three interpretations described below.

One interpretation of Xenophon's views on Sparta is that he was straight-forwardly and consistently pro-Spartan, perhaps even to the point of intro-ducing factual distortions and purposeful omissions in order to make certain that Sparta appeared in the best light possible.[5] From this perspective, chapter 14 of the *Lacedaimonion Politeia* is an affirmation of the praise of Lycurgus' laws found in the rest of the treatise – those laws were extremely effective so long as they were obeyed.[6] This interpretation, which has a long history that stretches back to an article published by B. G. Niebuhr in the 1820s,[7] was at one time widely held, but has become less popular in recent decades. The primary advantages of this interpretation are that it accounts easily for the praise for Sparta found in much of Xenophon's work and can be connected to details of his biography. A significant disadvantage is that Xenophon in some places, such as chapter 14 of the *Lacedaimonion Politeia*, overtly criticizes Sparta. Furthermore, it is difficult to justify the idea that authors' biographies condition their work in clear, predictable ways.

A second interpretation is that Xenophon's views on Sparta evolved over the course of time: he was in his early years strongly pro-Spartan but was

[5] See, for example, the notes in Cawkwell 1979.
[6] Dorion 2010: 288–9; Gray 2007: 217–21.
[7] Niebuhr 1828: 1.464–82.

progressively disillusioned by the Spartans' frequently questionable behavior as the hegemon of much of the Greek world in the early decades of the fourth century. Moreover, he would have been under no significant obligation to Sparta after his expulsion from Scillus in 371.[8] From this perspective chapter 14 of the *Lacedaimonion Politeia* is a postscript to a work produced at an earlier date. This interpretation has been particularly prominent among Francophone scholars, most notably François Ollier, and continues to have numerous adherents.

The primary advantages of this interpretation are that it easily accounts for both the praise and the criticism of Sparta found in Xenophon's work and can be connected to details of his biography. The disadvantages are, again, that the idea that authors' biographies condition their work in clear, predictable ways is difficult to justify, and, perhaps more importantly, that the chronology of Xenophon's work is unclear. This can lead to the dangerously circular habit of dating specific works and passages on the basis of the attitude towards Sparta found in that work or passage, and thus finding specious confirmation of the idea that Xenophon's attitude towards Sparta became increasingly negative over time.[9]

A third interpretation has its roots in a series of articles and books produced by Leo Strauss starting in 1939. Strauss sought to show that what previous scholars had seen as sometimes clumsy praise for Sparta was in fact brilliantly disguised satire and that Xenophon had from the outset a consistent, highly negative view of Sparta and its leaders. From this perspective chapter 14 of the *Lacedaimonion Politeia* is an overt statement of a bitingly critical understanding of Sparta that is expressed by means of delicate irony in the remainder of the treatise.[10]

A primary advantage of the interpretive approach pioneered by Strauss is that, in its more nuanced forms, it is capable of accounting for both the praise and criticism of Sparta offered by Xenophon without resorting to untestable chronological arguments. In addition, it encourages careful attention to the details of Xenophon's work, because it assumes Xenophon to be a writer capable of considerable subtlety. The primary disadvantage is that the portrayal of Xenophon as someone prone to dissimulation can lead to wild flights of interpretive fancy; any given passage can be taken to mean almost anything since the only meaning that can be easily excluded is the one that is most readily apparent.[11]

---

[8] See, for example, Delebecque 1957: 501; Ollier 1933: 372–440; Richer 2007; Riedinger 1991: 123–72; Schepens 2005: 43–62; Tigerstedt 1965–78: 1.159–79.

[9] See, for example, Riedinger 1991: 152–3 and Tigerstedt 1965–78: 1.160–77.

[10] Strauss 1939; see also Higgins 1977: 60–75; Humble 2004a; Proietti 1987: 44–79.

[11] See Dorion 2010 and Gray 2011: 56–7, 171–7, 268–9, 364–8 for acute critiques of Strauss's interpretive approach; cf. Johnson 2012a.

Strauss's reading of Xenophon has become increasingly influential in recent decades, particularly among Anglophone scholars, but the scholarship inspired directly or indirectly by Strauss has become quite heterogeneous because there is considerable, unresolved disagreement about how Xenophon went about articulating his views. Strauss believed that critical thinkers such as Xenophon were compelled to write in a cryptic fashion to avoid persecution, with the result that the true meaning of Xenophon's words is frequently, perhaps typically, the reverse of what it seems to be. Other scholars take the position that Xenophon says as much between the lines as in them, but are not prepared to accept that Xenophon says the opposite of what he means or means the opposite of what he says.

There are, in addition, disagreements about the extent of Xenophon's distaste for Sparta. Strauss believed that Xenophon saw little in the way of redeeming qualities in Sparta. Other scholars take the position that, throughout his life, Xenophon had a relatively balanced view of Sparta and that he found much to criticize, but also much that was laudable.

The reading of Xenophon's views on Sparta presented here might be described as neo-Straussian or perhaps Straussian-lite. It assumes that Xenophon was a subtle writer who crafted the wording, content, and structure of his narratives to suggest conclusions that he does not explicitly proclaim. Xenophon is not, however, understood as an author who engaged in elaborate games of literary subterfuge in which clever readers are expected to decipher an intended meaning that is the reverse of what it appears to be. Xenophon's writings as interpreted in this essay contain both praise and blame for Sparta and its leaders.

In the discussion that follows no attempt is made to link Xenophon's views on Sparta to specific aspects of his biography. Xenophon's long-running involvement with Sparta was an undeniably important part of his life, and that involvement made him an unusually well-informed observer of Spartan life. It is, however, difficult to demonstrate in a convincing fashion strong causal connections between specific facets of his biography and specific facets of his portrayal of Sparta. We can speak with considerable confidence about at least some aspects of Xenophon's views of Sparta, but we step onto much trickier ground when we seek to explain why Xenophon held the views that he did.

In a similar vein, Xenophon's attitude towards Sparta likely did evolve over time, but it is impossible to trace that evolution in a reliable fashion because we lack precise chronological information about what Xenophon wrote when. This is a particular problem since it seems likely that at least some of Xenophon's individual works were written in stages over the course of years if not decades. Moreover, scholars have found it impossible to achieve consensus on whether there are clear differences in Xenophon's portrayal of Sparta in different works within his corpus of writings (with the possible exception of the *Agesilaus*, on which see below). There is, therefore, no straightforward way of assigning absolute or relative dates to comments about Sparta found in any given passage written by Xenophon. As a result, establishing exactly what Xenophon thought about Sparta at any given point of his life presents major, perhaps insuperable, challenges. In the discussion that follows Xenophon's work is interpreted synchronically, which is to say that his attitude towards Sparta is understood as not evolving significantly over the course of time. This approach is not without its problems, but it is preferable to making untestable assumptions about the trajectory of Xenophon's views on Sparta and then reading his work in line with those assumptions.

Two key interpretive principles are employed in an attempt to reach an understanding of Xenophon's views of Sparta that is firmly grounded in his own words. The first such principle is that the recurrence of attitudes, themes, and motifs in different works within Xenophon's corpus is a strong sign that those attitudes, themes, and motifs reflect ideas that were important to Xenophon.[12] This is a significant issue because certain facets of Spartan life had been emphasized by Xenophon's predecessors such as Herodotus, and it is, as a result, always possible that Xenophon was in any given passage simply repeating established characterizations of Sparta and Spartans rather than expressing his own views. A second interpretive principle is that Xenophon tends to praise and blame specific traits regardless of whether they are displayed by individuals or collectivities such as armies or states.[13] It is, as a result, possible to assess his views on Sparta by comparing Sparta as depicted by Xenophon with his portrayal of individuals whom he clearly admired, Socrates most of all, but also Agesilaus, and the fictionalized Cyrus the Great and Persia described in the *Cyropaedia*.[14]

We will begin by exploring four traits of Sparta and Spartans that Xenophon seems to have found particularly praiseworthy: military competence, dedication to physical fitness, respect (*aidôs*), and self-restraint

---

[12] Gray 2011: 44–51.

[13] In part this was because, according to Xenophon, "whatever the character of the rulers is, such also that of the people under them for the most part becomes" (*Cyr.* 8.8.5). On the alignment of individuals and states in Xenophon's work, see Dillery 1995: 236–7; Gray 2007: 3–4; Higgins 1977: 30–1.

[14] Due 1989: 147–84 and *passim*; Gray 2011: 7–32, 51–3, 246–90, and *passim*; cf. Higgins 1977: 21–59; Tamiolaki 2012. Due and Gray argue that the *Cyropaedia* presents a relatively positive view of Cyrus and how he goes about governing, particularly in his early years. For a contrary view, that the *Cyropaedia* presents a thoroughly flawed ruler and state, see Carlier 1978/2010, Nadon 2001, and Tatum 1989.

(*enkrateia*). We will then consider what Xenophon saw as three crucial flaws in Sparta and Spartans: a predilection for coerced rather than willing obedience, a lack of prudence (*sôphrosynê*), and a tendency to privilege their own interests at the expense of their allies (*pleonexia*). In Xenophon's opinion, those flaws proved disastrous when Sparta found itself in the position of hegemon of much of the Greek world after the end of the Peloponnesian War.

The reader should remain aware throughout that the relative brevity of this chapter, the considerable extent of Xenophon's writings about Sparta, and the endless scholarly disputes about the meaning of virtually every passage make it impossible to produce anything resembling an exhaustive analysis of Xenophon's views on Sparta in the present context. For instance, there are other traits of Sparta and Spartans of which Xenophon seems to have approved (e.g. respect for elders, see *Memorabilia* 3.5.15) that are not treated here because they were, in the judgment of this author, less significant in the larger context of Xenophon's overall understanding of Sparta. Another subject that is not treated is the omission in the *Hellenica* of events of obvious significance (e.g. the foundation of the second Athenian naval confederacy, the liberation of Messenia, and the creation of the Arcadian League). These omissions were in the past habitually ascribed to a strong pro-Spartan, anti-Theban bias on the part of Xenophon, but they are now more commonly seen as a product of the nature of the *Hellenica* and the narrative strategies pursued in that work.[15] They are, therefore, not immediately relevant to the subject of this chapter.

Military Competence

For Xenophon one of Sparta's distinguishing and laudable traits was military competence. That competence, according to Xenophon, sprang from practices that fostered courage and discouraged cowardice as well as from careful attention to the technical aspects of warfare ranging from training in marching in formation to encampment procedures.[16] In the *Lacedaimonion Politeia* Xenophon writes that:

> Another measure of Lycurgus worthy of admiration is this: he brought it about in Sparta that an honorable death was preferable to a life of disgrace ... To speak truly, safety on the battlefield generally follows upon bravery rather than cowardice ... He clearly arranged happiness for the brave, misery for cowards. (9.1–3; cf. 3.3)

[15] For a list of omissions, see Underhill 1900: xxi–xxxv. On the omissions pertaining to Sparta, see Riedinger 1991: 41–60. On the omissions pertaining to Boeotian history, see Jehne 2004 and Sterling 2004.
[16] Tuplin forthcoming a.

Xenophon goes on to catalog a series of punishments that were inflicted on men who had proved themselves to be cowards. Shortly thereafter he proclaims that "if someone wishes, it is also possible to learn how military practices are arranged better here than in the rest of the other cities" (11.1) and launches into a lengthy, detailed discussion of those practices (11.2–13.11). The *Agesilaus* praises the king for his courage (6.1–2), his tactical and strategic capacities (1.9–22, 28–35; 2.1–8, 18–19), and his skill in recruiting and training soldiers (1.23–8, 2.7–8). In the *Symposium* Socrates counsels an ambitious acquaintance in Athens that "it is necessary to discover what sort of things the Spartans practice that give them the reputation of being the most capable military commanders" (8.39).

An enduring interest in practices that fostered courage and discouraged cowardice and in technical aspects of warfare is evident throughout Xenophon's corpus of work. Courage and cowardice are identified in the *Memorabilia* as subjects that received regular attention from Socrates (1.1.16), and that work includes an exchange in which Socrates lays out a definition of courage (4.6.10–11). In the *Hellenica* Xenophon at various points singles out for praise military units that displayed valor on the battlefield (e.g. 7.4.32, 7.5.16; cf. *Cyr.* 4.4.3). Xenophon's interest in the technical aspects of warfare is immediately evident from the fact that his writings include a treatise offering detailed suggestions to Athenian cavalry commanders (the *Hipparchikos*), and from frequent comments on military organization in his other works (e.g. *Por.* 4.42). In addition, it has been suggested that the *Cyropaedia* was intended in part as an outline of a military reform program that would revitalize the Spartan army.[17]

All of this material is important because it indicates that Xenophon's discussion of military competence with respect to Sparta is grounded in his own views and is not simply a reflection of characterizations of Sparta found in the writings of his predecessors or beliefs about Sparta held by his contemporaries. Furthermore, it also leaves little doubt that Xenophon saw military competence as a defining and laudable trait of Sparta and Spartans.

Dedication to Physical Fitness

The Spartans as portrayed by Xenophon are dedicated to maintaining a high degree of physical fitness.[18] After a brief preface, the first topic covered in the *Lacedaimonion Politeia* is the behavior expected of women in Sparta; Xenophon states that, in hopes of engendering stronger children,

---

[17] Christesen 2006.
[18] Humble 2006: 224–5; Ollier 1933: 404–5; Tuplin forthcoming a.

Lycurgus "ordered that women should train their bodies no less than men ... and established contests against each other in running and strength for women just as also for men" (1.4). This set Sparta apart from the rest of the Greek world, in which the athletic activities of females were sharply circumscribed. Rigorous physical training of various kinds was a fundamental part of the educational program imposed on Spartan boys (2.3, 3.2, 4.6), and adult men were required to stay fit through hunting (4.7) and exercising in the gymnasium (5.8–9; cf. 9.4–5). The requirement to train regularly extended to military campaigns, during which Spartans exercised twice a day (12.5–6). An athletic physique was a source of status among the Spartans who, according to Xenophon, "adorn themselves not with expensive clothes but with the excellent condition of their bodies" (7.3). All of this had the results one might expect: "not easily would someone find men healthier and with more capable bodies than the Spartans" (5.9; cf. 1.9).[19]

Xenophon leaves little doubt about his own enthusiasm for physical fitness. In both the *Hellenica* (3.4.16–18) and *Agesilaus* (1.25–7) he recounts in glowing terms the measures Agesilaus took to encourage physical training among his (mostly non-Spartan) army at Ephesus in Asia Minor in the winter of 395.[20] In the *Memorabilia* Xenophon writes that Socrates "approved of getting as much exercise as the soul sweetly welcomed, for he said that the habit contributed to good health and did not impede care of the soul" (1.2.4; cf. *Smp.* 2.3–4, 2.15–21). That same work includes a lengthy passage in which Socrates admonishes a young man for being in poor physical condition and urges him to take regular exercise so he will be prepared to do his part on the battlefield and will have a sounder body and mind (3.12.1–8; cf. 1.2.19, 2.1.28; *Oeconomicus* 11.12–18). In the *Cyropaedia* Cyrus the Great is raised in an educational system that privileges hunting as a form of exercise (1.2.10; cf. 1.4.5–15). His father advises him that he must ensure that his soldiers get regular physical training (1.6.17, 2.1.20, 2.1.29, 2.3.8, 2.3.23, 3.3.9), and as king he regularly takes his subordinates hunting in order to keep them fit and ready for battle (8.1.34–6). It thus seems safe to conclude that Xenophon emphasized the physical fitness of Spartans because he saw it as characteristic and praiseworthy.

[19] On sport in Sparta, see Christesen 2012 and 2013.
[20] On these passages, see Dillery 1995: 30. For other passages in the *Hellenica* in which Xenophon expresses enthusiasm, implicit or explicit, for physical fitness, see 5.3.17, 6.2.27, 6.4.11.

Respect

Respect is another trait that features prominently in Xenophon's description of Sparta. The relevant term in ancient Greek, *aidôs*, presents some difficulties because it can have a range of meanings and has no precise equivalent in English. For Xenophon *aidôs* seems typically to connote an appropriate degree of respect displayed by the young in dealing with their elders, and by subordinates in dealing with their superiors.[21]

In the *Lacedaimonion Politeia* Xenophon identifies instilling *aidôs* as one of the primary goals of the Spartan educational system. He writes that, "I have spoken about the educational systems of both the Spartans and of the rest of the Greeks. Whoever wishes to do so, let him judge for himself which one of these systems produces men who are more obedient, more respectful (*aidêmonesteroi*), and more self-controlled (*enkratèsteroi*) with respect to their needs" (2.14). He notes that a high-ranking Spartan magistrate, the *paidonomos*, had the power to punish any boy he felt was negligent, with the result that "great respect (*aidôs*) there stands beside great obedience" (2.2). According to Xenophon, Lycurgus wanted adolescents "to be imbued with a strong sense of respect (*to aidesthai*)" and to that end he prescribed that they walk silently, with their hands under their cloaks and their eyes on the ground (3.4). He describes the regulations for dining clubs (see below) as intended to avoid situations in which *aidôs* is absent (5.5). In Xenophon's *Symposium* Socrates discusses the chaste behavior expected between the partners in homoerotic relationships in Sparta and states that, "the goddess they worship is not Shamelessness but Respect (*Aidôs*)" (8.35).

Positive statements about *aidôs* are found throughout Xenophon's corpus. In the *Symposium* Socrates states that if the older male in a pederastic relationship conducts himself properly, he will help make his younger partner restrained and modest (*enkratês kai aidoumenos*, 8.27). Cyrus the Great displays *aidôs* as a young man (*Cyr.* 1.4.4, 1.5.1) and as king shows himself capable of inspiring respect from his subordinates (8.1.28, 33). Conversely, one of the commanders of the mercenary force assembled by Cyrus the Younger is criticized because he was incapable of inspiring either fear or respect (*aidôs*) in the men under his command (*Anab.* 2.6.19).

Self-Restraint

Xenophon portrays the Spartans as notable for their ability to practice self-restraint (*enkrateia*) and for the concomitant capacity to endure under

---

[21] On *aidôs* in Sparta, see Humble 1997: 187–240; Humble 1999; Richer 1999. On *aidôs* in general, see Cairns 1993.

difficult conditions (*karteria*).²² For Xenophon this self-restraint revolved around desires for physical comfort, food and drink, and sex.

The *Lacedaimonion Politeia* includes a considerable amount of discussion about how the system of laws and customs constructed by Lycurgus taught Spartans self-restraint. Xenophon claims that children were required to go barefoot (2.3), wear the same cloak in winter and spring (2.4), and consume limited quantities of food (2.5). The amount of time that newly married couples could spend together was restricted (1.5), thus limiting their sexual contact, and any sort of sexual activity between males in pederastic relationships was considered shameful (2.13–14). Adult male citizens were required to belong to and eat supper daily at a dining club where their intake of food and wine was regulated (5.1–4). Xenophon claims that the Spartan educational system produced men who were "more … self-controlled (*enkratesteroi*) with respect to their needs" (2.14).

The same sort of self-restraint figures prominently in the *Agesilaus*. The Spartan king is praised for his "self-control with respect to possessions" (*enkrateia chrêmatôn*, 4.3) and his abstemiousness in all forms of physical pleasure including drinking, eating, and sleeping (5.1–2). His immunity to the temptations of sexual pleasures (*aphrodisiôn enkrateia*) is discussed at length (5.4–7). According to Xenophon Agesilaus thought that "it beseems a ruler to surpass private citizens not in weakness but in endurance (*karteria*)" (5.2).

Elsewhere in his corpus of writings Xenophon strongly signals his approval of self-restraint and the ability to endure difficult conditions. In the *Memorabilia* Xenophon states that Socrates was "the most self-restrained (*enkratestatos*) of men with respect to desires for sex and food; further he was the most hardened (*karterikôtatos*) in enduring heat and cold and toil of every kind" (1.2.1; cf. 1.2.14, 1.3.5–8, 1.3.14–15, 1.5.6). Elsewhere in the same work Xenophon's Socrates describes *enkrateia* as the "foundation of all virtue" (1.5.4), identifies self-restraint and endurance as highly desirable traits in generals and people occupying any position of responsibility (1.5.1–5, 2.1.3, 2.1.6–7, 2.6.5, 4.5.1–12), and strives to instill *enkrateia* in others (2.1.1, 4.5.1). In the *Cyropaedia* one of the virtues that Cyrus pursues as king is self-restraint (*enkrateia*, 8.1.32; cf. 1.6.25, 2.3.13).

---

²² Xenophon's use of these terms is not entirely consistent and in some places he seems to subsume *karteria* under the heading of *enkrateia*. On Xenophon's views about *enkrateia*, see Dillery 1995: 134–8; Due 1989: 170–81; Lipka 2002: 18–19.

Coerced Obedience

Despite the fact that he found much in Sparta to admire, Xenophon by no means saw Sparta as an ideal state. From Xenophon's perspective, one of the major flaws in the Spartan system was that it instilled obedience through coercion.[23] This was problematic for Xenophon, who placed a high value on what he terms, in many places in his corpus of writings, "willing obedience."[24] In order to understand what Xenophon has to say on that subject, it is important to bear in mind that Xenophon typically touches on willing obedience when discussing the behavior of individual leaders, but in various places he makes it clear that willing obedience was something that could be generated by societal systems in general and educational systems in particular.

> "It seems to me that in all things the chief incentive to obedience is to both praise and honor those who obey, and to both dishonor and punish those who disobey." "This at any rate, my son, is the road to compulsory obedience. But there is another road, a shortcut, that leads to something much mightier, namely to willing obedience. For people very gladly obey someone whom they believe takes wiser thought for their interests than they themselves do." (*Cyr.* 1.6.20–1)

This exchange, which takes place between Cyrus the Great and his father, nicely expresses a sentiment that Xenophon repeats in numerous places in various works (see, for example, *Cyr.* 1.1.3, 3.1.28, 4.2.11; *Mem.* 1.2.10, 3.4.8; *Oec.* 21.4–5, 21.12).

For Xenophon willing obedience came into being when people were properly motivated and trained. As Cyrus' father indicates, a key factor in motivation was that people needed to believe that their leaders were genuinely concerned about the well-being of their followers. (See, for example, *Ages.* 6.4; *Anab.* 1.9.11–12; *Cyr.* 1.6.24, 1.6.42, 2.4.10, 8.7.13; *Hipp.* 6.2–3; *Oec.* 7.37.) Proper training entailed teaching through example. (See, for instance, *Cyr.* 1.2.8, 8.1.21–33; *Mem.* 1.2.3, 1.2.20.)

Willing obedience had many advantages. In a negative sense it did not require constant vigilance and punishment, which provoked resentment and, ultimately, disobedience. That cycle led to a downward spiral of further punishment, more resentment, and further disobedience. In an environment in which obedience was coerced through punishment, individuals who were confident that their actions would escape observation would consistently misbehave. (See, for example, *Hell.* 6.1.7.) Moreover, as soon as the

---

[23] Higgins 1977: 60–75; Humble 1997: 46–107; Millender forthcoming.
[24] Gray 2007: 4–9; Gray 2011: 15–18; Wood 1964: 52–4. On Xenophon's views on leadership, see Buxton in this volume.

individual or state imposing coerced obedience showed signs of vulnerability, subordinates would seize the opportunity to desert them.

In a positive sense, people who obeyed willingly were energetically cooperative, rather than sullenly acquiescent. As Ischomachus says in the *Oeconomicus*, "They are ashamed to do anything disgraceful, think it better to obey, and take pride in obedience, working with spirit, every man and all together, when it is necessary to work" (21.5; cf. *Cyr.* 3.3.59, *Mem.* 2.6.27).

Furthermore, willing obedience translated into loyalty even when the individual or state in command was vulnerable. In the *Oeconomicus* Socrates praises Cyrus the Younger for his ability to command such loyalty: "I think that this is a great piece of evidence of the excellence of a ruler, when men obey him willingly and wish to stand by him in moments of danger" (4.18–19; cf. *Anabasis* 1.9.29–31).[25]

Xenophon strongly emphasizes that obedience, to the laws and to magistrates, was one of the defining characteristics of Sparta (*Hell.* 7.1.8; *Lac. Pol.* 2.2, 2.14, 8.1–2; *Mem.* 3.5.16, 4.4.15).[26] Moreover, he identifies obedience as one of the praiseworthy traits possessed by Agesilaus (*Ages.* 1.36). Xenophon repeatedly signals his belief that obedience is a good and necessary thing (e.g. *Cyr.* 8.1.2; *Mem.* 4.4.1; *Hell.* 3.4.18), but he also saw something deeply problematic in the way obedience was secured in Sparta.

The content of the *Lacedaimonion Politeia* strongly suggests that Xenophon saw Sparta as a place where obedience was coerced. There was, as in the Persia described in the *Cyropaedia*, some element of teaching obedience through exemplary behavior (8.1–2). However, that was a minor part of a system in which Spartans, both young and old, were under constant observation and incessant threat of punishment. Xenophon notes that:

> In order that the boys might never be without a leader, even when the *paidonomos* [the magistrate in charge of the educational system] was absent, Lycurgus ordained that any one of the citizens who happened to be present would always be in charge and could order the boys to do whatever seemed proper and could punish them if they did anything wrong ... In order that the boys might never be without a leader, even if no adult citizen should be present, he decreed that the sharpest of the prefects [older boys in a position

---

[25] The diametric opposite of a benevolent leader such as Cyrus was a despotic ruler who looked solely to his own interests and who maintained control on the basis of force. Such a ruler, whom Xenophon describes at length in the *Hiero*, not only fails to inspire willing obedience and loyalty, but also inspires an inveterate hatred such that he lives at constant risk of assassination (see, for example, *Hier.* 2.7–11). The same is true of the Thirty, a junta that ruled Athens briefly after the Peloponnesian War. Xenophon provides a detailed and vituperative account of the Thirty in the *Hellenica* (2.3.1–4.43). For the Thirty as a negative paradigm of rulership, see Dillery 1995: 138–63.

[26] Humble 2006: 223–5; Tuplin forthcoming a.

of authority over younger boys] in each group of boys would be in charge. The result is that the boys are never left without a leader. (*Lac. Pol.* 2.10–11; cf. 6.1–2)

Adult men were compelled to eat in public, in their dining clubs, rather than in private, in order to ensure that "the laws would be least infringed" (5.2). Those same men were expected to spend a good deal of time at the gymnasium, where Lycurgus arranged that "the oldest man present would always supervise each one in attendance" (5.8). Hanging over all of this surveillance was the threat of punishment. The *paidonomos* was accompanied by young men carrying whips "so that they could mete out punishment whenever it was necessary. As a result, great respect (*aidôs*) there stands beside great obedience" (2.2; cf. 6.2). In addition to corporal punishment, there was a heavier penalty that could be imposed on both young and old: disenfranchisement (3.3, 10.7; cf. 8.3–4).

The predominance of coerced obedience in Sparta brings us back to the interpretively challenging passage from the *Lacedaimonion Politeia* (14.1–7) discussed in the introduction to this chapter. In that passage Xenophon accuses the Spartans of disobedience to Lycurgus' laws. Given his views on the difference between coerced and willing obedience, Xenophon's critique is not particularly surprising.[27] The Spartan system had flaws and as a result produced individuals with a tendency and capacity for disobedience in the absence of strict supervision and coercion. As we shall see shortly, in Xenophon's opinion the Spartans' penchant for coerced obedience also had a poisonous influence on their relationships with their allies.

An Absence of Prudence

Another major flaw in the Spartan system as described by Xenophon was that it inculcated respect (*aidôs*) and self-restraint (*enkrateia*), but not prudence (*sôphrosynê*).[28] As we have seen, for Xenophon *aidôs* was associated with the young and people in a subordinate relationship of some kind, and *enkrateia* was the "foundation of all virtue" (*Mem.* 1.5.4). *Aidôs* and *enkrateia* were valuable traits in and of themselves, and helped foster *sôphrosynê*, but were by no means adequate substitutes for *sôphrosynê*, which was the hallmark of the truly virtuous individual. Someone who possessed *sôphrosynê* was restrained in indulging in physical pleasures, but also

---

[27] Its placement within the work, however, remains difficult to explain.

[28] This section of text builds directly on the argumentation presented in Humble 1999 (cf. Humble 2002a). Skepticism about Humble's argumentation is expressed in Azoulay 2007a.

and more importantly he or she showed good sense and wisdom in dealing with intellectual, moral, and spiritual matters. Hence Xenophon writes that Socrates did not distinguish between wisdom (*sophia*) and prudence (*sôphrosynê*) because "if a man knew what is good and noble, and what is shameful, and practiced the former and avoided the latter, that man he judged to be both wise and prudent (*sophon te kai sôphrona*)" (*Mem.* 3.9.4).

The importance of *sôphrosynê* to Xenophon is evident from its close association with Socrates, who both embodies this trait and strives to engender it in others. In the *Memorabilia* Xenophon states that Socrates' "conduct was always prudent (*sôphronôn*)" (1.2.28), and in the *Apology* Socrates says at his trial that the Delphic oracle had proclaimed that, "no man was more free than I, or more just, or more prudent (*sôphronesteron*)" (14). Socrates' eagerness to nurture *sôphrosynê* in the people with whom he interacts is a repeated motif of the *Memorabilia* (1.1.16, 1.2.17–18, 4.3.1–2, 4.3.17–18).

Xenophon was certain that *sôphrosynê* could be taught; he states in the *Memorabilia* that "all good and honorable conduct is the result of training; this is especially true of prudence (*sôphrosynê*)" (1.2.23; cf. *Cyr.* 7.5.75). In the *Cyropaedia* Xenophon sketches an educational system that has the capacity to instill not just *aidôs* and *enkrateia*, but also *sôphrosynê* (1.2.2–16). Cyrus the Great goes through this educational system and, like Socrates, both embodies and teaches *sôphrosynê* (6.1.47, 8.1.30). In the *Anabasis*, Xenophon explicitly aligns Cyrus the Great and Cyrus the Younger and states that the latter was educated at the Persian court, "where one may learn *sôphrosynê* in full measure" (1.9.3).

Xenophon's discussion of the values instilled by Lycurgus' laws and customs in the *Lacedaimonion Politeia* is a study in delicacy in that, while he has much to say about how Spartans are notable for *aidôs* and *enkrateia*, he never mentions *sôphrosynê* and uses cognate words only twice. After discussing regulations about posture and silence intended to instill *aidôs* in boys, Xenophon adds that, "In this way it was manifest that the male sex was stronger with respect to *sôphrosynê* (*eis to sôphronein ischyroteron*) than the female sex" (3.4). In describing religious sacrifices made while on campaign, Xenophon notes that magistrates are present to ensure that the people in attendance behave prudently (*sôphronizô*) (13.5). The first passage makes the minimal claim that Spartan males were more prudent than Spartan females, and the second passage applies to behavior in a very specific context.

In the rest of his corpus of writings, Xenophon, with one notable exception, does not associate *sôphrosynê* with Spartans, either individually or collectively. The exception is Agesilaus, who, according to Xenophon, gave ample evidence of his *sôphrosynê* (*Ages.* 5.4, 5.7, 11.10). This anomaly has been explained in various ways. One explanation is that it is a matter of genre: the *Agesilaus* is an encomium, and contemporary sources show that *sôphrosynê* was regularly attributed to the subjects of encomia.[29] A second explanation is that Xenophon is not so much writing an encomium as a description of an ideal leader that is loosely based upon the Spartan king.[30] A final alternative is that Xenophon's feelings about Agesilaus on one hand and all other Spartans on the other diverged in significant ways. Regardless of how one assesses these various possibilities, it is clear that Xenophon is virtually silent on the subject of *sôphrosynê* in his extensive discussions of Sparta and Spartans. This is a significant silence, given the importance of *sôphrosynê* in the *Memorabilia*, which shows Socrates as an ideal role model and teacher, and in the *Cyropaedia*, which shows Cyrus the Great as an ideal leader.

Sparta's (Inevitable) Failure as Hegemon

In 404 Sparta emerged as the victor in the Peloponnesian War, and the undisputed leading power in the Greek world. In 371 the Spartans suffered a crushing defeat at the hands of the Thebans at the battle of Leuctra, a defeat that permanently shattered their hegemony. The reasons for the Spartans' spectacular rise and fall were, as one might expect, a subject of great interest to the people, including Xenophon, who watched these events unfold.

Xenophon highlights a number of factors that contributed to Sparta's collapse. Divine vengeance, set in motion by the Spartans' violation of oaths they swore to ratify treaties, looms large in his account of events (*Hell.* 5.4.1).[31] He also emphasizes flaws in the Lycurgan system of laws and customs that instilled a penchant for coerced obedience and that failed to inculcate *sôphrosynê*. He suggests that the Spartans in their dealings with their allies were incapable of securing willing obedience and, because they lacked prudence, were unable to resist selfishly pursuing their own interests at the

---

[29] Humble forthcoming; cf. Cartledge 1987: 55–66 and Schepens 2005: 43–62.

[30] Tigerstedt 1965–78: 1.175.

[31] Spartan impiety is not discussed at length here, despite the fact that piety was clearly an issue of crucial importance to Xenophon (see, for example, Due 1989: 156–8). This is because, although there is good reason to believe that there were a number of unusual features of religious life in Sparta (Parker 1989), Xenophon does not consistently portray the Spartans as markedly different from other Greeks in the details of their religious practice or in the depth of their religious beliefs. A discussion of Spartan (im)piety is thus not appropriate in the context of this particular chapter. Moreover, Xenophon does not offer a clear and consistent explanatory framework for the course of events in the early decades of the fourth century either in the *Hellenica* or elsewhere, with the result that discussions of his views on causation are necessarily complex and lengthy.

expense of their allies. They behaved with an increasing lack of restraint, turning friends into enemies in the process, and in the end this brought about their downfall.[32]

The Spartans as portrayed by Xenophon instinctively turn to coercion when dealing with subordinates and allies, and their inability to secure willing obedience produces resistance that in some cases has serious consequences. A particularly clear example of this can be found in Xenophon's description of Clearchus in the *Anabasis*. Clearchus was a Spartan commander who was a key leader in the mercenary army assembled by Cyrus the Younger. After recounting Clearchus' death, Xenophon adds:

> He used to punish severely, sometimes in anger ... He also punished on principle, for he believed that there was no good in an army that went without punishment ... In times of danger ... the men under his command were ready to obey him implicitly ...
>
> But when the danger was past, and they could go off to serve under another commander, many would desert him ... He never, therefore, had men following him out of friendliness and goodwill ... (2.6.9–13; cf. 1.3.1, 1.5.11–12)[33]

Other Spartan leaders described by Xenophon have the same problematic tendency. For example, in the *Hellenica* when the Spartan commander Mnasippus capriciously refuses to pay the mercenaries under his command, their officers complain, and Mnasippus responds by beating them. A battle is fought soon thereafter, and Xenophon dryly remarks that, "when his men marched out of the city with him, they were all dispirited and hating him, something that is least suited to fighting a battle" (6.2.19). The fashion in which Xenophon portrays Spartan commanders treating the non-Spartan soldiers under their command can easily be read as an implicit and critical comment on the ways Spartans in general interacted with non-Spartans, both at home and abroad.[34]

Xenophon goes out of his way to show that there was a great deal of resistance to the Spartan sociopolitical system within Sparta itself, thereby suggesting that the coerced obedience characteristic of Sparta caused major internal problems. He does this by relating in considerable detail a conspiracy to overthrow the Spartan government that was launched early in the fourth century by someone named Cinadon (*Hell.* 3.3.4–11).[35] There were in Sparta a restricted number of full male citizens (Spartiates or *homoioi*),

---

[32] The best single discussion of the relevant issues can be found in Tuplin 1993: 125–46 and *passim*.

[33] On obituaries in the *Anabasis* in general and of Clearchus in particular, see Gray 2011: 71–9; cf. Humble 1997: 78–80.

[34] See, for instance, Millender 2012 and forthcoming.

[35] On this part of the *Hellenica*, see Tuplin 1993: 52.

a substantial number of males with limited political rights who lived within the Spartan state but not in Sparta itself (*perioikoi*), and a large number of slaves (helots). There were in addition free men (other than the *perioikoi*) whose status was inferior to that of the Spartiates, but whose origins, numbers, and rights are poorly understood; Cinadon belonged to this group. According to Xenophon, Cinadon said that when the Spartiates were mentioned to any of the socially disadvantaged members of the Spartan state, "no one was able to conceal the fact that he would gladly eat them, even raw" (3.3.6). The Spartan authorities learned of Cinadon's conspiracy before it could be put into motion and successfully suppressed it, but its very existence points to a dangerously high level of disaffection within the Spartan state. Moreover, Xenophon's decision to recount Cinadon's conspiracy in the *Hellenica* is noteworthy in and of itself since in the remainder of that work he says little about the internal workings of the Spartan government. Xenophon draws no overt conclusions about the significance of the conspiracy, but the narrative suggests that there was something fundamentally wrong with the Spartan sociopolitical system. It seems likely that Xenophon intended his readers to draw the conclusions that the Spartan sociopolitical system inherently required coerced obedience in order to maintain a steep social hierarchy with a small number of elites at the top and that this coerced obedience created a situation in which the stability of the state was at constant risk.

The same dynamic is played out at the level of interstate relations. In the *Hellenica* Xenophon sketches a Sparta that claims to champion the idea that all Greek city states should be independent while simultaneously coercing friends and enemies alike into adhering to its wishes.

Xenophon presents with particular clarity the sentiments of Sparta's allies in a series of speeches delivered at a peace conference between Sparta and Athens just before the battle of Leuctra. As is generally the case with direct speeches reproduced by ancient Greek historians, it is nearly certain that the text is as much or more a product of Xenophon than an accurate transcription of the original speeches.[36] One of the speakers is an Athenian named Autokles who boldly admonishes the Spartans:

> You always say that the cities must be autonomous, but you yourselves are the greatest impediment standing in the way of their autonomy. For the first stipulation in your treaties with allied cities is that they follow where you might lead them. And yet how is this consistent with autonomy? You make enemies without taking counsel with your allies, and lead the allies against

---

[36] On the speeches in the *Hellenica*, see Gray 1989: 79–140 and Baragwanath in this volume.

those enemies, with the result that frequently so-called autonomous cities are compelled to take the field against men very friendly to them. Furthermore – and this is of everything the most contrary to autonomy – you establish governments ruled by groups of ten men here, groups of thirty men there, and your concern when it comes to these rulers is not that they rule in accordance with the law, but that they be able to hold the cities by force. (6.3.7–8)

The negative effects of the Spartans' tendency to secure obedience through coercion were, according to Xenophon, compounded by their tendency to pursue their own interests without much regard for the well-being of others. As we have seen, concern for the well-being of followers was a key component in obtaining willing obedience. For Xenophon, the failure to see to the well-being of followers had, in the long run, serious effects because it made them disobedient and disloyal. Intelligent leaders were, therefore, capable of understanding that while unapologetic pursuit of self-interest might in the short term redound to their benefit, it was in the long run likely to bring them to ruin (see, for instance, *Cyr.* 1.6.45). Indeed, Cyrus is praised by one of his allies in the *Cyropaedia* because he seemed "to take more pleasure in doing us kindnesses than in enriching himself" (5.1.28; cf. 8.4.7–8).

The Spartans as portrayed by Xenophon have a pernicious habit of behaving in a recklessly self-serving fashion.[37] In the *Hellenica* Xenophon characterizes the Spartans as prone to taking more than their fair share, something for which he employs the noun *pleonexia* and the verb *pleonektein*.[38] Towards the end of his speech attacking Spartan behavior, Autokles levels just that charge at them:

> It is necessary that those who are going to be friends do not expect to meet with justice from everyone else while showing themselves disposed to lay claim, as much as they are able, to more than their fair share (*pleista dunôntai pleonektountas phainesthai*). (6.3.9)

In an earlier section of the *Hellenica* that covers events in 395, Xenophon supplies a speech delivered by a Theban ambassador sent to Athens to seek an alliance against Sparta. The Theban says:

> The greedy rule (*pleonexia*) of the Spartans is much easier to overthrow than was your own empire … The Spartans are greedily taking advantage

---

[37] On this aspect of the *Hellenica*, see Dillery 1995: 195–237, 251; Higgins 1977: 28–30, 99–127; Sterling 2004; Tuplin 1993: 43–146, 165.

[38] The exception, as was the case with *sôphrosynê*, is Agesilaus, whom Xenophon describes as being unwilling to take more than his fair share (*pleonektein*) of anything except hardships and hard work (*Ages.* 5.3). Xenophon's treatment of *pleonexia* includes a significant nuance: he recognizes that *pleonexia* can be a positive trait in a military commander seeking to get the better of an enemy (*Cyr.* 1.6.27–41, *Mem.* 3.1.6).

(*pleonektousi*) of men who are much more numerous than they are and in no way inferior to them in arms. (3.5.15)

The wording of this passage is remarkable: Xenophon substitutes *pleonexia* in place of a term for hegemony such as *archê*; this is a highly unusual usage of *pleonexia* and is implicitly damning of Spartan rule.[39]

A particularly egregious episode occurred in 382, when a dissident party within Thebes volunteered to turn over the Theban acropolis, the Cadmea, to Spartan troops that happened to be in the vicinity of Thebes en route to northern Greece (*Hell.* 5.2.25–31, though cf. the somewhat divergent accounts given in Diodorus 15.20.2 and Plutarch *Ages.* 23–4). The Spartan commander, Phoebidas, proceeded to seize the Cadmea, even though Sparta and Thebes were at that time at peace and the Thebans had done nothing to provoke an attack on their territory. This blatant violation of Theban sovereignty was subsequently confirmed by the Spartan government, which made the decision to retain control of the Cadmea. Agesilaus played a leading role in this decision; he deployed the argument that the sole standard of judgment of Phoebidas' actions should be whether they were advantageous or disadvantageous to Sparta (*Hell.* 5.2.32).[40]

The Spartans' actions with respect to the Cadmea are portrayed by Xenophon as the most spectacular and ill-judged example of a general pattern of behavior that led to their downfall (see in particular *Hell.* 5.4.1). In part this was because in constantly and selfishly seeking their own aggrandizement the Spartans created enemies and engaged in hostilities that could easily have been avoided. This is most evident in their relations with the Thebans, who ultimately became the authors of Sparta's downfall. At the peace conference before the battle of Leuctra, an Athenian named Callistratus delivers a speech immediately after Autokles. Callistratus says that he hopes that the Spartans will change their behavior now that they have learned the dangers of *pleonexia*: "I hope now that, having been taught that seeking selfish gain (*pleonektein*) is unprofitable, we will again be reasonable in our friendship with each other" (6.3.11). In the event, the Spartans do not learn

---

[39] The strongly negative connotations that Xenophon attaches to *pleonexia* are apparent from the fact that he associates this impulse with Critias, an Athenian political figure whom Xenophon abhorred. In the *Hellenica* Critias claims that "men who wanted to take more than their fair share (*pleonektein*) could not avoid doing away with those who were most able to prevent them" (2.3.16). In the *Memorabilia*, Critias is described as *pleonektistatos* (1.2.12).

[40] For a similar, particularly poignant example of the Spartans under Agesilaus' leadership acting in a fashion that was, in the short term at least expedient, but nevertheless far from just, see Xenophon's account of the meeting between Agesilaus and the Persian satrap Pharnabazus (*Hell.* 4.1.29–36).

their lesson, and aggressively push the Thebans into a battle that ends in catastrophic defeat.

In addition, Xenophon suggests that the Spartans' *pleonexia* proved harmful because it sowed deep discontent among their allies. Xenophon makes it clear that long before Leuctra, the Spartans' allies were restive. A Theban ambassador to Athens, seeking to form an alliance with Athens against Sparta in 395, predicts that Sparta's allies will revolt as soon as they find a powerful state to support them (*Hell.* 3.5.10–13). After the Spartans suffer a major military defeat in 390, Agesilaus leads his forces back to Sparta in such a way as to pass through cities as late in the day as possible in order to avoid the sight of people from communities such as Mantinea, which was allied with Sparta, rejoicing in Sparta's misfortune (4.5.18). When the Spartans find themselves in a position of near unchallenged supremacy in 386, they immediately set about brutally imposing their will on their allies, many of whom had showed themselves to be less than enthusiastic in their support of Sparta (5.2.1). On the battlefield at Leuctra, the Spartans consider renewing the fight after their initial defeat, but decide not to do so, in part because the allied troops present to support the Spartan forces "had no heart for more fighting, and some were not even displeased at what had happened" (6.4.15).

As might be expected, their allies, who had numerous grievances, desert the Spartans in droves as soon as they learn of their defeat at Leuctra (*Hell.* 6.5.3–9, 6.5.32). Indeed, in the *Hellenica* Xenophon inserts a digression in order to praise the city of Phlius for remaining loyal to Sparta after Leuctra (7.2.1).[41] The Spartans, weakened by the loss of their allies, are unable to resist the growing power of the Thebans (strongly reinforced by the Spartans' former allies), lose much of their territory, and are rendered largely impotent.

Xenophon in various places in his corpus of writings connects the capacity to occupy a position of leadership successfully to the possession of *sôphrosynê*. It is only through *sôphrosynê* that individuals and states that achieve power can steer clear of the temptation to take advantage of their position to take more than their fair share, which in turn creates dangerous disaffection. Hence Ischomachus declares in the closing lines of the *Oeconomicus* that:

> It seems to me that this gift, the ability to elicit willing obedience, is not altogether human but divine. It is clearly given to those who truly achieve the highest degree of prudence (*sôphrosynê*). The gods give, it seems to me, tyrannical rule over unwilling subjects to those whom they consider worthy of

---

[41] On Phlius as a model community in the *Hellenica*, see Dillery 1995: 130–8.

living a life like that of Tantalus, who is said to spend eternity in Hades fearing lest he die a second death. (21.12)

In the *Cynegeticus* Xenophon writes:

> Those who wish to take more than their fair share (*pleonektein*) in the city train themselves to win victories over their friends, whereas hunters train themselves to win victories over common enemies. This training makes the latter more effective, the former much worse, against all other enemies. The latter undertake the chase with prudence (*sôphrosynê*) as a companion, the former have shameful insolence as their companion. (13.15)

And in the *Cyropaedia*, Cyrus, after having acquired a vast empire, gathers together the leading men among the Persians to consider how they might hold onto their new-won gains. He muses that:

> To gain [an empire] often falls to the lot of one who has shown only daring, but to gain and hold, that is no longer possible without prudence (*sôphrosynê*), restraint (*enkrateia*), and great care. (7.5.76; cf. 4.2.44 and *Mem.* 4.3.1)

From this perspective, there was little surprising about the collapse of Spartan power. Spartans were trained in coerced obedience, and the Spartan system instilled *aidôs* and *enkrateia*, which were both laudable traits, but neither of which was sufficient for a person or state occupying a position of leadership. *Aidôs* was suitable for the young or subordinates, and *enkrateia* restrained physical appetites; *sôphrosynê* was required if those in power were to behave in ways that did not provoke resistance from allies and subjects.[42] The Spartans' inability to inspire willing obedience and their lack of *sôphrosynê* made them particularly ill suited to be the hegemon of much of the Greek world.

Conclusion

If Xenophon was critical of the Spartans' failure as hegemons, and ascribed that failure to flaws in the Spartan sociopolitical system, he also saw their rise and fall as part of a larger pattern.[43] There was a long tradition in the Greek world of believing that success led to arrogance, arrogance led to

---

[42] Cyrus observes that those possessed of *aidôs* avoid offensive acts when they are under observation, whereas those possessed of *sôphrosynê* avoid offensive acts even when they are not under observation (*Cyr.* 8.1.31). In other words, *aidôs* only curbs misbehavior when the threat of detection and punishment is present. Insofar as those in power are, in the short term at least, immune to the threat of punishment from their subordinates it is only *sôphrosynê* that can constrain their behavior.

[43] There has been considerable scholarly discussion of this point. A key referent is Tuplin 1993: 163–8 and *passim*; see now also Hau 2012.

rash behavior, and rash behavior led to disaster; and Xenophon seems to have subscribed to this view. In the *Hellenica* an ambassador, who has come to seek Spartan help to fend off the attacks by an aggressively expansionist neighboring city, remarks that, "God, perhaps, made it such that as a people's power grows, so too does their pride" (5.2.18).

Xenophon suggests that Thebes and Athens were as susceptible to fall into this pattern of behavior as Sparta.[44] He is thus fundamentally pessimistic about the capacity of individuals and states that become powerful to maintain their position for extended periods of time. He nevertheless also displays a certain degree of optimism in that he intimates that people can learn from their mistakes and that, perhaps, those who have had power and then lost it are capable of behaving more prudently thereafter. As one of the characters in the *Cyropaedia* remarks:

> It seems to me, Cyrus, to be more difficult to find a man who can bear good fortune well than one who can bear misfortune well. For good fortune engenders arrogance (*hybris*) in most men, whereas misfortune engenders prudence (*sôphrosynê*) in all men. (8.4.14)

In a similar vein, Socrates in the *Memorabilia* sees Athens's weakened state after its defeat in the Peloponnesian War as an advantage:

> The city seems to me now to have a disposition more acceptable to a good ruler. For confidence breeds carelessness and slackness and disobedience, whereas fear makes men more attentive and more obedient and more amenable to discipline. (3.5.5)

A state that had suffered and learned the proper lessons from that suffering, most notably the importance of prudence in all things and all times, would not seek to take more than its fair share.

As the rule of the Thirty in Athens comes to an end, one of its opponents advises the member of the junta and its supporters to "know yourselves" (*Hell.* 2.4.40), to become better men as a result of their experience in gaining and losing power. It is possible that Xenophon had similar hopes that the Spartans, chastened by their fall from power and possibly even enlightened by Xenophon's musings, might re-emerge from the disaster at Leuctra wiser and capable of building the sort of stable, lasting alliances that would enable them to once again become hegemons of the Greek world.[45]

---

[44] See, for example, *Memorabilia* 3.5.2 on the Boeotians, and 3.5.13 on the Athenians.
[45] Daverio Rocchi 2007, Dillery 1995: 241–9, Gray 1989: 178–82, Higgins 1977: 99–127. It has been argued by some scholars that Xenophon envisaged an alliance between Athens and Sparta, both of which could draw on the lessons of the past as guide to future, more prudent conduct. See, for example, Dillery 1995: 16, Ollier 1933: 429, Riedinger 1991: 191–206.

Further Reading

The best place to begin a deeper exploration of Xenophon's views on Sparta is by reading those works produced by Xenophon that focus entirely or largely on Sparta and Spartans: the *Lacedaimonion Politeia*, the *Agesilaus*, and the *Hellenica*. A good translation of and commentary upon the *Lacedaimonion Politeia* can be found in Lipka 2002. (A translation without commentary can be found in the Penguin Classics volume with the title *Plutarch on Sparta*. Gray 2007 provides a commentary but no translation.) A good recent translation of the *Agesilaus* by Robin Waterfield, with useful notes by Paul Cartledge, can be found in a Penguin Classics volume with the title *Hiero the Tyrant and Other Treatises*. The *Hellenica* is now available in the Landmark series, in which translated texts are accompanied by an array of helpful maps and notes.

The best single starting place in terms of the relevant secondary literature is Powell and Richer (forthcoming), an edited volume replete with up-to-date articles focusing on Xenophon's writings about Sparta. Another collection of important essays can be found in Gray 2010a. The interpretation of Xenophon's views on Sparta presented in this chapter follows upon ideas and insights drawn from a number of sources, most notably Dillery 1995 and Tuplin 1993. Tuplin's extensive writings about Xenophon remain fundamental, and he has edited or co-edited two volumes of valuable articles (Hobden and Tuplin 2012a, Tuplin 2004a). On the subject of *sôphrosynê* and Spartans in Xenophon's work, Humble's work (1999, 2002a) is essential.

Those interested in methodologies for reading and interpreting Xenophon would be well served by consulting the scholarship of Vivienne Gray (1989, 2011). On the specific issue of Straussian readings of Xenophon, one should, in addition to Gray's work, look to Dorion 2010.

A relatively brief overview of the history of ancient Sparta can be found in Kennell 2010. For a more thorough exploration of the same subject, see Cartledge 2002 and Cartledge and Spawforth 2002. Cartledge 1987 remains the fundamental study of Sparta in the era of Xenophon and Agesilaus.

PART V

RECEPTION AND INFLUENCE

20

EWEN BOWIE

Xenophon's Influence in Imperial Greece

Introduction

Of the many texts that demonstrate the importance of Xenophon in the Greek literary culture of the Roman Empire, few do so better than Dio of Prusa's recommendations to a rising politician who already had a good education but apparently wanted to raise his oratorical game. After proposing that he study certain orators and historians, Dio recommends Xenophon as a model in several genres:

I shall now turn to the Socratics, writers who, I insist, are quite indispensable to every man who aims at oratory. For just as without salt no food is gratifying to the taste, so no genre of literature, it seems to me, could possibly be pleasing to the ear if it had no share in Socratic grace. It would be a long task to praise the others, and to read them is not something everybody can do. But I think that Xenophon, and he alone of the ancients, can suffice for a man in public life. Whether one is commanding an army in time of war, or is guiding the affairs of a city, or is speaking in a popular assembly or the council chamber, or even if one were addressing a court of law and desired, not merely as an orator, but as a city statesman or imperial figure, to say what is appropriate to such a person in a court case, the best model of all, it seems to me, and the most profitable for all these ends is Xenophon. For his ideas are clear and simple and can be seen easily by everyone, and the character of his style is attractive, pleasing, and convincing, carrying much conviction and exercising much charm and impact, so that his power seems not like cleverness but actually like magic.

If, for instance, you were willing to read his work on the *Anabasis* very carefully, you will find no argument among those which it is possible you will use which he has not analyzed and could present as a kind of norm to any man who wishes to go in his direction or imitate him. If it is useful for the city statesman to encourage those who are seriously demoralized, he often shows how one ought to do this; or if the need is to incite and exhort, nobody with a command of the Greek language could not be aroused by Xenophon's hortatory speeches. My thoughts, indeed, are moved and sometimes I weep as I read his account so many years later. He also has the answer on how to associate circumspectly with men who are proud and conceited and neither to come to some harm at their hands because they are displeased nor indecorously to enslave one's own mind to them and do their pleasure at every turn. And also how to hold secret discussions both with generals apart from the multitude, and with the multitude in a different way; how to converse with imperial figures; and how to deceive enemies so as to harm them and friends so as to benefit them; how to tell the truth persuasively to those who are groundlessly disturbed without distressing them; how not glibly to trust those in authority, and the means by which men outmaneuver others and are outmaneuvered – all these points the composition covers adequately. For I imagine that it is because he blends deeds with words, not taking over something he has heard or imitating, but both doing things himself and narrating them, that he made his words most convincing in all his compositions and above all in this one which I happened to recall. And be assured that you will in no way regret it, but that both in the Council and before the People you will be aware of this man reaching out his hand to you if you approach the challenge of reading him with enthusiasm.

τρέφομαι δὲ ἤδη ἐπὶ τοὺς Σωκρατικούς, οὓς δὴ ἀναγκαιοτάτους εἶναί φημι παντὶ ἀνδρὶ λόγων ἐφιεμένῳ. ὥσπερ γὰρ οὐδὲν ὄψον ἄνευ ἁλῶν γεύσει κεχαρισμένον, οὕτως ⟨λόγων⟩ οὐδὲν εἶδος ἔμοιγε δοκεῖ ἀκοῇ προσηνὲς ἂν γενέσθαι χάριτος Σωκρατικῆς ἄμοιρον. τοὺς μὲν δὴ ἄλλους μακρὸν ἂν εἴη ἔργον (14) ἐπαινεῖν καὶ ἐντυγχάνειν αὐτοῖς οὐ τὸ τυχόν. Ξενοφῶντα δὲ ἔγωγε ἡγοῦμαι ἀνδρὶ πολιτικῷ καὶ μόνον τῶν παλαιῶν ἐξαρκεῖν δύνασθαι· εἴτε ἐν πολέμῳ τις στρατηγῶν εἴτε πόλεως ἀφηγούμενος, εἴτε ἐν δήμῳ λέγων εἴτε ἐν βουλευτηρίῳ, εἴτε καὶ ἐν δικαστηρίῳ μὴ ὡς ῥήτωρ ἐθέλοι μόνον, ἀλλὰ καὶ ὡς πολιτικὸς καὶ βασιλικὸς ἀνὴρ τὰ τῷ τοιούτῳ προσήκοντα ἐν δίκῃ εἰπεῖν· πάντων ἄριστος ἐμοὶ ⟨δοκεῖ⟩ καὶ λυσιτελέστατος πρὸς ταῦτα πάντα Ξενοφῶν. τά τε γὰρ διανοήματα σαφῆ καὶ ἁπλᾶ καὶ παντὶ ῥᾴδια φαινόμενα, τό τε εἶδος τῆς ἀπαγγελίας προσηνὲς καὶ κεχαρισμένον καὶ πειστικόν, πολλὴν μὲν ἔχον πιθανότητα, πολλὴν δὲ χάριν καὶ ἐπιβολήν, ὥστε μὴ λόγων δεινότητι μόνον, ἀλλὰ καὶ γοητείᾳ ἐοικέναι τὴν δύναμιν.

(15) εἰ γοῦν ἐθελήσειας αὐτοῦ τῇ περὶ τὴν Ἀνάβασιν πραγματείᾳ σφόδρα ἐπιμελῶς ἐντυχεῖν, οὐδένα λόγον εὑρήσεις τῶν ὑπὸ σοῦ λεχθῆναι δυνησομένων, ὃν οὐ διείληπται καὶ κανόνος ἂν τρόπον ὑπόσχοι τῷ πρὸς αὐτὸν ἀπευθῦναι ἢ μιμήσασθαι βουλομένῳ. εἴτε γὰρ θαρρῦναι τοὺς σφόδρα καταπεπτωκότας χρήσιμον πολιτικῷ ἀνδρί, καὶ πολλάκις ὡς χρὴ τοῦτο ποιεῖν δείκνυσιν· εἴτε προτρέψαι καὶ παρακαλέσαι, οὐδεὶς Ἑλληνικῆς φωνῆς ἐπαΐων οὐκ ἂν ἐπαρθείη (16) τοῖς προτρεπτικοῖς Ξενοφῶντος λόγοις (ἐμοὶ γοῦν κινεῖται ἡ διάνοια καὶ ἐνίοτε δακρύω μεταξὺ ⟨διὰ⟩ τοσούτων ἐτῶν τοῖς λόγοις ἐντυγχάνων) μέγα φρονοῦσι καὶ ἐπηρμένοις ὁμιλῆσαι φρονίμως καὶ μήτε παθεῖν τι ὑπ' αὐτῶν δυσχερανάντων μήτε ἀπρεπῶς δουλῶσαι τὴν αὑτοῦ διάνοιαν καὶ τὸ ἐκείνοις κεχαρισμένον ἐκ παντὸς ποιῆσαι, καὶ ταῦτα ἔνεστιν. καὶ ἀπορρήτοις δὲ λόγοις ὡς προσήκει χρήσασθαι καὶ πρὸς στρατηγοὺς ἄνευ πλήθους καὶ πρὸς πλῆθος ⟨οὐ⟩ κατὰ ταὐτό, καὶ βασιλικοῖς

τίνα τρόπον διαλεχθῆναι, καὶ ἐξαπατῆσαι ὅπως πολεμίους μὲν ἐπὶ βλάβῃ, φίλους δ' ἐπὶ τῷ συμφέροντι, καὶ μάτην ταραττομένοις ἀλύπως τἀληθὲς καὶ πιστῶς εἰπεῖν, καὶ τὸ μὴ ῥᾳδίως πιστεύειν τοῖς ὑπερέχουσι, καὶ οἷς καταστρατηγοῦσι καὶ καταστρατηγοῦνται ἄνθρωποι, πάντα ταῦτα ἱκανῶς τὸ σύνταγμα περιέχει. (17) ἅτε γὰρ οἶμαι μιγνὺς ταῖς πράξεσι τοὺς λόγους, οὐκ ἐξ ἀκοῆς παραλαβὼν οὐδὲ μιμησάμενος, ἀλλ' αὐτὸς πράξας ἅμα καὶ εἰπών, πιθανωτάτους ἐποίησεν ἐν ἅπασί τε τοῖς συντάγμασι καὶ ἐν τούτῳ μάλιστα, οὗ ἐπιμνησθεὶς ἐτύγχανον. καὶ εὖ ἴσθι, οὐδένα σοι τρόπον μεταμελήσει, ἀλλὰ καὶ ἐν βουλῇ καὶ ἐν δήμῳ ὀρέγοντός σοι χεῖρα αἰσθήσῃ τοῦ ἀνδρός, εἰ αὐτῷ προθύμως καὶ φιλοτίμως ἐντυγχάνοις.

Dio *Oration* 18.13–17

Dio's prescription of Xenophon's works, foregrounding the *Anabasis* as a mine of oratorical models in a wide variety of situations, is but one of a vast range of testimonies to his impact between the fourth century BC, beginning during his own lifetime, and the Byzantine period. Another very different testimony from some decades later is the circulation of a work entitled *Araspas in Love with Panthea* whose ascription to the Hadrianic sophist Dionysius of Miletus is confidently rejected by Philostratus on stylistic grounds.[1] The large topic of Xenophon's reception in antiquity was brilliantly explored by Münscher almost a century ago.[2] This chapter does not try to replace any part of Münscher's work: indeed any attempt to update its concise and sometimes breathless exposition could only take the form of a book-length study. Instead it offers two case studies of Xenophontic influence of different sorts on the Greek literary culture of the Roman Empire. The first addresses one field where Münscher's study was deficient, the Greek novels. The second moves into the nexus of literary production and an active military and political life exemplified by Arrian of Nicomedia, a theme that carries us beyond the purely literary frontiers that Münscher adopted.[3]

It is not surprising that as a Stoic Dio opens his recommendation of Xenophon with the *Memorabilia* (*Memoirs about Socrates*), but for many educated readers in the early imperial period it was probably their representations both of Socrates the man and of his philosophical positions that sparked an interest in Xenophon, the person and his writings alike. Others may have been drawn by Xenophon's style alone. His key place as a model for writing marked by charm (χάρις) and simplicity (ἀφέλεια) was already evident in the essay *On Expression* (περὶ ἑρμηνείας) of a Demetrius,[4]

---

[1] ὁ Ἀράσπας ὁ τῆς Πανθείας ἐρῶν, Philostr. *VS* 1.22.524.

[2] Münscher 1920.

[3] Another area in which Münscher's focus was too narrow is that of portraits of Xenophon in this period, on which see Minakaran-Hiesgen 1970.

[4] Among Demetrius' citations those from Xenophon come third in frequency, after Homer and Plato, and ahead of (in order) Aristotle, Demosthenes, and Thucydides; see Apfel

probably a work of the first century B C. His status as an example of Atticism was also endorsed in that century by Caecilius of Caleacte and Dionysius of Halicarnassus.[5] But it was a work of Xenophon much admired for its presentation of the virtues required in a leader, not named by Dio but probably in his mind alongside the *Anabasis*, that proved fundamental for the creation of an influential new genre by Greek writers of the early empire – the *Cyropaedia* (*Education of Cyrus*).

Romantic Fiction in a Xenophontic Mold

The eight-book *Cyropaedia*, itself in some sense a historical novel,[6] was manifestly one of the most important of the parents and foster parents of the novels of romantic adventure whose earliest example to survive complete is almost certainly Chariton's *Callirhoe*.[7] *Callirhoe*'s eight-book structure and largely oriental setting are the most obvious such genetic features. Just as the world of Xenophon's Cyrus is wholly Persian – indeed Plutarch refers to the *Cyropaedia* as "the Persian history" (τὰ Περσικά)[8] – so too Chariton's couple, albeit starting and ending their story in Syracuse, undergo most of their tribulations within the Persian Empire. These tribulations have an educative impact on each of them, especially on Chaereas, who admittedly starts with much more to learn, to the extent that one might see the book as a *Chaereou paideia* (*Education of Chaereas*).[9] Alongside emulation of the *Cyropaedia*, however, Chariton also exploits Xenophon's *Anabasis*. Once Callirhoe and Chaereas have successively reached the Aegean coast of Asia Minor, each is taken on a journey upcountry to the Persian Empire's capital, which Chariton represents as Babylon. For Callirhoe leaving the sea is as traumatic as its resighting was exhilarating for Xenophon's Ten Thousand.[10]

1935. Xenophon is in fact *named* eighteen times, more often than Plato (seventeen) and Homer (sixteen).

[5] For Caecilius' quotations from *Cyr.*, *Mem.*, and (probably) *Lac. Pol.* see Münscher 1920: 108–9.

[6] Zimmermann 2009.

[7] For the case for putting Xenophon's *Ephesiaca* earlier than Chariton see O'Sullivan 1994. For Chariton's priority see Tilg 2010.

[8] Plut. *mor.* 1093b.

[9] For the novels as education see Lalanne 2006; for the development of the protagonists' characters De Temmerman 2014. The inner debates of Dionysius, Mithridates, and Artaxerxes also have a claim to a Xenophontic pedigree.

[10] Callirhoe exclaims "I am being taken away beyond the Euphrates and imprisoned in the depths of Persia – I, an island girl – where there is no longer any sea" (ὑπὲρ τὸν Εὐφράτην ἀπάγομαι καὶ βαρβάροις ἐγκλείομαι μυχοῖς ἡ νησιῶτις, ὅπου μηκέτι θάλασσα, Chariton 5.1.6). Note too how both Callirhoe ("sea," θάλασσα, 3.10.8) and Chaereas ("O sea," ὦ θάλασσα, 3.5.9, 6.6) address the sea. The key Xenophontic intertext is the soldiers' cry at *Anab.* 4.7.24 "Sea, sea" (Θάλαττα θάλαττα).

Moreover the temporal setting, imprecise or self-contradictory though it may be,[11] must be taken to be in the two decades after the Syracusan leader Hermocrates' defeat of the Athenian expedition to Sicily in 413 BC and during the reign of Artaxerxes II,[12] i.e. roughly contemporary with the action of the *Anabasis*.

Within Chariton's narrative many details evoke the *Cyropaedia*. Panthea's incomparable beauty is a model for Callirhoe's. Xenophontic too is the description of the Persian king, as he struggles to master his passion for Callirhoe, setting off to hunt – a remedy for his plight suggested by his eunuch Artaxates "especially since you take particular pleasure in hunting" (μάλιστα δὲ κυνηγεσίοις ἐξαιρέτως χαίρεις, 6.3.9), perhaps a gesture towards the *Cynegeticus*.[13]

Of course the place of *eros*, sexual desire, in Chariton's new genre is quite different from its role in the *Cyropaedia*. There it is confined to the story of Abradatas and his faithful wife Panthea, an inset tale within the narrative of Cyrus' military achievements, whereas for Chariton it is the narrative's mainspring, to which travel and martial activity are subordinate.

This cocktail that blends important ingredients drawn from both the *Cyropaedia* and the *Anabasis* is served up again in other early novels. The author of the *Ephesiaca* has his couple start in western Asia Minor: much of their travel happens within a timeless version of the Persian Empire, although Habrocomes (a name that might seem to be a Greek calque on the Persian Abradatas) gets as far west as south Italy and even Nuceria in southern Campania.[14] This novelist abandons the eight-book structure, but he has, or gives himself, the name Xenophon.

Two others of the early generation of novels, the *Ninus* and *Metiochus and Parthenope*, are preserved only in fragments, in the latter case helpfully contextualized by a later adaptation in Persian.[15] This adaptation gives little sign that either the Greek hero Metiochus or the heroine Parthenope, fictitious daughter of Polycrates tyrant of Samos, left the Herodotean Greek world in which they originated, but Herodotus (3.120–5) had presented Polycrates as murdered by the Persian Oroetes, and at least the shadow of

---

[11] For the problem of Chariton's conflicting markers of his story's date see an unpublished paper by S. Trzaskoma "The First Alternate History Novel: Chariton's *Callirhoe* and History that Never Happened."

[12] For Artaxerxes as king, Chariton 4.6.3 etc.

[13] Panthea's beauty, *Cyr.* 5.1.7. The king goes hunting, Chariton 6.4.1–2, cf. *Cyr.* 6.4.1–3: see Bowie 2006 (noting such unusual words as ὑακινθινοβαφής, "dyed the colour of hyacinths").

[14] For the importance of Habrocomes' visit to Nuceria for Xenophon's date see Coleman 2011.

[15] Full discussion in Hägg and Utas 2003.

the Persian Empire must often have been visible. The *Ninus* – often, but probably wrongly, thought to be earlier than Chariton's *Callirhoe* – may have stood closer than *Metiochus and Parthenope* to Xenophon's works: a young eastern prince goes off to battle an enemy in a snowy mountainous region whose description has verbal echoes of the *Anabasis*,[16] and he approaches the delicate matter of proposing to a young princess with a Cyrus-like self-control.

Thus it seems that at least three of our earliest prose fictional texts are playing with Xenophontic models in different ways, and this cannot with certainty be excluded for *Metiochus and Parthenope* either. It must be remembered, however, that there were other games in town: the *Incredible Things beyond Thule* of Antonius Diogenes, perhaps written in the same Carian city as *Callirhoe*, Aphrodisias, and even in the same decade,[17] gave priority to another of the novel's ancestors, the *Odyssey*, at least in scale and structure (twenty-four books). It took its brother and sister protagonists north and west, not east, and may have confined its hints of Xenophontic DNA to locating their family home in Tyre and having their story buried there in a grave and discovered by a soldier in Alexander's army that conquered Persia.

The strong Xenophontic color of many of the first novels left its mark on several that followed. The diverse parodic features of Achilles Tatius, writing in the early decades of the second century, are calculated to tease the reader of Plato rather than of Xenophon, but his *Clitophon and Leucippe* reverts to an eight-book structure, its geographical context is chiefly once-Persian Phoenicia, Egypt, and Ephesus, and Leucippe's mother is given the romantically resonant name Panthea and a strong commitment to chastity, albeit vicariously her daughter's. Iamblichus, writing around 170, gave his *Babylonian Histories* (*Babyloniaca*) an entirely eastern, and chiefly Mesopotamian, location and cast: one of its fortuitously transmitted fragments has clear linguistic echoes of Xenophon.[18]

A century or more later Heliodorus offered readers a new take on the figure of a noble "barbarian" whose virtues exemplified Greek philosophical ideals – the Egyptian priest Calasiris – and a journey upcountry (this

---

[16] With *Ninus* fr. B 9–11 "and there was fear concerning the cold temperatures and snows on the mountain passes" (καὶ φόβος μὲν ἦν κρυμῶν καὶ χιόνων περὶ τὰς ὀρείους ὑπερβολάς) cf. "the passes of the mountain" (τὰς ὑπερβολὰς τοῦ ὄρους) *Anab.* 4.6.7 and the snow of *Anab.* 4.4.11.

[17] Bowie 2002 and 2007 on dating Antonius Diogenes, Bowersock 1994: 34–40 on his probable origin in Aphrodisias.

[18] Münscher 1920: 146, noting the fragment "On how the Babylonian king goes forth" (περὶ προόδου τοῦ Βαβυλωνίων βασιλέως) fr. 1 Habrich, transmitted in *codd. Laurentianus* 57,12 and *Vaticanus* 1354 and reworking *Cyr.* 8.3.9–14.

time through Egypt to Ethiopia) by a youth Greek by birth, Theagenes, and a girl Greek by education, Charicleia. Alongside this reworking of the *Cyropaedia* and *Anabasis* the contrast between the virtue (ἀρετή) of the major characters and the vice (κακία) of the world initially inhabited by the Athenian Cnemon, a contrast especially important to Heliodorus' early books,[19] is a version of the choice offered Heracles between virtue and vice in the fable attributed by Socrates to Prodicus, one of the passages of Xenophon best known throughout antiquity. It is not by chance that Heliodorus gives Cnemon's father the name Aristippus,[20] precisely that of the similarly hedonistic pupil to whom Socrates addresses Prodicus' fable in the opening section of *Memorabilia* book 2. So far as I know the *Aethiopica* has not been carefully trawled for Xenophontic *mimesis*, and more doubtless awaits discovery.[21]

Of surviving novels only Longus' *Daphnis and Chloe* seems to eschew hints at the Xenophontic strand of the genre's ancestry, though Daphnis' first kiss from Chloe might allude to the end of the *Symposium*,[22] and the important scene in which Methymnan youths fail to control their hunting dogs (2.13.4) could at a pinch be read as homage to the *Cynegeticus*.

Philosopher, Historian, and Man of Action: the "New Xenophon" (ὁ νέος Ξενοφῶν)

The career and writings of Arrian present us with a quite different testimony to the influence of Xenophon in the early centuries A D. As with his older contemporary, Dio of Prusa, also Bithynian, Arrian's point of entry to the life and works of Xenophon was probably his *Memorabilia*, but this hangs on chronology, and hence that issue receives particular attention in the following discussion.

Lucius Flavius Arrianus was from Nicomedia in Bithynia, born (perhaps towards A D 90) into a family more probably descended from Italian settlers

---

[19] See Morgan 1989.

[20] Hld. 1.9.1 etc. The relevance of Aristippus' role in *Mem.* book 2 was missed by Bowie 1995.

[21] We might guess, for example, that Theagenes' people, the Aenianes, whose cavalrymen process so beautifully at Delphi (3.3) owe something to the Aenianes of *Anab.* 1.2.6 whose skillful dancing is picked out at 6.1.7.

[22] With "and partly because she had long desired to kiss Daphnis, she leapt up and gave him a kiss that was without training or artifice" (τὰ δὲ πάλαι ποθοῦσα φιλῆσαι Δάφνιν, ἀναπηδήσασα αὐτὸν ἐφίλησεν, ἀδίδακτον μὲν καὶ ἄτεχνον ...) *D&C* 1.17.1, compare "for they seemed like people who had not been taught their movements but who were eager to do what they had long desired" (ἐῴκεσαν γὰρ οὐ δεδιδαγμένοις τὰ σχήματα ἀλλ' ἐφιεμένοις πράττειν ἃ πάλαι ἐπεθύμουν) at *Smp.* 9.6 (of the simulated lovemaking of "Dionysus" and "Ariadne").

than one Greek for many generations.[23] His Asia Minor origins may have given him a particular interest in the *Anabasis* and *Cyropaedia*, probably read at school with a *grammaticus* and then studied for style and diction with a *rhetor*.[24] Where he studied rhetoric is unclear: there is little indication of high-quality rhetoric being taught in Nicomedia or Nicaea at this time:[25] he possibly went to one of the illustrious centers in the province of Asia, Ephesus, Smyrna, or Pergamum, but more probably to Athens. It could have been at Athens, then, that his plan to emulate Xenophon germinated, if not earlier – nothing in his few statements about his own career and interests sheds light on this.[26] The last stage in his formal education may have been his attendance at the lectures in Nicopolis (like Athens, in the Roman province of Achaea) of the Stoic ex-slave from Hierapolis in Phrygia, Epictetus. Arrian's fellow students included young men from senatorial families, and sometimes passing senators such as the Maximus who was *en route* to a post as financial controller (*corrector*, διορθωτής) of cities in Achaea: his appearance in the *Discourses* probably belongs to 107 or 108, offering a date for Arrian's own presence.[27] Such connections may have facilitated his first documented public position, participation in the advisory council (*consilium*) of the province's governor Gaius Avidius Nigrinus, meeting at Delphi between 111 and 114 to resolve a question of land ownership in Phocis.[28] It did not, of course, require an interest in Socrates to find a visit to Delphi rewarding, but such an interest would have enhanced Delphi's attractions.

The next stages in Arrian's career are obscure. A claim in the *Indian History* (*Indice* 4.15) to have seen the rivers Inn and Save has suggested a post in Noricum. He wrote about Trajan's Parthian War as if a participant, perhaps holding a junior command, but this is documented by nothing in epigraphy or his surviving writings. It is only a guess that he became a friend of Hadrian, now or earlier, or was adlected by Trajan or Hadrian to the senate.[29]

---

[23] Syme 1982: 210 canvasses 82 or 83 and suggests (184) that the now secure *praenomen* Lucius goes back to a grant of citizenship to his ancestors by Lucius Flavius *cos. suff.* 33 BC, while allowing that the names Flavius and Arrianus are "common and indistinctive."

[24] For Xenophon's place in curricula by the early empire see Münscher 1920: 140. For such education in general see Morgan 1998.

[25] See Bowie 2014b.

[26] E.g. Arrian, *Cyneg.* 7.4, asserting interest in war, philosophy, and hunting from an early age. See also the *Bithynica* quoted below, n. 41.

[27] Assuming the Maximus of *Diss.* 3.9 to be that of Plin. *Epp.* 8.24.2, identified by Syme 1982: 184–5 with Sex. Quinctilius Maximus from Alexandria Troas, *quaestor* in Bithynia-Pontus in AD 99/100.

[28] *Syll.*³ 827, republished by Plassart in *FdD* iii 4 (1970) no. 290.

[29] Syme 1982: 190 assumed he was adlected at praetorian level (*inter praetorios*): but even tribunician level (*inter tribunicios*) should not be excluded, cf. C. Iulius Severus of Ancyra, *ILS* 8826.

His next sighting is in Baetica, an "unarmed" province, where a puzzling poem inscribed at Cordoba marks a dedication by a proconsul Arrianus to Artemis, perhaps of the mid-120s.[30] Late in the 120s, probably in 129, he was suffect consul with a Severus as his colleague,[31] and from 131 to 137 imperial governor (*legatus pro praetore*) of Cappadocia, commanding two legions and auxiliary troops, with which he either fought off or deterred an Alan invasion in AD 135.[32] His last appearance is in 145/6 as archon in Athens,[33] where he had probably long had citizenship.

The Cappadocian command was the context for three literary works. The *Periplous* of the Black Sea, a Greek literary version of a report sent formally to Hadrian in Latin, belongs early in Arrian's governorship and is suffused with Xenophontic resonances. The *Order of Battle against the Alans*, in or soon after AD 135, evokes passages in the *Cyropaedia*, and presents Arrian simply calling himself "Xenophon," probably never part of his official nomenclature.[34] Finally the extant portion of his *Essay on Tactics*, dated explicitly to Hadrian's twentieth imperial year (136/7), deals only with cavalry and is some sort of descendant of Xenophon's *Hipparchus*.

As well as these technical works, and in the context of much time devoted to public offices,[35] Arrian composed major works which in varying degrees performed *mimesis* of Xenophon's oeuvre. Their dates are debated, and decisions on chronology have implications for the route by which Arrian proceeded to Xenophontic self-fashioning and for the works of Xenophon that were most important to it.

The earliest work is probably his *Discourses of Epictetus*, a collection manifestly modeled on Xenophon's *Memorabilia* and claimed in his prefatory letter to Lucius Gellius to have been published because unauthorized

[30] Cf. Bosworth 1976, Koenen 1977 (with references to the dozen preceding papers): *editio princeps* Tovar 1971: 401–12.
[31] Brick stamps *CIL* XV 244; 252.
[32] On date cf. Syme 1982: 200.
[33] *IG* II² 2055.
[34] *Ectaxis* 10, 21. At *Cyn.* 1.4 Arrian writes of himself as "having the same name as him (sc. Xenophon) and belonging to the same city and having had the same enthusiasms from my youth, hunting and military leadership and wisdom" (ὁμώνυμός τε ὢν αὐτῷ καὶ πόλεως τῆς αὐτῆς καὶ ἀμφὶ ταὐτὰ ἀπὸ νέου ἐσπουδακώς, κυνηγέσια καὶ στρατηγίαν καὶ σοφίαν: cf. the phrase at 16.7 "that other Xenophon" (ἐκείνῳ γε τῷ Ξενοφῶντι); at *Peripl.* 12.5 the name is implied by the sentence "this is told by the older Xenophon" (ταῦτα Ξενοφῶντι τῷ πρεσβυτέρῳ λέλεκται). Thus the Suda s.v. Ἀρριανός A 3868 claims Arrian "had the further name" (ἐπικληθείς) Xenophon, cf. Photius *Cod.* 58 (the *Parthica*) "and they gave him the additional name 'the new Xenophon'" (ἐπωνόμαζον δὲ αὐτὸν Ξενοφῶντα νέον). But "Xenophon" never appears in Arrian's name in an inscription, e.g. most recently the statue base from Comana published by Baz 2007 (now *I Comana* 63, cf. *SEG* 58.1665), where he is simply Φλ(άβιον) Ἀρριανόν.
[35] Cf. the *Bithynica* quoted below, n. 41.

versions of Arrian's lecture notes were circulating. Epictetus was a very different sort of philosopher from the Platonic Socrates, eschewing his aporetic stance and his patient luring of his interlocutor through a series of agreed propositions to a self-contradictory or absurd conclusion. But he was closer to Xenophon's Socrates, and the Stoic doctrines which Arrian's Epictetus preached were legitimate descendants of Socratic thought. Four books of *Discourses* (Διατριβαί) were thus a fair bid to establish their writer as a new Xenophon.[36] That Arrian did not entitle them *Memorabilia* (or *Memoirs*: Ἀπομνημονεύματα is the Greek title of Xenophon's work) is perhaps surprising: but at least one work so entitled, recording lectures and dicta of Epictetus' teacher, Gaius Musonius Rufus, had been published after his death not later than AD 101/2.[37] And if Arrian's publication of the *Discourses* is late, after his senatorial career, the waters may have been further muddied by Favorinus' recent use of the title *Memorabilia* for a work that apparently combined material concerning the history of the Academy with anecdotes about his own philosophical and sophistic career. But one reason for putting the *Discourses* earlier than his historical works is a statue base from Corinth on which a Lucius Gellius Menander honors a legate of Cappadocia, probably Arrian, precisely as a philosopher.[38]

Yet in theory, at least, the *Anabasis of Alexander*, with title and seven-book structure recalling Xenophon's, might compete with the *Discourses* for the status of Arrian's first major work. Bosworth thought it no later than AD 125.[39] It can hardly be earlier, given Arrian's boast that his claims to greatness rest not on his career "in his own city" (Nicomedia? Athens? Rome?) but on his pre-eminence in Greek letters:[40]

---

[36] The four books of *Discourses* transmitted are generally held only to be part of an eight-book work, but the evidence is shaky. For the relation between Epictetus' doctrines and Arrian's presentation see Brunt 1977.

[37] *Memorabilia of Musonius the Philosopher* (Ἀπομνημονεύματα Μουσωνίου τοῦ φιλοσόφου) are credited to Asinius Pollio of Tralles by the confused Suda entry Π 2165, but suggested by Münscher 1920: 122 rather to be by the Alexandrian Valerius Pollio, given a Hadrianic date by the Suda Π 2166.

[38] *AE* 1968, 473. *Corinth* VIII 3 n. 124: 3 [φιλ]όσοφ[ον(?) . . . . . .] ‖[πρεσ]βευτὴν [Αὐτοκρά τορος]‖Καί[σα]ρος Τραια[νοῦ Ἀδρ]ι[ανοῦ]‖5 [Σ]εβα[σ]τοῦ, ἀντιστ[ράτηγ]ον [τῆς]‖ ἐπαρχ[είας τῆς Καππαδ]οκ[ίας. Λ.]‖[Γ]έλλιος Μ[ένανδρος καὶ Λ. Γέλλιος]‖ [Ἰο]ῦστος υ(ἱὸς) το[ῦ Γελλίου Μενάνδρου]‖εὐεργ[εσίας ἕνεκεν]. Cf. Bowersock 1967. For Gellius see Arrian's introductory letter to the *Discourses*.

[39] Bosworth 1972, cf. Bosworth 1980: 6. Badian, in *Der Neue Pauly* "Arrianus [2]," thought such a claim for the importance of the *Anabasis* unlikely later in Arrian's literary career. Syme 1982: 206 n. 146 saw his use of the name Xenophon in *Peripl.* as indicating that the *Anabasis* had already been published – perhaps, or perhaps simply conceived?

[40] For excellent discussions see Moles 1985, Marincola 1989, and Strazdins 2012: 166–77.

But as to who I am to form these judgments about myself, I have no need to set down my name, for it is by no means unknown in the world, nor what my country is or my family, nor if I have held some high office in my city: but what I do set down is this, that these writings are for me my country and family and offices, and have been ever since my youth. And on this basis I do not think myself unworthy of the first rank in the Greek language, if indeed we also consider Alexander first in things military.

ὅστις δὲ ὢν ταῦτα ὑπὲρ ἐμαυτοῦ γιγνώσκω, τὸ μὲν ὄνομα οὐδὲν δέομαι ἀναγράψαι, οὐδὲ γὰρ οὐδὲ ἄγνωστον ἐς ἀνθρώπους ἐστίν, οὐδὲ πατρίδα ἥτις μοί ἐστιν οὐδὲ γένος τὸ ἐμόν, οὐδὲ εἰ δή τινα ἀρχὴν ἐν τῇ ἐμαυτοῦ ἦρξα· ἀλλ' ἐκεῖνο ἀναγράφω, ὅτι ἐμοὶ πατρίς τε καὶ γένος καὶ ἀρχαὶ οἵδε οἱ λόγοι εἰσί τε καὶ ἀπὸ νέου ἔτι ἐγένοντο. καὶ ἐπὶ τῷδε οὐκ ἀπαξιῶ ἐμαυτὸν τῶν πρώτων ἐν τῇ φωνῇ τῇ Ἑλλάδι, εἴπερ οὖν καὶ Ἀλέξανδρον τῶν ἐν τοῖς ὅπλοις.

Arrian, Anabasis 1.12.5

The issue is complicated by Arrian's similar claim in his eight-book history of Bithynia, as we know from Photius' summary, a claim that he had worked on it since his youth.[41] But just as that history was plausibly seen by Photius as belonging to Arrian's later years, so too the *Anabasis*' "second preface" counts against its being the work of a young writer.

This *Bithynian History* was, then, a sort of thank-offering to his native land when it had become clear that the years after his active senatorial career would be spent in Athens rather than, or more than, in Nicomedia. Later, probably, than the *Anabasis* were also his ten-book

---

[41] Photius, *Cod.* 93, p. 71a32: "The same writers's (i.e. Arrian's) *Bithynica* was read, eight books, in which he elegantly records mythical events concerning Bithynia and the rest of its history, offering an account of his country's history to his country. For in his work he establishes his own family as from Nicomedia, and that he was born and raised and educated there, and that he acted as priest of Demeter and her daughter, to whom, he says, the city is actually dedicated; and in this history he also mentions other works ... and he clearly composed the exposition of his country fourth; and it is after his works on Alexander, Dio, and Timoleon, after these three histories that he brought this composition to completion, although right from the beginning, from the point he had the capacity to write, he wanted to apply himself to and put together this theme, but its preparation was protracted by his lacking sufficient time – for this is the reason he gives himself for his tardiness in this" (ἀνεγνώσθη τοῦ αὐτοῦ (sc. Ἀρριανοῦ) τὰ Βιθυνικά, ἐν βιβλίοις ὀκτώ, ἐν οἷς τά τε μυθικὰ τὰ περὶ Βιθυνίας καὶ τἆλλα, ὅσα συνέστη περὶ αὐτήν, εἰς λεπτὸν ἀναγράφει, τῇ πατρίδι δῶρον ἀναφέρων τὰ πάτρια. Νικομήδειον γὰρ τὸ γένος αὐτοῦ ἐν ταύτῃ τῇ συγγραφῇ διορίζει, ἐν αὐτῇ τε γεννηθῆναι καὶ τραφῆναι καὶ παιδευθῆναι, καὶ ἱερέα τῆς Δήμητρος καὶ τῆς παιδὸς αὐτῆς, αἷς καὶ τὴν πόλιν ἀνακεῖσθαί φησι, χρηματίσαι. μέμνηται δὲ ἐν ταύτῃ τῇ συγγραφῇ καὶ ἑτέρων πραγματειῶν ... φαίνεται δὲ τετάρτην γράφων τὴν τῆς πατρίδος ἀφήγησιν. μετὰ γὰρ τὰ περὶ Ἀλέξανδρον καὶ Τιμολέοντα καὶ Δίωνα, μετὰ τὰς περὶ αὐτοὺς ἱστορίας, ἥδε αὐτῷ ἡ συγγραφὴ ἐξεπονήθη, καὶ ἐξ ἀρχῆς μὲν, ἀφ' οὗ γράφειν ἴσχυσε, ταύτην ἐνστήσασθαι καὶ συντάξαι τὴν ὑπόθεσιν βουληθέντι, τῆς δὲ παρασκευῆς τῷ ἐνδεῶς αὐτὸν ἔχειν παρατεινάσης τὸν χρόνον· ταύτην γὰρ αὐτὸς τῆς ἐπὶ τούτῳ βραδυτῆτος ἀποδίδωσιν αἰτίαν).

history of Alexander's successors and his seventeen-book *Parthian History* (*Parthica*). This substantial work – seven books on earlier history and geopolitics, ten on Trajan's war – falls as much in the tradition of Herodotus (the Persian Empire, Persian wars) and Thucydides (an account of a single war) as that of Xenophon. Thus although we also find *mimesis* of Xenophon in another minor work, the *Cynegeticus*, which explicitly updates that of Xenophon, and although there may well have been emulation of the *Agesilaus* in Arrian's lost lives of *Dio* and of *Timoleon*, in most of his major historical works Arrian has cut the umbilical cord with his Athenian hero and writes history (as stylistic analysis shows he wrote his Greek) as much under the influence of Herodotus and Thucydides. That Herodotus-*mimesis* was attractive is shown by the Ionic dialect he chose for his account of the return of Alexander's fleet from the Indus to Susa in his *Indian History* (*Indice*).

The sequence *Discourses – Anabasis –* other historical works constructs an Arrian on whom Xenophontic influence was in the first instance that of the *Memorabilia* – primarily, perhaps, a by-product of his youthful exposure to philosophy. There followed emulation of the *Anabasis*, with necessary transposition from autoptic history, albeit always presented by Xenophon in the third person, to a narrative fatally dependent on often contradictory sources. This may have encouraged Arrian to tackle other types of history, including the *Parthica* and *Alanice* that we have lost, each of which will have allowed some element of autopsy.[42]

This reconstruction would change if the *Anabasis* were earlier than the *Discourses*, but the former would probably remain Arrian's historiographic début.[43] We might conjecture that Xenophon's personal loyalties, torn between Athens and Sparta, and his literary schizophrenia, oscillating between admiration of Greece and of Persia, enhanced his appeal to a descendant of Latin settlers in Bithynia who grew up Greek and was among the relatively small number of Greek speakers from the East to rise to the consulate and have a military career in the service of Rome.[44]

Further Reading

No monograph in English has been devoted to Dio of Prusa since Jones 1978, but aspects of Xenophon's impact are touched on in Swain 2000 and Gangloff 2006. In the voluminous scholarship on the Greek novel in the last

[42] But note the caution of Syme 1982: 189.
[43] But cf. speculatively Syme 1982: 181–2.
[44] Vidal-Naquet 1984 follows through aspects of the dichotomy, noting in particular the interracial marriages at Susa in *Anabasis* 7.4.4–8.

fifty years Reardon 1991 remains an excellent introduction (with English translations of the novels and major fragments in Reardon 2008) and a flavor of work since then can be found in Whitmarsh 2008. Illuminating recent work on Chariton includes Smith 2007 and Tilg 2010. Arrian too has had no recent monograph, but Stadter 1980 (one of the catalysts for Syme 1982) remains an excellent introduction.

21

NOREEN HUMBLE

Xenophon and the Instruction of Princes

The reception of Xenophon in the early modern period is complex. His fourteen extant works cross numerous generic boundaries and therefore appealed, then as now, to different interests. Further, appreciating his corpus as a whole for some time depended upon the ability to read Greek, along with access to manuscripts containing the texts. Not many were in this position. It took more than a century from the recovery of Xenophon's works in the West (ca. 1400) before his whole corpus had been translated into Latin – the earliest complete edition of Latin translations appeared in 1534 while a complete edition of the Greek texts only appeared in 1540[1] – and it was much longer again before all the works had been translated into the various vernaculars. It is clear, however, that the most popular of his works to start with were the *Hiero*, *Cyropaedia*, and *Oeconomicus*. It is also clear that, regardless of the way we tend to read these works now, all three were mined for supportive material by those writing instructional handbooks for rulers, *specula principum* ("mirrors-for-princes"), a genre of writing that had been in existence for a long time and was constantly evolving as it was adapted to new political realities.[2] Of the three, however, it is the *Cyropaedia* that had the widest reach as an instructional guide, not just for princes but eventually in a broader sense for anyone who would potentially hold a position of power (e.g. priests, teachers, magistrates, etc.). Accordingly, the majority of this chapter will be concerned with examples of how the *Cyropaedia*, in particular, was received and appropriated, with an emphasis on the early modern period.

Once the Greek text of the *Cyropaedia* began circulating in the quattrocento, there was little chance that the work was going to be read in any

---

[1] Marsh 1992: 82. In 1525 a Greek edition was published that was missing only the *Apology*. The first of Xenophon's works to be translated into Latin was the *Hiero* by Leonardo Bruni in 1403 (see further below), the last was the *Hellenica* in the first quarter of the sixteenth century.

[2] See Skinner 1988.

other way than as an advice book for leaders because Cicero had praised it and recommended it on those grounds in two works which had rapidly become core texts in fifteenth-century schools.[3] In his first letter to Quintus (1.1.23) he writes:

> Such is that famous Cyrus, described by Xenophon, not according to historical truth, but as a representation of just rule. By that philosopher there were united in Cyrus the greatest dignity and a remarkable courtesy. Indeed, not without reason was our renowned Africanus accustomed to keep those books in his hands. For in them no duty of a diligent and moderate ruler is passed over. And if that person, who was destined never to be a private individual, so cultivated these things, in what way do you think ought they to be practised by those to whom authority has been so given that they must give it back, and given by those laws to which they must return?[4]

And in a letter to Paetus (*Epistulae ad Familiares* 9.25.1) he presents himself, with his characteristic lack of modesty, as benefiting also from reading the work: "The *Cyropaedia*, which I have worn out by reading, I have thoroughly exemplified during my command."

Indeed, Lorenzo Valla (ca. 1401–57), who was the first to translate any portion of the work, dedicating in 1438 his Latin translation of *Cyropaedia* 1.1.1–1.4.15 to Alfonso V of Naples and his son Ferdinand, is in no doubt about how it should be read. He says, of Alfonso: "for you recall Cyrus and represent him as though in a mirror (*quasi in speculo*)."[5] At no point with any of the subsequent translations is there any real deviation from this line. Though none will again specifically use the word *speculum* when referring to the text, almost all who translate the work refer to the fact that Scipio and Cicero kept the book close at hand in order to justify their translation project by pointing to the general usefulness of the work.

For those who could read Greek and were able to get hold of a manuscript of the *Cyropaedia*, access to the work could be had – and indeed was sought – from as early as the beginning of the fifteenth century.[6] By the middle of the century (1447) an abbreviated six-book Latin translation was available, the work of Poggio Bracciolini (1380–1459), also made for Alfonso V. Though it was never printed it achieved a certain popularity, to judge both from the number of extant manuscripts and from the fact that his Latin version was the basis for the first French and Italian translations of

---

[3] See Sancisi-Weerdenburg 1990: 38 on Cicero's positive advance broadcasting of Xenophon's *Cyropaedia*, and Black 2001: 352–7 for the prominence of these Ciceronian works on school curricula.
[4] All translations are my own unless otherwise noted.
[5] On Valla's translation see Marsh 1984.
[6] See Sancisi-Weerdenburg 1990: 37–9 and Botley 2010: 92.

Figure 21.1. This vignette appears on the initial page of a presentation copy (1470) of Francesco Filelfo's translation into Latin of the *Cyropaedia*. The recipient, Federico da Montefeltro, is depicted on horseback approaching the seated Cyrus. Vatican Library, ms Urb. lat. 410, f. 1r.

the work in the 1470s.[7] The first complete Latin translation of the work, by Francesco Filelfo (1398–1481) and dedicated in 1469 to Pope Paul II, was the first in any language to make it into print, in 1477.[8] The initial page of the Latin translation in the lavish presentation copy of Filelfo's edition made for Federico da Montefeltro in 1470 features a miniature vignette: Federico himself is shown on horseback approaching the seated Cyrus (Figure 21.1).

As mentioned above, all these translators promoted the work as a *speculum principis*, though in all cases they were careful to note that their princely dedicatees actually had no need of the lessons found in the text, since they had already reached the height of perfection achieved by Cyrus. Too much, of course, cannot be read into this type of rhetoric; excessive praise of a dedicatee was a standard feature of dedication letters.[9] But the fact that sole and powerful rulers or rulers-to-be were invariably the dedicatees of this work testifies to the way in which it was initially read and promoted and how readily and easily it meshed with contemporary thinking.

Given that Cicero had pigeonholed the *Cyropaedia* as an ancient *speculum* and that the early modern translators all marketed the work in a similar vein, we might reasonably expect to find early modern *specula* engaging with the *Cyropaedia*, and, indeed, we do. Authors of this type of writing did not pass up the opportunity to add the authority of Xenophon's Cyrus to their arguments once they became aware of it. However, while it is often noted that Xenophon's *Cyropaedia* had a significant influence on this type of writing, what precise form this influence took is less frequently examined, with one exception.

"Xenophon's Best-Known and Most-Devoted Reader":[10] the Case of Machiavelli

Though Niccolò Machiavelli (1469–1527) is far from being the first humanist to make use of the *Cyropaedia*, he makes a good starting point for the discussion, partly because his use of Xenophon has attracted some scholarly attention, and partly because the complicated reception of his own works mirrors the problems of studying the reception of ancient authors in this period. The plethora of views on Machiavelli tends to suggest that readers find what they are looking for in his works,[11] just as early modern readers

---

[7] See Marsh 1992: 118–20 on Poggio's translation, and 81 for a brief survey of early vernacular translations.
[8] On Filelfo's Latin translation of the *Cyropaedia*, see the recent edition by De Keyser 2012.
[9] On common topoi in dedication letters see Gualda Rosa 1973.
[10] As Nadon 2001: 6 refers to Machiavelli.
[11] Berlin 1972 discusses this tendency.

of ancient Greek texts tended to find what they were looking for in the texts that they were reading.

Generally discussion is confined to *The Prince* (*Il principe*, finished by 1513 but not published until 1532) and *The Discourses* (*Discorsi sopra la prima deca di Tito Livio*, probably written ca. 1516–19 but not published until 1531). Between these two works Xenophon's *Cyropaedia* is explicitly referenced five times. In *The Prince*, Machiavelli closes chapter 14 with an exhortation to rulers to read historical works and to imitate eminent men who themselves imitated others, as Scipio imitated Cyrus:

> Anyone who reads the life of Cyrus, written by Xenophon, will realise, when he considers Scipio's life and career, how greatly Scipio's imitation of Cyrus helped him to attain glory, and how much Scipio's sexual restraint, affability, humanity and generosity derived from his imitating the qualities of Cyrus, as recorded in this work by Xenophon. (trans. Skinner and Price 1988: 53–4)

The other four occurrences can be found in the *Discourses*, where Xenophon's Cyrus is brought in in support of diverse points. First, Cyrus provides a historical precedent to support the use of deceit (2.13.1; trans. Gilbert 1989: 1.357): "with deception and not with force he gained his kingdom. No other conclusion is to be drawn from such an action than that a prince who wishes to do great things must learn to deceive." Secondly, after showing how Camillus took the town of the Falisci by showing decency and integrity, and how Scipio gained renown for his continence when he returned a young wife to her husband unmolested and so won over all Spain as a result, Xenophon's Cyrus is held up as an example of all these qualities (3.20.2–3). Thirdly, in comparing the severity of Manlius Torquatus to the sociability of Valerius Corvinus, Machiavelli argues that the latter quality is more useful for a prince and again brings in Xenophon's Cyrus as a model precursor of Valerius because of his fidelity to the constitution, his reputed virtue, and his affability, kindliness, and compassion (3.22.6, 9). And finally, Xenophon's Cyrus is given as an example of a leader who very much appreciated the importance, in wartime, of skills learned in hunting (3.39.1). These examples do not by any means exhaust references to Cyrus in these two works of Machiavelli. He is quite happy too to make use of the less sunny portrait known from Herodotus and in some instances the portrait he draws seems an amalgam.[12]

What are we meant to make of the way Machiavelli draws on Xenophon? Scholars who have taken their inspiration from Leo Strauss, who himself worked both on revivifying Xenophon's reputation as a serious political

[12] See Sancisi-Weerdenburg 1990: 47–9 for a brief and complementary overview of Machiavelli's composite portrait of Cyrus.

philosopher and on situating Machiavelli as the first political philosopher to break decisively with the past, argue that Machiavelli, though seemingly favorable to the *Cyropaedia*, is actually at the same time engaging in an extended critique of it which goes far beyond the explicit references to the work. Machiavelli, so one reading goes, could see that Xenophon had the right idea – force and deceit being necessary for successful political rule – but he felt that Xenophon left this message too much in the background. Hence, Scipio's ultimate failure (*Prince* 17), particularly, on this reading, compared to Hannibal (*Discourses* 3.21).[13]

Whether or not we agree that Machiavelli engaged with Xenophon's text in such a sustained way, it would have been surprising had he made no reference at all to the *Cyropaedia*. However radical Machiavelli's advice is in *The Prince*, for example, he is still couching his ideas within a well-established generic form of writing, the *speculum principis*.[14] Further, in separating out his discussions of principalities (*The Prince*) and republics (*The Discourses*), regardless of a certain amount of overlap, he is again following in the footsteps of others.[15] Within these types of writing it was customary to appropriate ancient exempla, frequently with a disregard for the original context, for authoritative support, and "it was the applicability of these ideas that was important, not their historical truth."[16] Thus once knowledge of Xenophon's *Cyropaedia* was acquired, it was appropriated as needed as an authoritative exemplar, more easily perhaps in advice books aimed at princes, but also in discussions of other types of governments.

So, for example, several decades prior to Machiavelli's *Prince*, Giovanni Pontano (1429–1503) in his *De principe* (*On the Prince*, 1468), which was written in the style of a letter to Alfonso, Duke of Calabria, is actually much more forthright than Machiavelli in his recommendation of Cyrus as a model and anticipates him in linking Camillus, Scipio, and Cyrus as exemplars of piety:

> A person will be considered to have justice when everyone bears his authority patiently and when they even submit themselves to his restraint willingly. This is what we read about Cyrus, who is thought to have been an example not only of justice but of all the royal virtues [cf. *Cyr.* 1.1.3] ... The aforementioned Cyrus, as well as Camillus, Scipio Africanus, and all very eminent

---

[13] See, e.g., Newell 1988; similarly Nadon 2001: 13–25.

[14] See Gilbert 1938: 8–9 on Machiavelli's awareness of the tradition in which he writes. See also the salutary remarks of Quentin Skinner in a recent article in the *New York Review of Books* (July 5, 2014).

[15] See Hankins 2009: ix–x for a succinct overview.

[16] Rummel 1985: 118 is commenting on Erasmus here but the observation applies more broadly.

men have been distinguished in this virtue [i.e. piety], and your grandfather Alfonso surpassed every king of his own age and of many earlier centuries. (trans. Kraye 1997: 70)

Kindness also brings many benefits. Since you excel in that virtue, you are not only assured of being loved by your friends, but also by everyone else. Cyrus, whom I particularly want you to imitate, at a time when he was least able to be generous, owing to his own poverty, used to try to obtain the goodwill of his followers through kindness, assisting them in their work and sharing their labors. When afterwards he acquired the kingdom of Assyria, he was unstinting in every type of generosity, since it was not money but his friends, to whom he had given considerable wealth, which he regarded as his treasure. He took so much pleasure in the prosperity not only of his friends and household but also of each one of his subjects that he said it was the duty – and in fact a requisite – of a good king to make communities happy as well [cf. *Cyr.* 3.3.6–7]. (trans. Kraye 1997: 77, slightly modified)

Likewise, Platina (Bartolomeo Sacchi, 1421–81) in his *De principe* (*On the Prince*, 1471), which was dedicated, like Pontano's work, to one of his princely tutees, Federico Gonzaga of Mantua, makes extensive use of the *Cyropaedia* as an exemplary text, not just recommending it and Cyrus as exemplars for others, but remarking that he himself used it as a model for his own work (see the proem to his third book on military matters).[17] And he repeats points almost all the translators make in their dedicatory epistles:

Cicero confirms that Scipio was accustomed to keep the *Cyropaedia* of Xenophon constantly to hand; and Cicero, having worn out his copy through frequent reading, exemplified the entire book during his command. Nothing stirs our hearts as much towards virtue, courage, temperateness and true glory as seeing the names of deserving, learned men committed to writing for all time. This incentive is entirely lacking to those who are without knowledge and experience of literary pursuits. (trans. Kraye 1997: 102)

Recalling Cicero's comments about Scipio reading the *Cyropaedia* tripled the weightiness of the exemplum: it would be hard to find an ancient author in the period better and more widely known than Cicero, and Scipio, though generally held up as a great Republican hero, had also been *the* model of sexual restraint, affability, humanity, and generosity (even without the comparison with Cyrus) since the time of Petrarch.[18]

If, however, Machiavelli was aiming to counter earlier wholehearted recommendations that rulers read the *Cyropaedia* by suggesting instead that

---

[17] Ferrau 1979 notes eleven instances in which the *Cyropaedia* is drawn upon in an unambiguously positive way throughout this work.

[18] The story Machiavelli reports in the *Discourses* of Scipio's continence and sexual restraint had long been celebrated in prose, poetry, and art. See Cast 1974.

ancient historical works like the *Cyropaedia* needed to be read with care (as the example of Scipio, who on this reading was not ruthless enough, shows),[19] he is not alone in this either. In his *Institutio principis christiani* (*Education of a Christian Prince*, 1516), dedicated to the young Prince Charles (later Charles V), Erasmus of Rotterdam (1466–1536) makes a similar point much more forthrightly:

> See that you are not misled by the names of writers and leaders celebrated by the agreed judgment of the ages. Both Herodotus and Xenophon were pagans and very often depict the worst image of a prince, even if in doing so they were writing history, whether telling an enjoyable story or painting a picture of an outstanding leader … When you hear of Achilles, Xerxes, Cyrus, Darius and Julius, do not be at all overwhelmed by the enormous prestige of their names; you are hearing about great raging bandits, for that is what Seneca calls them several times. (trans. Cheshire and Heath 1986: 251)

In expressing such reservations both Erasmus and Machiavelli are much more likely to be engaging with the blanket approval given works like the *Cyropaedia* by predecessors and contemporaries than engaging in an extended critique of the *Cyropaedia* itself.

Later in the work Erasmus's more positive comment, about Xenophon's *Cyropaedia* wisely teaching about the importance of educating the young,[20] is neither contradictory nor does it negate the admonition above. Erasmus does not deny that there is material of value in works like the *Cyropaedia* and that a wise reader, forearmed and reading with discretion, will gain some value from the work – he himself is such a reader – but his engagement with the text is due to the fact both that his predecessors in this genre engaged with it and that it has some points he can usefully re-present. To assert, therefore, that the *Cyropaedia* was of central importance to Erasmus, as there is a tendency to do,[21] is not quite accurate. Indeed, Erasmus in his preface views himself in composing the *Institutio* as being in competition with another ancient *speculum*, Isocrates' *To Nicocles*, a work he himself had translated into Latin in 1516, dedicating it also to the future Holy Roman Emperor, Charles V.[22]

---

[19] Benner 2013: 173–5.
[20] "The prince who is about to take up office must bear this fact especially in mind, that the chief hope for the state is founded in the proper training of its children – something which Xenophon wisely taught in his *Cyropaedia*" (trans. Cheshire and Heath 1986: 259).
[21] E.g. Gilbert 1938: 13 and Rummel 1985: 16.
[22] "I have taken Isocrates' work on the principles of government and translated it into Latin, and in competition with him I have added my own, arranged as it were in aphorisms for the reader's convenience, but with considerable differences from what he laid down" (trans. Cheshire and Heath 1986: 204).

The *Hiero* and *Oeconomicus*: Exemplary Sententiae

There has been a modern tendency to regard only the *Cyropaedia* as a model for the mirror-for-princes genre in the early modern period. Two other works of Xenophon, however, also functioned as authoritative ancient sources for political philosophers to draw upon to reinforce pertinent points in their treatises: the *Hiero* and the *Oeconomicus*. Here perhaps we can see more easily the tendency of Renaissance political philosophers to cherry pick and decontextualize points in order to hammer home their own theories: useful material, no matter what its context, was readily appropriated without any real concern for its original context.

The *Hiero* was, in fact, the first of Xenophon's works to be translated into Latin, in 1403 by the learned Florentine humanist Leonardo Bruni (1370–1444). He dedicated it to his friend Niccolò Niccoli. This translation circulated widely (even now ca. two hundred manuscripts are extant) and indeed it was not superseded until Erasmus sat down to provide a new Latin translation, which he dedicated in 1530 to the banker Anton Fugger. The *Oeconomicus*, on the other hand, was translated several times in the fifteenth century. But contrary to the fate of Bruni's *Hiero*, extant manuscript evidence does not suggest wide circulation, and the first version to make it into print, in 1506, was the somewhat inaccurate translation of Raphael Maffei (1451–1522), who dedicated it to his wife, Minuccia.[23]

As might be expected, of the two treatises the *Hiero* had the bigger impact on political writing. Erasmus, in his dedicatory letter, makes a point of arguing that Xenophon uses the word tyrant in the archaic sense of king, and that although "this material does not in every respect fit the state of these times ... there are in the work many things which will be not useless for our princes also to know." But it is telling that neither he nor the work's first translator, Bruni – who in fact entitled the work *De vita tirannica*, in an age when the word tyrant did not carry any positive connotations at all – ventured to dedicate the work to a princely ruler, in the way that all translators of the *Cyropaedia* did. It has been shown, though, that Bruni ably used ideas from the *Hiero* to bolster his own views about kingship,[24] as did that early translator of the *Cyropaedia*, Poggio Bracciolini, in his *De infelicitate principum* (*On the Misfortune of Princes*).[25] Pontano considered the work important enough to copy out himself,[26] and Machiavelli in arguing that a tyrant "alone profits from his conquests, not his country" refers his reader

[23] See Marsh 1992: 149–56 (on the *Hiero*), 177–80 (on the *Oeconomicus*).
[24] Maxson 2009.
[25] Kajanto 1994 and Canfora 1996.
[26] De Nichilo 2013: 336–7.

to Xenophon's *Hiero* (*Discourses* 2.2.3). The work even becomes a mirror-for-tyrants in Etienne de la Boétie's (1530–63) *Discours sur la servitude volontaire* (*Discourse on Voluntary Servitude*), published in 1548:

> Xenophon, grave historian of first rank among the Greeks, wrote a book in which he makes Simonides speak with Hiero, tyrant of Syracuse, concerning the anxieties of the tyrant. This book is full of fine and serious remonstrances, which in my opinion are as persuasive as words can be. Would to God that all despots who have ever lived might have kept it before their eyes and used it as a mirror! (trans. Kurz 1942: 30–1)

The *Oeconomicus*, despite the evidence of the manuscript tradition, seems likewise to have been well known early on in the fifteenth century and from the start was used to provide an weighty exemplary model for female behavior in treatises about women and marriage, that is, as a sort of mirror-for-wives. Francesco Barbaro's (1390–1454) *De re uxoria* (*On Wifely Duties*) of 1416,[27] and Leon Battista Alberti's (1404–72) *I libri della famiglia* (*Books Concerning the Family*) of 1434 both make ample use of it.[28] And while Juan Luis Vives (1493–1540) may have drawn more heavily on the pseudo-Aristotelian *Economics* than Xenophon's work for his later (1523) *De institutione feminae christianae* (*On the Education of a Christian Woman*),[29] there is no doubt that he knew the value of Xenophon's work as an exemplary forebear of this type of writing. In his preface to Catherine of Aragon he writes:

> Moreover, when Xenophon and Aristotle transmitted rules for the management of domestic affairs, and Plato for the state, they made some observations pertaining to the duty of the woman. (trans. Fantazzi 2000: 45–6)

Clearly the intended audience for such treatises, in the main, was male, and they in no way challenge the contemporary male-female hierarchy; but not all translators and appropriators were content to leave the status quo unchallenged – at least in the imaginative world of print. It has been argued, for example, that Alessandro Piccolomini's (1508–79) Italian translation of the *Oeconomicus* in 1540 levels the balance between men and women even more than in the original, and certainly more than what is found in texts like those of Barbaro and Alberti, the latter of whom in particular presents a far more misogynistic picture than does Xenophon.[30]

---

[27] Barbaro also draws on the story of Panthea from the *Cyropaedia*; on his *De re uxoria* see Kohl 1978.
[28] See most recently Cabrini 2007. In the preface to book 3 Alberti writes: "I wished to try as much as I could to imitate that sweetest and most pleasant writer, Xenophon" (for the Italian text see Pellegrini and Spongano 1949: 234).
[29] Fantazzi 2000: 28–9. See also, briefly, Pomeroy 1994: 77–80.
[30] Robin 2013.

While the *Oeconomicus* was not itself viewed as a mirror-for-princes, it did contain material which could be easily adapted to the purposes of such treatises as well as to those of political writings more widely. It is, for example, the second (only to Aristotle) of a whole host of ancient authorities mentioned by Erasmus in the dedication letter accompanying his *Education of a Christian Prince*:

> Wisdom in itself is a wonderful thing, Charles greatest of princes, and no kind of wisdom is rated more excellent by Aristotle than that which teaches how to be a beneficent prince; for Xenophon in his *Oeconomicus* rightly considers that there is something beyond human nature, something wholly divine, in absolute rule over free and willing subjects. (trans. Cheshire and Heath 1986: 203)

That the point was to find some way to use ancient authors as authoritative ballast for contemporary arguments is well illustrated by an example from Justus Lipsius's (1547–1606) *Politica* (*Political Matters*, 1589). A reader would have been hard-pressed to imagine that the excerpted nugget "a well-arranged army is most pleasant to behold for friends, and most hateful to the enemy" (*Politica* 5.13.3) was, in its original context, one among a number of examples used by Ischomachus to teach his wife the importance of order in the household (*Oec.* 8.6).[31]

Entrenchment and Expansion: Prudential Economics, Poetics, and Pedagogy

As the sixteenth century progressed more and more of the literate population had access to ancient Greek authors as printing became fully established and vernacular translations were circulated. The *Oeconomicus* now comes to be appropriated as a "model for the eloquent legitimation of the application of thrifty and prudential principles of resource management."[32] The title given to the first French translation of the work in 1531 encapsulates this reception strand: *Science, pour senrichir honestement & facilement intitulee l'economic* (*Science for Enriching Oneself Honestly and Easily, Entitled The Oeconomicus*).

The reception of the *Cyropaedia* too becomes increasingly complex.[33] Already in the late fifteenth century, Cicero's comment marking it out as a fictive model of just rule was influencing other strands of interpretation, including a broader debate about the purposes of literature and specifically

---

[31] Waszink 2004: 60.
[32] Hutson 1994: 41.
[33] The story of Panthea, for example, takes on a life of its own in novellas, plays, and art.

about the power of poetry as the genre that could best incite emulation to virtue. In this debate the fictive exemplariness of the *Cyropaedia* can be found coupled with Virgil's *Aeneid*.[34] Further, Baldassare Castiglione (1478–1529), in his enormously influential mirror-for-courtiers, *Il cortegiano* (*The Courtier*) published in 1528, left his audience in no doubt about how he was reading the work. In his letter of dedication to Don Michel de Silva, he writes:

> Others say that since it is so very hard and well nigh impossible to find a man as perfect as I wish the Courtier to be, it was superfluous to write of him, because it is folly to teach what cannot be learned. To these I make answer that I am content to have erred in company with Plato, Xenophon and Marcus Tullius, leaving on one side all discussions about the Intelligible World and Ideals, among which, just as are included (according to those authors) the ideal of the perfect State, of the perfect King and of the perfect Orator, so also is the ideal of the perfect Courtier. (trans. Opdycke 2000: 7)

It has also been argued that Castiglione regarded his work as a sort of "Francesco-paedia" for his patron Francesco Maria della Rovere, Duke of Urbino, who was aged seventeen at the dramatic date of the dialogue and was one of the imaginary interlocutors in the work.[35]

The fundamental development, however, that ensured that the *Cyropaedia* became entrenched as an exemplary text for those in power or destined for powerful positions, was its adoption as a suitable text for learning Greek, particularly in Reformed circles. This is nicely illustrated in a work from 1559 entitled *Große Kirchenordnung* (*Great Church Organization*), which set out church and educational regulations for the Duchy of Württemberg. The document describes in copious detail the curriculum for the first five years of schooling. In the fifth year, when the students begin to study Greek, Xenophon's *Cyropaedia* and Aesop's Fables are listed as the texts of choice.[36] The first three years of the curriculum were clearly modeled on Philip Melanchthon's (1497–1560) *Visitation Articles* of 1528 and it is not a stretch to see the hand of the man who will come to be called the *praeceptor Germaniae* ("the teacher of Germany") in the choice of the Greek texts as well.[37] Melanchthon's knowledge of and positive opinion of the *Cyropaedia* are evident, for example, in his very significant revision in 1558 of a work that became the standard historical textbook in universities in the sixteenth

---

[34] See Wilson-Okamura 2010: 59–60, 208 for brief discussion.
[35] Albury 2011.
[36] Methuen 1994.
[37] See Springer 2011: 188 on Melanchthon's role in establishing Aesop's Fables on the educational curriculum.

century, *Carion's Chronicle*.[38] To the section on Cyrus, Melanchthon added the following:[39]

> It was to be wished that more things about Cyrus were in the book of Daniel but let us read as much as antiquity has handed down to us and contemplate diligently the virtues of Cyrus in Xenophon. In the whole history he never gets angry, he does not vie through ambition, he yields to Cyaxares, and he says that he has not rejoiced over much. So great was his diligence that he did not give his commands to unnamed people as a negligent paterfamilias says: "let someone go to fetch water, let someone cut wood"; but he gave commands by name to individuals who were known and he remembered their names. He ordered proclamation to be made in wartime that farmers were to be spared and were to be as little as possible part of the war. He ordered victory to be such that possessors should remain in charge of their possessions. He wished armed enemies to be repressed and a people which desired peace to be saved.

For Melanchthon historical events were first and foremost opportunities to present moral lessons,[40] and pagan narratives were promoted insofar as they could fulfill this purpose. It is no coincidence that a significant number of the sixteenth-century translations and commentaries of the *Cyropaedia* were produced by Melanchthon's friends and pupils, most notably his close friend Joachim Camerarius (1500–74), whose translation and commentary, dedicated to Count Anton von Ortenburg in 1572, was widely read.

Establishment of the text's authority was occurring in English Protestant circles around the same time.[41] Thomas Elyot (1490–1546) recommended it wholeheartedly in his popular political and educational handbook *The Book Named the Governor* of 1531, a work dedicated to Henry VIII but aimed also more broadly at young English noblemen (1.11):

> Xenophon, being both a philosopher and an excellent captain, so invented and ordered his work named *Paedia Cyri*, which may be interpreted the Childhood or Discipline of Cyrus, that he leaves to the readers thereof an incomparable sweetness and example of living, especially for the conducting and well ordering of hosts or armies. (Croft 1883: 84; silently modernized)

But perhaps more important for its promulgation was a coterie at Cambridge led by John Cheke (1514–57), the first Regius Chair of Greek in Cambridge in 1540 and subsequently tutor to Prince Edward from 1544 to 1549. Some

---

[38] This work chronicled world history from creation up to the sixteenth century. It was composed first by Johann Carion and printed in 1532. From the start, Melanchthon was involved as an advisor. The work was reprinted many times and translated into all the vernaculars; see Lotito 2011.

[39] For the Latin text see *Corpus Reformatorum* 12.784.

[40] See Ben-Tov 2009.

[41] For a general overview of the *Cyropaedia* in the English renaissance see Grogan 2007.

of those connected to Cheke in various ways themselves became influential schoolteachers, particularly Thomas Ashton (at Shrewsbury) and Richard Mulcaster (at Merchant Taylors in London), who taught Greek to Philip Sidney and Edmund Spenser, respectively.[42] Both pupils drew upon the *Cyropaedia* for their poetical purposes. Sidney, in setting forth his theory of poetics in his *Defense of Poesy* (1583), tapped into the now long-standing tradition of appropriating the *Cyropaedia* as an exemplar of the power of fiction over history:

> But if the question be for your own use and learning, whether it be better to have it set down as it should be, or as it was, then certainly is more doctrinable the feigned Cyrus of Xenophon than the true Cyrus in Justin, and the feigned Aeneas in Virgil than the right Aeneas in Dares Phrygius. (Maslen 2002: 92)

And Spenser declares in a letter to Walter Ralegh that Xenophon's *Cyropaedia* is to be preferred, as a model for *The Faerie Queene* (1590), to Plato's *Republic* because it presents "doctrine by ensample [example]," and he uses it as a model for his own fictive knights.[43]

A third Protestant group needs to be added to the mix here as well. Humanists of Calvinist persuasion were in fact responsible for the bulk of the editorial and commentary tradition on Xenophon's works during the sixteenth century, the most notable of the group being the scholar/publisher Henri II Estienne (1531–98). In 1561 Estienne published a bilingual *Opera omnia* of Xenophon's works (dedicated to Camerarius, who was working on his own translation of the *Cyropaedia* at the same time). The revised edition of 1581 was dedicated to James VI of Scotland (1566–1625). In the dedication letter Estienne explicitly compares James to Cyrus:

> Therefore may God greatest and best bestow upon you this ornament of your realm and all the other things by means of which you may carry its glory far and wide, and may he bring it about that the whole world may admire in you an image painted for our times of that Cyrus whom our Xenophon so graphically painted. For he (Cyrus) brought back to their fatherland God's people who had been in exile for so many years. Just as to you while still a boy it was granted to pull back into your realm the Christian religion that had been left out in the cold.

The comparison hinges on the actions of the biblical Cyrus and his restoration of the Jews (*Ezra* 1:2–4) – a point about Cyrus not mentioned in the

---

[42] On these pedagogical connections see Rhodes 2013.
[43] See Grogan 2014: 58–62 for Sidney's and Spenser's appropriation of the *Cyropaedia*.

Cyropaedia – and refers to the establishment of the Church of Scotland in the 1560s. James, however, perhaps saw himself more as a Xenophontic Cyrus. We know that as a boy, when he was under the tutelage of the eminent Scottish humanist George Buchanan (1506–82), and Peter Young (1544–1628),[44] that he read at least some of the *Cyropaedia*, because we have in Young's hand some notes about his pupil's reaction to some of the texts they read, which he entitles "Apophthegmata Regis" ("Sayings of the King"). There is one on the *Cyropaedia*:[45]

> While reading in Xenophon [*Cyr.* 5.2.28] how Gadates had been castrated for the fact that the concubine of the King looked at him with approval, the King [James] said that the woman should have been castrated instead.

In 1599 when James came to compose his own work of princely instruction, the *Basilikon Doron* (*Royal Gift*), for his young son Henry (aged four at the time), this is not a passage that made the cut, though it had obviously caught the attention of the youthful royal tutee. But for James, who "combined absolutist principles with the emphasis on the monarch's duty to rule according to law and in the public good,"[46] there could be no better exemplar than Xenophon's Cyrus, particularly after 1603 when he also became King James I of England and Ireland, and hence the ruler of an empire:[47]

> But because I would not be thought a partial praiser of this sport [hunting], I remit you [Henry] to *Xenophon*, an old and famous writer, who had no mind of flattering you or me in this purpose and who also set down a fair pattern for the education of a young king under the supposed name of *Cyrus*. (From book 3; Sommerville 1994: 56, silently modernized)

During this century, therefore, though the work does not lose its authority as an exemplar for princes, the establishment of the text as suitable for educational purposes in Protestant circles and schools ensured it became part of the fabric of knowledge of all learned men and as a mirror not just for princes but for future leaders of all sorts. These included, among others, magistrates, church leaders, diplomats, and teachers.

---

[44] Young is less well known than Buchanan but as the younger of the two tutors spent more time with James. When the latter became king, Young carried out diplomatic missions for him. For further information see the entries on both men in the *Oxford Dictionary of National Biography*.

[45] Warner 1893: lxxiii.

[46] Sommerville 1994: xv.

[47] On the *Cyropaedia* and the *Basilikon Doron*, see further Cramsie 2006: 49–53 and Grogan 2014: 57–60.

Signs of Waning Interest: the Eighteenth Century

Xenophon's *Cyropaedia* remained embedded in the education system for approximately three centuries, not always, but often, in the position in which Melanchthon and others had placed it, as an appropriate text for those at the early stages of their Greek studies. For example, in Daniel Waterland's *Advice to a Young Student with a Method of Study for the First Four Years*, first published in 1706, and with many reprints, Xenophon's *Cyropaedia* is the second classical author, after Terence, to be read in the first year of study "as being pure and easy Greek." Numerous diverse sources in this century note it as a text that one is recommended to have read before entering university in the British Isles and the young American republic, though it also at the same time appears on university curricula.[48] Furthermore, it continues to be drawn upon in various ways in the tradition of educating princes, which still existed though was waning with the growth of republicanism. Thus Andrew Michael Ramsay (1686–1743) in his *Les voyages de Cyrus* (*The Voyages of Cyrus*, 1727), a mirror-for-princes crafted in the form of an educational novel, and Henry St. John, Viscount Bolingbroke (1678–1751) in his *The Idea of a Patriot King* (1738), an advice book dedicated to Frederick Prince of Wales, while both anti-Machiavellian by conviction, like Machiavelli make use of Xenophon's Cyrus as an authoritative figure to enhance their own agendas.[49]

Yet, it is also in this century that we find arising more frequently less positive strands of reception of the *Cyropaedia* as an educative text whether for princes or more broadly speaking in the schools. Laurence Sterne's well-known parody in his novel *Tristram Shandy* of 1751 is often quoted as representative of the watershed in terms of the *Cyropaedia*'s popularity:

> The first thing which entered my father's head, after affairs were a little settled in the family … was to sit down coolly, after the example of Xenophon, and write a Tristra-*paedia* or system of education for me; collecting first for that purpose his own scattered thoughts, counsels, and notions; and binding them together, so as to form an Institute for the government of my childhood and adolescence. (book 5, chapter 16)

It has been argued that Sterne's "Trista-*paedia*" is in part aimed at the petrification of the curriculum at this time, but also, and perhaps more so, at the petrification of pedagogical practice, that is, the "overly scrupulous, nitpicky reading endorsed in public schools and universities."[50] Thus it becomes

---

[48] See, e.g., Clarke 1959: 71, 161–2, and Winterer 2013.
[49] Ahn 2008. See also briefly Tatum 1989: 27–9.
[50] Matuozzi 2013: 505, who has also shown that Waterland's curriculum was used in Sterne's school at the time he was there.

representative of what was important in a bygone age. Thomas Hutchinson, in his 1785 school edition of the *Anabasis*, argued that that text was a much more interesting read than the *Cyropaedia*, and across the ocean a young John Quincy Adams grumbled that the *Cyropaedia*'s style was too simple, its events uninteresting.[51]

Yet its influence did not wane completely. Most of the US founding fathers had a copy in some language or other. Thomas Jefferson, for example, was looking for an Italian copy while he was in France in 1787 just before drawing up the US Constitution. For them Cyrus could be regarded as a benevolent despot ruling over willing subjects, and thus in this way the *Cyropaedia* could be appropriated as a mirror-for-presidents.

And though we find a significant increase in publications of Xenophon's *Anabasis* as a school text in the nineteenth century,[52] the *Cyropaedia* does not altogether disappear. Bishop Huntingford, in a postscript to his *Introduction to the Writing of Greek* (1811), which makes use of excerpts from the *Cyropaedia*, justifies his use of this text as follows:[53]

> There is so much invention in the plan; such just conception of the endowments requisite towards constituting an illustrious and good character, in the virtues ascribed to Cyrus; so much propriety in the words and actions of the several personages introduced; so many exquisite strokes of true politeness; so much Attic festivity in the symposiac parts; and so much civil, military, political and religious wisdom in the more serious dialogues, that for genius and useful knowledge and instruction, the *Cyropaedia* perhaps is superior to any work whatever either of Plato or Aristotle.

It is not really until the middle of the nineteenth century that the *Anabasis* completely supplants the *Cyropaedia* as the text of choice for early Greek learning.[54]

A Modern Mirror-for- ... Managers?

Filelfo was apoplectic about Poggio's abbreviated version of the *Cyropaedia*. One wonders what he would have made of Larry Hedrick's *Cyrus the Great: The Arts of Leadership and War* (2006). Hedrick not only condenses the work nearly beyond recognition, but also turns it into a first-person

---

[51] Winterer 2013 for this information on Adams as well as that on Jefferson below.
[52] First springing up in Germany after Humboldt's reform of the education system in the early part of that century; on which see Rijksbaron 2002.
[53] Huntingford 1811: 294–5. Winterer 2002: 12–13 shows the *Cyropaedia* still being used at some US colleges in the late eighteenth and early nineteenth centuries.
[54] Rood 2004c: 44–7 in general for the shift from the *Cyropaedia* to the *Anabasis*.

account so that he has Cyrus speaking directly to today's reader with tips for managing others successfully. The promotional material states the following:[55]

> A new generation of readers, including business executives and managers, military officers, and government officials, can now learn about and benefit from Cyrus the Great's extraordinary achievements, which exceeded all other leaders' [sic] throughout antiquity.

The way for this particular strand of appropriation had been paved back in 1954 when management guru Peter F. Drucker lauded the work for its usefulness in imparting leadership skills.[56] He, however, unlike most of those now commenting favorably on Hedrick's work online, likely read the *Cyropaedia* in Greek as part of his education in the rigorous system of the Austrian gymnasium. One can only wonder what he, also, would have made of Hedrick's rewriting of the work.

But Hedrick is doing nothing very different from the early modern humanists. As Quentin Skinner has so adeptly shown, humanists wrote their advice books to suit the political contexts within which they found themselves, and constantly adapted and refigured ancient authorities to provide ballast for their own views. Xenophon and his *Cyropaedia* are no less authoritative for Hedrick than they were for Pontano, Platina, Machiavelli, Melanchthon, Camerarius, Sidney, Spenser, and King James VI and I. That in our postmodern world, in radically different political and economic circumstances, new and unexpected ways are being found of adopting and re-presenting as an exemplar this ancient *speculum principis* attests to the enduring power and adaptability of *Cyropaedia*. With the internet now providing unprecedented accessibility to the text, it will be intriguing to track the creative appropriations that will undoubtedly continue to be made in the future.[57]

Further Reading

Though he does not deal with the reception of Xenophon, Skinner 1988 is essential reading for an overview of the political contexts within which

[55] www.amazon.com/Xenophons-Cyrus-Great-Arts-Leadership/dp/0312364695.
[56] Drucker 1954: 159.
[57] A good portion of the work for this chapter was carried out at the Huntington Library in San Marino where I was fortunate to hold a Mayers Fellowship in 2014. I am grateful to the staff there for their unfailing help and good humor. Thanks are also due to Jeroen De Keyser, Jane Grogan, Keith Sidwell, Michael Ullyot, and the editor of this volume, who have all improved the chapter in different ways.

the mirror-of-princes genre operated. On the reception of the *Cyropaedia*, Tatum 1989: 3–35 provides a selective overview from the ancient world to the twentieth century, Sancisi-Weerdenburg 1990 surveys fourteenth- and fifteenth-century Italy, and Grogan 2007 discusses it in relation to the English Renaissance. For the translation history of the *Cyropaedia* in the early modern period see Marsh 1992.

22

TIM ROOD

Xenophon's Changing Fortunes in the Modern World

Almost autobiographical: the advantages of having a country seat in the neighbourhood of a big town. Here we feel the MODERNISM of XENOPHON.

H. G. Dakyns, marginal note on *Cyr.* 5.4.34[1]

The aim of this chapter is to provide an overview of some of the main ways in which the figure of Xenophon and his writings have been interpreted over the course of the last three centuries. It will start with an attempt to capture recent images of Xenophon by means of the stereotypes through which he has been interpreted. It will then set this range of modern views against the changing fortunes of Xenophon and his works since the eighteenth century.

Stereotyping Xenophon

An extraordinary number of different Xenophons have surfaced in the centuries since he wrote. The last century alone can attest a baffling variety of readings of his character. A Greek classical scholar writing under the regime of the Colonels in the early 1970s regarded Xenophon as "a conceited lover of display" and "a self-centred individual" – the "'hippie' of the fourth century."[2] A quarter of a century earlier, in the immediate aftermath of World War II, the American economist Alvin Johnson had more sympathetically seen Xenophon as "the first American" – "blithe and gallant and resourceful" and "often charged with superficiality" because, like Americans, he "fail[ed] to see the things that aren't there." Johnson recalled in particular Xenophon's account in the *Anabasis* of how he encouraged the despondent Greeks after the capture of their generals by assuring them that they had nothing to fear from the Persians. Xenophon had even warned them that

[1] Dakyns 1914: 187.
[2] Soulis 1972: 189.

435

if they did not hurry away from the long-limbed women of Mesopotamia "they would become as lotus-eaters, forgetting their beloved fatherland" (3.2.25): "Doesn't that sound like a Yankee?"[3]

Xenophon has also been made to fit a very different national stereotype – the honorary Englishman. His description, slightly earlier in the same scene in the *Anabasis*, of how he clothes himself in his finest gear before addressing the troops (3.2.7) has irresistibly called to mind the self-destructive bravado of one of the great English heroes, Nelson, at the battle of Trafalgar.[4] But the Xenophon who has most often called an English stereotype to mind is the country squire living and writing in retirement at Scillus in the Peloponnese, where he had been settled by the Spartans after returning from Asia. A striking example of this Xenophon can be found in a review in the *Times Literary Supplement* in May 1930. The book under review, A. J. Butler's *Sport in Classic Times*, features Xenophon so often that his index entry simply reads "*passim*." It led the reviewer – George Forrester Scott, an Oxford-educated journalist who contributed frequently to the *TLS* on classics, cricket, and the countryside – to thoughts of this writer of "great charm" who had the gifts of "simplicity and humanity," and who was himself "a noble character – soldier, country gentleman, philosopher, sportsman, in whom, risking a charge of smugness, we may venture to claim a resemblance to a not uncommon English type."[5]

The English Xenophon reappeared in the *Times Literary Supplement* in a very different guise later in the century when Terence Irwin, a young philosophy lecturer at Harvard, was given the task of reviewing Leo Strauss's *Xenophon's Socrates*. It was the third monograph on Xenophon by an émigré German Jewish scholar who was at the time, through his teaching at the University of Chicago, one of the most influential political philosophers in the United States. Strauss's Xenophon was a far more complex figure than the noble character celebrated by George Forrester Scott. He was an adept exponent of irony – a writer who cultivated the art of concealment and had to be read slowly for the philosophical message missed by most readers to be grasped. Strauss created this Xenophon as part of his project of rewriting the history of philosophy. He wanted to move beyond historicism and return to what he saw as the Socratic conception of philosophy – a continual inquiry into the question of how to live, an inquiry that was in itself a way of living. In elaborating this conception of the philosophical life, Strauss rejected all attempts to relate the thought of writers like Xenophon to their

[3] Johnson 1948: viii.
[4] E.g. Smith 1824: 171 n.; Howell, 1949: 5.
[5] Scott 1930: 455.

historical situations: "this is not the natural way of reading the work of a wise man and, in addition, Xenophon never indicated that he wanted to be understood that way."[6]

Terence Irwin would have none of this attempt to recuperate an esoteric Xenophon. He dismissed *Xenophon's Socrates* as "almost valueless" – "a tedious paraphrase" that "merely reminds us how unexciting Xenophon can be." Irwin preferred to resurrect the figure of the country squire: Xenophon, he wrote, "quite closely resembles a familiar British figure – the retired general, staunch Tory and Anglican, firm defender of the Establishment in Church and State, and at the same time a reflective man with ambitions to write edifying literature." Himself born in Northern Ireland and educated at Oxford, Irwin did not risk the charge of smugness: he added that "American Xenophons do not seem to be so common."[7]

Irwin was by no means alone in his contempt for Xenophon. In the same year that his review was published, similar remarks appeared in the *Times Literary Supplement* in a review of J. K. Anderson's *Xenophon* (still the most recent biography of Xenophon). Apart from his best work, the *Anabasis*, the reviewer crowed, "the rest of Xenophon is seldom read – and rightly." He went on to isolate Xenophon's two main defects – "unoriginality and a simple belief in the virtues of military leadership" – and to write scathingly of Xenophon's shortcomings as a philosopher. The arguments of Xenophon's dialogue on tyranny, the *Hiero*, were dismissed as "so unconvincing that only Leo Strauss has been able to take them seriously" – "by the simple expedient of claiming that Xenophon intended to ridicule the position he actually holds." This reviewer was even prepared to praise Strauss's "fascinating and perceptive essay" as a way of damning Xenophon even more: "the opposite of Xenophon was bound to be more interesting than Xenophon himself." "The world is full of retired generals like Xenophon," the reviewer concluded: "Let them stick to memoirs."[8]

These snooty condemnations of Xenophon have themselves met with a hostile reception in some quarters. Among those who rallied to his defense was the Cambridge classicist Simon Goldhill. Reviewing a more recent book on Xenophon's depiction of Socrates, Goldhill quoted Irwin's hostile description of Xenophon and set about overturning his phrases one by one:

> "firm defender of the Establishment in Church and State" scarcely represents a man who was exiled from his democratic country to live in the community of its worst military and political enemies, and who fought (and wrote about

---

[6] Strauss 1948: 4.
[7] Irwin 1974: 409, 410.
[8] Anon. 1974: 927.

his fighting) for a charismatic barbarian revolutionary. Nor does "staunch Tory and Anglican" ... help us get close to the man who boldly developed literary forms, who wrote a founding text of erotic fiction, and who passionately defended and memorialized a fashionable philosopher put to death by the state for religious and political crimes. Indeed, for contemporary cultural historians Xenophon should be seen as a figure of exemplary importance and attractively transgressive social positioning: the man who crosses the boundaries of engagement between Greek and barbarian, Athens and Sparta; who argues his dissent within and against democracy through his writing; whose texts innovate in form and genre, and play with the voices of first and third person expression; whose interests spread from the key cultural institutions of hunting and fighting, to political biography, trendy philosophy, and tourism. Xenophon is ripe for rehabilitation.[9]

Goldhill scores some good hits as he reacts against the twentieth-century tendency "to denigrate Xenophon in ideological and literary terms as a sort of Colonel Blimp" – even if "charismatic barbarian revolutionary" smacks more of Fidel Castro or Ché Guevara than of Cyrus the Younger, the Persian prince Xenophon served. Yet even as he pokes fun at Irwin's hackneyed characterization of Xenophon, Goldhill himself constructs a quasi-mythical image of Xenophon the breaker of boundaries, a slippery, elusive, liminal figure constructed under the sign of *différance*.

Goldhill does succeed in bringing out the aspect of Xenophon's writings that has done most to revive his reputation in recent decades – namely their extraordinary range. Xenophon's main rivals, Thucydides and Plato, wrote only works of history and philosophy, respectively. But in addition to those two genres Xenophon also covered historical fiction (the *Cyropaedia* – which has an erotic subplot, at least), biography (the *Agesilaus* – perhaps better classed as panegyric), estate and household management (the *Oeconomicus* – one of the Socratic works), economic advice (the *Ways and Means*), hunting (the didactic *Cynegeticus*), not to mention the new literary form of the war (or tourist?) memoir, the *Anabasis* itself. This spectacular range has even led to Xenophon being praised as "the most inventive and in many ways the most influential generic innovator"[10] in ancient Greece – a far cry from Irwin's stodgy writer.

Actual followers of Leo Strauss were no more persuaded by Irwin's attack on the Straussian image of Xenophon. The earlier idealistic image of Xenophon the country gentleman lives on in a new chapter on Xenophon that the political philosopher Christopher Bruell added in 1987 to a textbook on the history of political philosophy that Strauss had co-edited. In this

---

[9] Goldhill 1998.
[10] Pelling 1999: 331.

chapter Bruell explored an opposition that he saw as central to Xenophon's ethical thought – the opposition between Socrates the man of philosophy and Cyrus the man of politics. He argued that Xenophon's Socratic education enabled him to confront political life with a "grace and dignity" deriving from "an inner freedom not shared by Cyrus" – and to return in time to a rich enjoyment of private life:

> Country life ... would have appealed to him as allowing more leisure for contemplation and writing – especially since that contemplation might embrace, as we know from the *Anabasis* that it did, his own political experiences among other things. For a man like Xenophon, the contemplative reliving of experience was sure to be a deepening of them ... promising a more profound enjoyment than the original experiences themselves.[11]

Bruell seems to offer a rich reading of Xenophon – but it is a reading created largely by recourse to the potential ("would have appealed," "was sure to be") and to questionable categories ("for a man like Xenophon"). The very boldness of Bruell's recourse to the potential may suggest merely that Xenophon's writings – the only evidence we have for his character – are full of pitfalls for anyone trying to extract autobiographical nuggets. These pitfalls are so great, indeed, precisely because Xenophon's writings are intimately bound to his own experiences – not least his relationship with Socrates, his participation in the Ten Thousand's march through Asia, and the life of farming, hunting, and religious observances he led at Scillus. The only evidence for this final aspect of Xenophon's life is a prolepsis in the *Anabasis* (5.3.7–13) – a brief passage that reveals very little but has nonetheless fomented the image of Xenophon the country gentleman.[12]

This sketch has revealed some of the conflicts in the modern view of Xenophon and also the slenderness of some of the evidence even for a character whose writings are so well preserved as Xenophon. It is time now to see whether these conflicts are reflected in the shifts in Xenophon's fortunes since the eighteenth century.

From Moral Exemplum to Unpatriotic Villain

The high status of Xenophon's writings in the early modern period is shown by the fact that, up to the end of the eighteenth century, the only Greek authors to receive more English editions were Homer and Aesop.[13] Xenophon himself was also presented extremely positively. An identical

---

[11] Bruell 1987: 114.
[12] Rood 2012c discusses the reception of this passage.
[13] Wilson 2004: 274.

repertoire of biographical information passed from one reference work or literary history to another: thus a historical dictionary in 1703 described him as a "General, Philosopher, and Historian," noted two nicknames mentioned in ancient sources ("Grecian bee" and "Attic muse"), and recounted the story of how Xenophon responded when, in the middle of a sacrifice, he heard the news of his son Gryllus' death (he first took off his garland, then put it back on when he heard that his son had died nobly).[14] Towards the end of the century, a fuller account in Lemprière's *Bibliotheca classica* presented much the same image, ending in the same way with Gryllus' death, while also suggesting that Xenophon "shewed that he was a true disciple of Socrates" both in his military leadership and in his sentiments on religion: "he supported the immortality of the soul, and exhorted his friends to activate those virtues which ensure the happiness of mankind, with all the zeal and fervor of a christian."[15]

One indication of the great prestige enjoyed by Xenophon is his presence in alphabet rhymes, which were first found in written form in the seventeenth century, and which became an increasingly popular way of spreading literacy in children in the course of the eighteenth. Admittedly one reason for Xenophon's prominence was that he did not have much competition: Xerxes tended to be either a rival (as in the nonsense alphabets of Edward Lear) or a colleague ("Xerxes, Xenophon," in the popular *New England Primer*, or "X is for Xenophon, and Xerxes the king"). The bare combination of Xerxes and Xenophon was also deployed in guides to pronunciation, which would note that their names were actually pronounced "*Zerxses, Zenophon*" ("*Zenophon*" was also a common spelling of the name in the eighteenth and early nineteenth centuries).[16]

More ambitious examples of the alphabet rhyme point to how Xenophon could fit the genre's pedagogic concerns:

> X is a letter little used,
> And hard to write upon;
> It stands, here, for two famous men
> Xerxes and Xenophon.
> The first, he was a warrior bold,
> A king of mighty fame;
> The latter was a learned man,
> In Greece well known his name.[17]

---

[14] Anon. 1703: n.p.
[15] Lemprière 1788: n.p.
[16] Walker 1821: 69.
[17] Anon. 1851: 121.

Figure 22.1. The letters W and X from "[The] paragon of alphabets" (London: John Harris, ca. 1815). Cotsen Children's Library, Department of Rare Books and Special Collections, Princeton University Library.

The teaching of literacy was similarly combined with implicit moral exhortation in verses such as "X was one *Xenophon*, prudent and learn'd" and "X for old Xenophon, noted for sense."[18] Patriotic military themes could also be embraced: "W for Wellington, who won at Waterloo; X is for Xenophon, a great leader, too."[19] And we can see from Figure 22.1 that alphabet rhymes (which would typically be read aloud by women) also played a role in the creation of gender identities.

Alphabet rhymes typically removed Xenophon and Xerxes from much contact with history. In "X is a letter little used," the surprisingly positive portrayal of Xerxes leads to an arbitrary separation of Xenophon's philosophical and military interests. But the fortunate combination of Xenophon and Xerxes could nonetheless feed into their broader reception as paradigms of success and failure: the lingering influence of the nursery was felt during Sherman's March to the Sea in the closing stages of the US Civil War when a London newspaper wrote that Sherman "will either be a Xerxes or a Xenophon."[20]

[18] Opie and Opie 1951: 49 (from T. W.'s *A Little Book for Little Children*); Welch 1901: 163.
[19] B. 1893.
[20] See Rood 2010a: 176.

441

Part of the pedagogical usefulness of alphabet rhymes lay in their suggestive juxtapositions. What did it mean to read "X for old Xenophon, noted for
sense" straight after "W for Wealth in gold, silver and pence"? The injunction to "ev'ry Son" to "read the works of Xenophon" (Figure 22.1) followed
an encounter with "Wandering Willy": "That wand'ring far from home is
silly / Is often prov'd, – and now in Willy." Any child who remembered these
lines when they encountered the actual works of Xenophon would be aware
that Xenophon himself wandered far from home – and that his wandering
very nearly proved silly, until a lucky windfall brought him Wealth.

The tensions in Xenophon's life that lay below the surface of these alphabet rhymes came to be fully explored in nineteenth-century scholarship.
That Xenophon served first with a foreign prince and later with the Spartans
raised questions about his commitment to Athens. One of the first major
attacks on Xenophon's patriotism was made in a short and vitriolic article
written by the German scholar B. G. Niebuhr in 1827. Niebuhr (who had
served in the Prussian government in the war against Napoleon) was the
first scholar to develop the thesis that the *Hellenica* was in fact two separate
works. Part of his argument was based on the attitude to Athens supposedly
found in the two parts of the work: the loyalty shown in the first two books
(written, in Niebuhr's view, soon after the return of the Ten Thousand) contrasts with the second part, where "we meet at every turn with the odious
malignity of the renegade, grown old in his offensive idolatry of the mummy
into which the Spartan constitution had then withered": "Verily a more
degenerate son was never cast out by any state than this Xenophon!" – an
"old driveller, with ... the lisping naïveté of a little girl!"[21] Niebuhr's attack
on Xenophon soon met with a response by Ferdinand Delbrück, and the
controversy was picked up by "C. T." – the historian Connop Thirlwall – in
the first volume of a short-lived British journal, *Philological Museum*. For
Thirlwall, it was enough to contrast Xenophon's attitude to Athens with
that of Socrates: "He who thought it impious to attempt even to elude the
execution of an unjust sentence passed according to the laws of his country,
would surely have scrupled to revenge one by arms. He who refused to sell
even his instruction, would not have envied Xenophon that delightful retreat
in which he enjoyed the pension he had earned by his – love to Athens."[22]

Niebuhr and Thirlwall were trying to overturn the admiration felt by most
eighteenth-century writers for two of the jewels in Xenophon's crown – his
praise of Sparta and his friendship with Socrates. Even if Plutarch played a
larger role in shaping attitudes to Sparta at this time, Xenophon's apparent

---

[21] Niebuhr 1832: 487.
[22] Delbrück 1829; Thirlwall 1832: 530.

philo-Laconianism was one source of his popularity. It is true that Athens was much praised in the eighteenth century, but it was a Plutarchan image of Athens at the time of Solon and the Persian Wars that was found most congenial. Xenophon's writings about Athens after her fall from power did not, then, detract from his own standing. As the stock of the Athenian democracy later in the fifth and in the fourth century rose, however, Xenophon's apparent anti-democratic leanings meant that his reputation began to decline. George Grote could even lay stress on Xenophon's pro-Spartan tendencies in order to read him against the grain, as attesting, despite his own political instincts, to the superiority of Athenian to Spartan institutions.[23]

Xenophon's standing fell further in the nineteenth century owing to the greater professionalization of the academic discipline. Plato and Thucydides were now admired as model philosophers and historians, and Xenophon seen as inferior to both. The lowering of his academic reputation was combined with further charges against his morality. In 1893 Félix Dürrbach argued that Xenophon's proleptic account of the sanctuary he bought for Artemis at Scillus fitted the apologetic intention of the *Anabasis*: Xenophon, he suggested, was defending himself against the charge of improper appropriation of sacred funds. And in 1910, in an article designed to undermine the historical credibility of Xenophon's portrayal of Socrates, Léon Robin castigated Xenophon's "trickery" in asking the Delphic oracle not whether or not he should join Cyrus in Asia but to which gods he should sacrifice in order to return safely; he then argued that Xenophon's account of the foundation of the sanctuary shows "Xenophon's cleverness degenerat[ing] into a sort of hypocritical sharp practice."[24] Far from being a model of Christian piety, then, Xenophon has become aligned with clerical hypocrisy.

As we have seen, similarly dismissive views of Xenophon have been expressed by scholars over the course of the last century. At the same time, attention has tended to shift away from the character of Xenophon and onto the qualities of his writings. It is to the story of their reception that we now turn.

The Changing Fortunes of Xenophon's Works

Xenophon's works have varied greatly in popularity over the centuries. Before the eighteenth century, Xenophon was most admired for didactic works such as the *Cyropaedia* and *Oeconomicus*, which could be read as offering useful advice about how to exercise rule, whether over an empire

---

[23] Grote 1888, e.g. 8.58.
[24] Robin 1910: 13–14.

or a household. In the eighteenth century itself, the *Memorabilia* was generally seen as his most important work.[25] The form of the Socratic dialogue was imitated in works such as Thomas Amory's *Dialogue on Devotion*, composed "after the manner of Xenophon" and itself prefixed by "a conversation of Socrates on the being and providence of God" (a translation of *Memorabilia* 1.4). Amory captures some of the reasons for Xenophon's renown when he writes that Plato, for all his virtues, "must yet be own'd inferiour to XENOPHON in Clearness, and in a natural convincing way of Reasoning."[26]

The *Memorabilia* was famous above all for the Choice of Heracles (2.1.21–34) – the story (taken from the sophist Prodicus) of how Heracles was approached by two women, Vice and Virtue, who offered him the choice between an easy and luxurious life and a hard life devoted to toil. This fable was adapted in numerous ways in the eighteenth century: to name a few, it was paraphrased by Addison in the second volume of *Tatler*; turned into poems by William Shenstone and Bishop Lowth; painted by Benjamin West and imitated by Hogarth; represented in the gardens at Stowe; and set to music by Handel and by Anton Schweitzer, with a libretto by Christoph Martin Wieland.[27] Its literary qualities were also praised in an influential essay on allegory by John Hughes: "This Fable is full of Spirit and Elegance; the Characters are finely drawn, and consistent; and the Moral is clear."[28]

One of the most influential advocates of the Choice of Heracles was the philosopher and statesman the Earl of Shaftesbury. Shaftesbury commissioned a painting of the fable from the Neapolitan Paolo de Matteis (Figure 22.2), and published his instructions to the painter in *A Notion of the Historical Draught or Tablature of the Judgment of Hercules*. This text offered precise guidance on which moment in the story should be chosen, concluding that the painting should show Hercules still drawn towards pleasure, but twisting his body round to face the figure of Virtue. It is a mark of Shaftesbury's influence that in Shenstone's poem, as in the painting, the figure of Virtue bears "an imperial sword."[29]

The value Shaftesbury placed on Xenophon's Socratic writings is also suggested by the engraved portrait by Closterman that appeared in the second edition of Shaftesbury's *Characteristicks*. The engraving shows Shaftesbury in a classical portico opening behind him into an orderly rural backdrop. Next to Shaftesbury is a ledge with two books with spines facing

[25] Dorion 2000: viii–xviii.
[26] Amory 1733: 4.
[27] Bond 1987: ii.99–103; Shenstone 1741; Lowth 1834: 477–86.
[28] Hughes 1750: xxxix-xl.
[29] Shenstone 1741: 8; cf. Shaftesbury 1914: 42 ("the imperial or magisterial sword").

Figure 22.2. *The Choice of Heracles* by Paolo de Matteis, 1712, commissioned by Anthony Ashley Cooper, 3rd Earl of Shaftesbury. Ashmolean Museum, Oxford.

the viewer: a volume of Plato flat on its side and an upright volume of Xenophon. The image can be read as "a vindication of the active ideal of philosophy, embodied in the Xenophontic vision of Socrates,"[30] and again as a celebration of a balance between rural retirement and political commitment. The qualities for which Shaftesbury admired Xenophon are neatly expressed in a comment in *Characteristicks* on the benefits of "the early Banishment and long Retirement of a Heroick Youth out of his Native Country." It was to Xenophon's exile, he suggested, "that we owe an original System of Works, the politest, wisest, usefullest, and (to those who can understand the *Divineness* of a just *Simplicity*) the most *amiable*, and even the most elevating and exalting of all un-inspir'd and merely human Authors."[31] Particularly important for Shaftesbury, as for many other eighteenth-century readers, were the virtues of politeness and usefulness.

It was in the nineteenth century that the *Anabasis* came to be regarded as Xenophon's masterpiece. The fame of this work grew out of its adoption as

[30] Klein 1994: 108.
[31] Shaftesbury 1999: 2.247.

a school text. By the same token, however, its victory was far from straightforward. George Forrester Scott recognized that the fact that it had been "made a chopping-block for generations of schoolboys" had "served to conceal from many people" the nobility of Xenophon's character. Forced to read Xenophon's military memoir slowly, as an aid to learning Greek, not as an adventure story in its own right, schoolchildren did not appreciate the character of Xenophon. A vivid classroom scene in Thomas Wolfe's autobiographical novel *O Lost* (the original version of *Look Homeward, Angel*) suggests all the same that, however dull the teaching, the work could spark the imagination. The main character is taught by a teacher who "was simply the mouthpiece of a formula of which he was assured without having a genuine belief" – παρασάγγας πεντεκαίδεκα ("fifteen parasangs"). The passage continues with a pastiche of schoolmasterly pedantry ("'Anabasis' comes from two Greek words meaning to go up. The Greeks went up into Persia") before a sudden flourish: "O the sea! The sea! Θάλασσα, θάλασσα."[32]

Wolfe unerringly picks out in this passage the three motifs that are signposts of the fame achieved by Xenophon's account: the word "anabasis" itself, which has been taken to mean both an advance, in line with the proper Greek meaning of the word, and a retreat, after the most famous part of Xenophon's expedition; parasangs, the Persian unit of measurement repeatedly used by Xenophon; and the joyous shout of "*Thalatta! Thalatta!*" (often cited in the Ionic form "*Thalassa! Thalassa!*") raised by the Ten Thousand when they first catch sight of the Black Sea (4.7.21–4).

These motifs have appeared with countless permutations in numerous branches of modern culture. "Anabasis," for instance, has been the title of drawings by the American artist Cy Twombly and of modernist poems by the French writer Saint-John Perse and the American poet W. S. Merwin. In these poems (as in Wolfe's novel) the term is applied to a journey to the interior of the human spirit as well as a journey to the interior of a country. It is also thanks to Xenophon that parasangs have popped up in odd places – including Paris. Stephen Bonsal, a member of the American diplomatic corps at the Versailles peace conference, recounts in his memoir how he met some members of the Pontic Greek delegation (from the region where Xenophon's men reached the sea), and went on "a walk of several parasangs," talking about "the misnamed Anabasis"; and afterwards he "walked them another parasang or two to a boulevard café."[33] Part of Bonsal's wit here lies in his feigned ignorance about the length of a parasang – which is something like three miles or an hour's walk.

[32] Wolfe 2000: 248–9.
[33] Bonsal 1946: 181–2.

It is above all the shout of "The Sea! The Sea!" that has caught readers' imagination since the start of the nineteenth century. The words have been evoked in numerous poems, military memoirs, and travel books, and shouted on many a seaside holiday. Their widespread appeal was playfully exploited by James Joyce in his modernist masterpiece *Ulysses* (1922). In the opening scene, Joyce mocks the shout's romantic aura as he presents the pompous Buck Mulligan exclaiming "*Thalatta! Thalatta!* She is our great sweet mother" as he looks out on Dublin Bay. This shout is then picked up in a much less assertive register in Molly Bloom's concluding monologue: "O that awful deepdown torrent O and the sea the sea crimson sometimes like fire and the glorious sunsets." Joyce continued his playful use of Xenophon in *Finnegans Wake*, which is littered with puns such as "Galata! Galata!," "kolossa kolossa!," and "tha lassy! tha lassy!" Nor was this type of punning restricted to James Joyce. As a child, the satirist Ronald Knox is said to have been asked whether Xenophon's men had cried "Thalatta" or "Thalassa," and answered "The latter." Schoolmasters also developed helpful rhymes of their own: "Thalatta, thalatta, they made such a clatter, / Xenophon rode up to see what was the matter."[34]

Even if it is not currently much studied in schools, *Anabasis* continues to be Xenophon's most read work – an extraordinary ancient example of the adventure story, featuring model Greek soldiers stranded in an area of the Middle East that has been of immense geopolitical significance in recent years. While readers of *Anabasis* continue to wrestle with the ambiguities of Xenophon's portrayal of the Greek soldiers, works such as the *Cyropaedia* have attracted more scholarly controversy. A seemingly unbridgeable rift has developed between ironic and exemplary readings of Xenophon's political and philosophical writings, reflected within academia in institutional divisions between departments of Classics and Political Philosophy.

The Choice of Xenophons

When Simon Goldhill wrote in 1998 that Xenophon was "ripe for rehabilitation," he had been pre-empted by an American political philosopher, Richard C. Bartlett, who had suggested two years earlier that the "rehabilitation of Xenophon" was already well under way – thanks not least to Leo Strauss – but that his "full rehabilitation" would depend on readers bringing to his writings "the question … of the best way of life for a human being."[35] The repetition of the language of rehabilitation underlines that Xenophon

---

[34] See Rood 2004c for a full discussion of the reception of this shout.
[35] Bartlett 1996: 1, 6.

is still in some sense a figure of nostalgia, defined by the great reputation he enjoyed in earlier centuries. But the terms of Bartlett's rehabilitation are very different from Goldhill's: Xenophon is here not a paradigm of liminality, to be appreciated by cultural theorists, but a teacher of ethics, to be enjoyed by readers prepared to immerse themselves in his wisdom. This very diversity of cultural and philosophical approaches testifies all the same to the continuing appeal and even modernity of this beguilingly simple and strangely difficult writer.

Further Reading

There are two recent books specifically devoted to the afterlife of Xenophon's *Anabasis*: Rood 2004c discusses the reception of the shout of "Thalatta! Thalatta!" and also the adventures of travelers who have followed in the tracks of the Ten Thousand, while Rood 2010a explores the use of Xenophon in the USA, with a particular focus on the Mexican War and the Civil War. The reception of Xenophon's account of his life on his estate at Scillus is discussed by Rood 2012c and 2013b. School editions of Xenophon are analyzed in Rijksbaron 2002, while the use of Xenophon in Nazi education is treated in Roche 2016 and forthcoming. Rood 2015a focuses on the handling of Xenophon by Leo Strauss and his followers.

EDITH HALL

Epilogue: Xenophon: Magician and Friend

The editor of this volume, Michael Flower, concluded his Introduction with the hope that it will help to widen Xenophon's readership, because "his ideas still have the power to engage us in profound and useful ways." The cumulative effect of the chapters in this book is indeed to show how Xenophon's works, however wonderfully varied, all usefully explore the best ways of acting in the world. This is regardless of whether they consist of skilled reporting of the past or of advice for the present. Everything Xenophon wrote concerns ethical ideas as they are manifested and applied in practical living. The ancient Greeks and Romans did indeed believe that one of the two aims of art of any kind was to be useful to humans living in communities. But the other aim of art, they agreed, was to create pleasure – *hēdonē*. Xenophon merits our attention because he is morally edifying, to be sure. But his works also bestow delight. Who does not cheer at his touching reunion with his faithful horse, which he had been forced to sell when stranded, penniless, in Anatolia? His friends secretly raised the money to buy it back "because they heard he was fond of it" (*Anabasis* 7.8.2–3; see 8.8.6).

Bowie's chapter drew our attention to the praise lavished on Xenophon by Dio Chrysostom when drawing up a list of recommended reading for trainee orators. Dio certainly saw Xenophon's utility: he "is of all the ancient writers the most useful for the public man." But his writing partly convinces us, explains Dio, because it is "attractive and pleasurable" (*prosēnes kai kecharismenon*). The impact is not just that of wonderful wordplay, but actually of *magic* (*goēteia*, 18.14). Xenophon is a verbal magician: his works are spellbinding. Dio's paean illuminates the effect of Xenophon's wizardry by the addition of arresting details: the orator has a visceral emotional response to the *Anabasis*, actually feeling aroused by the hortatory speeches, and moved to tears by the deeds of valor (18.15–16). Writing at a distance of more than four centuries, Dio responds to Xenophon as if he were physically on the march upcountry alongside him. But, perhaps most importantly, Xenophon works as a *writer* because Xenophon was an *actor* in the events he narrates. His speeches are so effective because "he combines deeds with words, because he did not learn by hearsay nor by copying, but by doing deeds himself as well as telling of them" (18.18).

Abraham Lincoln once responded to the suggestion that powerful men didn't need to read books by saying "books serve to show a man that those original thoughts of his aren't very new, after all."[1] Part of Xenophon's magic, whether he is talking about morale in armies or kindness to animals, is that he makes us feel that there is little new under the sun. And the constituents of Xenophontic sorcery that Dio identified as making him the perfect model for the public speaker are precisely the same as those that make him the perfect reading for anyone discovering the ancient Greeks today: his accessibility, capacity to make his readers time-travel – feel that they are emotionally present and participating in the emotions of the events described – and his ability to come over as an appealing "real" person, a man of action, whom his audience regards as a friend. In this brief, closing chapter, I hope to entice any reader not yet convinced by the foregoing chapters to acquire a translation at least of the *Anabasis* forthwith,[2] and set out with Xenophon on his extraordinary adventure.

We are told that Alexander the Great's project of conquering Asia was inspired by reading the *Anabasis* (Eunapius, *Lives of the Sophists* 1.453), and countless other soldiers, adventurers, and colonialists have followed suit.[3] A vivid illustration of this text's appeal to the imagination occurs in H. G. Wells's semi-autobiographical *Tono-Bungay* (1909), in which the narrator, George, reminisces about life at English boarding school. His favorite reading there was "penny dreadfuls" with "ripping stuff, stuff that anticipated Haggard and Stevenson."[4] But the best game the boys played had been invented by George himself:

> We found a wood where 'Trespassing' was forbidden, and did the 'Retreat of the Ten Thousand' through it from end to end, cutting our way bravely through a host of nettle beds that barred our path, and not forgetting to weep and kneel when at last we emerged within sight of the High Road Sea. So we have burst at times, weeping and rejoicing, upon startled wayfarers. Usually I took the part of that distinguished general Xenophon and please note the quantity of the o ... Well, – if I met those great gentlemen of the past with their accents carelessly adjusted I did at least meet them alive, as an equal and in a living tongue.[5]

[1] See Gallaher 1898: 54.
[2] There are many translations available, of which Warner 1972, much reprinted, and Waterfield 2005 both come highly recommended.
[3] See especially Rood 2004c and 2010a.
[4] Wells 2005 [1909]: 29.
[5] Wells 2005 [1909]: 31.

The implicit comparison of the *Anabasis* with the adventure fiction of Robert Louis Stevenson and the imperial-lands fantasies of H. Rider Haggard, the subversive trespassing, the walls of nettles, the emotional intensity, the jibe at pedantic schoolmasters – all these signal the psychological appeal of a group adventure in a faraway land; the imagination can enhance history there, and we can all be heroes for an hour. It is hardly surprising that individuals who have in childhood read Xenophon's foundational example of this story type often lend it almost metaphysical reverberations later.

In April 1941, while Yugoslavia and Greece were surrendering to Germany, the poet and classicist Louis MacNeice produced a rousing, straightforward adaptation of the *Anabasis* for BBC Radio's Overseas Service.[6] He thus demonstrated the endless susceptibility of ancient literature to adaptation in modern media and to modern purposes. But the story haunted him. In a prescient poem written two decades later, not long before his premature death in 1963, MacNeice associates memories of his youth, and an intimation of mortality, with the first glimpse of the Black Sea by Xenophon's exhausted comrades:

> Round the corner was always the sea. Our childhood
> Tipping the sand from its shoes on return from holiday
> Knew there was more where it came from, as there was more
> Seaweed to pop and horizon to blink at. Later
> Our calf loves yearned for union in solitude somewhere
> Round that corner where Xenophon crusted with parasangs
> Knew he was home ...[7]

We are all travelling on the journey of a lifetime where the sea – whether it means infinity, death, sexual union, or home – is always just "round the corner." In that memorable phrase, "encrusted with parasangs," MacNeice evokes the magical thrill of the reader of Xenophon's first encounter with the exotica of the Persian Empire, the resonant Old Iranian nouns "encrusting" the surface of his lucid prose.

Dio praises Xenophon because what he says is clear and can be understood by anybody. His sheer accessibility is still a key component of his capacity to enchant. His use in elementary stages of training in the ancient Greek language – by smaller boys even than those who are given Herodotus – has contributed historically to his appeal to women. Although until as late as the twentieth century females were kept well away from the "manly" Thucydides on account of his perceived intellectual rigor and austerity,[8] they will have

---

[6] Under the title *The March of the 10,000*. See Wrigley and Harrison 2013: 31–42.
[7] MacNeice 1963: 13.
[8] Hall forthcoming a.

encountered Xenophon in their role as mothers and sisters of quite young boys. Sarah Fielding, sister of Henry and herself an established novelist, in 1762 published a fine translation, entitled Xenophon's *Memorabilia and Apology of Socrates*. (This was several times reprinted; her version of the *Apology* was still being reused as late as the *Socratic Discourses* edited by A. D. Lindsay for the Everyman series, first published in 1904 but reprinted until 1937.[9]) And three decades after Fielding's Xenophon translation, Lady Sophia Burrell published a blank-verse epic on just one embedded tale in the *Cyropaedia*.[10]

Sarah Fielding is anxious in her translation to demonstrate that any reader could enjoy the pagan Xenophon without compromising her Christian beliefs. Xenophon did believe in a providential divine (at *Hellenica* 5.4.1. he notoriously asserts that "the gods neglect neither impious persons nor those who do wicked deeds"),[11] and this colored his interpretation of history in a way compatible with Christianity of most denominations. When his works were first printed during the Renaissance, ancient pagan Greeks were routinely identified as the cultural and spiritual ancestors of the Christian west, while the Asiatic, eastern barbarians, as described by historians such as Herodotus and Xenophon, were systematically – and anachronistically – conflated with Muslims, especially Turks.[12] During the decades leading up to the Greek War of Independence in the late eighteenth and early nineteenth centuries, it was therefore inevitable that the *Anabasis* informed the many "escape-from-the-Seraglio" poems, plays, and operas so voguish at that time.[13] Wiffen's "The Captive of Stamboul" (1820), for example, laments the Ottoman occupation of the land

> o'er which Minerva's Xenophon,
> from red Cunaxa called his heroes on;
> the baffled Persian barred his way in vain,
> and idly round him shook his empty chain;
> in all, through all, he mocked th' insidious foe,
> the Median sling and the barbaric bow;
> chill, faint with famine, bleeding, wasted, wet,
> firm, though betrayed, and conquering, though beset.[14]

Christians have approvingly perceived Xenophon's religious outlook as a simple, sensible, ethical piety – a characterization best expressed in Landor's

---

[9] See Hall 2016.
[10] Burrell 1794.
[11] Dillery 1995: 193.
[12] Hall 2007a and Hall 2013: ch. 8.
[13] Hall 2013: chs. 9–10.
[14] Wiffen 1820: 142.

two imaginary conversations between Xenophon and Cyrus the Younger and Xenophon and Alcibiades.[15] To the latter, Xenophon describes his world-view: "Hesitation and awe become us in the presence of the gods; resolution and courage in presence of mortal men."[16] His Socratic works were even used as models for explicitly Christian devotional works in dialogue form.

When it comes to social class, however, the politics of Xenophon's reception are more complicated. He indeed has a centuries-old association with the elite curriculum, as the first ancient Greek prose author usually encountered by privileged boys. In English-speaking countries, this became inevitable after Xenophon was prescribed in Dr Johnson's "Scheme for the Classes of a Grammar School" as the supreme exemplar of Attic prose.[17] Tony Harrison, a working-class boy born in 1937 who won a place at Leeds Grammar School, remembers reading Xenophon there:

> Tugging my forelock fathoming Xenophon
> grimed Greek exams with grease and lost me marks,
> so I whisper when the barber asks Owt on?
> No, thank you! YES! Dad's voice behind me barks.[18]

While taking any classically educated reader straight back to those childhood moments construing sentences in Xenophon, the image of that ancient author's text becoming smeared with proletarian hair pomade also represents the sense of class difference beginning to dawn on Harrison's youthful self.

Yet Xenophon, for all his emblematic curricular power, has (like Herodotus) penetrated deeper into popular culture than, for example, either Thucydides or Polybius. This is partly because he was translated into Latin at a very early date in the Renaissance, guaranteeing wide circulation,[19] and illustrated versions of the *Anabasis* have been produced for children with no knowledge of ancient languages.[20] But he is also one of the few ancient authors who – in modern-language translations – have routinely been found on the shelves of workers' libraries, since the very first in Europe were founded in Scotland in the 1750s.[21] Moreover, for all Xenophon's own

---

[15] Landor 1891: 121–39.
[16] Landor 1891: 133.
[17] Boswell 2008 [1791]: 59.
[18] Harrison 1984: 140.
[19] Botley 2004: 9–10.
[20] Havell 1910.
[21] The first workers' libraries opened in the 1750s at Leadhills and Wanlockhead. They were brought to a fine art in the libraries of the South Wales miners in the later nineteenth century. The catalogues show that Xenophon, Caesar, and Augustine, usually in translation, were three of the classical authors most often available, along with the Stoics whose writing might be classed as spiritual autobiography, Epictetus and Marcus Aurelius. See Hall and Stead forthcoming.

aristocratic birth, and questionable attitude to democracy, he has enjoyed a
high reputation amongst democrats and levelers. The Dorset poet William
Barnes composed a mid-Victorian socialist poem, "Fellowship," about the
local peasants' intuitive contentment with poverty. They believed, said Barnes,
that the poor, because they are less isolated and can rely on each other's soli-
darity, have more fun than the rich, who "must live in lonesome states /
With none for mates in fellowship." Barnes's note to this poem explains that
"Xenophon, in his *Hiero*, chap. vii, makes the king say to Simonides: – 'I
wish to show you those pleasures which I enjoyed while I was a common
man; and now, since I have been a king, I feel I have lost. I was then among
my fellows, and happy with them as they were happy with me.' "[22]

When the "common man" and common woman wanted to enjoy themselves, they could access stories from Xenophon in entertaining theatrical
and musical forms. Xenophon's literary versatility has led to several individual episodes acquiring such status that they have produced a whole series
of responses and a reception history of their own. The story of "The Choice
of Heracles" was often extracted from its context, and retold, even sung and
danced, on early modern and Enlightenment stages, culminating in Handel's
1751 oratorio.[23] The *Cyropaedia* is the ultimate source of the romance-unto-
death of Panthea and Habrodates, often adapted for the stage, for example
in John Bankes's 1696 *Cyrus the Great, or the Tragedy of Love* at Lincoln's
Inn Fields. Greekless readers could read the same story in James Hurdis's
epyllion *Panthea* (1790).[24]

But the extent of Xenophon's influence is not only a result of the pleasure
with which new works responding to his could provide. A specific form
of the *usefulness* identified by Dio has been instrumental, too. The sheer
number of topics Xenophon covered means that he turns up in an astonishing variety of factual publications encompassing wider fields than any
other ancient Greek thinker except Aristotle. Socrates' confession in his
Symposium that he takes dancing lessons, as well as the sexy pantomimic
performance at the end of the party (9.2–7), have dominated discussions
of the morality of dancing since the earliest Puritan debates on the topic.[25]
Xenophon's *Ways and Means* was central to early treatises on mining technology, especially Georgius Agricola's seminal *de Re metallica* (1556),[26] and
on economics.[27] His historical works permeate eighteenth-century invective

[22] Barnes 1868: 170 and 171.
[23] See also, e.g. Whyte 1772.
[24] Hurdis 1790: 69–227.
[25] E.g. Gosson 1582: 86–7. See Hall 2010.
[26] See the translation of Hoover and Hoover 1950: 6, 26, 28.
[27] Davenant 1698, on whom see further Hall and Macintosh 2005: 36–40.

454

against the use of mercenaries in British imperial territories,[28] and his *On Household Management* crops up in numerous contexts, including (along with the *Cyropaedia*) discussions of gardening.[29] When Georgian showmen advertised their exotic fauna to the London public, they were sure to mention Xenophon when describing their fabulous ostriches.[30]

Along with accessibility, Dio specifies Xenophon's virtue of making the reader feel the emotions of the moment he is describing. It is this quality which has led two scenes in particular to appeal to painters. The first is his idyllic description of the sanctuary he built for Artemis at his new home in Skillos near Olympia, where he settled with his wife and children some time after his adventures abroad. He would hold annual festivals there, with sumptuous banquets and hunting expeditions (*Anabasis* 5.3.7–10). This passage became a favorite of Italian Renaissance noblemen as offering an exemplary image of bountiful leadership; painters strove to capture the happiness of the moment. *Sacrificio di Senofonte a Diana* in the Palazzo Barberini in Rome, attributed to Pietro da Cortona, shows a bearded Xenophon standing in front of his temple and organizing the other men as they bring back their spoils from the hunt; to the right is his wife, with their little sons, one of whom is playing with a sheep. This painting was much imitated.[31] The other intensely paintable episode is of course the first sighting of the Black Sea, famously captured by Benjamin Haydon in a canvas first exhibited at the Egyptian Hall in Piccadilly in 1832, allowing late Georgian viewers to fancy themselves transported in time back to the turn of the fourth century BC.[32]

But there is another sense in which Xenophon has, more than any other ancient historian, encouraged "time travel," and that is in his close relationship with fiction. His traces linger not only in the North American novel of the frontier (his influence on J. Fenimore Cooper is palpable[33]) but also in science fiction and fantasy writing. The importance of the *Anabasis* in this

[28] See e.g. Callender 1795: ch. 2.
[29] Addison 1794: 271.
[30] "The most astonishing and largest OSTRICH ever seen in Europe" is advertised as on display at the Pastry-Cook Mr. Patterson's, 37 Haymarket. The playbill (John Johnson Collection of Handbills *Animals on Show* I (7) in the Bodleian Library) informs the reader that "Dr. YOUNG observes from Xenophon, that Cyrus had horses which overtake the goat and wild ass, but none could reach this creature." See *Anabasis* 1.5.3.
[31] On the cultural context in which the painting was created, see Rood 2013a. There is a copy, for example, at the National Trust property The Vyne in Sherborne St. John, Basingstoke, viewable online at http://artuk.org/discover/artworks/ xenophons-sacrifice-to-diana-220133.
[32] Anon. 1832.
[33] There are references to the *Anabasis* in several of his novels. See, e.g. Cooper 1840: 263.

category of novel was forever guaranteed when the much reprinted 1877 English-language version of Jules Verne's *Journey to the Center of the Earth* inserted a resounding reference to the Cyreans' first glimpse of the sea. This is how Axel recalls his arrival, with Uncle Liedenbrock, at the "new *mare internum*":

> A vast sheet of water, the commencement of a lake or an ocean, spread far away beyond the range of the eye, reminding me forcibly of that open sea which drew from Xenophon's ten thousand Greeks, after their long retreat, the simultaneous cry, "Thalatta! thalatta!" the sea! the sea! The deeply indented shore was lined with a breadth of fine shining sand, softly lapped by the waves, and strewn with the small shells which had been inhabited by the first of created beings.[34]

There have been many futuristic stories based on the *Anabasis* subsequently, of which one, *Star Guard* (1955) by Alice Mary Norton, writing under the male pseudonym Andre Norton, is foundational in the genre. Its political landscape, despite the setting in the fourth millennium AD, is clearly that of the USA at the dawn of the civil rights movement; the soldier-hero Kana Karr is a mixed-race human, and the "evil empire" he opposes with his fellow mercenaries is an intergalactic Central Control which refuses to allow earth-dwellers equal citizenship rights.[35]

Earlier we quoted Abraham Lincoln. The words of another US president, Woodrow Wilson, sum up how many of Xenophon's admirers feel about him: "I would never read a book if it were possible for me to talk half an hour with the man who wrote it."[36] Xenophon was on close terms with Socrates, and witness to several momentous historical events. The diplomat Sir Thomas Elyot, one of his earliest English admirers, described him as "bothe a philosopher and an excellent capitayne."[37] A Victorian enthusiast put it another way: we can learn about Socrates from Plato, but also from "the scarr'd hand of gallant Xenophon."[38] Yet our gallant captain leaves so many frustrating silences about his life that in his resurrected presence it would difficult to decide which questions to ask (besides the obvious

---

[34] Anon. 1872, opening of ch. 30. The previous chapter is simply entitled "Thalatta! Thalatta!" The author of this famous translation, with illustrations by Édouard Riou, which is far more melodramatic than Verne's 1864 original French edition, remains unidentified.

[35] One other such novel likely to have staying power is Paul Kearney's well-written *The Ten Thousand* (2008).

[36] Whittlesey 1934.

[37] Elyot 1531: 39.

[38] "Socrates" in Tupper 1860: 62.

one articulated by Flower in the introductory essay: why did he *write* so much, and on such diverse topics?). One thing is certain, however. We may be bewildered by the mysteries surrounding his adventures abroad and his experiences in Greece, including his family life and his compromised relationships with both the Athenians and the Spartans. But that bewilderment paradoxically coexists with a sense that we know the man better than any ancient Greek author before him, and better than most who came afterwards. In this respect, reading Xenophon often feels similar to reading Montaigne or Walter Raleigh,[39] and with that sense of familiarity there comes affection.

There have been several skillful examinations in this volume of the problematic nature of the authorial presence, whether in the first or third person, in all Xenophon's works. I leave aside the question of whether Leo Strauss was correct in hearing Xenophon as satirical (with which I do not personally concur). But Flower is correct in insisting that, for the scholar, "Xenophon" – whether as "I" or "he," as narrator, subject, historian, panegyrist, or teacher of practical arts – always "requires careful analysis."[40] Our feelings of intimacy with Xenophon are not exactly artificial but they are deceptive. They exist partly, to be sure, because (as Dio insisted) Xenophon was not just a writer – he had participated in the events and situations he describes. Yet, despite all the important information that he omits, it is his habit of sporadically offering insights into his own feelings that makes him seem intensely real. The notion of psychological "identification" with characters in art has, since Freud, become one of the most fraught in literary theory. But there is no denying that Xenophon extends noisy invitations to his reader to identify with him by sharing his aesthetic perceptions and inward thoughts.

From many examples, I choose just one, the banquet held by the fearsome Thracian king Seuthes II (*Anabasis* 7.3.26–33). Xenophon is a guest of honor and challenged to present a gift to the king. But he has come emptyhanded, and, we are told, "had already been drinking a little." Nervously, we read on to see how he solves his problem. He takes the drinking horn and delivers an impromptu speech declaring his comrades to be the best gift Seuthes could desire. Then the barbarian monarch drinks with Xenophon, scatters the last wine drops with him, and – dangerous moment passed – the party continues uproariously. There is an orchestra of trumpets, Seuthes

---

[39] Xenophon was of course a favorite of Montaigne (see Green 2012: 193); he is compared with Raleigh by, e.g., Campbell 1756: letter 7.

[40] See above, p. 4.

practices his war cry, and a troupe of comedians performs. This episode would be exciting enough in itself – it is a vivid and unparalleled glimpse into the court life of the eastern Balkan barbarians – but seeing it through Xenophon's slightly tipsy eyes invites us to sympathize with his predicament and feel intense relief when he finds a way out.

Flower notes that the only time that Xenophon seems to have dropped seriously out of fashion since the Renaissance was in the middle of the twentieth century. One reason for this is certainly that the revulsion against militarism and the accelerated decolonization that followed World War II threw a shadow over some aspects of ancient Greek imperial and colonial history that had previously been celebrated. It is revealing that the role that the *Anabasis* has recently played on BBC Radio has been anything but warmongering: in Colin Teevan's *How Many Miles to Basra?* (2006), Xenophon's retreat functions as an antecedent of the plight of traumatized British soldiers stranded during an unpopular war in Iraq.[41] But the other reason why Xenophon lost favor is surely that it was in the aftermath of World War II that the very concept of "the author" came under attack in the Academy.

The first challenge to the importance of the writer as an individual in literary history came in a 1946 article by two American practitioners of the New Criticism, who stressed that literature is the possession of its readership.[42] The emphasis on the consumers of the text and of its role in cultural discourse, rather than on its creator, was developed theoretically by French poststructuralists, above all Roland Barthes, Michel Foucault, and Jacques Derrida.[43] The "death of the author" was announced. It became profoundly unfashionable, even in Classics, where literary theory was initially viewed with suspicion, to talk about *any* author's "intentions," let alone his or her "reality" or "lived experience." It is only recently that the author has been reinstated, albeit as just one amongst several agents and factors that can usefully be taken into account in textual analysis.[44] This comes as a welcome development to those of us who have always shared the feeling of H. G. Wells's George, that we have met Xenophon "alive, as an equal and in a living tongue."

---

[41] The radio play was subsequently developed into a full stage play and published as Teevan 2006. The proximity of Cynaxa to Fallujah, scene of a terrible battle in December 2004, prompted the drawing of parallels between the events of the Iraq War and those described in the *Anabasis*.

[42] Wimsatt and Beardsley 1946.

[43] For full bibliography and discussion see Burke 1998.

[44] See, e.g., Grethlein 2012.

IMPORTANT DATES IN THE LIFE OF XENOPHON

All dates are BC	
431	Outbreak of Peloponnesian War between Athens and Sparta
430–425	Birth of Xenophon
413	Athenian expedition to Sicily destroyed; Spartans occupy Athenian countryside
411–410	Athenian democracy overthrown; oligarchic rule at Athens
410	Democracy restored at Athens
406	Battle of Arginusae and trial of the Athenian generals
405	Spartans destroy Athenian fleet at Aegospotami and blockade Athens
September 405–April 404	Death of Darius II of Persia; accession of Artaxerxes II
404	Athens surrenders to Sparta
Summer 404–Spring 403	Rule of the Thirty at Athens (8 months). Xenophon serves in the cavalry under the Thirty (?)
403	Democracy restored at Athens
401	Xenophon joins the expedition of Cyrus the Younger; battle of Cunaxa near Babylon and death of Cyrus
401–399	Xenophon becomes a general and helps lead Cyrus' mercenaries (the Ten Thousand) back from Mesopotamia to Asia Minor
400	Agesilaus becomes one of Sparta's two kings
399	Trial and execution of Socrates
399–395	Xenophon and the remnants of the Ten Thousand serve various Spartan commanders in Asia Minor

(*cont.*)

All dates are BC	
396–395	Xenophon campaigns with King Agesilaus in Asia Minor
395	Outbreak of Corinthian War; Athens, Corinth, and Thebes ally against Sparta
Spring 394	Xenophon returns to Greece with Agesilaus
August 394	Xenophon present at the battle of Coronea in Boeotia; decree of exile passed against Xenophon at Athens (now or earlier)
ca. 390	Spartans grant Xenophon an estate at Scillus
386	The King's Peace; Sparta secures hegemony in Greece
382	Sparta seizes the Acropolis of Thebes
Winter 379/8	Liberation of Thebes from Spartan contol
378	Second Athenian League formed
376	Athenians defeat a Spartan fleet off Naxos
371	Thebans defeat a Spartan army at Leuctra; Xenophon is expelled from Scillus and moves to Corinth
370–369	Thebans invade the Peloponnese and liberate Messenia from Sparta
362	Battle of Mantinea; Xenophon's son Gryllus killed in a cavalry skirmish; Athenians pardon Xenophon (now or earlier)
360	Death of King Agesilaus
359/8	Death of Artaxerxes II
ca. 350	Death of Xenophon

BIBLIOGRAPHY

Aalders, G. J. D. (1953) "Date and intention of Xenophon's Hiero," *Mnemosyne* 6: 208–15.

Abbott, H. P. (2008) *The Cambridge Introduction to Narrative*, 2nd edn. Cambridge.

Adams, C. D. (1912) "Are the political 'speeches' of Demosthenes to be regarded as political pamphlets?" *AJP* 43: 5–22.

Addison, J. (1794) *Interesting Anecdotes, Memoirs, Allegories, Essays, and Poetical Fragments, Tending to Amuse the Fancy, and Inculcate Morality*. Vol IV. London.

Ahn, D. (2008) "The politics of royal education: Xenophon's *Education of Cyrus* in early eighteenth-century Europe," *The Leadership Quarterly* 19: 439–52.

Akrigg, B. (2007) "The nature and implications of Athens' changed social structure and economy," in *Debating the Athenian Cultural Revolution: Art, Literature, Philosophy, and Politics, 430–380 BC*, ed. R. Osborne. Cambridge: 27–43.

Albury, W. R. (2011) "Castiglione's *Francescopaedia*: Pope Julius II and Francesco Maria della Rovere in *The Book of the Courtier*," *Sixteenth Century Journal* 42.2: 323–47.

Allan, R. J. and M. Buijs (eds.) (2007) *The Language of Literature*. Leiden.

Allen, R. E. (1959) "Anamnesis in Plato's *Meno* and *Phaedo*," *The Review of Metaphysics* 13: 165–74.

Aloni, A. (2001) "The proem of Simonides' Plataea Elegy and the circumstances of its performance," in *The New Simonides: Contexts of Praise and Desire*, eds. D. Boedeker and D. Sider. Oxford: 86–105.

Alonso-Núñez, J. M. (2002) *The Idea of Universal History in Greece: From Herodotus to the Age of Augustus*. Amsterdam.

Althoff, J. (2005) "Form und Funktion der beiden hippologischen Schriften Xenophons Hipparchicus und De re equestri (mit einem Blick auf Simon von Athen)," in *Antike Fachtexte: Ancient Technical Texts*, ed. T. Fögen. Berlin and New York: 235–52.

Alvey, J. E. (2011) "The ethical foundation of economics in ancient Greece, focussing on Socrates and Xenophon," *International Journal of Social Economics* 38: 714–33.

Ambler, W. H. (1996) "On the *Oeconomicus*," in *Xenophon: The Shorter Socratic Writings*, ed. R. C. Bartlett. Ithaca, NY: 102–31.

Ameling, W. (1984) "L. Flavius Arrianus neos Xenophon," *Epigraphica Anatolica* 3: 119–22.

Amory, T. (1733) *A Dialogue on Devotion, after the Manner of Xenophon; in which the Reasonableness, Pleasure and Advantages of it are Considered*. London.

Anderson, J. K. (1974a) *Xenophon*. New York.

(1974b) "The battle of Sardis in 395 BC," *CSCA* 7: 27–53.

Andreades, A. M. (1933) *A History of Greek Public Finance*. Vol. I. Cambridge, MA.

Andrewes, A. (1970) "Lysias and the Theramenes papyrus," *ZPE* 6: 35–8.

Ankersmit, F. (2010) "Truth in history and literature," *Narrative* 18: 29–50.

Annas, J. (1981) *An Introduction to Plato's Republic*. Oxford.

Anon. (1703) *An Universal, Historical, Geographical, Chronological and Poetical Dictionary*. London.

(1815) *The Paragon of Alphabets*. London.

(1832) "Exhibition at the Egyptian Hall," *The Original: A New Miscellany*, no. 1, Saturday March 3, 126.

(1851) *The Rhyming Alphabet; or, Sarah Bell and Fanny Blake*. Philadelphia.

(1872) *A Journey to the Centre of the Earth, from the French of Jules Verne*. London.

(1974) Review of J. K. Anderson, *Xenophon*, *Times Literary Supplement* 3782 (August 30): 927.

Apfel, H. V. (1935) *Literary Quotation and Allusion in Demetrius' περὶ ἑρμηνείας and Longinus' περὶ ὕψους*. Diss. Columbia.

Ash, R., J. Mossman, and F. B. Titchener (eds.) (2015) *Fame and Infamy: Essays for Christopher Pelling on Characterization in Greek and Roman Biography and Historiography*. Oxford.

Asper, M. (2007) *Griechische Wissenschaftstexte: Formen, Funktionen, Differenzierungsgeschichte*. Stuttgart.

Atak, C. (forthcoming) "Plato's *Statesman* and Xenophon's Cyrus," in Danzig and Alon (eds.) (forthcoming).

Azoulay, V. (2004a) *Xénophon et les grâces du pouvoir: de la charis au charisme*. Paris.

(2004b) "The Medo-Persian ceremonial: Xenophon, Cyrus and the King's body," in Tuplin (ed.) (2004a): 147–73.

(2004c) "Xénophon, la *Cyropédie* et les eunuques," *Revue française d'histoire des idées politiques* 11: 3–26.

(2006a) "L'*Archidamos* d'Isocrate: une politique de l'espace et du temps," *REG* 119: 504–31.

(2006b) "Isocrate, Xénophon ou le politique transfiguré," *REA* 108: 133–53.

(2007a) "Sparte et la *Cyropédie*: du bon usage de l'analogie," *Ktèma* 32: 435–56.

(2007b) "Panthée, Mania et quelques autres: les jeux du genre dans l'oeuvre de Xénophon," in *Problèmes du genre en Grèce ancienne*, eds. V. Sébillote-Cuchet and N. Ernoult. Paris, 277–87.

"B.", S. (1893) "Hero Alphabet," *St. Nicholas: An Illustrated Magazine for Young Folks* 20: 558.

Badian, E. (1993) "Thucydides and the outbreak of the Peloponnesian War," in *From Plataea to Potidaea: Studies in the History and Historiography of the Pentekontaetia*. Baltimore: 125–62.

(1995) "The ghost of empire: reflections on Athenian foreign policy in the fourth century BC," in *Die athenische Demokratie im 4. Jahrhundert v. Chr.: Vollendung oder Verfall einer Verfassungsform?*, ed. W. Eder. Stuttgart: 79–106.

(2004) "Xenophon the Athenian," in Tuplin (ed.) (2004a): 33–53.

Bakker, E. J. (1997a) *Grammar as Interpretation*. Leiden.

(1997b) "Verbal aspect and mimetic description in Thucydides," in Bakker (1997a): 7–54.

(ed.) (2010) *A Companion to the Ancient Greek Language*. Malden, MA, Oxford, and Chichester.

Balot, R. K. (2006) *Greek Political Thought*. Malden, MA and Oxford.

(ed.) (2009) *A Companion to Greek and Roman Political Thought*. Malden, MA, Oxford, and Chichester.

Baragwanath, E. (2012a) "A noble alliance: Herodotus, Thucydides, and Xenophon's Procles," in *Thucydides and Herodotus*, eds. E. Foster and D. Lateiner. Oxford: 316–44.

(2012b) "The wonder of freedom: Xenophon on slavery," in Hobden and Tuplin (eds.) (2012a): 631–63.

Barnes, J. (ed.) (1984) *The Complete Works of Aristotle: The Revised Oxford Translation*. 2 vols. Princeton.

Barnes, W. (1868) *Poems of Rural Life*. London.

Bartlett, R. C. (1996) "Editor's Introduction," in *Xenophon: The Shorter Socratic Writings: Apology of Socrates to the Jury, Oeconomicus, and Symposium*. Ithaca, NY.

Baz, F. (2007) "Ein neues Ehrenmonument für Flavius Arrianus," *ZPE* 163: 123–7.

Bearzot, C. (2001) "Il 'papiro di Teramene' e le Elleniche di Ossirinco," *Sileno* 27: 9–32.

Beck, H. (2001) "'The Laws of the Fathers' versus 'The Laws of the League': Xenophon on federalism," *CP* 96: 355–75.

Benner, E. (2013) *Machiavelli's Prince: A New Reading*. Oxford.

Ben-Tov, A. (2009) *Lutheran Humanists and Greek Antiquity: Melanchthonian Scholarship between Universal History and Pedagogy*. Leiden.

Berlin, I. (1972) "The originality of Machiavelli," in *Studies in Machiavelli*, ed. M. P. Gilmore. Florence: 147–206.

Bers, V. (2010) "Kunstprosa: philosophy, history, oratory," in Bakker (ed.) (2010): 455–67.

Beversluis, J. (1993) "Vlastos's quest for the historical Socrates," *Ancient Philosophy* 13: 293–312.

Bigalke, J. (1933) *Der Einfluß der Rhetorik auf Xenophons Stil*. Diss. Greifswald.

Billows, R. (2009) "The authorship of the 'Hellenika Oxyrhynchia'," *Mouseion* 9: 219–38.

Black, R. (2001) *Humanism and Education in Medieval and Renaissance Italy: Tradition and Innovation in Latin Schools from the Twelfth to the Fifteenth Century*. Cambridge.

Blanchard, K. C., Jr. (1994) "The middle road of classical political philosophy: Socrates' dialogues with Aristippus in Xenophon's *Memorabilia*," *Review of Politics* 56: 671–96.

Bleckmann, B. (2006) *Fiktion als Geschichte: neue Studien zum Autor der Hellenika Oxyrhynchia und zur Historiographie des vierten vorchristlichen Jahrhunderts*. Göttingen.

Bloch, H. (1940) "Studies in historical literature of the 4th Century BC," in *Athenian Studies Presented to W. S. Ferguson*. HSCPh Supplement 1. Cambridge, MA: 303–76.

Bobonich, C. (2011) "Socrates and eudaimonia," in *The Cambridge Companion to Socrates*, ed. D. R. Morrison. Cambridge: 293–332.

Bodei Giglioni, G. (1970) *Xenophontis De Vectigalibus*. Florence.

Boeckh, A. (1886) *Die Staatshaushaltung der Athener*. 3rd edn. 2 vols. Berlin.

Boedeker, D. (2001) "Paths to heroization at Plataea," in *The New Simonides: Contexts of Praise and Desire*, eds. D. Boedeker and D. Sider. Oxford: 148–63.

Bona, G. (1974) "ΛΟΓΟΣ e ΑΛΗΘΕΙΑ nell' *Encomio* di *Elena* di Gorgia," *RFIC* 102: 5–33.

Bond, D. F. (1987) *The Tatler*. 3 vols. Oxford.

Bonsal, S. (1946) *Suitors and Suppliants: The Little Nations at Versailles*. New York.

Boswell, J. (2008 [1791]) *The Life of Samuel Johnson*. Harmondsworth.

Bosworth, A. B. (1972) "Arrian's literary development," *CQ* 22: 163–85.

(1976) "Arrian in Baetica," *GRBS* 17: 55–64.

(1980) *A Historical Commentary on Arrian's History of Alexander*. Vol. I. Oxford.

Botley, P. (2004) *Latin Translation in the Renaissance*. Cambridge.

(2010) *Learning Greek in Western Europe, 1396–1529*. Philadelphia.

Bourriot, F. (1996) "*Kaloi kagathoi, kalokagathia* à Sparte aux époques archaiques et classiques," *Historia* 45: 129–40.

Bowden, H. (2004) "Xenophon and the scientific study of religion," in Tuplin (ed.) (2004a): 229–46.

Bowen, A. J. (ed.) (1998) *Xenophon: Symposium*. Warminster.

Bowersock, G. W. (1967) "A new inscription of Arrian," *GRBS* 8: 279–80.

(1994) *Fiction as History*. Berkeley and Los Angeles.

Bowie, E. L. (1995) "Names and a gem: aspects of allusion in the *Aethiopica* of Heliodorus," in *Ethics and Rhetoric: Classical Essays for Donald Russell on his Seventy-fifth Birthday*, eds. D. C. Innes, H. M. Hine, and C. B. R. Pelling. Oxford: 269–80.

(2002) "The chronology of the earlier Greek novels since B. E. Perry: revisions and precisions," *Ancient Narrative* 2: 47–63.

(2006) "Viewing and listening on the novelist's page," in *Authors, Authority and Interpreters in the Ancient Novel: Papers in Honour of Gareth Schmeling. Ancient Narrative*, Supplementum 5, eds. S. N. Byrne, E. P. Cueva, and J. Alvares. Groningen: 69–82.

(2007) "Links between Antonius Diogenes and Petronius," in *The Greek and the Roman Novel: Parallel Readings. Ancient Narrative*, Supplementum 8, eds. M. Paschalis, S. Frangoulidis, S. J. Harrison, and M. Zimmerman. Groningen: 121–32.

(2014a) "Becoming Wolf, staying sheep," in *Roman Rule in Greek and Latin Writing*, eds. R. Rees and J. M. Madsen. Leiden: 39–78.

(2014b) "Greek culture in Arrian's Bithynia," in *Le monde d'Arrien de Nicomédie*, eds. S. Lalanne and A. Hostein, *Ktèma* 39: 37–49.

Bradeen, D. W. (1974) *The Athenian Agora XVII. Inscriptions: The Funerary Monuments*. Princeton.

Bradley, P. (2001) "Irony and the narrator in Xenophon's *Anabasis*," in *Essays in Honor of Gordon Williams*, eds. E. I. Tylawsky and C. G. Weiss. New Haven: 59–84, reprinted in Gray (ed.) (2010a): 520–52.

(2011) "Xenophon's *Anabasis*: reading the end with Zeus the Merciful," *Arethusa* 44.3: 279–310.

Braun, T. (2004) "Xenophon's dangerous liaisons," in Lane Fox (ed.) (2004): 97–130.

Breebaart, A. B. (1983) "From victory to peace: some aspects of Cyrus' state in Xenophon's *Cyropaedia*," *Mnemosyne* 36: 117–34.

Breitenbach, H. R. (1950) *Historiographische Anschauungsformen Xenophons*. Freiburg.

(1967) "Xenophon von Athen," *RE* 2nd series, vol. IX: 1567–2052.

Briant, P. (1990) "Hérodote et la société perse," in *Hérodote et les peuples non-grecs*, ed. M. Narcy. Geneva: 69–104.

(ed.) (1995) *Dans le pas des Dix-Mille: peuples et pays du Proche-Orient vus par un grec*. Toulouse.

(1996) *Histoire de l'empire perse*. Paris.

(2002) *From Cyrus to Alexander: A History of the Persian Empire*. 2nd edn. Tr. P. T. Daniels. Winona Lake, IN.

Brickhouse, T. C. and N. D. Smith (1989) *Socrates on Trial*. Princeton.

(2000) *The Philosophy of Socrates*. Boulder, CO.

Brock, R. (2004) "Xenophon's political imagery," in Tuplin (ed.) (2004a): 247–57.

(2013) *Greek Political Imagery from Homer to Aristotle*. London.

Browning, E. A. (2011) Review of Gray (2011), *BMCR* 2011.09.35.

Bruce, I. A. F. (1967) *An Historical Commentary on the Hellenica Oxyrhynchia*. Cambridge.

Bruell, C. (1987) "Xenophon," in *History of Political Philosophy*, eds. L. Strauss and J. Cropsey. 3rd edn, orig. pub. 1963. Chicago: 90–117.

Brulé, P. (2003) *Women of Ancient Greece*. Tr. A. Nevill. Edinburgh.

Bruns, I. (1896) *Das literarische Porträt der Griechen*. Berlin.

Brunt, P. A. (1977) "From Epictetus to Arrian," *Athenaeum* 55: 19–48.

(1980) "On historical fragments and epitomes," *CQ* 30: 477–94.

Buckler, J. (1980) *The Theban Hegemony, 371–362 BC*. Cambridge, MA.

(2003) *Aegean Greece in the Fourth Century BC*. Leiden.

(2004) "The incident at Mount Parnassus, 395 BC," in Tuplin (ed.) (1990): 397–411.

Buckler, J. and H. Beck (2008) *Central Greece and the Politics of Power in the Fourth Century BC*. Cambridge.

Bugh, G. R. (1988) *The Horsemen of Athens*. Princeton.

Buijs, M. (2005) *Clause Combining in Ancient Greek Narrative Discourse: The Distribution of Subclauses and Participial Clauses in Xenophon's Hellenica and Anabasis*. Leiden.

(2007) "Aspectual differences and narrative technique: Xenophon's Hellenica and Anabasis," in Allan and Buijs (eds.) (2007): 122–53.

Bundy, E. L. (1986) *Studia Pindarica*. Berkeley and Los Angeles.

Burke, E. M. (1984) "Eubulus, Olynthus and Euboea," *TAPA* 114: 111–20.

Burke, S. (1998) *The Death and Return of the Author: Criticism and Subjectivity in Barthes, Foucault, and Derrida*. Edinburgh.

Burnet, J. (1911) *Plato's Phaedo*. Oxford.

(1914) *Greek Philosophy: Thales to Plato*. London.

Burrell, S. (1794) *The Thymbriad (from Xenophon's Cyropoedia [sic])*. London.

Buxton, R. F. (2016) "Novel Leaders for Novel Armies: Xenophon's Focus on Willing Obedience in Context," *Histos* Supplement 5: 163–97.

Cabrini, A. M. (2007) "Alberti e Senofonte," in *Alberti e la tradizione: per lo smontaggio dei mosaici albertiani*, eds. M. Regoliosi and R. Cardini. Florence: 19–44.

Cairns, D. (1993) *Aidos: The Psychology and Ethics of Honour and Shame in Ancient Greek Literature.* Oxford.

Callender, J. T. (1795) *The Political Progress of Britain; or, An Impartial History of Abuses in the Government of the British Empire, in Europe, Asia, and America.* Philadelphia and London.

Campbell, J. (1756) *The Rational Amusement, Comprehending a Collection of Letters on a Great Variety of Subjects.* Cork.

Canfora, D. (1996) "La topica del 'principe' e l'uso umanistico delle fonti in Poggio Bracciolini," *Humanistica Lovaniensia* 45: 1–92.

Canfora, L. (1970) *Tucidide continuato.* Padova.

(1990) "Eduard Meyer tra Cratippo e Teopompo," in *Eduard Meyer: Leben und Leistung eines Universalhistorikers,* eds. W. M. Calder and A. Demandt. Leiden: 74–96.

(2013) "PSI 1304," in *Teopompo: Elleniche, Libro II,* eds. L. Canfora and R. Otranto. Bari: 75–100.

Carlier, P. (1978/2010) "The idea of imperial monarchy in Xenophon's *Cyropaedia,*" in Gray (ed.) (2010a): 327–66 (= "L'idée de monarchie imperiale dans la *Cyropédie* de Xénophon," *Ktèma* 3 (1978): 133–63).

Carlsen, J. (2002) "Estate managers in ancient Greek agriculture," in *Ancient History Matters: Studies Presented to Jens Erik Skydsgaard on his Seventieth Birthday,* ed. K. Ascani. Rome: 117–26.

Carlucci, G. (2013) "Vita di Teopompo di Chio: una ipotesi di ricostruzione," in *Teopompo: Elleniche, Libro II,* eds. L. Canfora and R. Otranto. Bari: 7–24.

Cartledge, P. (1987) *Agesilaos and the Crisis of Sparta.* Baltimore.

(1999) "The Socratics' Sparta and Rousseau's," in *Sparta: New Perspectives,* eds. S. Hodkinson and A. Powell. Swansea: 311–37.

(2002) *Sparta and Lakonia: A Regional History 1300–362 B.C.* 2nd edn. London.

(2004) "What have the Spartans done for us? Sparta's contribution to the western civilization," *G&R* 51/2: 164–79.

(2009) "Spartan government and society" in Strassler (ed.) (2009): 347–58.

Cartledge, P. and A. Spawforth (2002) *Hellenistic and Roman Sparta: A Tale of Two Cities.* 2nd edn. London.

Cast, D. (1974) "Aurispa, Petrarch and Lucian: an aspect of Renaissance translation," *Renaissance Quarterly* 27: 157–73.

Cavenaile, R. (1975) "Aperçu sur la langue et le style de Xénophon," *Les études classiques* 43: 238–52.

Cawkwell, G. (1963) "Eubulus," *JHS* 83: 47–67.

(1972) "Introduction," in *Xenophon: The Persian Expedition,* tr. Rex Warner. Harmondsworth: 9–48.

(ed.) (1979) *Xenophon: A History of My Times.* London.

(1997) "The Peace between Athens and Persia," *Phoenix* 51: 115–30.

(2004) "When, how, and why did Xenophon write the *Anabasis*?" in *The Long March: Xenophon and the Ten Thousand,* ed. R. Lane Fox. New Haven: 47–67.

Chambers, M. (ed.) (1993) *Hellenica Oxyrhynchia: Post Victorium Bartoletti.* Stuttgart and Leipzig.

Chantraine, P. (1949) *Xénophon: Économique.* Paris.

Chernyakhovskaya, O. (2014) *Sokrates bei Xenophon: Moral – Politik – Religion.* Tübingen.

Cheshire, N. M. and M. J. Heath (trs.) (1986) *"The Education of a Christian Prince,"* in *Collected Works of Erasmus.* Vol. XXVII, ed. A. H. T. Levi. Toronto: 199–288.

Christ, M. R. (2012) *The Limits of Altruism in Democratic Athens.* Cambridge.

(2013) "Demosthenes on *philanthropia* as a democratic virtue," *CP* 108: 202–22.

Christesen, P. (2006) "Xenophon's *Cyropaedia* and military reform in Sparta," *JHS* 126: 47–65.

(2012) "Athletics and social order in Sparta in the Classical period," *CA* 31: 193–255.

(2013) "Sport and society in Sparta," in *A Companion to Sport and Spectacle in Greek and Roman Antiquity,* eds. P. Christesen and D. Kyle. Malden, MA, Oxford, and Chichester: 146–58.

Christophides, L. N. (1992) "On share contracts and other economic contributions of Xenophon," *Scottish Journal of Political Economy* 39: 111–22.

Chroust, A.-H. (1945) "Socrates: a source problem," *The New Scholasticism* 19: 48–72.

Clarke, M. L. (1959) *Classical Education in Britain 1500–1900.* Cambridge.

Classen, C. J. (1984/1986) "Xenophons Darstellung der Sophistik und der Sophisten," *Hermes* 112: 154–67, reprinted in *Ansätze: Beiträge zum Verständnis der frühgriechischen Philosophie* (1986). Amsterdam: 175–90.

Clay, D. (1994) "The origins of the Socratic dialogue," in Vander Waerdt (ed.) (1994a): 23–47.

Coleman, K. M. (2011) "Sailing to Nuceria: evidence for the date of Xenophon of Ephesus," *Acta Classica* 54: 27–41.

Connor, W. R. (1984) *Thucydides.* Princeton.

Cooper, J. (1999) "Notes on Xenophon's Socrates," in *Reason and Emotion: Essays on Ancient Moral Psychology and Ethical Theory.* Princeton: 3–28.

Cooper, J. F. (1840) *The Pathfinder; or, The Inland Sea.* Paris.

Cramsie, J. (2006) "The philosophy of imperial kingship and the interpretation of James VI and I," in *James VI and I: Ideas, Authority, and Government,* ed. R. Houlbrooke. Aldershot: 43–60.

Croft, H. H. S. (ed.) (1883) *The Boke Named the Gouernour, devised by Sir Thomas Elyot, Knight.* London.

Csapo, E. and W. J. Slater (1994) *The Context of Ancient Drama.* Ann Arbor.

Curtis, J. (2013) *The Cyrus Cylinder and Ancient Persia: A New Beginning for the Middle East.* London.

Dakyns, H. G. (1914) (tr.) *The Education of Cyrus.* London and New York.

Dalby, A. (1992) "Greeks abroad: social organisation and food among the Ten Thousand," *JHS* 112: 16–30.

Danzig, G. (2002) "La prétendue rivalité entre Platon et Xénophon," *Revue française d'histoire des idées politiques* 2.16: 351–68.

(2003) "Why Socrates was not a farmer: Xenophon's *Oeconomicus* as a philosophical dialogue," *G&R* 50: 57–76.

(2004) "Apologetic elements in Xenophon's *Symposium,*" *Classica et Mediaevalia* 55: 17–48.

(2005) "Intra-Socratic polemics: the *Symposia* of Plato and Xenophon," *GRBS* 45: 331–57.

(2009) "Big boys and little boys: justice and law in Xenophon's *Cyropaedia* and *Memorabilia,*" *Polis* 26.2: 271–95.

(2010) *Apologizing for Socrates: How Plato and Xenophon Created Our Socrates.* Lanham, MD.

(2012) "The best of the Achaemenids: benevolence, self-interest, and the 'ironic' reading of the *Cyropaedia*," in Hobden and Tuplin (eds.) (2012a): 499–539.

(2013) "Plato's *Charmides* as a political act: apologetics and the promotion of ideology," *GRBS* 53: 486–519.

(2014a) "Xenophon on virtue, happiness and the human *telos*," paper presented at the conference "Plato and Xenophon: Comparative Studies," Bar-Ilan University, Israel.

(2014b) "The use and abuse of Critias: conflicting portraits in Plato and Xenophon," *CQ* 64: 507–24.

(2014c) "Alcibiades versus Pericles: apologetic strategies in Xenophon's *Memorabilia*," *GR* 61: 7–28.

(forthcoming) "Nature, culture and oligarchic rule in Xenophon's Socratic theory of friendship: *Memorabilia* Book Two," in *Socrates and the Socratic Dialogue*, eds. A. Stavru and F. de Luise.

Danzig, G. and N. Alon (eds.) (forthcoming) *Plato and Xenophon: Comparative Studies* (proceedings of a conference held at Tzuba in June 2014).

Daryaee, T. (2006) "The construction of the past in late antique Persia," *Historia* 55.4: 493–503.

Davenant, C. (1698) *Discourses on the Publick Revenues, and on the Trade of England. In Two Parts ... To which is Added, a Discourse upon Improving the Revenue of the State of Athens by Xenophon, now Made English.* London.

Daverio Rocchi, G. (2007) "La présentation de Sparte par Xénophon dans les *Hélleniques*, la *République des Lacédémoniens* et l'*Agésilas*," *Ktèma* 32: 391–404.

David, E. (1979) "The pamphlet of Pausanias," *PP* 34: 94–116.

Davidson, J. (1990) "Isocrates against imperialism: an analysis of the *De Pace*," *Historia* 39: 20–36.

Davies, J. K. (1971) *Athenian Propertied Families, 600–300 B.C.* Oxford.

(2007) "Classical Greece: production," in *The Cambridge Economic History of the Greco-Roman World*, eds. W. Scheidel, I. Morris, and R. P. Saller. Cambridge: 333–61.

Davies, P. (2013) "'Kalos kagathos' and scholarly perceptions of Spartan society," *Historia* 62: 259–79.

de Jong, I., R. Nünlist, and A. Bowie (eds.) (2004) *Narrators, Narratees, and Narratives in Ancient Greek Literature.* Studies in Ancient Greek Narrative 1. Leiden.

De Keyser, J. (2012) *Francesco Filelfo: Traduzioni da Senofonte e Plutarco.* Alexandria.

De Luise, F. and A. Stavru (eds.) (2013) *Socratica III: Studies on Socrates, the Socratics, and the Ancient Socratic Literature.* Sankt Augustin.

De Nichilo, M. (2013) "Fortuna e tradizione della versione bruniana dello Ierone di Senofonte," *Cahiers de recherches médiévales et humanistes* 25: 327–40.

De Romilly, J. (1954) "Les modérés athéniens vers le milieu du IVe siècle: échos et concordances," *REG* 67: 327–54.

(1992) *The Great Sophists in Periclean Athens.* Tr. J. Lloyd, orig. pub. 1988. Oxford.

De Temmerman, K. (2014) *Crafting Characters: Heroes and Heroines in the Ancient Greek Novel.* Oxford.

Delatte, A. (1933) *Le troisième livre des Souvenirs Socratiques de Xénophon*. Liége and Paris.
Delbrück, J. F. F. (1829) *Xenophon: zur Rettung seiner durch B. G. Niebuhr gefährdeten Ehre*. Bonn.
Delebecque, E. (1957) *Essai sur la vie de Xénophon*. Paris.
Deman, T. (1942) *Le témoignage d'Aristote sur Socrate*. Paris.
Demont, P. (2003) "L'Enquête de Xénophon sur le pouvoir de Cyrus (*Cyropédie* VII, 5, 57–VIII)," in *Grecs et Romains aux prises avec l'histoire: représentations, récits et idéologie*, eds. G. Lachenaud and D. Longrée. Rennes: 189–202.
   (2006) "Xénophon et les homotimes," *Ktèma* 31: 277–90.
Dik, H. H. (1995) *Word Order in Ancient Greek: A Pragmatic Account of Word Order Variation in Herodotus*. Leiden.
Dillery, J. (1993) "Xenophon's Poroi and Athenian imperialism," *Historia* 42: 1–11.
   (1995) *Xenophon and the History of His Times*. London and New York.
   (1996) "Reconfiguring the past: Thyrea, Thermopylae and narrative patterns in Herodotus," *AJP* 117: 217–54.
   (2001) "Introduction," in *Xenophon: Anabasis*. Reprinted with corrections. Cambridge, MA: 1–37.
   (2004) "Xenophon, the military review and Hellenistic pompai," in Tuplin (ed.) (2004a): 259–76.
   (2009) "Building a house: I Cor. 3.6ff., Xenophon's Memorabilia, and the persistence of an image," in Ἀντιφίλησις: *Studies on Classical, Byzantine and Modern Greek Literature and Culture. In Honour of John-Theophanes A. Papademetriou*, eds. E. Karamalengou and E. Makrygianni. Stuttgart: 414–16.
   (2015) *Clio's Other Sons: Berossus and Manetho. With an Afterword on Demetrius*. Ann Arbor.
Dobski, B. (2009) "Athenian democracy refounded: Xenophon's political history in the *Hellenika*," *Polis* 26: 316–38.
Dodds, E. R. (1960) *Euripides Bacchae*. 2nd edn. Oxford.
Donlan, W. (1973) "The origin of καλὸς κἀγαθός," *AJP* 94: 365–74.
Dorati, M. (2007) "Alcune ambiguità del narratore dell'*Anabasi*," *QUCC* 85:105–13.
Döring, K. (2011) "The students of Socrates," in *The Cambridge Companion to Socrates*, ed. D. R. Morrison. Cambridge: 24–47.
Dorion, L.-A. (2000) "Introduction," in *Xénophon: Mémorables*, eds. L.-A. Dorion and M. Bandini. Vol. I. Paris: vii–cclii.
Dorion, L. (2006) "Xenophon's Socrates," in *A Companion to Socrates*, eds. S. Ahbel-Rappe and R. Kamtekar. Malden, MA and Oxford: 93–109.
   (2008) "Socrate *oikonomikos*," in *Xénophon et Socrate: actes du colloque d'Aix-en-Provence (6–9 novembre 2003)*, eds. M. Narcy and A. Tordesillas. Paris: 253–81.
   (2009) "Xenophon's Socrates," in *A Companion to Socrates*, eds. S. Ahbel-Rappe and R. Kamtekar. Oxford: 93–109.
   (2010) "The Straussian exegesis of Xenophon: the paradigmatic case of *Memorabilia* IV 4," in Gray (ed.) (2010a): 283–323 (= "L'exégèse straussienne de Xénophon: le cas paradigmatique de Mémorables IV 4," *PA* 1 (2001): 87–118).
   (2011) "The rise and fall of the Socratic Problem," in *The Cambridge Companion to Socrates*, ed. D. R. Morrison. Cambridge: 1–23.
   (2013a) *L'autre Socrate: études sur les écrits socratiques de Xénophon*. Paris.

(2013b) "La responsabilité de Cyrus dans le déclin de l'empire perse selon Platon et Xénophon," in Dorion (2013a): 393–412.

(2014) "Le statut et la fonction de la rhétorique dans les écrits socratiques de Xénophon," in Pontier (ed.) (2014): 17–40.

(2016) "L'influence des chapitres théologiques des *Mémorables* (I 4 et IV 3) sur le livre II du *De natura deorum* de Cicéron," *Philosophie Antique* 16: 181–208.

(forthcoming) "Plato and Xenophon on the different reasons why Socrates always obeys the Law," in Danzig and Alon (eds.) (forthcoming).

Dorion, L.-A. and M. Bandini (eds.) (2000) *Xénophon: Mémorables. Tome I: Introduction génerale, Livre I*. Paris.

(2011a). *Xénophon: Mémorables. Tome II: Livres II–III*. Paris.

(2011b). *Xénophon: Mémorables. Tome III: Livre IV*. Paris.

Dover, K. J. (1968) *Lysias and the Corpus Lysiacum*. Berkeley and Los Angeles.

(1981) "Appendix 2: strata of composition," in *A Historical Commentary on Thucydides*, eds. A. W. Gomme, A. Andrewes, and K. J. Dover. Vol. V. Oxford: 384–444.

(1997) *The Evolution of Greek Prose Style*. Oxford.

Dow, S. (1965) "The greater *demarkhia* of Erchia," *BCH* 89.1: 180–213.

Drucker, P. F. (1954) *The Practice of Management*. New York.

Due, B. (1983) "The trial of the generals in Xenophon's *Anabasis*," *C&M* 34: 33–44.

(1989) *The Cyropaedia: Xenophon's Aims and Methods*. Aarhus.

Ellis, A. (2014) "A Socratic history: theology and didacticism in Xenophon's rewriting of the Herodotean Croesus *Logos*," paper presented at the conference "Plato and Xenophon: Comparative Studies," Bar-Ilan University, Israel.

Elyot, T. (1531) *The Boke Named the Gouernour*. London.

Engels, J. (1993a) "Der Michigan-Papyrus über Theramenes und die Ausbildung des 'Theramenes-Mythos'," *ZPE* 99: 125–55.

(1993b) "Die Ὑπομνήματα-Schriften und die Anfänge der politischen Biographie und Autobiographie in der griechischen Literatur," *ZPE* 96: 16–36.

Erbse, H. (1961) "Die Architektonik im Aufbau von Xenophons *Memorabilien*," *Hermes* 89: 257–87.

Erler, M. (2002) "Stoic *oikeiosis* and Xenophon's Socrates," in *The Philosophy of Zeno*, eds. T. Scaltsas and A. S. Mason. Larnaka, 241–57.

Euben, J. P. (1994) "Democracy and political theory: a reading of Plato's *Gorgias*," in Euben et al. (eds.) (1994): 198–226.

Euben, J. P., J. R. Wallach, and J. Ober (eds.) (1994) *Athenian Political Thought and the Reconstruction of American Democracy*. Ithaca, NY.

Fantazzi, C. (ed.) (2000) *Education of a Christian Woman: A Sixteenth Century Manual by Juan Luis Vives*. Chicago.

Farber, J. J. (1979) "The *Cyropaedia* and Hellenistic kingship," *AJP* 100.4: 497–514.

Farrell, C. A. (2012) *Xenophon in Context: Advising Athens and Democracy*. Diss. King's College London.

Fehling, D. (1969) *Die Wiederholungsfiguren und ihr Gebrauch bei den Griechen vor Gorgias*. Berlin.

(1979) *Herodotus and his "Sources": Citation, Invention, and Narrative Art*. Tr. J. G. Howie, orig. publ. 1971. Leeds.

Ferrari, G. R. F. (ed.) (2007) *The Cambridge Companion to Plato's Republic*. Cambridge.

Ferrario, S. (2012) "Historical agency and self-awareness in Xenophon's *Hellenica* and *Anabasis*," in Hobden and Tuplin (eds.) (2012): 341–76.

(2014) *Historical Agency and the 'Great Man' in Classical Greece*. Cambridge.

Ferrau, G. (ed.) (1979) *Bartholomaei Platinae De principe*. Palermo.

Field, L. K. (2012) "Xenophon's *Cyropaedia*: educating our political hopes," *Journal of Politics* 74.3: 723–38.

Figueira, T. J. (2012) "Economic thought and economic fact in the works of Xenophon," in Hobden and Tuplin (eds.) (2012a): 665–87.

Fine, G. (1992) "Inquiry in the *Meno*," in Kraut (ed.) (1992): 200–26.

Finkel, I. (ed.) (2013) *The Cyrus Cylinder: The King of Persia's Proclamation from Ancient Babylon*. New York.

Finley, M. I. (1973) *The Ancient Economy*. Berkeley and Los Angeles.

(1975/1990) *The Use and Abuse of History*. Reprinted with corrections 1990. London.

(1977) *The World of Odysseus*. 2nd edn. New York.

Flower, H. I. (1992) "Thucydides and the Pylos Debate (4.27–29)," *Historia* 41: 40–57.

Flower, M. A. (1994) *Theopompus of Chios: History and Rhetoric in the Fourth Century* BC. Oxford.

(2000) "From Simonides to Isocrates: the fifth-century origins of fourth-century panhellenism," *CA* 19: 65–101.

(2012) *Xenophon's Anabasis; or, The Expedition of Cyrus*. New York.

(2015) "Implied characterization and the meaning of history in Xenophon's *Hellenica*," in Ash et al. (eds.) (2015): 110–27.

(2016) "Piety in Xenophon's theory of leadership," in *Aspects of Leadership in Xenophon*, ed. R. F. Buxton. *Histos* Supplement 5: 85–119.

Flower, M. and J. Marincola (2002) *Herodotus: Histories Book IX*. Cambridge.

Ford, A. (2011) *Aristotle as Poet: The Song of Hermias and Its Contexts*. Oxford and New York.

Fornara, C. W. (1983) *The Nature of History in Ancient Greece and Rome*. Berkeley and Los Angeles.

Forsdyke, S. (2009) "The uses and abuses of tyranny," in Balot (ed.) (2009): 231–46.

Foster, E. (2012) "Some recent work on direct and indirect discourse in the ancient historians," *Histos* 6: 329–42.

Gagarin, M. and D. M. MacDowell (1998) *Antiphon & Andocides*. Austin, TX.

Gaile-Irbe, A. (2011) *Réformer la tyrannie: étude de Hiéron de Xénophon*. 2 vols. Diss. Strasbourg.

Gallaher, J. E. (1898) *Best Lincoln Stories Tersely Told*. Chicago.

Gangloff, A. (2006) *Dion Chrysostome et les mythes*. Grenoble.

Garlan, Y. (1994) "Warfare," in *Cambridge Ancient History*, 2nd edn, VI: 678–92.

Gauthier, P. (1976) *Un commentaire historique des Poroi de Xénophon*. Geneva and Paris.

(1984/2010) "Le programme de Xénophon dans les *Poroi*," *Rev. Phil.* 58: 181–99, reprinted as "Xenophon's programme in the *Poroi*," in Gray (ed.) (2010a): 113–36.

Gautier, L. (1911) *La langue de Xénophon*. Geneva.

Gavins, J. (2007) *Text World Theory: An Introduction*. Edinburgh.

Gemoll, W. (1932) "Zu Xen. An. I 8, 18," *Philologische Wochenschrift* 2: 62–4.

Georges, P. (1994) *Barbarian Asia and the Greek Experience: From the Archaic Period to the Age of Xenophon.* Baltimore and London.

Gera, D. L. (1993) *Xenophon's Cyropaedia: Style, Genre, and Literary Technique.* Oxford.

Giannantoni, G. (1990) *Socratis et Socraticorum reliquiae.* Naples.

Gigante, M. (1957) "Un nuovo frammento politico (P. Heid. 182)," *Maia* 9: 68–74.

Gilbert, A. (1938) *Machiavelli's Prince and Its Forerunners: The Prince as a Typical Book De regimine principum.* New York.

   (1989) *Machiavelli: The Chief Works and Others.* Vol. I. 1st edn publ. 1958. Durham, NC.

Gilula D. (2002) "Entertainment at Xenophon's *Symposium*," *Athenaeum* 90: 207–13.

Gini, A. (1993) "The manly intellect of his wife: Xenophon, 'Oeconomicus' ch. 7," *CW* 86: 483–6.

Giraud J. M. (1999) *Xenophon et l'histoire.* Villeneuve d'Ascq.

Gish, D. (2012) "Defending *dêmokratia*: Athenian justice and the trial of the Arginusae generals in Xenophon's *Hellenica*," in Hobden and Tuplin (eds.) (2012a): 161–212.

Gish, D. and D. Ambler (2009) *The Political Thought of Xenophon* = *Polis* 26 (2009): 181–410.

Glazebrook, A. (2009) "Cosmetics and *sôphrosunê*: Ischomachus' wife in Xenophon's *Oikonomikos*," *CW* 102: 231–46.

Goldhill, S. (1995) *Foucault's Virginity: Ancient Erotic Fiction and the History of Sexuality.* Cambridge.

   (1998) Review of Gray (1998), *BMCR* 1998.12.08.

   (2002) *The Invention of Prose.* Oxford.

Gomme, A. W. (1956) *A Historical Commentary on Thucydides.* Vol. II. Oxford.

Gomme, A. W., A. Andrewes, and K. J. Dover (1981) *A Historical Commentary on Thucydides.* Vol. V. Oxford.

Gosling, J. C. B. and C. C. W. Taylor (1982) *The Greeks on Pleasure.* Oxford.

Gosson, S. (1582) *Playes Confuted in Fiue Actions: Prouing that they are not to be Suffred in a Christian Common Weale.* London.

Gould, J. (1989) *Herodotus.* London and New York.

Gray, V. J. (1979) "Two different approaches to the battle of Sardis in 395 B.C.," *CSCA* 12: 183–200.

   (1981) "Dialogue in Xenophon's *Hellenica*," *CQ* 31: 321–34.

   (1985) "Xenophon's 'Cynegeticus'," *Hermes* 113: 156–72.

   (1986) "Xenophon's *Hiero* and the meeting of the wise man and tyrant in Greek literature," *CQ* 36: 115–23.

   (1989) *The Character of Xenophon's Hellenica.* London.

   (1991) "Continuous history and Xenophon, *Hellenica* 1–2.3.10," *AJP* 112: 201–28.

   (1998) *The Framing of Socrates: The Literary Interpretation of Xenophon's Memorabilia.* Stuttgart.

   (2000) "Xenophon and Isocrates," in *The Cambridge History of Greek and Roman Political Thought*, eds. C. Rowe and M. Schofield, with S. Harrison and M. Lane. Cambridge: 142–54.

   (2003) "Interventions and citations in Xenophon, *Anabasis* and *Hellenica*," *CQ* 53: 111–53, reprinted in Gray (ed.) (2010a): 553–72.

(2004a) "Le Socrate de Xénophon et la démocratie," *Les études philosophiques* 2 (*Les écrits socratiques de Xénophon*): 141–76.

(2004b) "Historiography: Xenophon," in de Jong et al. (eds.) (2004): 129–46.

(2004c) "Philosophy: Xenophon," in de Jong et al. (eds.) (2004): 377–88.

(2004d) "Biography: Xenophon," in de Jong et al. (eds.) (2004): 391–401.

(2006) "The linguistic choices of Prodicus in Xenophon's Choice of Heracles," *CQ* 56: 426–35.

(2007) *Xenophon on Government*. Cambridge.

(ed.) (2010a) *Xenophon*. Oxford Readings in Classical Studies. Oxford.

(2010b) "Introduction," in Gray (ed.) (2010a): 1–28.

(2010c) "Work in progress on Xenophon's language," in *Proceedings of the New Zealand Universities Classics Conference*, ed. E. A. Mackay (web).

(2011) *Xenophon's Mirror of Princes: Reading the Reflections*. Oxford.

(2014) "Le style simple de Xénophon," in Pontier (ed.) (2014): 319–37.

Grayson, A. K. (1975) *Babylonian Historical-Literary Texts*. Toronto.

Grayson, C. H. (1975) "Did Xenophon intend to write history?," in *The Ancient Historian and His Materials: Essays in Honour of C. E. Stevens on His Seventieth Birthday*, ed. B. Levick. Westmead: 31–43.

Green, F. (2012) *Montaigne and the Life of Freedom*. Cambridge.

Green, P. (1994) "Text and context in the matter of Xenophon's exile," in *Ventures into Greek History*, ed. I. Worthington. Oxford: 215–27.

(2010) *Diodorus Siculus: The Persian Wars to the Fall of Athens. Books 11–14.34 (480–401 BCE)*. Austin, TX.

Gregory, J. (1999) *Euripides: Hecuba. Introduction, Text, and Commentary*. Atlanta.

Grethlein, J. (2012) "Xenophon's *Anabasis* from character to narrator," *JHS* 132: 23–40.

(2013) *Experience and Teleology in Ancient Historiography: 'Futures Past' from Herodotus to Augustine*. Cambridge.

Gribble, D. (1999) *Alcibiades and Athens: A Study in Literary Presentation*. Oxford.

Griffiths, A. (2006) "Stories and storytelling in the *Histories*," in *The Cambridge Companion to Herodotus*, eds. C. Dewald and J. Marincola. Cambridge: 130–44.

Grissom, D. (2012) *Thucydides' Dangerous World: Dual Forms of Danger in Classical Greek Interstate Relations*. Diss. University of Maryland, College Park.

Grogan, J. (2007) "'Many Cyruses': Xenophon's *Cyropaedia* and English Renaissance humanism," *Hermathena* 183: 63–74.

(2014) *The Persian Empire in English Renaissance Writing, 1549–1622*. Basingstoke.

Grote, G. (1872/1888) *A History of Greece*. 10 vols. London.

Gruen, E. S. (2011) *Rethinking the Other in Antiquity*. Princeton and Oxford.

Gualdo Rosa, L. (1973) "Le lettere di dedica nelle traduzioni dal greco nel '400: appunti per un'analisi stilistica," *Vichiana* n.s. 2: 68–85.

Guthrie, W. K. C. (1978) *A History of Greek Philosophy*. Vol. V: *The Later Plato and the Academy*. Cambridge.

Haake, M. (2013) "Illustrating, documenting, make-believe: the use of *psephismata* in Hellenistic biographies of philosophers," in *Inscriptions and their Uses in Greek and Latin Literature*, eds. P. Liddel and P. Low. Oxford: 79–124.

Hackforth, R. (1913) *The Authorship of the Platonic Epistles*. Manchester.

Hadot, P. (2002) *What is Ancient Philosophy?* Cambridge, MA.

Hägg, T. (2012) *The Art of Biography in Antiquity*. Cambridge.

Hägg, T. and B. Utas (2003) *The Virgin and Her Lover: Fragments of an Ancient Greek Novel and a Persian Epic Poem*. Leiden.

Hall, E. (1989) *Inventing the Barbarian: Greek Self-definition through Tragedy*. Oxford.

(2007a) "Aeschylus' *Persians* via the Ottoman Empire to Saddam Hussein," in *Cultural Responses to the Persian Wars*, eds. E. Bridges, E. Hall, and P. J. Rhodes. Oxford: 167–79.

(2007b) "Greek tragedy 430–380 BC," in *Debating the Athenian Cultural Revolution: Art, Literature, Philosophy, and Politics, 430–380 BC*, ed. R. Osborne. Cambridge: 264–87.

(2010) "Heroes of the dance floor: the missing exemplary male dancer in ancient sources," in *The Ancient Dancer in the Modern World*, ed. F. Macintosh. Oxford: 145–68.

(2013) *Adventures with Iphigenia in Tauris: A Cultural History of Euripides' Black Sea Tragedy*. New York.

(2016) "Intellectual pleasure and women translators in 17th- and 18th-century England," in *Unsealing the Fountain: Women Classical Scholars from the Renaissance to Jacqueline de Romilly*, eds. R. Wyles and E. Hall. Oxford: 103–31.

(forthcoming) "'Romantic poet-sage of history': Herodotus and his Arion in the long 19th Century," in *Herodotus in the Nineteenth Century*, ed. T. Harrison.

Hall, E. and F. Macintosh (2005) *Greek Tragedy and the British Theatre 1660–1914*. Oxford.

Hall, E. and H. Stead (forthcoming) *Classics and Class in Britain 1789–1917*.

Hamilton, C. D. (1979) *Sparta's Bitter Victories: Politics and Diplomacy in the Corinthian War*. Ithaca, NY.

(1991) *Agesilaus and the Failure of Spartan Hegemony*. Ithaca, NY.

Hankins, J. (ed.) (2009) *Aurelio Lippo Brandolini: Republics and Kingdoms Compared*. Cambridge, MA.

Hansen, M. H. (1984) "Two notes on Demosthenes' symbouleutic speeches," *C&M* 35: 57–70.

(1989) *The Athenian Ecclesia II: A Collection of Articles 1983–89*. Copenhagen.

(1999) *The Athenian Democracy in the Age of Demosthenes*. 2nd edn. Norman, OK.

Harding, P. (tr. and ed.) (1994) *Androtion and the Atthis*. Oxford.

Harman, R. (2008) "Viewing, power and interpretation in Xenophon's *Cyropaedia*," in *The Children of Herodotus*, ed. J. Pigon. Newcastle: 69–91.

(2012) "A spectacle of Greekness: panhellenism and the visual in Xenophon's Agesilaus," in Hobden and Tuplin (eds.) (2012a): 427–53.

(2013) "Looking at the Other: visual mediation and Greek identity in Xenophon's *Anabasis*," in *Ancient Ethnographies*, eds. E. Almagor and J. Skinner. Edinburgh: 79–96.

Harrison, T. (1984) *Selected Poems*. Harmondsworth.

Hartog, F. (1988) *The Mirror of Herodotus: The Representation of the Other in the Writing of History*. Tr. J. Lloyd. Berkeley and Los Angeles.

Harvey, D. (1984) "The wicked wife of Ischomachus," *EMC* 28 (n.s. 3): 68–70.

Hatzfeld, J. (1946) "Note sur la date et l'objet du Hiéron de Xénophon," *REG* 59/60: 54–70.

Hau, L. 2012. "Does pride go before a fall? Xenophon on arrogant pride," in Hobden and Tuplin (eds.) (2012a): 591–610.

Havell, H. L. (1910) *Stories from Xenophon*. London.

Haywood, J. (2016) "Divine narratives in Xenophon's *Anabasis*," *Histos* 10: 85–110.

Hedrick, L. (2006) *Xenophon's Cyrus the Great: The Arts of Leadership and War.* New York.

Henry, W. P. (1967) *Greek Historical Writing: A Historiographical Essay Based on Xenophon's Hellenica.* Chicago.

Herchenroeder, L. (2008) "Plutarch's *Gryllus* and the so-called Grylloi," *AJP* 129.3: 347–79.

Hicks, R. D. (ed.) (1925) *Diogenes Laertius*. Vol. I. Cambridge, MA.

Higgins, W. E. (1977) *Xenophon the Athenian: The Problem of the Individual and the Society of the Polis.* Albany, NY.

Hindley, C. (1999) "Xenophon on male love," *CQ* 89: 219–40, reprinted in Gray (ed.) (2010a): 72–110.

(2004) "*Sophron eros:* Xenophon's ethical erotics," in Tuplin (ed.) (2004a): 125–46.

Hirsch, S. W. (1985) *The Friendship of the Barbarians: Xenophon and the Persian Empire.* Hanover, CT and London.

Hirzel, R. (1895) *Der Dialog.* 2 vols. Reprinted 1963. Hildesheim.

Hobden, F. (2005) "Reading Xenophon's *Symposium*," *Ramus* 34.2: 93–111.

(2013) *The Symposion in Ancient Greek Society and Thought.* Cambridge.

Hobden, F. and C. Tuplin (eds.) (2012a) *Xenophon: Ethical Principles and Historical Enquiry.* Leiden.

Hobden, F. (2012b) "Introduction," in Hobden and Tuplin (eds.) (2012a): 1–41.

Holzapfel, L. (1882) "Über die Abfassungszeit der dem Xenophon zugeschriebenen Πόροι," *Philologus* 41: 242–69.

Hoover, H. C. and L. H. Hoover (1950) *Georgius Agricola, De re metallica, Translated from the First Latin Edition of 1556.* New York.

Horn, G. (1926) *Quaestiones ad Xenophontis elocutionem pertinentes.* Diss. Halle.

Hornblower, S. (1991/2008) *A Commentary on Thucydides.* 3 vols. Oxford.

(1994) "Introduction," in *Greek Historiography*, ed. S. Hornblower. Oxford: 1–72.

(1995) "The fourth century and Hellenistic reception of Thucydides," *JHS* 115: 47–68.

(2004) "'This was decided' (*edoxe tauta*): the army as *polis* in Xenophon's *Anabasis* – and elsewhere," in Lane Fox (ed.) (2004): 243–63.

(2006) "Herodotus' influence in antiquity," in *The Cambridge Companion to Herodotus*, eds. C. Dewald and J. Marincola. Cambridge: 306–18.

Howell, E. (1949) "Meet General X," *G&R* 18: 1–13.

Hughes, J. (1750) "An essay on allegorical poetry, with remarks on the writings of Spencer," in *The Works of Spencer*. Vol. I. London: xix–xli.

Humbert, J. (1967) *Socrate et les petits Socratiques.* Paris.

Humble, N. (1997) "*Xenophon's View of Sparta: A Study of the Anabasis, Hellenica, and Respublica Lacedaemoniorum.* Diss. McMaster.

(1999) "*Sôphrosynê* and the Spartans in Xenophon," in *Sparta: New Perspectives*, eds. S. Hodkinson and A. Powell. Swansea: 339–53.

(2002a) "Was *sôphrosynê* ever a Spartan virtue?," in *Sparta: Beyond the Mirage*, eds. A. Powell and S. Hodkinson. Swansea: 85–109.

(2002b) "The limits of biography: the case of Xenophon," in *Pleiades Setting: Essays for Pat Cronin on his 65th Birthday*, ed. K. Sidwell. Cork: 66–87.

(2004a) "The author, date and purpose of chapter 14 of the *Lakedaimonion Politeia*," in Tuplin (ed.) (2004a): 215–28.

(2004b) "Xenophon's sons in Sparta? Perspectives on *xenoi* in the Spartan upbringing," in *Spartan Society*, ed. T. Figueira. Swansea: 231–50.

(2006) "Why the Spartans fight so well, even if they are in disorder: Xenophon's view," in *Sparta and War*, eds. S. Hodkinson and A. Powell. Swansea: 219–33.

(2008) "Re-dating a lost painting: Euphranor's battle of Mantineia," *Historia* 57.4: 347–66.

(forthcoming) "True history: Xenophon's *Agesilaos* and the encomiastic genre," in Powell and Richer (eds.) (forthcoming).

Humphreys, S. C. (1978) *Anthropology and the Greeks*. London.

Hunnings, L. (2010) "Paradigms of execution: managing slave death from Homer to Virginia," in *Reading Ancient Slavery*, eds. R. Alston, E. Hall, and L. Proffitt. Bristol: 51–71.

Hunt, P. (1998) *Slaves, Warfare and Ideology in the Greek Historians*. Cambridge.

Hunter, R. L. (2004) "Homer and Greek literature," in *The Cambridge Companion to Homer*, ed. R. Fowler. Cambridge: 235–53.

Huntingford, G. I. (1811) *Introduction to the Writing of Greek in Two Parts: For the Use of Winchester College*. 8th edn. Oxford.

Hurdis, J. (1790) *Poems*. London.

Huss, B. (1999a) *Xenophons Symposion: Ein Kommentar*. Stuttgart.

(1999b) "The dancing Sokrates and the laughing Xenophon, or the other 'Symposium'," *AJP* 120.3: 381–409.

Hutchinson, G. (2000) *Xenophon and the Art of Command*. London.

(2009) "Read the instructions: didactic poetry and didactic prose," *CQ* 59: 196–211.

Hutson, L. (1994) *The Usurer's Daughter: Male Friendship and Fictions of Women in Sixteenth-Century England*. London.

Irwin, T. H. (1974) Review of L. Strauss, *Xenophon's Socrates, Philosophical Review* 83: 409–13.

(1992) "Plato: the intellectual background," in Kraut (ed.) (1992): 51–89.

Jacoby, F. (1949) *Atthis: The Local Chronicles of Ancient Athens*. Oxford.

(1950) "The authorship of the *Hellenica* of Oxyrhynchos," *CQ* 44: 1–8, reprinted in Jacoby (1956) Abhandlungen zur greichischen Geschichtsschreibung. Leiden: 322–33.

Jansen, J. N. (2007) *After Empire: Xenophon's Poroi and the Reorientation of Athens' Political Economy*. Diss. University of Texas at Austin.

(2012) "Strangers incorporated: outsiders in Xenophon's *Poroi*," in Hobden and Tuplin (eds.) (2012a): 725–60.

Jehne, M. (1994) *Koine Eirene: Untersuchungen zu den Befriedungs- und Stabilisierungsbemühungen in der griechischen Poliswelt des 4. Jahrhunderts v. Chr.* Stuttgart.

(2004) "Überlegungen zu den Auslassungen in Xenophons *Hellenika* am Beispiel der Gründung des Zweiten Athenischen Seebunds," in Tuplin (ed.) (2004a): 463–80.

Joel, K. (1893–1901) *Der echte und der xenophontische Sokrates*. 3 vols. Berlin.

Johnson, A. (1948) "On Xenophon and Dr Strauss," in Strauss (1948): vii–ix.

Johnson, D. M. (2003) "Xenophon's Socrates on justice and the law," *Ancient Philosophy* 23: 255–81.

(2005a) "Xenophon's Socrates at his most Socratic (*Mem.* 4.2.)," *Oxford Studies in Ancient Philosophy* 29: 39–73.

(2005b) "Persians as centaurs in Xenophon's 'Cyropaedia'," *TAPA* 135: 177–207.

(2009) "Aristippus at the crossroads: the politics of pleasure in Xenophon's *Memorabilia*," *Polis* 26: 204–22.

(2012a) "Strauss on Xenophon," in Hobden and Tuplin (eds.) (2012a): 123–59.

(2012b) "Why the *Cyropaedia* is so dull," comment posted in www.cyropaedia.org.

Johnson, W. A. (2000) "Towards a sociology of reading in Classical antiquity," *AJP* 121: 593–627.

Johnstone, S. (1994) "Virtuous toil, vicious work: Xenophon on aristocratic style," *CP* 89: 219–40, reprinted in Gray (ed.) (2010a): 137–66.

Johnstone, C. L. (2009) *Listening to the Logos: Speech and the Coming of Wisdom in Ancient Greece.* Columbia, SC.

Jones, C. P. (1978) *The Roman World of Dio Chrysostom.* Cambridge, MA.

Kahn, C. H. (1981) "Did Plato write Socratic dialogues?" *CQ* 75: 305–20.

(1996) *Plato and the Socratic Dialogue: The Philosophical Use of a Literary Form.* Cambridge.

Kajanto, I. (1994) "Poggio Bracciolini's *De infelicitate principum* and its classical sources," *International Journal of the Classical Tradition* 1.1: 23–35.

Kakridis, J. (1961) *Der Thukydideische Epitaphios.* Munich.

Keller, W. J. (1911) "Xenophon's acquaintance with the History of Herodotus," *CJ* 6.6: 252–9.

Kelly, D. (1996) "Oral Xenophon," in *Voice into Text: Orality and Literacy in Ancient Greece,* ed. I. Worthington. Leiden: 149–63.

Kennell, N. (2010) *Spartans: A New History.* Malden, MA, Oxford, and Chichester.

Kermode, F. (1983) *The Art of Telling.* Cambridge, MA.

Kindt, J. (2012) *Rethinking Greek Religion.* Cambridge.

Klein, L. E. (1994) *Shaftesbury and the Culture of Politeness: Moral Discourse and Cultural Politics in Early Eighteenth-century England.* Cambridge.

Kleingünther, A. (1933) *ΠΡΩΤΟΣ ΕΥΡΕΤΗΣ: Untersuchungen zur Geschichte einer Fragestellung.* Philologus Supplement 26.1. Leipzig.

Koenen, L. (1977) "Cordoba and no end," *ZPE* 24: 35–40.

Kohl, B. G. (1978) "Francesco Barbaro," in *The Earthly Republic: Italian Humanists on Government and Society,* eds. B. G. Kohl, R. G. Witt, and E. B. Welles. Manchester: 179–230.

Konstan, D. (1997) *Friendship in the Classical World.* Cambridge.

Kraus, C. S. (ed.) (1999) *The Limits of Historiography: Genre and Narrative in Ancient Historical Texts.* Leiden, Boston, and Cologne.

Kraut, R. (ed.) (1992) *The Cambridge Companion to Plato.* Cambridge and New York.

Kraye, J. (ed.) (1997) *Cambridge Translations of Renaissance Philosophical Texts.* Vol. II: *Political Philosophy.* Cambridge.

Krentz, P. (1982) *The Thirty at Athens.* Ithaca, NY.

(ed.) (1989) *Xenophon: Hellenika I–II.3.10.* Warminster.

(ed.) (1995) *Xenophon: Hellenika II.3.11–IV.2.8.* Warminster.

Kroeker, R. (2009) "Xenophon as a critic of the Athenian democracy," *HPTh* 30: 197–228.

Kroll, J. H. (1977) "An archive of the Athenian cavalry," *Hesperia* 46: 83–140.

Kronenberg, L. (2009) *Allegories of Farming from Greece and Rome: Philosophical Satire in Xenophon, Varro and Virgil*. Cambridge.

Kuhrt, A. (1984) "The Achaemenid concept of kingship," *British Institute of Persian Studies* 22: 155–60.

(2007) "Cyrus the Great of Persia: images and realities," in *Representations of Political Power: Case Histories from Times of Change and Dissolving Order in the Ancient Near East*, eds. M. Heinz and M. H. Feldman. Winona Lake, IN: 169–91.

Kurz, H. (ed.) (1942) *Anti-Dictator: The Discours sur la servitude volontaire of Etienne de La Boétie*. New York.

Laforse, B. (1997) *Xenophon and the Historiography of Panhellenism*. Diss. University of Texas at Austin.

(1998) "Xenophon, Callicratidas, and panhellenism," *AHB* 12: 55–67.

(2000) "Xenophon's Clearchus," *SyllClass* 11: 74–88.

Lalanne, S. (2006) *Une éducation grecque: rites de passage et construction des genres dans le roman grec ancien*. Paris.

Landor, W. S. (1891) *Imaginary Conversations*, ed. Charles G. Crump. Vol. I. London.

Lane, M. (2001) *Plato's Progeny: How Plato and Socrates Still Captivate the Modern Mind*. London.

Lane Fox, R. (ed.) (2004) *The Long March: Xenophon and the Ten Thousand*. New Haven.

Latacz, J. (1977) *Kampfparänese, Kampfdarstellung und Kampfwirklichkeit in der Ilias, bei Kallinos und Tyrtaios*. Munich.

Lazenby, J. F. (2004) *The Peloponnesian War: A Military Study*. London and New York.

Lee, J. W. I. (2007) *A Greek Army on the March: Soldiers and Survival in Xenophon's Anabasis*. Cambridge.

Lefèvre, E. (1971/2010) "Die Frage nach dem *BIOS EUDAIMWN*: die Begegnung zwischen Kyros und Kroisos bei Xenophon," *Hermes* 99: 283–96, reprinted as "The question of the *BIOS EUDAIMWN*: the encounter between Cyrus and Croesus in Xenophon," in Gray (ed.) (2010a): 401–17.

Lemprière, J. (1788) *Bibliotheca Classica; or, A Classical Dictionary, Containing a Full Account of All the Proper Names Mentioned in Ancient Authors*. Reading.

Lendle, O. (1995) *Kommentar zu Xenophons Anabasis (Bücher 1–7)*. Darmstadt.

Lendon, J. E. (1989) "The Oxyrhynchus historian and the origins of the Corinthian War," *Historia* 38: 300–13.

(2006) "Xenophon and the alternative to realist foreign policy: *Cyropaedia* 3.1.14–31," *JHS* 126: 82–98.

Lévy, E. (1990) "L'art de la déformation historique dans les Helléniques de Xénophon," in *Purposes of History*, eds. H. Verdin, G. Schepens, and E. de Keyser. Louvain: 125–57.

Lewis, D. M. (1977) *Sparta and Persia*. Leiden.

Lewis, J. D. (2009) "Xenophon's *Poroi* and the foundations of political economy," *Polis* 26: 370–88.

Liddell, H. G. and R. Scott (1996) *A Greek–English Lexicon*. 9th edn. Oxford.

Lipka, M. (2002) *Xenophon's Spartan Constitution: Introduction, Text, Commentary*. Berlin and New York.

Livingstone, N. (2001) *A Commentary on Isocrates' Busiris*. Leiden.

Loftus, A. (2000) "A new fragment of the Theramenes Papyrus (P. Mich. 5796b)," *ZPE* 133: 11–20.

Long, A. A. (1988) "Socrates in Hellenistic philosophy," *CQ* 38: 150–71, reprinted in *Stoic Studies* (1996). Cambridge: 1–33.

Loraux, N. (1986) *The Invention of Athens: The Funeral Oration in the Classical City*. Trans. A. Sheridan, orig. publ. 1981. Cambridge, MA.

Lotito, M. A. (2011) *Wittenberg Historiography: Philipp Melanchthon and the Reformation of Historical Thought*. Diss. University of Michigan.

Low, P. (2007) *Interstate Relations in Classical Greece*. Cambridge.

Lowry, S. T. (1987) *The Archaeology of Economic Ideas*. Durham, NC.

Lowth, R. (1834) *Sermons; and Other Remains of Robert Lowth, Sometime Bishop of London*. London.

Luccioni, J. (1947a) *Les idées politiques et sociales de Xénophon*. Paris.
  (1947b) *Xénophon: Hiéron*. Paris.

Luppino Manes, E. (1991) "L'Agesilao di Senofonte: tra encomio e commiato," *Miscellanea greca e romana* 16: 133–63.

Luraghi, N. (2013) "Lo storico e la sua guerra: Tucidide e la grande strategia della Guerra del Peloponneso," in *American Legacy: Quaderno della Società Italiana di Storia Militare*, ed. V. Ilari. Rome: 75–92.
  (2014) "Ephorus in context: the return of the Heraclidae and fourth-century Peloponnesian politics," in Parmeggiani (ed.) (2014): 133–51.

Ma, J. (2003) "Kings," in *A Companion to the Hellenistic World*, ed. A. Erskine. Malden, MA and Oxford: 177–95.
  (2004) "You can't go home again: displacement and identity in Xenophon's *Anabasis*," in Lane Fox (ed.) (2004): 330–45, reprinted in Gray (ed.) (2010a): 502–19.

Mably, G. B. de (1783) *Two Dialogues Concerning the Writing of History*. London.

MacDowell, D. M. (1962) *Andocides: On the Mysteries*. Oxford.

Mackenzie, D. C. (1985) "The wicked wife of Ischomachus again," *EMC* 29 (n.s. 4): 95–6.

Mackil, E. (2013) *Creating a Common Polity: Religion, Economy, and Politics in the Making of the Greek Koinon*. Berkeley and Los Angeles.

MacLaren, M. (1979) "A supposed lacuna at the beginning of Xenophon's *Hellenica*," *AJP* 100: 228–38.

MacNeice, L. (1963) *The Burning Perch*. New York.

Magnelli, A. (2007) "Lo storico di Ossirinco: il più antico continuatore delle *Storie* di Tucidide?" *RAL* 17: 41–73.

Maidment, K. J. (1941) *Minor Attic Orators: Antiphon, Andocides*. Cambridge, MA.

Maier, H. (1913) *Sokrates, sein Werk und seine geschichtliche Stellung*. Tübingen.

Malkin, I. (2011) *A Small Greek World: Networks in the Ancient Mediterranean*. Oxford and New York.

Mallowan, M. (1972) "Cyrus the Great (558–529 B.C.)," *British Institute of Persian Studies* 10: 1–17.

Mansfield, J. (1986) "Aristotle, Plato, and preplatonic doxography and chronography," in *Storiografia e dossografia nella filosofia antica*, ed. G. Cambiano Turin: 1–59, reprinted in *Studies in the Historiography of Greek Philosophy* (1990). Assen: 22–83.

Marincola, J. M. (1989) "Some suggestions on the proem and 'second preface' of Arrian's *Anabasis*," *JHS* 109: 186–9.

(1997) *Authority and Tradition in Ancient Historiography*. Cambridge.

(1999) "Genre, convention, and innovation in Greco-Roman historiography," in Kraus (ed.) (1999): 281–324.

(ed.) (2007a) *A Companion to Greek and Roman Historiography*. Malden, MA and Oxford.

(2007b) "Speeches in classical historiography," in Marincola (ed.) (2007a): 118–32.

(2010) "The rhetoric of history: allusion, intertextuality, and exemplarity in historiographical speeches," in Pausch (ed.) (2010): 259–89.

(2014) "Rethinking Isocrates and historiography," in Parmeggiani (ed.) (2014): 39–62.

Markle, M. M. (1976) "Support of Athenian intellectuals for Philip: a study of Isocrates' Philippus and Speusippus' letter to Philip," *JHS* 96: 80–99.

Marr, J. L. and P. J. Rhodes (2008) *The 'Old Oligarch': The Constitution of the Athenians Attributed to Xenophon*. Oxford.

Marsh, D. (1984) "Lorenzo Valla in Naples: the translation from Xenophon's *Cyropaedia*," *Bibliothèque d'Humanisme et Renaissance* 46.2: 407–20.

(1992) "Xenophon," in *Catalogus Translationum et Commentariorum*. Vol. VII, eds. V. Brown, P. O. Kristeller, and F. E. Cranz. Washington, DC: 75–196.

Masaracchia, E. (1996) "La 'Ciropedia' di Senofonte e l'ideologia imperiale persiana," *QUCC* 54.3: 163–94.

Maslen, R. W. (ed.) (2002) *An Apology for Poetry (or The Defence of Poesy): Sir Philip Sidney*. 3rd edn. Manchester.

Matuozzi, J. (2013) "Schoolhouse follies: Tristram Shandy and the male reader's tutelage," *ELH* 80.2: 489–518.

Maxson, B. J. (2009) "Kings and tyrants: Leonardo Bruni's translation of Xenophon's *Hiero*," *Renaissance Studies* 24.2: 188–206.

McCoy, M. (2007) *Plato on the Rhetoric of Philosophers and Sophists*. Cambridge.

McKechnie, P. and S. J. Kern (eds.) (1988) *Hellenica Oxyrhynchia*. Warminster.

McNamara, C. (2009) "Socratic politics in Xenophon's *Memorabilia*," *Polis* 26: 223–45.

McPherran, M. (1996) *The Religion of Socrates*. University Park, PA.

Meissner, B. (1992) *Historiker zwischen Polis und Königshof:Studien zur Stellung der Geschichtsschreiber in der griechischen Gesellschaft in spätklassischer und frühhellenistischer Zeit*. Hypomnemata 99. Göttingen.

Meister, K. (1990) *Die griechische Geschichtsschreibung von den Anfängen bis zum Ende des Hellenismus*. Stuttgart, Berlin, and Cologne.

Mejer, J. (1978) *Diogenes Laertius and His Hellenistic Background*. Wiesbaden.

Merkelbach, R. and H. C. Youtie (1968) "Ein Michigan-Papyrus über Theramenes," *ZPE* 2: 161–9.

Methuen, C. (1994) "Securing the Reformation through education: the Duke's scholarship system of sixteenth-century Württemberg," *The Sixteenth Century Journal* 25.4: 841–51.

Millar, F. G. B. (1965) "Epictetus and the imperial court," *JRS* 55: 141–8.

Millender, E. (2001) "Spartan literacy revisited," *CA* 20: 121–64.

(2012) "Spartan 'friendship' and Xenophon's crafting of the *Anabasis*," in Hobden and Tuplin (eds.) (2012a): 377–425.

(forthcoming) "Foxes at home, lions abroad: Spartan commanders in Xenophon's *Anabasis*," in Powell and Richer (eds.) (forthcoming).

Miller, M. C. (1997) *Athens and Persia in the Fifth Century* BC: *A Study in Cultural Receptivity.* Cambridge.

Miller, W. (ed.) (1914) *Xenophon, Cyropaedia.* 2 vols. Cambridge, MA.

Minakaran-Hiesgen, E. (1970) "Untersuchungen zu den Porträts des Xenophon und Isokrates," *Jahrbuch des Deutschen Archäologischen Instituts* 85: 112–57.

Mingay, J. M. and R. R. Walzer (1991) *Aristotelis Ethica Eudemia.* Oxford.

Missiou, A. (1992) "*Doulos tou basileos*: the politics of translation," *CQ* 43: 377–91.

Mitchell, L. G. (1997) *Greeks Bearing Gifts: The Public Use of Private Relationships in the Greek World, 435–323* BC. Cambridge.

(2007) *Panhellenism and the Barbarian in Archaic and Classical Greece.* Swansea.

(2013) *The Heroic Rulers of Archaic and Classical Greece.* London and New York.

Moles, J. L. (1985) "The interpretation of the 'second preface' in Arrian's *Anabasis*," *JHS* 105: 162–8.

(1992) "Review of Gray (1989)," *CR* 42: 281–4.

(1993) "Truth and untruth in Herodotus and Thucydides," in *Lies and Fiction in the Ancient World*, eds. C. Gill and T. P. Wiseman. Austin, TX: 88–121.

(1994) "Xenophon and Callicratidas," *JHS* 114: 70–84.

Möller, A. (2007) "Classical Greece: distribution," in *The Cambridge Economic History of the Greco-Roman World*, eds. W. Scheidel, I. Morris, and R. P. Saller. Cambridge: 362–84.

Momigliano, A. (1936a) "Per l'unità logica del Lakedaimonion Politeia di Senofonte," *RFIC* 14: 170–3 = (1966) Vol. I: 341–5.

(1936b) "Per la storia della pubblistica sulla Koινὴ Eἰρήνη nel IV secolo A.C.," *ANSP* n.s. 5: 97–136 = (1966) Vol. I: 481–7.

(1966) *Terzo contributo alla storia degli studi classici e del mondo antico.* 2 vols. Rome.

(1975) *Alien Wisdom: The Limits of Hellenisation.* Cambridge.

(1982) *La storiografia greca.* Turin.

(1993) *The Development of Greek Biography.* Expanded edn. 1st edition 1971. Cambridge, MA.

Morgan, J. R. (1989) "The story of Knemon in Heliodorus' *Aithiopika*," *JHS* 109: 99–113.

Morgan, K. (2004) "The education of Athens: politics and rhetoric in Isocrates and Plato," in *Isocrates and Civic Education*, eds. T. Poulakos and D. Depew. Austin, TX: 125–54.

Morgan, T. (1998) *Literate Education in the Hellenistic and Roman Worlds.* Cambridge.

(1999) "Literate education in Classical Athens," *CQ* 49: 46–61.

Morrison, D. (1994) "Xenophon's Socrates as a teacher," in Vander Waerdt (ed.) (1994a): 181–208, reprinted in Gray (ed.) (2010a): 181–208.

(2007) "The Utopian Character of Plato's Ideal City," in *The Cambridge Companion to Plato's Republic*, ed. G. R. F. Ferrari. Cambridge: 232–55.

(2008) "Remarques sur la psychologie morale de Xénophon," in *Xénophon et Socrate*, eds. M. Narcy and A. Tordesillas. Paris: 11–27.

Mueller-Goldingen, C. (1995) *Untersuchungen zu Xenophons Kyrupaedie.* Stuttgart and Leipzig.

Münscher, K. (1920) *Xenophon in der griechisch-römischen Literatur. Philologus* Supplementband 13.11. Leipzig.

Murnaghan, S. (1988) "How a woman can be more like a man: the dialogue between Ischomachus and his wife in Xenophon's *Oeconomicus*," *Helios* 15: 9–22.

Murphy, D. J. (2013) "Isocrates and the dialogue," *CW* 106: 311–53.

Murray, O. (1967) "Aristeas and Ptolemaic kingship," *JTS* 18: 337–71.

Nadon, R. (2001) *Xenophon's Prince*. Berkeley and Los Angeles.

Näf, B. (1997) "Vom Frieden reden – den Krieg meinen? Aspekte der griechischen Friedensvorstellungen unter der Politik des Atheners Euboulos," *Klio* 79: 317–40.

Nails, D. (1985) "The shrewish wife of Socrates," *EMC* 29 (n.s. 4): 97–9.

(2002) *The People of Plato: A Prosopography of Plato and Other Socratics*. Indianapolis.

Narcy, M. and A. Tordesillas (eds.) (2008) *Xénophon et Socrate: actes du colloque d'Aix-en-Provence (6–9 novembre 2003)*. Paris.

Natali, C. (2001) "Socrate dans *L'Économique* de Xénophon," in *Socrate et les Socratiques*, eds. G. Romeyer Dherbey and J.-B. Gourinat. Paris: 263–88.

Natoli, A. F. (2004) *The Letter of Speusippus to Philip II: Introduction, Text, Translation and Commentary*. Historia Einzelschriften 176. Stuttgart.

Nee, L. D. (2009) "The city on trial: Socrates' indictment of the gentleman in Xenophon's *Oeconomicus*," *Polis* 26: 246–70.

Newell, W. R. (1981) *Xenophon's Education of Cyrus and the Classical Critique of Liberalism*. Diss. University of Michigan.

(1988) "Machiavelli and Xenophon on princely rule: a double-edged encounter," *The Journal of Politics* 50: 108–30.

Nestle, W. (1939/1948) "Xenophon und die Sophistik," *Philologus* 94: 31–50, reprinted in *Griechische Studien: Untersuchungen zur Religion, Dichtung, und Philosophie der Griechen* (1948). Stuttgart: 430–50.

Nicolai, R. (1992) *La storiografia nell'educazione antica*. Pisa.

(2004) *Studi su Isocrate: la communcazione letteraria nel IV sec. a.C. e i nuovi generi della prosa*. Seminari Romani di Cultura Greca 7. Rome.

(2006) "Thucydides continued," in *Brill's Companion to Thucydides*, eds. A. Rengakos and A. Tsakmakis. Leiden: 693–719.

(2014a) "Cyrus orateur et ses maîtres (grecs)," in Pontier (ed.) (2014): 179–94.

(2014b) "At the boundary of historiography: Xenophon and his corpus," in Parmeggiani (ed.) (2014): 63–87.

Niebuhr, B. G. (1828) *Kleine historische und philologische Schriften*. 2 vols. Bonn.

(1832) "On Xenophon's *Hellenica*," tr. C. Thirlwall, *Philological Museum* 1: 485–98.

Nielsen, T. H. (2004) "Triphylia," in *An Inventory of Archaic and Classical Poleis*, eds. M. H. Hansen and T. H. Nielsen. Oxford: 540–6.

Nietzsche, F. W. (1967) *Werke*. Vol. IV. Eds. G. Colli and M. Montinari. Berlin.

Nightingale, A. W. (1995) *Genres in Dialogue: Plato and the Construct of Philosophy*. Cambridge.

Norden, E. (1909) *Antike Kunstprosa*. 2 vols. Leipzig, reprinted Stuttgart 1983.

Norton, A. (1955) *Star Guard*. San Diego and New York.

Nussbaum, G. B. (1967) *The Ten Thousand: A Study in Social Organization and Action in Xenophon's Anabasis*. Leiden.

Ober, J. (1989) *Mass and Elite in Democratic Athens: Rhetoric, Ideology, and the Power of the People*. Princeton.

(1998) *Political Dissent in Democratic Athens: Intellectual Critics of Popular Rule*. Princeton.

O'Connor, D. K. (2011) "Xenophon and the enviable life of Socrates," in *The Cambridge Companion to Socrates*, ed. D. R. Morrison. Cambridge: 48–74.

O'Flannery, J. (2003) "Xenophon's (The Education of Cyrus) and ideal leadership: lessons for modern public administration," *Public Administration Quarterly* 27.1–2: 41–64.

O'Mahoney, P. (2011) "On the 'hiccuping episode' in Plato's *Symposium*," *CW* 104: 143–59.

Oost, S. I. (1977/1978) "Xenophon's attitude towards women," *CW* 71: 225–36.

O'Sullivan, J. N. (1994) *Xenophon of Ephesus*. Berlin.

Oliver, G. J. (2011) "Before 'Lykourgan Athens': the origins of change," in *Clisthène et Lycurgue d' Athènes*, ed. V. Azoulay. Paris: 119–32.

Ollier, F. (1933) *Le mirage spartiate: étude sur l'idéalisation de Sparte dans l'antiquité grecque de l'origine jusqu'aux Cyniques*. Paris.

(1961) *Xénophon Banquet, Apologie de Socrate*. Paris.

Opdycke, L. E. (2000) *Count Baldesar Castiglione: The Book of the Courtier*. Ware.

Opie, I. A. and P. Opie (1951) *The Oxford Dictionary of Nursery Rhymes*. Oxford.

Opitz, A. (1913) *Quaestiones Xenophonteae: De Hellenicorum atque Agesilai necessitudine*. Breslau.

Osborne, R. (1985) *Demos: The Discovery of Classical Attika*. Cambridge.

(2004) *The Old Oligarch: Pseudo-Xenophon's Constitution of the Athenians*. 2nd edn. London.

(2010) "Democratic ideology, the events of war and the iconography of Attic funerary sculpture," in *War, Democracy and Culture in Classical Athens*, ed. D. Pritchard. Cambridge: 245–65.

Ostwald, M. (1986) *From Popular Sovereignty to the Sovereignty of Law: Law, Society, and Politics in Fifth-Century Athens*. Berkeley and Los Angeles.

Ostwald, M. and J. P. Lynch (1994) "The growth of schools and the advance of knowledge," *Cambridge Ancient History*, vol. VI.2: 592–633.

Pellegrini, F. C. and R. Spongano (eds.) (1949) *Leon Battista Alberti: i primi tre libri della Famiglia*. Florence.

Pangle, T. L. (1985) "The political defense of Socratic philosophy: a study of Xenophon's 'Apology of Socrates to the Jury'," *Polity* 18: 98–114.

(1994) "Socrates in the context of Xenophon's political writings," in Vander Waerdt (ed.) (1994a): 126–50.

Parker, R. (1989) "Spartan religion," in *Classical Sparta: Techniques Behind Her Success*, ed. A. Powell. London: 142–72.

(2004) "One man's piety: the religious dimension of the *Anabasis*," in Lane Fox (ed.) (2004): 131–53.

Parker, V. (2007) "Sphodrias' raid and the liberation of Thebes: a study of Ephorus and Xenophon," *Hermes* 135: 13–33.

Parmeggiani, G. (2011) *Eforo di Cuma: studi di storiografia greca*. Bologna.

(2012) "Sui fondamenti della tesi antica della paternità anassimenea del *Tricarano*: mimesi stilistica e analogia tra i proemi storiografici di Anassimene di Lampsaco e di Teopompo di Chio (ad Anaximenes *FGrHist* 72 TT 6, 13; F 1)," *Histos* 6: 214–27.

(ed.) (2014) *Between Thucydides and Polybius: The Golden Age of Greek Historiography*. Cambridge, MA.

Parpola, S. (2003) "Sakas, India, Gobryas, and the Median royal court: Xenophon's *Cyropaedia* through the eyes of an Assyriologist," in *Continuity of Empire (?): Assyria, Media, Persia*, eds. G. Lanfranchi, M. Roaf, and R. Rollinger. Padua: 339–50.

Parsons, P. (2001) "These fragments we have shored against our ruin," in *The New Simonides: Contexts of Praise and Desire*, eds. D. Boedeker and D. Sider. Oxford: 55–64.

Patzer, A. (1999/2010) "Der Xenophontische Sokrates als Dialektiker," in *Der fragende Sokrates*, ed. K. Pestalozzi. Stuttgart: 50–76, reprinted as "Xenophon's Socrates as dialectician," in Gray (ed.) (2010a): 228–55.

Pausch, D. (ed.) (2010) *Stimmen der Geschichte: Funktionen von Reden in der Antiken Historiographie*. Berlin and New York.

Peek, W. (1957) *Attische Grabschriften II: unedierte Grabschriften aus Athen und Attika*. Berlin.

Pelling, C. B. R. (1999) "Epilogue," in Kraus (ed.) (1999): 325–60.

(2000) *Literary Texts and the Greek Historian*. London and New York.

(2006) "Speech and narrative in the *Histories*," in *The Cambridge Companion to Herodotus*, eds. C. Dewald and J. Marincola. Cambridge: 103–21.

(2007) "Ion's Epidemiai and Plutarch's Ion," in *The World of Ion of Chios*, eds. V. Jennings and A. Katsaros. Leiden: 75–109.

(2009) "Tacitus' personal voice," in *The Cambridge Companion to Tacitus*, ed. A. J. Woodman. Cambridge: 147–67.

(2013) "Xenophon's and Caesar's third-person narratives – or are they?" in *The Author's Voice in Classical and Late Antiquity*, eds. A. Marmodoro and J. Hill. Oxford: 39–73.

Perlman, S. (1976) "Panhellenism, the polis and imperialism," *Historia* 25: 1–30.

(1976–7) "The Ten Thousand: a chapter in the military, social and economic history of the fourth century," *RSA* 6–7: 241–84.

Petrocelli, C. (2001) *Senofonte: Ipparchico. Manuale per il commandante di cavalleria*. Bari.

Pitcher, L. (2009) *Writing Ancient History: An Introduction to Classical Historiography*. London.

(2014) "Themistogenes of Syracuse (108)," in *Brill's New Jacoby Online*.

(forthcoming) "Thucydides in Greek and Roman historiography," in *The Cambridge Companion to Thucydides*, ed. P. Low.

Polanyi, K. (1977) *The Livelihood of Man*. New York, San Francisco, and London.

Pomeroy, S. B. (1994) *Xenophon: Oeconomicus. A Social and Historical Commentary*. Oxford.

Pontier, P. (2006) *Trouble et ordre chez Platon et Xénophon*. Paris.

(2010) "L'Agésilas de Xénophon: comment on réécrit l'histoire," *CEA* 47: 359–83.

(2012) "Xenophon and the Persian kiss," in Hobden and Tuplin (eds.) (2012a): 611–30.

(ed.) (2014) *Xénophon et la rhétorique*. Paris.

Poulakos, T. and D. Depew (eds.) (2004) *Isocrates and Civic Education*. Austin, TX.

Powell, A. and S. Hodkinson (eds.) (1994) *The Shadow of Sparta*. London and New York.

Powell, A. and N. Richer (eds.) (forthcoming) *Xenophon and Sparta*. Swansea.

Powers, N. (2009) "The natural theology of Xenophon's Socrates," *Ancient Philosophy* 29: 249–66.

Pownall, F. S. (2000) "Shifting viewpoints in Xenophon's *Hellenica*: the Arginusae episode," *Athenaeum* 88: 499–513.

(2004) *Lessons from the Past: The Moral Use of History in Fourth-Century Prose.* Ann Arbor.

(2012) "Critias in Xenophon's *Hellenica*," *SCI* 31: 1–17.

Prandi, L. (1985) *Callistene: uno storico tra Aristotele e i re macedoni.* Milan.

Prinz, W. (1911) *De Xenophontis Cyri institutione.* Göttingen.

Proietti, G. (1987) *Xenophon's Sparta.* Leiden.

Purves, A. C. (2010) *Space and Time in Ancient Greek Narrative.* Cambridge and New York.

Raaflaub, K. A. (1983) "Democracy, oligarchy, and the concept of the 'free citizen' in late fifth-century Athens," *Political Theory* 11: 517–44.

(2004) *The Discovery of Freedom in Ancient Greece.* Chicago.

Radermacher, L. (1896/1897) "Über den Cynegeticus des Xenophon," *RhM* 51: 596–627 and 52: 13–41.

Rahn, P. J. (1971) "Xenophon's developing historiography," *TAPA* 102: 497–508.

Ready, J. (2011) *Character, Narrator and Simile in the Iliad.* Cambridge and New York.

Reardon, B. P. (1991) *The Form of Greek Romance.* Princeton.

(ed.) (2008) *Collected Ancient Greek Novels.* With a new foreword by J. R. Morgan. Berkeley and Los Angeles.

Reeve, C. D. C. (tr. and ed.) (1998) *Aristotle: Politics.* Indianapolis.

Reichel, M. (1995/2010) "Xenophon's Cyropaedia and the Hellenistic novel," in *Groningen Colloquia on the Novel.* Vol. VI, ed. H. Hofmann. Groningen: 1–20, reprinted in Gray (ed.) (2010a): 418–38.

Reisert, J. R. (2009) "Ambition and corruption in Xenophon's *Education of Cyrus*," *Polis* 26: 296–315.

Rhodes, N. (2013) "Marlowe and the Greeks," *Renaissance Studies* 27: 199–218.

Rhodes, P. J. (1981) *A Commentary on the Aristotelian Athenaion Politeia.* Oxford.

(2010) *A History of the Classical Greek World.* 2nd edn. Malden, MA, Oxford, and Chichester.

Rhodes, P. J. and R. Osborne (eds.) (2003) *Greek Historical Inscriptions: 404–323 BC.* Oxford.

Richards, H. (1897) "The minor works of Xenophon. VI, VII The Constitutions," *CR* 11: 229–37.

(1898) "The minor works of Xenophon. XI The Cynegeticus," *CR* 12: 285–92 and 383–90.

(1899) "The minor works of Xenophon. Conclusion," *CR* 13: 342–9.

Richer, N. (1999) "*Aidôs* at Sparta," in *Sparta: New Perspectives*, eds. S. Hodkinson and A. Powell. Swansea: 90–115.

(2007) "Le modèle lacédémonien dans les oeuvres non historiques de Xénophon," *Ktèma* 32: 405–34.

Riedinger, J.-C. (1991) *Etude sur les Helléniques de Xénophon et l'histoire.* Paris.

Riemann, K.-A. (1967) *Das herodoteische Werk in der Antike.* Munich.

Rijksbaron, A. (2002) "The Xenophon factory: one hundred and fifty years of school editions of Xenophon's *Anabasis*," in *The Classical Commentary: Histories, Practices, Theory*, eds. R. K. Gibson and C. S. Kraus. Leiden: 235–67.

Rinner, W. (1981) *Untersuchungen zur Erzählstruktur in Xenophons Kyrupaedie und Thukydides, Buch VI und VII*. Diss. Graz.

Roberts, J. T. (1994) *Athens on Trial: The Antidemocratic Tradition in Western Thought*. Princeton.

Robertson, N. (1990) "The laws of Athens, 410–399 BC: the evidence for review and publication," *JHS* 110: 43–75.

Robin, D. (2013) "A Renaissance feminist translation of Xenophon's *Oeconomicus*," in *Roman Literature, Gender and Reception: Domina Illustris*, eds. D. Lateiner, G. K. Gold, and J. Perkins. London: 207–21.

Robin, L. (1910) "Les *Mémorables* de Xenophon et notre connaissance de la philosophie de Socrate," *Année philosophique* 21: 1–47.

Roche, H. (2016) "Xenophon and the Nazis: a case study in the politicization of Greek thought through educational propaganda," *Classical Receptions Journal* 8: 79–81.

(forthcoming) "Classics and education in the Third Reich: *Die Alten Sprachen* and the Nazification of Latin and Greek teaching in secondary schools," in *Brill's Companion to the Classics, Fascism and Nazi Ideology*, eds. K. Demetriou and H. Roche. Leiden.

Rodgers, B. B. (1930) *The Knights of Aristophanes*. London.

Rood, T. C. B. (2004a) "Panhellenism and self-presentation: Xenophon's speeches," in Lane Fox (ed.) (2004): 305–29.

(2004b) "Xenophon and Diodorus: continuing Thucydides," in Tuplin (ed.) (2004a): 341–95.

(2004c) *The Sea! The Sea!: The Shout of the Ten Thousand in the Modern Imagination*. London.

(2006) "Advice and advisers in Xenophon's *Anabasis*," in *Advice and Its Rhetoric in Greece and Rome*, eds. D. Spencer and E. Theodorakopoulos. Bari: 47–61.

(2007) "Xenophon," in *Time in Ancient Greek Narrative*. Studies in Ancient Greek Narrative 2. *Mnemosyne* Supplement 291, eds. I. J. F. de Jong and R. Nünlist. Leiden: 147–63.

(2010a) *American Anabasis: Xenophon and the Idea of America from the Mexican War to Iraq*. London.

(2010b) "Xenophon's parasangs," *JHS* 130: 51–66.

(2011) "Black Sea variations: Arrian's *Periplus*," *Cambridge Classical Journal* 57: 137–63.

(2012a) "The plupast in Xenophon's *Hellenica*," in *Time and Narrative in Ancient Historiography: The 'Plupast' from Herodotus to Appian*, eds. J. Grethlein and C. Krebs. Cambridge: 76–94.

(2012b) "Xenophon," in *Space in Ancient Greek Narrative*. Studies in Ancient Greek Narrative 3. *Mnemosyne* Supplement 339, ed. I. J. F. de Jong. Leiden: 161–78.

(2012c) "A delightful retreat: Xenophon and the picturesque," in Hobden and Tuplin (eds.) (2012a): 89–121.

(2013a) "Xenophon and the Barberini: Pietro da Cortona's *Sacrifice to Diana*," *Journal of the Warburg and Courtauld Institutes* 77: 1–22.

(2013b) "Redeeming Xenophon: historiographical reception and the transhistorical," *Classical Receptions Journal* 5: 199–211.

(2014) "Space and landscape in Xenophon's *Anabasis*," in *Space, Place, and Landscape in Ancient Greek Literature and Culture*, eds. K. Gilhuly and N. Worman. Cambridge: 63–93.

(2015a) "Political thought in Xenophon: Straussian readings of the *Anabasis*," *Polis* 32: 141–63.

(2015b) "Self-characterization and political thought in Xenophon's *Anabasis*," in Ash et al. (eds.) (2015): 97–109.

Roscalla, F. (2004) "*Kalokagathia e kaloi kagathoi* in Senofonte," in Tuplin (ed.) (2004a): 115–24.

Rosetti, L. (2011) *Le dialogue Socrate*. Paris.

Rummel, E. (1985) *Erasmus as a Translator of the Classics*. Toronto.

Rung, E. (2004) "Xenophon, the Oxyrhynchus historian and the mission of Timocrates to Greece," in Tuplin (ed.) (2004): 413–26.

Ruzicka, S. (2012) *Trouble in the West: Egypt and the Persian Empire, 525–332 BC*. Oxford and New York.

Sancisi-Weerdenburg, H. (1985/2010) "The death of Cyrus: Xenophon's *Cyropaedia* as a source for Iranian history," *Acta Iranica* 25: 459–71, reprinted in Gray (ed.) (2010a): 439–53.

(1987) "The fifth Oriental monarchy and Hellenocentrism," in *Achaemenid History II: The Greek Sources*, eds. H. Sancisi-Weerdenburg and A. Kuhrt. Leiden: 117–130.

(1990) "Cyrus in Italy: from Dante to Machiavelli. Some explorations of the reception of Xenophon's *Cyropaedia*," in *The Roots of the European Tradition*, eds. H. Sancisi-Weerdenburg and H. J. W. Drijvers. Leiden: 31–52.

Sanders, K. R. (2011) "Don't blame Socrates (Xen.Mem.1.2.40–46)," *CP* 106: 349–56.

Sandridge, N. B. (2012) *Loving Humanity, Learning, and Being Honored: The Foundations of Leadership in Xenophon's Education of Cyrus*. Cambridge, MA.

Santas, G. X. (1979) *Socrates: Philosophy in Plato's Early Dialogues*. London.

Saunders, T. J. (1992) "Plato's later political thought," in Kraut (ed.) (1992): 464–92.

Scaife, R. (1995) "Ritual and persuasion in the house of Ischomachus," *CJ* 90: 225–32.

Scardino, C. (2007) *Gestaltung und Funktion der Reden bei Herodot und Thukydides*. Berlin and New York.

(2012) "Indirect discourse in Herodotus and Thucydides," in *Thucydides and Herodotus*, eds. E. Foster and D. Lateiner. Oxford: 67–96.

Schacht H. (1890) *De Xenophontis studiis rhetoricis*. Diss. Berlin.

Schepens, G. (1977) "Historiographical Problems in Ephorus," in *Historiographia Antiqua: Commentationes Lovanienses in Honorem W. Peremans Septuagenarii Editae*, eds. T. Reekmans, E. Van 't Dack, and H. Verdin. Leuven: 95–118.

(1993) "L'apogée de l'archè spartiate comme époque historique dans l'historiographie grecque du début du IVe siècle av. J.-C.," *AncSoc* 24: 169–204.

(2001) "Who wrote the *Hellenica Oxyrhynchia*? The need for a methodological code," *Sileno* 27: 201–24.

(2004) "Ἀρετή e ἡγεμονία: i profili storici di Lisandro e Agesilao nelle *Elleniche* di Teopompo," in *Il Peloponneso di Senofonte*, eds. G. Daverio Rocchi and M. Cavalli. Milan: 1–40.

(2005) "A la recherche d'Agésilas le roi de Sparte dans le jugement des historiens du IVe siècle av. J.-C," *REG* 118: 31–78.

(2007) "Tucidide 'in controluce': la Guerra del Peloponneso nella storiografia greca del quarto secolo a.C.," in *Il dopoguerra nel mondo antico: politica, propaganda, storiografia*, ed. L. Santi Amantini. Rome: 59–99.

(2012) "Timocrates' mission to Greece – once again," in Hobden and Tuplin (eds.) (2012a): 213–41.

Schleiermacher, F. (1818/1879) "Ueber den Werth des Sokrates als Philosophen," in *Abhandlung der philosophischen Klasse der Königlich-Preussischen Akademie aus den Jahren 1814–1815*. Berlin: 51–68, reprinted in *ΠΛΑΤΩΝ: The Apology of Socrates, the Crito and Part of the Phaedo*, ed. W. Smith. London: 1–27.

Schmitz, T. A. (2010) "The Mytilene debate in Thucydides," in Pausch (ed.) (2010): 45–65.

Schnayder, J. (1966) "Hyperbaton Xenophontis exemplo illustratur," *Eos* 56: 53–9.

Schofield, M. (2006) *Plato: Political Philosophy*. Oxford.

Schöll, R. (1890) *Die Anfänge einer politischen Literatur bei den Griechen*. Munich.

Schorn, S. (2008) "Die Vorstellung des xenophontischen Sokrates von Herrschaft und das Erziehungsprogramm des *Hieron*," in *Socratica 2005*, eds. L. Rossetti and A. Stavru. Bari: 177–203.

(2012) "The philosophical background of Xenophon's *Poroi*," in Hobden and Tuplin (eds.) (2012a): 689–723.

Scott, D. (1987) "Platonic anamnesis revisited," *CQ* 37: 346–66.

Scott, G. F. (1930) Review of A. J. Butler, *Sport in Classic Times, Times Literary Supplement* 1478 (May 29): 455.

Seager, R. (2001) "Xenophon and Athenian democratic ideology," *CQ* 51: 385–97.

Sealey, R. (1975) "Pap. Mich. inv. 5982: Theramenes," *ZPE* 16: 279–88.

Sedley, D. (2005) "Les origines des preuves stoïciens de l'existence de Dieu," *Revue de métaphysique et de morale* 48: 461–87.

(2007) *Creationism and Its Critics in Antiquity*. Berkeley and Los Angeles.

Sekunda, N. (1988) "Persian settlement in Hellespontine Phrygia," in *Achaemenid History 3: Method and Theory*, eds. A. Kuhrt and H. Sancisi-Weerdenburg. Leiden: 175–96.

Shaftesbury, Earl of (1914) *Second Characters, or The Language of Forms*. Ed. B. Rand, orig. pub. 1711. Cambridge.

(1999) *Characsticks of Men, Manners, Opinions, Times*. 2 vols. ed. P. Ayres. Oxford.

Shalev, D. (2006) "The role of εὑρήματα in the 'Lives' of Diogenes Laertius and related literature," *Hermes* 134: 309–37.

Shayegan, M. R. (2012) *Aspects of History and Epic in Ancient Iran from Gaumāta to Wahnām*. Washington, DC.

Shear, J. (2011) *Polis and Revolution: Responding to Oligarchy in Classical Athens*. Cambridge.

Shenstone, W. (1741) *The Judgment of Hercules, a Poem*. London.

Sicking, C. M. J. and P. Stork (1997) "The grammar of the so-called historical present in ancient Greek," in Bakker (ed.) (1997a): 131–68.

Skinner, Q. (1988) "Political philosophy," in *The Cambridge History of Renaissance Philosophy*, eds. C. B. Schmitt and Q. Skinner. Cambridge: 387–452.

Skinner, Q. and R. Price (eds.) (1988) *Machiavelli: The Prince*. Cambridge.

Smith, N. S. (tr.) (1824) *Xenophon: The Expedition of Cyrus into Persia, and the Retreat of the Ten Thousand Greeks*. London.

Smith, S. D. (2007) *Greek Identity and the Athenian Past in Chariton: The Romance of Empire*. Groningen.

Sommerstein, A. H. (ed.) (1981) *The Comedies of Aristophanes*. Vol. II: *Knights*. Warminster.

Sommerville, J. P. (ed.) (1994) *King James VI and I: Political Writings*. Cambridge.

Soulis, E. M. (1972) *Xenophon and Thucydides*. Athens.

Sourvinou-Inwood, C. (1989) "Assumptions and the creation of meaning: reading Sophocles' *Antigone*," *JHS* 109: 134–48.

(2006) "Tragedy and anthropology," in *A Companion to Greek Tragedy*, ed. J. Gregory. Malden, MA and Oxford: 293–304.

Spence, I. G. (1993) *The Cavalry of Classical Greece: A Social and Military History with Particular Reference to Athens*. Oxford.

Spencer, M. G. (2013) *David Hume: Historical Thinker, Historical Writer*. University Park, PA.

Springer, C. E. (2011) *Luther's Aesop*. Kirksville, MO.

Stadter, P. A. (1976) "Xenophon in Arrian's *Cynegeticus*," *GRBS* 17: 157–67.

(1980) *Arrian of Nicomedia*. Chapel Hill, NC.

(1991/2010) "Fictional narrative in the *Cyropaideia*," *AJP* 112: 461–91, reprinted in Gray (ed.) (2010a): 367–400.

(2009) "Character in politics," in Balot (ed.) (2009): 457–70.

(2012) "Staying up late: Plutarch's reading of Xenophon," in Hobden and Tuplin (eds.) (2012a): 43–62.

Stalley, R. F. (1983) *An Introduction to Plato's Laws*. Oxford.

Sterling, N. (2004) "Xenophon's *Hellenica* and the Theban hegemony," in Tuplin (ed.) (2004a): 453–62.

Stevens, J. (1994) "Friendship and profit in Xenophon's *Oeconomicus*," in Vander Waerdt (ed.) (1994a): 209–37.

Stokes, M. C. (1992) "Socrates' mission," in *Socratic Questions: New Essays on the Philosophy of Socrates and Its Significance*, eds. B. S. Gower and M. C. Stokes. London: 26–81.

(2012) "Three defenses of Socrates: relative chronology, politics, and religion," in Hobden and Tuplin (eds.) (2012a): 243–67.

Stoll, O. (2010) *Zum Ruhme Athens: Wissen zum Wohl der Polis. Xenophons Ideal einer Führungspersönlichkeit und Athens Reiterei im Hipparchikos <Logos>*. Berlin.

(2012) "For the glory of Athens: Xenophon's Hipparchikos <Logos>, a technical treatise and instruction manual on ideal leadership," *Studies in History and Philosophy of Science* 43: 250–7.

Strassler, R. (tr. and ed.) (2009) *The Landmark Xenophon's Hellenika*. New York.

Strauss, B. (1997) "The problem of periodization: the case of the Peloponnesian War," in *Inventing Ancient Culture: Historicism, Periodization, and the Ancient World*, eds. M. Golden and P. Toohey. London and New York: 165–75.

Strauss, L. (1939) "The spirit of Sparta, or the taste of Xenophon," *Social Research* 6: 502–36.

(1948/2000) *On Tyranny: An Interpretation of Xenophon's Hiero*. New York. Corrected and expanded edition, including the Strauss-Kojève Correspondence, eds. V. Gourevitch and M. S. Roth (2000) Chicago.

(1970) *Xenophon's Socratic Discourse: An Interpretation of the Oeconomicus.* Ithaca, NY.

(1972) *Xenophon's Socrates.* Ithaca.

Strazdins, E. (2012) *The Future of the Second Sophistic.* Diss. Oxford.

Stronk, J. (1995) *The Ten Thousand in Thrace: An Archaeological and Historical Commentary on Xenophon's Anabasis, Books VI.iii–vi–VII.* Amsterdam.

Swain, S. C. R. (ed.) (2000) *Dio Chrysostom.* Oxford.

Syme, R. (1982) "The career of Arrian," *HSCPh* 86: 181–211.

Tamiolaki, M. (2008) "Les *Helléniques* entre tradition et innovation: aspects de la relation intertextuelle de Xénophon avec Hérodote et Thucydide," *Cahiers des études anciennes* 45: 15–52.

(2010) *Liberté et esclavage chez les historiens grecs classiques.* Paris.

(2012) "Virtue and leadership in Xenophon: ideal leaders or ideal losers?" in Hobden and Tuplin (eds.) (2012a): 563–89.

(2013) "A citizen as a slave of the state? Oligarchic perceptions of democracy in Xenophon," *GRBS* 53: 31–50.

(2014a) "A l'ombre de Thucydide? Les discours des *Helléniques* et l'influence thucydidéenne," in Pontier (ed.) (2014): 121–38.

(2014b) "Is Xenophon 'dark'? Towards a typology of readings in the *Cyropaedia*," unpublished paper delivered at Princeton University.

Tatum, J. (1989) *Xenophon's Imperial Fiction: On the Education of Cyrus.* Princeton.

Taylor, A. E. (1911) *Varia Socratica.* Oxford.

(1932) *Socrates.* London.

Teevan, C. (2006) *How Many Miles to Basra?* London.

Thesleff, H. (1978) "The interrelation and date of the *Symposia* of Plato and Xenophon," *Bulletin of the Institute of Classical Studies* 25: 157–70.

Thiel, J. H. (1922) ΞΕΝΟΦΩΝΤΟΣ ΠΟΡΟΙ. Diss. Amsterdam.

Thillet, P. (1957) "Note sur le 'Gryllos,' ouvrage de jeunesse d'Aristote," *Revue philosophique de la France et de l'Étranger* 147: 352–4.

Thirlwall, C. (1832) "Xenophon, Niebuhr, and Delbrueck," *Philological Museum* 1: 498–536.

Thomas, D. (2009a) "Introduction," in Strassler (ed.) (2009): ix–lxvi.

(2009b) "Chronological problems in the continuation (1.1.1–2.3.10) of Xenophon's *Hellenika*," in Strassler (ed.) (2009): 331–9.

Thraede, K. (1962) "Das Lob des Erfinders: Bemerkungen zur Analyse der Heuremata-Kataloge," *RhM* 105: 158–86.

Thumiger, C. (2013) "Vision and knowledge in Greek tragedy," *Helios* 40: 223–45.

Tigerstedt, E. N. (1965–78) *The Legend of Sparta in Classical Antiquity.* 3 vols. Stockholm.

Tilg, S. (2010) *Chariton of Aphrodisias and the Invention of the Greek Love Novel.* Oxford.

Tober, D. (2010) "Politeiai and Spartan local history," *Historia* 59: 412–31.

Too, Y. L. (1995) *The Rhetoric of Identity in Isocrates: Text, Power, Pedagogy.* Cambridge.

(1998) "Xenophon's *Cyropaedia*: disfiguring the pedagogical state," in *Pedagogy and Power: Rhetorics of Classical Learning,* eds. Y. L. Too and N. Livingstone. Cambridge: 282–302.

(2001) "The economies of pedagogy: Xenophon's wifely didactics," *PCPhS* 47: 65–80.

(2008) *A Commentary on Isocrates' Antidosis.* Oxford.

Tovar, A. (1971) *Estudios sobre la obra de Americo Castro.* Madrid.

Tsagalis, C. (2009) "Personal names and narrative techniques in Xenophon's Anabasis," in *Narratology and Interpretation: The Content of the Form in Ancient Texts*, eds. J. Grethlein and A. Rengakos. Berlin and New York: 451–79.

Tucker, A. (2004) *Our Knowledge of the Past: A Philosophy of Historiography.* Cambridge.

Tuplin, C. (1987) "Xenophon's exile again," in *Homo Viator: Classical Essays for John Bramble*, eds. M. Whitby, P. Hardie, and M. Whitby. Bristol: 59–68.

(1990) "Persian decor in Cyropaedia: some observations," in *The Roots of the European Tradition: Achaemenid History V*, eds. H. Sancisi-Weerdenburg and J. W. Drijvers. Leiden: 17–31.

(1993) *The Failings of Empire: A Reading of Xenophon Hellenica 2.3.11–7.5.27.* Stuttgart.

(1994) "Xenophon, Sparta, and the *Cyropaedia*," in Powell and Hodkinson (eds.) (1994): 127–81.

(1996) "Xenophon's *Cyropaedia*: education and fiction," in *Education in Greek Fiction*, eds. A. H. Sommerstein and C. Atherton. Bari: 65–162.

(ed.) (2004a) *Xenophon and His World: Papers from a Conference held in Liverpool in July 1999.* Stuttgart.

(2004b) "The Persian Empire," in Lane Fox (ed.) (2004): 154–83.

(2004c) "Xenophon, Artemis and Scillus," in *Spartan Society*, ed. T. J. Figueira. Swansea: 251–79.

(2007a) "A foreigner's perspective: Xenophon in Anatolia," in *The Achaemenid Impact on Local Populations and Culture in Anatolia*, ed. I. Delemen. Istanbul: 7–31.

(ed.) (2007b) *Persian Responses: Political and Cultural Interaction with(in) the Achaemenid Empire.* Swansea.

(2007c) "Treacherous hearts and upright tiaras: the Achaemenid King's head-dress," in Tuplin (ed.) (2007b): 67–97.

(2007d) "Continuous histories (*Hellenica*)," in Marincola (ed.) (2007a): 159–70.

(2010) "Xenophon and Achaemenid courts: a survey of evidence," in *Der Achämenidenhof*, eds. B. Jacobs and R. Rollinger. Wiesbaden: 189–230.

(2012) "Xenophon," in *Oxford Classical Dictionary*. 4th edn, eds. S. Hornblower, A. J. Spawforth, and E. Eidinow. Oxford: 1580–3.

(2013) "Xenophon's *Cyropaedia*: fictive history, political analysis and thinking with Iranian kings," in *Every Inch a King: Comparative Studies on Kings and Kingship in the Ancient and Medieval Worlds*, eds. L. Mitchell and C. Melville. Leiden: 67–90.

(2014a) "Le salut par la parole: les discours dans l'*Anabase* de Xénophon," in Pontier (ed.) (2014): 69–120.

(forthcoming a) "Spartans in Xenophon's *Anabasis*," in Powell and Richer (eds.) (forthcoming).

(forthcoming b) "Plato, Xenophon and Persia," in Danzig and Alon (eds.) (forthcoming).

Tupper, M. F. (1860) *Three Hundred Sonnets.* London.

Underhill, G. (1900) *A Commentary with Introduction and Appendix on the Hellenica of Xenophon*. Oxford.

van Berkel, T. (2010) "Pricing the invaluable: Socrates and the value of friendship," in *Valuing Others in Classical Antiquity*, eds. R. R. Rosen and I. Sluiter. Leiden: 249–77.

van der Eijk, P. J. (1997) "Toward a rhetoric of ancient scientific discourse," in Bakker (ed.) (1997a): 77–129.

(2007) *Greek Technical Writings*. Stuttgart.

Vander Waerdt, P. A. (ed.) (1993) "Socratic justice and self-sufficiency: the story of the Delphic Oracle in Xenophon's *Apology of Socrates*," *Oxford Studies in Ancient Philosophy* 11: 1–48.

(ed.) (1994a) *The Socratic Movement*. Ithaca, NY.

(1994b) "Socrates in the *Clouds*," in Vander Waerdt (ed.) (1994a): 48–86.

Vanderpool, E. (1965) "The location of the Attic deme Erchia," *BCH* 89.1: 21–6.

Vannini, L. (2012) "Note sul 'papiro di Teramene'," *Studi di Egittologia e di Papirologia* 9: 88–95.

Vela Tejada, J. (2004) "Warfare, history and literature in the Archaic and Classical periods: the development of Greek military treatises," *Historia* 53: 129–46.

Vidal-Naquet, P. (1984) "Flavius Arrien entre deux mondes," in *Arrien, Histoire d'Alexandre: l'Anabase d'Alexandre le Grand et l'Inde*, ed. Pierre Savinel. Paris: 309–94.

Vlassopoulos, K. (2013a) *Greeks and Barbarians*. Cambridge.

(2013b) "The stories of the Others: storytelling and intercultural communication in the Herodotean Mediterranean," in *Ancient Ethnography: New Approaches*, eds. E. Almagor and J. Skinner. London: 49–75.

Vlastos, G. (1971) "The paradox of Socrates," in *The Philosophy of Socrates: A Collection of Critical Essays*, ed. G. Vlastos. Garden City, NY: 1–21.

(1991) *Socrates: Ironist and Moral Philosopher*. Ithaca, NY.

(1994a) "The historical Socrates and Athenian democracy," in Vlastos (1994b): 87–108.

(1994b) *Socratic Studies*. Cambridge.

von Fritz, K. (1949) "The so-called historical present in early Greek," *Word* 5: 186–201.

Von Reden, S. (2007) "Classical Greece: consumption," in *The Cambridge Economic History of the Greco-Roman World*, eds. W. Scheidel, I. Morris, and R. P. Saller. Cambridge: 385–406.

Walbank, F. W. (1996) "Two Hellenistic processions: a matter of self-definition," *SCI* 15: 119–30.

(2002) *Polybius, Rome and the Hellenistic World: Essays and Reflections*. Cambridge.

Walker, A. D. (1993) "*Enargeia* and the spectator in Greek historiography," *TAPA* 123: 353–77.

Walker, J. (1821) *A Critical Pronouncing Dictionary and Expositor of the English Language*. 23rd edn. London.

Wareh, T. (2012) *The Theory and Practice of Life: Isocrates and the Philosophers*. Washington, DC.

Warner, G. F. (ed.) (1893) *The Library of James VI, 1573–1583, from a Manuscript in the Hand of Peter Young, his Tutor*. Edinburgh.

Warner, R. (tr.) (1972) *Xenophon: The Persian Expedition*. Harmondsworth.
(tr.) (2004) *The Persian Expedition*. Introduction by G. Cawkwell. Harmondsworth.
Waszink, J. (ed.) (2004) *Justus Lipsius: Politica. Six Books on Politics or Political Instruction*. Assen.
Waterfield, R. (tr.) (1990) *Xenophon: Conversations of Socrates*. London.
(tr.) (1997) *Xenophon: Hiero the Tyrant and Other Treatises*. Introduction and notes by P. Cartledge. Harmondsworth.
(2004) "Xenophon's Socratic mission," in Tuplin (ed.) (2004a): 79–113.
(tr.) (2005) *The Expedition of Cyrus*. Oxford.
(2009) *Why Socrates Died: Dispelling the Myths*. New York.
(2012) "Xenophon on Socrates' trial and death," in Hobden and Tuplin (eds.) (2012a): 269–305.
Waters, M. (2014) *Ancient Persia: A Concise History of the Achaemenid Empire, 550–330 BCE*. Cambridge and New York.
Weissenberger, M. (2003) "Cephisodorus (5)," in *Brill's New Pauly*. Vol. III. Leiden: 136.
Welch, C. (1901) *A Book of Nursery Rhymes*. Boston, New York, and Chicago.
Wellman, R. (1976) "Socratic method in Xenophon," *JHI* 37: 307–18.
Wells, H. G. (2005 [1909]) *Tono-Bungay*. Harmondsworth.
Wendland, P. (1910) "Beiträge zu athenischer Politik und Publicistik des vierten Jahrhunderts," *Gött. Nachr.* 3–4: 123–82, 287–323.
Whidden, C. (2007) "The account of Persia and Cyrus's Persian education in Xenophon's 'Cyropaedia'," *The Review of Politics* 69.4: 539–67.
Whitby, M. (2004) "Xenophon's Ten Thousand as a fighting force," in Lane Fox (ed.) (2004): 215–42.
White, H. (1978) *Tropics of Discourse: Essays in Cultural Criticism*. Baltimore.
(1980) "The value of narrativity in the representation of reality," *Critical Inquiry* 7.1 (*On Narrative*): 5–27.
Whitehead, D. (1990) *Aineias the Tactician: How to Survive under Siege*. Oxford.
Whitmarsh, T. G. W. (ed.) (2008) *The Cambridge Companion to the Greek and Roman Novel*. Cambridge.
Whittlesey, W. L. (1934) "Panacea politics: a book review," *Today: An Independent National Weekly* 3: 17.
Whyte, S. (1772) "The choice of Hercules: an ode, for music," in *The Shamrock; or, Hibernian Cresses*. Dublin: 41–5.
Wiater, N. (2010) "Speeches and historical narrative in Polybius' *Histories*: approaching speeches in Polybius," in Pausch (ed.) (2010): 67–107.
Wickersham, J. M. (1994) *Hegemony and Greek Historians*. Lanham, MD.
Widdra, K. (1964) *Xenophontis De re equestri*. Leipzig.
Wiffen, J. H. (1820) *Julia Alpinula. With The Captive of Stamboul and Other Poems*. London.
Wilamowitz-Moellendorff, U. von (1905) "Lesefrüchte," *Hermes* 40: 116–53.
Wilson-Okamura, D. S. (2010) *Virgil in the Renaissance*. Cambridge.
Wilson, P. (2004) "Homer and English epic," in *The Cambridge Companion to Homer*, ed. R. Fowler. Cambridge: 272–86.
Wimsatt, W. and M. C. Beardsley (1946) "The intentional fallacy," *Sewanee Review* 54: 468–88. Revised version in W. Wimsatt (1954), *The Verbal Icon: Studies in the Meaning of Poetry*. Lexington, KY: 3–18.

Winterer, C. (2002) *The Culture of Classicism: Ancient Greece and Rome in American Intellectual Life, 1780–1910*. Baltimore.

(2013) "The U.S. Founders and Cyrus the Great of Persia," www.cyropaedia.org/2013/06/01/the-u-s-founders-and-cyrus-the-great-of-persia/.

Wolfe, T. (2000) *O Lost*. Columbia, SC.

Wolpert, A. (2002) *Remembering Defeat: Civil War and Civic Memory in Ancient Athens*. Baltimore.

Wolfsdorf, D. (2008) "Hesiod, Prodicus and the Socratics on work and pleasure," *Oxford Studies in Ancient Philosophy* 35: 1–18.

Wood, N. (1964) "Xenophon's theory of leadership," *C&M* 25: 33–66.

Wormell, D. E. W. (1935) "The literary tradition concerning Hermias of Atarneus," *YCS* 5: 55–92.

Wrigley, A. and S. J. Harrison (eds.) (2013) *Louis MacNeice: The Classical Radio Plays*. Oxford.

Wüst, F. R. (1938) "Bericht über die Forschungen zur Griechischen Geschichte des 4. Jahrhunderts v. Chr.," *Die Welt als Geschichte* 4: 328–35.

Wylie, G. J. (1992) "Agesilaus and the Battle of Sardis," *Klio*: 74: 118–30.

Wyllie, P. J. (2001) *Xenophon's Art of Horsemanship*. MA thesis University of Virginia.

Yunis, H. (1997) "Thrasymachus B1: discord, not diplomacy," *CP* 92: 58–66.

Zarghamee, R. (2013a) *Discovering Cyrus*. Washington, DC.

(2013b) "Xenophon's *Cyropaedia* and Persian oral history (Part one, Part two, Part three)," comments posted on www.cyropaedia.org.

Zimmermann, B. (1989) "Roman und Enkomion: Xenophons *Erziehung des Kyros*," *WJA* 15: 97–105.

(2009) "The historical novel in the Greek world: Xenophon's *Cyropaedia*," in *Fiction on the Fringe: Novelistic Writing in the Post-Classical Age*, ed. G. A. Karla. Leiden: 95–103.

INDEX

life and times, Xenophon's (*cont.*)
old age, in 98–99
religion *see* religion
Scillus years (ca. 392–371) *see*
Scillus years
volume and nature of works 10, 15–16
Life of Henry Brulard, The (Stendhal) 1–2
Lincoln, Abraham 450
Lipsius, Justus 426
Lives and Opinions of Eminent Philosophers
(Diogenes Laertius) 45, 53
Longinus 229, 240
Longus 409
Lycurgus 200, 377–378, 382–383, 386

Macaulay, Lord 3
Machiavelli, Niccolo 3, 174–175, 431
Cyropaedia, and 419–423
appropriating ancient exempla for
authoritative support 421–422
critique of 420–421
referring to 420
suggesting ancient works be read with
care 422–423
tyrants 424–425
MacNeice, Louis 451
Maier, H. 49, 52
managers, Xenophon instructing 432–433
Manual (Arrian of Nicomedia) 54
Marincola, John 8
Melanchthon, Philip 427, 431
Memorabilia (Xenophon) 1, 2, 15
Aristippus conversing with Socrates 48–49
Aristotle, whether read
Memorabilia 49–53
art capturing both spiritual and physical
qualities 137
Athens
Athenian affairs, reflecting
disappointment with 70–71
political society sustaining/improving
way of life, as 66, 67–68
references to 66, 67–68, 70–71, 346
authorial voice 250–254
building narrator's authority 251
diminishing use of 'I' 252–253
knowledge, sources of 251
personal and adversarial note in final
paragraph 253–254
personal tone coming back more
explicitly 253
rhetorical questions implying reader
shares writer's indignation 250, 253

setting for more elaborate versions of
encounters 251
strong first-person, opening with 250
third-person 'he-Xenophon',
introduction of 252
benefits, pleasure, and subtlety 128–131
demonstrating Socrates' usefulness
through wide range of topics
128–129
pleasure 129–130
Socrates' mixture of philosophy and
practicality 129–130
subtlety 129–131
'Choice of Heracles' 444–445, 454
date of 33–34
defense of Socrates 189
audience, tone and history 119–123
democracy
freedom 66–67
obedience to laws 66–67
Socrates' ideas on positive cultivation of
democratic citizenry 66–67
tyranny, and 356–357
fictional devices in 9
friendship
good friends actually being useful
partners 334
mutually beneficial partnership between
peers, as 333–334
qualities of the ideal friend 334
law
creation of 61
obedience to 61, 66–67
purpose of 61
leadership
investigating leadership through
problematic case 346
qualities of leaders 327–328
universal scope of Xenophon's
management model 330–331
monarchy 62–63
oligarchy 354–355
Persia, references to 360–361
popularity in 18th century 3, 444–445
Presocratics, references to 37–41
contradictory theses defended by
philosophers, citing 39–40
setting positions in opposition to each
other 39
Socrates' attitude towards
research 38–39
Socrates condemning interest in 'divine
things' 38

INDEX

Cambridge Companions to...

AUTHORS

TOPICS